Language Intervention Series
Volume VIII

THE ACQUISITION OF COMMUNICATIVE COMPETENCE

THE ACQUISITION OF COMMUNICATIVE COMPETENCE, edited by Richard L. Schiefelbusch, Ph.D., and Joanne Pickar, M.A., is the eighth volume in the **Language Intervention Series**—Richard L. Schiefelbusch, series editor. Other volumes in this series include:

Published:
Volume I   **BASES OF LANGUAGE INTERVENTION**   edited by *Richard L. Schiefelbusch, Ph.D.*
Volume II   **LANGUAGE INTERVENTION STRATEGIES**   edited by *Richard L. Schiefelbusch, Ph.D.*
Volume III   **LANGUAGE INTERVENTION FROM APE TO CHILD** edited by *Richard L. Schiefelbusch, Ph.D., and John H. Hollis, Ed.D.*
Volume IV   **NONSPEECH LANGUAGE AND COMMUNICATION Analysis and Intervention**   edited by *Richard L. Schiefelbusch, Ph.D.*
Volume V   **EMERGING LANGUAGE IN AUTISTIC CHILDREN**   by *Warren H. Fay, Ph.D., and Adriana Luce Schuler, M.A.*
Volume VI   **EARLY LANGUAGE   Acquisition and Intervention**   edited by *Richard L. Schiefelbusch, Ph.D., and Diane Bricker, Ph.D.*
Volume VII   **DEVELOPMENTAL LANGUAGE INTERVENTION Psycholinguistic Applications**   edited by *Kenneth F. Ruder, Ph.D., and Michael D. Smith, Ph.D.*

In preparation:
TEACHING FUNCTIONAL ACADEMICS   edited by *Steven Warren, Ph.D., and Ann Rogers-Warren, Ph.D.*
COMMUNICATIVE COMPETENCE   Assessment and Intervention   edited by *Richard L. Schiefelbusch, Ph.D.*

Language Intervention Series
Volume VIII

THE ACQUISITION OF COMMUNICATIVE COMPETENCE

Edited by
Richard L. Schiefelbusch, Ph.D.
University Professor
and
Director, Bureau of Child Research;
Chairman, Child Language Graduate Program
University of Kansas
Lawrence, Kansas

and

Joanne Pickar, M.A.
Department of Human Development
and Family Life
and
Bureau of Child Research
University of Kansas

University Park Press
Baltimore

UNIVERSITY PARK PRESS
International Publishers in Medicine and Allied Health
300 North Charles Street
Baltimore, Maryland 21201

Copyright © 1984 by University Park Press

This book is protected by copyright. All rights, including that of translation into other languages, are reserved. No part of this book may be reproduced, stored in a retrieval system, or transmitted, in any form or by any means, electronic, mechanical, photocopying, recording, or otherwise, without the prior written permission of the publisher.

Sponsoring editor: Janet S. Hankin
Production editor: Megan Barnard Shelton
Text design by: S. Stoneham, Studio 1812, Baltimore

Typeset by: Maryland Composition Company, Inc.
Manufactured in the United States of America by:
Halliday Lithograph

Library of Congress Cataloging in Publication Data
Main entry under title:

The acquisition of communicative competence.

(Language intervention series ; v. 8)
Includes index.
1. Language acquisition. 2. Communicative competence.
I. Schiefelbusch, Richard L. II. Pickar, Joanne.
III. Series.
P118.A14   1984   401'.9   84-2286
ISBN 0-8391-1989-5

contents

Contributors vii
Preface ix

Introduction 1

Section I   **Developmental Factors and Functions**

chapter 1   **The Development of Preverbal Communication:** Its Contribution and Limits in Promoting the Development of Language
             Susan Sugarman 23

chapter 2   **Parent-Child Interaction and the Development of Communicative Ability**
             Catherine E. Snow 69

chapter 3   **Children's Play and Communicative Development**
             Jacqueline Sachs 109

chapter 4   **Cognitive Aspects of Communicative Development**
             Mabel Rice 141

Section II   **Dimensions of Communicative Competence**

chapter 5   **Form and Force Interactions:** The Development of Negatives and Questions
             Jill G. de Villiers 193

chapter 6   **Children's Acquisition of Presuppositional Usages**
             Ganie DeHart and Michael Maratsos 237

chapter 7   **The Structure of Children's Requests**
             David Gordon and Susan Ervin-Tripp 295

chapter 8   **Grammatical Devices for Sharing Points**
             Brian MacWhinney 323

Section III **Children across Cultures**

chapter 9   **Cultural Variation in Children's Conversations**
             Bambi B. Schieffelin and Ann R. Eisenberg 377

v

Section IV	**Developmentally Different Children**	
chapter 10	**Communicative Competence in Children with Delayed Language Development** *Lynn S. Snyder*	423
chapter 11	**Communication in Infancy and the Emergence of Language in Blind Children** *Cathy Urwin*	479
Afterword	**Assisting Children To Become Communicatively Competent** *Richard L. Schiefelbusch*	525
	Index	534

contributors

Ganie DeHart, M.S.
Institute of Child Development
University of Minnesota
51 East River Road
Minneapolis, Minnesota 55455

Jill G. de Villiers, Ph.D.
Psychology and Philosophy
  Departments
Smith College
Northampton, Massachusetts 01063

Ann Eisenberg, Ph.D.
Division of Behavioral and Cultural
  Sciences
University of Texas at San Antonio
San Antonio, Texas 78285

Susan Ervin-Tripp, Ph.D.
Institute of Human Learning
University of California at Berkeley
Building T-4
Berkeley, California 94720

David Gordon, Ph.D.
Institute of Human Learning
University of California at Berkeley
Building T-4
Berkeley, California 94720

Brian MacWhinney, Ph.D.
Department of Psychology
Carnegie-Mellon University
Pittsburgh, Pennsylvania 15213

Michael Maratsos, Ph.D.
Institute of Child Development
University of Minnesota
51 East River Road
Minneapolis, Minnesota 55455

Mabel Rice, Ph.D.
Bureau of Child Research
University of Kansas
Lawrence, Kansas 66045

Jacqueline Sachs, Ph.D.
Departments of Communication
  Sciences and Psychology
University of Connecticut
Storrs, Connecticut 06268

Richard L. Schiefelbusch, Ph.D.
Bureau of Child Research
University of Kansas
Lawrence, Kansas 66045

Bambi B. Schieffelin, Ph.D.
Graduate School of Education
University of Pennsylvania
3700 Walnut
Philadelphia, Pennsylvania 19104

Catherine E. Snow, Ph.D.
Graduate School of Education
Harvard University
7th Floor Larsen Hall
Cambridge, Massachusetts 02138

Lynn S. Snyder, Ph.D.
Department of Speech Pathology
  and Audiology
University of Denver
Denver, Colorado 80208

Susan Sugarman, Ph.D.
Department of Psychology
Princeton University
Princeton, New Jersey 08540

Cathy Urwin, Ph.D.
Child Care and Development Group
University of Cambridge
Free School Lane
Cambridge, England CB2 3RF

preface

This book concerns *how* children acquire knowledge about language forms, functions, and contextually appropriate usages. It also concerns *what* forms, functions, and usages must be acquired in order for a child to be considered communicatively competent. The term communicative competence refers to the child's knowledge and skills of both the formal and functional aspects of language. As such it includes: *linguistic competence**—competence in producing and understanding phonetically, grammatically and semantically correct utterances; and *social* or *interactional competence*—competence in the social and cultural rules for the appropriate use of language in different social situations. The editors and authors feel that the study of communicative competence has created a more adequate scientific base for studying language acquisition. Nevertheless, *knowledge* of how to communicate competently does not assure competence. Knowledge about how to perform is not equivalent to performance.

The most apparent aspect of knowledge-based competence is that it is assessed through performance. Otherwise, one must infer the existence of knowledge and how it was formed. Fortunately, it is possible to observe much of what a child does in learning a language—the way the child maps the relationships among objects, persons, and events and, at the same time, the contingent effects of his or her participation in cultural contexts. From these observations we are able to document many of the competence assumptions. Nevertheless, we must still *infer* that the complex knowledge gained from these transactions forms the basis of the child's competence. Apparently, this competence includes both knowledge of *rules* and knowledge of *performance*—the understanding and the production of utterances appropriate to the context in which they occur. Thus, *communicative competence is the totality of experience-derived knowledge and skill that enables a speaker to communicate effectively and appropriately in social contexts.*

According to this definition, the study of *communicative competence* concerns the way humans perform with language and the cultural conditions that influence how they perform. In the broadest sense there is a "learn by doing" strategy in language acquisition.

Our efforts in this book have produced a synthesis of information that researcher and clinician alike can draw on in studying children in social contexts. The context includes information contributed by cross-cultural linguists, cultural anthropologists, developmental psycholinguists, language-communication specialists, and many others.

The book is divided into four sections: 1) Developmental Factors and Functions; 2) Dimensions of Communicative Competence; 3) Children across Cultures; and 4) Developmentally Different Children. The content highlights major issues for developmental and educational disciplines serving normal and handicapped children. Several authors have discussed research pertaining to both language acquisition and language intervention. The intention is to present current research findings and to identify areas of needed study for both researchers and practitioners.

Credit should be given to the authors for accepting the charge for writing

---

* See Chomsky, N. 1965. Aspects of the Theory of Syntax. MIT Press, Cambridge, MA.

to both familiar and unfamiliar audiences; to the publisher for remaining optimistic throughout the extended period of manuscript preparation; and to Marilyn Fischer, Mary Beth Johnston, Jean Roberts, Lori Llewellyn, and Thelma Dillon for expert support and assistance.

R. L. S.

Introduction

Richard L. Schiefelbusch

Bureau of Child Research
University of Kansas
Lawrence, Kansas

contents

DEVELOPMENT OF COMMUNICATIVE COMPETENCE 3
PLAN OF THE BOOK 5
OVERVIEW 6
    Developmental Factors and Functions 6
    Dimensions of Communicative Competence 10
    Children across Cultures 12
    Developmentally Different Children 12
DISCUSSION AND SUMMARY 16
REFERENCES 19

Language is a system for communication. Although it has most often been studied out of an interest in its formal properties, language must be seen as a system of use to be understood fully. The need to understand the uses of language is especially great when considering language development, because children acquire language in order to communicate.

Emphasis on the uses of language led to the recognition that the notion of "grammatical competence" was an inadequate characterization of knowledge about language. In addition, one needs to describe the development of *communicative competence* (Hymes, 1964)—the ability to use language not just correctly but also effectively. An approach to language acquisition that recognizes the centrality of communicative competence to development enables us to understand language as a culturally situated social behavior.

DEVELOPMENT OF COMMUNICATIVE COMPETENCE

The "modern" study of child language began with Chomsky's published theoretical formulations (1957, 1959, 1965). Two of the issues he raised have had special impact on research in language structure and language acquisition. The first is that fluent speech stems from a set of rules that underlie sentence construction. According to this view, the language-learning child is exposed to a limited sample of speech but must arrive at a set of rules that will enable him to produce and comprehend an infinite number of possible sentences.

Chomsky's second issue relates to the child's innate knowledge of (and capacity for) linguistic universals. This capacity, he posits, explains the structural principles that are common to all languages. The assumption is that universals are found in the acquisition history of children across languages and cultures.

Bowerman (1982) pointed out that during the 1960s Chomsky's formulations induced most language investigators to be interested primarily in linguistically relevant knowledge—knowledge of the linguistic code. However, by the late 1960s a small number of investigators— including Hymes (1964, 1971); Slobin (1967); and Campbell and Wales (1970)—had begun to voice objections to the preoccupation with linguistic competence. They pointed out that linguistic knowledge represented only one component of what a language user must know to be competent, and that Chomsky was overlooking what a speaker must know to produce utterances appropriate to the particular cultural contexts in which they occur. Their assumption was that there also should be formalized rules for language *use*. This assumption led Slobin (1967) and Gumperz and Hymes (1964) to characterize communicative competence as the totality of knowledge that enables a speaker to produce utterances that are structurally well formed, referentially accurate, and contextually appropriate, and to understand the speech of others as a joint function of its structural characteristics and social context.

This definition of communicative competence includes a much more comprehensive range of knowledge while preserving the *competence* construct advanced by Chomsky. The important dimension added by the new competence definition is that *knowledge* extends beyond the rules for selecting well-formed utterances and includes referentially accurate and contextually appropriate use. Thus, the definition includes knowledge of both semantic reference and pragmatic functions. In addition, the stipulations include both production and comprehension.

This expansion of Chomsky's original meaning of *competence* includes a cognitive and a pragmatic emphasis. However, even with this expansion of the competence concept, the term remains philosophically similar to Chomsky's position, which is that the speaker possesses knowledge of the rules requisite to appropriate language. Nevertheless, the philosophical differences appear to be greater when language is studied in cultural contexts.

An important development in the cultural analysis of language acquisition was the 1967 publication of *A Field Manual for Cross-Cultural Study of the Acquisition of Communicative Competence*. This volume was edited by Slobin, and included contributions by several psychologists and anthropologists at the University of California at Berkeley. The manual detailed the range of phenomena that should be studied and included suggestions for the conduct of cross-cultural research on language acquisition.

The shift from linguistic to communicative competence marked an important theoretical change in the way in which most child language researchers thought about language. The shift emphasized the belief that the language-acquiring child is learning not only linguistic structure, but also the social values and rules underlying language in social interaction. As Gumperz and Hymes (1964) and others have pointed out, rules for speaking are different from those that govern language as an abstract system. Interpretation of spoken language requires an understanding not only of referential meaning, but also of conveyed and situated meaning. Conveyed meaning refers to the meaning of an utterance according to its use in different semantic contexts. Situated meaning involves the features of context or situation, and emerges as an interaction unfolds and is negotiated by the participants, drawing on their shared knowledge of social and cultural conventions. Children as well as adults actively use their knowledge of all three of these levels of meaning in order to interpret what is being communicated in an interaction. Knowledge of these three levels and the ability to negotiate meaning in an interaction are part of one's communicative competence. Knowledge develops within interactions that are culturally shaped and culturally meaningful.

In order to address this issue Hymes (1971) considered language users and actual events. He suggested that the goal of a broad theory of competence is to show the ways in which what is systematically possible, feasible, and appropriate are linked to produce actually occurring communicative behavior. He proposed that competence includes knowledge that goes with the performance of appropriate speech. In addition to competence determined by a repertoire of rules, we should also consider the speaker's experience in behaving in specific contexts where communication must accomplish multiple purposes simultaneously. The dimensional nature of communication contexts can be understood and responded to appropriately only through cultural experience. Appropriate comprehending and responding should be part of our definition of competence.

Let us now attempt to restate the definition. *Communicative competence* is the totality of experience-derived knowledge and skill that enables a speaker to produce utterances that are structurally well formed, referentially accurate, and socially appropriate in culturally determined communication contexts, and to understand the speech of others as a joint function of structural characteristics and social context. According to this definition, *communicative competence* enables speakers to use language appropriately in environmental contexts. Thus, the functions affecting competence are both person center and context centered.

In summary, environmental influences on communicative competence may have been obscured for a time by the distinction between *competence* (the speaker-hearer's knowledge of his language) and *performance* (the use of language in representative situations). However, by the late 1960s a number of linguists had pointed out that linguistic knowledge constitutes only *one* component of what the speaker must know to be competent with language. We now propose that knowledge of linguistic rules in combination with knowledge and skills of the speaker in environmental contexts forms the competences essential for communication.

PLAN OF THE BOOK

This is a book on language development from a communication competence perspective. The authors and editors share a common view that a competent communicator must possess relevant knowledge and must have appropriate strategies and skills for transacting language in representative contexts. Such a view requires that the authors and editors explain *how* the child acquires the requisite knowledge and skills and *what* comprises the requisite knowledge and skills.

This chapter provides an overview of the various sections, chapters, and themes of the book. Editorial license has been exercised in interpreting chapters to bring out and amplify issues relevant to the *how* and *what* and to provide an integrated statement about the development of communicative competence. Finally, a summary discussion at the end of the book attempts to extend the developmental perspectives toward intervention themes.

OVERVIEW

The book includes four sections: 1) developmental factors and functions, 2) dimensions of communicative competence, 3) children across cultures, and 4) developmentally different children.

Developmental Factors and Functions

Section I contains four chapters, each of which presents a topic that is assumed to be important to the acquisition of communicative competence: preverbal communication, parent-child interaction, children's play, and cognitive mapping. In Chapter 1 Sugarman focuses on the infant's intention to communicate. Actions that are initially directed toward single objects or persons evolve in late infancy into coordinated person-object interchanges. These coordinated transactions are followed by the child's first word.

Several important issues are highlighted by the study of preverbal communication. First, the infant's object and person schemata may convey intention when presented sequentially. Second, the infant learns to encode intentions that are instrumental in communicative transactions prior to the emergence of words. Third, the child's attention to objects and to persons evolves into more complex object-object and person-object schemata at about the same time (near the end of the first year). Fourth, the infant's strategy of using an object to relate to another object or using a person to gain an object (as discussed by Sugarman) may indicate a stage of cognitive development that immediately precedes first words.

Sugarman strongly implies that prelinguistic communication events are functionally prerequisite to subsequent language development, and Snow, in Chapter 2, begins with this assumption: "Social interaction with warm and caring adults is undeniably a prerequisite to normal cognitive and social development" (p. 71). However, Snow's issue is broader than Sugarman's. Sugarman focuses on the structure of communication transactions of the first months prior to early words, whereas Snow describes the adult-infant social experiences in their full range. Snow points out that adults interpret infant behaviors as attempts to communicate even when it is obvious that no explicit intention to communicate exists. At the same time infants search for contingencies among objects, persons, and events and the behavior of their caregivers. Snow suggests that these two principles form the bases for caregiver-child transactions during the prelinguistic period.

Snow presents a number of excerpts from the 3-, 4½-, 6-, and 12-month age periods to illustrate prespeech interactions. Games during the first year provide rich contexts for the mutual sharing of intentions and contingencies. A major advantage of games is that they can be expanded and complicated to stay at or just beyond the child's level of competence. Snow finds that much of the child's early ability to comprehend speech and produce early words develops from games and other social routines. The social routines such as greeting, thanking, requesting, and acknowledging enable the child to be a full participant in social functions.

During the second and third years the child continues to look for correspondences between his own focus of attention and the adult's utterances. Now the child uses a greater variety of devices, including comments, questions, and requests, to signify intentions. The child's verbal devices also create possible semantic contingencies to guide adult responding. This means that the child directly cues the adult to respond to his focus of attention. Cueing is not possible for the prelinguistic infant who cannot express semantic intent. Snow emphasizes that semantically contingent speech facilitates children's learning of language. She provides a tabular overview of various studies of semantic contingency. The studies show that a great proportion of the speech addressed to small children is semantically contingent on the child's previous utterances and that the more semantically contingent speech a child hears the greater the facilitation of his language acquisition. Snow emphasizes, however, that the 3- to 6-year-old child is affected by a wide range of influences and that there is a relationship between the quality of the home environment and the development of literacy skills. At this stage the crucial factor seems to be parental responsiveness to child interests and to the child's literacy-related activities.

Both Sugarman and Snow also examine the early language of handicapped children. Sugarman analyzes early person-object schemata and Snow considers the divergent patterns of parent-child transactions.

Their special observations are discussed in the section on impaired development.

In Chapter 3, Sachs considers the influences of play in the development of communicative competence. Play is examined through three stages, beginning with caregiver-infant *social* play and extending through *symbolic* play and *role* play. Social play, as discussed by Sachs, might help a child acquire the foundations of communication and discover the combinational nature of language. The foundations may include vocabulary, turntaking, reciprocal semantic relations, and signals of readiness (cueing). The combinational nature of language may involve learning that variations in adult utterances signal a change in meaning.

Symbolic play is also referred to as pretend play. Such play begins by the middle of the second year when the child uses objects (cups, brushes, dolls) in representative fashion. The pretend play evolves by 3 years into pretend actions that may involve a fantasy narrative and may include plans for sequences of play. Current research on pretend play is establishing a close relationship between evolving play and evolving language. The involvement of child and parent in symbolic play is discussed from the perspective of each participant. Apparently the parent contributes by showing the child how to play and how to construct narratives. Both contributions are usually made in a manner of fun and enjoyment.

Role play provides the means for studying the child's adapted utterances in discourse. These adaptations are frequently referred to as register variations. The child's knowledge of registers begins very early, and young children are able to reflect role variations with vocal, inflectional, and gestural changes when playing roles, e.g., mother, sister, brother, father, doctor, nurse, or baby.

Sachs regards the role-playing activities as buffers that allow a child to pretend to be other social agents and to extend knowledge of discourse beyond the here and now. Also, the child can employ speech devices before being expected to use them. Such experience is especially meaningful as the child grows and is expected to communicate in new and expanded ways.

In Chapter 4 Rice provides a comprehensive model of language-related conceptual knowledge that includes person knowledge, social categories, and event knowledge. She regards these knowledge categories to be additional to the object-related understandings that are basic to referential knowledge. However, she considers person knowledge to be linked with object knowledge in the way children acquire their understanding of both. The person-object knowledge discussed by Sugarman (Chapter 1) and by Snow (Chapter 2) suggests that both have their origins in early stages of prelinguistic communications. Beyond the early knowledge schemata, person knowledge describes how persons represent the world. The key issue is the child's increasing understanding of the social perspectives of others. Such social perspectives are linked also to knowledge of social categories and to event knowledge. Social categories combined with knowledge of object categories provide understanding of the dimensional meanings of social context. These categories are static, whereas event knowledge relates to familiar sequences. Knowledge of these events, in turn, enables the child to understand how persons act upon each other to produce social events. The knowledge categories discussed by Rice are especially meaningful when considered in light of presuppositional knowledge, discussed by DeHart and Maratsos in Chapter 6.

None of the four chapters reveals *how* children learn a language. However, in aggregate, they provide a wealth of essential information about the acquisition process. Interpersonal processes begin early in infancy when adults respond to the object- or person-related behavior of the infant. Early intentions (or assumed intentions) of the infant set in motion the response chain of the adult. The infant's object-object and person-object schemata emerge by the end of the first year. During the early months the adult is prone to interpret a wide range of infant physical movements and vocalizations as intentions to communicate, while the infant seems to be actively searching for contingencies among objects, persons, and events and the behavior of his caregivers. This behavior precedes and continues during the child's transition to word use.

All of the child's gestural, postural, vocal, and observational skills are brought into play in the games that infants and adults play. These games extend into a range of social, symbolic, and role play that children engage in during the preschool and early school years.

Several assumptions can be made about the early acquisitional periods. First, the process builds from stable relationships that involve frequent exchanges—a substantial amount of time is given to communication transactions. Second, the adult often attributes specific meanings and interactions to the child's prelinguistic behaviors. Third, transactions become more complex as the child's comprehensions and response repertoires permit the expansion of the range of game playing. Fourth, the adult adapts his communication style, including the modeling, imitating, and prompting, to the child's level. Fifth, the child's communicative competencies develop in a highly individualized manner so that exact sequences of acquisition are difficult to establish across children. For this reason, instead of standard, step-by-step acquisition of form and function, we find individualized sequences for each child.

Dimensions of Communicative Competence

Section II includes discussion of negatives and interrogatives (de Villiers), presuppositions (DeHart and Maratsos), point sharing (MacWhinney), and requests (Gordon and Ervin-Tripp). Each chapter concerns the child's emerging competence. Whereas the first section concerns *how* language is learned, the second section relates generally to *what* is learned.

Chapter 5 (de Villiers) provides a partial bridge between the *how* and *what* issues. The chapter sets up a framework for analyzing the grammatical *form*, which conveys the propositional content, and illocutionary *force*, which indicates the speaker's intention in making the utterance. Six hypotheses are presented to aid the study of these form and force components. The bridging functions are apparent in the hypotheses. For instance, the first hypothesis focuses on precursors and the second on the possible order of precursor functions. Although de Villiers considers the issues raised by Sugarman and Snow, she begins from the standpoint of form (negatives and interrogatives) and proceeds to study the precursor functions indicated in such research. In like fashion de Villiers covers form-function mappings, parent-child transactions, social and event knowledge, and indirect expressions.

Perhaps de Villiers's main contribution to the discussion is to highlight the need for further research on form and force functions. Nevertheless the analysis provides interesting implications for the continuity of development in the first two years and limited evidence for precursor functions. There is evidence that form-function mappings broaden with age. De Villiers's chapter provides an interesting confirmation of the conclusions drawn in the first four chapters and, by introducing the analysis of negatives and questions, provides an entrée to the descriptive dimensions in the chapters that follow.

DeHart and Maratsos's (Chapter 6) discussion of presuppositions is in some respects a continuation of Rice's discussion. Presuppositions are essentially the "semantic or pragmatic assumptions of a speaker, as reflected in the words, linguistic forms, and sentential devices he uses" (p. 239). The assumptions include the person knowledge, social category knowledge, and event knowledge discussed by Rice as well as the object knowledge and person knowledge discussed by Sugarman.

Presuppositions, according to DeHart and Maratsos, may include assumptions about word meaning, assumptions about what the listener knows, or assumptions about the social context in which the speaker and listener find themselves. The authors believe that some rudimentary form of presupposition exists in the child's early use of language and that the child gradually develops sophistication in a wide range of word choices, sentential devices, and social roles.

Chapter 6 concerns the basic presuppositions associated with communication, presuppositions carried by particular linguistic forms, and presuppositions carried by general linguistic devices. The authors suggest that the appropriate question is not how children learn to presuppose, but rather how children learn to understand and express the particular presuppositions carried by various words and linguistic devices. They also suggest that the mastery of many presuppositional devices depends on and parallels the acquisition of other cognitive and linguistic skills.

Gordon and Ervin-Tripp (Chapter 7) provide a structure for analyzing children's requests. In so doing, they analyze social and situational variables and provide a design for analyzing instrumental language. Instrumental language gets a hearer to cooperate with or carry out a goal of a speaker. Social relationships and situational variables affect which strategy is selected, which in turn affects the type of instrumental act (e.g., request) expressed. Requests are either conventional (obtain cooperation by asking for it) or nonconventional (cite reasons, goals, or obstacles). Conventional and nonconventional requests may be directed to exactly the same purpose, but may express different strategies. The discussion of these strategies takes us beyond form to the nature of the child's instrumental concepts of social motivation and social interaction.

In Chapter 8 MacWhinney provides a comprehensive account of what a child must learn to be a competent "point sharer." MacWhinney's point-sharing system includes both the speaker (the point sharer) and the listener (the point user). Twelve of the most prominent devices for point sharing are presented along with their polysemic structure. (A polyseme is an alternative reading of a lexical item; many English words have dozens of alternative minor readings with a common thread of meaning.) To share points effectively, the child must acquire the various point-sharing devices and their polysemes.

MacWhinney does not discuss the development of point sharing in children. Instead, he presents a dictionary of devices and polysemes. In a brief analysis at the end of his chapter he explains that the child, in order to make successful use of the devices of the point-sharing system, "must construct the basic structures of a dictionary, a grammar, and encyclopedia, a diary with a lexical, referent, and discourse memory, and a rhetoricon" (p. 363). This analysis of five systems constitutes an extension to the theory of functionalist grammar found in

Bates and MacWhinney (1982). MacWhinney provides a structure for a system of point sharing to which can be added more complex elaborations.

Children across Cultures

In Chapter 9, Schieffelin and Eisenberg provide a useful analysis of cultural variations and suggestions for studying the problems a child from another culture might encounter in his new setting. The school adjustment of the child from another culture may be complicated by the difference in discourse style used in the school and in the home. This is in contrast to other schoolchildren whose discourse styles at work and at home are similar. It is suggested that we analyze the difficulties that minority children have in adjusting to the style of discourse used by the dominant culture. The primary issue is that faulty communication can occur when individuals from different cultural groups interact.

The authors point out that societies differ greatly in the amount of verbal interaction that occurs between adults and children. Also, they differ as to who does the talking, who does the listening, and who is expected to initiate a conversation. Are children encouraged to maintain a conversation? How is turn taking accomplished? Finally, there are numerous performance differences in interactive behavior. For instance, do adults respond freely to children and expand their responses? Are children expected to be direct or indirect in making requests? Are interactions supported by nonverbal signs such as direction of gaze?

Schieffelin and Eisenberg imply that the tools and methods of ethnographic research should be utilized in educational planning for cultural minorities. Such planning might improve the quality of education for minority children. The prospects are that such work could lead adult caregivers and teachers to combine efforts in adapting better to children who have communication styles that may differ from those used at school.

Developmentally Different Children

The preceding discussion was related to normal language-learning children. The focus has been upon the antecedents, precursors, and sequences of the development of communicative competence together with a discussion of forms and strategies children use to communicate. However, the language of developmentally different children is also examined, with two purposes in mind. The first is to provide contrastive information on the development of communicative competence. The second is to provide a perspective for intervention. The latter is the topic of the discussion section at the end of the book.

Language-Disordered Children Rice points out that language-disordered children pose serious assessment problems because they have difficulty formulating grammatically complex and socially appropriate responses. She suggests that we need new methods for inferring communicative competence, methods that are based upon nonlinguistic means of deducing conceptual knowledge. Improved methods of assessment would greatly facilitate our understandings of the ways both disordered and normal children communicate.

Rice finds the research data about language-disordered children difficult to interpret. She speculates that children who do not adjust their language to social contexts may fail to do so because they have not yet acquired the corresponding social knowledge. Perhaps children are insensitive to subtleties of socially based linguistic variations because they do not understand the structures of verbal language. These speculations can be answered reliably only through further research.

Synder, like Rice, finds language-disordered children to be variable. Some have deficits in performative skills and others do not. However, generally, "they could not formulate request forms with the range of strategies and devices that are available to normal children" (p. 434). Also, the findings suggest that the presuppositions of older language-disordered children enable them to consider their listener and to mobilize language to effectively inform a listener. However, they seem to use less complex forms and have more difficulty in revising messages than do normal children. Language-disordered children may have difficulty recalling narratives and integrating ideas. In addition, they have difficulty separating their own reality from the fictions in the story. Finally, they seem to be less assertive and active in conversational exchanges.

From the information presented by Snyder and Rice one is inclined to speculate that many language-disordered children have more comprehension of social contexts and devices than they have expressive conversational skills. Perhaps the challenge to caregivers and teachers is to provide a range of responsive experiences leading to more active conversational devices.

Mentally Retarded Children Although mentally retarded children are delayed in the development of communicative competence when compared with age peers, the picture is less clear when they are matched with younger normal children at a comparable stage of cognitive development. Oller, Tharp, and Coleman (1978) found that such groupings produced similar semantic information and syntactic constructions, but that the normally developing children used a higher proportion of advanced speech act strategies.

Greenwald and Leonard (1979) found that Stage 5 (Piaget's sensorimotor stage) Down's syndrome children did not perform as well on declarative tasks as did normal children at the same stage of development. Also, they found that the Down's syndrome group did not combine vocalizations with gestures as often as did the normal children. However, the retarded group showed higher functional performance as compared to the matched group. The investigator attributed this finding to the relatively longer period of time spent in the sensorimotor stage. Miller, Chapman, and Bedrosian (1977) made a similar observation. The assumptions made by these investigators are that the longer period gives the retarded child more communicative experience and that this additional experience can enhance some retarded children. However, for others the interactions may lead to dysynchronous development.

Longhurst and Berry (1975) found a relationship between IQ and the style of transaction. Children with higher IQs attended more to the needs of listeners and to listener cues. Also, they made more informative revisions based on these cues. However, other investigators have found that retarded children are sensitive to listeners.

Autistic Children Autistic children display dramatic problems in communication. Prominent among the behavioral descriptors are impaired interpersonal relationships resulting from lack of eye contact and decreased physical contact, deficient social play and self-help behaviors, stereotyped behaviors, and disturbance of speech and language (Simmons and Tynchuk, 1973). The statements of autistic children often seem to bear little relation to the context or the situation. Their utterances often appear to be delayed echolalia. Consequently, their verbalizations have been considered to be devoid of communicative intent.

These observations suggest that autistic children do not consider their listeners and do not seek to evoke interest in their listeners. Thus, their communicative efficiency appears to be low. They convey and attend inefficiently in a communication context. Recent research suggests that their deviant behavior might be reduced if we investigate the informativeness of their delayed echolalia. Baltaxe and Simmons (1975), Schuler (1980), and Prizant (1978) found primitive communicative functions in such utterances and suggested that the autistic child's echolalic utterances are more informative than our casual observations lead us to believe. Careful observation by Prizant (1978) of the conceptual conditions in which echolalia occurs revealed as many as four communicative functions. Thus, studies of the speech acts of the autistic highlighted both their communicative deficits and their previously overlooked abilities.

One of the more revealing analyses of the early communication behavior of an autistic child is provided by Sugarman (this volume).

She found that one autistic child did not progress smoothly from object-object to person-object routines, but learned them separately and integrated them later. Also, the child's slow development of social initiatives seemed to be limited largely to interpersonal rituals. Improvements in socialization emerged by a process of elaborating these routines.

Blind Children Urwin (Chapter 10) finds some early transaction problems also for young blind children. They do not invite reciprocal gazing nor direct the adult's attention to objects by pointing nor otherwise convey intentions in the visual modes as do normal infants. They may not invite adult attention. Consequently, the blind infant may experience fewer preverbal communication events. Studies of normal infants have placed great emphasis upon visually based communication systems. Parents of blind children must adjust to other receptive and expressive modes if they are to monitor their infant's attention. To avoid delays in their acquisition of language, blind children must be encouraged to develop alternative means for expressing intentions and engaging in the mutual signaling of intent. Unless this is done a blind child may be delayed in social transactions and object exploration during the early years.

Fraiberg (1977) found that blind children vocalize less than sighted children at a similar age. They are delayed in the development of attachment behavior, sensorimotor intelligence, and symbolic play. In general, parents of blind children wait longer for the emergence of language than do parents of sighted children.

Communication Problems with Early Impairment In normal infant-caregiver transactions, the infant's active visual and movement cues provide the adult with sufficient inducements to play. In contrast, the handicapped child—e.g., autistic, retarded, blind—may present limited or seemingly nonrelevant cues. The adults' task then must be to learn to "read" these less functional repertoires and to respond appropriately to them. They must be more active initiators to evoke communication in the absence of spontaneous infant responding. Adults must cultivate nonstandard responses to fit the unique channeling capabilities of the infant. The blind infant provides a good illustration of this need. Because the child does not invite eye contact and reciprocal gazing nor call mutual attention to distal objects nor point to communicate interactions, the adult is faced with constraints in trying to fashion play sequences. Other means for engaging in transaction sequences must be found.

This visual constraint on early communication is contrastive in many ways to the problems posed by deaf infants. Deaf infants have the visual cuing features lacking in the blind infant but do not attend to sound cues provided by the caregiver. Consequently, the deaf infant has difficulty with vocal responding, vocal imitation, and subsequent formation of wordlike responses.

Other impairments, such as cerebral palsy (motor responding and motor cuing problems), retardation (attentional and sensorimotor delays), or autism (limited social responses), pose serious limitations for early communication exchanges. The caregiver in each instance is faced with constraints in arranging social transactions. The probability that parents can provide alternative functional responses and engage in expanding play activities may be low unless they are given direction and encouragement. However, additional research is needed to guide the professional in providing optimal instructions and in understanding how to facilitate and augment the impaired infant through the early stages of preverbal communication. Similarly, there is an urgent need for optimal procedures to help impaired infants acquire a functional symbol system so that both input (a problem for deaf and severely retarded infants) and output (a problem for cerebral palsied and severely retarded children) can be combined for effective communication. In this stage of development the blind infant, who can both hear and vocalize, may have difficulties with shared environmental orientations essential for communication. The autistic child who has limited social contact may not participate socially and so does not experience frequent communication events.

In all instances of early impairments, the daily relationships with adult caregivers provides the means for subsequent communicative competences. This general observation applies to children across nations and cultures.

DISCUSSION AND SUMMARY

How do children learn to communicate competently? Sugarman explains that infants first interact separately with persons and objects. Next, they combine person- and object-oriented activity in a single exchange, using a person to obtain an object, and using an object to solicit the attention of a person. Sugarman also observes that coordinated person-object activities provide for a range of play activities in which the child increasingly signals his intentions. All of this precedes the emergence of the first word. The extensive communicative experiences that take place coordinately with adult caregivers may prompt the search for a more effective means of communication. Thus, Sugarman introduces the probability that communication experiences precede the emergence of language and, in addition, may create the contexts and the incentives for symbolic behaviors.

This possibility is also considered by Snow, who finds that the first words express the same intentions that the child expresses nonverbally and that both the verbal and the nonverbal expressions are embedded in the social context. Both expressions may communicate intentions and needs. The nonverbal expressions are antecedent to the verbal and may be prerequisite to them. Snow points out that turn-taking and event sequences are also taught in play.

Sachs divides play activities into social play, symbolic play, and role play. Each is assumed to make an important contribution to the child's social and cognitive development: "language and play are closely related to each other as well as to the child's cognitive development" (p. 134).

The play activities enable the child to explore and experience a range of make-believe and real-world roles on the way to learning how to question (de Villiers), request (Gordon and Ervin-Tripp), and share points (MacWhinney). The conventional and the nonconventional forms of requesting may be learned from play experiences during the preschool and early school years.

One gains the impression that the developing child usually has a rich environment in which to learn how to be competent. As Snow and Sachs point out, the normal child is buffered from adverse developmental outcomes. There are more than enough favorable experiences to enable the child to learn the culturally expected styles of communication. As Schieffelin and Eisenberg point out, the styles will reflect the beliefs and values of the particular culturally embedded speech community. However, for handicapped children the picture changes. The realities for each child may call for an optimized environment in which a greatly increased amount of social stimulation is required. The determination of each child's special needs may enable the adults to provide the additional instrumental experience. In the absence of this special assistance the handicapped child may fail to achieve expected levels of competence.

What do children learn that makes them communicatively competent? The content of this book would suggest that children learn how to: 1) match forms and forces flexibly (de Villiers); 2) make presuppositions about linguistic forms, devices, and the roles of speaker and listener (DeHart and Maratsos); 3) make requests so that their purposes will be achieved (Gordon and Ervin-Tripp); 4) use a system of grammatical devices for sharing points (MacWhinney); and 5) use these devices of language effectively in their cultural contexts (Schieffelin and Eisenberg).

These discussions about dimensions of language knowledge and skill cover a range of issues. However, they do not describe the full range of communicative competence, and at present it probably is not feasible to propose such a description. However, the discussions may be useful for clinicians and intervention researchers (see Afterword) and for helping the reader to understand the development of communicative competence. The content provides numerous suggestions about the gaps in knowledge. These suggestions highlight the need for continued research.

REFERENCES

Baltaxe, C., and Simmons, L. 1975. Language patterns of autistic adolescents. *In* P. Mittler (ed.), Research to Practice in Mental Retardation. University Park Press, Baltimore.

Bates, E., and MacWhinney, B. 1982. Functionalist approaches to grammar. *In* L. Gleitman and E. Wanner (eds.), Language Acquisition: The State of the Art. Cambridge University Press, New York.

Bowerman, M. 1982. Language development. *In* H. Triandis and H. Heron (eds.), Handbook of Cross Cultural Psychology, Vol. 4: Developmental Psychology. Allyn & Bacon, Inc., Boston.

Campbell, R., and Wales, R. 1970. The study of language acquisition. *In* J. Lyons (ed.), New Horizons in Linguistics. Penguin Books, Harmondsworth, England.

Chomsky, N. 1957. Syntactic Structures. Mouton, The Hague.

Chomsky, N. 1959. Review of Skinner. Language 35:26–58.

Chomsky, N. 1965. Aspects of the Theory of Syntax. MIT Press, Cambridge, MA.

Fraiberg, S. 1977. Insights from the Blind. Souvenir Press, London.

Greenwald, C., and Leonard, L. 1979. Communicative and sensorimotor development in Down's syndrome children. Am. J. Ment. Defic. 84:296–303.

Gumperz, J., and Hymes, D. 1964. The ethnography of communication. Am. Anthropol. 66(6), Pt. 2.

Hymes, D. 1964. Formal discussion. *In* U. Bellugi and R. Brown (eds.), The Acquisition of Language. Monogr. Soc. Res. Child Dev. 29(1, Serial no. 92).

Hymes, D. 1971. Competence and performance in linguistic theory. *In* R. Huxley and E. Ingram (eds.), Language Acquisition: Models and Methods. Academic Press, London.

Longhurst, T., and Berry, C. 1975. Communication in retarded adolescents: Response to listener feedback. Am. J. Ment. Defic. 80:158:164.

Miller, J., Chapman, R., and Bedrosian, J. 1977. Defining developmentally disabled subjects for research: The relationship between etiology, cognitive development, language and communicative performance. Paper presented at the Second Annual Boston University Conference on Language Development, Boston.

Oller, D., Tharp, T., and Coleman, D. 1978. A natural logic of pragmatic function of language. Paper presented at the Third Annual Boston University Conference on Language Development, Boston.

Prizant, B. 1978. An analysis of the functions of immediate echolalia. Unpublished Ph.D. dissertation, State University of New York, Buffalo.

Schuler, A. 1980. The interaction of social linguistic and cognitive development in childhood autism. *In* W. Fay and A. Schuler (eds.), Emerging Language in Autistic Children. University Park Press, Baltimore.

Simmons, J., and Tynchuk, A. 1973. The learning deficits in childhood psychosis. Pediatr. Clin. North Am. 20:665–679.

Slobin, D. 1967. A Field Manual for the Cross-Cultural Study of the Acquisition of Communicative Competence. A.S.U.C. Bookstore, Berkeley, CA.

Section I

Developmental Factors and Functions

The Development of Preverbal Communication
Its Contribution and Limits in Promoting the Development of Language

Susan Sugarman

Department of Psychology
Princeton University
Princeton, New Jersey

Editors' Note

There are significant developments in communication prior to the onset of language. After a period during which they tend to focus on persons or objects in their interactions, children gradually bring these two pursuits together. The result is that an intent to communicate becomes increasingly evident in the children's behavior, before they begin to speak.

Topics included here are theoretical and methodological issues involved in studying preverbal communication, a combined longitudinal and cross-sectional study of preverbal communication in normal infants, a study of the communicative development in institutionalized infants, and a study of a young autistic child. The final section addresses the significance of preverbal communication in the development of a first language.

All the studies reveal the same sequence of preverbal communicative developments. Intentional communication develops prior to language—that is, the discovery of communication occurs prior to the emergence of first words. However, the existing data do not indicate unequivocally that preverbal communication is prerequisite to language. Rather, the data show preverbal communication, as operationalized here, to be antecedent to and linked with the emergence of language in a higher order cognitive-developmental chain. Still, the data do strongly suggest a prerequisite status for preverbal communication and, consequently, an instrumental role for early preverbal experience in subsequent language acquisition.

contents

CONCEPTUAL AND METHODOLOGICAL ISSUES IN THE STUDY OF PREVERBAL COMMUNICATION 26

    The Object of Inquiry: The Intention to Communicate 27
    Inferring Communicative Intent in the Preverbal Child 27
    Cognition and Communicative Development:
        The Predicted Sequence 29

STUDY 1: DEVELOPMENT OF PERSON-OBJECT COORDINATION IN NORMAL INFANTS IN A HOME ENVIRONMENT 30

    Procedure 31
    Results 36
    Discussion 44

STUDY 2: DEVELOPMENT OF PERSON-OBJECT COORDINATION IN INSTITUTIONALIZED INFANTS 46

    Methods 47
    Results 47
    Discussion 49

STUDY 3: COMMUNICATIVE DEVELOPMENT IN AN AUTISTIC CHILD 51

    Etiology 52
    Technique 53
    Observations 54
    Discussion 58

GENERAL DISCUSSION: IMPLICATIONS OF DEVELOPING THE ABILITY TO COMMUNICATE BEFORE LANGUAGE 60

ACKNOWLEDGMENTS 64

REFERENCES 64

It is claimed that human language is so complexly and uniquely structured that we would be unable to acquire it without some innate predisposition toward linguistic structure (Chomsky, 1968). It is also claimed that prelinguistic developments, such as sensorimotor intelligence and nonlinguistic symbolization, prime children for acquiring language (see Rice, this volume).

Although these claims are often opposed, they are both very likely true and are merely at cross-purposes. If prelinguistic developments do contribute to language acquisition, this fact does not refute the claim that language is constrained to develop in a particular direction, and it leaves much of linguistic structure unaccounted for. Conversely, the presence of an innate component of language, if there is one, does not explain *how* children acquire language (Chomsky, 1968, p. 76 and note 19; Luria, 1974/1975). That is, the claim that the system is constrained to develop in a particular direction does not implicate any particular set of mechanisms by which this development might occur. Prelinguistic developments must be among the factors that condition children to acquire language, at least insofar as they motivate children to look for a language to learn.

This chapter is concerned with the development of communication prior to speech. The working hypothesis is that communication develops prior to speech and might prompt the search for increasingly efficient means of communicating, including, eventually, language. This hypothesis is more difficult to demonstrate than it might appear. However, is necessary to begin with a more basic question: does communication begin when children start to talk, or are there significant developments in communication prior to the onset of language?

The thrust of recent developmental research is that: 1) infants do communicate before they begin to talk; and 2) this communicative ability evolves over the first year of life (see selections in Bullowa, 1979, and Lock, 1979a; also see Bates, 1976, 1979; Bruner, 1975a, 1975b; Dore, 1974; Ryan, 1974; Sugarman, 1978). The import of this development for language is not yet clear. What is ambiguous is not whether preverbal communication is related to language at all, but how, and exactly which, preverbal communicative abilities affect language development. The search for strategies of language intervention, toward which this volume is directed, highlights these uncertainties. Ultimately one wants to know what skills to cultivate in order to facilitate the development of language in problem cases. This task is greatly aided by knowing what skills are necessary, or likely to be necessary, to the development of language in nonproblem cases. Definitive iden-

---

Preparation of this manuscript was supported by NICHHD grant HD 05951. Portions of the data were collected while the author held a Hampshire College Fellowship from the Calder Foundation.

tification of prerequisites to language is problematic for reasons that are given later. However, the available evidence can be critically examined for what can and cannot be fairly confidently said about the relation between preverbal communication and language.

The first section of this chapter attempts to clarify some of the theoretical and methodological issues involved in studying preverbal communication. It establishes a working definition of communication that is applicable to the preverbal period and considers in principle the relation between communication and cognition. The second section examines in detail a combined longitudinal and cross-sectional study of preverbal communication and cognition in normal home-reared infants (Sugarman, 1973, 1978). The third section of the chapter explores a cross-sectional study of communicative development in institutionalized infants, and the fourth reviews a case study of communicative development in a young autistic child. Because the latter two studies were undertaken in part as pilot projects for the study of normal development, they are incomplete in many ways. They are included here to highlight the potential contribution of studies of atypical development to our understanding of the relation between preverbal communication and language. The final section addresses the significance of preverbal communicative development for the development of a first language.

All three studies reveal the same sequence of preverbal communicative developments. The observed behavior patterns indicate that intentional communication develops prior to language. The normal home-reared children and the autistic child began to speak shortly after reaching the final step in the preverbal sequence, but the institutionalized children did not begin to speak until several months later. Consequently, intentional communication may be a necessary stepping stone to language, but it is not a sufficient one.

CONCEPTUAL AND METHODOLOGICAL ISSUES IN THE STUDY OF PREVERBAL COMMUNICATION

The notion that communication precedes the development of language is not new. The evidence originally cited in support of this position consists of the infant's prespeech *sounds*, which were thought to serve a nonintellective or expressive function (e.g., DeLaguna, 1963; Jesperson, 1964; Vygotsky, 1962). Although the insight that speaking evolves from a prespeech communicative source is reasonable, two problems inhere in identifying that source simply as sounds.

First, the data base is overly restrictive. Although speech is vocal, there is no obvious reason why the behaviors relevant to prespeech communication should be limited to vocalizations, unless one is studying the phonetic transition to language; and, if that is the case, then one is arguably not studying communication per se (see below). It is even overly restrictive to limit the relevant repertoire to behaviors with high social potency, such as smiling and eye-to-eye contact. The ontogeny of a particular function is at issue, not the ontogeny of a particular behavior or class of behaviors. (See de Villiers' review of the research on negation, in this volume, for more discussion of this issue.)

The second problem is more conceptual. It is not clear that the uttering of expressive sounds by itself constitutes communication (it should be admitted here that, with the possible exception of DeLaguna, the early writers were not making claims about communication as such, but were concerned with the "origins of speech"). Communication involves more than the emitting of a behavior with a high social potency.

The Object of Inquiry: The Intention to Communicate

Communication involves the *intention* to convey an idea to someone else. This is what distinguishes communication from the production simply of expressive or other interpretable behaviors. On many occasions we may infer the desires, feelings, or intentions of another individual by watching that person's behavior. Indeed, before they talk, normal children growing up in a normal environment engage in varied exchanges with their caregivers during which the caregivers readily interpret the children's behaviors (Ryan, 1974; Snow, this volume). However, the fact that an act is interpretable, even if the interpretation is universal or culture wide, does not mean that the actor intended to communicate (Weiner et al., 1972). The intention to communicate is something distinct from the intention to accomplish something, however visibly evident the intention to accomplish something might be (Sugarman, 1978).

It is the development of the intention to communicate that is of interest in the present chapter. Our principal question was whether the intention to communicate could be said to exist prior to talking, and, if so, how this intention develops and when it appears relative to the emergence of language.

Inferring Communicative Intent in the Preverbal Child

The identification of communicative intent is more complicated with a preverbal child than it is with a child who talks. Talking involves conventional, specialized behavior that almost automatically signals communicative intent (an exception would be autistic speech). In contrast, when we have the impression that a (preverbal) 10-month-old is attempting to communicate, the particular behaviors in which the child is engaged are behaviors that can also serve practical ends; they are not reserved just for communication. An example would be the child's reaching for something.

What is it about the child's nonverbal behavior that might make an intent to communicate increasingly clear? The present studies addressed this question by focusing on the way children organize sequences of relatively neutral behaviors (unritualized behaviors that serve a variety of social and pragmatic ends) in social contexts. It was necessary first to determine how a preverbal child might be able to make clear both his intentions regarding some state of affairs and the fact that he is communicating. Expression of both functions in one single act would require representational-symbolic intelligence (see Halliday, 1975, for a related argument), which children below 1 year of age are believed not to possess (see, e.g., Fischer, 1980; Piaget, 1963). Children below 1 year of age who lack representational intelligence might, however, express this two-faceted intentionality sequentially. They could do this by juxtaposing actions concerning some external state of affairs, for example an object, with bids (actions or vocalizations) made toward a person.

An example of what we later refer to as a "coordinated person-object" interaction would involve a child who solicits his mother's attention by touching her arm and looking at her face, and subsequently reaches for an object on her lap. This sequence contrasts with the behavior of the child who strains to pull an object from his mother's lap and who devotes his full attention to the object. The communicative "valence" of each sequence is the same: in each one the child's desire to possess something is equally clear (see de Villiers, this volume, for a similar point). The difference between these sequences lies, then, not in how visibly evident the children's practical goals are, but in the way those intentions are conveyed. By combining explicit bids toward the mother with efforts to obtain the object, the first child appears to be *indicating* his intentions (to obtain the object) to someone else, rather than simply pursuing them. It could be said that this child marks behaviorally, if globally, what action or reaction is expected of whom regarding what thing.

Two aspects of this analysis should be clarified. First, one might question what looks like unabashed empiricism in the selection of criteria to index "intentional communication," i.e., actions directed toward an external object combined with actions directed toward a person. One can easily imagine cases in which such coordination is not obvious but in which an intent to communicate is still present. Conversations between adults frequently do not involve objects, and, when adults ask for an object, they may do so while looking away from the intended provider. Adults and older children, however, use conventional codes that act as social signals even when the individual using them is not explicitly oriented toward his interlocutor (see Bates, 1979). In the absence of such codes, the explicit coordination of person and object orientations serves to identify probable cases of communicative intent.

A second, related, point concerns exactly what is being claimed about the child's intentions in these episodes. On the one hand, the notion of intentionality is central to any account of communication (see, e.g., Austin, 1962; Searle, 1969). On the other hand, it is precarious and fruitless to try to specify when a child does and does not possess certain intentions (Bruner, 1975b; Nelson, 1978). This is not what is being attempted here. Instead the *visibility* of certain intentions is being characterized from the *observer's point of view*. This emphasis on visibility not only permits an objective research strategy, but also highlights a central criterion for successful communication.

Cognition and Communicative Development: The Predicted Sequence

The communicative feats of which children are capable should reflect their level of cognitive development. The above discussion already alluded to one of the ways in which the cognitive competency of preverbal children must constrain their communicative interactions. A child who has not yet developed mental representation will not be able to draw upon means of communication that are dependent upon mental representation. However, it was also suggested that, despite this limitation, prerepresentational children should be able to demonstrate an intent to communicate that is distinct from an intent simply to accomplish something.

It is possible to ground this claim more specifically in the kinds of intelligent coordination children are known to develop during the prerepresentational period. As is argued in detail later, the "coordinated person-object" sequence described above, which was presented as a reasonable index of intentional communication, involves instrumental coordination. The child who solicits his mother's attention and then reaches for an object on her lap uses one means (bidding toward the mother) for obtaining a discretely different end (obtaining the object). Because the "means" are indirectly, rather than directly, related to the goal, instrumental behavior is involved. A second, more widely documented, type of instrumental coordination involves two physical objects, as opposed to a person and an object. Examples of this "object-object" coordination include using a cushion to pull a watch forward and using a stick to bat a toy forward. Because object-object coordination is known to appear toward the end of the first year (Duncker, 1945; Piaget, 1963), it is reasonable to expect other kinds of instrumental coordination, including instrumental relations involving people, to appear at about the same age. In other words, it is reasonable to expect intentional communication, operationalized as person-object coordination, to appear by the end of the first year—that is, prior to speech.

The presence of instrumental behavior in both person-object and object-object coordination would lead one to expect that the steps involved in achieving one type of coordination are similar to those involved in achieving the other. Instrumental coordination of two physical objects is preceded by a series of developments in which objects are used or pursued separately by the child. During this time children develop a rich and differentiated repertoire for dealing with individual objects. In fact, prior to the time when children coordinate two objects instrumentally, their intentions with respect to some goal object may be abundantly clear, yet still fail; and despite repeated failures to reach this goal, they do not bring a second object to their aid (Duncker, 1945; Piaget, 1963). A major hypothesis in the studies below was that the development of person-object coordination in social interaction follows a developmental course similar to that of object-object coordination. This hypothesis follows from the assumption that both patterns are subject to the same cognitive-developmental constraints. Thus, it was expected that children would first interact separately with persons and objects, even in contexts in which persons and objects were both present. They would then begin to engage in increasingly differentiated behavior patterns within each type of pursuit. Next, they would begin to combine person- and object-oriented activity in a single exchange, e.g., using a person to obtain an object, and using an object to solicit the attention of a person. It was expected that this series of developments would coincide with analogous developments in instrumental object-object coordination, at least in normal development.

STUDY 1: DEVELOPMENT OF PERSON-OBJECT COORDINATION IN NORMAL INFANTS IN A HOME ENVIRONMENT

A large body of spontaneous social-interactive behavior data was obtained from the observation of seven first-born infants. The study began with two girls and one boy 4 to 5 months of age, and with two girls and two boys 8 to 9.5 months. Subjects were solicited on the basis of their Amherst, Massachusetts birth records. Initial contact with parents was made by mail, and final arrangements were made by phone. Families were informed that the infant's communicative behavior and play were to be observed.

Procedure

All subjects were observed in their homes, usually with only the mother present. Subjects were observed monthly for 5 months. Each session consisted of three parts: an observation period, a communication elicitation task, and two of the Uzgiris-Hunt (1975) scales that measure instrumental coordination according to Piagetian (Piaget, 1963, 1971) stages. Observation of spontaneous social-interactive behavior was normally terminated after an hour. Prolonged observation was necessary in only three of 35 sessions. If the infant was drowsy, the observer remained present until a minimum of 45 sequences had been recorded. The communication task and the Uzgiris-Hunt scales were administered by the observer after the observation hour, so as not to bias the observations.

Spontaneous Social-Interactive Behavior Social-interactive behavior of both infant and mother was recorded with pencil and paper by the otherwise passive observer. When the child approached the observer, the observer responded minimally and recorded the interaction. Ongoing activity—for example, diaper changing—was also noted. A special notational system was used to record all interactions. A list of notational symbols appears in Table 1 and a representative data sheet appears in Table 2.

The joint satisfaction of two criteria determined an instance of social interaction for recording purposes: 1) activity by two people, and 2) at least one participant oriented at least partially toward the other. Sequences of interaction were considered terminated when either of these two criteria was no longer being met. However, instances in which one participant remained oriented toward the other were noted, e.g., mother disappears and child looks in direction of exit.

Social interactive behaviors were recorded during the session, but were not scored until afterward. Immediately after each observation session, the child's behavior in each sequence of interaction was scored. The scoring categories were based on the orientation and the complexity of the child's activity.

Two orientation categories were used: *single orientation* toward person *or* object, and *coordinated person-object orientation*. In a single person-oriented exchange, the child focuses only on the person and treats her socially by directing a gesture, eye contact, and/or vocalization to her. In a single object-oriented interaction, the child directs his behavior toward an object external to both child and adult. Another person is present in object-oriented interactions (the presence of another person is required for the sequence to be counted), but no obvious social bidding occurs. Thus, the adult simply serves as the location or

Table 1. Notation symbols for social-interactive behavior

Referent	Symbol
Participants	
participants in interaction	a, b, c, etc.
Objects	
object	ob
objects (alternative to *ob*)	bottle, car, etc.
object of action or glance unclear	x
Actions	
looks at	O
smiles	S
laughs	L
touches	T
holds	H
reaches	R
pulls	P
points	N
approaches	A
recedes	D
gives	G
takes, receives	C
frets, cries	F
vocalizes	V
pulls self up	U
global, diffuse activity	Z
all other actions[a]	(written out as necessary)
Sequence	
sequential behaviors	(A)—(B)
simultaneous behaviors	(A)·(B)
Context	
ongoing behaviors, noted separately	diapering, feeding, etc.

Reprinted by permission from Sugarman, S. 1978. Some organizational aspects of preverbal communication. *In* I. Markova (ed.), The Social Context of Language. John Wiley & Sons, Inc., New York.

[a] In some cases in which subjects were becoming capable of increasingly complex behavior, a more global notation was employed, e.g., *mother demonstrates act* (stacking rings on pole)—*child watches act—child reproduces act.*

occasion of the child's activity, rather than as a social partner. In contrast, in coordinated person-object interaction the child combines behavior directed toward a person with behavior directed toward an object.

A simple-complex distinction was made within the single-orientation category. This distinction was intended to reflect how visible the children's intentions were. It is analogous to Piaget's (1963, 1971) distinction between unitary actions applied to an external object (sec-

Table 2. Consecutive sequences observed for subject MM at 9.5 Months

Sequences	Context notes
	m = mother
	c = child
	s = observer
1. mV·Oc—cSm—mVc—mSc	(in living rm.; m on
2. mOc—cOm	couch; c on floor; s in chair)
3. mA·Oc—cOm—mV·Oc—cV·Om	(m off couch)
4. cOs—sOc	
5. cOs—sOc	
6. cOs—sOc	
7. cAm—cTm—cPm—mOc—m(Lift)c—mVc—cV·S·Om	
8. m(Kiss)c—cV·Om	
9. m(Roll)ball c—cH ball—cOm—mV·Oc—cOm—mV·Oc—cOm—mO·Vc—c(Roll)ball	(m and c at opposite ends of room; m saying "Roll the ball . . .")
10. cOm—mS·Vc—cSm—cV	
11. cH ball (toward)m—mO·V·Sc—cH ball (toward)m—mO·Vc—cZ·O·Vm	

Reprinted by permission from Sugarman, S. 1978. Some organizational aspects of preverbal communication. *In* I. Markova (ed.), The Social Context of Language. John Wiley & Sons, Inc., New York.

a See notational symbols in Table 1.

ondary circular schemata) and the combination of several such actions, which permits construction of a clear means-end relation. Once able to combine acts, children can combine their initial action toward some object goal with a second action (for example, the removal of an obstacle) in order to further goal attainment (Piaget, 1963). Similarly, in the scoring of social interactions, sequences that involved a series of discrete behaviors oriented toward the same target were considered to be better reflections of goal-directed effort than were unitary action schemes.

Theoretically, the complex single (object)-orientation category could include instances in which a child actually used a material intermediary, for example a stick, to obtain a result or another object. This would make it analogous to coordinated person-object interaction, in which the child might appeal to a person to get an object. It will be recalled that one of the objectives of the study was to determine when and how person-object coordinations emerge relative to object-object coordinations.

A description of each social-interactive scoring category is provided below.

Simple single orientation: Unitary actions directed toward either a person or an object:

1. Simple person-oriented acts. These sequences involve a behavior (other than, or in addition to, looking) directed to a person. Examples: 1) child looks and/or smiles at adult; 2) adult looks at and vocalizes to child—child smiles at adult. These exchanges can be repeated several times in succession.
2. Simple object-oriented acts. The child manipulates or turns his attention to an external object. Another person is involved only incidentally. Behavior clusters are limited to unitary, largely repetitive acts, e.g., beating, mouthing. Example: adult holds object over child's cot—child beats at object, orienting solely toward that object—adult continues to dangle object.

Complex single orientation: Series of different discrete behaviors directed toward either a person or an object:

1. Complex person-oriented acts. These include approaches or responses to another person involving a combination of different behaviors directed to that person. Examples: 1) child looks, smiles at adult—child touches, tugs at adult clothing—adult lifts child; 2) adult vocalizes to, touches child—child looks, vocalizes, and reaches out toward adult—adult touches, shakes child.
2. Complex object-oriented acts. Different discrete behaviors are combined and directed exclusively toward an external object. The child does not direct his attention to the adult, nor does he clearly solicit the adult's assistance if he needs it. Examples: 1) child attempts to pull object from adult's lap—adult holds object on lap—child continues to pull, twist object—adult removes object; 2) adult gives child a box and lid—child takes objects without acknowledging adult—child puts lid on box.

Coordinated person-object orientation: The child makes clear his objective regarding the object and socially approaches the adult involved. Examples: 1) child looks up, touches adult's arm—adult acknowledges child—child reaches toward object in adult's lap; 2) child holds jar toward adult, looks at adult and vocalizes—adult takes jar from child, vocalizes to child; 3) adult jangles bell in front of child—child reaches toward bell, laughs at adult, touches adult's arm—adult jangles bell; 4) child vocalizes to adult, reaches toward chair—adult places child in chair.

Some exchanges that we ultimately categorize as complex person-oriented exchanges might appear to meet the criteria for coordinated person-object orientation exchanges. Consider, for instance, the child who approaches the adult, looks up, reaches, and tugs at the adult's arms. This episode resembles a coordinated exchange insofar as the child has marked his objective and how the other person is to help accomplish it. However, the approach and goal-oriented behaviors are continuous: they are all focused on the adult. Thus, the constituents of the child's bid are less differentiated than they would have to be if an external object (or a third person), as well as the adult interactee, were involved. Because it was the *visible* distinction between social contact and goal behaviors that was criterial to the coordinated person-object category, all sequences with no external object were excluded from that category and categorized among the complex single (person) interactions instead.

The present typology accommodated most of the interactive sequences that were recorded for every subject. The remaining sequences, those that were deemed unscorable, were noted separately. These included sequences in which the orientation of the infant's activity was not clear (e.g., flailing arms and legs upon being tickled by the adult), sequences in which the infant's activity or attention was directed elsewhere while the mother made social contact, and sequences in which fretting was the child's only activity. These diffuse sequences were excluded because the scoring categories depend upon the existence of a distinct orientation in the child's behavior. Additional unscored sequences included exchanges in which both the person and object orientations were present, but in which: 1) the adult clearly elicited each focus in succession (e.g., adult dangles object before child's face, then adult removes object and looks into child's face); or 2) the relation between the two foci was otherwise ambiguous (e.g., child manipulates object, suddenly looks up at adult across the room, returns to manipulating object). A final unscored group of sequences contained rituals (e.g., "peekaboo"), that is, reciprocal exchanges between the adult and the child that are built up over time and consist of a fixed set and order of actions. These sequences often involve a training element or a reliance on the mother's stereotyped behaviors. For a variety of reasons it was decided that these sequences would ultimately require a different kind of analysis. However, we acknowledge the potential contribution of these routines to the child's communicative development (see Ratner and Bruner, 1977; Urwin, 1978), particularly in cases in which the child and caregiver elaborate, rather than simply repeat, these routines. Exchanges of this sort are discussed anecdotally later in this chapter.

In summary, spontaneous social-interactive behaviors were categorized in terms of their orientation, and the integration of different orientations; for the single-orientation categories, the number of different actions involved was also a factor (length of sequence was not). An independent rater scored seven consecutive sequences from the middle of each session for three subjects. Together, these subjects spanned the entire age range observed. Agreement between this rater and the observer for these 105 sequences was 98%; the reliability of the original recording was not assessed.

Communication Elicitation Task The child's interest in a novel object was elicited while the child was seated. The object was then abruptly withdrawn; it was held away from the tester's head and out of the child's reach, but in his visual field. This procedure was repeated at least five times per session. Subjects' responses to the removal of an object were scored using categories that are slightly more differentiated than those applied to the naturalistic data (see Table 3).

Uzgiris-Hunt Scales The Uzgiris-Hunt (1975) scales for "Means of Achieving Desired Events" and "The Development of Causality" were administered. Subjects were assigned to a stage of sensorimotor intelligence (with respect to instrumental coordination) on the basis of their performance on both tests. In cases in which performance differed across tests, the scores were combined. However, performance on one scale was always within one stage of performance on the other (Sugarman, 1973, Appendices III.4 and IV.4), and the one-stage discrepancy occurred in only five out of the 35 test sessions.

Results

Children's social-interactive behavior developed in the order predicted. The youngest subjects' repertoires were dominated by unitary, repetitive actions directed toward a person or toward an object. Next to appear were differentiated actions toward a person or object in which the children's immediate goal was often clearly marked. Finally, integrated person-object activity emerged. With this final step, the children began to coordinate their pursuit of an object with social entreaties toward people. Each of these steps was associated with an analogous advance in object-object instrumental coordination.

Base Rate for Spontaneous Social Interaction The mean frequency of interactive sequences recorded per session was 64.1 for the entire sample. The means for individual subjects ($N = 7$) range from 52.6 to 74.8; frequencies for individual sessions ($N = 35$) ranged from 45 to 113. The frequency of recorded interactive sequences was not significantly correlated with age for any subject and did not differentiate the younger and older age groups.

Table 3. Communication Elicitation Task

No. of trials _____   Subject: _____
                                Age: _____
                                Date: _____

Seat the child in a high chair next to a table. Interest the child in an object; engage in play with child and object momentarily. Abruptly move the object out of reach, but still in the visual field of the child.

If the child indicates a desire for the object, make no response; if the child ceases activity, indicate a need for clarification, by saying, for example, "What's the matter?" Respond appropriately to the child's ensuing response, e.g., if the child wants the object, give it to him/her.

Mark the child's response for each trial on the appropriate line (indicate trial #: 1–5).

CHILD RESPONSE:
A. *Diffuse fuss or no reaction*   _____
B. *Simple, singly oriented activity*   _____
   B1. Looks at adult, only   _____
   B2. Looks at, reaches for object, only   _____
C. *Complex, singly oriented activity*   _____
   C1. Looks at and fusses (etc., multiple gestures) at   _____
       adult
   C2. Reaches for object, points, vocalizes, etc. in di- _____
       rection of object
   C3. Looks at and reaches for adult *hand*   _____
D. *Coordinated orientation activity, unadapted*   _____
   D1. Points at/reaches for object, and then looks (etc.) _____
       at adult
   D2. Points at/reaches for object, and then looks (etc.) _____
       at adult hand
E. *Coordinated orientation activity, adapted*   _____
   E1. Solicits adult's attention and then points at/   _____
       reaches for object
   E2. Repetition of D1 or E1.   _____

Note any language used by child.

The proportion of sequences in each category was computed for each session, based on the total number of sequences of interaction for that session. The data presented below contain trends in these proportions for each subject. A combined index of mother-child and observer-child interactions was used in the analysis because similar trends were found in the two sets of data. Although the appearance of locomotion (at about 8 months) added approach behaviors (e.g., crawling) to the child's repertoire, this had no effect on the frequency with which children engaged in "complex" exchanges, that is, exchanges involving combinations of several different behaviors. Thus, the results for locomotive and nonlocomotive sequences are combined below.

Categorized sequences accounted for an average of 79% of the sequences recorded in a session ($s = 10.57$). For all subjects but one there was no trend with age in the proportion of categorized/uncategorized sequences. A more pervasive circumstantial effect involved an inflated proportion of simple person-oriented interactions at the outset of each session. Subjects repeatedly studied the observer and then the mother, as if to compare them. However, because this effect appeared in all five sessions, and hence across age, it should not have affected the trend in any of the proportions. It merely made the proportions in the remaining categories smaller than might otherwise have been the case.

Trends in Person-Object Coordination: Spontaneous Performance
Figures 1A and 1B present for each infant the proportion of sequences falling into the different social-interactive categories at each observation session. The data from session 4 are not plotted for subject AF of the older group because this infant was recovering from illness at the time and was cranky and tired.

The combined graphs indicated that simple single-orientation sequences were present before the age at which the youngest children were studied in this investigation. The time of onset for complex single-orientation sequences ranged from 4.5 months (LF) to 7 months (CF). The first signs of coordinated person-object interaction were exhibited by infants between 8 and 10 months.

The peak or marked rise in each category occurred in the same order as the emergence of each category. Simple single-orientation sequences reached their peak first. This peak occurred between 4.5 and 7 months in the younger group. When they reached peak performance in this category, the younger infants engaged in larger proportions of simple single-orientation sequences than did the older children who were tested initially at 8.5–9.75 months. This suggests that the older infants (especially AF and JM) had surpassed their peak in activity of this sort. In the entire sample, complex single-orientation sequences were the next activity to peak or rise markedly. Except for two of the older subjects (AF and JM), this occurred between 7.75 and 10.5 months. It is not clear when the marked rise occurred for AF and JM because these subjects demonstrated the same (20–26%) proportion of complex single-orientation activity across all the sessions. Coordinated person-object orientation sequences were last to show a distinctive increase. The younger subjects engaged in only a negligible proportion of these

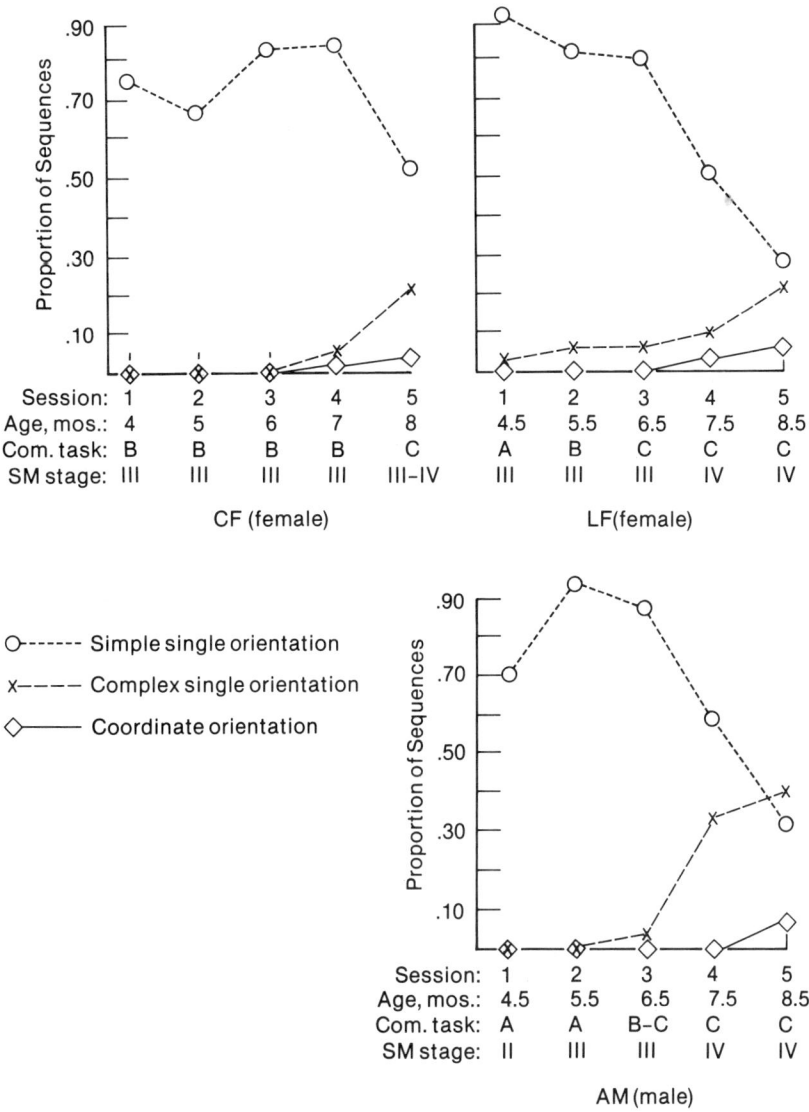

Figure 1A. Proportion of sequences observed in individual social-interactive categories, Communication Elicitation Task (Com. task) performance, and sensorimotor (SM) stage for younger home-reared sample. Younger group was first observed at 4–5 months of age. Key for Communication Elicitation Task: A = diffuse reaction or no response; B = simple single orientation; C = complex single orientation; D, E = coordinated person-object orientation (see Table 3). (Adapted from Sugarman, S. 1978. Some organizational aspects of preverbal communication. In I. Markova (ed.), The Social Context of Language. John Wiley & Sons, Inc., New York.)

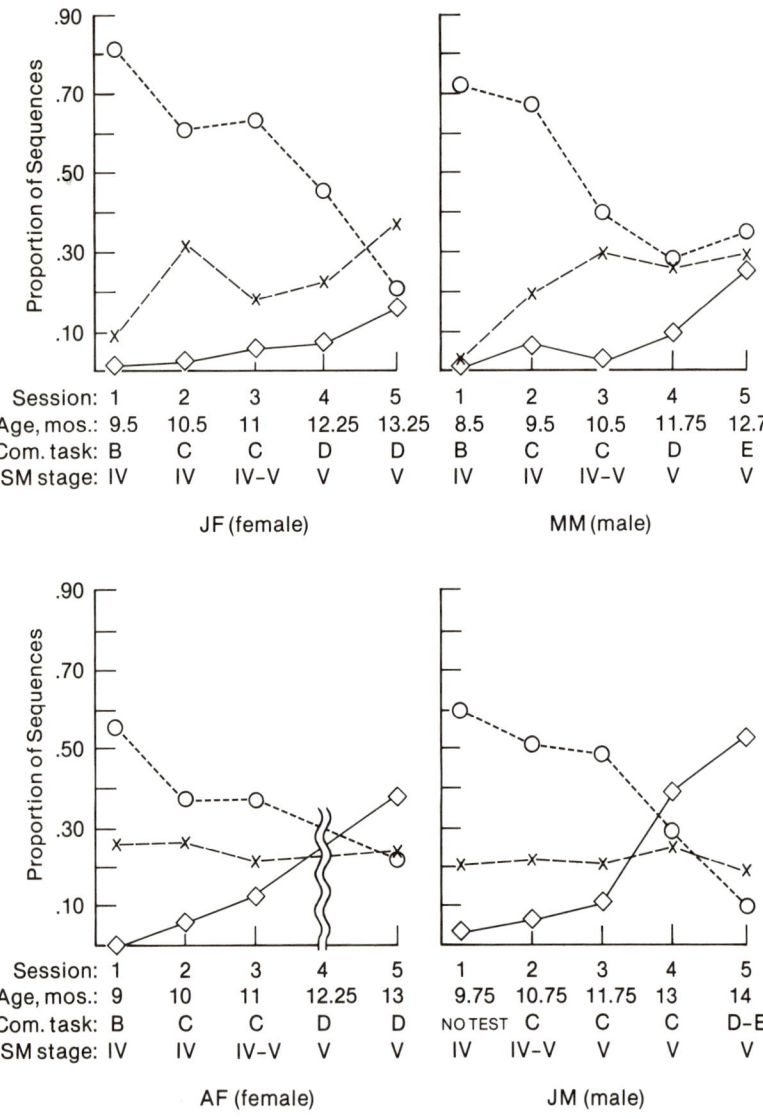

Figure 1B. Proportion of sequences observed in individual social-interactive categories. Communication Elicitation Task (Com. task) performance, and sensorimotor (SM) stage for older home-reared sample. Older group was first observed at 8.5–9.5 months of age. Keys for graphs and Communication Elicitation Task same as for Figure 1A. For subject AF, data from session 4 are omitted (see text). (Adapted from Sugarman, S. 1978. Some organizational aspects of preverbal communication. *In* I. Markova (ed.), The Social Context of Language. John Wiley & Sons, Inc., New York.)

sequences (2–5%) by the final observation session. However, the older subjects showed a steady increase in this behavior across the five sessions. The three older infants with plots for each session (JF, MM, and JM) showed a marked rise in coordinated interactions after 11.75 months. By 13 months, the two consistently more advanced infants, AF and JM, showed an actual dominance of coordinated interactions over all other types of interactions.

It is of interest to note the performance of AF during the (unplotted) session in which she was ill. Her behavior pattern deviated from what would be expected on the basis of her performance during the other sessions (see graph), and from the performance of her agemates. Simple single-orientation interactions increased dramatically during this session (12.25 months), while complex single-orientation and coordinated interactions decreased. The inflated proportion of simple single-orientation interaction (60% of all sequences recorded during this session) was due almost entirely to an increase in simple bids directed to the mother. This finding is consistent with Ainsworth's (1969) observations. Ainsworth also found increases in simple contact-maintaining behaviors in infants at times of illness and stress.

Trends in Person-Object Coordination: Elicited Performance Subjects' performance on the communication elicitation task directly reflected the trends in spontaneous interaction. The results for each session for each infant are presented in Figures 1A and 1B below each graph. A "B" score corresponds to simple single orientation, "C" to complex single orientation, and "D" and "E" to coordinated person-object orientation (see Table 3). The highest score attained in each session is shown. The scores on the elicitation task roughly correspond to the age ranges associated with the peak or marked rise in the respective category during the spontaneous interactions. In other words, most of the "B"s were obtained between 4.5 and 7 months, most of the "C"s between 7.75 and 10.5 months, and most of the "D"s and "E"s after 11.75 months. In addition, the order in which the categories appeared on the elicitation task corresponds to the order of their appearance in the spontaneous data, i.e., no reversals occurred.

Person-Object and Object-Object Coordination Each category of social-interactive behavior reached its peak or rose markedly when subjects were demonstrating the equivalent level of coordination in their encounters with physical objects on the Uzgiris-Hunt tasks (see Figures 1A and 1B). Simple single-orientation social interactions reached their peak when the infants were engaging in simple repetitive schemes with individual physical objects (sensorimotor stage III). These schemes involved actions, such as hitting or pulling, in order to produce various effects, such as noise or rhythmic movement. As already noted, social interaction at this stage involved either simple social contact with an adult or behavior directed exclusively toward an object located on or around the adult. Thus, if the caregiver held a toy over the infant, the infant would engage himself with the object alone (for example, beating it) or with the adult alone (for example, vocalizing back and forth). In both instances the infant repeated an effect by repeating the action associated with it. What further connection, if any, the infant might have seen or intended between his action, the adult, and the object was not clear from his behavior.

The peak of complex single-orientation interaction occurred when children were demonstrating simple goal-directed behavior with respect to physical objects (sensorimotor stage IV). In early instances of this goal-directed activity, a child might push aside an intervening obstacle—for example, a pillow—in the course of reaching for an object. However, the children would not attempt to use an intervening object as a tool in their efforts to reach the goal object, nor would they enlist the help of an adult to obtain the object. Although person-oriented interactions remained separate from object-oriented ones, the children's approach to persons and to objects in social contexts did become more varied. In person-oriented interactions the children would combine various behaviors—for instance, tugging at the adult's clothing and then reaching up toward the adult's face—in order to obtain or maintain social contact. Although not formally considered in the present analysis, elaborate play rituals between mother and child also appeared during this period. During this play a specific bid became the cue for a specific response or for a specific sequence of exchanges, rather than for social contact in general.

A means-end structure was more apparent in the children's object-oriented interactions than in their person-oriented ones. In his object-oriented interactions, a child might first try a direct approach to obtaining some goal, e.g., pulling an object from the adult's hand; if this failed, he might then try an action indirectly related to the goal, e.g., removing the adult's hand from the object. If the child were to meet with resistance from the adult he might persist by pulling at the object with his mouth, adjusting his grasp, and so on. What is striking about these object-oriented exchanges is that, despite the immediate availability of the adult and despite the children's propensity for making social entreaties, no social contact was apparent. Children would look only at those parts of the adult's body that were impeding, or facilitating, the action. This peculiar dichotomy becomes more comprehensible in the light of subjects' concurrent manipulations with physical objects. In solitary object manipulations, as in object-oriented social interactions, the children themselves had to act directly on the objects they wanted. It seems that they had not yet learned to set in motion either instruments or agents to help them reach their goals.

It was when the children began to subordinate the use of one physical object to maneuvering a second (sensorimotor stage V) that they showed a coordination of object pursuit and social focus in their interpersonal exchanges. The earliest object-object instrumental activity involved: 1) using a string or a support, i.e., something physically attached to the goal object, in order to reach the object; and 2) using a nearby stick to retrieve an object. These developments in object-object coordination were accompanied by analogous developments in person-object coordination. The children would now use an adult to obtain something in their transactions with the environment. They could accomplish this by first signaling the adult (e.g., by looking, touching, and/or vocalizing), and then pointing out the goal object or attempting the desired maneuver (e.g., reaching toward the object, or trying to twist off a lid). In both cases the children used some means (e.g., maneuvering a stick in object-object coordination, or touching an adult and pointing to the goal object in person-object coordination) that produced an effect (the approach of the object, or action by the adult) that led to attainment of the goal.

Hence subjects made analogous and contemporaneous progress toward instrumental coordination in social and physical object contexts at this stage. However, there were some differences between physical and social-instrumental maneuvers. Maneuvers with physical objects involved direct manipulation of the intermediary at 1 year, but most social or coordinated-orientation interactions were not direct at this time. When the children began to invoke adult aid in maneuvering objects, they usually cued the adult without physically manipulating her. Some interesting transitional interactions occurred in this regard. Subjects occasionally used part of the adult as an instrument, as when pushing the adult's hand toward an object that was out of reach (see also Piaget, 1971, pp. 295–296). However, most of the transitional interactions that were observed in this study approximated social bidding more closely. The children usually brought the object to the adult's hand, rather than bringing the adult's hand to the object (see also Piaget, 1971, pp. 311–312). In Piaget's account such transitional social behaviors are exhibited by children who are entering sensorimotor stage V.

Language As early as 7 months, subjects turned in response to their names; and shortly thereafter they responded to routinized questions and commands given in context. Elicited imitations of single words (e.g., "Hi," "Mama") were reported as of 10 months. All four older subjects began to produce single words spontaneously, although sparsely, at around 12 months.

Spontaneous speech began at about the time (12 months) that subjects began to coordinate person and object foci with any frequency in their nonverbal social interactions. All (older) subjects also had achieved some degree of object-object instrumental coordination by this point.

Discussion

In view of the small sample observed in this initial study, it is reassuring that evidence of the same developmental sequence exists elsewhere. Bates, Camaioni, and Volterra (1975), Bates et al. (1977), Gray (1979b), Lock (1979b), and Trevarthen and Hubley (1979) have all reported a gradual merging of social and object schemes during the first year, and the trend is implicit in at least two other accounts (Blount, 1971; Sander, 1969). Furthermore, Bates and her colleagues also observed the correspondence between coordinated social-object exchanges and object-object instrumental coordination found in the present study (see also Harding and Golinkoff, 1979; Snyder, 1975).

The Interactive System and the Marking of Intentions At all three phases of communicative development identified in the present study, interactions between mother and child "work." Mother and child are engaging one another and responding appropriately to one another. It is the extent to which the child marks his intentions in these interactions that changes. Even in the first phase, when unitary (simple single-orientation) actions predominate in the infant's repertoire, the caregiver makes reliable adjustments to the infant and the infant responds in kind (Bruner, 1968; Lewis and Goldberg, 1969; Piaget, 1971; Richards, 1974; Trevarthen, 1979). In the next phase, when the child has moved beyond merely repeating efficacious behaviors, he employs different discrete behaviors directed toward a particular goal (complex single orientation), thereby lending clarity to the expression of his intentions (Ainsworth, 1969; Bell and Ainsworth, 1972). With the advent of socially focused goal-directed activity (coordinated orientation), what the child ultimately wants, and what the child ultimately gets, may be the same as what he wants and gets during the preceding phase, but a new feature is added to these exchanges. The child *signals* his intent to someone else, at least insofar as such signaling may be inferred from the sequencing of socially directed and object-directed actions. One could say that the child has begun in a practical way to *encode* his desires for someone else, rather than simply to display his intent. In other words, the mother's (or the observer's) role has begun to change, from interpreter to communicative partner.

Preverbal Communication and Cognition In the present study developments in preverbal communication were closely associated with developments in object-object instrumental coordination. The intent of having sought this relationship, and the implications of having found it, now must be clarified.

As indicated earlier, cognition broadly defined was taken to be a limiting condition for various kinds of transactions with the environment. The ability to construct or appreciate instrumental relations is one such limiting condition. Both nonverbal interaction with people and object manipulation are particular kinds of transactions with the environment. To the extent that cognitively based instrumental coordination is required for a certain pattern of social interaction (e.g., integrating persons and some external state of affairs) and for a certain pattern of object manipulation (object-object instrumental coordination), one would expect these two patterns to develop in analogous ways. That is, at some level of generality, they should pass through the same developmental phases, and in the same order. One would also expect rough temporal coincidence of analogous stages in the normal population, but not necessarily in any individual case. The results from this study were consistent with these expectations. It was found that: 1) social interactions could be analyzed with relative ease according to levels of instrumental coordination; and 2) developments in person-object coordination were in temporal synchrony with developments in object-object coordination. These findings suggest that preverbal social interaction is dependent in part on the child's ability to construct instrumental relations.

Despite the overwhelming (specific behavioral and general organizational) similarity of the person-object and object-object coordination sequences, there were also some differences that must be explored to uncover other possible factors that might affect the development of preverbal social interactions. One area of divergence occurred on the behavioral, as opposed to the organizational, level. Some behaviors occurred almost exclusively in interaction with persons, e.g., smiling and vocalizing. Other researchers also have noted that in the first few months of life infants begin to reserve a special repertoire of individual behaviors for persons (Ainsworth, 1969; Bruner, 1968; Trevarthen, 1974). Precisely what cognitive distinction between persons and objects can be attributed to the child on the basis of this discrimination is unclear. Theorists such as Piaget (1971) maintain that animate and inanimate (or human and nonhuman) classes of objects initially are not conceptually differentiated by the child, but this view is not universal (see, e.g., Trevarthen, 1979; Werner and Kaplan, 1963). Regardless of children's initial level of differentiation, however, their subsequent interactive patterns clearly indicate that they eventually do treat people as external agents who can act at their own discretion, but who may be solicited as "instruments" in achieving some end. Objects, meanwhile, are physical instruments that must be manipulated directly in order to be put into action; they cannot be "solicited." Evidence of this differentiation between animate agents and inanimate instruments is apparent in person-object coordinated interactions in which the child solicits the adult's help in reaching some objective by approaching the adult without materially manipulating her.

Generally, then, preverbal "intentional" communication may develop from the intersection of a number of trends, *one* of which is instrumental coordination, and another of which has to do with developing particular schemes pertinent only to people. Ultimately, these schemes must include the understanding that people act at their own will, although they may be influenced from the outside. Communication is not tantamount to manipulation either literally or figuratively.

Preverbal Communication and Language Both Halliday (1975) and Bruner (1975a) suggested that the development of a general social-regulatory function is an essential step in language development. Person-object integration in social interaction could be considered a nonverbal instance of that function. The fact that the children in the present study engaged in this kind of interaction just prior to talking supports the Halliday-Bruner hypothesis. However, as the next sections show, studies of communicative development in atypical settings currently make it necessary to qualify this hypothesis.

STUDY 2: DEVELOPMENT OF PERSON-OBJECT COORDINATION IN INSTITUTIONALIZED INFANTS

Institutions traditionally have been cited as environments in which social input is deficient for normal development in a number of areas (see, e.g., Provence and Lipton, 1963). Language, particularly production, is one area of development that is often delayed under these circumstances. One of the features cited as a possible retardation factor is the lack of caregiver responsiveness to infants' crying and noncrying signals both before and after language develops. Investigators of normal infants have found that such responsiveness is critical to the infant's development of a differentiated repertoire of noncrying modes of communication in the first year of life (Bell and Ainsworth, 1972). Although close study has not been made of prespeech communicative development among institutionalized infants, especially not in the kinds of terms set forth here, the existing findings would suggest that preverbal (as well as verbal) communication is delayed in institutionalized infants. However, preliminary data from an investigation similar to the one discussed in the last section indicates that this is not the case, at least not for all aspects of preverbal communication.

Methods

Subjects were six infants who had been in residence at a metropolitan institution since birth or from some point within the first 6 months of life. The infants were 5.5 (male), 6 (female), 8 (female), 17 (female), 17 (male), and 19 (female) months old when observed. These children were reported to have no medical complications. Each child was observed over three consecutive sessions for a total of an hour. Both adult-child and child-child interactions were recorded during these sessions, but only the adult-child interactions are reported here.

The infant-caregiver ratio was approximately 3:1. On any given day each child was in contact with four adults, one of whom was a full-time staff member and permanently assigned to a particular group of infants; other staff rotated among groups. The turnover of these other staff was frequent.

With a few exceptions, the methods used for recording and scoring spontaneous social interaction were the same as those used in the study of home-reared infants. The principal difference is that the category of object-oriented interactions was not divided into simple and complex interactions; the person-oriented category, however, did retain this distinction. Because of this discrepancy, and because of the overall low incidence of object-oriented interactions in both the institutionalized ($\bar{x} = 5\%$) and home-reared ($\bar{x} = 10\%$) samples, object-oriented episodes are omitted from the analysis below.

Results

The results of this study must be seen as tentative for a number of reasons. The total number of subjects observed and the total number of observation sessions conducted were few. Furthermore, although a substantial number of interactive sequences was scored ($\bar{x} = 43$ per institutionalized subject), that number varies widely between subjects ($s = 25.73$) and correlates significantly with age.

Despite these limitations, the essential features of the more carefully controlled home-reared study were preserved in the institutionalized study. The combined performance of all six subjects reveals trends in person-object coordination very much like those found for the home-reared infants (see Figure 2). The two youngest children engaged in predominantly simple single-orientation interaction and virtually no complex single-orientation or coordinated person-object interaction. The 8-month-old engaged in a moderate proportion of

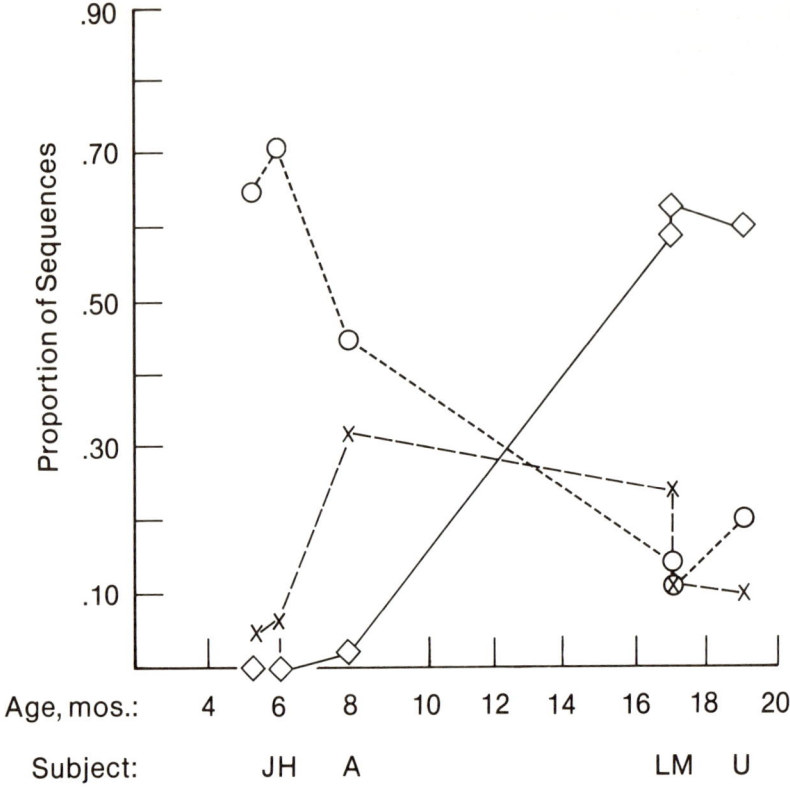

Figure 2. Proportion of sequences in social-interactive categories at different ages for institutionalized sample. The data are discontinuous across age. Line graphs are being used to facilitate comparisons with the home-reared sample (Figures 1A and 1B). Key for Communication Elicitation Task: A = diffuse reaction or no response; B = simple single-orientation; C = complex single-orientation; D, E = coordinated person-object orientation (see Table 3).

complex single-orientation interaction and a negligible proportion of coordinated person-object interaction. The three oldest children engaged predominantly in coordinated interaction.

The permanent staff members' records indicated that the three oldest children had only recently begun to talk. The first word was recorded at 16 months. I recorded 10–15 different words for each of the three children over the 3-day observation period (when two children were 17 months old and one was 19 months old). Utterances consisted of single words, and many of these were elicited directly by one of the caregivers (who would say, for example, "Say 'hello,'" or, while pointing to a picture, "what's that?"). Words used spontaneously included "Ah, no!" when one of the 17-month-olds was informed that it was time for a diaper change, and "Hi!" when the 19-month-old encountered another child during floor play. The home-reared children, by contrast, uttered their first words at around 12 months.

Comprehension was not assessed in the institution, and no record had been kept of it. Informal observation suggested that the three older children responded appropriately to most questions and commands directed explicitly to them, as was the case with the older home-reared children during their later sessions.

Although these data are scant, they suggest that language production was delayed in the institutionalized sample. This result would be consistent with the delay in language production that has been observed among institutionalized infants in other studies (Ainsworth, 1966; Provence and Lipton, 1963; Tizard and Joseph, 1970; Tizard et al., 1972).

Discussion

The data obtained from the institutionalized infants and the home-reared children indicate that the two groups of children may have developed preverbal communicative skills in the same sequence and on the same schedule. However, in comparison to the home-reared infants, the institutionalized children were late in beginning to talk. The tentative nature of these findings must be emphasized because no institutionalized child was available for observation at the most crucial age for these developments, 12 months. Nevertheless, other findings offer circumstantial support for the proposed pattern of development.

Consistent with the present findings on preverbal communicative development, other studies of institutionalized children have failed to find substantial lags in sensorimotor development, but have found delays in representational functioning (Ainsworth, 1966; Paraskevopoulos and Hunt, 1971). Secondly, when Tizard et al. compared differently structured institutional environments, they found that, although early language comprehension and production were sensitive to the setting, nonverbally measured intelligence was insensitive (1972, Table 5). Finally, some authors have observed a social precocity and seductiveness among institutionalized infants (Bridges, 1933; Robertson and Robertson, 1971). Given the present results, this last finding makes sense. The ability to seduce and manipulate other people is of considerable adaptive value in an institutional setting. As seen above, it can be accomplished without language or other symbolic-representational skills.

Although based on a diversity of measures, the preceding studies suggest that various aspects of preverbal or "sensorimotor" (Piaget, 1963) competence may be able to develop normally in institutional environments, but that certain early representational skills, notably language, may be delayed. (Tizard et al., 1972, found evidence, however, that this lag in language development disappears by 3 years of age.) Unfortunately, the lack of formal testing of cognitive development in this study precludes firm conclusions about the relation of representational functioning and various input factors to language (or, for that matter, to preverbal communicative) development. That is, it is not clear whether the language delay, if it indeed existed, stemmed directly from deficiencies in aspects of the social-interactive environment or whether the delay resulted from deficient input in combination with deficiencies in representational functioning. Moreover, even the knowledge that the social-linguistic input to the child is inadequate for normal language development would leave unanswered the question of how it is inadequate. There simply might not have been enough social and linguistic input. There might also have been qualitative abnormalities in the interactive situation—for example, a lack of response to infant noncrying output, or a general lack of consistent and contingent response to that output. (See Snow, this volume, for a discussion of the social and linguistic input given to normal and delayed children.)

Whatever factors were responsible for the language delay, these factors did not delay the development of preverbal interactions in which a child integrates social bidding and pragmatic pursuits (person-object coordination). However, one aspect of preverbal communicative development that may have been lacking in the institution is the development of special routines and function-specific codes between caregivers and infants (these routines and codes are not necessary for person-object integration). Investigators of normal home-reared children (e.g., Bruner, 1975a) have claimed that the preverbal child is functionally primed for language by the elaborate calibration process through which these routines evolve. Other investigators (Blount, 1971; Ryan, 1974) have stressed the importance of repeated exchanges with at least one central interpreting figure. What is important is not necessarily the correctness of the caregiver's interpretation, but the continued treatment of the infant as a communicator who expresses particular meanings (Ryan, 1974). In most institutions, the rotating staff, the high infant-caregiver ratio, and the consistently enforced schedule of feeding, napping, and other activities all reduce the tendency to establish elaborate signal systems (but see Tizard and Tizard, 1971, 1974, for significant variations within institutions in these activities). It is premature to draw conclusions about the precise contribution of these kinds of signal systems to verbal or preverbal communicative development, but the present array of results does suggest that these systems ought to be systematically examined in studies of language development in non-normal settings.

In summary, the study of institutionalized infants revealed the same sequence of preverbal communicative developments as the home-reared study. Moreover, the timing of these preverbal developments appeared to be the same in the two settings. However, in comparison to the home-reared children, the institutionalized children were delayed in the acquisition of language. The development of coordinated person-object exchanges coincided with the home-reared children's production of their first words, but the institutionalized children did not begin to speak until several months after coordinated exchanges had developed. Thus, these data leave open the possibility that the development of socially focused, or coordinated person-object, exchanges may be necessary for the development of language, but they also imply that such exchanges are insufficient for language development.

STUDY 3: COMMUNICATIVE DEVELOPMENT IN AN AUTISTIC CHILD

Our study of institutionalized infants suggested that some features of preverbal communication may develop at a normal pace in cases where language onset is delayed. Infantile autism poses the opposite possibility. The criterial symptoms of autism (Kanner, 1973) suggest that the development of preverbal intentional communication should be difficult for autistic children. This raises the question of whether or not these children will start to talk without, or before, achieving person-object coordination. Cases of autism thus ought to allow further investigation of the extent to which preverbal communicative development is a prerequisite to language.

Kanner (1973) identified aloneness as one of the cardinal features of autism. "Aloneness" involves an avoidance of social contact, and in some cases the avoidance may be nearly total. In the extreme, this syndrome would rule out: simple social contact exchanges (referred to here as "simple single-person–orientation" exchanges); complex social exchanges ("complex single-person orientation"); and exchanges in which the child focuses his pragmatic pursuits on other people, signaling behaviorally his intentions to them ("coordinated person-object orientation"). At the same time, this syndrome would not preclude the occurrence of both simple and complex interactions with objects, either in the presence or absence of other people.

Kanner's own observations affirm the existence of simple exchanges involving physical objects. In these exchanges an adult furnishes the occasion for the encounter but is not dealt with socially:

> When a hand was held out before him so that he could not possibly ignore it, he played with it briefly as if it were a detached object. He blew out a match with an expression of satisfaction with the achievement, but did not look up to the person who had lit the match. (p. 11)

Kanner also reported instances of more complex involvements with objects in which the child removes the adult as an obstacle but does not make social contact:

> ... he was never angry at the interfering *person*. He angrily shoved away the *hand* that was in his way or the *foot* that stepped on one of his blocks. (p. 5, emphasis in original)
>
> When the book was taken away from him, he struggled with the hand that held it, without looking at the *person* who had taken the book. When he was pricked with a pin .... He looked timidly at the pin, shrank from further pricks, but at no time did he seem to connect the pricking with the *person* who held the pin. (pp. 26–27, emphasis in original)

These observations raise two intriguing questions. First, to the extent that autistic children develop greater communicative competence than is evident in these sequences, the question arises as to how such competence develops. More specifically, if these children come to coordinate their pragmatic pursuits with an orientation toward people, do they build this coordination directly from the complex object-oriented activities in which they engage at the outset? Or, is it necessary to develop *socially* (person-) oriented exchanges from their simplest beginnings and progress through a phase of complex purely social involvement before social exchanges can incorporate pursuits pertaining to an external state of affairs? A second question concerns the point in autistic children's communicative development at which language emerges.

Systematic data bearing on these questions are virtually nonexistent. However, several years ago I had the opportunity to interact for over a year with a young child diagnosed as autistic. Detailed notes are available from that encounter, although the observations were made prior to the refinement of the categories that were employed in the two preceding studies. Nevertheless, the notes contain sufficient detail to permit some insight into the questions raised above.

Etiology

Lee C. received therapy for 1 year and 3 months, beginning at the age of 2 years, 2 months, and ending at the age of 3 years, 5 months. Therapy was given during hourly play sessions that were conducted weekly.

Lee's delivery at birth was uncomplicated, and he suffered no major illnesses in infancy. However, his parents noted peculiar behavioral symptoms, such as staring and rocking, as early as 6 months. At 19 months Lee was diagnosed as being at least partially autistic. His symptoms included delayed language development, unresponsiveness toward persons, rocking, hand flapping, and a preoccupation with objects, sounds, and light. Prognosis was considered good. He was brought in for therapy at 26 months because he had become difficult to manage at home.

Technique

My interactions with Lee were reactive and supportive, rather than directive. The approach, by coincidence, bears some similarity to the "incidental teaching" strategy described by Hart (in press), in which the therapist responds to the child's initiation of contact and then prompts an elaboration of the interaction. The present approach differed from Hart's in the identification of behaviors to be followed up, and in the fact that the burden of elaboration was left more with the child.

An attempt was made throughout the sessions to identify the child's *typical* ways of interacting with the environment, that is, his predominant "schemes" (Piaget, 1963). These schemes were used as the basis for intervention. At the outset Lee's schemes concerned only the nonhuman environment, for example, scratching the side of tin cans, or spilling crayons from a container and then lining them up on the floor. Rather than capitalizing, as Hart proposes, on the child's few moments of apparent social contact (e.g., looking at the therapist), I gradually introduced myself into Lee's prevailing object schemes. The object world was the world in which he felt comfortable. It therefore seemed better to use his involvement with objects as the foundation for the gradual integration of people into his interactive sphere than to use his precarious, and probably frightening, social contacts as the foundation.

Because Lee clearly found social contact aversive in the early sessions, I initially introduced myself more to have my presence discovered than to elaborate Lee's actions. Hence my initial involvements were either imitative with slight modifications, or they complemented Lee's actions. Thus, for example, I imitated and slightly altered the hand flapping in which Lee engaged when he was excited by something. I also participated in his routine of lining up crayons by handing him crayons once he had begun lining them up himself. Later on, as Lee began to *expect* my involvement, I began to elaborate my reactions (e.g., scribbling with a crayon on a piece of paper before handing him the crayon), primarily to draw attention to my existence as a separate person who was ultimately independent of his direct control. Drawing attention to my autonomy seemed important, because one of Lee's problems was his treatment of people as "things" to be manipulated or avoided.

This approach may seem counterintuitive because it does not directly model socially adaptive behavior, but appears to reinforce distinctly nonadaptive behavior, (e.g., hand flapping, compulsively lining up crayons). However, the approach, at least in this one case, did lead within a few months to spontaneous elaboration on the child's part and unhesitating initiation of social contact; eventually, the child also integrated his object and social involvements. This outcome suggests that, when children like Lee interact with a therapist, they extract something far more general than specific behaviors. They discover something about human exchange itself. In other words, children develop a prototype of human interaction based partly on these socially isolated exchanges engaged in during therapy. Like normal children, they may acquire in due course those specific behaviors or behavior systems best suited to the interactive or communicative needs they have developed. Should things go well, they should eventually need a means of communication as flexible as language (see Luria and Yudovich, 1971).

Observations

Lee demonstrated no language production or comprehension when first seen at 26 months, and his parents reported that they had observed no evidence of these abilities. Left to his own devices, Lee remained occupied exclusively with objects. To the extent that circumstances required that he deal with a person, parts of the person were handled as though they were objects (e.g., tugging my hand, removing it from something); but in most cases, Lee engaged himself exclusively with an object that I had presented. By the end of therapy, however, Lee often engaged in interactions in which he focused his pragmatic pursuits around me in a social, non-mechanical fashion. Importantly, in the interim, he progressed through phases of social interaction that are characteristic of normal development during the first year of life.

Early Developments At 2–3 years of age (i.e., during the first 8–10 months of therapy) Lee remained involved primarily with objects, even when he and I were engaging in some kind of joint activity. Although simple social contact occasionally did appear, it remained separate from object involvement. Each type of simple orientation exchange gradually became more complex and showed increasing initiative on Lee's part.

During this early period, Lee and I slowly built up collective rituals involving physical objects. These exchanges were initially the result of my introducing myself into one of Lee's object schemes:

> Lee approached the table and reached toward a stack of pads and a box of crayons, both out of his reach. After I had placed the paper and crayons on the floor, Lee began to remove the crayons from the box one by one and line them up. I began adding crayons to his line, and whether I placed my crayon next to his or a few inches away, he placed his crayon next to mine, thus filling in the gap, if there was one.

Once this procedure had been repeated several times, I introduced a variation:

> When a few crayons were still left in the box, I picked them out one by one and handed them to Lee. He took them from my hand, made a few strokes with each one on the paper (we had spent several minutes scribbling last week), and then placed them in the row of crayons on the floor.

This crayon routine was repeated in one form or another nearly every week for several weeks. Before long Lee began to pause for me to hand him something, and later on he spontaneously handed crayons to me.

During this initial period, Lee also began to exchange glances with me, mainly during pauses from his activity. Furthermore, a set of ritualized social exchanges evolved. Many of these exchanges consisted of reciprocal imitation with no external object involved. As with the preceding early object routines, the exchange aspect of the imitative social routines was almost invariably initiated by me. Nevertheless, the imitative sequences were clearly sustained by Lee, even after I began to modulate my actions:

> Lee spotted a small toy on the floor. He flapped his hands in the air vigorously, at about ear level, and then picked up and scratched the toy. He put the object down and flapped his hands again. Once his hands dropped toward each other. I responded by moving mine apart. Lee moved his hands apart and I moved mine together. We went back and forth this way three or four times. Lee grinned and clapped his hands together. I clapped mine, and we clapped in alternation another few times before Lee turned to walk toward the table.

Variations of this sequence, e.g., slapping the floor in between bouts of clapping hands, continued over the next several weeks.

Some of these purely social routines began to take on a codelike quality. For example, Lee's walking to the window came to stand for a lengthy episode that involved my joining him at the window and naming things outside, Lee touching my face, and me touching Lee's face. As in the preceding example, Lee himself initiated these routines by enacting a portion of the routine. In one instance, he initiated one of these routines with the clear intention of getting something done. In the first few months of therapy, it usually happened that Lee had an object in his hands when it was time to leave the playroom. On such occasions I would request the object as I coaxed Lee to the door. For quite a while this terminal object happened to be a Scribbage can. However, some time after this had ceased to be the case, Lee abruptly picked up the Scribbage can and handed it to me. I placed the can on the table. Lee extended the can three more times while whimpering. Finally, as he was extending the can, he looked beyond me to the door. It was clear then that he wanted to leave and had been enacting the routine that was previously associated with leaving.

Later Developments More dramatic changes occurred after Lee's third birthday. His interactions with objects were now frequently punctuated with simple social contact, such as eye-to-eye contact or smiling. In addition, a build-up of more complicated person-centered exchanges, notably social games, occurred. Most importantly, Lee began to initiate these games on his own:

> While I was sitting in a chair, Lee approached, extended his arms to me, pulled back until our arms were tense, and then flopped toward me. Then he ran backwards still holding on, and repeated the sequence. I caught on and let him drop back and then pulled him forward.

In a similar episode:

> Lee began beating his fingers rhythmically on the floor while we were sitting on the floor facing each other. He looked in my direction, reached for my hand, and then resumed tapping. We began to beat rhythms on the floor simultaneously and in alternation. Lee re-initiated this game three more times during the session by tapping and reaching toward my hand.

Lee also converted the hand-flapping routine to a new game, during the same session:

> Lee began to flap his hands over a large tower of blocks that we had built. When I imitated him he paused, smiled broadly at my face, reached for my hands, and began to shake my arms while continuing to smile and laugh. Within a few weeks he would initiate this new game by reaching for my hands without waiting for me to imitate his flapping.

Consultation with Lee's parents suggested that these exchanges originated in the playroom rather than at home. Nevertheless, the exchanges still represented progress.

In summary, at around his third birthday, Lee initiated exchanges not only by reenacting old rituals, but by creating new ones. Moreover, he solicited my involvement in these games by doing more than executing a game component (e.g., tapping the floor in the second example above). He also cued me in a separate, distinctly social way (looking at me, reaching for my hand, and *then* tapping). This format resembles person-object coordination insofar as solicitation of the person to be engaged is distinct from and coordinated with the "object" of the exchange (the game).

After his third birthday, Lee made further progress toward integrating his pursuit of physical-object goals with social contact. Whereas I initially participated in Lee's object schemes by inserting myself into them (e.g., handing him crayons or blocks unsolicited), Lee now began to solicit my aid, not just in an instrumental way, but in a social way. The following two examples, 2 months apart (around Lee's third birthday), show this transition:

> As on several preceding weeks, Lee began to build a tower of yellow blocks. He stood one block up and then handed me the next one without looking at me. I hesitated. Still without looking at me he handed me another block and impulsively uttered, "Mmnn." Before I responded, he picked up a third block and matched it end to end with the blocks in my hand without looking at me or at the tower that he had begun to build on the shelf. He then turned to the shelf and began to cry. I immediately placed the blocks on the stack.

> Lee began building a tower. After stacking three blocks while I was watching, he handed me a fourth block, looked at my face, and then turned toward the tower.

The next set of excerpts, abstracted from several months of therapy, illustrate a more protracted development of socially focused pragmatic pursuits:

> Lee rose to the table and reached vaguely toward a large cardboard can with a picture on it. Before he touched it, he flapped his hands over it and peered inside.

> During the above and subsequent sessions, Lee demonstrated a fascination for the form of the can and also came to enjoy playing with the clay inside. During a session shortly afterwards, Lee found the can within his reach, picked it up, and began to cry (there was a lid on the can). I removed the lid, and Lee stopped crying and removed the contents.

After the fact, it appears that Lee had a specific goal in mind regarding the object, but made clear neither the goal nor the manner in which it was to be achieved. He merely expressed discomfort. However, by judging from the context and past experience, I could infer what Lee wanted.

> Several weeks later Lee located the can, extended his arm toward it, but could not reach it. Still reaching toward the can he produced a drawn-

out sound. I walked to the table, handed him the can, and returned to my former location.

In this session Lee made his goal clear by engaging in more differentiated behavior than he had previously done under similar circumstances. He combined wanting something with expressing the desire, but not with "requesting" what he wanted. A few sessions later, however:

> ... Lee reached for the can. After failing to obtain it, he *looked at my face and vocalized*, and reached for the can once again. Later, after an unsuccessful attempt at opening the lid, Lee walked toward me, fingered the lid, made the sound "uh-uh-uh," and *looked at my face*. I opened the can for him and placed it back in his outstretched hands.

Instances of this sort became more prevalent as time went on, particularly during the last 5 months of observation.

Language Midway through therapy, Lee began to respond at home and in the playroom to simple routine questions and commands given in context. His productive language, on the other hand, was almost entirely nonexistent throughout the course of treatment. Lee's sound production and sound combinations gradually became more fluid, but they did not materialize into words. Sometimes, however, his parents could coax him to imitate a few words such as "Hi." Remarkably, at the very last observation session (before I was to leave the area permanently), Lee approached me with his arms outstretched and said "Up!" He was reported to have done the same thing spontaneously at home. Follow-up reports by another therapist indicate that Lee used a few more single words in this fashion during the next few months.

Discussion

This allegedly autistic child progressed from an involvement purely with the object world to a coordination of object and person involvement. He clearly demonstrated this coordination by 3 years of age, whereas normal children demonstrate it by 1 year. However, like a normal child, he began to speak (spontaneously) shortly after he began to coordinate nonverbal person- and object-oriented bids. Moreover, Lee went through the same steps as normal children in developing person-object coordination. Specifically, he did not build person-object coordination from his already complex involvements with objects. Instead, he developed a separate domain of social exchange, and gradually integrated that domain into his transactions with the physical environment.

At first Lee's socially oriented exchanges were very fleeting. His predominant mode of interacting with a person was a purely impersonal one. Next, he elaborated social exchanges that did not involve physical objects or the physical manipulation of people. He subsequently began initiating novel social exchanges, and coordinating his pragmatic pursuits (for example, opening a lid) with social involvement (for example, explicitly soliciting help through some form of social approach) in order to achieve a goal.

Lee's cognitive development was not formally tested. Anecdotal observation suggests that he had an appreciation of object premanence from the earliest testing sessions. Object-object instrumental acts are not apparent in the case record. However, this does not necessarily mean that they did not occur. There may have been insufficient opportunity for them to occur, or they may have been overlooked in the preparation of the case record, or the child might not have been capable of such acts. In any event, it is not clear whether this child was capable of object-object coordination substantially before he developed person-object coordination or whether the two types of coordination evolved at the same time. It should be noted that some language-delayed children are delayed in instrumental (object-object) coordination, but not in other symptoms of late sensorimotor intelligence, such as object permanence (Snyder, 1975).

Clarification of the interplay of physical-cognitive and social-cognitive skills in cases such as this has important consequences for remediation. If it turns out that a child is capable of object-object instrumental coordination long before he exhibits similar coordination in bringing his social and object worlds together, then he has the *cognitive* capacity to bring the worlds together but does not do so. If, on the other hand, person-object and object-object instrumental coordination are both delayed, then a broader cognitive deficit is implicated, and not just the absence of the social mapping of a given cognitive ability.

In summary, the present case study of communicative development in an autistic child further supports the hypothesis that the development of some form of intentional communication is necessary for the onset of language. Intentional communication, operationalized as person-object coordinated exchanges, in turn appears to depend specifically on the development of differentiated *social* exchanges, and not simply on a build-up of complex involvements with objects. In this particular case, it also appears that the elaboration of interpersonal rituals played a prominent role in the child's social-interactive development. This may be because autistic children rely heavily on routines in their engagements with the environment (see, e.g., Kanner, 1973), and such routines therefore provide the only way to break through the autistic net. On the other hand, as several researchers (e.g., Bruner, 1975a; Ryan, 1974) have claimed, it may be the case generally that such exchanges functionally prime a child for developing language and other social skills. Lee's language, however, did not appear to emerge within the context of a previously established routine. Rather, it was through the execution and elaboration of these rituals that the child made his clearest progress in social interaction prior to uttering his first communicative word. The closing discussion considers in greater depth the proposed relations between preverbal communication and the emergence of language.

GENERAL DISCUSSION: IMPLICATIONS OF DEVELOPING THE ABILITY TO COMMUNICATE BEFORE LANGUAGE

It is evident in the three studies discussed that children develop the ability to engage in exchanges that may properly be called communicative prior to the time they begin to speak. Preverbal children can pragmatically "encode" their intentions for someone else. They do this by engaging in goal-appropriate (goal-expressive or goal-corrected) behavior, and by orienting this behavior explicitly toward another person. This coordination evolves in late infancy, along with equivalently complex instrumental coordinations involving physical objects.

In every context observed, the development of coordinated person-object interchanges was preceded by a series of developments in which object-oriented and person-oriented interactions evolved separately. Furthermore, the advent of coordinated person-object interchanges was in every case followed by the child's first words. Importantly, "every context" includes not only normal children living in a normal home environment, but also otherwise-normal children in an institutional environment and an autistic child living at home. The institutionalized sample progressed through the same sequence of preverbal communicative developments, and did so at the same rate, as the home-reared children. These children began to speak after passing through the sequence, but did so considerably later than the home-reared children. The autistic child also progressed through the preverbal communicative sequence, but at a much slower rate than did the institutionalized and home-reared normal children. Limited data suggest that the autistic child began to speak shortly after he reached the endpoint of the preverbal sequence, the development of person-object coordinated exchanges. Hence, speech onset intersected the sequence at the point that it did in the home-reared sample and (relatively) earlier than it did in the institutionalized sample.

The observation that the development of preverbal communication consistently precedes even the barest language use in substantially different contexts might suggest that the development of preverbal communication is a prerequisite to language. Although intuitively satisfying on theoretical grounds and empirically plausible in view of the data presented, this conclusion needs closer scrutiny. The issue of whether preverbal communication (operationalized as person-object coordination) is normally necessary to the development of language has important implications for remediation. Suppose, for example, that the behavioral coordination of person- and object-oriented interaction prior to language is not absolutely necessary for the development of language. Under such circumstances one would not automatically decide to cultivate person-object coordination in a child who had not learned to talk. On the other hand, even if we cannot definitively document that person-object coordination is a prerequisite to normal language development, the cultivation of person-object coordinated interaction might still facilitate language development in children with particular kinds of problems. These issues are elaborated below.

Consider first the notion of a prerequisite. To say that skill A is a prerequisite to skill B means not only that skill B follows skill A in development, but that skill B builds in some way from skill A. The first condition, that of a precedence, is clearly met in the present studies. Fully developed preverbal communication, in the sense of person-object coordinated interaction, preceded children's first words in every study; and analogous findings are reported elsewhere (Bates et al. 1975, 1977). The more important, and more difficult, question is whether preverbal communication *must* precede language onset so that language can build from it.

The pattern of results that we have seen, particularly in the study of the autistic child, suggests the presence of a strong relationship between preverbal communication and language. In the case of the autistic child, both the development of preverbal intentional communication and language onset were delayed relative to normal development. This suggests the possibility that language depends on the prior development of communicative schemes. Unfortunately, the present data on this point, although highly suggestive, are not conclusive and relevant data from other sources are not available. We would have conclusive evidence of a strong relation between preverbal communication and language if we could show that the initial delay was specific to preverbal communication, and not applicable more generally to its cognitive concomitants. If it turns out, as some have suggested (e.g., Snyder, 1975), that the initial delay is a more pervasive cognitive one, then there may be only a weak link between preverbal and verbal communication. Starting to speak may presuppose certain very general cognitive skills and a minimal orientation toward social exchange. It may not require fully developed preverbal communication. Preverbal communication may develop prior to language to the extent that it does because the child is ready cognitively and socially (through a history of reliable interchanges with others around him) to develop that ability. Language may emerge subsequently because it depends on additional developments. Preverbal communication and language may appear when they do, and in the order they do, not because they are two direct links on the same chain, but because they are the normal symptoms of two links in a higher-order chain.

Another set of considerations also suggests caution in drawing strong links between preverbal communication and language on the basis of the present data. Autism is a syndrome that pervasively affects sociability and communication. It may be that the only way an afflicted child becomes oriented toward language is through the development of an interest and competence in communication. The same may be true of children with other kinds of delay. For example, in her extensive study of language development in blind children, Urwin (1978, this volume) emphasizes the importance of rich caregiver-child exchanges and the development of an explicit coordination of social and object schemes. Urwin also maintained that the blind child's particular cognitive and social problems may necessitate his use of alternative routes to language. Thus, cases of non-normal development can clarify aspects of normal development, but at the same time they may present problems of their own.

Turning this around, positive—rather than negative—consequences follow for remediation. With delayed children, the facilitation of certain preverbal competencies may facilitate language even when those same preverbal competencies play a lesser role in normal language acquisition.

This separation of what develops and what may be facilitative has been demonstrated in other contexts. For example, Bower (1974) reported instances in which very young infants were trained to exercise behaviors that do not normally appear spontaneously in infants' repertoires. Training of this sort appears to facilitate the development of later, plausibly related skills. Thus, toddlers may walk early if neonatal walking is elicited and exercised in the first month or so of life. Given that these neonatal experiences rarely occur in normal development, it can hardly be argued that they normally serve as stepping stones to the later acquisitions. However, this does not preclude the possibility that exercise of the earlier behavior may facilitate the development of the later one.

To summarize thus far, the development of nonverbal interpersonal exchanges involving a coordination of person and object foci precedes speech onset across a variety of contexts. However, there is no conclusive evidence that this coordination is a necessary condition for language, although such a relation is strongly suggested by the data. The development of person-object coordinated interactions may turn out to be a necessary stepping stone to language in the normal population, or it may be an optional stepping stone. Either way, however, cultivation of this type of social-interactive organization in cases of a disorder may at least prompt the children to pay attention to language.

Interestingly, this differentiation and coordination of social and object components appears to be the very basis from which children with no language input at all begin to evolve natural symbolic gestural systems for communication. Goldin-Meadow and Feldman (1977) found that deaf toddlers who are not being taught sign language began to evolve their own gestural systems for representing ideas at around the time that hearing children begin to speak. Moreover, the structural features of these natural symbol systems share some features with very early spoken language. Goldin-Meadow and Feldman isolated natural symbols from their subjects' behavior stream by searching for attempts by the children to make social contact with the "listener" through bidding (for example, through eye contact) that was clearly distinct from both the message conveyed and the behaviors through which the message was conveyed. The gestures also had to be symbolic, rather than simply direct actions on objects (Feldman, Goldin-Meadow, and Gleitman, 1979). Although these investigators do not furnish an account of presymbolic communication as it is outlined here, the basic differentiation and coordination of person and object (goal) orientations is clearly prefigured in their account of gestural-symbolic communication.

The argument that person-object coordinated bids may not be prerequisite to language (or other symbolic communication) may seem unwieldy and unparsimonious at this point. The intent of the argument, however, is simply to stress the limits of empirical inquiry, and the need for very careful a priori consideration of what skills are necessarily entailed in later ones, and what skills *may* figure in later ones or may be used to foster later ones (see Sachs, this volume, for a similar point regarding social play and language).

The specific behavioral developments described in this chapter may be among those skills that *may* figure in language acquisition but that need not do so. That is, it is not yet clear whether the intention to encode experience for someone else, i.e., to communicate, must be displayed nonverbally, and in the precise manner described, before a child can begin to speak.

However, if communication is more broadly construed, then children's communicative experience in the preverbal period *must* figure in language acquisition. Before children can use language to communicate they must learn what communication is. They must learn that there is a purpose not only to making clear their experience, but to intentionally presenting that experience for, or as though it were for, someone else. The studies we have considered indicate that at least some of this learning occurs prior to language. This could be in part what prompts the search for new, more effective means of communication—a first language.

ACKNOWLEDGMENTS

Robert Bell, Sam Glucksberg, Mimi Whei-Ping Lou, and James Wertsch are gratefully acknowledged for comments on an earlier version of this manuscript.

REFERENCES

Ainsworth, M. D. S. 1966. Reversible and irreversible effects on maternal deprivation on intellectual development. In O. J. Harvey (ed.), Experience, Structure, and Adaptability. Springer Publishing Co., New York.
Ainsworth, M. D. S. 1969. Object relations, dependency, and attachment: A theoretical review of the infant-mother relationship. Child Dev. 40:969–1025.
Austin, J. S. 1962. How To Do Things with Words. Oxford University Press, Oxford, England.
Bates, E. 1976. Language and Context: The Acquisition of Pragmatics. Academic Press, Inc., New York.
Bates, E. 1979. The Emergence of Symbols: Cognition and Communication in Infancy. Academic Press, Inc., New York.
Bates, E., Benigni, L., Bretherton, I., Camaioni, L., and Volterra, V. 1977. From gesture to the first word: On cognitive and social prerequisites. In M. Lewis and L. Rosenblum (eds.), Interaction, Conversation, and the Development of Language. John Wiley & Sons, Inc., New York.
Bates, E., Camaioni, L., and Volterra, V. 1975. The acquisition of performatives prior to speech. Merrill-Palmer Q. 21:205–226.
Bell, S., and Ainsworth, M. D. S. 1972. Infant crying and maternal responsiveness. Child Dev. 43:1171–1190.
Blount, B. 1971. Socialization and prelinguistic development among the Luo of Kenya. Southwestern J. Anthropol. 20:41–50.
Bower, T. G. R. 1974. Development in Infancy. W. H. Freeman and Co., San Francisco.
Bridges, K. 1933. A study of social development in early infancy. Child Dev. 4:36–49.
Bruner, J. S. 1968. Processes of Cognitive Growth: Infancy. Heinz Werner Lecture Series. Clark University Press, Worchester, MA.
Bruner, J. S. 1975a. The ontogenesis of speech acts. J. Child Lang. 2:1–19.
Bruner, J. S. 1975b. From communication to language: A psychological perspective. Cognition 3:255–287.
Bullowa, M. (ed.). 1979. Before Speech: The Beginning of Interpersonal Communication. Cambridge University Press, New York.
Chomsky, N. 1968. Language and Mind. Harcourt, Brace, and World, New York.

DeLaguna, G. 1963. Speech: Its Function and Development. Indiana University Press, Bloomington, IN.
Dore, J. 1974. A pragmatic description of early language development. J. Psycholinguistic Res. 4:343–350.
Duncker, K. 1945. On problem solving. Psychol. Monogr. 58, Whole No. 270, No. 5.
Feldman, H., Goldin-Meadow, S., and Gleitman, L. 1979. Beyond Herodotus: The creation of language by linguistically deprived deaf children. *In* A. Lock (ed.), Action, Gesture, and Symbol: The Emergence of Language. Academic Press, Inc., New York.
Fischer, K. W. 1980. A theory of cognitive development: The control and construction of hierarchies of skills. Psychol. Rev. 87:477–531.
Goldin-Meadow, S., and Feldman, H. 1977. The development of language-like communication without a language model. Science 197:401–403.
Gray, H. 1979. Learning to take an object from the mother. *In* A. Lock (ed.), Action, Gesture, and Symbol: The Emergence of Language. Academic Press, Inc., New York.
Halliday, M. A. K. 1975. Learning How to Mean: Explorations in the Development of Language. Elsevier, New York.
Harding, C., and Golinkoff, R. 1979. The origins of intentional vocalizations in prelinguistic infants. Child Dev. 50:33–40.
Hart, G. Incidental strategies. *In* R. L. Schiefelbusch (ed.), Communicative Competence: Assessment and Intervention. University Park Press, Baltimore. (in press)
Jesperson, O. 1964. Language: Its Nature, Development, and Origins. W. W. Norton & Company, Inc., New York.
Kanner, L. 1973. Childhood Psychosis: Initial Studies and New Insights. John Wiley & Sons, Inc., New York.
Lewis, M., and Goldberg, S. 1969. Perceptual-cognitive development in infancy: A generalized expectancy model as a function of mother-child interaction. Merrill-Palmer Q. 15:89–101.
Lock, A. (ed.). 1979a. Action, Gesture, and Symbol: The Emergence of Language. Academic Press, Inc., New York.
Lock, A. 1979b. The emergence of language. In A. Lock (ed.), Action, Gesture, and Symbol: The Emergence of Language. Academic Press, Inc., New York.
Luria, A. R. 1974/1975. Scientific perspectives and philosophical deadends in modern linguistics. Cognition 3/4:377–386.
Luria, A. R., and Yudovich, F. 1971. Speech and the Development of Mental Processes in the Child. Penguin Books, Baltimore.
Nelson, K. 1978. Early speech in its communicative context. *In* F. Minnifie and L. Lloyd (eds.), Communicative and Cognitive Abilities: Early Behavioral Assessment. University Park Press, Baltimore.
Paraskevopoulos, J., and Hunt, J. McV. 1971. Object construction and imitation under differing conditions of rearing. J. Genet. Psychol. 119:301–321.
Piaget, J. 1963. The Origins of Intelligence in Children. W. W. Norton & Company, Inc., New York.
Piaget, J. 1971. The Construction of Reality in the Child. Ballantine Books, New York.
Provence, S., and Lipton, R. 1963. Infants in Institutions. International Universities Press, New York.

Ratner, N., and Bruner, J. S. 1977. Games, social exchange, and the acquisition of language. Unpublished manuscript, Oxford University, Oxford, England.

Richards, M. P. M. 1974. First steps in becoming social. In M. P. M. Richards (ed.), The Integration of a Child into a Social World. Cambridge University Press, Cambridge, England.

Robertson, J., and Robertson, J. 1971. Young children in brief separation: A fresh look. In R. S. Eissler (ed.), The Psychoanalytic Study of the Child, Vol. 26. The Hogarth Press, London.

Ryan, J. 1974. Early language development. In M. P. M. Richards (ed.), The Integration of a Child into a Social World. Cambridge University Press, Cambridge, England.

Sander, L. W. 1969. The longitudinal course of early mother-child interaction: Cross-case comparison in a sample of mother-child pairs. In B. M. Foss (ed.), Determinants of Infant Behavior, IV. Methuen, London.

Searle, J. R. 1969. Speech Acts: An Essay in the Philosophy of Language. Cambridge University Press, Cambridge, England.

Snyder, L. S. 1975. Pragmatics in language-deficient children: Pre-linguistic and early verbal performatives and presuppositions. Unpublished doctoral dissertation, University of Colorado, Boulder.

Sugarman, S. 1973. A description of communicative development in the pre-language child. Unpublished B. A. thesis, Hampshire College.

Sugarman, S. 1978. Some organizational aspects of preverbal communication. In I. Markova (ed.), The Social Context of Language. John Wiley & Sons, Inc., New York.

Tizard, B., Cooperman, O., Joseph, A., and Tizard, J. 1972. Environmental effects on language development: A study of young children in long-stay residential nurseries. Child Dev. 43:337–358.

Tizard, B., and Joseph, A. 1970. The cognitive development of young children in residential care. J. Child Psychol. Psychiatry 11:177–186.

Tizard, J., and Tizard, B. 1971. The social development of two-year-old children in residential nurseries. In H. R. Schaffer (ed.), The Origins of Human Social Relations. Academic Press, Inc., New York.

Tizard, J., and Tizard, B. 1974. The institution as an environment for development. In M. P. M. Richard (ed.), The Integration of a Child into a Social World. Cambridge University Press, Cambridge, England.

Trevarthen, C. 1974. Infant responses to objects and persons. Paper presented at the spring meeting of the British Psychological Society, Bangor.

Trevarthen, C. 1979. Communication and cooperation in early infancy: A description of primary intersubjectivity. In M. Bullowa (ed.), Before Speech: The Beginning of Interpersonal Communication. Cambridge University Press, New York.

Trevarthen, C., and Hubley, P. 1979. Secondary intersubjectivity: Confidence, confiding, and acts of meaning in the first year. In A. Lock (ed.), Action, Gesture, and Symbol: The Emergence of Language. Academic Press, Inc., New York.

Urwin, C. 1978. The development of communication between blind infants and their parents: Some ways into language. Unpublished D. Phil. thesis, Cambridge University, Cambridge, England.

Uzgiris, I., and Hunt, J. McV. 1975. Assessment in Infancy: Ordinal scales of Psychological Development. University of Illinois Press, Urbana.

Vygotsky, L. S. 1962. Thought and Language. MIT Press, Cambridge, MA.
Weiner, M., Devoe, S., Rubinow, S., and Geller, J. 1972. Nonverbal behavior and nonverbal communication. Psychol. Rev. 79:185–214.
Werner, H., and Kaplan, B. 1963. Symbol Formation. John Wiley & Sons, Inc., New York.

chapter

Parent-Child Interaction and the Development of Communicative Ability

Catherine E. Snow

Harvard University
Graduate School of Education
Larsen Hall
Cambridge, Massachusetts

Editors' Note

Children learn language in the context of interaction with older children and adults. Face-to-face social exchanges with 3–6-month-old infants, organizing joint attention to objects with older infants, and structuring conversations with 1–2-year-olds so that adult responses are semantically contingent on child utterances all contribute to children's development of communicative abilities. Common to this set of facilitative social behaviors is the feature of *contingency* on child behaviors.

Language-delayed children benefit from the same set of facilitative interactions as children learning language normally. However, language-delayed children may require an optimal, rather than just facilitative, social environment, because their capacity to benefit from each facilitative encounter may be reduced. Examples of language intervention strategies for various diagnostic groups of language-delayed children are included; if such children are identified early, provision of an optimal social and linguistic environment can prevent severe language problems.

contents

**SOCIAL INTERACTIONS WITH NORMALLY
DEVELOPING CHILDREN** 72
   The First Year of Life 72
   The Second and Third Years of Life: The Period of Early
      Language Acquisition 84
   Language Development after Age Three 91

**SOCIAL INTERACTION WITH
LANGUAGE-HANDICAPPED, -DELAYED, AND
-DISORDERED CHILDREN** 93
   Language-Handicapped Children 93
   Language-Delayed and Language-Disordered Children 95
   Imitation and Modeling 95

CONCLUSIONS 99

REFERENCES 101

Social interaction with warm and caring adults is undeniably a prerequisite to normal cognitive and social development. The necessity of such social experiences throughout the first years of life is evident from the case studies of Victor, the "wild boy of Aveyron" (Lane, 1976), and Genie, a present-day "wild child" (Curtiss, 1977). Both of these children, although probably normal at birth, suffered severe cognitive and emotional deficits later in life as a result of their early isolation from normal social environments.

Even when caretaking and social interaction with adults are sufficient for normal cognitive and emotional development, the absence of linguistic interaction with adults can lead to specific deficits in language acquisition. For example, hearing children of deaf parents have been reported to show severe language deficits (Bard and Sachs, 1977; Sachs and Johnson, 1976) except in cases where access to interaction with hearing adults or older siblings was available (Bard and Sachs, 1977; Jones and Quigley, 1979). Similarly, deaf children raised orally frequently show language retardation even when they are given much explicit language instruction. One reason for this retardation may be that much of the language in the environment is inaccessible to these children. Children raised in institutions, where access to interaction with adult caretakers is limited, also show retarded language development (DuPan and Roth, 1955; Pringle and Bossio, 1958; Pringle and Tanner, 1958; Tizard et al., 1972), as do children who are cared for more by peers or older siblings than by adults (Bates, 1975; Harkness, 1977).

Thus, social contacts with caring adults are crucial to normal development and linguistic interaction with adults is prerequisite to normal language acquisition. Beyond these effects, certain types of social interaction with adults facilitate language acquisition, both in normally developing children and in various groups of children showing language delay. These facilitative adult behaviors have been identified not only for the period when the child is actively acquiring language, but also during the prelinguistic period, before the child has started to talk or even communicate.

The purpose of this chapter is to: 1) review and evaluate the available literature on how social interaction with caretakers contributes to normal language acquisition; 2) review the small number of available studies that have attempted to apply these findings to intervention with language-delayed children; and 3) make some further suggestions for language intervention with various diagnostic groups of language-delayed children.

SOCIAL INTERACTIONS WITH NORMALLY DEVELOPING CHILDREN

It is important to consider two major conclusions to be drawn from studies of the acquisition of language. First, the child's development of language is a late stage in communicative development, and a refinement of earlier stages in the development of that ability. Children acquire the ability to communicate meanings, which can be paraphrased as *I want X, Look at X,* and *Pay attention to me,* before they have any language (Carter, 1978; Halliday, 1975), and their first words usually express precisely those same meanings (see de Villiers, this volume, for a more complete discussion of this progression). Second, the acquisition of expressive as well as receptive language is fully embedded in and dependent upon the social context in which the child develops. Expressively, the child's acquisition of semantic-syntactic constructions and simple morphology is guided by his communicative needs in the social context. Receptively, his performance is guided by his world knowledge and communicative expectations, not by syntactic analyses (see, for example, Bohannon, 1976; Shatz, 1978). Accordingly, language acquisition and communicative competence appear to be identical during the early stages of normal development. For the young child language *is* communication, except in cases of severe pathology (see, e.g., Blank, Gessner, and Esposito, 1979) when some linguistic forms are acquired independent of communicative intent. Only with the development of metalinguistic functions do most children start to deal with language forms independent of their interpersonal meaning.

The First Year of Life

Two principles are especially obvious during the first year:

1. Adults interpret child behaviors as attempts to communicate, even in situations where it is quite obvious that no explicit intention to communicate exists.
2. Children search for contingencies between salient objects, persons, and events in the world and the behavior of their caregivers.

These two principles, operating together, create a situation in which maximum correspondence is attained between the child's focus of attention and the caretaker's communicative behaviors. A number of excerpts from my own observations of mother-infant interaction are presented, in order to illustrate the nature and potential effect of caretaker-child interaction during the prelinguistic period. These observations were carried out as part of a study of 10 English mother-infant pairs, observed and videotaped when the children were about 3, 4½, 6, and 12 months old. Further information on the study can be found in Snow, deBlauw, and Van Roosmalen (1978).

Antony at Three Months Antony's mother is a housewife, and his father is a graduate student. Antony is their second child; he has an older brother named Richard. The following 2½-minute interchange between Antony and his mother took place when Antony was 3 months, 2 weeks, and 4 days old. It occurred during a 10-minute period of videotaping, taken during the same week as a 90-minute audiotaped observation. Clearly, Antony's mother interpreted the videotaping as a special situation, one that called for extra effort on her part to get Antony to "perform." However, her behavior during this session was not different in quality from her behavior during the longer observation; the only difference was that, when videotaped, she was more persistent in attempting to evoke responses.

Antony is lying face up on a blanket on the floor. His mother is kneeling on the floor directly in front of him, often leaning forward so that she is positioned above him. She is using a "lively" speech style, high-pitched voice, and frequent rising intonation (indicated in the transcripts by a question mark).

M: Now you're getting in the mood. Are you getting in the mood? All right? You keep it up. Do some more. All right? Now you do some more of that. Mmm? You talk some more. Come on. You kick and talk some more. Mmm. You kick and talk some more. That's right. That's right. Come on. Come on. You talk some more. Talk some more. Come on. Come on.
A: (broad smile)
M: That's better. Come on. Say some more. Say some more. Come on.
A: (stretches)
M: That's a big stretch.
A: (coughs)
M: Oh dear. Oh dear. Come on.
A: (vocalizes, smiles)
M: That's better. And some more. Come on.
A: (stretches)
M: What a big stretch. What a big stretch. What a big stretch. More coming out? Is there more coming out? Come on, say some more.
A: (vocalizes)
M: That's right.
A: (vocalizes)
M: That's better. Come on. That's better. That's better. Say some more. Come on. Say lots more. You keep on talking. Yes you do.
A: (burps)
M: Oh dear me. Oh dear me. Oh goodness yes. Oh dear.
A: (vocalizes)
M: That's right. Come on. More. More. Come on.
A: (stretches, opens mouth)
M: Nothing's coming out. Nothing's coming out. Come on. More. Come on. Lots more talking. Come on. Lots more talking.
A: (vocalizes)
M: Lots more talking.

A: (vocalizes)
M: Lots more talking. That's right. That's better. That's better.
A: (turns head away from M)
M: This way. More? More? More? Come on. (kisses A)
A: (vocalizes)
M: That's right. More? (kisses A)
A: (vocalizes)
M: I know, it's very exciting. Come on. (kisses A three times) More?

I have reproduced this exchange at such length because it illustrates so well the first principle of communicative development mentioned above—that caretakers search for communicative responses in the behavior of their children. This principle is especially obvious in this exchange precisely because the child involved is so young. The fact that Antony is only 3 months old, and clearly is not capable of understanding what his mother is asking him nor of responding in any true sense, does not deter his mother from requesting him to talk or from responding to his vocalizations as speech.

Antony's mother's speech in the above passage also illustrates some of the frequently noted characteristics of "baby talk." She used short, grammatically simple, and highly repetitive utterances that had strong ties to the here and now or the baby's current experiences and surroundings (see Snow, 1977b, for a review of the studies on mothers' speech to children).

The first studies of mothers' speech to children were done with children who were just starting to talk, and it was generally assumed that maternal speech modifications were adjustments to the limited language comprehension capabilities of the children. However, later studies with younger, prelinguistic children (e.g., Kaye, 1980; Snow, 1977a; Stern, 1974; Sylvester-Bradley and Trevarthen, 1978) showed that maternal speech to infants from birth onward is simple, concrete, and repetitive. These findings led many researchers to conclude that the child's level of comprehension does not control the modifications found in caretaker speech. Instead, it was suggested that baby talk is the result of caretakers' beliefs about appropriate ways of treating infants who are assumed to be capable of participating in reciprocal interactions. It was pointed out that extensive amounts of talk and play with young infants are characteristic of only some cultures (Snow, 1981); in other cultures, caretakers respond to infants' distress signals, but think it unnecessary or silly to talk or play with prelinguistic children (see Schieffelin and Eisenberg this volume, for a more complete discussion of cultural variation in mother-child interaction). In Western cultures, the typical baby talk speech style has been explained as the results of: 1) caretakers' attempts to impose conversational forms of interaction on the child (Snow, 1977a); 2) adaptations to the child's form of communication (Sylvester-Bradley and Trevarthen, 1978); and/or 3) efforts to construct a theory of who the baby is (Kaye and Charney, 1980). Central to these alternate explanations of the origin of baby talk is the notion that caretakers attempt to communicate with infants even before the infants are capable of performing true communicative acts.

However, the fact that baby talk modifications seem to be affected by caretakers' notions about the importance of communicating with infants should not blind us to the role of the addressee's linguistic ability in controlling the nature of those modifications. Bohannon and Marquis (1977) found that a child could control the amount of repetition and the degree of simplicity in the speech addressed to him by demonstrating different levels of comprehension. When children are old enough to respond differentially to content and linguistic form in adult speech, they give cues both by how they talk and by how well they comprehend. Both modes help to regulate the type and level of modifications in speech addressed to them.

For prelinguistic children, other features of their behavior contribute to caretakers' speech modifications. For example, Snow (1977a) found that the proportion of maternal references to the baby and his needs decreased while references to objects and events increased at about 7 months, when the babies were showing greatly increased attention to nonhuman visual stimuli and were starting to manipulate toys and other objects. It has been suggested that the timing parameters and the high level of repetitiveness in maternal speech to infants represent a response to the rhythmic and repetitive bursts of activity shown by the infants themselves (Kaye, 1980; Stern et al., 1983), and that some of the paralinguistic and phonetic features of baby talk can be seen as adaptations to the infant's perceptual capabilities and preferences (Sachs, 1977). It seems, then, that the modifications found in caretaker speech to infants and young children can be understood only if we keep two factors in mind: 1) caretakers' cultural beliefs about the appropriateness of interacting and establishing communication with infants, and 2) caretakers' responsiveness to the child's communicative, precommunicative, and attentional behaviors.

Antony at Six Months The following exchanges were extracted from a 90-minute observation session of Antony at 6 months, 4 days of age. The entire session was audiotaped, but handwritten observational notes were taken to supplement the tape transcriptions. During most of the 90-minute observation, Antony's mother was involved in feeding him. First, she fed him solids with a spoon, and then from a bottle.

> *M:* Pop it in.
> *A:* (vocalizes with mouth closed) Mmmm.
> *M:* Mmmm, lucky boy.
> *A:* Mmmm.
> *M:* Mmmm. Lucky boy. Pop it in, that's right. Pop it in. Go on. Eat it.

In the preceding exchange, Antony's mother both imitates and interprets his closed-mouth vocalization, relating it to the meaningful adult form *mmmm* for "delicious." This is another example of how mothers search for communicative intention in an infant's behavior. In this case, the search was supported by the infant's production of a vocalization that resembles a meaningful adult vocalization.

However, the child's production of a vocalization that resembles an adult utterance is not necessary for the attribution of communicative intent. As the first example demonstrated, smiles and even burps are considered indicative of communicative intent when the child is 3 months old. Similarly, in the following example, Antony's mother attributed communicative intent to the infant based on his crying.

> Antony's mother was spoon-feeding him. Meanwhile, his 2-year-old brother Richard had, unnoticed, crawled onto a rather high bookcase. Richard fell suddenly from the bookcase; his resulting scream startled Antony.
> *M:* (to Richard) Up you get. What a silly place to climb up on. Better now? Shall we go . . . shall we go upstairs and find what the mouse brought you?
> *R:* (crying) Yes.
> *M:* (to Richard) I think we better had.
> *M:* (to A, who has been crying since Richard's first scream) It's quite all right now, he's better.
> *F:* (to A, who is still crying) Come on, little fella. Hey! Wasn't that a surprise! He'll be all right.

In this exchange, both parents respond to Antony's crying as if it was occasioned by Richard's fall, and as if it expressed concern for Richard. Although it seems likely that Antony did start crying because he was startled or frightened by Richard's screams, it is unlikely that he was crying out of sympathy for Richard's pain. Thus, both parents were finding highly sophisticated communicative intentions in Antony's behavior. In addition, both were relating his behavior to a highly salient event in their common surroundings.

It is important to note that, when Antony's parents related his behavior to a salient event in the environment, the parents themselves referred to and nonverbally responded to this salient event. Repeated instances of this sort may facilitate the child's compliance with the second principle of development, that children attempt to relate the behaviors of their caretakers to salient objects, persons, and events.

A similar facilitative situation occurs when parents initiate discussion about salient objects and events. For instance, in the next example, Antony's mother initiates conversation about what, to the child, must be the most salient events in his surroundings—Richard's disappearance and sudden reappearance.

> *M:* (to Richard) Why don't you run away and hide someplace and then come back and see what he does.
> *R:* (runs to kitchen)
> *M:* (to A) Where's Richard? Where's he gone, Toti? Is he coming?
> *A:* (vocalizes)
> *R:* (runs back)
> *M:* Is he coming? Where is he? Is he coming? There he comes! Goodness!

In the preceding example, the mother only guessed that Antony's vocalization was related to Richard's disappearance and eventual reappearance. However, there were also instances in which the child's gaze makes the focus of his attention more explicit. Note that in the forthcoming example, the need for guesswork is minimized when Antony looks and smiles at the observer.

> (Observer sneezes)
> *A:* (looks at Observer, smiles)
> *M:* That was funny, wasn't it? Sneezing.

This sort of maternal talk creates a situation in which the child's focus of attention matches the available verbal input. Macnamara (1972), Cross (1977, 1978), and Wells (1980) have all hypothesized that this correspondence is a prerequisite to language development.

The preceding two examples also illustrate what Gleason (1973) has called the "language of socialization." Parents use this language to tell children or indicate to them what they should do, think, and feel in different situations. In the first example, the mother literally took Antony's role in the game. She put into words the reactions he was expected to have at Richard's actions: interest at Richard's disappearance, surprise and joy at his reappearance. In the second example, the mother provided a label for both the event, *sneezing*, and the infant's experience, *funny*. In both of these examples, the mother verbalized Antony's expected reaction to a salient event. Gleason gives similar examples with somewhat older children, e.g., mothers saying "Oh what a *heavy* pail!" in regard to ordinary-sized pails.

Adults' comments on salient objects and events isolate those experiences for the infants, help focus the infants' attention on them, and provide labels and verbal responses that the infants can, after many exposures, themselves use for such experience. It has been confirmed repeatedly in research on caretaker speech that the semantic content of maternal speech is controlled by the concrete perceptual world of the child. Snow (1977a) found that 65-70% of mothers' referential utterances to 6-month-olds referred to the infants' immediate surroundings. Collis (1977) and Collis and Schaffer (1975) reported that 51% of the maternal utterances addressed to 10-month-olds referred to objects that the child was actually looking at. Messer (1978), in a study of 11-24-month-olds, found that between 73% and 96% of mothers' references to toys concerned objects that, at the time of the utterance, were actually being manipulated either by the mother or the child.

Caretakers succeed in talking about the events and objects that are salient to their prelinguistic children only to the extent that they can correctly identify the current perceptual experiences of their children. The caretaker's ability to give the child labels for objects and events is limited by the match between the adult's and the child's preceptions of what is going on. We have already shown how the child's gaze can facilitate such a match. The match improves when the child reaches the stage of being able to direct the adult's comments by asking questions like "What's that?", "What's happening?", and "What's he doing?" When a prelinguistic child looks at a particular doll, the adult can reasonably assume that the child's attention is focused on the doll, not the nearby truck; but the adult must still guess that the child's interest is in the doll's name (Raggedy-Ann), not its color (red), its facial expression (smiling), its number (one), labels for its part (head, leg, arm, body), its possessor (baby), its position (sitting), or any of the many other things one might say about a Raggedy Ann doll.

Greenfield and Smith (1976) pointed out the importance of a similar perceptual organization for adults and children in the early stages of language acquisition. Similarly, Nelson (1973) offered evidence suggesting that children whose mothers matched them in their typical ways of perceiving events acquired language faster than children whose mothers' speech was not matched to the child's own semantic organization. One might well ask, however, whether the labeling of events and objects that goes on at 10, 9, and even 5 or 4 months of age, long before the child himself starts to produce words, has any effect on the child's eventual vocabulary development. Two studies suggest that hearing their mothers produce labels for objects and experiences might well improve children's ability to later remember and articulate those labels themselves. Mann and Baer (1971) showed that, when 4-year-olds were given receptive training only on nonsense words, the children articulated those words better than control words that they had not heard. These results suggest that hearing his mother repeat words like *bottle, doll, ball,* and *bed* throughout the first year of life may contribute to the 1-year-old's ability to pronounce those words. Even more relevant, Vasta et al. (1978) showed that words heard as labels for objects were articulated more accurately than words not heard or words heard equally often but not in association with objects. Because both these studies were done with older children, further research is necessary before the results can be extrapolated to children in the prelinguistic period. However, it seems likely that, for some children at least, purely passive exposure to words helps them analyze the acoustic properties of a word, so that a better attempt can be made at pronouncing it.

Antony at One Year The two principles mentioned in the last section also apply to the 1-year-old child's interactions. Adults continue to interpret a child's behaviors as attempts to communicate even when it is obvious to observers that no effort to communicate was made; and children still attempt to relate the behaviors of their caretakers to salient objects, persons, and events. The following exchanges illustrate the relevance of these principles to the 1-year-old child's interactions. These exchanges were taped during a 90-minute observation session when Antony was 13 months, 2 weeks, and 4 days old.

Antony is eating lunch, using his hands to feed himself.
M: Well, what do you think about it?
A: (vocalizes)
M: Yes, it's nice, isn't it?
A: (vocalizes)
M: Are you going to eat it?
A: (vocalizes)
M: No? You going to have a drink? You have a drink first, and then think about it.

According to the mother, Antony did not use any real words at this time. However, the absence of standard lexical items does not stop the mother from attributing communicative intent to the child in accord with the first principle. Indeed, the mother interprets Antony's vocalizations quite readily and distinctively, although none of them approaches a standard adult lexical item. Very similar sounding (to the observer) vocalizations are interpreted first as a statement that the food is nice, and then as a denial that Antony will eat it.

Another important point to notice about this exchange is the high frequency with which Antony vocalizes. The alternation of speaking turns between Antony and his mother is very frequent; no longer does the mother need to talk for a long time, waiting for Antony to answer. This decrease in the mean length of the maternal turn during the first year of life has been documented (e.g., Snow, 1977a), and reflects the fact that children achieve considerable communicative and conversational competence long before their linguistic achievements are even measureable.

The 1-year-old's considerable communicative competence is also reflected in his use of gestures. At about 12 months, children start to communicate through gestures–such as reaching, pointing, and offering—sometimes accompanied by vocalizations (Bates, Camaioni, and Volterra, 1975; Carter, 1978; Rheingold, Hay, and West, 1976). These communicative gestures often originate in the context of shared games or routines; when responded to as meaningful, however, they develop very quickly into the conventionalized signs characteristic of sophisticated communication systems. How children use gestures to communicate and how adults respond to them is illustrated in the following episode.

M: Look here. You going to have some more?
A: (holds grape out to M)
M: No thanks, you have it. Pop it in. Pop it in.
A: (puts grape in mouth)
M: There!
A: (vocalizes)
M: Yes! (imitating the intonation of A's vocalization) Put it in. That's a good boy.
A: (vocalizes)
M: Nice, isn't it?
A: (playing with food)
M: That's what's called messing about with your lunch. Put it in. Come on. Don't think you really want any more. Come on. Quick. Quick quick quick. One two three whee.
A: (fusses)
M: No more? All right. You finish your drink then. Drink it up.

Notice Antony's mother's response to his gesture of holding out a grape: "No thanks, you have it." In accord with the first principle, she interpreted his gesture, which may or may not have been meant as an offer to give the grape, as if it had been a completely executed speech act. Furthermore, as in the first example given in this section, she responded to his minimally articulated vocalizations as if they were not just words, but various speech acts. Considering both the mother's response to Antony's gesture and her response to Antony's vocalizations, this 1-minute exchange contains three examples of how mothers ascribe specific communicative intents to a child before there is any clear evidence of those intents. Antony's mother interpreted his holding out a grape as an offer, she interpreted his vocalizations as "yes," and she interpreted his fussing as an expression of not wanting any more lunch.

Finally, as in the early stages of the prelinguistic period, parents infer that a child's vocalizations concern salient objects/events, and they tailor their own contributions to involve those same objects/

events. This process, together with the ever-present ascription of communicative intent, is illustrated in the following episode.

> A: (crawls to M, onto her lap)
> M: And what do you want, hmm? You're not having my coffee. No. Mum mum mum. Say it!
> A: (looks at observer's coffee)
> M: You're not having her coffee either. Mum mum mum. No you're not!

In this case, his mother models for Antony his own expression of anger—*Mum mum mum*. This example of the language of socialization resulted from a whole chain of inferences that began with Antony looking at the coffee: his look at the coffee indicates that he wants the coffee, therefore he is requesting the coffee, therefore he will be angry at her refusal to give it to him.

As the above observations illustrate, normally developing children grow up in a situation in which their own search for contingencies and their caretakers' search for communicative intentions conspire to create correspondences between the child's desire or focus of attention and the adult's simultaneous or successive utterance. The occurrence of these correspondences is a prerequisite to language acquisition, because the very young child is clearly incapable of figuring out the structure of language unless presented with linguistic input that is decipherable on nonlinguistic grounds. The child assumes that the adult utterance encodes what he himself is observing about the situation; he then uses his knowledge of the structure of the event observed, plus whatever receptive knowledge he has of the lexical items used by the adult, to figure out how to express the relevant relationships linguistically. If the child heard the same utterance but could not predict what aspect of the event was being described, he would have no basis for deciding what relationship was being expressed, and thus he would have no opportunity for learning how to express that relationship himself (Macnamara, 1972).

Games during the First Year of Life Game playing is a seemingly minor, but potentially very important, aspect of parent-child interaction during the first year of life. When successful, it provides a concentration of many of the aspects of interaction discussed above: mother and child direct their attention to the same event, the child is given maximum opportunity to take his turn, and minimal or diffuse child responses are interpreted as adequate and specific.

> M: Oh goodness me. Oh goodness me. (lifts Matthew above her head, looking at him) You like that?
> (lifts again) Is that funny?
> (lifts again) Is that funny?

(lifts again)	Are you flying? Are you flying? Are you? Hmm?
(lifts again)	Are you flying? Whee!
(lifts again)	Whee! Are you flying?
(lifts again)	What can you see up there? What can you see?
(lifts again)	Ho! Hooo!

The above sequence, in which the mother of 3-month-, two-week-old Matthew initiated the game she called "airplane," illustrates the potential benefits of game playing. Bruner (1975a, 1975b, 1977; Bruner and Sherwood, 1976; Ratner and Bruner, 1978) has identified the following skills and bits of information that could be acquired in the context of game playing:

1. *The nature of a signal*—When playing bouncing games like "Ride a cock horse" or the "airplane" game demonstrated above, mothers often pause expectantly at crucial points in the game. This pause gives the child an opportunity to produce some behavior—typically a jiggle, a laugh, or a vocalization—that can be taken as a signal to continue. More importantly, when the mother makes her behavior contingent upon the child's behavior, the latter's behavior will eventually develop into a true, intentionally produced signal within the context of the game.
2. *Agent-action-patient relationships*—In games like "give and take" and "hide and find," the mother and the child alternately give and receive, hide and look for objects. Thus, the roles of "agent" and "recipient" (patient) are abstracted from an individual's performance in much the same way that the deictic expressions (e.g., *you* and *I*) are abstracted from the person but identified with specific roles within specific conversational situations. In the experience of the preverbal child, the most crucial activities probably involve familiar actors—e.g., the child eating, drinking, pounding, and throwing; and the caretaker feeding, changing, and picking up. Outside the context of games like "Give and take," the child may have very little chance to notice the separability of actions like *eating* from the agent of the action, a distinction that is, of course, crucial to linguistic expression.
3. *Reference*—In "give and take" games, as in "hide and find" games, the major object of the exercise is to maintain the child's attention on the object attended to by the mother. This exercise in joint attention is a prerequisite to meaningful reference, and thus to teaching the child labels for objects.
4. *Phonological patterns*—The highly predictable and repetitive structure of games provides the child with many opportunities to attach meaning to the adult utterances used at crucial junctures in

games, and eventually to imitate and use those utterances in his own initiation of, or participation in, games. A high proportion of the first expressions used by children—e.g., *"Peek-a-boo," "Where is it?", "All gone,"* and *"What's that?"*—can be accounted for by the game routines that they have experienced (Benedict, 1979; Nelson, 1973).

A great advantage of games and other such teaching routines is that they can be expanded and complicated to stay at or just beyond the child's level of competence. "Pat-a-cake" can be played with a 9-month-old, whose passive hands are taken through the requisite gestures, and with a 3-year-old, who sings the words himself. "Where's your (body part)?" routines can be carried out with 10-month-olds, who respond by pointing correctly to a few parts of their own bodies; with 2-year-olds, who can point correctly to several parts of their own, their parents', their siblings', and their dolls' bodies; and with 3-year-olds, who solemnly quiz their parents on their knowledge of body parts. The importance of such games and routines is evident from their by-products rather than from their frequency of occurrence. Although these activities seem to represent an insignificant amount of the social and linguistic interaction to which the child is exposed, much of the child's early ability to comprehend speech and a large proportion of his early words develop from such routines. (See Sachs, this volume, for a more complete discussion of games and their benefits.)

Social Routines during the First Year of Life In contrast to the preceding playful routines, a large amount of parental training and teaching is devoted to social routines such as *hello, goodbye, excuse me, please,* and *thank you* (Gleason, 1980; Greif and Gleason, 1980). The study of how these social routines are acquired is important for two reasons. First, their mastery enables the child to function as a full participant in the social order. Adequate performance of the basic social tasks of greeting, thanking, requesting, and acknowledging represents an important step to parents, especially to the parents of language-handicapped or otherwise retarded children (Gleason, 1980). Children who possess these simple skills have acquired the ability to get adults to talk to them, and thus are fostering their own language acquisition.

Second, the way in which social routines like *hello* and *goodbye* are taught and learned may not be so dissimilar from the way in which a great deal of language acquisition occurs. It has been thought that the learning of such memorized routines is irrelevant to the acquisition of the rules governing most language use. However, it has become increasingly clear that: 1) explicit teaching does occur for all aspects of language acquisition; 2) many of the child's early multiword utterances may be acquired initially as memorized chunks, not as the result of applying productive rules; and 3) many early utterances may be acquired first as fillers for slots in social routines, i.e., as units with purely communicative function rather than as semantically analyzed units.

The Second and Third Years of Life:
The Period of Early Language Acquisition

During the second and third years of life, the child's act of assuming and looking for correspondences between his own focus of attention and the adult's utterance continues to support his language acquisition. However, the child's role in the process expands and becomes more active as he grows. The mother no longer has to rely on eye contact, gaze direction, gestures, and socializations to determine the focus of the child's attention. By 18 months the child is able to identify that focus by issuing comments, questions, and requests. These utterances not only provide much better clues to his intentions than did his preverbal behavior, but, in comparison to the latter, they also impose stronger obligations on the adult to respond.

Consider the following example, in which a 30-month-old named Nathaniel manages to control the topic of conversation gesturally and verbally using only his rather simple interrogative form and much imitation of the adult's utterances.

N: This a this?
Who's this?
Da this?
M: This is a special tape recorder, Nathaniel.
N: Special tape recorder.
Mummy's tape recorder.
M: Mummy's special tape recorder.
It's a . . . like a television.
N: Television tape recorder.
M: It takes pictures too.
N: Makes tapes too.
Makes tapes too.
M: Makes tapes too?

Even during the period after the development of speech, breakdown can occur in the process of providing correspondences. Consider the situation of the child whose articulation is relatively unclear. The following exchange between Nathaniel, at 31 months, and his parents was recorded on a Saturday morning at the breakfast table. The parents' conversation for the previous few minutes dealt with their plans for the day, and with making a list of needed groceries.

M: Cold in here, isn't it?
F: Um-hmm.
M: Nathaniel, are you cold?
N: Go to the supermarket.
M: What, sweetie?
N: Go the supermarket. Go the supermarket.
M: I don't understand you.
N: Go to the supermarket. Go the supermarket. Go to the super . . . (noticing his own spoon) Nathaniel spoon itchy. Nathaniel spoon itchy.
M: Nathaniel's spoon is itchy?
F: Grapefruit spoon.

In this conversation, Nathaniel demonstrated considerable conversational and cognitive competence. He contributed in a relevant way to the conversation between his parents, and demonstrated knowledge of his family's Saturday routine and of how and where groceries are obtained. All of this competence was short circuited in its communicative effectiveness by his parents' inability to decipher his (admittedly rather deviant) pronunciation of the word supermarket. As a result of this inability, the conversation broke down, and Nathaniel lost his opportunity to receive 1) confirmation of his prediction that the family would be visiting the supermarket; 2) any further information about the proposed visit; 3) a model for improving his pronunciation of the word supermarket, or 4) a model of a more complex or correct utterance about visiting the supermarket.

The sort of communicative frustration experienced frequently by Nathaniel during his third year is probably quite similar to what all children experience sometimes, especially during the early stages of language acquisition, and what language-delayed or language-disordered children experience regularly. Nathaniel's experience represents a breakdown of precisely the kind of semantic contingency between child speech and adult speech that is generally recognized to be crucial to normal language acquisition. The importance of semantically contingent speech during the period of rapid language acquisition, from about 18 months to about the fourth birthday, is discussed more fully in this section.

Semantic contingency refers to the relationship of adult speech (in semantic context) to the immediately preceding child speech. Semantically contingent speech is therefore contingent on the child's speech not just temporally or acoustically, but in terms of the topic being discussed. Semantically contingent speech thus provides an even stronger set of correspondences between a child's behavior or focus of attention and verbal input than is possible during the first year of life, when many of the correspondences have to be created by the adult on the basis of rather minimal cues from the child. The prelinguistic child cannot be assumed to express any semantic intent, so the adult cannot be semantically contingent. The adult interacting with the 2-year-old, on the other hand, can use the child's utterances as a basis for finding semantic contingency.

Of course, the adult will be much more successful in achieving semantic contingency if he or she is familiar with the child, with the child's experiences and interests, and with the child's linguistic and cognitive level. The familiar caretaker can combine knowledge of what the child knows and is likely to be talking about with knowledge from the child's utterances to ensure maximum semantic contingency.

The most striking and reproducible finding about social interaction and language acquisition is the finding that semantically contingent speech facilitates children's learning of language (Cross, 1978; Wells, 1980). Semantically contingent speech includes, but is not limited to, a number of types of adult speech that have been mentioned in the child language literature for the last 15 years as likely to support language acquisition: adult repetitions of child utterances, expansions of child utterances, response to child questions, clarification questions (also called occasional questions and contingent queries), and acknowledgments or confirmations of child assertions. It contrasts precisely with those types of speech that have a negative effect on language acquisition: expressions of rejection or disapproval of child utterances, directives to initiate new actions, sudden changes of topic, and negative commands. In short, during the early stages of language acquisition, adult speech that extends conversational topics initiated by the child facilitates the child's acquisition of language, whereas adult speech that introduces new conversational topics, which requires the child to shift the focus of his attention to something entirely different, or directs him to initiate new activities unrelated to his current activities, does not support fast and easy language acquisition.

Table 1 presents an overview of the various studies that have looked at some aspect of semantic contingency in speech to children. These studies are not reviewed here individually; taken together, they demonstrate that 1) a great proportion of the speech addressed to children is semantically contingent on the children's previous utterances, and 2) the more semantically contingent speech a child hears the greater the facilitation of his language acquisition. The centrality of the notion of semantic contingency in normal social interaction with language-learning children poses an important problem to those dealing with language-delayed populations. To a large extent, semantic contingency is maintained for the 2-year-old because his language development and his cognitive development are paced together. Without here going into the very important issues of whether and how cognitive development steers language development (see, e.g., Bowerman, 1978, for an excellent discussion of these issues), it is clear that the 2-year-old's language is closely tied to his or her cognitive development. Brown (1973) pointed out that the "prevalent semantic relations" that appear repeatedly in Stage I speech encode precisely the notions—agency, action, location, attribution—that are being worked on in the cognitive domain during the sensorimotor period of development. Similarly, maternal speech to 2-year-olds is largely limited to discussions of actions, locations, attributes, and the other prevalent relations (Snow, 1977b), and thus is in general pitched at the right semantic level for the interests and abilities of the 2-year-old child. In the best case, maternal speech is also semantically contingent on the child's thoughts and interests in an utterance-by-utterance analysis (Cross, 1978; Wells, 1980).

Semantically contingent speech in the very strict sense—use of expansions, repetitions, and semantic extensions, and avoidance of initiation of new conversational topics—is probably facilitatory only during the early stages of language development, when children's comprehension abilities are sufficiently limited that they cannot process both new complex linguistic structures and new content. Second, even during the early stages of language development, it seems that normally developing children receive a significant amount of input that is *not* strictly semantically contingent nor finely tuned to their own cognitive-linguistic level.

In American homes, fathers evidently often have the function of introducing new, more complex linguistic material to children, perhaps because they are less familiar with their children's abilities and limitations. Gleason and her colleagues (Gleason, 1980; Greif and Gleason, 1980; Masur, 1979; Masur and Gleason, 1979; Weintraub, 1976) have found that fathers are responsible for introducing rare vocabulary items to their 2-year-old children, and Engle (1979) found that fathers speak more complexly than mothers to 2-year-olds, but less complexly to 3-year-olds. Both Engle (1980) and Masur (1979) found that fathers were more likely to initiate and dominate play activities, whereas mothers followed the children's activities more. Fathers may, by failing to adjust their speech level to their children's abilities as finely as mothers can, force their children to expand their abilities, thus providing a transition to contacts with teachers, casual acquaintances, and strangers, who are even more "out-of-tune" with the child.

It has been suggested (Cross, 1977; Snow, 1977b) that semantic limitations on maternal speech account to some extent for the widely noted characteristics of syntactic simplicity and repetitiveness. In addition, however, parents do seem to monitor their children's language

Table 1. Studies of semantically contingent speech

Study	Measure of semantic contingency	Age of addresses	N	Nature of findings
Cazden (1965)	Expansions	28–38 mos	12	Experimental manipulation; no effect of expansions over greater exposure to conversations with adults
Cherry (in press)	Clarification questions	30–48 mos 2 years	37 12	Clarification requests constitute 9% of adult-to-child utterances; their form is adjusted to child's language level
Cross (1978)	Expansions, semantic extensions, conversational initiatives	19–33 mos	16	Linguistically accelerated children received more semantically contingent speech, fewer conversational directives
Hovell, Schumaker, and Sherman (1978)	Expansions	22–24 mos	4	Operant paradigm; expansion of noun phrases helped more than modeling noncontingently in teaching adjectives
Howe (1980)	Initiation of exchanges, provision of extended replies	20–25 mos	24	Greatest progress over 3 months in children whose mothers provided extended replies to their initiations
Kaye and Charney (1980)	Response, turnabout	26 mos 30 mos	27 26	Mothers control the maintenance of conversation even at 30 months; no effects of conversational structure on language development found

...on and Loud (1972)	Expansions	6;3–7;8	83	Operant paradigm; imitation + expansion superior to simple exposure in teaching adjective ordering rule
Nelson (1977)	Recastings illustrating complex verbs or questions	28–31 mos	12	Experimental manipulation; selective effect of recastings on production of verbs and questions
Nelson, Carskaddon, and Bonvillian (1973)	Expansions, recastings	32–40 mos	27	Experimental manipulation; recastings and expansions significantly improved children's language over control group, especially verb measures
Sachs (1979)	Reference to earlier past	20–29 mos (MLU = 1.0–4.0)	1	Parental reference to earlier past was infrequent until child started to show comprehension, then jumped abruptly in frequency
Schachter (1979)	Responsive speech	22–34 mos	30	Responsive speech more typical of high socioeconomic status groups; explicit teaching did not differentiate groups
Schumaker (1976)	Expansions	±2 years	?	Children were successfully trained using expansions to produce formulas and novel utterances

continued

90 Snow

Table 1. (*Continued*)

Study	Measure of semantic contingency	Age of addresses	N	Nature of findings
Snow (1983)	Related to child activity, vocalization, or utterance	17 mos	10	Correlation of 0.70 between numbers of semantically related maternal utterances and child's vocabulary
Stella-Prorok (1981)	Maternal pointing, showing, describing present objects and events	13–36 mos	15	Observational; maternal pointing, showing, and labeling present objects correlated with child's level of development
Wells (1980)	Imitations, expansions, extensions, locus of reference	MLU = 1.5	33	Significant correlation with child's language level 9 months later found for maternal imitations, extensions, and references to adult and child
Whitehurst and Novak (1973)	Expansions	3;5–4;7	4	Operant paradigm; best learning rate for types of modeling phrases that child imitated and received contingent feedback on

abilities, probably by assessing comprehension rather than production, and to adjust both the topics discussed and the formal complexity of their utterances accordingly (Bohannon and Marquis, 1977; Cross, 1977; Longhurst and Stepanich, 1975; Moerk, 1974; Sachs, 1979; Wells, 1980). This fine tuning may not be as precise syntactically as it is semantically, simply because topic selection falls more easily under the control of the speaker than does selection of syntactic form, but it does nonetheless ensure that there is a reasonable match between the comprehension abilities of the child and the complexity of the syntax to which he is exposed.

Relatively little attention has been paid to the question of how social interaction supports vocabulary acquisition. It is clear that some explicit and much implicit teaching occurs (Anglin, 1976; Rogers, 1978, 1979), at least in middle-class homes. Recent research suggests, in fact, that the first word combinations rely on rules for single words or very small classes of words (see, e.g., Braine, 1971), not on fully productive rules. If this is true, then the child's vocabulary size and content is crucial to his syntactic level, and interactions that teach vocabulary can have direct consequences for syntactic development (Furrow, Nelson, and Benedict, 1979). Book reading is a prime context for vocabulary acquisition (see Goldfield and Snow, in press, for a review). Ninio (1980) has analyzed social interactions around picture books of middle-class and working-class mothers, and has demonstrated that the nature of the book reading routine adhered to by the mother predicts whether children learn their picture book vocabulary receptively or productively. If children start out comprehending adult sentences primarily by looking for reasonable relations among the lexical items they know, then vocabulary learning may be more crucial to syntactic acquisition than has traditionally been recognized or acknowledged.

Language Development after Age Three

During the early stages of language acquisition, the most facilitative adult interactions with children are contingent on and responsive to the children's utterances. However, after the early stages of language development, it is possible that children's language and cognitive development are better facilitated by parental behaviors that go beyond simply responding to, accepting, and extending the child's own intentions. Once children are capable of processing moderately complex speech, they should be exposed to new information about how the world is organized, and encouraged to expand their imaginations to deal with fantasy, humor, and deceit. In other words, because children in the early and late stages of language acquisition need to learn different skills, a style of interaction that is optimal for the young child may not be optimal for the older one. Optimal styles of interaction for a child in the later stages of language acquisition are geared to promote his vocabulary and world knowledge, the ability to use language playfully and creatively, the development of literacy-related language skills, and the ability to reflect on language and use it noncommunicatively in games and puzzles.

Studies of how the 3–6-year-old child's social interactions are related to his language growth have focused on: 1) the relationship between the home environment of the child and his early development of literary skills; and 2) social class differences in social interaction and school-related skills. In regard to the first issue, researchers who have studied preschool, largely self-taught spellers and readers have identified a constellation of parental behaviors that seem to be associated with early literacy: presence of books in the home, use of literacy skills in ways that are relevant to the child; positive responsiveness to the child's interest in hearing stories; and willingness to answer the child's questions about how to read letters and words as well as how to spell words. On the other hand, high levels of parental motivation for early literacy and parental attempts to teach children to read are not sufficient for successful preschool achievement of literacy (Clark, 1976; Durkin, 1966; Söderbergh, 1971). As with language, the crucial factor seems to be parental responsiveness to children's interests: responding to the child's interest in literacy-related activities promotes the development of literacy better than does parental initiation of literacy training.

It may seem that the development of reading ability is not a topic that should properly be treated in a discussion of the relationship between social interaction and language acquisition. However, reading can be seen as a stage in language acquisition because it depends heavily on the development of certain linguistic skills—specifically, the skills of phoneme abstraction and symbolization (Calfee, Lindamood, and Lindamood, 1973; Liberman et al., 1974). A second reason to consider the development of reading ability in this chapter is that the language-disabled population and the reading-disabled population overlap considerably (see, e.g., Hutson, 1974). Another reason is that reading can be used as a language remediation tool for some populations of language-handicapped children. A successful program utilizing reading as the primary channel for teaching language to hearing-impaired children has been initiated in Sweden (Söderbergh, 1981). Thus, input via reading could be a major factor in improving the language skills of severely hearing-impaired school-age children.

It is clear that reading failure is often a phenomenon associated with low family income, low levels of parental educational achievement, poor housing, and other indicators of low social status. The nature of the social interaction in families whose children are at high risk for reading failure has been described by Hess and Shipman (1965) and Bee et al. (1969). The long-term effects of impoverished home environments have been described (Bradley and Caldwell, 1976; Elardo, Bradley, and Caldwell, 1977; Walters, Connor, and Zunich, 1964), as have the positive effects of training mothers in different methods of interaction with their children (Madden, Levenstein, and Levenstein, 1976). Low socioeconomic status parents do engage their children in many of the types of semantically contingent and literacy-related behaviors we have identified as facilitative (see Andersen, Teale, and Estrada 1980; Miller, 1982; Schachter, 1979), but the frequency or consistency of such interactions may be less (see Schachter, 1979) in families who have relatively few resources of time, money, and leisure available for devotion to their children.

SOCIAL INTERACTION WITH LANGUAGE-HANDICAPPED, -DELAYED, AND -DISORDERED CHILDREN

Language-impaired children may have special handicaps or they may have specific language disorders in the absence of apparent handicaps. In either event, language-impaired children have problems developing appropriate language usage.

Language-Handicapped Children

Consider the situation of the child who suffers from hearing loss, blindness, or Down's syndrome. The child who has a moderate to severe hearing loss sees what is going on around him and what his mother is looking at, pointing at, or manipulating, but he does not hear clearly what she has to say about those objects and events. Thus the level of correspondence between objects and events that the child observes and the parental speech he hears is much less than for a hearing child. Furthermore, the playful routines, such as those that Antony's mother frequently initiated when he was 3 months old, and that parents usually find very rewarding, do not arouse much attention or excitement in a child with a hearing loss. Finally, if the child's parents are committed to an oral education, they might ignore and possibly discourage the child's use of the early communicative gestures that provide an important channel of contact even for hearing children (LeGrand, 1979; Snow, 1981a). Thus, parents committed to an oral education may respond less frequently and may be less exploitative of their children's early communicative behaviors than are parents of hearing children or parents who advocate Total Communication for children with hearing losses.

In contrast to the hard-of-hearing child, the blind or severely visually handicapped child hears what his parents say to him and responds to playful routines; but he fails to relate the adult utterances to what is going on unless his parents are extremely skilled in identifying the child's focus of attention. The blind child does not orient visually to an object evoking his attention; nor does he orient toward adults with whom he is playing. This inability to give the cues normally associated with attention focus makes it difficult to sustain games of object-centered play routines with blind children (Fraiberg, 1977; Urwin, 1979, this volume). Eye contact is a potent early social signal that is used extensively in the very early playful routines of normal children. Its absence in blind children can lead to a feeling of frustration on the part of their parents, and may be interpreted by the parents as a sign that their child is disinterested in social contact and rejects them. Thus, it is not surprising that blind children typically show deficits in language acquisition (Burlingham, 1961; Urwin, 1979, this volume; Wood, 1970). However, blind infants can also show normal language acquisition if parents richly exploit their children's interest in object play and physical contact games in an effort to develop common foci of attention, interpretable signals, and social expressions (Urwin, 1979, this volume).

Finally, children with Down's syndrome typically show an increasing developmental deficit with age. In infancy, Down's syndrome children are generally passive and nondemanding. Moreover, they often are relatively unresponsive to attempts at social play and unwilling to establish eye contact with social partners (Corrigall, 1979; Jones, 1977). Consequently, Down's syndrome babies, like blind infants, tend to discourage and frustrate their potential social partners, thereby limiting their own access to precisely the kind of social interaction that is crucial to normal development. However, considerable success in arresting the children's developmental declines has been achieved by preschool programs that emphasize one-to-one contact between adult and child, explicit training devoted to linguistic and cognitive development, and parental training and support (Clunies-Ross, 1979; Hayden and Dmitriev, 1975; Hayden and Haring, 1977). Because the training given in these programs is achieved through the use of social games, imitation routines, and other techniques similar to the activities engaged in purely for fun with normal babies, these programs underscore the importance of such games and routines for the normal development of any infant. (However, see Sachs, this volume, for a somewhat different analysis of the progress achieved in these preschool programs as well as a discussion of play as a "prerequisite" for normal development.)

This is not to suggest, however, that normal amounts of access to social play would in itself ensure normal rates of development in various populations of language-handicapped children. If the child, by virtue of his handicap, shows a lessened ability to profit from each instance of social contact, then much more intensive, frequent, and programmed interactions with adults may be necessary to achieve the same degree of developmental support. For example, the hard-of-hearing child, who receives a degraded signal from each of his parents' utterances, may need many more repetitions of a word utterance or game sequence before he is capable of recognizing or imitating it. Similarly, the blind child, whose access to information about objects is grossly limited, may need a much more structured introduction to the world of objects, and to their names, than a seeing child. Whereas children with no handicaps are somewhat buffered against the potential negative effects of moderate neglect, disinterested caretaking, and unplayful caretakers, handicapped children require maximum responsiveness and extensive access to social interactions if they are to develop normally.

Language-Delayed and Language-Disordered Children

The language-delayed child's situation can be very different from that of the language-handicapped child. For instance, a retarded child whose cognitive development is, like his language development, slowed down presents much the same picture as a normally developing child. His play activities, his ability to function in the world, and his productive language all evoke adult speech of appropriate semantic complexity for him (Berry, 1976). The child with a specific language disorder, on the other hand, who at 5 has the linguistic ability of a 2-year-old, nonetheless possesses the nonlinguistic abilities and the interests of a much older child. This discrepancy makes it very hard for parents to talk to the child. When his parents try to talk about things that interest him, the complications of temporal sequence, cause and effect, conditionality, and so on must all be discussed—but these cannot be expressed without using complex syntactic constructions that are beyond the child's comprehension (Cromer, 1974).

Imitation and Modeling

An issue that has received considerable attention in the language acquisition literature, and that is of special interest to those dealing with language-delayed populations, is the role played by imitation in language acquisition. Imitation seems to be an obvious tool to use in language teaching and remediation; however, if it plays no part in normal language acquisition, then it probably should be used only as a last resort in language therapy, reserved for use with children with whom no other techniques are feasible. On the other hand, if imitation does play a role in normal language acquisition, then the way it functions should be examined more closely in order to maximize its effectiveness in therapy.

An early systematic study of imitation (Ervin, 1964) led to the conclusion that imitation was an epiphenomenon of language acquisition, not a learning strategy. This conclusion was based on the finding that imitations were not progressive, i.e., not more complex than spontaneous productions. Additional support for this conclusion included: 1) observations of children (e.g., autistic children) who imitated a great deal but failed to acquire significant productive linguistic ability; and 2) children who acquired language without producing any imitations.

However, more detailed analyses of the imitated and spontaneous utterances of children revealed that imitations did function, for some children at least, as ways of introducing new grammatical constructions or new vocabulary items into their productive repertoires (Bloom, Lightbown, and Hood, 1974; Moerk, 1977; Ramer, 1976; Snow, 1981b). The children in question first used the new structures or vocabulary items only in immediate imitations; however, after a period of imitating them, the children did start using them in their spontaneous speech, suggesting that the period of imitation promoted productive control over the items. It should be noted, however, that the imitations that had this effect were "spontaneous," i.e., not encouraged, demanded, or elicited by the adult. Furthermore, the children were selective, i.e., they imitated only some of the structures or words they heard. The selection of what to imitate probably occurred on the basis of the children's own linguistic systems and their needs to communicate particular ideas.

Another qualification to consider regarding the effects of imitation on normal language acquisition is that not all children do it. Bloom et al. (1974) found that 2 of the 6 children they studied imitated at consistently very low rates; for these children, immediate imitation could have played at most only a minor role in supporting their acquisition of productive language.

One problem with assessing the role of imitation in the language acquisition of all children, especially the "nonimitators" referred to previously, is that for methodological reasons only immediate or relatively immediate imitations have been studied. Bloom et al. argued that this was not a serious problem because greatly extending the interval over which children's utterances were counted as imitations did not affect their computed rate of imitation for nonimitators. However, Bloom et al. used a 5-utterance interval between the child imitation and the adult model as the basis for counting an utterance as an imitation in their first analysis, and a 10-utterance interval in the second analysis. Because they found that the longer interval yielded no significant increment in the proportion of child utterances that could be counted as imitations, they concluded that including delayed imitations in their analysis would not affect the results.

Before accepting or rejecting Bloom et al.'s conclusion, we need to consider how the function and situational context of an imitation might affect its timing. Imitations can serve pragmatic, conversational functions, such as signaling noncomprehension and keeping the conversation going (Keenan, 1977; McTear, 1978). In order to be successful, imitations serving these functions must occur directly after the adult model. Thus, their frequency should not increase by increasing the model-imitation interval from 5 to 10 utterances. However, there are some situations in which an immediate imitation would be functionally inappropriate. For example, when an imitation is associated with a particular activity, it could not be expected to occur until the activity is repeated. Such imitations may involve lags of several hours or days. Consider the following example:

> On a Tuesday evening, 35-month-old Nathaniel was put in a bath that was a bit too hot for his taste. In response to his protest, his mother said, "It's not too hot! But I'll just put some more in to make it colder, okay?" On Wednesday evening, stepping into the same bathtub, Nathaniel said to his mother, who was regulating the running water, "Not too hot just colder, okay?"

This complex utterance was clearly an imitation of his mother's utterance from the previous evening. It was used because it could be expected to have a desired communicative effect in that situation. At no point during the intervening 24 hours would there have been any point in producing that particular imitation. This sort of delayed imitation frequently occurs in connection with repeated caretaking activities, games, household routines, and book-reading routines (Ferrier, 1978; Moerk and Moerk, 1979), but it can be captured only by diary studies or extensive recording, not by the episodic recording normally used in child language research. Although extensive recording requires a great deal of time, the knowledge gained from such recording may be substantial, and clinically valuable if imitations can be incorporated into productive language (see, e.g., Clark, 1977, 1978; Moerk and Moerk, 1979).

Some evidence is available to suggest that both immediate and delayed imitation could play a role in a language therapy program.

Simply modeling new constructions for children, without even praising or otherwise reinforcing the children's immediate imitations of the modeled constructions, has been shown to increase the frequency with which the modeled constructions are used in spontaneous speech (Hursh and Sherman, 1973; Lahey, 1971; Nelson and Bonvillian, 1974; Whitehurst, 1972; Whitehurst, Ironsmith, and Goldfein, 1974; Whitehurst and Vasta, 1975). Combining modeling with instructions to imitate and reinforcement for correct imitations is even more effective in increasing the frequency of the modeled construction in children's spontaneous speech (Hursh and Sherman, 1973; Whitehurst, 1972). Indeed, this type of program constituted effective therapy for the language delay of one 3-year-old boy (Whitehurst, Novak, and Zorn, 1972).

However, the use of imitation in therapy for language-delayed children must be guided by an understanding of the language system available to the child and a realization that imitations that have a communicative function may be better candidates for incorporation into a productive language system than those whose use is limited to drills and therapy sessions. Clearly, even children who imitate a very high proportion of adult utterances do not imitate all possible adult utterances. Their imitations are selective, and the selection is based on: 1) their ability to (at least partially) comprehend the meaning of the structure in question; and 2) their recognition that it is an important structure for communication. Thus, incorporating imitation into a language therapy program should be undertaken only after the child's productive language system has been analyzed to determine: 1) what structures are just beyond his current productive capacity and thus good candidates for being facilitated; and 2) what messages the child needs to but cannot communicate. Models for imitation that serve the child's purposes and match his communicative needs will be more effective than models that are chosen because of their place in the therapist's agenda. Finally, the use of imitation in therapy should be restricted by the principle of contingency discussed previously. Models for imitation in normal adult-child conversations are frequently expansions of the child's own utterances (Folger and Chapman, 1978). Moreover, such contingent models are more effective than noncontingent models even when both are imitated (Whitehurst and Novak, 1973).

The findings regarding the facilitatory effects of maternal speech on children's language growth clearly have implications for preventive intervention and for therapy. However, questions concerning the *best* way to apply these findings in the clinical situation are still difficult to answer. Demonstration that a particular feature of interaction is normal or frequent in input to normally developing children does not necessarily imply that it will be useful with language-delayed children. It is rather at the more general level of understanding how the facilitatory features of normal interaction emerge from the communicative needs of both partners that this research may be most relevant to therapists. Children benefit more from speech that relates to their activities and interests than from speech designed to serve the teacher's or therapists's purposes. Negotiation of real communicative intents, created by real wants and needs on children's and caretakers' parts, creates the context for normal language acquisition and may well be the most potent context for effective language therapy as well.

Research findings more specifically relevant to training have been mentioned elsewhere in this chapter. Use of labels in the presence of the objects to which they refer supports vocabulary teaching, even if it occurs during the prelinguistic period (see page 78). Vocabulary acquisition is not only a prerequisite to, but often a direct channel to, the acquisition of syntax and morphology. If children can comprehend the vocabulary in adults' utterances, they can often divine for themselves the meaning and thereby the syntactic structure of those utterances. Finally, as discussed in the preceding section, use of imitation and routines is both typical of "normal" interactions and often useful in therapeutic settings.

CONCLUSIONS

Study of parental speech to children and of the nature of the social interaction available to children was originally motivated largely by the nature-nurture issue, and by the claims of linguists and developmental psycholinguists that the speech available to children was inadequately rich, structured, or informative to support language learning in the absence of a highly structured, innate language acquisition device. Despite the general findings that speech to children is syntactically simple, semantically concrete and relevant, repetitive, phonologically of high clarity and saliency, and presented in a nonlinguistic situational and social context by virtue of which its meaning is made unmistakable, it is still not universally accepted that the need to posit a structured, innate component specific to language acquisition has been lessened. Many linguists, and some developmental psycholinguists (e.g., Newport, Gleitman, and Gleitman, 1977), maintain that the data about language available to the child from the speech he hears are inadequate to support language learning.

Whatever one's position on the need for early communicative responsiveness, contingent speech, and supportive social environments,

I think it has become clear that the child who is, for whatever reason, at risk for language delay or disability cannot develop normally without optimum access to the crucial features of social interaction described previously. The normally developing child is buffered in many ways against various kinds of developmental risks and insults. Low levels or short periods of malnutrition, neglect, illness, psychological trauma, or parental rejection usually will not by themselves produce any pathology (Sameroff, 1975). Haphazard caretaking, intermittent social responsiveness, relatively short or infrequent episodes of play, contingent parental input, and peer interaction characterize a suboptimal language-learning environment, but may result in no noticeable deficits or delays in language acquisition. However, when a child is at risk for language delay or disability because of some deficit in language processing ability, or because of mental retardation, sensory impairment, or a psychodynamic disorder, he has lost his buffering. He may be able to develop language normally only in an optimum social environment, one with constant access to adult caretakers who are always able and willing to engage in contingent social interaction.

The normal child who is left to play alone for a few hours a day may still learn to talk with amazing rapidity, but the hearing-impaired child may need those extra few hours of exposure to adult speech for normal language development. The normal child may be left to amuse himself in his crib for an hour after waking with no adverse consequences, but the blind child may need that extra hour a day of playing with toys and hearing his mother talk about them to discover the principle of reference. The normal child may discover grammatical regularities from the contingent speech occasionally addressed to him while he is playing in the room in which his mother is cleaning and cooking. On the other hand, a retarded child may need 10 or 20 times as much exposure to contingent adult speech before he can discover the same regularities and begin to exploit them in his own speech. The child with normal language facility may be able to select for himself adult utterances that fit into his system, adult utterances that represent interesting structures to which he should attend, and adult utterances that should be ignored as too complex; but the child with a specific language disability may need exposure to language that is already filtered and programmed by his caretakers in order to avoid confusion and overload.

In conclusion, clinicians should attempt to: 1) identify those children who need extra social buffering because their biological buffering has failed them, putting them at risk for language disorders; and 2) train parents to provide social buffering so that normal development can occur, rather than waiting for the risk to actualize itself as a full-blown language problem.

REFERENCES

Andersen, A. B., Teale, W. H., and Estrada, E. 1980. Low income children's preschool literacy experiences: Some naturalistic observations. Q. Newsletter Lab. Comp. Hum. Cognition 2:59-65.

Anglin, J. 1976. Word, Object, and Conceptual Development. W. W. Norton & Co., New York.

Bard, B., and Sachs, J. 1977. Language acquisition in two normal children of deaf parents. Paper presented at the Second Annual Boston University Conference on Language Development, Boston. (ERIC # 150 868)

Bates, E. 1975. Peer relations and the acquisition of language. In M. Lewis and L. Rosenblum (eds.), Friendship and Peer Relations. John Wiley & Sons, Inc., New York.

Bates, E., Camaioni, L., and Volterra, V. 1975. The acquisition of performatives prior to speech. Merrill-Palmer Q. 21:205-226.

Bee, H. L., van Egeren, L. F., Streissguth, A. P., Nyman, B. A., and Leckie, M. S. 1969. Social class differences in maternal teaching strategies and speech patterns. Dev. Psychol. 1:726-734.

Benedict, H. 1979. Early lexical development: Comprehension and production. J. Child Lang. 6:183-200.

Berry, P. 1976. Language and Communication in the Mentally Handicapped. University Park Press, Baltimore.

Blank, M., Gessner, M., and Esposito, A. 1979. Language without communication: A case study. J. Child Lang. 6:329-352.

Bloom, L., Lightbown, P., and Hood, L. 1974. Imitation in language development: If, when, and why. Cognitive Psychol. 6:380-420.

Bohannon, J. 1976. Normal and scrambled grammar in discrimination. Child Dev. 47:669-681.

Bohannon, J., and Marquis, A. 1977. Children's control of adult speech. Child Dev. 48:1002-1008.

Bowerman, M. 1978. Semantic and syntactic development: A review of what, when and how in language acquisition. In R. L. Schiefelbusch (ed.), Bases of Language Intervention. University Park Press, Baltimore.

Bradley, R., and Caldwell, B. 1976. The relation of infants' home environments to mental test performance at 54 months: A follow-up study. Child Dev. 47:1172-1174.

Braine, M. 1971. Children's first word combinations. Monogr. Soc. Res. Child Dev. 41:1.

Brown, R. 1973. A First Language: The Early Stages. Harvard University Press, Cambridge, MA.

Bruner, J. 1975a. From communication to language: A psychological perspective. Cognition 3:255-285.

Bruner, J. 1975b. The ontogenesis of speech acts. J. Child Lang. 2:1-20.

Bruner, J. 1977. Early social interaction and language acquisition. In H. R. Schaffer (ed.), Studies in Mother-Infant Interaction. Academic Press, Inc., New York.

Bruner, J., and Sherwood, V. 1976. Early rule structure: The case of peekaboo. In J. Bruner, A. Jolly, and K. Sylva (eds.), Play: Its Role in Development and Evolution. Penguin, Harmondsworth, England.

Burlingham, D. 1961. Some notes on the development of the blind. In R. S. Eissler (ed.), Psychoanalytic Study of the Child, Vol. 16, pp. 121-145. International Universities Press, New York.

Calfee, R., Lindamood, P., and Lindamood, C. 1973. Acoustic-phonetic skills and reading—K-12. J. Educ. Psychol. 64:293-298.

Carter A. 1978. The development of systematic vocalisations prior to words: A case study. In N. Waterson and C. Snow (eds.), The Development of Communication. Wiley, London.

Cazden, C. 1965. Environmental assistance to the child's acquisition of grammar. Unpublished doctoral dissertation, Harvard University.

Cherry, L. The role of adults' requests for clarification in the language development of children. In R. Freedle (ed.), Discourse Processing: A Multidisciplinary Approach: Vol. II. Ablex Publishing Corp., Norwood, N. J. (in press).

Clark, M. M. 1976. Young Fluent Readers. William Heinemann, London.

Clark, R. 1977. What's the use of imitation? J. Child Lang. 4:341-359.

Clark, R. 1978. Some even simpler ways to learn to talk. In N. Waterson and C. Snow (eds.), The Development of Communication. Wiley, London.

Clunies-Ross, G. C. 1979. Accelerating the development of Down's syndrome infants and young children. J. Spec. Educ. 13:169-177.

Collis, G. M. 1977. Visual co-orientation and maternal speech. In H. R. Schaffer (ed.), Studies in Mother-Infant Interaction. Academic Press, Inc., New York.

Collis, G., and Schaffer, H. 1975. Synchronisation of visual attention in mother-infant pairs. J. Child Psychol. 16:315-320.

Corrigall, J. 1979. An observational study of the interaction between Down's Syndrome babies and their mothers. Unpublished doctoral dissertation, University of Cambridge.

Cromer, R. F. 1974. Receptive language in the mentally retarded: Processes and diagnostic distinctions. In R. L. Schiefelbusch and L. L. Lloyd (eds.), Language Perspectives: Acquisition, Retardation, and Intervention. University Park Press, Baltimore.

Cross, T. 1977. Mother's speech adjustments: The contribution of selected child listener variables. In C. Snow and C. Ferguson (eds.), Talking to Children. Cambridge University Press, Cambridge, England.

Cross, T. 1978. Motherese: Its association with the rate of syntactic acquisition in young children. In N. Waterson and C. Snow (eds.), The Development of Communication. Wiley, London.

Curtiss, S. 1977. Genie: A Psycholinguistic Study of a Modern-day "Wild Child." Academic Press, Inc., New York.

DuPan, R., and Roth S. 1955. The psychologic development of a group of children brought up in a hospital type residential nursery. J. Pediatr. 47:124-129.

Durkin, D. 1966. Children Who Read Early. Teachers' College Press, New York.

Elardo, R., Bradley, R., and Caldwell, B. 1977. A longitudinal study of the relation of infants' home environment to language development at age three. Child Dev. 48:495-603.

Engle, M. 1979. Do fathers speak motherese? An analysis of the language environments of young children. Unpublished manuscript, University of California-San Diego.

Engle, M. 1980. Language and play: A comparative analysis of parental initiatives. In H. Giles (ed.), Language: Social Psychological Perspectives. Pergamon Press, Ltd, London.

Ervin, S. 1964. Imitation and structural change in children's language. *In* E. Lenneberg (ed.), New Directions in the Study of Language. MIT Press, Cambridge, MA.

Ferrier, L. 1978. Some observations of error in context. *In* N. Waterson and C. Snow (eds.), The Development of Communication. Wiley, London.

Folger, J., and Chapman, R. 1978. A pragmatic analysis of spontaneous imitations. J. Child Lang. 5:25–38.

Fraiberg, S. 1977. Insights from the Blind: Comparative Studies of Blind and Sighted Infants. Basic Books, Inc., New York.

Furrow, D., Nelson, K., and Benedict, H. 1979. Mothers' speech to children and syntactic development: Some simple relationships. J. Child Lang. 6:423–442.

Gleason, J. B. 1973. Code switching in children's language. *In* T. Moore (ed.), Cognitive Development and the Acquisition of Language. Academic Press, Inc., New York.

Gleason, J. B. 1980. The acquisition of social speech: Routines and politeness formulated. *In* H. Giles (ed.), Language: Social Psychological Perspectives. Pergamon Press, Ltd, London.

Goldfield, B. A., and Snow, C. E. Reading books with children: The mechanics of parental influence on children's reading achievement. *In* J. Flood (ed.), Understanding Reading Comprehension. International Reading Association, Newark, Delaware. (in press)

Greenfield, P., and Smith, J. 1976. Communication and the Beginnings of Language. Academic Press, Inc., New York.

Greif, E. B., and Gleason, J. B. 1980. Hi, thanks, and goodbye: Some more routine information. Lang. Society 9:159–166.

Halliday, M. A. K. 1975. Learning How to Mean: Explorations in the Development of Language. Edward Arnold, London.

Harkness, S. 1977. Aspects of social environment and first language acquisition in rural Africa. *In* C. Snow and C. Ferguson (eds.), Talking to Children: Language Input and Acquisition. Cambridge University Press, Cambridge, England.

Hayden, A. H., and Dmitriev, V. 1975. The multidisciplinary preschool program for Down's syndrome children at the University of Washington Model Preschool Center. *In* B. Z. Friedlander, G. M. Sterritt, and G. E. Kirk (eds.), Exceptional Infant, Vol. 3: Assessment and Intervention. Brunner/Mazel, New York.

Hayden, A. H., and Haring, N. G. 1977. The acceleration and maintenance of developmental gains in Down's syndrome school-age children. *In* P. Mittler (ed.), Research to Practice in Mental Retardation, Vol. 1: Care and Intervention. University Park Press, Baltimore.

Hess, R., and Shipman, V. 1965. Early experience and the socialization of cognitive modes in children. Child Dev. 36:869–886.

Hovell, M., Schumaker, J., and Sherman, J. 1978. A comparison of parents' models and expansions in promoting children's acquisition of objectives. J. Exp. Child Psychol. 25:41–57.

Howe, C. 1980. Mother-child conversation and semantic development. *In* H. Giles (ed.), Language: Social Psychological Perspectives. Pergamon Press, Ltd, London.

Hursh, D., and Sherman, J. 1973. The effects of parent presented models and praise on the vocal behavior of their children. J. Exp. Child Psychol. 15:328–338.

Hutson, B. A. 1974. Language factors in reading disability. Paper presented to the American Educational Research Association, Chicago, April.
Jones, M., and Quigley, S. 1979. The acquisition of question formation in spoken Spanish and American sign language by two hearing children of deaf parents. J. Speech Hear. Disord. 44:196–208.
Jones, O. 1977. Mother-child communication with prelinguistic Down's syndrome and normal infants. In H. R. Schaffer (ed.), Studies in Mother-Infant Interaction. Academic Press, Inc., New York.
Kaye, K. 1980. Why we don't talk "Baby talk" to babies. J. Child Lang. 7:489–507.
Kaye, K., and Charney, R. 1980. How mothers maintain "dialogue" with two-year-olds. In D. Olson (ed.), The Social Foundations of Language and Thought. Essays in Honor of Jerome Bruner. W. W. Norton & Co., New York.
Keenan, E. 1977. Making it last: Repetition in children's discourse. In S. Ervin-Tripp and C. Mitchell-Kernan (eds.), Child Discourse. Academic Press, Inc., New York.
Lahey, B. 1971. Modification of the frequency of descriptive adjectives in the speech of Head Start children through modelling without reinforcement. J. Appl. Behav. Anal. 4:19–22.
Lane, H. 1976. The Wild Boy of Aveyron. Harvard University Press, Boston.
LeGrand, M. 1979. Koen, Annette & Els: De interaktie tussen een moeder en haar dove kind (Koen, Annette & Els: The interaction between a mother and her deaf child) (in Dutch). Unpublished master's thesis, University of Amsterdam.
Liberman, I. Y., Shankweiler, D., Fischer, F., and Carter, B. 1974. Explicit syllable and phoneme segmentation in the young child. J. Exp. Child Psychol. 18:201–212.
Longhurst, T., and Stepanich, L. 1975. Mothers' speech addressed to one-, two-, and three-year-old normal children. Child Study J. 5:3–11.
Macnamara, J. 1972. Cognitive basis of language learning in infants. Psychol. Rev. 79:143.
McTear, M. 1978. Repetition in child language: Imitation or creation? In R. Campbell and P. Smith (eds.), Advances in the Psychology of Language. Plenum Publishing Corp., New York.
Madden, J., Levenstein, P., and Levenstein, S. 1976. Longitudinal IQ outcomes of the mother-child home program. Child Dev. 47:1015–1025.
Malouf, R., and Dodd, D. 1972. Role of exposure, imitation, and expansion in the acquisition of an artificial grammatical rule. Dev. Psychol. 7:195–203.
Mann, R. A., and Baer, D. M. 1971. The effects of receptive language naming on articulation. J. Appl. Behav. Anal. 5:291–298.
Masur, E. 1979. Clues, strategies, rules and plans: Cognitive functions of parents' speech to preschool children. Paper presented to Stanford Child Language Forum, Stanford University.
Masur, E., and Gleason, J. 1979. Parent-child interaction and the acquisition of lexical information during play. Unpublished manuscript, Boston University.
Messer, D. 1978. The integration of mothers' referential speech with joint play. Child Dev. 49:781–787.
Miller, P. 1982. Amy, Wendy and Beth: Learning language in South Baltimore. University of Texas Press, Austin.

Moerk, E. 1974. Changes in verbal child-mother interactions with increasing language skills of the child. J. Psycholing. Res. 3:101–116.
Moerk, E. 1977. Processes and products of imitation: Evidence that imitation is progressive. J. Psycholing. Res. 6:187–202.
Moerk, E., and Moerk, C. 1979. Quotations, imitations and generalizations. Factual and methodological analyses. Int. J. Behav. Dev. 2:43–72.
Nelson, K. 1973. Structure and strategy in learning to talk. Monogr. Soc. Res. Child Dev. 38, No. 149.
Nelson, K. E., 1977. Facilitating children's syntax acquisition. Dev. Psychol. 13:101–107.
Nelson, K. E., and Bonvillian, J. 1974. Concepts and words in the 18 month old: Acquiring concept names under controlled conditions. Cognition 4:435–450.
Nelson, K. E., Carskaddon, G., and Bonvillian, J. 1973. Syntax acquisition: Impact of experimental variation in adult verbal interaction with the child. Child Dev. 44:497–504.
Newport, E., Gleitman, L., and Gleitman, H. 1977. Mother, I'd rather do it myself. *In* C. Snow and C. Ferguson (eds.), Talking to Children: Language Input and Acquisition. Cambridge University Press, Cambridge, England.
Ninio, A. 1980. Picture book reading in mother-infant dyads belonging to two subgroups in Israel. Child Dev. 51:587–590.
Pringle, M. L. K., and Bossio, V. 1958. A study of deprived children. Part II. Vita Humana 1:142.
Pringle, M. L. K., and Tanner, M. 1958. The effects of early deprivation on speech development: A comparative study of 4 year olds in a nursery school and in residential nurseries. Lang. Speech 1:269.
Ramer, A. 1976. The function of imitation in child language. J. Speech Hear. Res. 19:700–717.
Ratner, N., and Bruner, J. 1978. Games, social exchange and the acquisition of language. J. Child Lang. 5:391–402.
Rheingold, H., Hay, D., and West, M. 1976. Sharing in the second year of life. Child Dev. 47:1148–1158.
Rogers, D. 1978. Information about word meaning in the speech of parents to young children. *In* R. Campbell and P. Smith (eds.), Advances in the Psychology of Language. Plenum Publishing Corp., New York.
Rogers, D. 1979. How a child learns what a word means. Paper presented at Max-Planck Conference "Beyond Representation," Nijmegen, the Netherlands.
Sachs, J. 1977. The adaptive significance of linguistic input to prelinguistic infants. *In* C. Snow and C. Ferguson (eds.), Talking to Children: Language Input and Acquisition. Cambridge University Press, Cambridge, England.
Sachs, J. 1979. Topic selection in parent-child discourse. Discourse Processes 2:145–153.
Sachs, J., and Johnson, M. 1976. Language development in a hearing child of deaf parents. *In* W. von Raffler-Engel and Y. Lebrun (eds.), Baby Talk and Infant Speech. Swets & Zeitlinger, Lisse, The Netherlands.
Sameroff, A. 1975. Early influences on development: Fact or fancy? Merrill-Palmer Q. 21:267–294.
Schachter, F. F. 1979. Everyday Mother Talk to Toddlers. Academic Press, Inc., New York.

Schumaker, J. B. 1976. Mothers' expressions: Their characteristics and effects on child language. Unpublished doctoral dissertation, University of Kansas.

Shatz, M. 1978. Children's comprehension of question-directions. J. Child Lang. 5:39–46.

Snow, C. E. 1977a. The development of conversation between mothers and babies. J. Child Lang. 4:1–22.

Snow, C. E. 1977b. Mothers' speech research: From input to interaction. In C. Snow and C. Ferguson (eds.), Talking to Children: Language Input and Acquisition. Cambridge University Press, Cambridge, England.

Snow, C. 1981a. Social interaction and language acquisition. In P. Dale and D. Ingram (eds.), Child Language: An International Perspective. University Park Press, Baltimore.

Snow, C. E. 1981b. The uses of imitation. J. Child Lang. 8: 205–212.

Snow, C. E. 1982. Are parents language teachers? In K. Borman (ed.), Social Life of Children in a Changing Society. Erlbaum, Hillsdale, NJ.

Snow, C., deBlauw, A., and Van Roosmalen, G. 1978. Talking and playing with babies: The role of ideologies of childbearing. In M. Bullowa (ed.), Before Speech. Cambridge University Press, Cambridge, England.

Söderbergh, R. 1971. Reading in Early Childhood. Almquist & Wiksell, Stockholm.

Söderbergh, R. 1981. Teaching deaf preschool children to read in Sweden. In P. Dale and D. Ingram (eds.), Child Language: An International Perspective. University Park Press, Baltimore.

Stella-Prorok, E. 1981. Mother-child verbal interchanges: A field descriptive study with Brazilian children aged from one to three. In D. Ingram, F. Peng, and P. Dale (eds.), Proceedings of the First International Congress for the Study of Child Language. University Press of America, Lanham, MD.

Stern, D. 1974. Mother and infant at play: The dyadic interaction involving facial, vocal, and gaze behaviors. In M. Lewis and L. Rosenblum (eds.), The Effect of the Infant on Its Caregiver. John Wiley & Sons, Inc., New York.

Stern, D., Spieker, S., Barnett, R., and MacKain, K. 1983. The prosody of maternal speech: Infant age and context-related changes. J. Child Lang. 10:1–16.

Sylvester-Bradley, B., and Trevarthen, C. 1978. Baby talk as an adaptation to the infant's communication. In N. Waterson and C. Snow (eds.), The Development of Communication. Wiley, London.

Tizard, B., Cooperman, O., Joseph, A., and Tizard, J. 1972. Environmental effects on language development: A study of young children in long-stay residential nurseries. Child Dev. 43:337–358.

Urwin, C. 1979. The development of communication between blind infants and their parents. In A. Lock (ed.), Action, Gesture and Symbol: The Emergence of Language. Academic Press, Inc., New York.

Vasta, R., Andrews, D., Griffin, J., and Kwiatowski, B. 1978. Facilitating accuracy of imitative articulation through reception training. J. Exp. Child Psychol. 26:508–516.

Walters, J., Connor, R., and Zunich, M. 1964. Interaction of mothers and children from lower class families. Child Dev. 35:433–440.

Weintraub, S. 1976. Some sex differences in the language parents address to children. Paper presented to First Boston University Conference on Language Development, Boston.

Wells, G. 1980. Adjustments in adult-child conversation: Some effects of interaction. *In* H. Giles (ed.), Language: Social Psychological Perspectives. Pergamon Press, Ltd, London.
Whitehurst, G. J. 1972. Production of novel and grammatical utterances by young children. J. Exp. Child Psychol. 13:502–515.
Whitehurst, G., Ironsmith, E., and Goldfein, M. 1974. Selective imitation of the passive construction by young children. J. Exp. Child Psychol. 17:288–302.
Whitehurst, G., and Novak, G. 1973. Modeling, imitation training and the acquisition of sentence phrases. J. Exp. Child Psychol. 16:332–345.
Whitehurst, G., Novak, G., and Zorn, G. 1972. Delayed speech studied in the home. Dev. Psychol. 2:169–177.
Whitehurst, G. J., and Vasta, R. 1975. Is language acquired through imitation? J. Psycholinguistic Res. 4:37–59.
Wood, H. 1970. Problems in the development and home care of preschool blind children. Unpublished doctoral thesis, University of Nottingham.

chapter 3

Children's Play and Communicative Development

Jacqueline Sachs

*Departments of
Communication Sciences
and Psychology
University of Connecticut
Storrs, Connecticut*

Editors' Note

Language acquisition reflects both the nature of the child and the nature of the social setting in which language occurs. In discussing communicative competence the author draws from ethnolinguistics to emphasize that utterances must fit the surrounding discourse context and must be appropriate to an expanding range of communication events. However, the principal emphasis is placed on the relationship between the development of communicative abilities and play, especially caregiver-infant *social* play, *symbolic* play, and *role* play.

Social play allows the study of the social interactions that a child has with his caregivers as his cognitive functions develop. *Symbolic play* (pretend play) provides a further analysis of cognitive development. *Role play* reveals the child's ability to adapt his utterances to novel discourse in extended social contexts.

All forms of play supply a social and semantic context for language acquisition and cognitive growth. The relationship between play, language, and social development is analyzed relative to clinical application. The key variable in play may be responsiveness to social events. Intervention activities might be directed at maintaining social responsiveness as a means for increasing social skills along with further language and further play skills. The obverse of this favorable trend may well be the incompetence found in children with limited social engagements.

contents

**CAREGIVER-INFANT SOCIAL PLAY AND
LANGUAGE DEVELOPMENT** 114

    Acquiring the Foundations for Communication 115
    Discovering the Combinatorial Nature of Language 116
    Social Play: Necessary, Typical, or Optimal? 117

SYMBOLIC PLAY AND LANGUAGE DEVELOPMENT 118

    Play and Language: Reflections of the Same
        Underlying Abilities 120
    Parental Involvement in Symbolic Play 122

ROLE PLAY AND LANGUAGE USAGE IN CONTEXT 124

    Playing the Role of a Caregiver 125
    Playing the Role of a Baby 126
    Other Roles 127
    Comments on Methodology 127

**RELATIONSHIPS BETWEEN PLAY AND OTHER ASPECTS
OF DEVELOPMENT** 128

    How Research on Language Acquisition Might Enrich the
        Study of Play 129
    How Research on Play Might Enrich the Study of
        Language and Social Development 131
    Implications for Intervention 133

REFERENCES 135

> In truth, the young child is the hardest mental toiler on our planet. Fortunately, he does not even suspect this.
>
> K. Chukovsky, *From Two to Five*

This chapter focuses on the relationship between play and the development of communicative abilities. It includes discussions of caregiver-infant social play, the emergence of symbolic play, and role play.[1] Researchers studying language acquisition have recently shown increased interest in play. This interest reflects new ways of viewing the acquisition of language. A brief overview of both traditional and current viewpoints shows why the relationship between play and language, almost ignored in the past, is receiving more attention today.

As the field of developmental psycholinguistics emerged in the 1960s, it was largely motivated by Chomsky's (1959) criticisms of the behaviorists' explanations of mental phenomena. The major thrust of research was to find evidence refuting the behaviorists' model of language development. In the behaviorist framework, the child gradually built up a set of "linguistic responses" by imitating adults and being reinforced for successively closer approximations to the adult model (see, e.g., Mowrer, 1954; Skinner, 1957). Powerful evidence against such a model could be obtained by locating novel, productive structural patterns in a child's speech that were different from those in adult language. Because morphology and syntax often yielded good examples of such novel patterns, researchers focused on these two areas for many years (Braine, 1963; Brown and Fraser, 1963; Ervin and Miller, 1963).

The results of this early research on structural patterns encouraged investigators to consider language development as an interesting and "special" sort of process that cannot be explained simply by saying "children imitate what they hear." Instead of relying on an imitation-reinforcement model, researchers began to: 1) conceive of the child as an "inventor" of language; and 2) accept the notion that there is some biological specialization for language that gives the child a strong predisposition to acquire this complex system (Chomsky, 1965; McNeill, 1966).

In moving away from an imitation-reinforcement model of language acquisition, researchers in the 1960s generally ignored the influence of social-interactional factors and the possibility that cognitive skills underlying a child's nonlinguistic development might be responsible for linguistic achievements as well. However, the lack of attention

---

[1] Another aspect of play and language is not covered here: children's play with linguistic materials (e.g., sound play, rhymes, puns, and jokes) and the role these playful activities may serve for language mastery. A review of such phenomena and suggestions about their functions may be found in Garvey (1977b).

given to these ideas is being rectified. Researchers are now adopting broad models of language acquisition. Views on how the child acquires language have expanded to the point where investigators are reexamining the importance of a child's social interactions with his parents. Furthermore, instead of viewing the acquisition of language as a "special" sort of process requiring "special" cognitive abilities, researchers are now investigating parallels between linguistic and nonlinguistic behaviors in an effort to discover whether the underlying cognitive requirements are similar. In other words, researchers are now shifting away from models that are either strongly behaviorist (as in the 1950s) or strongly nativist (as in much of the 1960s).

Newer models of language acquisition might be called *constructive-interactional*. Most developmental psychologists now believe that the child brings with him biological specializations that may facilitate the acquisition of both linguistic and nonlinguistic skills. On the other hand, psychologists are also convinced that language is best acquired in a social, affective, and linguistic environment that is supportive of language learning. Thus, the pattern of acquisition reflects both the nature of the child and the nature of the social-interactional setting in which language is used. The following points are discussed to illustrate the broad framework now being adopted in acquisition studies.

1. After long ignoring the social setting for learning and the type of language input heard by the child, attention has again turned to assessing the support for language learning that children gain from those who interact with them. In speaking to children, adults modify the form, content, and discourse structure of their speech (Snow and Ferguson, 1977). Thus, many aspects of adult-child linguistic interaction seem well designed for the child who is learning to communicate. Moreover, there is evidence that characteristics of the child's social and linguistic environment affect the child's acquisition of language. For example, the rate at which children learn certain forms of expression can be accelerated either by concentrated exposure to those forms (Nelson, 1980) or by hearing the mother use them (Furrow, Nelson, and Benedict, 1979). Second, children of deaf parents may show abnormal language development if their primary exposure to language has been from noninteractional sources such as television (Sachs and Johnson, 1976; Sachs, Bard, and Johnson, 1981; but see Rice, this volume, for further discussion of this issue). The apparent need for interaction has led researchers to look at play because play often forms an important part of early caregiver-child interaction. Indeed, there is a rapidly growing body of research that describes minute details of "baby games" in an attempt to determine the role of this type of interaction in language acquisition. The first section of this chapter deals with social play and early language development.

2. Many theorists have attempted to account for some aspects of language development in terms of general cognitive development. For example, Macnamara (1972) suggested that the young child acquires nonlinguistic conceptual categories and then discovers the linguistic forms that express these concepts. Other researchers (e.g., Bloom, 1973; Brown, 1973; Sinclair, 1970) have noted a correspondence between the semantic content of a child's early utterances and characteristics of his sensorimotor intelligence (Piaget, 1954, 1960). This interest in a relationship between language and cognitive development has led to studies (Bates et al., 1979; Bloom, Lifter, and Broughton, in press; Corrigan, 1978; Dihoff and Chapman, 1977; Ingram, 1979; Menn and Hazelkorn, 1977; Miller et al., 1980) that attempt to relate changes in linguistic abilities to nonlinguistic behaviors (typically cognitive stages within a Piagetian framework). Accordingly, the second section of this chapter is devoted to a discussion of research on the relationship between stages in the development of language and changes in the use of objects in symbolic play.

3. The discussion so far has dealt with changes in the ways that researchers view *how* language is acquired. However, these changes have been accompanied by new ways of conceptualizing *what* is learned when language is acquired. Whereas developmental psycholinguists were concentrating on syntactic changes in children's language, researchers in a field now called *ethnolinguistics* began to study ways in which the context might affect a person's use of language. The results obtained from this new field of research indicated that people choose their utterances to fit a number of aspects of the communicative context. First, utterances must fit the surrounding discourse context, and be relevant to the topic established or in some way signal that a topic change is being introduced. Second, utterances must be appropriate to the situation, with some situations requiring more formal speech than others. Situational appropriateness also requires that the form of an utterance fit the knowledge, status, and sex of the listener. The term *communicative competence* (Hymes, 1967) is often used in discussing all of the aspects of language that a speaker must control in order to communicate effectively.

Given the importance of communicative competence and the findings of the ethnolinguists, traditional studies of syntax, semantics, and phonology are now being supplemented by research on the development of contextually appropriate language usage in naturally occurring contexts. Because play is a frequent and spontaneous form of interaction between the child and caregiver as well as between the child and his peers, researchers have used play—especially role play—as a context in which to observe the child's use of language. The third section of this chapter discusses connections between role play and the development of some aspects of language usage. It addresses such questions as "How does a child reveal knowledge about language usage in role play?" and "Does role play help a child learn to fit language forms and content to the communicative context?"

In summary, research on language acquisition has broadened significantly in the past decade. Researchers interested in how children acquire language now consider both the social interactions that a child has with his parents and the child's own cognitive development. The study of play affords researchers the opportunity to assess both factors. Parent-child interactions often take the form of social play as discussed in the first section of this review, and some aspects of the child's cognitive development are reflected in his symbolic play as discussed in the second section. Finally, aside from broadening their views on how children acquire language, researchers also have expanded their notions of what is acquired. Studies on phonological, syntactic, and semantic development are now being augmented by research on the child's ability to fit an utterance to the communicative context. This last ability can again be evaluated through play, specifically role play, as discussed in the third section of this chapter. The final section of this chapter is devoted to an analysis of the relationship between play, language, and social development. The direction of effects is discussed together with how this relationship affects both researchers and clinicians.

CAREGIVER-INFANT SOCIAL PLAY AND LANGUAGE DEVELOPMENT

Considerable attention has been given to the social interactions that occur between infants and caregivers. Observations of these interactions indicate that, as infants approach the age at which language begins, their interactions with caregivers become increasingly structured. Conventional "baby games" of the culture as well as games invented in the family begin to emerge. Some games involve the use of objects (e.g., "give and take" routines), but others do not (e.g., "pat-a-cake").

Research on caregiver-child interaction is based on the notion that communication that occurs before language may pave the way for later symbolic representation and linguistic interaction (see Snow, this volume). This notion applies to many kinds of caregiver-child interactions, including playful ones. Indeed, it has been suggested that certain characteristics of games seem to parallel aspects of language acquisition or in some way provide a basis for learning the necessary communicative skills. This section discusses how caregiver-child play might help a child acquire the foundations of communication and discover the combinatorial nature of language. It also analyzes whether such play is necessary, typical, or optimal for development.

Acquiring the Foundations for Communication

Bruner and his colleagues (Bruner, 1978; Bruner, Roy, and Ratner, 1982; Ratner and Bruner, 1978; Wood, Bruner, and Ross, 1976) have conducted a detailed study of mother-child interactions. Some of these interactions contained games such as "peek-a-boo" and playful routines such as "give and take" and "build and bash." Findings from this research indicate that play with adults is relevant for language learning in a number of ways:

1. Because play is less goal oriented than other situations in which language is used, it provides a language-learning context where there is little pressure or frustration.
2. Games such as "peek-a-boo" and "hide-and-seek" involve both a simple semantic domain and shared attention to objects and events. Thus, these games provide an ideal situation for the mother to teach the child vocabulary (see also Masur and Gleason, 1980).
3. Games have a reciprocal role structure and permit variations in the order of elements. These features are analogous to characteristics of language: both play and language contain options for representing reciprocal semantic relations, and both permit some variety in the sequencing of elements.
4. Games have a structure that promotes the acquisition and practice of turn-taking skills. At first, the mother initiates the game and carries out all activities herself. After the mother has involved her child in a particular game on repeated occasions, she begins to expect the child to be aware of the sequence of events in the game. Whereas she initially led the child at each step, she may later wait at certain points for the child to provide a response before she continues her actions. This pattern of acting and waiting is usually repeated, building on turn-taking abilities already acquired in infancy (Stern, 1977). Furthermore, Ratner and Bruner (1978) argued that the mother's expectation that the child will signal his readiness to take a turn helps the child acquire signals of readiness. Thus, games provide the child with opportunities to practice old turn-taking skills and encourage him to acquire new ones.

Finally, Snow (1977, this volume) has shown that what the

adult accepts as a turn is not constant in play involving language. As the child gets older, the adult begins to expect signals that are more in conformity with the cultural pattern of vocalization. Snow has provided dramatic examples of changes in a caregiver's perceptions of how an infant should fulfill his turn in a playful conversation. Initially, a smile or even a burp was responded to as if the child had "said something." Once the child typically fulfilled his turn by vocalizing (i.e., babbling), a smile or burp was ignored as not conversationally relevant. Thus, play and parental expectations regarding the ways in which children should participate in play may offer children incentives to improve their vocal skills.

Discovering the Combinatorial Nature of Language

In order to communicate effectively, children not only need to learn when and how to take a turn, but also that utterances are formed by combining meaningful elements. However, it seems that some children begin with another hypothesis about the nature of language. Toward the end of the first year, children often show jargon babbling (long strings of meaningless sounds with sentential intonation). A child may even mix jargon with a few well-known words, as my daughter did when "reading" from books at around 14 months of age. Although many children also acquire a few routines (utterances learned as wholes that consist of more than one word from the adult point of view), some children initially seem to operate with the belief that language learning *is* learning routines. The rate of early language acquisition is usually somewhat slower for such children (Nelson, 1973).

Sachs and Truswell (1978) suggested that play with adults can help the child discover the correct model of language. Such play may involve questions about variable items, such as "Where's your nose?" and "Where's your tummy?" At the beginning of this game a child can give a correct response by processing the question as a routine, but continued success requires that the child learn that variations within an utterance boundary signal a change in meaning.

Snow (1980) also argued that many children's games involve "filling slots." Such games may afford children opportunities to learn about word-word and word-action combinations. For example, in the game of "peek-a-boo," there is a slot after the reappearance of the person in which the word "peek-a-boo" must be inserted. Snow noted that mastering the game involves at least two aspects of learning: 1) learning the word or action, and 2) learning the sequence of events. A child might know something about the response but use it at the wrong time, as when Snow's 28-month-old son said "wee, wee, wee home" when his toe was touched.

Social Play: Necessary, Typical, or Optimal?

Recent descriptions of social play and language parallel Vygotsky's (1962, 1978) observations about the role of the parent in child development. In Vygotsky's view, the child functions under the guidance of the adult, and the adult makes it possible for the child to engage in actions that the child would not be able to perform alone. According to this view, the characteristics of caregiver-infant play should make play an ideal situation for learning certain communicative skills. However, there is no solid evidence that such experience in play activity actually contributes in an important way to the acquisition of communicative competence. Thus, the distinctions among necessary conditions, not necessary but optimal conditions, and not necessary but typical conditions for language acquisition are important ones.

Researchers generally have not had much success in identifying conditions that are necessary for language acquisition. To some extent, however, they have been able to limit the number of contenders by identifying conditions that are *not necessary*. One way to identify the latter conditions is to study atypical situations. For example, children with physical and sensory impairments are often denied certain types of input. If these children still manage to acquire language, then possession of the respective physical/sensory abilities is not necessary for language acquisition. Furthermore, exposure to the corresponding social inputs also is not essential. Several studies of hearing-impaired, blind (see Urwin, this volume), and physically handicapped children have been based on this rationale and have been helpful in identifying conditions that are not always necessary for language acquisition.

Studies of nonhandicapped children living in environments that provide unusually low levels of social support also have been very informative. Children in these environments are abused, rejected (see Turnbull, 1972, for an extreme example), and/or given few opportunities to engage in interaction and play with adults. The results obtained from these studies indicate that such children usually acquire linguistic skills despite their nonsupportive environments. Thus, extensive adult-infant play is not always necessary for language acquisition.

However, adult-infant play may be part of an environmental situation that is *optimal* for some aspects of cognitive growth and communicative development. This possibility has received a great deal of attention. Researchers have designed intervention programs in which mothers were encouraged to engage in play with their young children (see Madden, Levenstein, and Levenstein, 1976). The effects of increased mother-child play on the children's cognitive development were then measured. Unfortunately, the results of such intervention programs are still uncertain.

Other attempts to define the relationship between mother-child play and children's development have focused on assessing the correlation between the two variables. The problem with these studies is that, even when mother-child play is found to be significantly related to the child's cognitive development (see, e.g., Clarke-Stewart, 1973), the direction of the effects still cannot be determined. We do not know whether increased play results in enhanced cognitive development, or whether advanced cognitive development results in increased play. Indeed, the relationship could even operate both ways. For example, using a cross-lagged panel analysis, Bradley, Caldwell, and Elardo (1979) found that, during their subjects' first year of life, advanced cognitive abilities led to greater involvement with the mother; however, in the second year of life, more maternal involvement predicted faster-developing babies. Finally, the investigators qualified their finding of an apparent reversal by pointing out that, even with this statistical technique, great caution is warranted in drawing conclusions about the direction of causation. (See Rosenfeld, in press, for further discussion and some possible solutions to this problem.) In summary, much more work is needed before we know: 1) just what aspects of interaction enhance a child's development; and 2) whether social play has an effect on the acquisition of language and communicative competence.

SYMBOLIC PLAY AND LANGUAGE DEVELOPMENT

The second type of play to be discussed in this chapter is symbolic or pretend play. Piaget (1962), Vygotsky (1962), and Werner and Kaplan (1963) have all given pretend play a central place in cognitive development because it involves symbolization and transformations away from the "here and now." This section briefly discusses how these transformations develop in children's play. It also discusses recent research on the relationship between symbolic play and language. The notion that these behaviors reflect the same underlying abilities is analyzed as it pertains to the relationship between: 1) early play and the emergence of single word utterances; and 2) later play and the use of multiword utterances. Finally, the way in which parental involvement in symbolic play might contribute to children's development is discussed.

Looking at the child's play with objects in the first two years of life, we find a number of changes.[2] The earliest object play involves actions on one object (e.g., banging an object). This is then followed

---

[2] For a thorough review of stages in play, see Fein (1981) and Rubin, Fein, and Vandenberg (1983).

by play in which a child uses two objects together in combinatorial play (e.g., inserting an object into a container). Around the middle of the second year of life, the child may begin to use objects in a way that seems to represent the way they are typically used (Piaget, 1962). For example, the child might pick up a cup and appear to drink from it even though there is nothing in the cup. Such activities constitute the first pretend or symbolic acts of play. Initially, the child's use of objects in pretend play is self-directed (e.g., a child pretending to brush his hair); later, the child performs such pretend actions on substitute objects such as dolls (Fein, 1975; Lowe, 1975; Watson and Fischer, 1977). Eventually, the child plans a series of pretend actions (Nicolich, 1977). By 3 years of age, the child can use language to transform roles, objects, and actions into a fantasy narrative (Garvey, 1977a; Garvey and Berndt, 1977; Matthews, 1977) and to describe plans for sequences of play (see Gearhart, 1979, and Sachs, Goldman, and Chaille, 1984, for analyses of the speech used to plan episodes of play in a pretend setting).

There have been many studies of the development of pretend play in the young child, but only recently has attention turned to the possible relationship between play and language. Bates et al. (1979) attempted to discover whether play and several measures of cognitive functioning were related to the acquisition of language in 25 children who were between the ages of 9 and 13 months. The investigators found no significant overall relationship between language development and a composite of cognitive measures including spatial relations and object permanence. However, they did obtain a positive relationship between language development and play. The children's combinatorial play was related to their comprehension and production abilities. Furthermore, when measures of symbolic play were obtained by observing the child's actions, the investigators again found a positive relationship between play and language production. (However, no significant relationship between symbolic play and language was obtained when the play was evaluated from a maternal interview.)

Support for Bates et al.'s (1979) finding of a general correlation between symbolic play and language development can be obtained from a variety of sources (e.g., Dihoff and Chapman, 1977; Fein, 1978; Lowe and Costello, 1976). Moreover, the fact that Bates et al. obtained a significant relationship between play and language but failed to find such a relationship between a composite of cognitive measures and language is consistent with research findings from higher primates. Chevalier-Skolnikoff (1976) has shown that higher primates—which do not use linguistic means of communication in the natural situation—score well on measures of object permanence and spatial relations, but are not as well developed in areas of tool use, imitation, and symbolic play.

Play and Language: Reflections of the Same Underlying Abilities

In explaining their results, Bates and her colleagues suggested that the same or similar developmental skills might underlie both language and play. Similar suggestions have been made by Bloom (1973) and Sinclair (1971). (For a discussion of this proposal, including an evaluation of alternative possibilities, see Bates et al., 1977.) One example of a skill that might underlie both play and language is the ability to establish a relationship between a sign and its referent. In contrast to the acquisition of cognitive skills such as object permanence (see Corrigan, 1978), the development of both language and play requires the establishment of a relationship between a sign and a referent.

Bates et al. (1979) were primarily interested in the relationship between play and the emergence of single-word utterances. However, their suggestion—that certain developmental skills might be responsible for both play and language—applies to multiword constructions as well as to single-word utterances. Increases in utterance length seem to parallel changes in symbolic play; and recent research again has uncovered several developmental skills that might account for this parallel. One of these later developmental skills is the ability to think about a complete action, object, or goal; another underlying skill is the ability to function independently of the "here and now."

Nicolich (1975) investigated the relationship between play and the emergence of combinatorial speech in five children. The children were observed every month for a year beginning when they were 14 to 19 months of age. Each child's play behavior was scored during each session by assigning the most advanced behavior seen during that session to one of seven levels. The child's language was classified according to whether most of the utterances were single-word or multiword constructions. Nicolich found that the use of multiword constructions was related to the emergence of planned sequences of play behavior. Evidence of planning included: 1) instructing the mother to begin an activity; 2) announcing one's intentions; and 3) actively searching for an object needed in a game after one such object had already been located. Nicolich hypothesized that the appearance of multiword utterances and planned segments of play are dependent on the child being able to think about a complete action, object, or goal. Thus, the cognitive ability to mentally represent a complete event is reflected in both the verbal and nonverbal domains at about the same time.

Another characteristic of both symbolic play and language is that development in both areas is associated with an increasing independence from the "here and now." During the early stages of symbolic play, only objects are transformed; eventually, however, the child may transform both objects and roles to carry out elaborate make-believe sequences. In language development the earliest uses of language are again tied to the nonlinguistic context, but over time the child shows increasing independence from the context in both comprehension and production (Bates et al., 1984; Sachs, 1984). The degree to which facility with decontextualized language is attained may be predictive of academic success and literacy (Glucksberg, Krauss, and Higgins, 1975; Olson, 1977).

The existence of decontextualization in play and language has been studied by Rocissano (1979). She observed eight children between the ages of 16 and 24 months at the first observation. Rocissano scored each child's play behavior in terms of its independence from contextual support. At the highest level, the play did not reflect a property intrinsic to the perceptual characteristics of the objects used, nor did the activity imitate the play of a partner. For the analysis of language, Rocissano looked at both the mean length of utterance (MLU) and the relationships expressed in individual utterances. Utterances were classified as either "single-element relationships" or "multi-element relationships." Single-element relationships involved only one entity. For example, use of the word *this* suggests the existence of one entity; and the utterance *big boat* refers to an attribute of one entity. In contrast, multi-element relationships involve two or more entities in a relationship; for example, *eat cake* involves both a presupposed agent and an object. Rocissano argued that as the child's MLU and use of multi-element relations increases, so does his independence from the nonlinguistic context. By her third observation, when the children were between 20 and 29 months of age and had MLUs ranging from 1.19 to 2.15, Rocissano noted a significant correlation between MLU and environmentally independent play. In addition, MLU was significantly related to: 1) the child's tendency to act on another object rather than on himself; and 2) the performance of sequences of different actions in play. During this third observation, Rocissano also found that the use of multi-element relationships was strongly related to the occurrence of environmentally independent play, nonreflexive actions, and action sequences. She interpreted these results as indicating that higher levels of both language and play involve decreasing levels of contextual support.

In the various relationships between language and play described here, the claim is not that a step in language development is dependent upon a characteristic of play, but rather that both language and play reflect the same underlying cognitive changes. This distinction is illustrated by the work of Greenfield and her colleagues (Goodson and Greenfield, 1975; Greenfield, Nelson, and Saltzman, 1972). These investigators have found that the structural characteristics of construction/manipulative play parallel the development of language structure. Greenfield hypothesized that there are principles common to both action and language that should show developmental change, but the particular realizations of these features will differ because of differences in the medium of the behavior. "Because these principles are so general, they guide development over and over in many specific acquisitions" (Goodson and Greenfield, p. 745). A similar notion lies behind the Project Zero research on the development of symbol systems as expressed across various media such as language, symbolic play, art, music, and mathematics (see, e.g., Gardner and Wolf, 1979; Wolf and Gardner, 1981).

Parental Involvement in Symbolic Play

Although there is a large literature on symbolic or pretend play in children, little has been said about adult involvement in such play. In fact, researchers interested in the emergence of pretend play have often deliberately used methods that would enable them to observe behavior free of adult influence. Some investigators have evaluated the child's play without the child's mother being present. Although others like Nicolich (1977) felt that the mother's presence is important, they nevertheless instructed the mothers to avoid making suggestions or initiating play activities with their children. One exception is a study by Dunn and Wooding (1977). These investigators observed children playing both when their mothers had free time and when their mothers were busy with housework. It was found that children who were engaged in pretend play often attempted to involve their mothers in the play. On the other hand, nonpretend object play was often carried out alone. Given the fact that some children often attempt to involve their parents in pretend play, it would be helpful to know more about parental contributions to the development of pretend play and the relationships between pretend play and language. In short, we need to know what, if any, advantages pretend play with parental involvement has over pretend play without parental involvement. So far, the available research indicates that parents may contribute to the child's play and ultimately to his overall development by: 1) showing the child how to play and that it is enjoyable to play; and 2) imposing story lines on the child's play activities, thereby showing the child how narratives are constructed.

Learning How To Play   As pretend play emerges, adult models of such play may influence its development. A number of investigators (e.g., Bretherton et al., 1979; Garvey, 1977a; Johnson, 1978; Lieberman, 1977; Singer, 1973) have noted that, even in the early months of a child's life, adults perform activities that are not to be taken literally. Infants in this culture see adults playing with dolls, stuffed animals, cars, and certain other objects even before the infants can manipulate these objects themselves. The adults move the toys about, talk to them, make sounds for them, and describe their actions and motivations as if the objects were animate. It is as if the adult plays *for* the child before the child himself is able to play. In this play the adult: 1) shows the child that it is possible and enjoyable to use objects in nonliteral ways; and 2) transmits information about how to play. For example, adults may convey to children the common cultural constraints about what objects are viewed as animate, what activities are appropriate for various objects, and so on. We talk for dolls (human and animal) but typically not for cars; and we make noises for cars but typically not for trees. Some toys are frequently moved as part of the play, whereas others are held stationary to form the location of the play. Here again we think of Vygotsky's (1962, 1978) observation that children function under the guidance of adults. Although I know of no direct evidence that adult modeling of pretend play accelerates its development, the potential for adult behavior to influence the emergence of symbolic representation and symbolic systems in both play and language is great and clearly deserves further investigation.

Learning How To Construct Narratives   Parental involvement in pretend play also might facilitate a child's learning about the construction of narratives to accompany his play. The narrative functions of language that appear in storytelling and talk about past events are becoming recognized as important aspects of language usage. Such linguistic activities play a role in interpersonal communication and are crucial to the organization of reality for an individual's own thought. Given their importance, it is not surprising that the development of narrative abilities has received a good deal of attention.

Unfortunately, the earliest stages of narrative development are often overlooked in this research. Most of the research on the construction of narratives has focused on school-age children (see Cazden, 1979, for a review of this literature). However, narrative skills begin to develop long before the child enters school. Even very young children know something about the structure of stories. In analyzing the simple story "The baby cried; the mommy picked it up," Sacks (1972) showed that even a 2-year-old storyteller was aware that stories involve both a problem and a resolution of the problem.

The earliest narratives of children often accompany their pretend play. Furthermore, pretend play—especially if it includes an adult partner—may be an excellent context for the young child to learn about the construction of narratives. Just as parents model playing with toys, they also may model the telling of a story by imposing story lines on the child's play activities. In a longitudinal analysis of adult-child interaction during spontaneous doll-play sequences, Sachs (1980) found that the comments of the parents enriched the ongoing play by providing it with a rational structure. The adults were likely to describe the ongoing activity in terms of the actions and motivations of the dolls instead of simply describing the child's actions. For example, when a child put a blanket on a doll, the child was likely to say "Blanket on" but an adult was likely to say "The baby's tired." Moreover, adults often identified "problem elements" without telling children the potential solutions. However, problems were described in such a way that inferences about reasonable solutions could be made. For example, once when a child was putting her dolls in a sitting position, the adult made the play suggestion "Do they want something to eat?" These observations suggest that such interactions might help children learn about story construction. Similar results have been reported by Kavanaugh, Whittington, and Cerbone (1983). Other influences on narrative abilities include hearing stories read and past events retold.

ROLE PLAY AND LANGUAGE USAGE IN CONTEXT

In this section research in which role play is used to study a child's ability to adapt his utterances to both the discourse and social context is considered. Generally speaking, these adaptations or register variations are a frequent and widespread phenomenon. This does not mean, however, that all registers are readily observable. There are many different kinds of registers, some of which rarely occur.

Researchers who wish to observe several kinds of registers in real-life situations may waste a great deal of time waiting for the infrequent ones to occur. Consequently, some researchers have tried to accelerate the observational process by using role play (Ervin-Tripp, 1973). During this play the child may be encouraged first to play the role of a parent and then to play the role of a child. Other possible role contrasts include: teacher and learner, doctor and patient, and doctor and nurse. By asking a child to play contrasting roles, an observer can discover what the child knows about how each person speaks. Furthermore, because situations arise that would be rare or impossible in real life, role play gives an observer the opportunity to discover what a child knows about language use in novel situations.

Playing the Role of a Caregiver

The acquisition of speech styles or registers begins very early. Children as young as 1;9 have been observed using paralinguistic features such as softness and whispering in appropriate contexts (Weeks, 1971). Other paralinguistic features appear in children's early talk to babies. For example, one of Sachs' (1977) subjects used a high pitch at 2;1 when talking to her baby dolls.

Linguistic adaptations appear as children grow older. Sachs and Devin (1976) analyzed the baby talk of four children (3;9 to 5;5) using a variety of stylistic measures. When the children's speech to babies (live and dolls) was compared with their speech to mothers and peers, Sachs and Devin found that the first style was most consistently distinguished from the others by the use of a high pitch, exaggerated intonation, short utterances, less complex utterances, more names, and more imperatives. Other features characteristic of speech directed to babies included the use of endearments and certain kinds of routines. When speaking to babies, the preschoolers not only shifted their style of speaking; they also shifted the content of their speech. Differences in content between speech to babies and speech to peers and mothers were reflected in the type of questions addressed to these listeners. To babies, the children asked more questions about internal state (e.g., "You don't want any more?") than about the external world (e.g., "What color is that?"). The reverse was true of speech directed to mothers and peers.

Garvey (1979) studied the dyadic play of two girls who spontaneously adopted the roles of mother and baby. Her findings are generally consistent with those of Sachs and Devin. When the child playing the mother spoke to the child playing the baby, the "mother's" pitch increased and the length of her utterances decreased. The "mother" also asked many questions regarding the physical and attentional needs of the "baby." In comparing the amount of "mother"-initiated speech with the amount of "baby"-initiated speech, Garvey found that the "mother" talked more than the "baby."

Finally, in analyzing the discourse characteristics of the speech in these roles, Garvey found that the child playing the role of mother was very responsive to all of "baby's" utterances. The "mother" also attended to whether "baby" responded to her. When the "baby" did not respond, the "mother" repeated and modified her utterances as in the following example:

Here's a little motor car, a little motor car.
See that motor car?
This is your motor car. (pause 1 sec)
Your very own new motor car. Okay? (1979, p. 72)

Andersen (1977) studied both mother and father caregiver roles using a technique she called "controlled improvisation." Each of her 24 subjects (ages 3;9–7;1) was given two hand puppets to encourage the subject to play two roles while the experimenter played a third role. For example, a child might play the role of a mother with the puppet on his right hand and play a father with the puppet on his left hand; the experimenter in this case would play the role of a baby. As fathers, children spoke with a low pitch accompanied by backed and lowered vowels; "mothers" on the other hand, used a high pitch. "Mothers" also used longer utterances and talked more than did "fathers." "Mothers" were more polite in that they used endearments, qualifications, and indirect requests. Sometimes the "mothers" also used hints (e.g., "Now it's time for your naptime") in interacting with their "babies." "Fathers" tended to use direct imperatives without giving any explanation or reason for a request.

Playing the Role of a Baby

Children's awareness of how babies talk to caregivers has also been studied. Sachs and Devin (1976) compared the styles used by children in playing the role of baby to the styles used in playing adults and peers. The results indicated that the most consistent characteristics of the baby role were the use of a high pitch, phonetic substitutions, and short, simple utterances. The children did not have an entirely accurate conception of baby syntax, however. Although short utterances such as *hat on* and *no touch* were used, long complex utterances also appeared (e.g., "Could you put my sweater on?"). When playing the baby, the content of the children's speech centered on caregiving functions: many of their utterances were efforts to direct the caregiver to "baby" or to "baby's" needs. An analysis of pronoun use in the various roles showed that 49% of the utterances as "baby" contained a first person pronoun. In contrast, only 11% of the utterances in the role of caregiver contained this pronoun. Thus, the "babies" clearly reflected a self-orientation in their speech.

Andersen (1977) also reported that the utterances of "babies" tended to be shorter than those of "caregivers," but again the children were not consistent in their use of syntactic characteristics. Like Sachs and Devin, Andersen also found that the speech of "babies" was distinguished by the use of high pitch, phonetic modifications (such as palatalization and nasalization), and phonological substitutions. Other more subtle linguistic features revealing linguistic and social knowledge included the differential use of placeholders and boundary markers such as *well*. *Well* was almost never used by children when they were playing the role of a child speaking to a parent, but it frequently appeared in the speech of children role playing a parent speaking to a child.

Other Roles

Andersen (1977) asked her subjects to role play two other situations. The first situation involved a doctor, a nurse, and a patient, and the second contained a teacher, a student, and a foreign student. Although Andersen found that the family scene was easiest for her subjects to play, many children also revealed knowledge of the styles associated with these other roles. For example, doctors were portrayed with a low pitch. In one scene, a child was already using a puppet to role play a father when the doctor puppet was introduced. Because "father" had already been speaking with a low pitch, the child ingeniously marked the doctor's voice by using a German accent and a pitch that was even lower.

An especially dramatic instance of a speech style used in play that would not be observed in real life has been provided by Mitchell-Kernan (1979). She studied 5- to 12-year-old Afro-American children who were spontaneously presenting plays to an audience of other children. The children's speech in various roles was analyzed for a number of features of Black English (e.g., final [l] and [r] omissions, [d] for [ð] substitutions, and [a] for [ay] substitutions) and assigned a score based on the percentage of Black English features present. The results indicated that the use of Black English features varied according to the role played. For example, one 11-year-old girl enacted several roles: nurse, mother, adult daughter, father, and teenage brother. Mitchell-Kernan found that, although the child's non–role playing speech contained between 50% and 73% Black English features, her use of Black English features in play ranged from only 18% in the role of nurse to 93% in the role of brother. Furthermore, the use of Black English features changed with the emotional state of the character portrayed. More Black English features were used as the interaction became more intense. Such a study clearly shows that children know a great deal about the social role of speech characteristics; it also demonstrates the unique value of a study of play for revealing such knowledge.

Comments on Methodology

The studies described here range from situations in which play was completely spontaneous to situations in which play was evoked by the experimenter. Each research method has its advantages and disadvantages. The disadvantage in studying spontaneously occurring play is that large amounts of data often must be collected to find examples of the targeted behavior(s). If one has a specific question in mind, sometimes it is more efficient to construct a situation that will evoke the desired behavior. On the other hand, experimenters who arrange situations designed to evoke play should be aware that the behaviors evoked may differ from those that occur naturally. The advantage in studying spontaneously occurring play is that the behavior is natural and there is a greater likelihood of observing language that reflects the child's potential. The danger of evoking unnatural behaviors with prearranged role play is apparent from a study by O'Connor, Strage, and Ervin-Tripp (1979). These investigators attempted to use a role playing situation to find out whether children comprehended hints as requests. Children 3 to 7 years of age were asked to act out the ending of a story after an indirect request form had been used. Unfortunately, some of the developmental differences of interest seemed to be obscured by the older children's tendencies to create interesting, unexpected endings. The investigators concluded that role playing provided the children with too much freedom in responding.

The method used for research also may affect the age at which a linguistic ability is observed. Experimental techniques may contribute difficulties that mask the child's linguistic knowledge. For example, based on findings from research on spontaneous play (e.g., Sachs and Devin, 1976), Andersen tried to use 3-year-olds in a pilot study for her thesis, but found that her puppet task was too difficult for children of that age. Similarly, Garvey and Berndt (1977) noted that the narrative language they observed in the spontaneous play of preschoolers was much more advanced than would have been expected from the research reported by Sutton-Smith, Botvin, and Mahony (1976), in which 5- to 10-year-olds were asked to tell a story.

RELATIONSHIPS BETWEEN PLAY
AND OTHER ASPECTS OF DEVELOPMENT

Some writers distinguish linguistic from communicative competence. The first term, *linguistic competence*, is used to refer to a person's syntactic, semantic, and phonological abilities. On the other hand, the term *communicative competence* is used to suggest aspects of a person's performance that lie outside the traditional areas of syntax, semantics, and phonology. However, because the child is learning how to communicate, not merely how to produce sounds, arrange words in sentences, or get listeners to cooperate, in my view, it would be better if we used the term *communicative competence* to refer to all aspects of communicative ability. Subareas of this competence—phonology, syntax, semantics, speech acts, dialogue, register variation, etc.—should be defined loosely because their boundaries are not at all clear. This usage of the term *communicative competence* would then reflect the broad way in which the term was used in *A Field Manual for Cross-Cultural Study of the Acquisition of Communicative Competence* (Slobin, 1967).

The frequent distinction between linguistic and communicative competence illustrates the fragmentation that exists within the field. Researchers engaged in studies of discourse pay little attention to the study of syntax, and vice versa. As fields grow there is inevitable specialization, but this specialization should not cause researchers to ignore the important principles of language acquisition uncovered in the last 20 years. As new areas emerge, they should build on that principled foundation rather than ignore it.

In accord with the preceding recommendation, the next three sections are devoted to an analysis of the relationship between play, language, and social development. The first of these sections shows how findings from research on language acquisition might enrich the study of play. The subsequent section deals with the same relationship, but in the reverse direction, discussing how findings from the research on play might enrich the study of language and social development. Each of these sections concerns ways in which the research findings on one component might enhance the design of research on the other components. The third section deals with the clinical implications of a bidirectional relationship among the preceding three variables. A model of this relationship is presented and appropriate goals for intervention based on this model are suggested.

How Research on Language Acquisition Might Enrich the Study of Play

Many of the principles abstracted from research on language acquisition might also apply to the study of play. Five of these broad principles are discussed here in the hope that such a discussion will encourage researchers to move beyond the description and categorization of behavior.

Abstraction of Invariant Features One of the principles derived from 20 years of research on language acquisition is that the child has a powerful drive to infer regularities from the behavioral evidence that is presented. Research on role play also reveals this drive. Although a child comes into contact with various individuals in a particular role, he usually pulls out general characteristics. For example, in playing the role of a doctor, the child does not imitate any particular set of utterances that a doctor once used; instead, the child abstracts certain invariant features from his wide experience.

Overregularization When the child begins to perceive regularities in the speech of others, those perceptions lead to overregularizations in his speech. Examples from morphology, syntax, and semantics are readily available. The child applies regular past tense endings to words that he has never heard in that form (e.g., "baby comed" and "I doed it."). Similarly, when English-learning children perceive that most sentences follow a subject-verb-object pattern, their perceptions often lead to errors in the comprehension of passive sentences.

Given the preceding tendencies, it is not surprising to find that children at certain stages of development use highly stereotyped speech styles in representing roles. Popular stereotypes and the regularities that a child abstracts from his experiences may override the irregularities encountered. In other words, a child's behavior often reflects his conceptions of "the big picture." A little girl whose only personal experience with doctors has been with a female pediatrician may still use a "male" voice in acting out the role of a doctor. Such stereotyping of roles seems to be analogous to the pattern we find in other aspects of the study of language. An interesting question would be what determines these stereotypes—the child's peer group contacts? the media? The existence of these stereotypes might suggest some caution in the use of "play therapy." It is usually assumed that children act out what they have seen in their families. Thus, their play presumably reflects their own experiences. However, recent research suggests that this assumption is not always warranted.

Order of Development Stylistic features are abstracted from the speech of others in an order that is consistent with other aspects of language development. For example, it appears that children learn what prosodic devices are appropriate in different situations before they learn what content (e.g., talk about internal states versus the external world) is appropriate for different situations; and they learn the latter before they perceive syntactic regularities in the ways that people in different roles convey the same content. However, when their perceptions lead to overregularizations, young children have problems repairing their role play because the metalinguistic awareness needed for such repairs is late to develop.

This ordering is consistent with what we know about other areas of acquisition. Evidence of an awareness of intonation and other vocal characteristics appears even in prelinguistic infants via their responses to language and the prosodic features of their babbling. An understanding of content and a subsequent knowledge of syntax develop after the child has become aware of prosodic variations. Finally, a metalinguistic awareness of language (e.g., requests for clarification, verbal puns) is again late to develop.

Production Limitations There are limitations on how frequently and consistently children reveal a behavior pattern that is in the process of being mastered. Inherent restrictions in the child's attentional and processing capacities may be partly responsible for these limitations. Although these production limitations are not well understood, all levels of language learning show them. Language skills emerge gradually and there is a long period in which the skills can be easily disrupted. Language, like other behaviors, becomes "automatized" only after a period of steady use. Role play is interesting when viewed with this concept in mind. In accord with Piaget's (1970) description of the child as "egocentric," researchers until recently generally believed that children could not role play. One of the thrusts of recent work has been to show that children *can* play the role of another. However, what has actually been shown is that children can *sometimes* and under *some* circumstances take the role of another.

Emphasis on the "Here and Now" The earliest uses of language seem to center on acts in which the child demands/indicates objects present in the "here and now." Similarly, the child's early pretend play and the stories he constructs during that play are tied to the immediate nonlinguistic context. This general tendency to operate within the immediate context may indeed be fortunate in that it might lead the child to adopt certain strategies that can facilitate his early acts of play and communication.

One of these strategies is to use whatever is given in the immediate context. This strategy applies both to the recent linguistic behaviors of adults and to objects from the real world. Thus, the child's use of puppets and dolls associated with a role probably facilitates his role play. Second, the consistency in an adult's linguistic behavior affords the child solid structures that he can later incorporate profitably into his own speech.

Eventually, however, parental involvement together with the child's expanding cognitive capacities should afford the child increasing independence from the "here and now." This independence not only leads to talk about abstract topics and past events, it also leads to more complex themes in play, fantastic object transformations, and accurate as well as effective language in role enactment.

How Research on Play Might Enrich the Study of Language and Social Development

The preceding section contained suggestions for ways in which current research on play and language might be enhanced by a review of previous work on child language. This section suggests ways in which this relationship might operate in the reverse direction. Because researchers who study play and the language used during play are concerned with the child's use of language in social contexts, their research might be applicable to the study of syntactic, semantic, and phonological aspects of language development as well as to the study of children's social development.

Enriching the Study of Traditional Topics in Language Acquisition
One eventual goal in studying the language used in play is to develop a model of what children learn and how they learn to interact with others. This model would reflect two basic assumptions. The first is that social intentions are of primary importance. The individual's reasons for speaking affect his later choices of vocabulary, syntactic structure, and prosody. Consequently, in order to understand the ways in which a child uses a specific form, we need to understand how that form relates to the child's intentions (see de Villiers, this volume, for examples of how children map forms onto intentions).

The second assumption in this model is that children learn how to use specific forms and syntactic patterns by uncovering the social intentions conveyed by their partners during discourse. In other words, children learn how to communicate by interacting with others. In discussing the acquisition of reference to past events in parent-child discourse, Sachs (1984) argued that syntactic forms associated with references to the past originate in quite concrete discourse phenomena. The idea that discourse with adults provides a child with a foundation upon which he can build also appears in the work of Ervin-Tripp (1977) and Bruner et al. (1982). Ervin-Tripp suggested that the child might try out certain "production rules" in limited contexts of discourse. If the results are favorable, such rules would then be applied to other discourse contexts and eventually give rise to stable syntactic patterns. Bruner et al. have similarly suggested that, in acquiring grammatical rules, the child builds upon a functional system that is already in existence.

The preceding assumptions illustrate how research on discourse and the acquisition of communicative competence might contribute to a better understanding of traditional topics in psycholinguistics. Ervin-Tripp (1977) argued that "the analysis of discourse is not a distraction from the study of the development of syntax" (p. 18). In other words, individuals interested in the broader issues of communicative competence are not ignoring the important problems that motivated developmental psycholinguists in the 1960s. Indeed, they are really trying to solve some of the more persistent problems by using a new approach. This approach may lead researchers to observe phenomena that were not attended to earlier, but the results might provide a fuller explanation of development in the more traditional areas of language acquisition.

Enriching the Study of Social Development Work on play and language should also be relevant to researchers interested in areas other than language development. Research on play and the language used during play is especially relevant to the study of social development. Over the years, research on play has focused on finer and finer details of children's nonlinguistic behavior. Although researchers interested in play are just beginning to use the content and style of a child's speech to assess his awareness of appropriate social behavior, such research eventually will yield a powerful tool for studying social development. To give a concrete example, Andersen (1977) found that the children she studied associated a low pitch with high status. If we know from prior observation that a particular child marks status in this way, then we can make inferences about the child's perceptions of a character's status by noting whether a high or low pitch is used.

Similarly, Sachs and Devin (1976) found that, when children were asked to talk like babies or caregivers, the children reliably associated certain social characteristics with those roles (e.g., that babies are dependent and caregivers are nurturant). These characteristics were reflected in some obvious ways as well as in some rather subtle ways. For instance, requests made by "babies" referred to the "babies'" own needs, whereas requests made by "caregivers" were frequently probes about the state of the baby. Finally, in Mitchell-Kernan's (1979) study, the way in which children role played Black and white characters revealed information about their perceptions of Black and white adults that might not be revealed by other means of assessing attitudes. Thus, as we better understand the ways in which we express social intentions, the study of register variation will become increasingly useful to those interested in social development.

Implications for Intervention

At this time, I cannot cite any empirical evidence to show that role playing actually does facilitate development. Researchers clearly need to begin studying how different amounts and types of role play affect children's development. Without this research, we can only speculate that experience in role playing might help children learn to use language and carry out various social roles more effectively. Keeping this note of caution in mind, some specific ways in which a child might benefit from role play with adults and subsequently with other children are suggested here.

Play between parent and child seems to be a good way for the child to learn certain aspects of language use. By playing a variety of roles that are different from those held in real life, parents can: 1) expose their children to roles that perhaps the children have never encountered; and 2) model the use of register variation. Other kinds of parent-child play offer additional possibilities. For example, Schieffelin (1979) and Schieffelin and Eisenberg (this volume) found that mothers of Kaluli children in New Guinea use playful teasing to teach their children how to be assertive in the use of language.

As children grow older and begin to participate in child-child play, they again have an opportunity to engage in roles and activities that they might not experience in real life. Such play might further enhance the development of sociolinguistic skills (Rubin, 1980; Singer, 1973).

In both parent-child and child-child play, children are buffered from the consequences of their behaviors. This buffering applies to both the content and the style of interaction. An example of a speech style being used in play when it would not be possible in reality was given in Mitchell-Kernan's (1979) study. The Black child who spoke with standard English speech would probably receive negative feedback from peers in real life, but such speech could be used to convey a role in a play. Constraints on other aspects of style are also more flexible in play. For example, participants in play are allowed to violate the rules of politeness (Lakoff, 1973) to engage in play fights. Indeed, play fighting is common in both animals and children. More than once I have intervened when I overheard my daughter saying something outrageously impolite to a friend, only to be told "Mommy, we were only pretending!"

So far the discussion in this section has focused on how children's play might contribute to their language development, but the relationship between play and language also operates in the reverse direction. Play supplies a social and semantic context for language acquisition, but language may be necessary for the development of more advanced forms of play and cognitive growth (Garvey and Hogan, 1973; Pellegrini, 1982). Thus, language and play are closely related to each other as well as to the child's social and cognitive development.

An analysis of this bidirectional relationship indicates that the key variable might be the infant's responsiveness. Typical patterns of interaction, play, and affectional bonding in infancy might be disrupted by any disorder that limits the infant's responsiveness. Handicapped children[3] may show deficits in play, language, and cognitive development (Darbyshire, 1977; Hulme and Lunzer, 1966; Kaplan and

---

[3] My comments here are limited to intervention with handicapped children. However, the relationship between language development and play in environmentally disadvantaged children deserves further study. Smilanski (1968) claimed that the child's environment affects both his play and his language (also see Griffing, 1979). In research on advantaged and disadvantaged 3- to 6-year-old Israeli children, Smilanski found that there was more dramatic play in the advantaged group, and argued that intervention could improve the cognitive development of the disadvantaged.

McHale, 1979; Lovell, Hoyle, and Siddall, 1968; Mogford, 1977) as the result of a spiral that begins when their disorder leads to a disengagement from normal social interaction. This disengagement in turn limits the child's opportunities to learn and use communicative skills. The last step in the spiral is that poor communicative abilities may restrict the child's cognitive development and social interaction with peers (Mueller, 1972). Finally, the effects of this spiral are self-perpetuating. Inadequate social skills lead to further disengagement, which then causes the cycle to start all over again.

In conclusion, one goal of intervention should be to interrupt the downward spiral. Instruction in communicative skills will be of little benefit unless adequate attention is given to a child's social relationships. As we better understand the connections between language and play, perhaps we can find ways to help children improve their abilities in both of these important domains.

REFERENCES

Andersen, E. 1977. Learning to speak with style: A study of the sociolinguistic skills of children. Unpublished doctoral dissertation, Stanford University.

Bates, E., Benigni, L., Bretherton, I., Camaioni, L., and Volterra, V. 1977. From gesture to the first word: On cognitive and social prerequisites. In M. Lewis and L. Rosenblum (eds.), Interaction, Conversation, and the Development of Language. John Wiley & Sons, Inc., New York.

Bates, E., Benigni, L., Bretherton, I., Camainoi, L., and Volterra, V. 1979. Cognition and communication from nine to thirteen months: Correlational findings. In E. Bates (ed.), The Emergence of Symbols: Cognition and Communication in Infancy. Academic Press, Inc., New York.

Bates, E., Bretherton, I., Shore, C., and McNew, S. 1984. Names, gestures and objects: The role of context in the emergence of symbols. In K. E. Nelson (ed.), Children's Language, Vol. 4. Lawrence Erlbaum Assocs., Inc., Hillsdale, N.J.

Bloom, L. 1973. One Word at a Time: The Use of Single-word Utterances before Syntax. Mouton, The Hague.

Bloom, L., Lifter, K., and Broughton, J. The convergence of early cognition and language in the second year of life: Conceptualization and measurement. In M. Barrett (ed.), Children's Single Word Speech. John Wiley & Sons, Inc., New York. (in press)

Bradley, R. H., Caldwell, B. M., and Elardo, R. 1979. Home environment and cognitive development in the first two years: A cross-lagged panel analysis. Dev. Psychol. 15:246–250.

Braine, M. D. S. 1963. The ontogeny of English phrase structure: The first phase. Language 39:1–13.

Bretherton, I., Bates, E., Benigni, L., Camaioni, L., and Volterra, V. 1979. Relationships between cognition, communication and quality of attachment. In E. Bates (ed.), The Emergence of Symbols: Cognition and Communication in Infancy. Academic Press, Inc., New York.

Brown, R. 1973. A First Language: The Early Stages. Harvard University Press, Cambridge, MA.
Brown, R., and Fraser, C. 1963. The acquisition of syntax. In C. N. Cofer and B. Musgrave (eds.), Verbal Behavior and Learning. McGraw-Hill Book Company, New York.
Bruner, J. 1978. On prelinguistic prerequisites of speech. In R. N. Campbell and P. T. Smith (eds.), Recent Advances in the Psychology of Language: Language Development and Mother-Child Interaction. Plenum Publishing Corp., New York.
Bruner, J., Roy, C., and Ratner, N. 1982. The beginning of request. In K. E. Nelson (ed.), Children's Language, Vol. 3. Lawrence Erlbaum Associates, Inc., Hillsdale, N.J.
Cazden, C. 1979. Peekaboo as an instructional model: Discourse development at home and at school. Papers Rep. Child Lang. Dev. 17:1–29.
Chevalier-Skolnikoff, S. 1976. The ontogeny of primate intelligence and its implications for communicative potential: A preliminary report. In S. Harnad, H. Steplis, and J. Lancaster (eds.), Origins and Evolution of Language and Speech. New York Academy of Sciences, New York.
Chomsky, N. 1959. A review of B. F. Skinner's Verbal Behavior. Language 35:26–58.
Chomsky, N. 1965. Aspects of the Theory of Syntax. MIT Press, Cambridge, MA.
Chukovsky, K. 1963. From Two to Five. University of California Press, Berkeley.
Clarke-Stewart, K. A. 1973. Interactions between mothers and their young children: Characteristics and consequences. Monogr. Soc. Res. Child Dev. 38 (Serial No. 153).
Corrigan, R. 1978. Language development as related to stage six object permanence development. J. Child Lang. 5:173–190.
Darbyshire, J. O. 1977. Play patterns in young children with hearing impairment. Volta Rev. 79:9–26.
Dihoff, R., and Chapman, R. 1977. First words: Their origins in action. Papers Rep. Child Lang. Dev. 13:1–7.
Dunn, J., and Wooding, C. 1977. Play at home and its implications for learning. In B. Tizard and D. Harvey (eds.), The Biology of Play. William Heinemann Medical Books, Ltd, London.
Ervin, S., and Miller, W. 1963. Language development. 62nd Yearbook for the National Society for the Study of Education, Part I. University of Chicago Press, Chicago.
Ervin-Tripp, S. 1973. Children's sociolinguistic competence and dialect diversity. In A. Dil (ed.), Language Acquisition and Communicative Choice. Stanford University Press, Stanford, CA.
Ervin-Tripp, S. 1977. From conversation to syntax. Papers Rep. Child Lang. Dev. 13:K1–21.
Fein, G. 1975. A transformational analysis of pretending. Dev. Psychol. 11:291–296.
Fein, G. 1978. Imagination and play: Some relationships in early development. Paper presented at a meeting of the American Psychological Association, Toronto, August.
Fein, G. 1981. Pretend play in childhood: An integrative review. Child Dev. 52:1095–1118.

Furrow, D., Nelson, K., and Benedict, H. 1979. Mothers' speech to children and syntactic development: Some simple relationships. J. Child Lang. 6:423–442.
Gardner, H., and Wolf, D. 1979. Early Symbolization. Jossey-Bass, San Francisco.
Garvey, C. 1977a. Play. Harvard University Press, Cambridge, MA.
Garvey, C. 1977b. Play with language and speech. *In* S. Ervin-Tripp and C. Mitchell-Kernan (eds.), Child Discourse. Academic Press, Inc., New York.
Garvey, C. 1979. An approach to the study of children's role play. Q. Newsletter Lab. Comp. Hum. Cognition 1:69–73.
Garvey, C., and Berndt, R. 1977. The organization of pretend play. Catalog of Selected Documents in Psychology, 7, Ms #1589. American Psychological Association, Washington, D.C.
Garvey, C., and Hogan, R. 1973. Social speech and social interaction: Egocentrism revisited. Child Dev. 44:562–568.
Gearhart, M. 1979. Social planning: Role play in a novel situation. Paper presented at the Biennial Conference of the Society for Research in Child Development, San Francisco, March.
Glucksberg, S., Krauss, R., and Higgins, E. T. 1975. The development of referential communication skills. *In* F. D. Horowitz (ed.), Review of Child Development Research, Vol. 4. University of Chicago Press, Chicago.
Goodson, B. D., and Greenfield, P. M. 1975. The search for structural principles in children's manipulative play: A parallel with linguistic development. Child Dev. 46:734–746.
Greenfield, P. M., Nelson, K., and Saltzman, E. 1972. The development of rulebound strategies for manipulating seriated cups: A parallel between action and grammar. Cognitive Psychol. 3:291–310.
Griffing, P. 1979. The relationship between socioeconomic status and sociodramatic play among black kindergarten children. Paper presented at the Biennial Conference of the Society for Research in Child Development, San Francisco, March.
Hulme, I., and Lunzer, E. A. 1966. Play, language and reasoning in subnormal children. J. Child Psychol. Psychiatry 7:107–123.
Hymes, D. 1967. Models of the interaction of language and social setting. J. Social Issues 23:8–28.
Ingram, D. 1979. Sensorimotor intelligence and language development. *In* A. Lock (ed.), Action, Gesture and Symbol: The Emergence of Language. Academic Press, Inc., New York.
Johnson, J. E. 1978. Mother-child interaction and imaginative behavior of preschool children. J. Psychol. 100:123–129.
Kaplan, B., and McHale, F. J. 1979. Communication and play behaviors of a deaf preschooler and his younger sibling. Paper presented at the Biennial Conference of the Society for Research in Child Development, San Francisco, March.
Kavanaugh, R. D., Whittington, S., and Cerbone, M. J. 1983. Mother's use of fantasy in speech to young children. J. Child Lang. 10:45–55.
Lakoff, R. 1973. The logic of politeness: Or, minding your P's and Q's. Papers from the Ninth Regional Meeting of the Chicago Linguistic Society. Linguistics Department, University of Chicago, Chicago, IL.
Lieberman, J. N. 1977. Playfulness: Its Relationship to Imagination and Creativity. Academic Press, Inc., New York.

Lovell, K., Hoyle, H. W., and Siddall, M. Q. 1968. A study of some aspects of the play and language of young children with delayed speech. J. Child Psychol. Psychiatry 9:41–50.

Lowe, M. 1975. Trends in the development of representational play in infants from one to three years: An observational study. J. Child Psychol. Psychiatry 16:33–47.

Lowe, M., and Costello, A. 1976. Manual for the Symbolic Play Test (Experimental Edition). NFER Publishing Co., Ltd, London.

Macnamara, J. 1972. Cognitive basis for language learning in infants. Psychol. Rev. 79:1–13.

McNeill, D. 1966. Developmental psycholinguistics. *In* F. Smith and G. Miller (eds.), The Genesis of Language. MIT Press, Cambridge, MA.

Madden, J., Levenstein, P., and Levenstein, S. 1976. Longitudinal IQ outcomes of the mother-child home program. Child Dev. 47:1015–1025.

Masur, E. F., and Gleason, J. B. 1980. Parent-child interaction and the acquisition of lexical information during play. Dev. Psychol. 16:404–409.

Matthews, W. S. 1977. Modes of transformation in the initiation of fantasy play. Dev. Psychol. 13:212–216.

Menn, L., and Hazelkorn, S. 1977. Now you see it, now you don't: Tracing the development of communicative competence. *In* J. Kegl (ed.), Proceedings of the Seventh Annual Meeting of the Linguistic Society.

Miller, J., Chapman, R., Branston, M., and Reichle, J. 1980. Language comprehension in sensorimotor stages V and VI. J. Speech Hear. Res. 23:284–311.

Mitchell-Kernan, C. 1979. Social and sociolinguistic knowledge in the role-playing of Afro-American children. Paper presented at the Biennial Conference of the Society for Research in Child Development, San Francisco, March.

Mogford, K. 1977. The play of handicapped children. *In* B. Tizard and D. Harvey (eds.), The Biology of Play. William Heinemann Medical Books, Ltd, London.

Mowrer, O. H. 1954. The psychologist looks at language. Am. Psychol. 9:660–694.

Mueller, E. 1972. The maintenance of verbal exchanges between young children. Child Dev. 43:930–938.

Nelson, K. 1973. Structure and strategy in learning how to talk. Monogr. Soc. Res. Child Dev. 38 (1–2, Serial No. 149).

Nelson, K. E. 1980. Toward a rare-event cognitive comparison theory of syntax acquisition. *In* P. S. Dale and D. Ingram (eds.), Child Language: An International Perspective. University Park Press, Baltimore.

Nicolich, L. 1975. A longitudinal study of representational play in relation to spontaneous imitation and development of multi-word utterances. Final Report, National Institute of Education. (ERIC document number ED 103 133).

Nicolich, L. 1977. Beyond sensorimotor intelligence: Assessment of symbolic maturity through analyses of pretend play. Merrill-Palmer Q. 23:89–99.

O'Connor, M. C., Strage, A., and Ervin-Tripp, S. 1979. Elicited role playing of commands and requests. Paper presented at the Biennial Conference of the Society for Research in Child Development, San Francisco, March. (ERIC Document Number ED 171 418.)

Olson, D. 1977. From utterances to text: The bias of language in speech and writing. Harvard Educ. Rev. 47:257–281.

Pellegrini, A. D. 1982. The construction of cohesive text by preschoolers in two play contexts. Discourse Processes 5:101–107.

Piaget, J. 1954. The Construction of Reality in the Child. Basic Books, Inc., New York.

Piaget, J. 1960. The Psychology of Intelligence. Littlefield Adams, Patterson, N.J.

Piaget, J. 1962. Play, Dreams and Imitation in Childhood. W. W. Norton & Company, Inc., New York.

Piaget, J. 1970. The Language and Thought of the Child. Harcourt, Brace & World, New York.

Ratner, N., and Bruner, J. S. 1978. Games, social exchange and the acquisition of language. J. Child Lang. 5:391–402.

Rocissano, L. 1979. Object play and its relation to language in early childhood. Unpublished doctoral dissertation, Columbia University.

Rosenfeld, H. M. *In* R. L. Schiefelbusch (ed.), Communicative Competence: Assessment and Intervention. University Park Press, Baltimore. (in press)

Rubin, K. H. 1980. Fantasy play: Its role in the development of social skills and social cognition. *In* K. H. Rubin (ed.), Children's Play. Jossey-Bass, San Francisco.

Rubin, K. H., Fein, G. G., and Vandenberg, B. 1983. Play. *In* P. H. Mussen and E. M. Hetherington (eds.), Handbook of Child Psychology: Socialization, Personality, and Social Development. John Wiley & Sons, Inc., New York.

Sachs, J. 1977. The adaptive significance of linguistic input to prelinguistic infants. *In* C. Snow and C. A. Ferguson (eds.), Talking to Children: Language Input and Acquisition. Cambridge University Press, Cambridge, England.

Sachs, J. 1980. The role of adult-child play in language development. *In* K. H. Rubin (ed.), Children's Play. Jossey-Bass, San Francisco.

Sachs, J. 1984. Talking about the there and then: The emergence of displaced reference in parent-child discourse. *In* K. E. Nelson (ed.), Children's language, Vol, 4. Lawrence Erlbaum Assocs., Inc., Hillsdale, N.J.

Sachs, J., Bard, B., and Johnson, M. 1981. Langauge learning with restricted input: Case studies of two hearing children of deaf parents. Appl. Psycholinguistics 2:33–54.

Sachs, J., and Devin, J. 1976. Young children's use of age-appropriate speech styles in social interaction and role-playing. J. Child Lang. 3:81–98.

Sachs, J., Goldman, J., and Chaille, C. 1984. Planning in pretend play: Using language to coordinate narrative development. *In* A. Pellegrini and T. Yawkey (eds.), The Development of Oral and Written Language in Social Contexts. Ablex Publishing Corp., Norwood, N.J.

Sachs, J., and Johnson, M. 1976. Language development in a hearing child of deaf parents. *In* W. von Raffler Engel and Y. Lebrun (eds.), Baby Talk and Infant Speech. Swets & Zeitlinger, Lisse, The Netherlands.

Sachs, J., and Truswell, L. 1978. Comprehension of two-word instructions by children in the one-word stage. J. Child Lang. 5:17–24.

Sacks, H. 1972. On the analyzability of stories by children. *In* J. Gumperz and D. Hymes (eds.), Direction in Sociolinguistics. Holt, Rinehart & Winston, Inc., New York.

Schieffelin, B. 1979. How Kaluli children learn what to say, what to do, and how to feel: An ethnographic approach to the study of communicative competence. Unpublished doctoral dissertation, Columbia University.

Sinclair, H. 1970. The transition from sensory motor behavior to symbolic activity. Interchange 1:119–129.
Sinclair, H. 1971. Sensorimotor action patterns as a condition for the acquisition of syntax. *In* R. Huxley and E. Ingram (eds.), Language Acquisition: Models and Methods. Academic Press, Inc., New York.
Singer, J. L. 1973. The Child's World of Make-Believe: Experimental Studies of Imaginative Play. Academic Press, Inc., New York.
Skinner, B. F. 1957. Verbal Behavior. Appleton-Century, New York.
Slobin, D. (ed.). 1967. A Field Manual for Cross-Cultural Study of the Acquisition of Communicative Competence. A. S. U. C. Bookstore, Berkeley, CA.
Smilanski, S. 1968. The Effects of Sociodramatic Play on Disadvantaged Preschool Children. Wiley, Toronto.
Snow, C. 1977. The development of conversation between mothers and babies. J. Child Lang. 4:1–22.
Snow, C. 1980. Social interaction and langauge acquisition. *In* P. S. Dale and D. Ingram (eds.), Child Language: An International Perspective. University Park Press, Baltimore.
Snow, C., and Ferguson, C. A. (eds.). 1977. Talking to Children: Language Input and Acquisition. Cambridge University Press, Cambridge, England.
Stern, D. 1977. The First Relationship: Infant and Mother. Fontana/Open Books, London.
Sutton-Smith, B., Botvin, G., and Mahony, D. 1976. Developmental structures in fantasy narratives. Hum. Dev. 19:1–13.
Turnbull, C. M. 1972. The Mountain People. Simon & Schuster, New York.
Vygotsky, L. S. 1962. Thought and Language. MIT Press, Cambridge, MA.
Vygotsky, L. S. 1978. Mind in Society: The Development of Higher Psychological Processes. Harvard University Press, Cambridge, MA.
Watson, M. W., and Fischer, K. W. 1977. A developmental sequence of agent use in late infancy. Child Dev. 48:828–836.
Weeks, T. E. 1971. Speech registers in young children. Child Dev. 42:1119–1131.
Werner, H., and Kaplan, B. 1963. Symbol Formation: An Organismic-Developmental Approach to Language and the Expression of Thought. John Wiley & Sons, Inc., New York.
Wolf, D., and Gardner, H. 1981. On the structure of early symbolization. *In* R. L. Schiefelbusch and D. D. Bricker (eds.), Early Language: Acquisition and Intervention. University Park Press, Baltimore.
Wood, D., Bruner, J., and Ross, G. 1976. The role of tutoring in problem solving. J. Child Psychol. Psychiatry 17:89–100.

Cognitive Aspects of Communicative Development

Mabel Rice
Bureau of Child Research
University of Kansas
Lawrence, Kansas

Editors' Note

This chapter presents an overview of the relationship between cognition and language. *Mental representation* and *categorization* are used to explain children's emerging concepts.

In light of new perspectives about social interactions, however, referential knowledge is a relatively narrow slice of communicative competence. The key issue is the child's increasing understanding of the social perspectives of others. Three components of cognitive/social knowledge are discussed: person knowledge, social categories, and event knowledge. Each is a prominent part of a comprehensive model of concept knowledge that the child draws from his environment.

Environmental experiences are presented as a combination of direct interaction in which children are participants and indirect interaction in which they are observers. The latter (observational) experience includes television viewing and adult-to-adult conversations.

Discussion of the available information about language disorders does not provide comprehensive methods of assessment. Nevertheless, approaches to intervention are suggested, e.g., teaching in experientially diverse contexts, arranging events that require the uses of social alternatives, and using socially based modeling techniques in functional contexts.

Preparation of this manuscript was supported by grants from the Spencer Foundation and the National Institute of Mental Health to Aletha Huston and John Wright of the Center for Research on the Influences of Television on Children.

contents

CONCEPTUAL UNDERPINNINGS OF COMMUNICATIVE COMPETENCE 143
   Recent Trends 144
   New Perspectives 153

ENVIRONMENTAL SOURCES OF LANGUAGE-RELEVANT KNOWLEDGE 170
   Indirect/Observational Learning 171
   Television 175

CONCLUSIONS 178

IMPLICATIONS FOR INTERVENTION WITH CHILDREN HAVING DIFFICULTY ACQUIRING LANGUAGE 179
   Identification/Assessment 179
   Rehabilitation/Training 182

ACKNOWLEDGMENTS 184

REFERENCES 184

The sources of language take us out of language.

Susan Ervin-Tripp

The belief that language is rooted in more general kinds of knowledge has been a dominant theme in recent child language writings. When the study of grammar was preeminent, ten years ago, some investigators noted that the structural linguistic knowledge of young children was not an entirely unique kind of learning, but instead demonstrated striking parallels to children's sensorimotor knowledge of how to organize their world (e.g., Greenfield, Nelson, and Saltzman, 1972; Sinclair, 1971), thereby linking the acquisition of grammar with more general cognitive learning. The linkage became more explicit when the research emphasis shifted to semantics and the meanings expressed in children's earliest utterances. A cognition hypothesis was proposed asserting that underlying cognitive knowledge accounted for children's linguistic understandings. According to this account, language acquisition is a matter of children figuring out which linguistic devices to use to express what they already know nonlinguistically.

The idea that cognitive understandings are directly linked to a child's mastery of language has inspired a sizeable body of literature exploring the relationship between children's conceptual and linguistic knowledge. Recent findings have led to new insights about the interrelationship, most of which reveal a greater complexity than first presumed, even at the earliest stages of language acquisition.

Almost all the existing work has addressed cognition and language in the context of referential and propositional meanings, consistent with the prevailing emphasis on semantics. However, children's linguistic knowledge consists of more than grammar and referential meanings. Children also learn socially based rules for the use of alternate language forms appropriate to the social context. It is now widely accepted that, in order to communicate successfully, a child must be able to produce and comprehend utterances on the basis of social appropriateness as well as grammatical well-formedness and referential accuracy. This comprehensive model of linguistic knowledge, referred to as communicative competence (Gumperz and Hymes, 1964; Hymes, 1971, 1972; Slobin, 1967), is emerging as the predominant model in the current child language literature.

CONCEPTUAL UNDERPINNINGS OF COMMUNICATIVE COMPETENCE

The comprehensive nature of the communicative competence model calls for new perspectives regarding the conceptual underpinnings of linguistic communication and the ways in which the two areas of knowledge interact.[1] Among the issues in need of reconsideration are the nature of the conceptual underpinnings, how the conceptual underpinnings relate to language acquisition,[2] and the sources of environmental information and kinds of experiences that are relevant to how children learn to bridge cognition and language. These issues are addressed below, beginning with an overview of the current literature regarding the relationship between cognition and language, a delineation of informational limitations, and suggestions for expansions consistent with the notion of communicative competence.

Recent Trends

Most of the recent literature has dealt with the cognitive underpinnings of the referential, propositional meanings encoded in language, e.g., what the child means when he says "cup" or "that man is big." Just what is involved in the "cognitive underpinnings" of the "meanings" of language? On the most obvious level, children talk about what they know. This is evident at the very earliest stages of language. The words that children learn first and their first word combinations express their views of the world. Children talk about what is interesting to them and attracts their attention (see, e.g., Greenfield, 1979) and about what they know about people, objects, events, and relationships (see, e.g., Brown, 1973, pp. 198–201).

As Dore (1979, p. 129) notes, the observation that children talk about what they know is not the real issue for language acquisition. The pertinent issue is *how* children come to be able to express their nonlinguistic cognitive achievements in linguistic terms. Put another

---

[1] The distinction between conceptual knowing and linguistic knowing is rather muddled in the child language literature. Although some authors consistently maintain the distinction, it is often the case that such a differentiation is initially implied and then subsequently obscured with talk of "linguistic concepts," "semantic concepts," and "concepts" that are defined entirely in terms of word meanings (see Dore, 1979, and Campbell, 1979, for discussions of this problem). Campbell (1979) also reminded us that the distinction has roots in broader philosophical issues, a matter rarely acknowledged in the empirically descriptive child language literature. It will be assumed here that conceptual and linguistic knowledge can be distinguished, and the distinction will be consistently maintained throughout. However, explicit acknowledgment of the premise that conceptual and linguistic understandings are distinct domains of mental endeavor does not imply a formal commitment to the dualist philosophical position as espoused by Campbell (1979).

[2] The question of whether or not cognitive knowledge accounts for *all* of language acquisition is not pursued here. Instead, this discussion focuses on how the two mental domains interrelate. Although there is agreement that language and conceptual understanding are closely associated with each other, the role of cognition as the exclusive source of language is a matter of debate. For example, Cromer (1981) argued for specifically linguistic acquisition mechanisms, independent of conceptual knowing. (See Rice, 1983a, and Rice and Kemper, in press, for reviews.)

way, the question is one of how a child learns to map conceptual meanings into linguistic forms (discussed in detail in Clark, 1973a, 1977).

The mapping problem is illustrated in Figure 1. Nonlinguistic knowledge is placed on the bottom because it is the more fundamental. It is first ontogenetically and is the more robust of the two domains. The two domains are offset to indicate that they are not isomorphic. There are aspects of nonlinguistic knowledge that remain resistant to verbal expression, such as spatial or sensorimotor knowledge. Likewise, some kinds of linguistic knowledge, such as arbitrary grammatical rules, are not accounted for by cognitive understandings or meaning.

The dilemma for contemporary observers of children's language development is to determine which parts of a child's nonlinguistic understandings get linked with language. Of all the things that young children know about their world, which are relevant for language? The search for linkages requires specification of the targeted linguistic skills as well as the underlying concepts. The literature has focused on the expression of referential and propositional meanings. This dimension of linguistic knowledge has been linked to two kinds of nonlinguistic understanding: mental representation and categorization. The perspective for inferring the linkages has been observation of children's language. Given the problems of determining what young children know, it has been most expedient to describe children's linguistic competence (what they say about things and events) and then search for related conceptual underpinnings.

Mental Representation Mental representation has been advanced as a primary cognitive prerequisite for language (e.g., Morehead and Morehead, 1974; Sinclair, 1971). The general notion is that, before a child can use words to refer to objects and events, especially when the

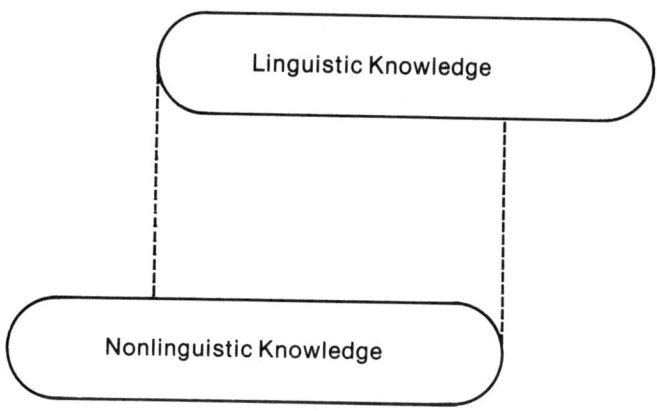

Figure 1. The mapping problem.

referents are not physically present, he must have the ability to represent reality mentally, including past and anticipated events. Piaget's theory has provided a cohesive model of the cognitive skills involved in a young child's mastery of mental representation (Mandler, 1983). Piaget introduced the object concept, a notion that has been the center of much attention in the language literature. Acquisition of the object concept involves the belief that people, objects, and places continue to exist when we are no longer in direct perceptual contact with them. The object concept evolves gradually during infancy, with full mastery not evident, according to Piaget, until sensorimotor Stage VI. Attainment of the concept is measured by performance on a graduated series of complex object permanence tests involving the invisible displacement of objects (e.g., Uzgiris and Hunt, 1975).

A closely related manifestation of mental representation is symbolic play, defined by Piaget (1962, p. 97) as the assimilation of a new object into schemes previously applied to other objects, evident in such behaviors as pretending that one object is another, or pretending to sleep. A number of investigations have explored whether or not mastery of the Piagetian tasks precede, co-occur with, or follow certain linguistic achievements, such as the appearance of first words or word combinations.

Two findings have emerged regarding these Piagetian measures of mental representation: first, they are evidently related to language acquisition in specific, localized ways rather than in more general, pervasive interrelationships, and, second, they are not necessarily acquired prior to allegedly related language skills. For example, Corrigan (1978) found in her longitudinal study of three young children that "object permanence is not related to all language development, and where there is a relation, the degree of correspondence varies depending upon the language variable in question" (p. 186). She reported that different types of object permanence tasks corresponded to different linguistic achievements, such as the onset of single-word utterances, an increase in children's total vocabulary, or comments on the disappearance or recurrence of objects. Within the localized correspondences there was no evidence that a particular level of object permanence knowledge was a firm prerequisite for acquisition of a particular language element. Although there was a general correspondence between a certain level of object knowledge and the onset of single-word utterances, individual children used several words before mastering this cognitive level.

Corrigan's study focused on the earliest stage of acquisition, the time of single word usage. Folger and Leonard (1978) reported similar findings for slightly different measures of object knowledge ("means-end" and "relating to objects," which included measures of symbolic play) and more advanced linguistic skill (two-word combinations). Neither the means-end scale nor the measure of symbolic play consistently differentiated between children who used single-word utterances and those who had learned to combine words.

Bates et al. (1979) did not regard it as surprising that different measures of sensorimotor skills demonstrate different temporal relationships with language achievements; they argued that both kinds of behavioral tasks tap into a common underlying cognitive structure. This deeper level of cognitive knowing may be manifested first in either kind of activity, language or nonlanguage. When Bates et al. (1979) analyzed the correlations among a number of measures of sensorimotor knowledge, communicative gestures, and referential and nonreferential language that they collected in a series of sessions with 25 infants during the interval between nine and 13 months of age, they concluded that the deeper cognitive framework relating sensorimotor cognition and language is localized, in skill-specific packages of "local homologies." They offered four reasons for this conclusion:

1. The sensorimotor cognitive measures did not correlate with each other (a finding also reported by Uzgiris and Hunt, 1975).
2. Some cognitive variables were good predictors of communicative development (i.e., imitation, tool use and symbolic play[3]) while others clearly were not (object permanence and spatial relations).
3. Each cognitive measure correlated with communicative development in different temporal patterns.
4. The cognitive scales tended to predict comprehension and production in slightly different ways. (pp. 128–129)

The findings and conclusions of Bates et al. (1979) are supported by other studies involving Piagetian measures (e.g., Miller et al., 1980). To suggest that the relationship between cognition and language is evident only in small bundles of tasks, and that these bundles change over time, still leaves unclear the nature of the interrelationship between the two emerging abilities. Important questions remain, such as why cognition and language tend to appear together at some times and not at others, and the direction of influence between the two types of knowledge. The ambiguities inherent in the findings are a function of the limitations of correlational data (discussed in Bates and Snyder, in press; Bates et al., 1982) and the nature of the measures. Piagetian tasks that were designed to tap broadly defined structures of cognitive

---

[3] Folger and Leonard (1978, pp. 525–526) attributed the difference between their findings and those of Bates et al. regarding symbolic play to differences in the criteria used for crediting a child with symbolic play.

knowledge are not suited to the detection of subtle linguistic and cognitive distinctions. In an attempt to resolve these ambiguities, recent studies have involved more precise measurements that include novel nonlinguistic tasks (reviewed in Bates and Snyder, in press).

One can conclude that the Piagetian measures of sensorimotor mental representation have limited explanatory power in regard to language acquisition. It is unlikely that some general sensorimotor cognitive structure, some kind of object-based real-world knowing (at least, as formulated by Piaget), precedes and accounts for how children around 12 months of age begin to manipulate words as symbols, or, somewhat later in development, begin to combine words to express object relationships. Furthermore, the Piagetian tasks do not illuminate whatever more restricted linkages there may be because the tasks do not correspond closely to language-specific meanings.

Categorization Categorization is another kind of nonlinguistic knowledge that has often been linked with the referential and propositional meanings of language. The abstraction of categories is an inherent part of the language-learning process. Bowerman (1981) characterized the child's problem as one of being able "to identify *recurrent regularities* and build a model isomorphic with the redundancy of the environment." She went on to describe the regularities:

> First are regularities or patterns in the linguistic signal itself. For example, recurrent sounds, words, intonational patterns, etc. must begin to be recognized as "the same" despite superficial variation. Restrictions on how linguistic forms are patterned must be discovered (e.g., *put the hat on*, *put on the hat*, *put it on*, but not *put on it*). Second are regularities in the child's social and physical environment and in her internal experiences or reactions. Identifying regularities of this second type entails nothing less than building up a complex system of *meanings*—ways of categorizing and interpreting the significance of events in the world. Third and most critical, the child must discover the *contingencies* between linguistic forms and physical and social meanings, that is, how the two sets of variables covary. For example, she must determine which linguistic variations are insignificant and which are linked in a regular way to variation in meaning. Conversely, she must learn which discriminable differences in meanings are matched by differences in language forms and which are not. And, most centrally, she must work out precisely what the connections are—i.e., what kinds of meanings are associated with given linguistic forms. (p. 99)

The kinds of linguistic knowledge that have been prominently linked to underlying categories of real-world information are word meanings and categories of semantic relations, such as "agent," "action," and "object." Considerations of categorical knowledge have focused on objects and their perceptual properties, such as the identification of objects and their attributes, the actions associated with an object, and strategies for grouping objects. For example, one line of work has mapped the real-world groupings that are correlated with the semantic organization of object words (Rosch et al., 1976). Other investigators who study how young children learn the meanings of words have explored the criteria for the application of words to novel objects, whether such generalizations are based on perceptual attributes (Clark, 1973b) or functional use (Nelson, 1974). The meanings expressed in children's earliest word combinations and the rules for combining words have been explained in terms of the child's knowledge of real-world objects, i.e., that objects exist, cease to exist, recur, can be acted upon, and are associated with people's activities (see, e.g., Bloom, 1973; Bloom, Lightbown, and Hood, 1975; Brown, 1973). Even the "agent" category has been defined in terms of a person's relationship to an object, e.g., as a "bottle-holder" (Schlesinger, 1977, p. 156) or a "box-opener" (p. 158).

The work regarding children's categories has had a broad impact on this area of inquiry. It has provided a new model of reference, has contributed to competing accounts of the direction of influence between the two domains, and has revealed unsuspected differences between production and comprehension. In regard to the first, Rosch's work on the internal organization of semantic categories has led to a major reformulation of the nature of reference (Brown, 1978). Three new principles have been established. First, the categories of real-world objects that correspond to object names are grouped according to probabilistic sets with overlapping boundaries instead of determinate, clearly delineated sets whose objects share common attributes (as the traditional experimental psychology experiments would lead one to expect). That is to say that some creatures may be "kind of like a bird," instead of "yes, definitely a bird," or "no, not a bird" (Lenneberg, 1957; Rosch and Mervis, 1975). Second, these categories are internally organized around a prototypic member; each member of the set shares one or more attributes with the prototype but not necessarily with other members (Anglin, 1977; Rosch and Mervis, 1975). Third, the level of abstraction at which the basic category cuts are made for the purpose of naming objects mirrors the correlational structure inherent in real-world objects (Rosch et al., 1976). That is, the belief that there is one truest name for things (e.g., "dog" instead of "German Shepherd" or "animal") is determined by physical reality. These three new principles of object reference have profound implications for how children go about organizing their world for the purpose of using words to refer to categories of objects.

One implication bears on the question of direction of influence. To the extent that the real world offers bundles of information that correspond to the categories of words, the child can rely on ready-made conceptual packages as a direct route to words. If this is the case, the mapping problems will be minimal. This possibility is countered by other considerations of categorical knowledge. Schlesinger (1977) argued that many of the regularities evident in linguistic categories are not fully revealed by real-world experience. For example, in order to determine the boundaries of linguistic concepts such as "agent," a child must receive clues from how the language he is learning expresses "agentness." According to Schlesinger, linguistic input is required for the acquisition of linguistically relevant categories. Bowerman (1976, pp. 135-136; 1977) presented a similar argument and suggested that the manner of mutual influence between language and cognition is quite intricate. Her position is that, although language can "get a concept started," the concepts are the child's own invention (not directed solely by linguistic input). Bowerman did acknowledge the possible influence of ready-made concepts in her observation that the child's system of creating equivalences may be constrained by certain "universally shared categorizational propensities" (1977, p. 26).

The study of categorical knowledge has revealed that the linkage between conceptual knowledge and linguistic understandings may differ as a function of the linguistic mode of performance. That is, successful production of language may tap into underlying cognitive meanings in a manner slightly different from that involved in the comprehension of language. That possibility is most strikingly demonstrated in findings reported by Rice (1980). Two groups of preschool children ages 2;3-3;4 were trained to correctly label the color of various red, green, and yellow objects. One group demonstrated an understanding of how to categorize objects according to color prior to the color word training; the other group did not. When the production training was completed (i.e., all children had learned to respond correctly when asked "What color is this?" in regard to an assortment of trained and untrained objects), the children with prior conceptual understanding spontaneously learned to comprehend color terms whereas the other children did not. That is, children who did *not* group objects according to color were able to correctly produce color terms at the conclusion of training, but did not respond correctly when asked to "Give me the red one." Two children demonstrated a consistent discrepancy between production and comprehension for 11 weeks.

A consideration of what one group of children knew that the other group did not know and the different demands of production and comprehension tasks led to the conclusion that the production and comprehension tasks tapped into different levels of conceptual knowledge; an understanding that objects could be categorized according to color was necessary for correct comprehension but not for production, allowing children without this knowledge to correctly produce color terms while simultaneously failing comprehension tasks (see Rice, 1980, pp. 85–116, for a more detailed account).

The conclusion that comprehension is linked with cognition in a manner somewhat unlike production is consistent with other evidence. Recall that Bates et al. (1979) found that the sensorimotor cognitive measures correlated with comprehension and production in slightly different ways. Another source of supportive evidence is the observation that the extensions of children's word meanings evident in comprehension tasks do not always coincide with those apparent in production tasks (e.g., Anglin, 1977; Gruendel, 1977; Nelson, Rescorla, and Gruendel, 1978). Gruendel (1977) speculated that "it is as if in comprehension the word functions to denote a concept or class instance, while in production it may also serve as a category term whose referents legitimately cross class boundaries" (p. 1575). Nelson et al. (1978, p. 966) concluded that the closest match between underlying concepts and word meanings will be evident in the child's comprehension meaning for a word.

The rich potential of the study of real-world categories that are linked with the referential meanings of language is constrained by a major methodological problem[4]: how to measure the real-world knowledge that is relevant to language in a manner independent of language. In almost all of the available writings, the existence of related categorical knowledge has been inferred from the extensions of the linguistic forms, that is, descriptions of the sets of ostensible referents. That state of affairs is not a problem if the purpose is to map the referential domain of certain linguistic forms. However, the conflation of linguistic and nonlinguistic categories does not illuminate *how* the child arrived at the linguistic mapping; the direction of influence is obscured. If the methods used to infer a child's knowledge are language-dependent, it cannot be determined if he recognized "recurrent regularities" in the world that eventually get linked to language *before* he actually made the linkage.

The problem of how to measure a child's appreciation of nonlinguistic recurrent regularities is a complex one with roots in deeper issues (see Campbell, 1979). However, it is not an entirely insurmountable difficulty; at least some kinds of underlying categorical knowledge can be operationally identified. For example, this has been accom-

---

[4] Closely related to but distinct from the known problems of conceptual confusions pointed out in the first footnote. Even in writings where conceptual distinctions are clear, measurement problems exist.

plished in two separate domains: color (Rice, 1980) and spatial relationships (Johnston, 1979; Levine and Carey, 1982). In both cases, an independent measure of nonlinguistic categorization strategies allowed for a close look at how cognitive and linguistic learning influence each other. The findings support the notion that cognitive understandings do tend to facilitate language acquisition, although the specifics of the interrrelationships seem to vary according to domain.

In those cases where it is possible to develop them, language-independent measures can clarify relationships and contribute to our ability to evaluate competing hypotheses. The pervasiveness of this possibility remains to be seen. Given our current state of measurement knowledge, it may well be possible only in certain localized areas. Yet the search for such specifiable linkages is certainly an appropriate research strategy. In the meantime, it is important to keep in mind that current assertions about the interplay between categorical and linguistic knowledge are usually based on observations made through a language lens.

To recapitulate, the mapping problem has been defined in particular ways (Figure 2). The dimension of language that has been studied is the expression of propositional meanings. The areas of putative cognitive linkage are mental representation and categorization, both of which are defined in terms of knowledge about objects. Piagetian measures of mental representation, such as object permanence, have con-

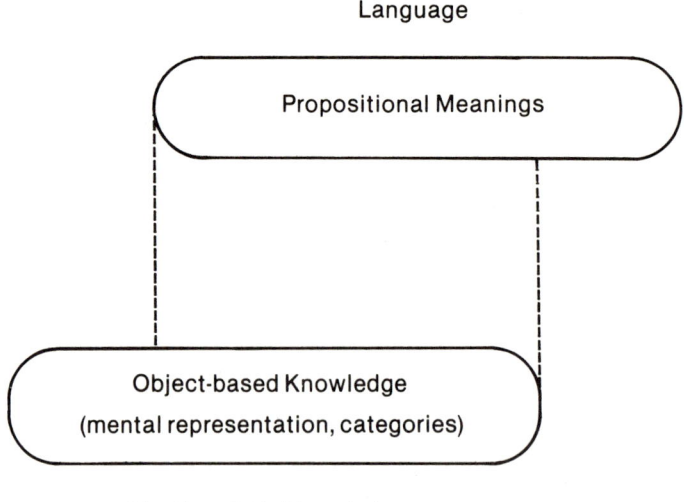

Figure 2. The mapping problem: current perspective.

tributed inconclusive patterns of evidence. On the other hand, the study of categories has led to important new insights regarding the nature of children's concepts and the parallels between the two domains. These contributions are limited by the "top down" perspective, the observation of cognition through a linguistic lens.

The available work is confined by the traditional concern with only the propositional meanings of language. Such a restricted model of children's linguistic knowledge does not capture the full and rich array of their communicative competence. Furthermore, such a narrow language window entails a relatively narrow slice of associated cognitive underpinnings. A broadening of the language lens to encompass socially and contextually based language rules allows for recognition of additional aspects of the cognitive base as well.

New Perspectives

What adjustments need to be made in existing notions of the conceptual underpinnings of language acquisition when the focus of child language inquiry shifts from the referential, propositional meanings of language to the way messages are realized in actual social interactions? A new kind of nonlinguistic knowledge must be accounted for, that of social knowledge.[5] As more is known about children's sociolinguistic knowledge, it is possible to infer more about the kinds of general social understandings that children acquire and the aspects of social awarenesses that become part of the system of communication rules. These social awarenesses are an integral part of the conceptual apparatus the child draws upon when learning language.

What kind of social awarenesses get linked up with linguistic communication? Our peephole to such awarenesses is how children use language, the regularities evident in children's adjustments of their patterns of communication to suit the social situation. As Shields (1979, p. 556) put it, a child's communicative skill is "an index of his knowledge of other persons." When a child adjusts his communication to accommodate the social context, "The child's image of the world is mirrored twice, once directly and again as a representation of the rep-

---

[5] Dore (in press) argued that the interpersonal nature of social knowledge requires a radically new theoretical perspective; the key to understanding pragmatic competence is a child's awareness of the personhood of himself and others, a knowledge qualitatively different from the usual notion of conceptual knowledge. Although it may well be that another, uncharted dimension of knowing is involved in interpersonal communication, the premise of this chapter is that the known dimension of representational knowledge is incompletely mapped. Increasing our awareness of the richness of the conceptual domain can enhance efforts to build all-encompassing theoretical models. In particular, any theory accounting for interpersonal subjectivity would have to deal with how persons are represented.

resentations of others. His image of himself is also mirrored twice, once with direct knowledge of his internal states, and again by his representations of his behavior in the eyes of others."

It is clear that children's social awareness and sociolinguistic/pragmatic knowledge are conflated in the existing literature. The measurement problems described above in regard to the referential uses of language are even more evident regarding the social dimensions of language. In the case of social/sociolinguistic knowledge we are slipping dangerously close to the circularity decried by Campbell (1979, p. 427), i.e., using facts about the nature of children's language to infer facts about social development that are in turn used to explain language development.

Nevertheless, given the present state of affairs, the point of entry into the maze is the linguistic phenomenon, the communication knowledge to be accounted for. The following discussion begins with an overview of the work describing children's pragmatic/sociolinguistic knowledge. Then the nature of underlying nonlinguistic social knowledge is addressed, followed by a return to the problems inherent in distinguishing the nature of the interaction between the two.

The Nature of Children's Pragmatic/Sociolinguistic Knowledge Researchers and lay persons alike observe that small children name objects and make statements such as "That's my dog!" Consequently, it was not necessary to document the fact that young children master referential/propositional meanings of language. However, sociolinguistic learning is not so obvious and, indeed, runs counter to Piaget's assumption that small children are egocentric. Insofar as the literature describing children's pragmatic competence includes many different topics and diverse perspectives, it is appropriate to clarify the perspective of interest here and to specify the kind of knowledge attributed to young children.

The linguistic phenomenon of pragmatic/sociolinguistic competence denotes alternative ways of saying the same thing. (See Ervin-Tripp, 1975, for a more detailed discussion of socially based linguistic alternatives.) Language use allows for different means of expressing the same ideas or functions. Bowerman (1981) noted that variation is possible at every level of language structure: "pronunciation (e.g., *eating* vs. *eatin'*, *What are you doing?* vs. *Whatcha doin'?*), lexicon (e.g., *woman* vs. *lady*, *Mr. Smith* vs. *Bob*, *Mary loves John* vs. *she loves him*), prosody (e.g., *Harry killed Jim* vs. *Harry killed Jim*), and syntax (e.g., *open the window* vs. *I wonder if there's some way to cool off this room?*)."

Closely related to the speaker's choice of how to say what he wants to say is the decision of when to say it. Certain comments are appropriate at some times and inappropriate at others. Answers are expected to follow questions; pronouns can be used after the referent has been established; "hello" does not belong in the middle of a telephone conversation.

The choice and timing of alternatives is rule governed, according to social context. Among the manifestations of rule-based alternatives are the use of address and polite forms, code switching (speaking in different ways to different people), the use of requests (direct, indirect, or hints), the alternation of turns, the maintenance of a given topic in a conversation, and the use of deictic words (words that indicate or point) such as pronouns, *here, there, come, go.*

Confirmation of the rule-governed nature of linguistic alternatives such as these is evident when the rules are broken, often with the consequence of embarrassment or humor. For example, in the movie "Being There," the central character, a lowly gardener, is introduced to the president of the United States. After observing his friend, who is also a personal friend of the president, address the president as "Bobby," the gardener does likewise. The inappropriate address term, a presumptuous indication of intimacy, friendship, and equal status, is amusing. On other occasions, the consequence of inadvertent violation of the rules can be embarrassment, such as when the secretary doesn't respond to the implied dismissal when the boss says "That is all I have for now."

Three major factors are involved in these rules: the linguistic code, the speaker's intent, and the social context. The interaction among the three is complex. The discussion that follows features the interrelations of these factors. Ervin-Tripp (1978) points out that "the same words can accomplish different acts or have different purposes, and the same acts can be expressed in different ways." For example, when an adult says to a child, "D'you wanna play on the swings?", the adult may be offering an activity, directing the child, or requesting information from the child. Any one of these intents could also be conveyed by other means. For example, if the adult were making an offer, he could have said, "It's OK to swing on the swings if you'd like" or "Let's swing."

A number of factors in the social context can influence the choice of alternatives, and, of course, the alternatives chosen can in turn influence the negotiable aspects of the social situation. Certain given characteristics of the participants and the social setting are especially important determinants of how a speaker chooses to express his message and how a listener may interpret it. Among the people attributes are relative status, sex, age, role, previous history of interpersonal relationships, and shared or common knowledge or experiences (established either prior to the conversation or within the conversation itself). Influential social variables are the kind of setting (school versus home, formal restaurant versus cafeteria) and the location (regional/geographical differences). In addition to these given variables, there are also influential negotiable social components, such as affect, task, and mood (Ervin-Tripp, 1978).

One must be sensitive to these social realities in order to behave according to the sociolinguistic rules. What evidence is there that children know about such rules? The recent literature abounds with data suggesting that children as young as 3 and 4 years of age, much younger than previously presumed, are quite aware of the need to adjust their language to the constraints of the social situation. Such knowledge is not limited to a few special cases, in some sort of isolated, fragmentary fashion, but is instead quite comprehensive, evident across a wide range of linguistic alternations and social factors. Some examples are:

Preschool children (3–5-year-olds) adopt a "baby talk" register when talking to younger children or pretending to be a baby (Sachs, this volume), and switch to sex- and role-differentiated registers, such as "mommy talk," "daddy talk," and "doctor talk," when acting out these roles (Andersen, 1977).

Children adjust their requests according to the rank or age of the addressee, softening requests via hints ("My tummy is hungry") and polite forms ("Please") for addressees of greater rank, status, or age (Ervin-Tripp, 1975; Gordon and Ervin-Tripp, this volume).

Preschool children manipulate the subtleties of the modal auxilliaries, pronouns, and deictic terms to take into account the listener's perspective and information shared with the speaker (Shields, 1979, pp. 543–548).

Very young children mark the distinction between new and old material in discourse in their use of *a* and *the* (Maratsos, 1976, 1979).

Children are able to carry on a conversation, following the rules for introducing, maintaining, and switching topics (e.g., Dore, 1977; Keenan, 1974).

Young children are able to describe sequences of everyday events (Nelson and Gruendel, 1979) and to relate stories (Kemper, 1984; Watson-Gegeo and Boggs, 1977).

Children learn setting-specific communication codes, such as the rules that apply to the school setting (Dore and McDermott, 1982).

Not only do children demonstrate knowledge of alternation and sequencing rules in their behaviors, they can sometimes explicitly call upon the rules. An observation of my daughter's behavior can serve as an illustration of the sociolinguistic subtleties that are within the grasp of very young children. When Mindy was 3, an acquaintance of mine babysat with her for a few hours one evening. After I had gone, Mindy, a very verbal little girl, proceeded to lace her comments with profanities, demonstrating a remarkable knowledge of when and where to insert obscene expletives. Because the babysitter was not familiar with how I handled such matters (and Mindy's facility seemed to indicate considerable practice), she chose to ignore the obscenities. Near the time when I was to return, Mindy produced another string of swear words, and then looked up at the babysitter and said, "My Mommy doesn't let me say those words." Obviously, Mindy had mastered several sociolinguistic rules. She knew where and how to use swear words, knew that her use of those words was not condoned by her mother, and knew that she had taken advantage of her babysitter's uncertainty as to how to respond, and I also believe that she knew that her reporting of the household rules served as a means of informing the babysitter that she had been taken advantage of by a 3-year-old.

It is clear that children's communicative survival skills are well developed by school age; they know how to manipulate language efficiently to serve social purposes. Of course, this is not to say that they have achieved a full adult competence. Many of the nuances of conversational interchanges and special types of discourse, such as insult, humor, and narration, are not evident until middle childhood or adolescence. Nevertheless, the richness and breadth of a preschool child's linguistic communication skills indicate complex social/cognitive underpinnings.

Beyond Present Models Three components of a comprehensive model of language-related conceptual knowledge can be discerned in recent writings: person knowledge, social categories, and event knowledge.

Person Knowledge Recall that object-related understandings have dominated current models of children's conceptual knowledge. However, a number of authors believe that understanding things is fundamentally different from knowing about people, and the latter may be more intimately linked with the development of communication skills (Bretherton, McNew, and Beeghly-Smith, 1981; Shields, 1979; Trevarthen and Hubley, 1979). Shields (1979) argued that in order to communicate a child must have more than representations of the world of things; he must also develop representations about people, including how they represent the world (including him) to themselves.

This claim contrasts sharply with Piaget's widely accepted characterization of preschool children as egocentric in nature, unable to appreciate the perspective of others in social interactions. Piaget's apparent disregard for what young children know about people is a consequence of his epistemological perspective, his concern with causality, time, and space, all notions rooted in objects and actions with objects. He focused on the development of logical mental structures essential for the organization of formal knowledge. The widespread adoption of the Piagetian perspective among developmental psychologists has perpetuated the assumption that preschoolers know little about other people.

Yet when the basic Piagetian methodology of analyzing the logical implicature of behavior is applied to children's conversational interactions, it is apparent that young children are not limited to an egocentric view of the world. Instead, "they show the beginnings of a model of human beings acting in a rule-governed social world" (Shields, 1979, p. 529). The basic level of knowledge is person knowledge. It is revealed in how children adjust their use of language to the social context, especially during the interpersonal exchanges in ongoing conversations. Shields unpacked the psychological awareness implicit in the superficially simple interchanges of nursery school children involved in play. She reasoned that the patterns of language use—such as modal auxilliaries (*shall, will, can*), deictic devices (*this, that*, pronouns), time reference, and ellipsis—indicate children's representations of the perceptions, intentions, experience, and memory of others. Furthermore, this person knowledge is fundamental, "the underlying substratum of his [a child's] success in interacting with persons," and precedes more differentiated knowledge such as social roles (p. 552).

Shields hypothesized a number of constant features in a child's psychological model of a person. These features are said to "have begun to form as the child builds up communicative skill" (p. 553):

1. Persons have identity over time despite changes in location, behavior, and appearance.
2. Persons are self-moving or animate, and influence over the course of their behavior has to be negotiated by invoking interest or a shared frame of constraint.
3. Persons identify each other and can react to each other.
4. Persons can see, feel, hear, touch, and smell, i.e., they have a perceptual field.
5. Persons intend their actions.
6. Persons conceptualize and construct their world in roughly similar ways.
7. Persons have moods and states such as anger and fear, and also wants, likes, and dislikes.
8. Persons can send and receive messages based on gestures and words that are related to context in stable ways.

9. Persons have an action potential, i.e., things they can and can't do.
10. Persons can retain previous experience and structure their present behavior by it.
11. Persons can replicate previous behaviors in new contexts.
12. Persons share sets of rules about what is appropriate within particular frames of action.

Shields' model is supported by Bretherton et al. (1981). They concluded that by two years of age children have an "explicit, verbally expressible theory of mind" evident most clearly in the ability of 20-month-old children to verbally represent internal states as experienced by themselves and others, e.g., *ouch/owie*, *sleepy*, *yucky*, or *nice*. Their data supported each of Shield's 12 points and suggested two additional ones:

13. Interpersonal behavior is regulated by reciprocal consent using words such as *let*, *may*, and *may not*.
14. The internal states of others are not always unambiguously expressed and may have to be inferred from statements such as: "Is T mad at me?" "Moo. D'ya hear?"

How does the notion of person knowledge fit with existing ideas of the conceptual underpinnings of language? A first impression is the strong parallel to Piaget's notions of object knowledge. Both are intended as a fundamental kind of knowledge, in the sense of conceptual organization at a deep level that forms the basis for later differentiations. The idea that some deeply rooted understanding of the psychological dimensions of people may account for how children quickly acquire communicative skill with language is appealing. Part of the attraction is based on the hope that nature operates in an elegantly simple fashion, whereby some general kind of basic knowing accounts for subsequent, more complex kinds of learning. Therefore, if we just look in the right place we will be able to identify the substratum from which local homologies spring. It is possible that person knowledge may account for the acquisition of communicative competence in the manner hoped for (but not fulfilled by) Stage VI sensorimotor intelligence (the full attainment of object permanence) in regard to the referential dimensions of language.

However, there are some grounds for caution. First, the assertions that person knowledge is separate from object knowledge and more fundamental in influence are open to debate. Uzgiris (1981) argued against both premises. She pointed out that children's experiences are not distinctly social or object based. Instead, experiences with objects are set in the context of interactions with persons and general cultural expectations and values, contrary to Piaget's relative denial of social experiences. Furthermore, she proposed that the two kinds of knowing interact and influence each other, with "considerable substitutability in the child's experiences with the world of persons and objects." Uzgiris' reciprocal support model suggests that efforts to link linguistic knowledge exclusively with person knowledge, without taking into consideration object-based mental structures, would underrepresent what is actually involved.

Another reason for caution is the matter of measurement. In the available studies, person knowledge is inferred from how children use language. Shield's (1979) major point is that, by careful observation and logical consideration of how children use language, we can deduce their social awarenesses, and, ultimately, the "growth of man's concept of man" (p. 556). Yet one cannot infer the directionality of influence under such circumstances (nor does Shields explicitly attempt to do so). Bretherton et al.'s (1981) assumption that the 12-feature person model proposed by Shields is a "minimum prerequisite for the occurrence of communication" is premature. It is not yet clear whether this set of psychological awarenesses precedes and is necessary for language, or if it develops concurrently with language acquisition in some complex interactive network (as Shields implied), or if language itself serves to signal some aspects of person awarenesses that are not fully realized until the child learns linguistic codes or rules for use.

A further caution is that, when the features of person knowledge are asserted to be directly related to a child's communicative skill, a fusion of a child's psychological understandings of other persons and his sociolinguistic knowledge is implied that may not actually occur for many years. A case in point is the claim that young children know that "persons intend their actions," and the implicit assertion that this knowledge is intimately linked to language acquisition. Such an assertion seems to be safely rooted in commonly accepted tenets of speech act theory. However, Ervin-Tripp (1978) presented data demonstrating that, in the case of directives, children as old as seven do not integrate attribution of speaker intent with linguistic interpretation or performance. She concluded that listeners often do not assess motive at all, and the internal consistency of linguistic responses, such as question/answer and comment/reply sequences, can be relatively independent of and even incongruent with simultaneous interpersonal negotiations.

The point is that a strong interpretation of the intent feature of children's person knowledge is not warranted, i.e., knowing that people intend their actions does not guarantee that a child brings this awareness to bear on his interpretation of the different surface realizations of speech acts. Instead, a less powerful interpretation is called for, such as one that postulates that in order to communicate effectively children must know about intentions in the basic sense of being able to take the view of the other, but that they can infer what the other has in mind regardless of the particular structure of the linguistic message. A child's ability to use and understand contextually appropriate linguistic alternatives can be attributed to less abstract ideational structures, such as localized rules based on contextual understandings.

These cautions notwithstanding, the idea that young children know about specifiable dimensions of their own and others' psychological functioning is a major contribution toward the identification of components of children's real-world knowledge that are essential to the acquisition of communicative competence. Whatever the nature of the interrelationship, it would be difficult to account for how children manage to adjust their language to social contexts without some kind of person knowledge. Not only does this notion have explanatory value for the interpersonal aspects of language use, it also sheds further light on the acquisition of reference.

Recall that the existing work describing children's referential knowledge has focused on the representation of objects and their attributes. Yet children early on refer to nonobject phenomena, such as mental states. Words like *want*, *hungry*, and *know* are among children's earliest words (Bretherton and Beeghly, 1982; Bretherton et al., 1981). It is clear that young children refer to aspects of personhood in addition to object-related knowledge. Much of the existing literature overlooks the fact that early referential language learning draws upon a conceptual base that includes an understanding of the psychological dimensions of people as well as the properties, functions, and causal relationships existing among objects.

Another sense in which person knowledge contributes to our understanding of referential knowledge is the explicit reminder of the interpersonal nature of the act of reference (Shields, 1979, pp. 546–548). In addition to learning the arbitrary symbols that a particular linguistic community uses to convey their mental representations of real-world information, children must also learn how to ensure that they and their interlocutors are referring to the same things, that they more or less share the same field of reference. The act of reference is more than a private matching of symbols with mental representations; it is an interpersonal sharing of this match. The shared nature of reference is evident in the communicative slippage that takes place when a mature speaker converses with a very young child who has learned only a few words. At the very beginning of a child's lexical acquisition, the match between symbol and signified often does not correspond to the adult lexical categories. For example, Braunwald's (1979) daughter used "ba" to mean *ball, milk,* or *more.* Adults readily assume the major burden of establishing the interpersonal field of reference in order to successfully communicate with the child. They attend to contextual cues, such as the needs, objects, and actions inherent in the situation, to infer what the child means to say. The beginnings of referential knowledge are acquired in interpersonal interactions with an adult who accommodates to the child's frame of reference (Veneziano, 1981).

With increased awareness of the perspective of others, young children become more proficient with the interpersonal context for reference. Shields (1979) provided two examples: children's use of nonspecific referents and reference to past or future events. Much of real-world conversation, including that of preschool children, is conducted with the liberal use of nonspecific referents, such as *this, that, one,* and personal pronouns. In order to successfully communicate what is meant by "here's one," or "that's him," as preschool children are able to do, the conversational participants must have established joint attention to the same referent. Similarly, reference to past or future events requires that attention be shifted to nonpresent events that are brought into present consideration by the participants in the conversation. It is clear that young children select linguistic alternatives that serve a referential function with the assumption that their interlocutors share their referential frame.

Social Categories Recall that the recent very productive work describing the real-world categories linked to word meanings has dealt with categories of objects and their attributes. However, just as referential meanings alone underrepresent a child's total linguistic knowledge, so do object categories underrepresent a child's ability to form categorical groupings. Just as a child can equate perceptually different objects, so can he equate superficially dissimilar social relationships, personal qualities, experiences or reactions, and interpersonal interactions. The detection of such regularities inherent in the social environment is intimately related to a child's ability to select socially appropriate linguistic alternatives. According to Ervin-Tripp (1978, p. 246), "When we address someone, or make a request, we do at least two things at once. We accomplish a communicative act such as calling out, or requesting, and we also convey our social categorizing of them and of our relationship."

Evidence of social categories influencing language use is not limited to the use of address or request alternatives, but is instead apparent across a wide range of sociolinguistic variants, such as polite forms, code switching, rules for carrying on a conversation, and setting-specific communication rules. The most obvious social categories linked to language are those based on age, sex, role, relative status, and familiarity. A child must adjust his choice of linguistic alternative to the perceived category of interlocutor. For example, children learn that "baby talk" is appropriate for a certain category of humans; that one can issue a direct command to a peer or someone of lesser social status, but hints or indirect requests are more appropriate for persons of greater status; that terms of endearment are appropriate for the category of personal intimates but not for less familiar persons; that some groups of women should be addressed as Dr., others as Miss, others as Mrs., and others by their first names; that formal talk is appropriate for the category of formal occasions but not for informal, personally intimate occasions; that social forms such as "Bless you" following a sneeze or cough are correct for humans but not animals; that special codes, such as slang, are appropriate for certain kinds of occasions or groups of participants and not others; and so on.

The relationship between social category and socially determined linguistic alternative rarely demonstrates a 1:1 correspondence, i.e., a single set of linguistic forms for a single social category. One of the reasons that matters are more complex is that in the real world social categories overlap, e.g., sex and status (males as dominants), sex and roles (women as mothers), age and status (older children have greater status than younger children), and familiarity and roles (familiar parents, unfamiliar astronauts). Given the interlocking nature of social categories, situations arise where the direction of influence of one counters another. For example, when a child encounters a familiar person in a formal role, such as a neighbor as his kindergarten teacher, he has to decide whether to address the neighbor as "Bob" or "Mr. Jones." A hierarchy of selection rules is developed, with the specifics of the rules varying with the particular context (Ervin-Tripp, 1975, pp. 133–135).

Certain linguistic alternations can correspond to an intersecting set of social variables—for example, the forms that signal male-female contrasts in Japanese also signal higher-lower. Ervin-Tripp (1975, pp. 145–149; 151–152) argued that these "equivalence structures" serve as cues to help a child learn the use of sociolinguistic rules. Children can metaphorically extend the meanings of clear-cut contrasts, such as sex and age, to infer how to mark status relationships.

How does the notion of social categories correspond to what is known about object categories? An obvious difference is that social categories lack the specificity of object categories. Social categories are inferred from subtle patterns of interactions and social behaviors, instead of objective groupings of things according to attributes. The nature of the categories themselves can be quite abstract. Some, such as sex and age, have physical correlates that can be readily discerned, but others, such as status and role, are not permanent qualities of the speakers, but are instead abstract properties.

Are the social categories associated with communicative competence vulnerable to the measurement problems discussed earlier? That is, is evidence of social categories inferred from observations of language use, and in turn used to account for the acquisition of those sociolinguistic rules? Not entirely, insofar as there are language-independent indications of some social categories. For example, dominance can be revealed by posture, eye contact, and physical distance. However, Gumperz (1972, p. 15) argued that some social concepts such as status and role are manifest only in the system of linguistic alternations: "The division between linguistic and social categories is thus obliterated." Ervin-Tripp (1975) observed that language may introduce social distinctions to a child, in that it may serve as an "instructional milieu for learners regarding the major social dimensions and categories of groups they join" (p. 152). Bowerman (1981, p. 153) concluded: "to the extent that socially important concepts can be inferred *only* through communicative interactions, and have no direct nonlinguistic correlates, acquisition of them could not take place independently of language." Notice that the conflating of social categories and sociolinguistic rules is not used to account for language development, as was the case with object and person knowledge, but is instead used to account for the acquisition of social categories.

The distinction between the idea that language may suggest social categories and the assertion that language is *necessary* for the awareness of certain social concepts rests on the premise that the social distinctions evident in communication patterns, such as roles, are not independent of language, in which case linguistic communication is the *only* manifestation of these subtle regularities in social interactions. This premise warrants explicit investigation. For example, careful observations of the nature of cues inherent in social settings may reveal subtle regularities in nonlinguistic variables, such as behavior, dress, and affective demeanor, that may signal the social distinctions evident in linguistic communication, or may confirm that such nonverbal variables are not sufficiently predictable to be helpful. Another source of useful information would be the social awarenesses demonstrated by children lacking verbal skills, such as the deaf. The stronger hypothesis would predict that such children would not be aware of the social distinctions evident only in rules for verbal language use. There is a hint of this possibility in the recent report of Kusché and Greenberg (1983). They found that deaf children were later than their normal peers in acquiring the concepts of good and bad, and that young deaf children were delayed in the acquisition of role-taking ability. Studies along these lines would contribute to our ability to sort out the direction of influence between social concepts and sociolinguistic rules.

Another issue that is not clear is the internal structure of the social categories linked with language, and the nature of their correspondence. Recent work (Cantor and Mischel, 1979) indicates that there may be close parallels to what is known about object categories. Social category groupings are not fully determined sets, i.e., some categories are more clearly identified as members than others. For example, some persons are clearly old whereas others are sort of old; some situations clearly indicate a status differential whereas others have elements of both status difference and equality. There is also evidence (Cantor, 1978) that social categories such as "extrovert" are internally organized around a prototypic member, with particular instances sharing one or more features or elements with the prototype but not necessarily with other members. One can readily imagine prototypic (i.e., stereotyped) role models for "teacher," "mother," or "boss," and a set of exemplars that share characteristics with the prototype but not each other. Furthermore, there is reason to suspect that the systems of linguistic markings correspond to real-world correlations. An example is the observation that in the real world social distance, unfamiliarity, and rank are highly correlated; Ervin-Tripp (1975, p. 152) reported that the same linguistic devices tend to be used to indicate each.

Just as the notion of person knowledge had relevance for both social and referential dimensions of language, so does the idea of social categories. The meanings of some words refer directly to social categories. When children learn the differences among *mother*, *woman*, and *wife* they must make categorical distinctions based on subtle differences in interpersonal relationships. Words like *want* and *need* correspond to abstract categories of social context combined with personal state. Reference to state words depends on knowledge of the psychological dimensions of people, as discussed in the preceding section, plus the ability to categorize that understanding into small parcels that correspond to the boundaries of the lexical forms. Any account of the referential knowledge of young children must be able to deal with the implicit social as well as object categories.

The categorical organization of conceptual knowledge has been a dominant construct in the literature, to the extent that one could erroneously conclude that all of the conceptual knowledge linked to language could be characterized as categorical in nature. Instead, another kind of conceptual organization, that is described as event knowledge, has direct ties to some dimensions of linguistic understandings.

Event Knowledge Event knowledge accounts for a way of representing real-world information that is unlike categorical organization. Categorical knowledge is generally regarded as a relatively static organization of abstract bundles of things that are similar in some way. The categories that have received the most study are those that are organized in a hierarchical fashion, such as robin/bird/animal. However, many of the regularities inherent in the world do not correspond to static categorical organization—for example, the established sequences of events involved in playing a game, relaying a message via the telephone, or preparing and eating a meal. Indeed, much of our real-world knowledge is organized in a sequential manner. Units are connected on the basis of temporal contiguities instead of static properties or attributes. These regularities are evident in ongoing activities that have a dynamic character as opposed to the more stationary nature of categories. Such sequentially organized knowledge is referred to as *event knowledge*. The notion has roots in schema theory, a holistic interpretation of how humans represent real-world knowledge. The idea of schema representation has a long tradition in social psychology.

More recently, schema theory has been influential in studies of memory (e.g., Mandler, 1979) and artificial intelligence (e.g., Schank and Abelson, 1977). Essentially, a schema is a mental structure whose elements are related to one another on the basis of spatial or temporal contiguities instead of class membership and similarity relationships (which are the framework of categories). According to Mandler (1979), a schema "consists of a set of (usually unconscious) expectations about what things look like and/or the order in which they occur." Schemata can be general or specific, and can be formed "for anything with which one is familiar, from the details of appearance of a Hepplewhite chair, to the procedure required to cook a souffle, or the events that occur during a trip to the theater" (Mandler, 1979). Two kinds of schemata have been differentiated, those based on spatial organization (such as knowledge of the normal appearance of a kitchen), and those based on sequential organization (such as knowledge of how to obtain, consume, and pay for food in a restaurant). It is the latter that is of interest here.

The specifics of how to characterize event knowledge are not clear. For example, possible levels of abstraction and the nature of hierarchical structuring are open to debate. The models that have been proposed (e.g., Schank and Abelson, 1977) are in the process of evolution (see, e.g., Abelson, 1979, 1981; Schank, 1979). However this knowledge is to be depicted, it is clear that young children have acquired some sort of general understanding of familiar sequences of events. Nelson (1981) concluded that script knowledge in young children is general in form, temporally organized, consistent over time, and socially accurate. Her conclusions are based on a number of studies with children ranging in age from 3 to 8 years. The children were asked to tell "what happens when . . ." they engaged in familiar activities such as eating dinner or going grocery shopping. Even 3-year-olds were able to relate reasonably accurate sequences of events. Another source of formal observation of children's sequential knowledge is their comprehension of stories. Elementary-age children rely heavily on familiar sequences for comprehension and recall of stories (see, e.g., Mandler, 1978). The formal evidence is consistent with informal observations of preschool children at play, where they often act out long sequences of familiar activities, such as the preparation of meals, telephone conversations, and trips to the grocery store (see, e.g., Garvey, 1977). Schank and Abelson (1977, pp. 222-237) reported that children as young as 2 years of age indicate knowledge of routine events and suggested that certain sequences may be learned as early as 4 months of age.

Event knowledge is alleged to be primary in several senses: it is the infant's first means of organizing and representing reality; it is the basis of subsequent categorical representations; and it remains a primary means of mental organization for adults (Mandler, 1979; Nelson, 1981; Schank and Abelson, 1977). Nelson (1981) argued that awareness of social roles derives from a child's representation of familiar sequences. As children experience the same person in the same role in different sequences, they are able to abstract the role category by generalizing similarities across contexts. According to Nelson, a child moves from a "rather direct representation of dynamically experienced relationships to an increasingly more general, abstract and therefore more static and categorical representation."

How does the recognition of children's event knowledge enhance our understanding of children's communicative competence? Several different points come to mind. First, the notion of a sequentially based representation is an appropriate way to characterize the conceptual underpinnings of some of the linguistic phenomena of interest. Some of a child's communicative knowledge is inherently sequential in nature. For example, the rules for maintaining a conversation are based on the ability to deal with temporally contiguous speech events. Indeed, some conversational settings, such as the telephone, consist of well-defined familiar sequences, such as starting a conversation with "hello," then determining the identity of the caller and the nature of the call, followed by a variable length of discourse in which turn-taking is closely maintained, and concluding by saying "good-bye." The mental representation and memory mechanisms involved in such interactive communicative exchanges are surely sequential in nature.

Other linguistic phenomena are linked with event knowledge indirectly. For example, Ervin-Tripp (1978) reported that children drew heavily upon their practical reasoning, their understanding of common event sequences, to infer the appropriate action response to an indirect request. If a mother says "Is the door open?" when she has her arms full of grocery bags, a child would open the door regardless of whether or not he understood the question to be a request. Ervin-Tripp suggested that such redundancies in natural context contribute to a child's mastery of indirect requests.

Another observation is that a consideration of sequentially organized knowledge can help clarify the nature of putative categorical knowledge. Recall that children's awareness of social categories, such as age, sex, and role, has been inferred from the manner in which children adjust their language to social context. However, the conceptual knowledge involved in such systematic adjustments may be less abstract than implied by the construct of categories. Instead, children's ability to use age-, sex-, or role-specific variants in their verbal interchanges may be accounted for by a more literal representation of familiar sequences or routines. Likewise, some of children's grammatical knowledge that is commonly attributed to rather static socially based categories, such as "agent" in the sense of "human actor," may in fact be based in event schemata. Slobin (1979) drew upon cross-linguistic evidence to argue that the child begins with the grammatical notion of "causal agent," which is in turn rooted in prototypical causal events in which an agent or instrument does something with a direct effect. He postulated (p. 19) that, contrary to current accounts, the child first learning language does not approach the task with categorical information but instead with "the basic events and parameters out of which the linguistic categories will be built."

The idea that social roles and linguistic manifestations of those roles are derived from event knowledge has implications for accounts of what is involved in the relationship between conceptual and linguistic knowledge. In the preceding discussion of social categories two assertions were reported: social concepts are indistinguishable from the patterns of linguistic alternations that signal them, and language introduces social concepts to children. These assertions are related to the claim presented above. *If* categories are rooted in event knowledge, it raises the possibility that the detection of the regularities represented in language (the process of categorization) originates in sequentially based experiences, that the common conceptual base is structured according to dynamically represented sequences of events, a construct unlike current models of the conceptual underpinnings of language. In that case, social categories and the linguistic patterns associated with them may arise from the same sequentially organized conceptual base, either concurrently or with one serving as a lever for the other. Although such relationships are possible, the primacy of event knowledge remains to be established. A central point in need of further clarification is how the sequential nature of event knowledge accounts for categorical learning.

Overall, the construct of event knowledge promises useful contributions to the study of the conceptual knowledge linked with language. It provides a model of the conceptual underpinnings of some kinds of sociolinguistic knowledge (those involving sequential dimensions) not readily accounted for by existing models; it clarifies the nature of contextual redundancies that contribute to language learning; it suggests an alternative explanation of young children's apparent sociolinguistic and grammatical knowledge that is more conservative than positing abstract categories; and it calls for a reconsideration of the nature of the fundamental conceptual structures and the basic processes of categorization, especially the abstraction of social categories.

Summary Person knowledge, social categories, and event knowledge—these three kinds of conceptual organization are all closely associated with a child's acquisition of communicative competence. The conceptual underpinnings of language are broader than much of the existing literature would suggest. The components of a comprehensive model of the interrelationship between cognition and communicative knowledge are illustrated in Figure 3. In order to manipulate socially influenced alternatives, engage in discourse, and interpret speech acts, young children call upon knowledge about people and groups of people as well as objects and object-based groupings; familiar sequences of happenings as well as static groupings.

Of course, the components do not interrelate in a 1:1 fashion, as might be implied by Figure 3. Children's knowledge includes mental representation, organization, and retrieval mechanisms that are called upon in the selection and sequencing of linguistic variants. How all these components of conceptual understanding interrelate and influence language acquisition or are shaped by language is unknown. For example, person knowledge is involved in all aspects of communicative competence; the sociolinguistic dimension draws upon each aspect of nonlinguistic knowledge. In the case of language learning the traditional distinctions among the different kinds of knowledge become blurred. A child seems to draw upon all facets of his understanding of the real world as he learns the codes and uses of verbal language, undoubtedly in some complex interactive fashion.

The next question is, how does the child come to know these things? What kinds of experiences does a child draw upon when acquiring linguistic communication skills? If we assume that a wide range of real-world knowledge is closely tied to a broad set of communication skills, then the sources of language-relevant information must also be

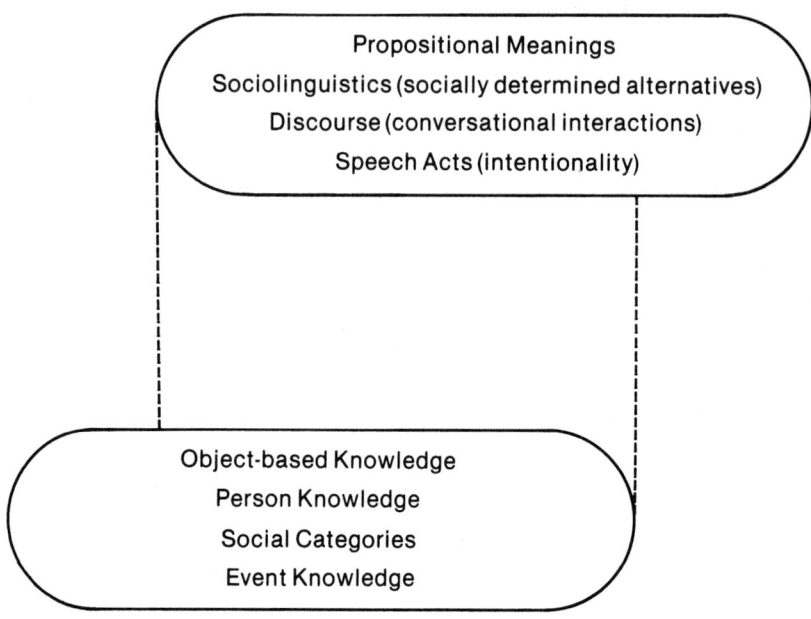

Figure 3. The mapping problem: expansions implicit in the communicative competence model.

evident across a wide spectrum of real-world happenings. However, the existing literature has recognized only a limited range of possible sources. That issue is the topic of the following section.

ENVIRONMENTAL SOURCES OF LANGUAGE-RELEVANT KNOWLEDGE

A young child learning to communicate by means of linguistic symbols has a rich kaleidoscope of real-world information that is constantly within his purview. Only a narrow slice of those experiences has been studied as a source of language-relevant information: direct communicative interchanges between a mature speaker (usually the mother) and a young child. Two features of the interaction have been emphasized: the immediate give-and-take of the interaction (i.e., the direct, one-to-one quality), and the tendency of mature speakers to adjust and simplify their communication patterns to correspond to the young child's level of linguistic competence (see Snow, this volume; Sachs, this volume). Although these features are no doubt facilitative of language acquisition, the extent to which they are necessary is unclear (see Sachs, this volume, for the distinction among necessary, typical, or optimal). Furthermore, the extent to which they represent the nature of experiences that children actually draw upon when learning language is questionable.

Indirect/Observational Learning

As children learn to communicate they have access to two kinds of occasions from which to learn: direct interactions, in which they are participants, and indirect interactions, in which they are observers. The available literature has focused on the former to the exclusion of the latter (Figure 4). Yet it is likely that most of a child's experiences are observational in nature. In the world that surrounds him, adults talk to other adults; children talk with other children, and there is a wide range of animate and inanimate actions, events, and interchanges that occur without regard to the presence of a youngster. The young

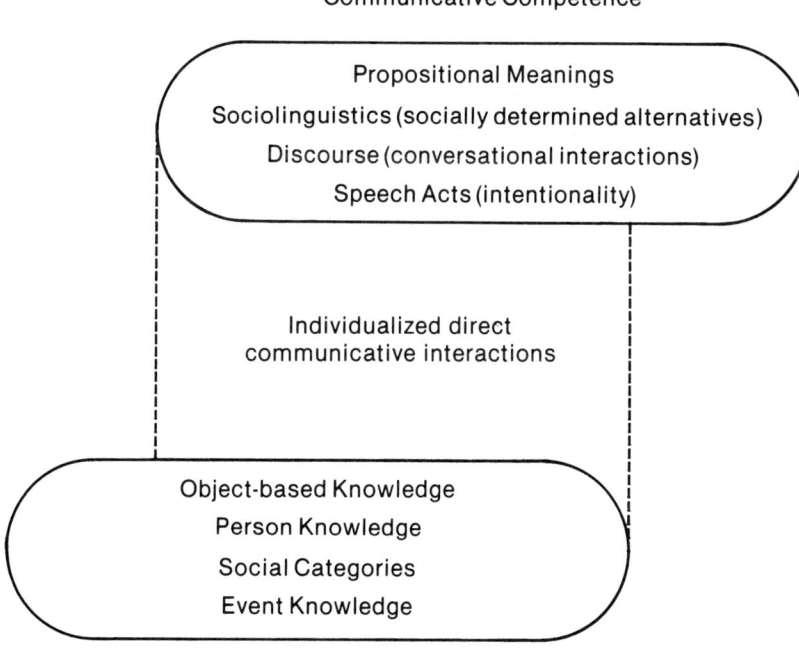

Figure 4. The means of transfer in the mapping problem: current perspectives.

language learner has ample opportunity to attend to, observe, and try to interpret the abundant and diverse real-world happenings that surround him.

There is reason to believe that indirect, observational learning may play an important role in a child's learning how to communicate. Two lines of reasoning support this belief. First, even at the earliest stages of acquisition, children are able to learn the basic structures and meanings of language with only minimal access to direct interchanges in which those linguistic forms are used. Second, some kinds of linguistic learning are most likely acquired in an observational context.

The first point is based on recent evidence that children who receive scant amounts of direct linguistic interaction manage to acquire the beginnings of language in much the same way as children in richer linguistic environments. Schiff (1979) studied five normal hearing children between the ages of 22 and 28 months whose parents were congenitally deaf. The parents communicated with each other with American Sign Language, and used both sign and oral language with their children. The children spent most of each day in the company of their mothers. Three of the five mothers' verbal communication was less than 15% intelligible, with mean lengths of utterance (MLUs) of less than 2.0. The amount of time the children spent in the company of hearing speakers fluctuated between 5 and 20 hours per week, depending upon the amount of time the children spent with their hearing grandparents on weekends. The children were observed longitudinally, for a minimum of 6 months. When their spontaneous utterances were compared to what has been reported for normal children, there were consistent parallels. "The results of this study indicate that two-year-old children from homes with limited linguistic input talk about the same kinds of things as do children from normal homes, and do so using many different syntactic combinations. They know something about ordering sentence constituents, learn some grammatical morphemes, are developing contingent speech and are not grossly delayed" (Schiff, 1979, p. 596).[6]

---

[6] In an earlier related study Schiff and Ventry (1976) concluded that several factors account for language acquisition in the case of hearing children and deaf parents. They studied 52 hearing children of deaf parents. Some of these children ultimately acquired normal language under the most adverse conditions, whereas others did not. Neither the amount of time spent with hearing adults during the preschool years nor the length of time spent watching television were related to speech and language skills. Instead, Schiff and Ventry concluded that "it may very well be that the quality of interaction with a child is more important than mere exposure to normal language" (p. 356). Findings from the 1979 study described above are consistent with this conclusion, i.e., very little time spent in direct interactions, coupled with indirect experience, was sufficient for young children to master the early stages of communicative competence.

What were the sources of such linguistic knowledge? Schiff suggested that some features may have been learned from the mothers' input, such as correct word order, but others, such as grammatical competence, could not be accounted for by mother's input, because the children actually demonstrated mastery of grammatical morphemes not acquired by their mothers. Presumably, the children were able to acquire language-relevant information from sources other than their mothers. The available sources included visits from hearing speakers, sometimes for as little as 5-10 hours weekly. The visiting time was the total time spent visiting, not the time the children were involved in direct interaction, so the actual time of direct involvement was considerably less. Another source of indirect information was television; the children watched television approximately 2 hours daily.

It is apparent that the children's exposure to normal patterns of language in an interaction specifically directed to them was indeed minimal. It is implausible that such limited occasions would account for *all* the spontaneous language acquisition demonstrated by the children, especially given the memory constraints operating with such young children. Instead, it is more reasonable to suppose that the children's indirect, observational learning experiences (overhearing adult-to-adult conversations and observing patterns of verbal communication presented on television) were also contributing significantly to their language learning.

The other line of reasoning suggesting the role of observationally acquired knowledge in children's language learning centers on how some kinds of linguistic learning seem to be inconsistent with the context of focused, directed interchanges with an adult interlocutor. For example, children as young as 3 learn when and how to use swear words, as the earlier example of Mindy's behavior illustrates. Observations of preschool children suggest that such learning is not trivial: these children know the functions associated with the linguistic forms, for example, to express chagrin, frustration, or indignation; they know when to insert swear words in the sequence of utterances; and they know that swearing is part of "adult talk" but not approved of by adults as "child talk." Only the latter, taboo aspect of the use of swear words is likely to be learned in a conversational interchange with an adult. It is unlikely that knowledge of adult use of swear words in context is the result of direct modeling or some sort of one-to-one interaction between a child and a mature speaker. Instead, it is far more plausible that children unobtrusively observe other speakers swear, and, later, in other circumstances, repeat what they overheard. Observational learning would also seem to play a primary role in the acquisition of role-specific linguistic patterns. For example, knowing how to talk like a daddy involves knowing how daddies talk to other people, in addition to how a daddy might talk to his own child. In a similar fashion, the personal pronouns *me*, *I*, and *you* require an ability to extract a speaker role-perspective different from that of the listener. Macnamara (1982, p. 43) suggested that children draw upon their observations of others' conversations as they master the pronouns.

Surely children draw upon such indirectly acquired information as they learn to map linguistic forms onto everyday events and social relationships. Although no one has argued otherwise, experiences beyond the immediate adult/child interactions have nevertheless been relegated to incidental or implicit status in our conceptions of the aspects of a child's environment that are relevant to his language learning. As our models of children's language expand to encompass "communicative competence," our recognition of all possible sources of relevant information must expand accordingly (Figure 5).

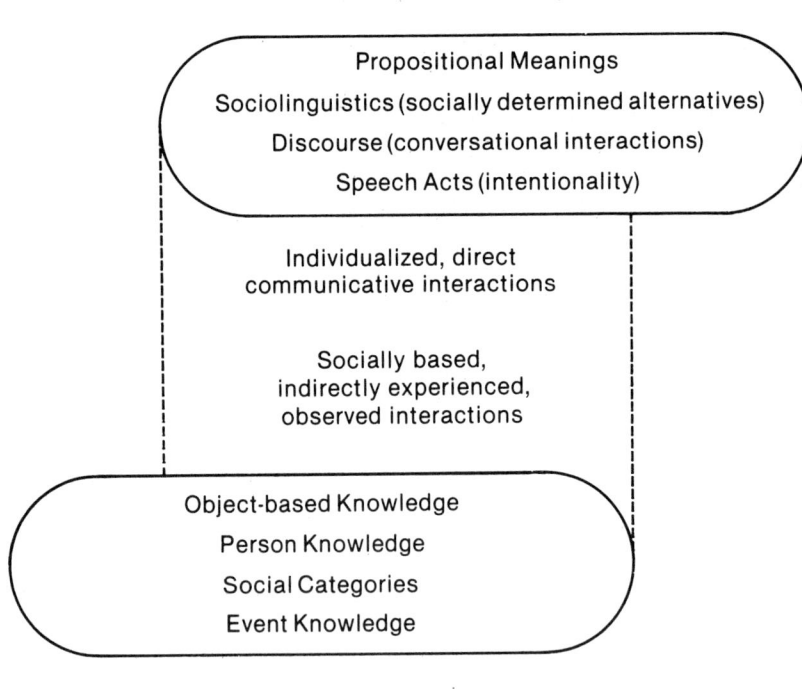

Figure 5. The mapping problem and means of transfer: a full model.

Television

One potentially rich source of information for a young child learning language is the communication medium of television (Rice, 1983). Although the medium has been dismissed by students of child language as an ineffectual environmental variable, the dismissal may be premature. The conclusion that television does not contribute to a child's mastery of language and its uses is based in part on the assumption that noninteractive sources of information are ineffective (Sachs, Bard, and Johnson, 1981), an assumption that is questionable.

The alleged ineffectiveness of television appeared to be confirmed in some reported observations suggesting that television viewing did not contribute substantially to children's language acquisition, observations that were confounded by extenuating circumstances. Nelson (1973) reported a negative correlation between amount of television viewing and language acquisition for children of approximately 18 months. However, she acknowledged that this relationship may be mediated by other environmental behaviors, such as the mother's behavior. She also noted that 18 months is younger than the expected age of television audiences. In fact, Anderson et al. (1979) reported that children do not begin purposive, systematic viewing until between 2 and 3 years of age. Snow et al. (1976, p. 2) mentioned that there are observed cases of Dutch children in eastern Holland who watch German television programs regularly and in preference to similar Dutch programs, but who neither achieve appreciable control of German nor really understand what the programs are about. Neither child variables nor program characteristics were specified in this observation. Ervin-Tripp (1971, p. 195) and Sachs and her colleagues (Sachs and Johnson, 1976; Sachs et al., 1981) reported that, contrary to the Schiff (1979) findings reported earlier, hearing children of deaf parents had deficient language development even though they watched television. However, additional factors may operate under such circumstances.[7]

Although the evidence regarding the role of television in children's language acquisition is indirect and quite limited, the operating assumption is that the negative findings are to be expected. Clark and Clark (1977, p. 330) seemed to sum up current opinion among many child language researchers in their assertion that "children seem not

---

[7] Johnston (1982a) reminded us that the evidence is still incomplete. She argued that more sophisticated descriptions of language patterns, such as ones that could capture the interrelationships between morphology and syntax, or lexical and syntactic competence, may reveal patterns of language acquisition unlike normal sequences. This suspicion is supported in a recently reported study (Johnston and Kahmi, 1980).

to acquire language from radio or television." They suggest two reasons why this is so: "even on television, people rarely talk about things immediately accessible to view for the audience. Children therefore receive no clues about how to map their own ideas onto words and sentences. Second, the stream of speech must be very hard to segment: they hear rapid speech that cannot easily be linked to familiar situations" (p. 330).

However, these alleged characteristics of televised language were not confirmed in a recent study describing the linguistic features of five children's television programs (Rice, in press; Rice, Huston, and Wright, 1982). In fact, some of the findings directly contradicted Clark and Clark's assumptions. The majority of comments in four of the programs were ones in which the speaker talked about things immediately accessible to view. Also, the stream of speech was not always rapid. In fact, the main characters of some programs had speaking styles consisting of a moderate, deliberate rate combined with a judicious use of pauses that distinctly marked linguistic units. Furthermore, there was considerable evidence of explicit attempts to adjust verbal messages to correspond to children's linguistic processing abilities, including various means of highlighting key linguistic messages. Another facilitative factor was the manner in which linguistic messages were combined with nonlinguistic production features. Overall, the impression is that, instead of presenting a complex jumble of verbal information, some television programs aimed at a child audience combine verbal messages with other content in a manner well suited to a preschool audience's language competencies. Just as it is premature to dismiss television on the grounds that children rely exclusively on immediate, interactive contexts for learning language, so is it inaccurate to dismiss it on the grounds that the verbal messages are always inappropriate for children.

The argument here is not that television viewing in and of itself would enable a young child to acquire linguistic communication. In fact, that is highly improbable. Even if the linguistic information itself were appropriate, the interactive and affective components of verbal communication—the qualitative aspects of young children's experience with language that surely play a vital role in how and why children learn to verbally communicate—would not be available to the child. Closely related to the need for interactive contexts at the very beginnings of language is the child's preference for them. Children who are younger than 30 months do not systematically monitor the TV screen but instead attend for only short periods of time to particularly salient events (Anderson et al., 1979). Of course, it is possible that children who have limited access to verbal interactions may be more attentive to television at younger ages than children who have frequent opportunities to verbally interact with others.

Even though television viewing is a secondary source of linguistically relevant information, it is premature to conclude that it has *no* influence on children's acquisition of communicative competence. Furthermore, there are sound reasons for carefully considering what children learn about language when they watch television. It is a powerful social force in the lives of children who live in industrialized nations, powerful in two senses: it attracts children's attention for literally hours of each day, and it influences several aspects of children's psychological development. Such behavioral variables as cognitive functioning (e.g., classification skills), aggressive behavior, prosocial behaviors (e.g., cooperation, helpfulness, delay of gratification, task persistence, creative use of fantasy), and social knowledge and stereotypes have all been linked to amounts of watching particular television content (see Stein and Friedrich, 1972, 1975, and Huston-Stein and Wright, 1979, for comprehensive reviews of the literature). Many of these behavioral variables are closely related to what is involved when children acquire communicative competence. Such findings suggest that television viewing may well influence children's acquisition of language. Support for this claim is found in reports that children learn word meanings when viewing (Ball and Bogatz, 1972; Meringoff et al., 1981), as well as verbal routines incorporated in play (Watson-Gegeo and Boggs, 1977).

Not only does television provide models of communication in social context, it also introduces children to a variety of experiences not available to them in their own immediate environment. Although they may never actually visit a courtroom, ranch, or spaceship, they may have TV-inspired ideas about the role of judges, ranch hands, and captains of spaceships, including the patterns of communication associated with each role. These examples could enhance children's awareness of such sociolinguistic variables as dialect differences, status indicators, styles of formal language, and conversational rules.

Television is an important part of a child's everyday language-learning laboratory, along with all the other rich and varied communicative interactions he observes in the world around him. We have recently heightened our awareness of the scope of children's communicative competence. Broader models of children's language-related abilities call for expanded models of conceptual underpinnings that in turn are derived from a wide range of real-world experiences. Given how little we know of the entire process, it is indeed premature to restrict our attention arbitrarily to only one type of interaction or one set of experiences.

CONCLUSIONS

As children acquire the system of language-based knowledge represented in the notion of communicative competence, they draw upon the totality of their experiences. Whereas existing models of this process are compartmentalized in nature and limited in scope, the reality is fluid, comprehensive, interactive in nature, and continuous even throughout adulthood.

The comprehensive model of what children learn, their communicative competence, allows for a view of the learning process that is broader, more integrative, and therefore more consistent with reality than previous models. Within the mental domain of language, the components that have been conceptually compartmentalized by scholars actually interrelate in an intimate fashion. In communication events, referential meanings, grammatical structures, and socially based rules for language use are each part and parcel of the whole. Likewise, a wide range of children's conceptual knowledge converges on the business of learning how to communicate with linguistic symbols. A child's understanding, mental representation, and memory of objects, persons, sequences of events, and categories of things, persons, and happenings are all involved in what he knows and learns about language.

The complexity and subtlety of the acquisition process rules out simple explanations. For example, the question of the direction of influence, i.e., cognition to language versus language to cognition, is undoubtedly cast in too broad a perspective. Instead, localized areas of interaction are more likely, such as understanding a particular conceptual domain and the linguistic means of expressing that understanding, or awareness of certain social distinctions and the system of linguistic alternation that corresponds to that social knowledge. It may well be that the interaction is content specific rather than domain (language versus cognition) specific.

Not only do children draw upon diverse kinds of knowledge in their acquisition of communicative competence, they do so in all possible contexts for learning. They learn by doing (participating) and by watching (observing). Although the very earliest stages of language learning probably depend upon some minimal amounts of participatory experiences, a great deal can be acquired in an indirect fashion. Indeed, some referential and sociolinguistic knowledge is probably picked up by the child mostly in observational contexts.

The diversity, richness, flexibility, and fluidity of the language-learning process undoubtedly contribute to its robustness. Children learn language under the most adverse circumstances (Schieffelin and Eisenberg, this volume; Schiff, 1979; Schiff and Ventry, 1976). Yet for reasons we often cannot identify, some children are unable to acquire communicative competence in the same effortless manner as their peers. The issues discussed above carry increased significance when applied to understanding the problems of these children.

IMPLICATIONS FOR INTERVENTION WITH CHILDREN HAVING DIFFICULTY ACQUIRING LANGUAGE

How do these broadened perspectives regarding the nature of language acquisition by normal children contribute to our ability to assist children who demonstrate atypical patterns of language acquisition? What do we already know about such children?

The literature addressing language-disordered children has dealt with two major issues. The first is identification/assessment, with an implicit concern with causality. The question is, how is the language-disordered child unlike the child who acquires language in a normal pattern, and does that difference account for the language problem? The second issue is rehabilitation/training. Here the questions deal with what to teach and how to teach it. Much more is known about the identification/description issue than about how to train. The following discussion regarding normal acquisition is related to both issues.

Identification/Assessment

A number of studies have compared the language patterns of children identified as having language disorders with those of children regarded as normal language learners. When phonology, syntax, grammatical morphology, or relational semantics are the dimensions of comparison, the only apparent difference between normal and language-disordered children is a slower rate of acquisition for the latter, i.e., their language is much like that of younger normal children (reviewed in Johnston, 1982a; Leonard, 1979; Rice, 1978).

In addition, there is preliminary evidence that language-disordered children perform differently from their normal peers on a variety of nonlinguistic conceptual tasks, such as visual imagery, symbolic play, classification tasks, and information processing (see Johnston, 1982a; Leonard, 1979). Overall, the findings suggest that a pattern of atypical language acquisition may be part of a more general representational deficiency (Johnston, 1982a; Leonard, 1979, 1980; Snow, this volume).

The import of this possibility is not clear. The evidence is not sufficiently robust to support a strong inference of causality. That is, it is too early to conclude that problems in acquiring language are caused by cognitive deficiencies and therefore all language-disordered children would demonstrate cognitive deficits. Instead, questions remain. The conceptual problems may be independent of the language difficulties. There is no evidence directly linking certain cognitive deficiencies with particular linguistic difficulties, e.g., visual imagery with linguistic forms that require taking the perspective of others. Leonard (1980) supported Bates' local homologies account (Bates et al., 1977). He reasoned that any relationship between language-disordered children's nonlinguistic and linguistic abilities is a function of some shared underlying mental structure, evident only in specific, localized skill areas. Johnston (1982a) pointed out that problems with process mechanisms, such as memory, attention, and/or perceptual exploration, may be implicated. If this is the case, language-disordered children may have acquired conceptual knowledge, but they are unable to use it efficiently.

In short, we understand little about the role of cognitive deficiencies in the problems some children have acquiring language. How does the discussion in the first two sections of this chapter promise to further our understandings of the nature of the problems? An initial observation is that the communicative competence model has just recently been extended to studies of language-disordered children (see Snyder, this volume). Johnston (1982a) concluded that what little evidence is available suggests that these children are effective and responsive conversationalists, although constrained by grammatical limitations, such as fewer question structures and pronouns. On the other hand, Leonard (1980) concluded that language-impaired children may have difficulties with pragmatic features, in that they use some features less frequently and acquire them at a later age than their normal peers. Snyder (this volume) emphasizes the difference in findings evident across different groups of language-disordered children and different tasks. Obviously, the limited findings are open to different interpretations.

Establishing the pragmatic/sociolinguistic knowledge of children with language difficulties poses some problems. Recall that the linguistic phenomenon of central interest is the existence of alternative ways of saying the same thing. These alternative ways may be at the level of phonology, lexicon, syntax, and/or prosody. Much of the normative literature is based on descriptions of what normal children say, their use of linguistic alternatives. However, the language-disordered child's use of alternatives is confounded by his difficulty in acquiring the other dimensions of language. For example, if he has an articulation problem, phonological alternations may not be helpful as indices of contextually based knowledge; similarly, if he has problems with syntax, the child may not be able to formulate grammatically complex yet socially appropriate alternatives. It will be necessary to rely on more subtle indices of sociolinguistic knowledge. Among the possibilities are: 1) variations within the individual child's communication patterns (how he chooses within his own range of alternatives); 2) systematic probing of his comprehension skills (the kinds of alternations he detects and understands in the verbal interactions of others); and 3) the use of nonlinguistic means of communicating. These indices are not as rich in information, as easy to observe, nor as objective to describe as are the spontaneous utterances of children in social context. Nevertheless, the goal is worth the attempt. The development of new methods of inferring pragmatic competence would enrich our understanding of both normal and atypical children.

The conceptual underpinnings of the social dimensions of the communication patterns of language-disordered children is an uncharted domain. The existing measures of their cognitive abilities are largely based on knowledge of objects. Yet the social dimensions (knowledge about people, social categories, and sequences of events) are important components of their conceptual knowledge: language-disordered children draw upon such knowledge in their use of language. If we can determine how and to what extent they do so, we will have a better idea of the nature of their problems.

The direction of influence within localized areas of social knowledge and sociolinguistic skills is an especially interesting issue. It may be that certain problems in language acquisition are linked with underlying conceptual deficiencies. For example, the reason some children never develop communication skills to any appreciable extent may be as much a matter of deficits in person-based knowledge as in object knowledge, or the particular patterns of language problems may be traceable to patterns of conceptual understanding. Children who do not adjust their language to social context may fail to do so because they have yet to master the corresponding social categories. Children who are unable to relate stories may not have the corresponding mental representation of event sequences (see Johnston, 1982b). An alternate possibility is that problems in language acquisition may contribute to problems in social learning. Consider the child who is insensitive to the subtleties of socially based linguistic variations because he does not understand the forms or structures of verbal language. The failure to distinguish between one linguistic variant and another may limit the youngster's ability to pick up the social distinctions those variations cue.

Another issue regarding the nature of language-disordered children's problems is how to conceptualize the difficulties they have acquiring certain forms or structures. Recall that the notions of person knowledge and social categories remind us that the referential aspect of language is also rooted in social context. It may be that the problems some children have acquiring ostensibly referential forms is a function of difficulties in mastering the associated social dimensions. For example, problems with personal pronouns or nonspecific referents may reflect an inadequate awareness of the interlocutor's perspective and state of knowledge. Likewise, those forms that refer to personal states or role status, such as *know* or *wife*, would be problematic for a child unaware of those dimensions or roles. A closer look at the nature of some children's problems in learning what appear to be linguistic skills involving reference may reveal that the difficulty is not solely in the symbol/signified relationship but also in the social dimensions of the relationship.

Obtaining information about *all* language-relevant dimensions of a language-disordered child's conceptual knowledge is complicated by the problems of measurement. It was pointed out in the earlier discussion that most of what is known about children's person knowledge, social categories, and event knowledge has been inferred from what children have to say. Obviously, that method poses not only theoretical but also practical problems in the case of children who have limited language abilities. Nonlinguistic means of deducing these dimensions of conceptual knowledge must be developed. Meeting this challenge will provide both an immediately useful clinical tool and a valuable research instrument for the study of all children.

Rehabilitation/Training

Some of the points presented earlier have immediate implications for language training procedures. Unfortunately, they do not resolve the question of whether the training of underlying cognitive knowledge should be explicitly incorporated into the language training program (see Rice, 1980, for discussions of this question, especially pp. 158–160). Three points suggest principles for training. The first is the reminder that children draw upon a wide range of their experiences and conceptual understandings as they acquire language. Yet many of our clinical paradigms restrict the range of experiences to those that can take place between a clinician and a child within the confines of one room. In contrast, intervention programs based on the home or classroom setting allow both a wider range of teaching experiences and the opportunity to infer the extent of a child's real-world experiences. Inasmuch as a child's communicative competence reflects his conceptual understandings, which are in turn drawn from a wide experiential base, therapy activities should correspond to the ideational richness and diversity represented in the targeted linguistic skills. It is time to move beyond the premise that a child can be taught all he needs to know about linguistic communication by means of activities that are limited to a small therapy room, the child and his clinician, and some toy object or pictures.

The second point with relevance for training is the role of event knowledge in children's language acquisition. Most existing clinical procedures emphasize static kinds of knowledge, such as categories of things. Even when sequences are used, such as pictures depicting a series of activities, they are usually used in ways unrelated to the sociolinguistic competencies discussed above (for example, story pictures are often used to elicit responses for the training of grammatical structures, or to elicit recall of the order of events within a particular set of activities). More enlightened use of sequences may be the most effective context for teaching sociolinguistic skills. Such commonplace and familiar sequences as visiting friends, going grocery shopping, baking cookies, or eating in a restaurant all call upon a variety of sociolinguistic rules. These rules may best be learned first embedded in a familiar sequence or routine and then later generalized to other, similar settings. For example, the use of polite forms may be combined with other status indicators, such as indirect requests, in one sequence and then later separated in contextually appropriate ways in other sequences. As the child learns the social alternatives appropriate for routine sequences, he will also have an immediate, if limited, competence to draw upon in his social interactions.

The third point to be considered, the value of observational learning, is closely associated with the preceding suggestion. A central feature of currently predominant clinical methods is the immediate participation of the child; an overt response is virtually always required. This feature undoubtedly reflects the heavy influence of operant learning theory on present clinical models. However, learning theory has also undergone recent changes. Just as underlying cognitive and perceptual factors are now recognized in behaviorally based accounts of language learning (Zimmerman and Whitehurst, 1979), so is the role of observational learning, including the ideas that overt responses are not required at the time of language learning and the form of subsequent responses need not mimic that of the model (Whitehurst, 1979).

A modeling technique for teaching language is especially appropriate for sociolinguistic rules. The full social context, involving the interactions of speakers, can be demonstrated. Little scenarios depicting familiar sequences of events and familiar social roles can serve to illustrate contextual adjustments in linguistic patterns. Some content can be more effectively presented to the child as observer instead of as participant, such as the use of first and second person pronouns, other deictic terms, and the rules governing interactions between mature speakers. It is doubtful that such demonstrations would suffice in and of themselves. After all, most language-disordered children have observed plenty of spontaneous communicative interactions and evidently have not benefited from the experience, insofar as they were not able to abstract the relevant regularities and/or match them with associated linguistic patterns. Therefore, demonstrations would need a full context, with explicit cuing from the clinician about what to look for with regard to kinds of social and linguistic features and their association. Observational circumstances may serve to introduce a sociolinguistic skill. They could then be followed by the child's participation, that is, acting out his own part and another's role in a simple sequence.

The therapy suggestions can be summarized as: 1) provide a variety of experiences; 2) explicitly teach socially appropriate communication embedded in familiar sequences of events; and 3) include observational as well as participatory learning contexts. These suggestions imply a more flexible clinical format than is traditional. In order to teach the broad array of skills involved in communicative competence, a correspondingly wide-ranging and flexible array of rehabilitation experiences is required.

ACKNOWLEDGMENTS

I would like to thank Aletha Huston, Sue Kemper, Judith Johnston, and Susan Sugarman for their helpful comments on earlier drafts of this manuscript.

REFERENCES

Abelson, R. P. 1979. The interaction of feelings and goals. Talk presented at Social Science Research Council Workshop on the Representation of Cultural Knowledge, San Diego, August 12.

Abelson, R. P. 1981. Psychological status of the script concept. Am. Psychol. 36(7):715–729.

Andersen, E. 1977. Learning to speak with style: A study of the sociolinguistic skills of children. Unpublished Ph.D. dissertation, Stanford University.

Anderson, D. R., Alwitt, L. F., Lorch, E. P., and Levin, S. R. 1979. Watching children watch television. In G. Hall and M. Lewis (eds.), Attention and the Development of Cognitive Skills. Plenum Publishing Corp., New York.

Anglin, J. 1977. Word, Object and Conceptual Development. W. W. Norton & Company, Inc., New York.

Ball, S., and Bogatz, G. A. 1972. Summative research of Sesame Street: Implications for the study of preschool children. In A. D. Pick (ed.), Minnesota Symposium on Child Psychology, Vol. 6. University of Minnesota Press, Minneapolis.

Bates, E., Benigni, L., Bretherton, I., Camaioni, L., and Volterra, V. 1977. From gesture to the first word: On cognitive and social prerequisites. In M. Lewis and L. Rosenblum (eds.), Interaction, Conversation, and the Development of Language, pp. 247–307. John Wiley & Sons, Inc., New York.

Bates, E., Benigni, L., Bretherton, I., Camaioni, L., and Volterra, V. 1979. Cognition and communication from 9-13 months: Correlational findings. *In* E. Bates (ed.), The Emergence of Symbols: Cognition and Communication in Infancy. Academic Press, Inc., New York.

Bates, E., Bretherton, I., Beeghly-Smith, M., and McNew, J. 1982. Social bases of language development: A reassessment. *In* H. W. Reese and L. P. Lipsitt (eds.), Advances in Child Development and Behavior, Vol. 16. Academic Press, Inc., New York.

Bates, E., and Snyder, L. The cognitive hypothesis in language development. *In* I. Uzgiris and J. McV. Hunt (eds.), Research with Scales of Psychological Development in Infancy. University of Illinois Press, Champaign-Urbana. (in press)

Bloom, L. 1973. One Word at a Time: The Use of Single-Word Utterances Before Syntax. Mouton, The Hague.

Bloom, L., Lightbown, P., and Hood, L. 1975. Structure and variation in child language. Monogr. Soc. Res. Child Dev. 40.

Bowerman, M. 1976. Semantic factors in the acquisition of rules for word use and sentence construction. *In* D. Morehead and A. Morehead (eds.), Directions in Normal and Deficient Child Language. University Park Press, Baltimore.

Bowerman, M. 1977. The structure and origin of semantic categories in the language learning child. Paper prepared for presentation at the Burg Wartenstein Symposium #74, Fundamentals of Symbolism, July 16-24, Wennergren Foundation for Anthropological Research, New York.

Bowerman, M. 1981. Cross-cultural perspectives on language development. *In* H. C. Triandis (ed.), Handbook of Cross-Cultural Psychology. Allyn & Bacon, Inc., Boston.

Braunwald, S. R. 1979. Context, word and meaning: Toward a communicational analysis of lexical acquisition. *In* A. Lock (ed.), Action, Gesture, and Symbol: The Emergence of Language. Academic Press, Inc., New York.

Bretherton, I., and Beeghly, M. 1982. Talking about internal states: The acquisition of an explicit theory of mind. Dev. Psychol. 18(6):906-921.

Bretherton, I., McNew, S., and Beeghly-Smith, M. 1981. Early person knowledge as expressed in gestural and verbal communication: When do infants acquire a "theory of mind?" *In* M. E. Lamb and L. R. Sherrod (eds.), Infant Social Cognition. Lawrence Erlbaum Assocs., Inc., Hillsdale, N.J.

Brown, R. 1973. A First Language: The Early Stages. Harvard University Press, Cambridge, MA.

Brown, R. 1978. A new paradigm of reference. *In* G. A. Miller and E. Lenneberg (eds.), Psychology and Biology of Language and Thought: Essays in Honor of Eric Lenneberg. Academic Press, Inc., New York.

Campbell, R. N. 1979. Cognitive development and child language. *In* P. Fletcher and M. Garman (eds.), Language Acquisition. Cambridge University Press, Cambridge, England.

Cantor, N. 1978. Prototypicality and personality judgments. Unpublished doctoral dissertation, Stanford University.

Cantor, N., and Mischel, W. 1979. Prototypes in person perception. *In* L. Berkowitz (ed.), Advances in Experimental Social Psychology, Vol. 12. Academic Press, Inc. New York.

Clark, E. V. 1973a. Non-linguistic strategies and the acquisition of word meanings. Cognition 2:161-182.

Clark, E. V. 1973b. What's in a word? On the child's acquisition of semantics in his first language. *In* T. E. Moore (ed.), Cognitive Development and the Acquisition of Language. Academic Press, Inc., New York.

Clark, E. V. 1977. Strategies and the mapping problem in first language acquisition. *In* J. Macnamara (ed.), Language Learning and Thought. Academic Press, Inc., New York.

Clark, H., and Clark, E. 1977. Psychology and Language. Harcourt Brace Jovanovich, Inc., New York.

Corrigan, R. 1978. Language development as related to Stage 6 object permanence development. J. Child Lang. 5:173–189.

Cromer, R. F. 1981. Reconceptualizing language acquisition and cognitive development. *In* R. L. Schiefelbusch and D. Bricker (eds.), Early Language: Acquisition and Intervention. University Park Press, Baltimore.

Dore, J. 1977. "Oh them Sheriff": A pragmatic analysis of children's responses to questions. *In* S. Ervin-Tripp and C. Mitchell-Kernan (eds.), Child Discourse. Academic Press, Inc., New York.

Dore, J. 1979. What's so conceptual about the acquisition of linguistic structures? J. Child Lang. 6(1):129–138.

Dore, J. The development of conversational competence. *In* R. L. Schiefelbusch (ed.), Communicative Competence: Assessment and Intervention. University Park Press, Baltimore. (in press)

Dore, J., and McDermott, R. 1982. Linguistic indeterminacy and social context in utterance interpretation. Language 57:374–398.

Ervin-Tripp, S. 1971. An overview of grammatical development. *In* D. Slobin (ed.), The Ontogenesis of Grammar. Academic Press, Inc., New York.

Ervin-Tripp, S. 1975. Speech acts and social learning. *In* K. Basso and H. Shelby (eds.), Meaning in Anthropology. University of New Mexico, Albuquerque.

Ervin-Tripp, S. 1978. Whatever happened to communicative competence? *In* proceedings of the Linguistic Forum, University of Illinois, Champaign-Urbana, September.

Folger, M. K., and Leonard, L. B. 1978. Language and sensorimotor development during the early period of referential speech. J. Speech Hear. Res. 21(3):519–527.

Garvey, C. 1977. Play. Harvard University Press, Cambridge, MA.

Greenfield, P. M. 1979. The role of perceptual uncertainty in the transition to language. Paper presented at a symposium on the transition from sensorimotor to linguistic communication at the Biennial Meeting of the Society for Research on Child Development, San Francisco, March.

Greenfield, P., Nelson, K., and Saltzman, E. 1972. The development of rulebound strategies for manipulating seriated cups: A parallel between action and grammar. Cognitive Psychol. 3:291–310.

Gruendel, J. 1977. Referential extension in early language development. Child Dev. 48(4):1567–1576.

Gumperz, J. J. 1972. Introduction. *In* J. J. Gumperz and D. Hymes (eds.), Directions in Sociolinguistics: The Ethnography of Communication. Holt, Rinehart and Winston, Inc., New York.

Gumperz, J. J., and Hymes, D. 1964. Ethnography of communication. Am. Anthropol. Special Issue No. 6.

Huston-Stein, A., and Wright, J. C. 1979. Children and television: Effects of the medium, its content, and its form. J. Res. Dev. Educ. 13:20–31.

Hymes, D. 1971. Competence and performance in linguistic theory. *In* R. Huxley and E. Ingram (eds.), Language Acquisition: Models and Methods. Academic Press, Inc., New York.

Hymes, D. 1972. On communicative competence. *In* J. B. Pride and J. Holmes (eds.), Sociolinguistics. Penguin, Harmondsworth, England.
Johnston, J. R. 1979. A study of spatial thought and expression: In back and in front. Unpublished Ph.D. dissertation, University of California, Berkeley.
Johnston, J. R. 1982a. The language disordered child. *In* N. Lass, J. Northern, D. Yoder, and L. McReynolds (eds.), Speech, Language and Hearing. W. B. Saunders Company, Philadelphia.
Johnston, J. R. 1982b. Narratives: A new look at communication problems in older language-disordered children. Lang. Speech Hear. Serv. Schools 13(3):144–155.
Johnston, J., and Kahmi, A. 1980. The same equals less: Syntactic and semantic aspects of the language of language disordered children. Paper presented at the Symposium on Research in Child Language Disorders, University of Wisconsin, Madison.
Keenan, E. O. 1974. Conversational competence in children. J. Child Lang. 1:163–183.
Kemper, S. 1984. The development of narrative skills: Explanations and entertainments. *In* S. J. Kuczaj (ed.), Discourse Development. Lawrence Erlbaum Assocs., Inc., Hillsdale, N.J.
Kusché, C. A., and Greenberg, M. T. 1983. Evaluative understanding and role-taking ability: A comparison of deaf and hearing children. Child Dev. 54:141–147.
Lenneberg, E. H. 1957. A probabilistic approach to language learning. Behav. Sci. 2:1–12.
Leonard, L. B. 1979. Language impairment in children. Merrill-Palmer Q. 25(3):205–232.
Leonard, L. B. 1980. Cognitive development and language impairment: Implications for intervention. Paper presented at Tenth Annual International Interdisciplinary UAP Conference on Piagetian Theory and Its Implications for the Helping Professions, University of Southern California, Los Angeles.
Levine, S. C., and Carey, S. 1982. Up front: The acquisition of a concept and a word. J. Child Lang. 9:645–657.
Macnamara, J. 1982. Names for Things: A Study of Human Learning. MIT Press, Cambridge, MA.
Mandler, J. M. 1978. A code in the node: The use of story schema in retrieval. Discourse Processes 1:14–35.
Mandler, J. M. 1979. Categorical and schematic organization in memory. *In* C. R. Puff (ed.), Memory, Organization and Structure. Academic Press, Inc., New York.
Mandler, J. M. 1983. Representation. *In* J. H. Flavell and E. M. Markman (eds.), Cognitive Development. Manual of Child Psychology, Vol. 2, (P. Mussen, ed.). John Wiley & Sons, Inc., New York.
Maratsos, M. 1976. The Use of Definite and Indefinite Reference in Young Children. Cambridge University Press, Cambridge, England.
Maratsos, M. 1979. Learning how and when to use pronouns and determiners. *In* P. Fletcher and M. Garman (eds.), Language Acquisition. Cambridge University Press, Cambridge, England.
Meringoff, L., Vibbert, M., Kelly, H., and Char, C. 1981. How shall you take your story, with or without pictures?: Progress report on a program of media research with children. Paper presented at a symposium on the Cognitive Impact of Media, Biennial Meeting of the Society for Research in Child Development, Boston, April.
Miller, J. F., Chapman, R. S., Branston, M. B., and Reichle, J. 1980. Language

comprehension in sensorimotor stages 5 and 6. J. Speech Hear. Res. 4:1–12.

Morehead, D. M., and Morehead, A. 1974. From signal to sign: A Piagetian view of thought and language during the first two years. In R. L. Schiefelbusch and L. L. Lloyd (eds.), Language Perspectives: Acquisition, Retardation and Intervention. University Park Press, Baltimore.

Nelson, K. 1973. Structure and strategy in learning to talk. Monog. Soc. Res. Child Dev. 149(38):1–2.

Nelson, K. 1974. Concept, word and sentence: Interrelations in acquisition and development. Psychol. Rev. 81:267–285.

Nelson, K. 1981. Social cognition in a script framework. In J. Flavell and L. Ross (eds.), Social Cognitive Development. Cambridge University Press, New York.

Nelson, K., and Gruendel, J. M. 1979. At morning it's lunchtime: A scriptal view of children's stories. Discourse Processes 2:73–94.

Nelson, K., Rescorla, L., and Gruendel, J. 1978. Early lexicons: What do they mean? Child Dev. 49(4):960–968.

Piaget, J. 1962. Play, Dreams, and Imitation in Childhood. W. W. Norton & Company, Inc., New York.

Rice, M. L. 1978. Identification of children with language disorders. In R. L. Schiefelbusch (ed.), Language Intervention Strategies. University Park Press, Baltimore.

Rice, M. L. 1980. Cognition to Language: Categories, Word Meanings and Training. University Park Press, Baltimore.

Rice, M. L. 1983a. Contemporary accounts of the cognition/language relationship: Implications for language clinicians. J. Speech Hear. Dis. 48(4):347–359.

Rice, M. L. 1983b. The role of television in language acquisition. Dev. Rev. 3:211–224.

Rice, M. L. The words of children's television. J. Broadcasting. (in press)

Rice, M. L., Huston, A. C., and Wright, J. C. 1982. The forms and codes of television: Effects on children's attention, comprehension, and social behavior. In D. Pearl, L. Bouthilet, and J. Lazar (eds.), Television and Behavior: Ten Years of Scientific Progress and Implications for the 80s. U.S. Government Printing Office, Washington, D.C.

Rice, M. L., and Kemper, S. Cognition and Language. University Park Press, Baltimore. (in press)

Rosch, E., and Mervis, C. B. 1975. Family resemblances: Studies in the internal structure of categories. Cognitive Psychol. 7(4):573–605.

Rosch, E., Mervis, C. B., Gray, W., Johnson, D., and Bayes-Braem, P. 1976. Basic objects in natural categories. Cognitive Psychol. 8:382–439.

Sachs, J., Bard., B., and Johnson, M. L. 1981. Language learning with restricted input: Case studies of two hearing children of deaf parents. Appl. Psycholing. (J. Child Lang.) 2(1):33–54.

Sachs, J. S., and Johnson, M. 1976. Language development in a hearing child of deaf parents. In W. von Raffler Engel and Y. LeBrun (eds.), Baby Talk and Infant Speech (Neurolinguistics 5). Swets and Zeitlinger, Amsterdam.

Schank, R. C. 1979. Language and memory. Talk presented at La Jolla Conference on Cognitive Science, August 15.

Schank, R., and Abelson, R. 1977. Scripts, Plans, Goals and Understanding. Lawrence Erlbaum Assocs., Inc., Hillsdale, N.J.

Schiff, N. B. 1979. The influence of deviant maternal input on the development of language during the preschool years. J. Speech Hear. Res. 22:581–603.

Schiff, N. B., and Ventry, I. M. 1976. Communications problems in hearing children of deaf parents. J. Speech Hear. Disord. 41:348–358.

Schlesinger, I. M. 1977. The role of cognitive development and linguistic input in language acquisition. J. Child Lang. 4:153–169.

Shields, M. M. 1979. The child as psychologist: Construing the social world. *In* A. Lock (ed.), Action, Gesture and Symbol: The Emergency of Language. Academic Press, Inc., New York.

Sinclair, H. 1971. Sensorimotor action patterns as a condition for the acquisition of syntax. *In* R. Huxley and D. Ingram (eds.), Language Acquisition: Models and Methods. Academic Press, Inc., New York.

Slobin, D. I. (ed.). 1967. A Field Manual for Cross-Cultural Study of the Acquisition of Communicative Competence. A.S.U.C. Bookstore, Berkeley, CA.

Slobin, D. I. 1979. The role of language in language acquisition. Unpublished paper, University of California, Berkeley.

Snow, C. E., Arlman-Rupp, A., Hassing, Y., Jobse, J., Joosten, J., and Vorster, J. 1976. Mothers' speech in three social classes. J. Psycholing. Res. 5:1–20.

Stein, A. H., and Friedrich, L. K. 1972. Television content and young children's behavior. *In* J. P. Murray, E. A. Rubinstein, and G. A. Comstock (eds.), Television and Social Behavior, Vol. 2. Television and Social Learning. Government Printing Office, Washington, D.C.

Stein, A. H., and Friedrich, L. K. 1975. The impact of television on children and youth. *In* E. M. Hetherington, J. W. Hagen, R. Kron, and A. H. Stein (eds.), Review of Child Development Research, Vol. 5. University of Chicago Press, Chicago.

Trevarthen, C., and Hubley, P. 1979. Secondary intersubjectivity: Confidence confiding, and acts of meaning in the first year. *In* A. Lock (ed.), Action, Gesture and Symbol: The Emergence of Language. Academic Press, Inc., New York.

Uzgiris, J. C. 1981. Experience in the social context: Imitation and play. *In* R. L. Schiefelbusch and D. Bricker (eds.), Early Language: Acquisition and Intervention. University Park Press, Baltimore.

Uzgiris, I., and Hunt, J. McV. 1975. Assessment in Infancy: Ordinal Scales of Psychological Development. University of Illinois Press, Champaign-Urbana.

Veneziano, E. 1981. Early language and nonverbal representation: A reassessment. J. Child Lang. 8:541–563.

Watson-Gegeo, K. A., and Boggs, S. T. 1977. From verbal play to talk story: The role of routines in speech events among Hawaiian children. *In* S. Ervin-Tripp and C. Mitchell-Kernan (eds.), Child Discourse. Academic Press, Inc., New York.

Whitehurst, G. J. 1979. Meaning and semantics. *In* G. J. Whitehurst and B. J. Zimmerman (eds.), The Functions of Language and Cognition. Academic Press, Inc., New York.

Zimmerman, B. J., and Whitehurst, G. J. 1979. Structure and function: A comparison of two views of the development of language and cognition. *In* G. J. Whitehurst and B. J. Zimmerman (eds.), The Functions of Language and Cognition. Academic Press, Inc., New York.

Section II

Dimensions of Communicative Competence

Form and Force Interactions
The Development of Negatives and Questions

Jill G. de Villiers

Psychology and Philosophy Departments
Smith College
Northampton, Massachusetts

Editors' Note

The literature on negatives and interrogatives in child language is used as a testing ground for six hypotheses on the relationship between the form and force components of speech acts. The hypotheses concerning the way form and force interrelate in acquisition are first described. A review of the acquisition of negative forms and functions follows and the hypotheses are tested against the available findings. The acquisition of interrogative forms and functions is then addressed and the hypotheses are assessed again. Finally, the two assessments are compared to see if general conclusions are possible in this area.

The author concludes that there is continuity in communicative development over the first 2 years of life; that the child begins with a limited set of form-function mappings that then broadens with age; that parents do not seem to use a limited set of mappings in their speech to small children; and, finally, that children respond well to indirect expressions of illocutionary force relying both on the content and on response strategies that initially bear little resemblance to the rules of conversation. However, the literature reveals a lack of parallel research on the two sentence modalities—in particular, on the range of forms that can serve negative functions.

contents

HYPOTHESES ABOUT FORM AND FUNCTION 196
NEGATION 196
    Form of Negatives 196
    Illocutionary Force of Negatives 199
    The Hypotheses Considered with Respect to Negation 203
INTERROGATIVES 212
    Form of Interrogatives 212
    Illocutionary Force of Interrogatives 219
    **The Hypotheses Considered with Respect
    to Interrogatives** 222
DISCUSSION 231
REFERENCES 233

Speech acts can be described as having two components: 1) a grammatical form, which conveys the propositional content; and 2) an illocutionary force, which indicates the speaker's intention in making the utterances—for example, to assert, promise, or request (Searle, 1969). Sometimes the illocutionary force is specified by an explicit performative verb, such as "I *ask* you . . . ," "I *request* that you . . . ," or "I *promise* . . . ." According to Katz (1977), one of the goals of semantic theory is to account for the illocutionary force of a sentence in the "null" situation, where there are no clues provided by nonverbal behaviors or discourse context to facilitate interpretation, rather as if it were printed in an anonymous letter.

Explicit statement of the speaker's communicative intention is rare in everyday discourse, however, and the more usual situation is one in which grammatical form is not a reliable indicator of illocutionary force. Questions are posed as declaratives, and commands masquerade as interrogatives. Thus, a listener cannot always use the form of a sentence—the words and their arrangement, or even the intonation—to decide what the speaker's intentions were in uttering it. Instead, a listener must rely on the prior discourse, or the nonverbal context, or the past history of his relationship with the speaker to work out the force of the utterance. A full account of how a listener arrives at the correct reading of a speaker's illocutionary force is a central problem for pragmatics rather than semantics, but it remains a remote goal. Nevertheless, studying the development of that interpretative ability in children has become a major research endeavor within the last 5 to 10 years.

The literature on pragmatics in child language is growing more rapidly than most researchers can digest it, especially because there are more theoretical arguments than empirical findings, and more anecdotes than statistically supported facts. However, there are many studies that do not warrant this bleak conclusion, and this review is biased toward them. To help synthesize this expanding research area, I have proposed six hypotheses about the development of form and function and their relationship. These hypotheses are not necessarily those that guided the research in the first place, but they have some intuitive plausibility and hence serve as an organizing framework for the selective review.

Two sentence modalities are the focus of discussion: negatives and interrogatives. It may seem peculiar to begin with sentence forms rather than with illocutionary forces, but there are two reasons for this choice. First, this was the direction of the field as a whole, with sentence forms being studied before functions became a popular topic of inquiry. Second, negative functions have not been studied independently of negative forms, so there is no way to start the other way around.

Following the presentation of the six hypotheses, there is a discussion of negative forms and functions. Then the hypotheses are assessed specifically with respect to negation. The development of interrogative forms and functions are then reviewed, and the hypotheses are examined again for this second modality. In the final section of the chapter the results of these two assessments are compared to see if more general conclusions can be drawn about present and future research on the interrelation of form and function in child language development.

HYPOTHESES ABOUT FORM AND FUNCTION

1. It is possible to identify in the behavior of preverbal children the communicative functions that are the precursors of illocutionary forces.
2. These precursor functions emerge in an order that is recapitulated when conventional expressions of these forces appear.
3. Children begin by using a limited set of form-function mappings, and this broadens until they are capable of using a variety of forms for any one function, and one form for a number of different functions.
4. In talking to young children, parents use a limited set of form-function mappings, which may facilitate the children's decoding of language. This usage changes as children become older and more linguistically mature.
5. Children at first understand the functions of only a limited set of "canonical" forms and have difficulty understanding indirect (i.e., "noncanonical") expressions of illocutionary force.
6. Children must rely on social and event knowledge in their interpretations of illocutionary force.

NEGATION

The study of negation has occupied researchers for well over a decade. Some of this research is discussed here before consideration of whether the six hypotheses apply to negation.

Form of Negatives

Bellugi (1967) was the first to report a detailed study of the development of negative syntax. She analyzed the negative sentences produced by Adam, Eve, and Sarah—the three children who were studied longitudinally by the Harvard group led by Brown (1973). Several stages in the development of negative forms were identified, which, Bellugi proposed, parallel the stages in the derivation of a negative sentence. According to the transformational grammar current at that time (Klima, 1964), the deep structure of a negative sentence consisted of a negative marker outside of the kernel sentence, i.e., NEG + S. Most of the earliest multiword negatives that the children produced consisted of a simple proposition preceded by the words *no* or *not*.

The next step in the derivation of the English negative consisted of placing the negative marker adjacent to the verb stem, that is, internal to the sentence. In the second stage of negation for the three children (mean lengths of utterance of 2.8 to 3.0), Bellugi identified four negative markers: *no, not, can't,* and *don't*; these were inserted adjacent to the verb in simple sentences. Because positive auxiliaries did not occur in the children's speech until some time later, *can't* and *don't* did not at this stage appear to be the negative versions of *can* and *do*. Instead, *can't* and *don't* functioned as unanalyzed wholes.

Modification of the auxiliary verbs constituted the next derivational step. The children exhibited a range of auxiliaries and their negative counterparts around mean lengths of utterance (MLUs) of 3.4 to 3.9, at which point most of the elementary syntax of negation appeared to be mastered. Of course, many more complex aspects, including the correct use of indefinites such as *not any* and *no one*, were not mastered for many months or even years after that.

Most subsequent work on the syntax of negation has focused on the first two stages identified by Bellugi. For instance, on the basis of his work on Japanese (McNeill and McNeill, 1968), Slobin's on Russian (1966), and Gregoire's study of French (1937), McNeill (1970) concluded that the development of negation begins with a negative marker external to the sentence not just in English but universally. McNeill proposed that this schema is part of a child's innate knowledge of linguistic structure, in keeping with his more general claim that children begin with the base structure and acquire transformational rules in the course of development.

An alternative source for these initial-*no* sentences was proposed by Wode (1977), who summarized data from German, Swedish, and English. He postulated four stages of early negation:

1. Single word negatives.
2. Multiword negatives with an initial negative marker that is *anaphoric* in meaning because it does not negate the proposition to which it is attached, but refers back to a previous utterance of the child or another speaker. For example, in the sequence "Let

Mommy tie it.—No Johnny tie," the *no* refers back to the previous speaker's proposal rather than negating the proposition "Johnny tie."
3. Multiword negatives with an initial nonanaphoric negative marker that does negate the proposition to which it is attached. Wode hypothesized that this stage is due to the child's overgeneralization of the negative form from stage 2. His evidence for this is that children use the forms reserved for anaphoric negatives to express the nonanaphoric meaning. For example, English children use *no* rather than *not* or *n't*. German children use *nein* rather than *nicht* or *kein*, and Swedish children use *nej* or *na* rather than *inte*. Wode suggested that the negative sentences found at this stage originate from the earlier use of anaphoric negatives rather than from an innate schema for negation.
4. The appropriate nonanaphoric negative morpheme is used internal to the sentence. Note that in this last step two problems appear to be solved simultaneously: the correct placement of the negative and the correct morpheme. Apparently the anaphoric negative never appears internal to the sentence.

When Wode proposed the preceding stages, he presented no distributional analysis of the children's speech but relied heavily on anecdotal examples from a small number of children. The lack of a distributional analysis together with the availability of evidence to refute the stages caused Park (1979) to doubt their reliability. Park's arguments were based on data he collected from one High German– and two Swiss German–speaking children. The High German–speaking child acquired nonanaphoric negative constructions before she acquired anaphoric constructions. Thus, stages 2 and 3 in Wode's system were reversed. Moreover, in the two Swiss German–speaking children, stages 2 and 3 never even appeared. The children progressed from using single-word negatives (stage 1) to using negatives—specifically, anaphoric negatives—internal to multiword constructions. Nonanaphoric negatives never occurred within sentence boundaries. Thus, in addition to skipping stages 2 and 3, the Swiss German–speaking children also used anaphoric negatives at stage 4, whereas Wode's subjects apparently used only nonanaphoric markers. After attempting to compare his results with those of Wode, Park concluded that "although the discrepancy cannot be accounted for at present, one thing is clear: Wode's theory is questionable" (p. 151).

Additional evidence to refute Wode's theoretical stages has been reported by Bloom (1970) and de Villiers and de Villiers (1979). These investigators, in contrast to Park, have objected primarily to Wode's third stage of negation—the use of multiword negatives with an initial nonanaphoric negative marker. Arguments for this stage (as well as for the one preceding it) depend heavily on sentences in which the subject is expressed, e.g.,

No the sun shining ("The sun's not shining"; Adam)
Not Fraser read it ("Fraser mustn't read it"; Eve)

Unfortunately these constructions are rarely used by very young children. In most instances of *neg + S*, the subject is not expressed, e.g., *no do that*, and it is not clear whether the subject has been "deleted" from the left or the right of the negative morpheme (Bloom, 1970). Bloom identified a small number of critical sentences in her own longitudinal study of three children, but in all cases the initial negative morpheme appeared to be anaphoric in function, negating a previous proposition. Bloom found no cases of nonanaphoric *neg + subject + predicate*. The absence of these constructions casts doubt upon Wode's third stage of negation.

De Villiers and de Villiers (1979) reanalyzed the negatives in the transcripts used by Bellugi. The results again indicated very few critical sentences in which the subject was produced and the negative was clearly intended to negate the proposition to which it was attached. There were none for Sarah, three for Adam, and two for Eve—scoring on the conservative side. We would have concluded that the evidence for Wode's third stage was equivocal, were it not for the fact that our own son, Nicholas, was bombarding us with examples of the critical sentences between the age of 23 and 29 months. These sentences, with expressed subjects and nonanaphoric initial negatives, are shown in Table 1.

In order to account for such disparate findings, we offer yet a third hypothesis regarding the source of nonanaphoric negative forms. They might derive from the input that certain parents provide, parents who engage in relatively polite negative discourse but reinforce their sentences with an initial *no*. In other words, a child's production of initial-*no* sentences during the third stage is neither the result of an innate schema nor an overgeneralization of the anaphoric *no*, but a hypothesis about the structure of negatives that derives from the sentences he hears adults use (for example, see Table 2). As such, it is not a universal stage but rather one option that some children may adopt for a limited time, and as shown below, for limited purposes.

Illocutionary Force of Negatives

The first systematic study of the semantics of negation was reported by McNeill and McNeill (1968) for two Japanese children. The authors

Table 1. Nicholas's negative sentences with the subject specified

Age and MLU		Rejection		Denial
25 m 2.2 MLU	7/21 8/2 8/13	No mummy do it. No Daddy change you. No Dampa sit on dat.	7/17 8/18	No Nana bought it. Weewee no strikes again.
26 m	8/23 9/8 9/18	No Safi pat it down. No my want one. No you tuts dat. No Eric come in my house.	9/9 9/10	My fweetie's no gone. Ticken's no need dars.
27 m 2.6 MLU	9/22 9/23 10/21	Not you have muffins. Not Sarah take it down. No your mummy buy one.	9/22 10/13	Nunu no like it. It's not. It's not, Daddy. You no need a pooh.
28 m 3.1 MLU	10/25 10/30 10/31 11/1 11/2 11/3 11/4 11/8 11/10 11/12 11/12 11/16 11/18	No Hanneke have tea. I don't like go in dat playground I don't like Daddy putting my socks on. I don't like to eat for five minutes. I don't like it half. Not you have toast. Not him come up wiff me. Not him come on here. Not him follow Nunu. I don't want watch the news. I don't want Hanneke come. Not Hanneke come in my house. I don't like Hanneke come in my house. Not Mummy do her fing. You can't eat it. I don't like go to sleep. I don't want to. I don't like medsin. You can't drink it. Not Nunu have it. Not you push it. I don't like you cut my hair.	10/28 11/7 11/13	It's not sharp. She's not having a shower. She's not upstairs. I not hurting Teddy.
3.1 MLU				

continued

Table 1. (*Continued*)

Age and MLU		Rejection	Denial
29 m 3.4 MLU	11/22	Not anybody eat it. You can't have it.	
	12/5	You not put me up in my room. (1st internal *no* rejection)	
	12/28	Don't eat a nose. (1st spontaneous *don't* imperative)	

argued that there were three dimensions of negative meaning involved. One concerns whether or not the speaker is denying the *truth* of a proposition versus the *existence* of some object. For example, "That isn't a car" (pointing to a truck) versus "There's no spoon" (looking at the place setting). The second dimension distinguishes between the denial of an *internal* wish and some *external* truth, e.g., "I don't like ice cream" versus "The door isn't open." The third dimension was called *entailment*, that is, whether or not the negative sentence entails the truth of a second proposition, e.g., "No, that's a felt-tip, not a ball point" versus "No, that's not a ball point."

The McNeills were interested in how forms and functions might relate to each other in development. Their analysis received its direction from the fact that Japanese has different negative markers associated with the different functions that the McNeills isolated. The simple forms in Japanese are as follows:

1. *Nai* as an auxiliary is used for nonentailing denial.
2. *Nai* as an adjective is used to assert the nonexistence of an object.
3. *Lya* is for internal denial, e.g., "I do not want."
4. *Liya* is used for entailing denial, i.e., the denial of a previous proposition plus an entailed assertion.

Table 2. Peter's negatives to his son Nicholas in a 15-minute interaction when Nicholas was 28 months old

See, it's not flat on the bottom.
No, you shouldn't make a hole in the bottom.
It's not a good idea to make a hole in the bottom.
No, let Daddy do it first.
No, I don't think you'll be able to cut straight.
No, don't cut too much on the front.
Why don't you cut a bit off here?
I don't want you to cut yourself with that knife.
You sure that knife's not too sharp?
No, I don't think you should put more holes in it.
No, don't cut two holes.
I hope you're not making a big mess back there.

McNeill and McNeill found that their subjects began by using one form—*nai* as an adjective—to express both external and internal denial. Later on, they used the *nai* adjective for external denials and *lya* for internal denials. Last to appear were entailing denials expressed by *liya*.

Pea (1979) pointed out the inadequacy of the preceding dimensional approach to the functions that negative sentences serve. In particular, he argued that the dimension *existence . . . truth* has a different logical status from the other two dimensions, in that only sentences can have truth values.

Bloom (1970) proposed a different framework for classifying the functions of negative sentences, one that appears to capture the important distinctions drawn by the McNeills, but in categories rather than binary dimensions. The major categories were:

1. *Nonexistence:* Some object does not exist in the context, or the child does not see it but has good reason to expect it. For example, a child at lunchtime might say, "There's no fork."
2. *Rejection:* The child opposes some object, action, or event that is either present, proposed, or imminent. For instance, a parent attempts to brush a child's hair and the child says, "Don't brush my hair."
3. *Denial:* The child negates the truth of a proposition stated by someone else or earlier by the child. For instance, someone accuses the child of being greedy and the child replies, "No, I'm not greedy."

Bloom found that these different negative functions were expressed in sentences at different points in development: nonexistence first, then rejection, then denial, for all three of her subjects.

In an illuminating discussion of the functions of negation, Pea (1979) described several functions that do not fit into Bloom's classification. Moreover, Bloom's original "nonexistence" category included a variety of phenomena: when a child expects to see a fork in a place setting and remarks, "no fork"; when a child hides a cookie under a cup and says, "no more cookie"; and when a child tries to push a broken car and says "not go." Although Bloom and Lahey (1978) proposed a further category of "non-occurrence" to deal with the last utterance, Pea suggested that the categories could be cut even finer than this.

One of the major problems for a functional analysis is to determine what are the psychologically real categories for the *child*, not the adult coder (de Villiers and de Villiers, 1978). Because Pea's concern was with the very earliest manifestations of negation, he could not use the child's differential use of linguistic markers as a clue to the psychological reality of the categories. Instead, Pea justified his categories by appealing to the nonverbal behavior of the child in the situation. His classification is slightly more differentiated than Bloom's:

1. *Rejection:* The child rejects an event, person, object, or activity that has been proposed or is imminent from the action context or the previous utterance. This includes responses to questions such as "Would you like a cookie?"
2. *Disappearance:* Some stimulus disappears or ceases, as when someone walks out of the room, or a record stops playing.
3. *Unfulfilled expectation:* The child expects something that does not happen, as when a Jack-in-the-box fails to pop up, or a child fails to find something in its usual place.
4. *Truth-functional negation:* These are a subset of Bloom's *denial* negatives in that the category includes only negatives in response to a proposition that is true or false given the truth conditions of the language, not the child's own motivations. So whereas the answer "no" to the question "Is that your brother?" would be classified as truth-functional negation, the answer "no" to the question "Do you want to go to the movies?" is classified as a rejection. This distinction is similar to McNeill's internal-external denial dimension.
5. *Self-prohibition:* Negatives occur in small children who sometimes reprimand themselves for engaging in some forbidden activity, as when a child approaches an electrical socket and says "No!" The utterance is not always effective in stopping the act, regardless of the speaker from who it originates.

The Hypotheses Considered with Respect to Negation

1. *It is possible to identify in the behavior of preverbal children the communicative functions that are the precursors of illocutionary forces.*

Many researchers, and all parents, have observed that the intention to communicate precedes the production of speech. Dore (1975), for example, has argued that prior to speech infants show evidence of attempting to communicate with adults, particularly when striving to achieve some goal. Bates, Camaioni, and Volterra (1975) maintained that the appearance of these prelinguistic communicative attempts characterizes the middle stage in a three-stage account of communicative development. The three stages are as follows:

a. A *perlocutionary* stage, in which the child has a systematic effect on his listener without having any intentional, conscious control over that effect.

b. An *illocutionary* stage, in which the child intentionally uses nonverbal signals to convey requests and to direct adult attention to objects and events.
c. A *locutionary* stage, in which the child constructs propositions and utters speech sounds within the same performative sequences that he previously expressed nonverbally.

Although this sequence seems indisputable, there is still considerable debate about when to attribute each stage to the child and whether they are stages in the strict sense of the term (Piaget, 1970). The difficulties are twofold. First, how can one tell when a child has moved from the *perlocutionary* to the *illocutionary* (intentional) stage of communication? Second, should we say that the illocutionary forces found during the illocutionary stage are like the forces expressed by an adult?

The first difficulty is pervasive not only within studies of child language but in the whole field of communication, including ethology. Within child language the arguments have reached an impasse. Investigators have demonstrated that mothers often ascribe communicative intent to infants whose entrance into the illocutionary stage is questionable. Moreover, mothers typically try to interpret the function of a vocalization from the earliest months of an infant's life (Wolff, 1969), but there is no way to know whether their interpretations are right or wrong. At a later point, the adult relies not only on the child's vocalizations but also on his nonverbal behaviors and the circumstances of the utterance (Ryan, 1974). The adult again acts as though the child were trying to communicate; and even if the interpretation is wrong, the child presumably learns something about the effect that his behavior produces. Distinguishing the perlocutionary from the illocutionary stage is very difficult because utterances from both stages have an effect on the adult. It is also very difficult to determine the function of an early utterance because there is no way to tell whether the effect on the adult was the one intended. It is apparent that adults continually make guesses as to the child's intentions. The rationale for using these guesses as data is that there is no more direct way of studying the child's communicative intentions.

A similar dilemma occurs within the study of animal communication. Communication is frequently defined rather broadly to include situations in which a signal from one animal to another provides information about the likely behavior of the sender. The problem then is how to distinguish intentional signals from other kinds of stimuli that provide information about future behavior. Is the noise of a stampeding herd a signal? When a bird spreads its wings to take flight, is that communication? Ethologists are in much the same position as developmental psychologists in that they are reluctant to grapple with the sticky question of intention or purpose on the part of the organism. Instead, they traditionally talk of signals as behaviors *specialized* (by evolution, usually) for the purposes of communication. That does not necessarily mean that the behaviors can serve no other function than a communicative one, but it does mean that the behaviors have undergone a process of formalization, becoming ritualized, abbreviated, or exaggerated so that their signal value is accentuated (Smith, 1977). For instance, some species of birds perform a rather elaborate display of wing spreading and neck extending. This display presumably serves as a signal of possible impending flight because the behavior is quite beyond what would be sufficient preparatory movements. Similarly, a dog bares its teeth as a signal of attack. "Intention movements" such as these frequently have become formalized as signals in a variety of animal species.

Bates (1976) argued that a similar process of ritualization accompanies the child's transition from perlocutionary to illocutionary communication. For instance, a 6-month-old baby might try to get an out-of-reach object by extending his arm toward it and whining or fretting. An adult who sees this behavior will attribute a clear intention to the child's behavior, and will probably pass the object to the child. The same baby at 9 months will extend his arm only a little way, fret, and look at the adult. The gesture evolves into a kind of pointing, which is a *formalized* version of the extended reach. It is abbreviated, falls short of achieving its goal, and is used communicatively. Thus it is analogous to the intention movements of other species. Perhaps the emergence of conventional signals accompanied by efforts to achieve eye contact with an adult marks the point at which we can claim that a child is *expressing* communicative functions prior to speech. Sugarman (this volume) argues that the point at which to begin the study of communication is when a child directs goal-appropriate behaviors toward another person. In other words, communication requires that a child contact a second person in an effort to engage him in an activity with an object. Thus, the child in the scenario on p. 34 is demonstrating the ability to communicate when he "holds jar toward adult—looks at adult and vocalizes—adult takes jar from child, vocalizes to child." At an earlier phase, the child does not direct these social signals to an adult, although the adult might nevertheless guess that the child needs help in achieving some goal. No one could deny that children have intentions or goals before this point, but we are concerned here with the communication of those intentions via conventionalized signals.

This point requires elaboration when we turn to the specific communicative functions of negation. Darwin (1955) claimed that the early negative is expressed universally with nasal sounds (Jesperson, 1917) and that the head shake is a "natural" expression of aversion, which perhaps is derived from turning the head away in rejection of food or an aversive stimulus. Hypothesizing that these natural expressions sometimes serve functions similar to those of words, Pea (1979) began his study of early negation when his subjects were 8 months of age. He traced the development of negation from the initial use of headshakes to the later use of words (including *stop, gone,* and *away*). Headshakes were first used around 1 year of age, with a range in Pea's six subjects of 10 to 14 months. In every case, the headshake was an expression of rejection when it first occurred. However, there was a gap of from 1 to 9 months between the first use of a headshake and the first use of negative words.

Examining Pea's functional data on gestural versus verbal expressions, it is apparent that gestural expressions were limited almost entirely to two categories: rejection and self-prohibition. There were no headshakes serving the function of truth-functional negation or disappearance negation. Does this mean that these functions do not appear prior to speech? This conclusion may be warranted for truth-functional negation. Early headshakes could not have served this function because truth-functional negation requires a response to the truth of a proposition, which in turn requires understanding the language. When children understand enough language to determine truth, they also have some spoken words and may choose to use speech instead of a headshake to convey their meanings.

The absence of headshakes as comments on disappearance/nonexistence is more puzzling and may require a different explanation. A headshake may not be the "natural" response to disappearance. An adult would more likely shrug or show some form of surprise. These behaviors could also be considered conventionalized, and one could search for their appearance in the responses of infants to unexpected events. In any case, by restricting his attention to headshakes as the only conventional expression of negation, Pea might have overlooked other gestural precursors of negation. I am not suggesting that the selection of other possible precursors is going to be easy. I am arguing that the choice of precursor *form* could bias the observation of precursor *function*, and that this is a serious problem in a study concerned with the order of emergence of these functions.

> 2. *These precursor functions emerge in an order that is recapitulated when conventional expressions of these forces appear.*

Pea (1979) analyzed three negative functions—rejection, disappearance/nonexistence, and truth-functional negation—in terms of their cognitive complexity. He argued that rejection negations are the simplest, because they "express inner attitudes of rejection toward behaviors, events or objects that are embedded in the child's very early motor-affective activities." Because the topic of rejection is right there in the context, there is no need for internal representation. In contrast, nonexistence/disappearance requires some cognitive representation because the object is not present to the child's senses. The child is remarking upon some discrepancy between his expectations and his sense experience. Finally, truth-functional negation demands internal representation of an even higher order, because it is concerned with the truth of propositions (see also Bloom and Lahey, 1978).

This seems like an eminently reasonable ordering for the child's cognitive development, but it is not obvious that cognitive development should predict the order in which negative functions are expressed, or that this order should be the same for conventional gestures, words, and sentences. Yet Pea presented evidence that the first gestures are indeed limited to conveying the hypothetically earliest function, rejection. It therefore becomes evident why it is important to know whether headshakes constitute the only conventional gesture of negation: it may be that the order of emergence reported by Pea is an artifact of choosing to study the gesture most well suited to the expression of rejection. Until further work on early gestures is available, it is not possible to accept Pea's hypothesis as proven.

Turning to the first words, Pea (1979) found that words serving the different functions emerged in an order that was consistent with the cognitive complexity of the functions. However, the size of the interval separating the first and second functions seems to be smaller than the one separating the second and third functions. In Pea's data, the temporal gap between rejection and disappearance/nonexistence was smaller than the one between disappearance/nonexistence and truth-functional negation. Bloom (1970) also reported that the single-word expression for rejection emerged first in her three subjects.

Even if rejection is the first function to emerge in single-word speech, we cannot assume that rejection will be the first function to appear in sentences. Indeed, Bloom (1970) found that sentences indicating nonexistence appeared before those expressing rejection, which appeared before those expressing denial. Furthermore, as these sentences grew in syntactic complexity, the order of development recapitulated the order in which the functions initially appeared in sentences. Variation in auxiliary forms occurred in sentences expressing nonexistence before it occurred in sentences expressing rejection (Bloom and Lahey, 1978).

De Villiers and de Villiers (1979) reported individual differences in the frequency with which various negative functions were expressed in sentences. These differences might interact with the order of syntactic elaboration. For instance, Nicholas had a clear preference for the expression of rejection, but the form of those rejections was rather stereotyped and primitive, namely *no + S.* In contrast, he produced rarer but well-formed expressions of denial during the same period. Thus, in a limited sense, his denials were more syntactically advanced than his rejections.

To summarize, the data concerning the order of emergence of negative functions are somewhat equivocal. In keeping with its complexity, truth-functional negation is the last to emerge. However, the claim that the order in which the functions emerge nonverbally corresponds to the order of their appearance in words and syntax does not seem to be well supported at present.

>   3. *Children begin by using a limited set of form-function mappings, and this broadens until they are capable of using a variety of forms for any one function, and one form for a number of different functions.*

It has already been pointed out that Pea's (1979) subjects reserved the headshake for a limited set of functions, but it is not known whether the use of the headshake later expands to incorporate truth-functional and disappearance negation. The children in Pea's study also reserved certain words for certain functions, but the significance is not clear. For instance, *gone, bye-bye,* and *stop* were reserved for disappearance, but these words are not multipurpose negatives. *No* and *don't* were the primary expressions of rejection, with *no* and *not* used for truth-functional negation. The children agreed on the uses of these conventional forms, but each child also had some idiosyncratic uses traceable to the parent's speech: *mustn't bite* in one child for self-prohibition, *I n't* (Oxfordshire slang) in another for rejection, and so on.

Developmentally, the word *no* is used first for rejection and self-prohibition. In explaining this restricted use of *no*, Edwards (1978) and Pea (1979) hypothesized that constraints on the child's actions provide the source for early negation. Later, negation becomes internally represented and truth-functional negation becomes possible. Hence, the initial use of *no* for purposes related to constraints on the child's behavior eventually expands to include the rejection of truth-statements.

However, it may take several years for a child to complete the transition from using *no* for action-based rejections and self-prohibitions to using *no* for logical truth-functional negation. Studies indicate that young children do not respond directly to truth-value but rather ask themselves "Would I say that?" For example, de Villiers and Tager-Flusberg (1975) uncovered a large effect of *plausibility* on the ability of their young subjects to respond correctly to negative sentences. Similarly, Kim (1980) found that 3- and 4-year-olds have great difficulty responding to the truth value of negative sentences that are true but not particularly plausible in the context. Therefore 2-year-olds cannot be said to have completed the transition from action-based to logical negation, which is a process that continues through the preschool years.

When the level of the sentence is considered, it again seems that children have preferred expressions for certain functions (de Villiers and de Villiers, 1979). Our son, Nicholas, used *no* + *S* almost exclusively to express rejection; however, internally positioned negatives did appear in sentences serving as denials. Adam, on the other hand, tended to use the initial *no* for denial, and *don't* for rejection. Eve, like Nicholas, rarely used *don't* in the early months. Both Eve and Nicholas preferred the initial *no* for rejection. As is shown below, these individual differences in form-function pairings are systematically related to the parent's use of negation.

Unfortunately, there are no data on later uses of negative forms. This would seem to be a fertile area for future research.

> 4. *In talking to young children, parents use a limited set of form-function mappings, which may facilitate the children's decoding of language. This usage changes as children become older and more linguistically mature.*

Our study showed that Adam's mother used sentences with an initial *no* predominantly for denial (deVilliers and deVilliers, 1979). Most of her rejection negatives were imperatives beginning with *don't*, which is the same pattern that occurs in Adam's speech. In contrast, Eve's mother and Nicholas' parents used initial *no* sentences for rejection, primarily the rejection of some aspect of their children's behavior. These sentences were usually polite negatives with an emphatic *no* at the beginning. Very few of these parental rejections were direct imperatives beginning with *don't*, and neither Eve nor Nicholas used any *don't* imperative rejections in this time period. In an effort to illustrate the different parental uses of *don't*, the speech directed to Adam is compared with the speech directed to Eve in Table 3. The sentences with *don't* that are cited in this table illustrate the various nonanaphoric uses of this marker that were recorded when the children's MLUs were below 2.6. The difference in the children's own use of *don't* is readily understandable from this table.

Turning to the use of anaphoric negatives, Adam and his parents as well as Eve and her parents again showed a restricted use of particular forms for particular functions. Adam's mother used anaphoric negatives to deny some earlier statement and so did Adam; Eve's mother used anaphoric negatives to reject actions, as did Eve.

Table 3. Comparison of parental uses of "don't"

Adam's mother's use of "don't"	Eve's mother's use of "don't"
Why don't you read *Shadow* yourself?	Why don't you call Grandma?
Why don't you look at some of the toys in the basket?	Oh, you don't wanna talk to Grandma.
Why don't you read to me?	You don't want milk, honey, you've just had some juice.
You don't need a pencil.	I don't think Mr. Fraser wants any water.
Why don't you take that over and show it to him?	I don't think so.
Don't pull Mommy.	I don't have it.
Don't take those out.	Why don't you put Rackety-Boom back in the toy box?
Don't jump.	Why don't you go lay down on the floor?
You don't have anything else to put in the box, do you?	You don't want anything to eat?
Don't hit his feet.	I don't think the man wants to taste it.
Why don't you come over here and play with the ball?	You don't need any more right now.
Don't touch.	Why don't you stay there?
I don't hear a horn.	You don't dance sitting down, you have to stand up to dance.
Why don't you write that?	Why don't you come in and sit in your chair, huh?
I don't know.	But you don't like tomato soup.
No, don't take his head off.	I don't know what you said.
Adam, you don't tell him what to write.	You don't want this.
Don't sit on that.	

What is currently lacking is a longitudinal study of form-function mappings in the negative sentences used by parents, to see if the forms broaden in use with the increasing ability or age of the child. From the data examined, it is doubtful that the results would be striking. An examination of Table 3 should persuade the reader that, at least by the time the children had MLUs of 2.6, their parents were providing a very rich input with regard to form-function mappings, despite the individual style variation. Even Adam's mother, who provided the clearest data on the use of *don't* in rejection imperatives, also used *don't* in lots of "*Why don't you . . .*" sentences, which do not even have a negative force, but rather make positive suggestions. Furthermore, Eve's mother used a variety of forms to convey rejections of her child's behavior. Most of these rejections, however, were disguised as denials: "I don't think Mr. Fraser wants any water"; "You don't want milk, honey, you've just had some juice."

In short, whereas some form-function pairings are systematic in these parents' speech, and their children adopt them readily, the overall impression is of diversity in the input. Some forms are used for widely different purposes (e.g., *don't*) and some functions are expressed by a variety of forms, some rather indirect.

> 5. *Children at first understand the functions of only a limited set of "canonical" forms and have difficulty understanding indirect (i.e., "noncanonical") expressions of illocutionary force.*

Dore (1977) proposed that illocutionary forces have associated with them a canonical sentence form, although they may also be expressed via noncanonical forms. Table 4 is taken from his paper, and illustrates the association of form and force in his model. Motivation for hypothesis 5 stems from Dore's two hypotheses concerning the listener's interpretation of illocutionary force:

> When a speaker uses the canonical sentence form of an illocutionary act, the expected illocutionary effect and the expected perlocutionary effect are unequivocally recognized by the hearer as a conventional pair, without inferences on the part of the hearer about the beliefs, expectations or motives of the speaker; but when the speaker uses a noncanonical sentence form of the same illocutionary act, the hearer will make inferences of varying degrees concerning the speaker's expected perlocutionary effect. (p. 236)

> If a hearer has some belief which makes him question the automatic illocutionary-perlocutionary effect relation of a speaker's illocutionary act of canonical sentence form, he will try to infer a different expected perlocutionary effect on the part of the speaker. (p. 237)

When these hypotheses are applied to negation, it would seem that the canonical form for expressing rejection is the negative imperative, and the canonical form for denial is the negative declarative. Consequently, one would predict that children might have some difficulty understanding rejections phrased noncanonically as declaratives. Sur-

Table 4. The relations between some basic illocutionary act types and the canonical and noncanonical forms used to realize the illocutionary act types

Sentence form	Illocutionary act types[a]			
	Assertive	Question	Requestive	Emotive
Declarative	X		O	
Interrogative		X	O	
Imperative			X	
Exclamatory			O	X

Reprinted by permission from Dore, J. 1977. Children's illocutionary acts. *In* R. Freedle (ed.), Discourse Production and Comprehension, p. 236. Lawrence Erlbaum Assocs., Inc., Hillsboro, N.J.

[a] X = canonical sentence form for corresponding illocutionary act type; O = noncanonical forms for the requestive type.

prisingly, there is no systematic work on this prediction. In the previously cited study of spontaneous speech, there is little evidence that children fail to understand indirect expressions of rejection. However, the parents who used indirect, polite rejections in these studies also tended to reinforce these expressions with an initial *no*, possibly as insurance against a failure of understanding. A full answer to the question of whether children have difficulty with noncanonical forms of negation must await further research.

> 6. *Children must rely on social and event knowledge in their interpretations of illocutionary force.*

Dore discussed the general form of this hypothesis, i.e., that hearers must use the context to interpret illocutionary forces. Clark and Lucy (1975) were also interested in this general hypothesis. They suggested that adults take longer to process indirect expressions because they go through certain steps:

1. Find a literal interpretation of the utterance.
2. Check its plausibility against the context.
3. If the literal interpretation is implausible, use certain "rules of conversation" to arrive at the intended meaning.

As Dore points out, we know very little about these rules of conversation for adults, and even less for children. However, the prediction is that children should fare better at interpreting the illocutionary force of an utterance when both the speaker and the context are familiar to them. Given such familiarity, children might recognize when a speaker is using an idiom, i.e., a form—even a noncanonical form—that consistently serves only one function, and consequently can be decoded without access to its literal interpretation.

INTERROGATIVES

The development of interrogatives has also been studied for well over a decade. Some of this research is reviewed before considering whether the six hypotheses apply to interrogatives.

Form of Interrogatives

The grammatical expression of questions in English involves three linguistic devices: rising intonation, *wh*-word fronting, and placement of the auxiliary in front of the subject noun phrase. Because the first device, rising intonation, is often considered the earliest hallmark of a question, it is important to consider the reliability and generality of this relationship. In comparing yes-no and *wh*- questions in adult speech, one finds that rising intonation marks the former questions more reliably than the latter (Crystal, 1978; Garvey, 1975). Otherwise, little is known about the use of intonation in yes/no and *wh-* questions. Crystal (1978) pointed out that intonation does not bear a simple relationship either to sentence modality or to discourse function. For example, the use of a rising intonation on yes-no questions occurs only on a probabilistic basis. Second, the judgment of intonation contour is not a simple matter. Finally, there might be individual differences among children in the use of intonation for certain functions (for a brief review, see de Villiers and de Villiers, 1978).

In their study of the speech of Adam, Eve, and Sarah, Klima and Bellugi (1966) described the use of rising intonation as well as *wh*-word fronting and auxiliary placement in questions. When the children's average MLU was 1.75, yes-no questions appeared as simple sentences with rising intonation. The three children had no auxiliary verbs in their speech at this time, so there were no other formal means of expressing the interrogative. The *wh*-questions that were produced during this period are characterized best as routines because the children had very few variants: "What's that?", "Where (NP) go?", and "What (NP) doing?" Furthermore, more complex *wh*-forms were not reliably comprehended.

Within a short time, Adam, Eve, and Sarah's use of *wh*-questions increased, and the *wh*-word began to function in place of a specific syntactic constituent that was absent from the sentence. The children at this point (average MLU of 2.75) seemed to understand many more of the *wh*-questions that were addressed to them. At least in natural conversation (but see below). However, auxiliary verbs were still absent in their own speech.

Klima and Bellugi (1966) reported that auxiliary verbs eventually did appear during the third period, that is, when the children's MLUs averaged 3.5. Furthermore, in yes-no questions, the children correctly "inverted" the subject and auxiliary, as in "Can I have a piece of paper?" and "Does the kitty stand up?" *Wh*-questions, however, appeared with incorrectly placed auxiliaries: "Why kitty can't stand up?" and "Where the other Joe will drive?" This discrepancy was taken as evidence that the children were learning transformational rules (such as auxiliary inversion), and that there was some limit on the number of transformational rules they could use in any one sentence. Thus, when the children fronted the *wh*-word, they failed to use auxiliary inversion.

A stage in which children invert subject NP and auxiliary in yes/no questions but not in *wh*-questions was not found in two other studies in the literature. Hecht and Morse (1974) tallied the percentage of inversion in the two types of questions in samples of speech collected from 12 children. The children were chronologically the same age (30 months), but varied widely in linguistic development. Despite the broad range of abilities studied, the results indicated that no child had a higher rate of auxiliary inversion for yes/no questions than for *wh*-questions.

Ingram and Tyack (1979) analyzed samples of questions collected by parents from 21 children with ages ranging between 2 and 4 years. Age and the upper boundary on utterance length were used to group the children into stages roughly corresponding to those of Klima and Bellugi. The two types of questions were then compared on the percentage of inversion. There again was no stage in which inversion occurred for yes/no but not for *wh*-questions; instead, overall rates of inversion were equivalent. Ingram and Tyack pointed out that the very few uninverted *wh*-questions that did appear involved uncontracted auxiliaries. This finding led them to suggest that some children might treat uncontracted and contracted auxiliaries differently with respect to inversion. Unfortunately, they do not publish any data that might support that proposal.

Both of these research teams used rather gross procedures to study developmental stages, and their methodologies might have obscured some subtle aspects of syntactic acquisition. Kuczaj and Maratsos (1975), however, undertook a more detailed longitudinal study of one child named Abe. They analyzed his developing knowledge of auxiliary verbs—specifically *can* and *will*—in declaratives, yes/no questions, and *wh*-questions. Their data were not obtained from spontaneous speech but from elicited imitation, a procedure that has received a mixed review within psycholinguistics (Bloom, 1973; Slobin and Welsh, 1973). Over a period of several months at the time when Abe was 2.5 to 2.9 years old (MLU 3.01 to 3.25), Kuczaj and Maratsos presented Abe with various model sentences to imitate. The models were of several types:

1. Ungrammatical declaratives with improperly tensed main verbs: "The monkey's mommy will yelled at the lion."
2. Ungrammatical declaratives with misplaced auxiliaries: "The boy push will the elephant."
3. Grammatical declaratives: "The nice monkey can kiss his little sister."
4. Ungrammatical yes/no questions with improperly tensed main verbs: "Will the mean turtle pushed the sand castle?"
5. Grammatical yes/no questions: "Can the little boy yell at the monkey?"

6. Ungrammatical *wh*-questions with misplaced auxiliaries: "Where the little boy's mommy will bake chocolate cookies?"
7. Grammatical *wh*-questions: "What can a skinny snake wiggle very fast?"

By studying Abe's correct and incorrect imitations, the researchers were able to uncover his developing knowledge of the auxiliary system of *can* and *will* before these forms appeared in his spontaneous speech.

The results revealed that Abe distinguished grammatical declaratives and yes-no questions from their ungrammatical counterparts. When given ungrammatical models of these forms, he often corrected the tense of the main verb even in his earliest imitations. He also corrected the auxiliary placement in ungrammatical declarative sentences. More important for our present discussion, however, was his imitation of grammatical yes-no and *wh*- questions. Like the subjects in Klima and Bellugi's study, Abe inverted auxiliaries in yes/no questions but not in *wh*-questions. At the same time that he imitated grammatical yes/no questions correctly, he imitated grammatical *wh*-questions by either omitting the auxiliary (6/10 times) or placing it after the subject (4/10 times). Furthermore, he echoically imitated *wh*-questions that contained misplaced (i.e., "uninverted") auxiliaries (8/10 times). It appears from these data that Abe preferred uninverted auxiliaries in *wh*-questions but inverted auxiliaries in yes/no questions. The authors noted that Abe went on to show this pattern in his own spontaneous speech, but they do not provide these data.

Given the discrepancies in the literature, it is worth taking a closer look at Kuczaj and Maratsos' (1975) study. The present author has some doubts about the use of elicited imitation because the models are contextually inappropriate, even when they are grammatical (see, e.g., Tager-Flusberg, de Villiers, and Hakuta, 1982). The problems are even greater when ungrammatical models are used because they also could distort the subject's data base. This latter possibility cannot be ruled out in the Kuczaj and Maratsos study. Notice that Abe received only correctly inverted yes/no questions as models, but that half of the *wh*-models were uninverted. Although it is interesting that Abe accepted the uninverted *wh*-questions so readily, it can be argued that he did not have an equivalent opportunity to demonstrate his acceptance of uninverted yes/no questions. Of course there was good reason not to present uninverted yes/no questions in that they are virtually identical to declaratives out of context, as they are in this procedure. However, suppose the ungrammatical *wh*-question models had consisted of sentences with *correct* auxiliary placement and improperly tensed main verbs. Then would Abe have shown the same phenomenon? To summarize, when the elicited imitation procedure is used to tap knowledge of the language that is not yet manifest in spontaneous speech, the influence of the models must be considered in assessing the findings.

Erreich (1980) carried out one of the most complete studies of inversion in which she corrected many of the flaws in earlier research. Her 18 subjects ranged in MLU from 2.66 to 4.26 and were preselected for being at an intermediate stage in the acquisition of auxiliaries. Subjects who never used auxiliaries or used them consistently correctly were excluded from the study. Erreich collected spontaneous questions as well as elicited questions over a series of one to three hour-long sessions with each child. For instance, the elicitation of yes/no questions consisted of saying to the child *Ask X if S*, e.g., "Ask Anne if she has any sisters." For *wh*-questions, there were two general forms: *Ask X NP*, e.g., "Ask Anne her mommy's name," and *Ask X wh-term infinitive NP*, e.g., "Ask Anne where to put the book." Notice that the eliciting prompts are biased in the opposite way to the models in Kuczaj and Maratsos' study: the yes-no eliciting prompts contain an uninverted auxiliary while the *wh*-prompts do not.

Results of Erreich's analysis indicated that the rate of inversion was equal for *wh*- and yes-no questions for 10 of the children. Five other children presented a pattern not yet reported: optional inversion in *wh*-questions but uninverted auxiliaries in yes/no questions. However, close inspection of the data does not suggest that this unusual pattern is a product of the elicitation prompts per se. Since the elicited questions of both types were inverted less often than spontaneous questions, Erreich attributed the difference to the relative difficulty of the elicitation task. Erreich concluded that children treat aux-inversion equivalently for the two question forms. The weight of existing evidence is certainly in favor of that conclusion.

Other studies have dealt with the development of auxiliaries in particular types of interrogative sentences. Kuczaj and Brannick (1979) used imitation and judgment tasks with preschool children to assess their knowledge of the auxiliary placement rule in different kinds of *wh*-questions. Because the psychological reality of auxiliary inversion has been questioned (e.g., Maratsos, 1978), Kuczaj and Brannick used the phrase auxiliary *placement* rather than auxiliary *inversion*. The results of this study indicate that the auxiliary placement rule is learned in a piecemeal fashion rather than across-the-board. For instance, questions beginning with *what* and *where* had correctly placed auxiliaries more frequently than did questions beginning with other *wh*-words (in particular *how long* and *how come*). Thus, the children imitated modal auxiliaries correctly in some kinds of *wh*-questions, but failed to do so in others.

Since their subjects did not apply the auxiliary placement rule to all questions simultaneously, Kuczaj and Brannick carefully analyzed each child's pattern of responding to uncover developmental stages in the correct use of the rule, as well as any overgeneralizations to *how come* questions in which the auxiliary should be in post-subject position: "How come he can go?" They uncovered several stages or patterns of responding to grammatical *wh*-sentences. Only three children consistently produced uninverted auxiliaries. All of the other children varied in their use of auxiliaries. Sometimes the children positioned the auxiliaries correctly, but other times they either positioned them incorrectly or omitted them, depending on the specific *wh*-word used. However, in contrast to the pattern Abe presented, ungrammatical *wh*-questions with uninverted auxiliaries were more difficult for the children to imitate than grammatical *wh*-questions. In other words, the children were much more likely to move auxiliaries from the uninverted position to the correct sentence position than to move them from the correct to the uninverted position.

Erreich (1980) also found different rates of auxiliary inversion/ placement in the presence of different *wh*-words, although there is little agreement across studies as to the order of difficulty. Erreich's subjects inverted more with *which* (one), *who, what,* and *where,* and less with *how, why,* and *when.* Labov and Labov (1976), in a study of *wh*-inversion in a single subject, found that *wh*-words influenced inversion in the following descending order: *how, which, who, where, what, when, and why.* The variability belies any simple account.

A broader question concerns the nature of the rule being learned. Kuczaj and Brannick (1979) favored the conclusion that children begin with rules of limited scope or generality. On the other hand, Erreich (1980) argued that the child could have a general rule from the start, but not necessarily know the entire domain of application of that rule. The child would have to learn, item by item, the membership of the category on which the rule operates. Unfortunately the empirical data do not easily distinguish between the two views, as can be seen in the following research.

Detailed information on the placement of auxiliaries in yes/no questions is available from Kuczaj and Maratsos (1983). They collected longitudinal data on the spontaneous speech of two children: Abe and his younger brother Ben. In addition, they analyzed cross-sectional samples from 14 other children. In the MLU range 3.0–6.5, the children reliably produced yes/no questions with auxiliaries in sentence-initial position; declaratives also showed correct auxiliary placement. It can be argued that by this time children know general rules involving a broad grammatical category of "auxiliary." However, the authors made two observations that call this hypothesis into question. First, some auxiliaries such as *haven't* and *couldn't* appeared in declaratives several months before they were used in interrogatives. If young children have only a broad undifferentiated auxiliary category, then why did this occur? Second, Maratsos and Chalkley (1980) argued that children learn syntactic classes by observing correlations in the behavior of terms in different contexts. This hypothesis implies that: 1) children should be able to use the declarative context to predict which elements can occur in the initial position of interrogatives; and 2) children ought to make predictable errors because some terms that behave like auxiliaries in declaratives cannot be the initial elements of yes/no questions. For example, the child who says, "I better do this" should be prone to say, "Better I do this?" Kuczaj and Maratsos, however, found no such overgeneralizations.

An alternative position might be that children learn the auxiliary placement rule in a piecemeal fashion for yes/no interrogatives just as they seem to do for *wh*-questions. Perhaps their knowledge is not of a general sort, but rather like a memorized list of exemplars of auxiliaries that can or cannot appear in the initial position. Unfortunately, this hypothesis also is not well-supported. Kuczaj and Maratsos (1983) reported, surprisingly, that various initial auxiliaries emerged simultaneously and not word-by-word. This simultaneity has also been reported by Bellugi (1971) and Miller and Ervin (1964). These findings suggest that children *do* have some abstract representation of the class of auxiliaries. Apparently, however, it is a representation that fails to include some auxiliaries such as *haven't* or *wouldn't*, but correctly excludes certain other words such as *better*.

Turning to the *wh*-forms themselves, there is a large body of research on the order of acquisition of different *wh*-forms in production as well as comprehension. *What* and *where*, for example, frequently appear long before *why* and *when*. One view is that it is the cognitive complexity of the concepts that determines the order of acquisition. This view receives some support from the fact that *when* and *why* do encode somewhat more abstract concepts than do *what* and *where*. However Wootten et al. (1979) pointed out that linguistic complexity also contributes to the acquisition sequence. The earlier emerging forms in their data—*what, where,* and *who*—are *wh*-pronominals that ask for the major sentence constituents that they replace. Consequently, they are rather simple syntactically. In contrast, *why, how,* and *when* ask for information concerning the semantic relations in the sentence as a whole, and do not simply replace a major sentence constituent. Wootten et al. referred to the latter group as *wh*-sententials. These sententials emerged later than did *what, where,* and *who.* Furthermore, when they did emerge, they appeared in more complex constructions than did *what, where,* and *who.*

Other researchers have analyzed the order of comprehension for *wh*-questions. Studies by Ervin-Tripp (1970), Tyack and Ingram (1977), and Cairns and Hsu (1978) differ in detail, but demonstrate that both the structure of the question and the transitivity of the verb influence comprehension, over and above any effects that cognitive complexity may have.

Winzemer (1981) suggested a further important influence on the child's comprehension of *wh*-questions that might account for the variability across studies. She argued that children may know initially that a *wh*-word replaces a constituent but not know which constituent. The semantics of the verb in the sentence provide the clue as to which constituents are likely to be specified. Her model proposes that verbs have as components of their meaning certain implied constituents. For example, the verb *eat* has an object as an expected constituent, but not a location. Hence the question "What is the boy eating?" fits these expectations better than "Where is the boy eating?" On the other hand, the verb *drive* does imply a location, hence the question "Where is the boy driving?" conforms to expectations.

In keeping with Winzemer's predictions, the children in her study were able to answer expected questions more readily than unexpected questions. In addition, they often made the error of answering with an expected component to an unexpected question. It remains to be determined how prevalent this strategy is in real discourse, where other contextual clues might override the expectations based on the lexical properties of the verb.

Two trends in research on syntax acquisition are exemplified within this subfield of research on the syntax of the interrogative. First, data analysis has become more sophisticated, quantitative, and concerned with individual differences. Second, there is considerably more doubt than there was 10 years ago (McNeill, 1970) that transformational grammar offers a suitable description of syntax acquisition. These trends combine, making it very difficult to reach a simple general conclusion about how children acquire syntactic forms. The field is in need of a new integrative theory. That is undoubtedly one of the reasons the area of pragmatics is attracting more attention.

Illocutionary Force of Interrogatives

Holzman (1972) analyzed the functions of interrogatives in the speech of three mothers and their children—Adam, Eve, and Sarah. She classified interrogatives into five functions or communicative intentions, as follows:

1. Requests for information, e.g., "What are you writing?"
2. Requests for behavior, e.g., "Would you ask Colin if he'd like some coffee?"
3. Questions designed to display or test the knowledge of the hearer, e.g., "What kind of truck is it?" (asked when the speaker is in full knowledge of the answer).
4. Interrogatives in which the thing that is questioned is not in the verbalization, e.g., the use of "What?" either to indicate a lack of understanding or to ask "Is that really what you said?"
5. Use of the interrogative for purposes other than questioning. The examples Holzman provided for this category include a variety of illocutionary forces such as threats, suggestions, and more subtle requests for behaviors than those in category 2. For example, an interrogative suggestion, as in "What are you waiting for, Adam?" might be used with the force of "Go ahead!" Other interrogatives in this category served as negative evaluations of the child's behavior. Examples include: "What do you keep asking me for?" and "What's the matter with you?" When asking such questions, the parent does not sincerely want an answer. Finally, some questions in this category were really statements in interrogative disguise, as when Sarah's mother said, "Doesn't he look like Uncle George?"

It is evident from even this brief description that interrogatives—especially the last category of interrogatives—are used for a large number of purposes in communication.

Shatz (1979) also studied the interrogatives that mothers directed to their children. She identified 11 functional categories of interrogatives. Parallel to Holzman's categories are: requesting information, requesting behavior, test questions, and requests for clarification. However, the existence of the seven other categories suggests that even these overlapping categories may have been more narrowly defined than were Holzman's. For instance, Shatz has a category called *challenge* in which the mother encourages the child to defend or alter a prior statement. An example she gives is the following:

    C: Go in, too.   [C puts block in wrong hole]
    M: Does it go in there? [M looks at C and C's block. C stops action]
    M: No.   [M shakes head and C tries a different hole]

A sixth category of interrogatives defined by Shatz contains questions that serve to call attention to something, as in "Hey, do you see this?" The status of this as a separate category from "requests for behavior" is questionable, given that any different act that the child is requested to perform could, in principle, have its own category. The familiar problem that occurs here is, how finely should one slice the categories? If it is merely a question of convenience for a coder, then the problem is not so severe. The categories should be broad enough so that there are sufficient exemplars, but narrow enough to make the exemplars homogeneous with respect to major functions. However, if, like Shatz, we are interested in questions such as how do function and form interrelate in maternal speech, then it is much more important to classify functions in some optimally revealing manner.

The other five categories identified by Shatz have much less obvious intent in that they serve as various kinds of conversational "fillers." They include:

7. Requesting confirmation, e.g., "Maybe we'd better get the top back on the tent, do you think?"
8. Giving encouragement, e.g., "Is that easier?"
9. Expressing empathy, e.g., "That's good, isn't it?"
10. Maintaining contact, e.g., "You making the camel again?"
11. Floor offer—a general question that gives the child the opportunity to direct the question, e.g., "Well, who's gonna make lunch?"

Rather surprisingly, given the subtleties of this analysis, coder agreement was around 80%. It would be interesting to know what it would be for a subset of the functions, in particular the last five categories.

It is likely that neither Holzman's nor Shatz's analysis exhausts the functions served by interrogatives, particularly in adult speech. Furthermore, although Holzman provided some data on how young children use the interrogative, much more research needs to be done in this area.

Of all the interrogative functions, requests have been subjected to the most complete analysis (Bates, 1976; Ervin-Tripp, 1977; Gordon and Ervin-Tripp, this volume; Gordon and Lakoff, 1971; Searle, 1975). Austin (1962) and Searle (1969, 1975) identified certain "felicity conditions" that must be met for a request to be considered sincere. Suppose speaker A requests speaker B to tell him the time. In order to do this, A must:

1. Believe B has the ability to tell time.
2. Have the desire that B should tell A the time.
3. Believe that B will tell the time if requested.
4. Have good reasons for B to tell the time.

These conditions are reflected in the polite forms that requests can take, for instance:

1. Ability: "Can you tell me the time?"
2. Desire: "Do you want to tell me the time?"
3. Future action: "Would you tell me the time?"
4. Reasons: "Why don't you tell me the time?"

The four interrogative forms for making a request coincide with the social conventions that make a request sincere. Of course, requests also can be issued in forms other than the interrogative. Requests can be disguised as declaratives or conveyed directly with imperatives. Thus, a person can, for example, request the time by using: 1) an interrogative such as "What time is it?", 2) an imperative such as "Tell me the time!" or 3) a declarative hint such as "I wonder what time it is?" or "I bet it's getting late" (Ervin-Tripp, 1977). Although the concern in this chapter is with the interrogative form and the preceding examples vary in form, it is still important to keep in mind that the function of *requesting* is common to all of the examples just given.

The Hypotheses Considered with Respect to Interrogatives

1. It is possible to identify in the behavior of preverbal children the communicative functions that are the precursors of illocutionary forces.

When one analyzes the functions that interrogatives serve in mature speech, it is very difficult to imagine many of them occurring prior to speech. For instance, "test" questions, "floor offers," and "requests for confirmation" all require an existing dialogue of some linguistic complexity. However, one function of the interrogative does appear prior to the onset of words, and that function is the *request*.

Perhaps it would be more correct to use the neutral term *directive* to label the request function in early child language. Both commands and requests are directives in that they are used to get someone to do something. Although the use of a command implies an authority relationship among participants that differs from that of the request, there is no evidence that children differentiate these two speech acts (Griffiths, 1979). Even though a parent may gloss a child's utterance on one occasion as "Give me that" and on another occasion as "Can I have that?", there is nothing to suggest that infants have an awareness of the social structures on which the distinction depends. Furthermore, infants do not mark the difference with any formal device such as intonation. On the contrary, Halliday (1975) reported that his subject, Nigel, marked all directives with the same intonation. A rising pattern was used on all "pragmatic" utterances (commands, questions, demands, etc.) and a falling intonation was used for all "mathetic" (referential) utterances. For this reason it would be preferable to use the term *directive* rather than *request*, but unfortunately researchers have consistently used the latter term. Consequently, with the above reservation, the different types of "requests" that have been identified in early communication are discussed here.

Carter (1974) studied one child, David, throughout his second year. She divided his communicative acts into nine categories of intention based on the following: "The primary criterion for assessing various types of intentionality in each instance was the goal, which, once achieved, resulted in the child's quieting or adopting a new mode or direction of behavior" (Carter, 1974, pp. 60–61). This criterion is very similar to the one adopted by Bates et al. (1975), except that the latter researchers required some evidence of an intention to involve another person in the achievement of the goal (e.g., child alternating eye contact between an object and an adult while vocalizing). The presence of some conventionalized signal, either vocal or gestural, is necessary to preserve the distinction between perlocutionary and illocutionary communication (Bates, 1976).

Since Carter's subject, David, was clearly beyond the age of perlocutionary communication, his vocalizations and gestures could be classified with some reliability. However, when David was 12–16 months of age, his gestures were classified more reliably than his vocalizations. Interjudge reliability for gestures was 97% versus 69% for vocalizations. Judges could reliably recognize instances of the "request object" category—open-handed reaching gestures accompanied by [m]-initial syllables.

A second category of requests reported by Bloom (1973), Dore (1975), and Halliday (1975) is "request action." One type of action request is the "request for transfer." Carter reported that David differentiated requesting an object from requesting an adult to transfer an object by accompanying each with a distinct vocalization. Otherwise, there is little evidence at this time to suggest that young children have any formal means of distinguishing requests for objects from requests for action.

In addition to requesting objects and actions, young children often call an adult's attention to some object or event. These calls for attention may originate as vocalizations marked by a rising intonation. Leopold (1949) reported that his daughter used a rising intonation at 15 months to call attention to an object or event. Later on, however, calls for attention often are conveyed by interrogatives.

The last type of request is the request for information. This too is conveyed first by the use of a rising intonation and later by interrogatives. Unfortunately, this similarity to forms serving other functions often makes it difficult to determine when a child is requesting information. For example, utterances in which a child calls attention to an object are often difficult to distinguish from attempts to gain information about an object. An adult might convey some information about an object in response to a child's utterance, but did the child actually request this information or was he simply calling the adult's attention to the object? Griffiths (1979) believed that true requests for information come in relatively late. He claimed that children initially use forms such as "What's that?" and "That?" either to call attention to an object or to request an object. Moreover, when requests for information such as "What's that?" do finally emerge, it seems that the utterances serve two functions simultaneously: "Tell me what that is, and can I have it?" As evidence for this double function, Holzman (1972) cited dialogues such as the following:

Eve: What's that?
Eve's mother: That belongs to the fireplace and you're not to play with it.

It is possible, however, that the parent infers the second function in such a case.

The major communicative functions found in preverbal and holophrastic children that later are served by interrogatives are requests of various kinds and attempts to direct attention. Although judges can classify these functions with some reliability for a particular child, the conventional signals seem to be much more varied and unpredictable than those used for negation. As a result, the continuity from gestural to vocal or verbal communication that has been reported in elaborate detail for a small number of children (Bates et al., 1975; Carter, 1974; Halliday, 1975) does not lend itself easily to the kind of analysis performed for negative functions.

> 2. *Precursor functions emerge in an order that is recapitulated when conventional expressions of these forces appear.*

The kind of data available are not well suited to address the hypothesis. Griffiths (1979) argues that the function of questioning ("requesting an answer") emerges later than the functions of requesting or calling attention to something. Unfortunately, there are no systematic data on early child speech that examine *both* form and function of interrogatives, in the same manner as for negation. So there is no answer at present to the question of whether requests are first to be elaborated syntactically, with questions emerging later. The question is more complex than it is for negation, because the function of *request* is not served by interrogative forms until much later (Bates, 1976). Young children express requests using imperatives or declaratives, so a complete evaluation of the hypothesis would require an analysis of the functions served by all such forms. Hence it is unlikely that the hypothesis will be revealing about form-function relationships *within* the interrogative, in contrast to its utility in analyzing negation.

Although we cannot offer a complete assessment of this hypothesis, a few preliminary steps have been taken toward this end. Holzman (1972), for example, studied the functions served by interrogatives as a general class. This study provided no data on the emergence of these functions over time, but it did give researchers a clue to the range of functions acquired by the time a child has an MLU of 3.0. Unfortunately, it is the only study of its kind and consequently is the only source of data on the functions served by interrogative forms in young children. Holzman's results indicated that children with an MLU of 3.0 use many but not all of the major functions of the interrogative. Interrogatives that served to request information, indicate a lack of understanding, and suggest behavior were all in evidence. "Test" questions were common for two of the subjects but not for a third, Sarah, whose mother also did not ask many test questions. However, the children did not use interrogatives to request behavior or to convey negative evaluations of another person's behavior. The absence of interrogative evaluations probably reflects only the different roles of parent and child.

In contrast to Holzman's study of the different functions served by one form (i.e., the interrogative), Garvey (1975) studied the different forms that serve one function (i.e., requests for actions/objects). Using dyads of preschool children, Garvey analyzed the way in which each child requested actions or objects from the other child during play. Her results indicate that, as children reach the age of 4 or 5 years, the interrogative form is used increasingly often for the purpose of making requests. The number of imperative or direct requests issued by Garvey's younger group (42-52 months) slightly exceeded that of her older group (55–67 months), but the older group used many more interrogative and declarative forms to phrase their requests indirectly.

Although Garvey and Holzman have provided some of the information needed to address our second hypothesis, much more information is needed before the hypothesis can be adequately evaluated. Garvey's project needs to be extended to cover other types of requests, including calls for attention and requests for information; and Holzman's study needs to be replicated longitudinally so that researchers can discover how the functions served by interrogatives might change with age and linguistic development. Finally, researchers need to explore the order in which different kinds of requests emerge in the nonverbal behaviors of young children, and whether requesting is the only communicative function that is later served by interrogatives that also appears prior to the onset of speech.

> 3. *Children begin by using a limited set of form-function mappings, and this broadens until they are capable of using a variety of forms for any one function, and one form for a number of different functions.*

Surprisingly, there is little direct work that examines this claim. For instance, in her work on interrogative functions, Holzman did not analyze the range of forms used for any of the functions reported. Thus, there is no way to tell if Holzman's subjects showed stereotyped form-function pairings within the interrogative category. Moreover, data related to the other half of this hypothesis—the use of one form for a number of different functions—is also unavailable. The work on syntax discussed previously makes no mention of the uses to which the forms were put. However, a report by Johnson (1980) on the ontogenesis of *wh*-question words in children's speech indicates that such words may originate in highly restricted interaction routines. The child's usage then gradually broadens until his words eventually become free of their limited contexts of use.

Although we do not yet know whether there is a one-to-one mapping between specific interrogative forms and functions in early child language, we do have some evidence indicating that, in contrast to declaratives and imperatives, interrogatives—as a broad class—serve a range of functions at least by MLU 3.0 (Holzman, 1972). This range expands to incorporate requests when children are around 4 years of age. Thus, the term *limited* does not really apply to the initial range of functions served by interrogative forms.

The term *limited* also may not apply to the forms that serve each function. Looking at broad form-function relationships from this second perspective, the earliest verbal requests are conveyed by imperatives. Requests in the form of declaratives and interrogatives do not emerge until later (Garvey, 1975), although perhaps not as late as one might expect. When Newcombe and Zaslow (1981) analyzed samples of discourse between 30-month-old children and adults, they uncovered a variety of oblique requests phrased as declaratives and interrogatives. Thus, the term *limited* also may not apply to the forms used for requests.

Finally, Garvey's data illustrate the fact that, within the domain of interrogative requests, 4-year-old children use a variety of forms similar to those used by adults. For example, her subjects issued requests by questioning the hearer's ability (e.g., "Can you hold this?"), his desires (e.g., "Do you want to catch me?"), his future actions (e.g., "Will you get me one?"), and reasons (e.g., "Why don't you hold it?"). These forms served the same functions as earlier direct requests. The shift seems to be in the variety of indirect interrogative forms available for the function of requesting.

> 4. *In talking to young children, parents use a limited set of form-functioning mappings, which may facilitate the children's decoding of language. This usage changes as children become older and more linguistically mature.*

Shatz (1979) studied the questions that 17 mothers addressed to their preschool children during a play session. The children were divided into two groups: a low group containing children who generally spoke in 2-word sentences or less, and a high one in which the children's mean length of sentences was 3 or 4 words. Using the functional categories described earlier in this chapter, Shatz analyzed the type and diversity of sentence forms used to express each function. The analysis of form consisted of identifying regularly occurring question frames, such as:

$$\left\{ \begin{array}{l} \text{Who} \\ \text{What} \end{array} \right\} \text{ is } \left\{ \begin{array}{l} \text{that} \\ \text{this} \\ \text{it} \end{array} \right\}$$

and

$$\left\{ \begin{array}{l} \text{Do} \\ \text{Does} \end{array} \right\} \text{NP V X}$$

The stereotypicality of the form-function pairing was then investigated. Stereotypical or "characteristic" pairings were those in which: 1) a given form (or frame) was associated with one function more frequently than with others; and 2) that pairing occurred at least once in the speech of more than half of the mothers in the group. Shatz justified the latter seemingly arbitrary criterion by arguing that her objective was not to uncover pairings that might enhance understanding of only one particular mother's speech, but rather to uncover those that might facilitate decoding of language in general. Given Shatz's objective, this approach seems reasonable. However, it does obscure individual patterns of form-function pairings that might provide a child with a valid entry point into the language as a whole. Furthermore, data on individual form-function pairings did prove interesting with respect to children's negation.

Although Shatz's definition of "characteristic pairing" limited her to analyzing group trends, these trends are highly relevant to a discussion of the fourth hypothesis. Shatz found that the questions produced by mothers of low-group children served as many different functions as those produced by high-group mothers. Both groups employed an equal frequency of "test" questions and questions serving conversational maintenance functions. Mothers of low-group children issued significantly more interrogative requests for action than high-group mothers, but high-group mothers issued more interrogative requests for information than low-group mothers. Most important, low-group mothers used characteristic form-function pairings more frequently than did high-group mothers (38% to 25%, $P < 0.01$). However, the variability of form-function pairings in questions addressed to even the low-group children was more striking than the significant group difference. Shatz argued that the mothers facilitated their children's analysis of language by exposing the children to a wide variety of form-function pairings, not by exposing them to a limited, systematic set.

Shatz's study provides the most direct data on the hypothesis at hand. However, Bellinger's (1979) research on directives also speaks to the issue. Bellinger studied how mothers give directives to children of different ages. Thus, whereas Shatz started with interrogative forms and analyzed the functions they served, Bellinger began with the functional category "directive" and looked at the forms used to express it.

Bellinger (1979) reported that the form of parental directives changed from imperative to interrogative as the children increased in age. We can consider the imperative to be the "canonical" form for a directive (Dore, 1977), with interrogatives being an indirect way of achieving the same goal. Bellinger found that imperatives comprised 67.4% of the directives given to the youngest children (1.0 to 1.8 years), with full interrogatives comprising only 19.6% of the directives given to this group. For children between 1.8 and 2.3 years, use of the interrogative form increased (65.1%) while use of the imperative form decreased (62.8%). Unfortunately, the picture subsequently becomes complicated by an increasing use of declaratives as "hints," with the result being a decline in the use of the interrogative as a directive to older children. In general, however, the mother's directives become increasingly indirect, and the form-function pairing did seem to become more elaborate as the children's age increased.

In conclusion, some of the results reported by Shatz (1979) and Bellinger (1979) initially might seem to support hypothesis 4. However, a combination of factors mitigates against drawing a simple conclusion about the truth of the hypothesis with respect to interrogatives. Shatz and Bellinger used very different schemes for analysis, and it is difficult to know whether their studies are contradictory or complementary. Shatz's use of the term "form" meant *within* the grammatical form of the interrogative, whereas Bellinger's meant the choice of sentence modality. Moreover, Shatz examined a variety of functions served by interrogatives, whereas Bellinger focused on directives.

5. *Children at first understand the functions of only a limited set of "canonical" forms, and have difficulty understanding indirect (i.e., "noncanonical") expressions of illocutionary force.*

This hypothesis actually concerns two separate but related issues: 1) whether canonical forms are easier to interpret than noncanonical forms; and 2) whether "characteristic pairings" are easier to interpret than "noncharacteristic pairings."

Consistent with the first part of the hypothesis, Ervin-Tripp (1977) proposed that children understand direct requests before they understand indirect ones. The proposed lag was based on the assumption that, in order to understand an indirect request, a child must first figure out the propositional content of the sentence, and then recognize that all sentences do not mean what they say. Similarly, Dore (1977) contended that children have direct access to the illocutionary force of a canonical form, but not to a noncanonical form. Shatz (1978a, 1978b) has the most direct data on this issue. She examined the responses of young children to their mothers' indirect and direct requests. The results indicate that 2-year-old children make surprisingly few errors in understanding requests. The children understood commands phrased as interrogatives and responded to them as appropriately as they did to imperatives. Holzman (1972) also reported that her subjects rarely misinterpreted their mothers' interrogatives when they served indirect functions.

One possible explanation for the findings reported by Shatz and Holzman is that children identify regular idioms or characteristic pairings in their mothers' speech. Because each of these idioms serves only one function, the child does not have to consider whether the sentence means what it says. Consequently, even noncanonical expressions of an illocutionary force can be understood if they appear regularly in the mother's speech. Although this explanation is appealing, the evidence to support it is limited. When Shatz (1979) investigated whether children generally understand characteristic pairs better than noncharacteristic pairs, her analyses revealed the following interesting, albeit not statistically significant, trends. Shatz's high group of children tended to have more success with characteristic directives than with noncharacteristic directives, but the same relationship did not apply to the low group. The low group, however, did seem to respond better to characteristic test questions than to noncharacteristic ones. Finally, a statistically significant trend limited to the low group was obtained when the response patterns of each child were compared with the mother's style of questioning. Within the low group, mothers who tended to produce more characteristic test questions had children who understood them more readily.

In summary, there is a small amount of support for the idea that children's comprehension is better for forms that have a restricted use, but the generality of this conclusion is not impressive in Shatz's (1979) data because the supporting evidence is limited to low-group children's responses to test questions and high-group children's responses to directives. Moreover, when the children's responses to characteristic questions were compared with their mothers' style of questioning, significant results were limited to test questions.

6. *Children must rely on social and event knowledge in their interpretations of illocutionary force.*

As discussed earlier, the assumption is that a listener first computes the literal meaning of an utterance. When this meaning is discrepant with the discourse context, the listener then searches for an alternative, indirect meaning. If young children succeed in understanding the illocutionary force of indirect speech acts, does this mean they have mastered all of these steps? Given the 2-year-old's cognitive, linguistic, and social knowledge, it seems unlikely that they can succeed by such a route. Shatz (1978a) argued that very young children get by with a simple heuristic that bypasses the above sequence. She proposed that children have a tendency to respond with action to their mothers' requests no matter how the requests are phrased. The children search the utterance for the mention of an action or an object to be acted upon, and indicate their understanding by engaging in the action. This would explain the result that 2-year-olds are as successful at responding to interrogative requests as they are to imperatives despite the difference in their directness. It also accounts for Shatz's (1978b) finding that children often respond with action to "information" questions such as "Do you brush your teeth?" and "Do you know how to draw?"

Thus, young children's surprising comprehension of indirect requests is not so much due to their learning the meaning of particular idioms in their parents' speech as it is to their tendency to respond with action whenever possible. The proposed sequence of steps to arrive at the illocutionary force, if it is true of adults (Clark and Lucy, 1975), must come into play at some later age. How older children infer indirect meaning from the context is now being studied experimentally (e.g., Ackerman, 1978), but the developmental picture is far from complete.

DISCUSSION

In comparing negatives and questions, one finds that some of the hypotheses fare differentially well in the two accounts. Consequently, it is difficult to come up with firm conclusions about their generality. Because most of the problems reside in the lack of parallel work in the two domains, it seems worth reiterating these problems in the hope that repetition might stimulate the necessary research.

First, the discussion of negatives focused on the issue, what are the functions of negative forms? In attempting to answer this question, a need for information concerning the reverse issue, what forms can serve negative functions, is repeatedly encountered. Unfortunately, this second question so far has received little attention in the literature. Few writers have mentioned the possibility that forms other than negatives might serve negative functions. Among the "negative" forms usually admitted for consideration are such words as *gone* and *stop*; but surely there are other forms that serve negative functions. For instance, the following dialogues both contain rejections: 1) "Give me one."—"You can't have more."; 2) "Give me one."—"You had one already." The rejection in the first dialogue is explicitly negative; the rejection in the second one is indirectly negative.

Very little attention has been paid to these indirect negatives. Consequently, the form-function analysis for negation is impoverished compared to the corresponding analysis with interrogatives. What we presently have for negation is research on the range of form-function mappings that is analogous to Shatz's (1979) work on the range of functions served by the general class of interrogative forms. Other work on interrogatives uses a broader level of analysis, i.e., whether or not there is a canonical sentence form for a particular illocutionary force (Dore, 1977), and how development might affect the use of specific pairings by a child (Garvey, 1975) and by adults speaking to a child (Bellinger, 1979). The equivalent broader picture for negative functions is not available, and, in particular, systematic research is needed on the use of noncanonical negatives.

The lack of parallel research also made it difficult to discuss the second hypothesis, whether precursor functions emerge in an order that is recapitulated when conventional expressions of these forces appear. Although this issue seemed straightforward for the case of the negative, difficulties were encountered with the interrogative. One reason for these difficulties is that requests are not expressed in interrogative form until relatively late, although they are the function most reliably identified in early communication. Furthermore, most other interrogative functions are defined in a way that makes the discovery of prelinguistic precursors unlikely.

Although there has been extensive work on the syntax of interrogatives, little research is available on children's form-function mappings. It has been reported that, at the earliest stages, children have particular forms that serve very limited functions. For example, Halliday (1975) reported that Nigel's expression "more meat" was initially used only as a request, but later generalized to serve the function of reporting. *Within* the interrogative, however, there has been no systematic research on form-function mappings for children that is comparable to the work of Pea (1979) and de Villiers and de Villiers (1979) on negation.

Let me now make some final comments about each of the hypotheses:

1. An analysis of the functions of child language indicates continuity in communicative development over the first two years of life. However, there are still unsolved methodological problems that plague research in this area.
2. There is limited evidence indicating that precursor functions emerge at different times in development; but the order in which these functions emerge does not seem to be recapitulated when conventional expressions appear.
3. Several studies confirm the hypothesis that the child begins with a limited set of form-function mappings that then broadens with age. This seems to be true within negation, and in the broader sense for interrogative functions such as the request.
4. Parents, on the other hand, do not reveal a limited set of form-function mappings in their speech to children. Evidence for the use of limited mappings was more favorable for negatives than for interrogatives, primarily because of methodological differences in the later studies—i.e., whether consistent form-function pairings idiosyncratic to one parent, or only common patterns, were deemed of interest. However, for both negatives and interrogatives, the variability of forms for particular functions is striking.
5. Children seem to respond surprisingly well to indirect expressions of illocutionary force. They rarely give literal interpretations in natural discourse situations.
6. To interpret indirect expressions, children seem to rely not only on the context, but also on response strategies that initially bear little resemblance to the rules of conversation by which adults supposedly understand illocutionary force.

REFERENCES

Ackerman, B. P. 1978. Children's understanding of speech acts in unconventional directive frames. Child Dev. 49:311–318.
Austin, J. L. 1962. How To Do Things with Words. Oxford University Press, New York.
Bates, E. 1976. Language and Context. Academic Press, Inc., New York.
Bates, E., Camaioni, L., and Volterra, V. 1975. The acquisition of performatives prior to speech. Merrill-Palmer Q. 21(3):205–226.
Bellinger, D. 1979. Changes in the explicitness of mother's directives as children age. J. Child Lang. 6:443–458.
Bellugi, U. 1967. The acquisition of negation. Unpublished doctoral dissertation, Harvard University.
Bellugi, U. 1971. Simplification in children's language. In R. Huxley and E. Ingram (eds.), Language Acquisition: Models and Methods. Academic Press, Inc., New York.
Bloom, L. 1970. Language Development: Form and Function in Emerging Grammars. MIT Press, Cambridge, MA.
Bloom, L. 1973. One Word at a Time: The Use of Single Word Utterances before Syntax. Mouton, The Hague.
Bloom, L., and Lahey, M. 1978. Language Development and Language Disorders. John Wiley & Sons, Inc., New York.
Brown, R. W. 1973. A First Language—The Early Stages. Harvard University Press, Cambridge, MA.
Cairns, H. S., and Hsu, J. R. 1978. Who, why, when and how: A developmental study. J. Child Lang. 5:477–488.
Carter, A. 1974. The development of communication in the sensorimotor period: A case study. Unpublished doctoral dissertation, University of California, Berkeley.
Clark, H., and Lucy, P. 1975. Understanding what is meant from what is said: A study in conversationally conveyed requests. J. Verbal Learn. Verbal Behav. 14:56–72.
Crystal, D. 1978. The analysis of intonation in young children. In D. Minifie and L. L. Lloyd (eds.), Communicative and Cognitive Abilities: Early Behavioral Assessment. University Park Press, Baltimore.
Darwin, C. 1955. The Expression of the Emotions in Man and Animals. The Philosophical Library, New York. (Original published in 1872.)
de Villiers, J. G., and de Villiers, P. A. 1978. Semantics and syntax in the first two years: The output of form and function and the form and function of the input. In F. D. Minifie and L. L. Lloyd (eds.), Communicative and Cognitive Abilities: Early Behavioral Assessment. University Park Press, Baltimore.
de Villiers, P. A., and de Villiers, J. G. 1979. Form and function in the development of sentence negation. Papers Rep. Child Lang. 17:57–64.
de Villiers, J. G., and Tager-Flusberg, H. 1975. Some facts one simply cannot deny. J. Child Lang. 2:279–286.
Dore, J. 1975. Holophrases, speech acts and language universals. J. Child Lang. 2:21–40.
Dore, J. 1977. Children's illocutionary acts. In R. Freedle (ed.), Discourse Production and Comprehension. Lawrence Erlbaum Assocs., Inc., Hillsboro, N.J.

Edwards, D. 1978. Constraints on actions: A source of early meanings in child language. *In* I. Markova (ed.), The Social Context of Language. John Wiley & Sons, Inc., New York.

Erreich, A. 1980. The acquisition of inversion in wh-questions: What evidence the child uses? Unpublished doctoral dissertation, City University of New York.

Ervin-Tripp, S. 1970. Discourse agreement: How children answer questions. *In* J. R. Hayes (ed.), Cognition and the Development of Language. John Wiley & Sons, Inc., New York.

Ervin-Tripp, S. 1977. Wait for me, rollerskate! *In* C. Mitchell-Kernan and S. Ervin-Tripp (eds.), Child Discourse. Academic Press, Inc., New York.

Garvey, C. 1975. Requests and responses in children's speech. J. Child Lang. 2:41–63.

Gordon, D., and Lakoff, G. 1971. Conversational postulates. *In* Papers from the Seventh Regional Meeting of the Chicago Linguistic Society. Chicago Linguistic Society, Chicago.

Gregoire, A. 1937. L'Apprentissage de Langage. 1. Les Deux Premières années. Droz, Paris.

Griffiths, P. 1979. Speech acts and early sentences. *In* P. Fletcher and M. Garman (eds.), Language Acquisition. Cambridge University Press, Cambridge, England.

Halliday, M. 1975. Leaning How To Mean: Explorations in the Development of Language. Edward Arnold, London.

Hecht, B. F., and Morse, R. 1974. What the hell are dese? Unpublished paper, Harvard University.

Holzman, M. 1972. The use of interrogative forms in the interaction of three mothers and their children. J. Psycholing. Res. 1:311–336.

Ingram, D., and Tyack, D. 1979. Inversion of subject NP and aux in children's questions. J. Psycholing. Res. 8:333–341.

Jesperson, O. 1917. Negation in English and Other Languages. Copenhagen.

Johnson, C. 1980. The ontogenesis of question words in children's language. Paper presented at the Fifth Annual Boston University Conference on Language Acquisition, October.

Katz, J. J. 1977. Propositional Structure and Illocutionary Force. Harvester Press, Hassocks, Sussex, England.

Kim, K. 1980. Development of the concept of truth-functional negation. Unpublished doctoral dissertation, Harvard University.

Klima, E. S. 1964. Negation in English. *In* J. Fodor and J. J. Katz (eds.), The Structure of Language: Readings in the Philosophy of Language. Prentice-Hall, Inc., Englewood Cliffs, N.J.

Klima, E. S., and Bellugi, U. 1966. Syntactic regularities in the speech of children. *In* J. Lyons and R. J. Wales (eds.), Psycholinguistic Papers. Edinburgh University Press, Edinburgh.

Kuczaj, S. A., and Brannick, N. 1979. Children's use of the *Wh* question modal auxiliary placement rule. J. Exp. Child Psychol. 28:43–67.

Kuczaj, S. A., and Maratsos, M. P. 1975. What children *can* say before they *will*. Merrill-Palmer Q. 21:89–111.

Kuczaj, S. A., and Maratsos, M. P. 1983. The initial verbs of yes-no questions: A different kind of general grammatical category. Dev. Psychol. 19:440–444.

Labov, W., and Labov, T. 1976. Learning the syntax of questions. Paper presented at the Conference on Psychology of Language, Stirling, Scotland.

Leopold, W. F. 1949. Speech Development of a Bilingual Child: A Linguist's Record. Vol. 3: Grammar and General Problems in the First Two Years. Northwestern University Press, Evanston, IL.

McNeill, D. S. 1970. The Acquisition of Language. Harper & Row Pubs., Inc., New York.

McNeill, D. S., and McNeill, N. B. 1968. What does a child mean when he says "no"? *In* E. M. Zale (ed.), Proceedings of the Conference on Language and Language Behavior. Appleton-Century-Crofts, New York.

Maratsos, M. P. 1978. New Models in linguistics and language acquisition. *In* M. Halle, J. Bresnan, and G. Miller (eds.), Linguistic Theory and Psychological Reality. MIT Press, Cambridge, MA.

Maratsos, M. P., and Chalkley, M. A. 1980. The internal language of children's syntax: The ontogenesis and representation of syntactic categories. *In* K. E. Nelson (ed.), Child Language, Vol. 2. Gardner Press, New York.

Miller, W., and Ervin, S. 1964. The development of grammar in child language. *In* U. Bellugi and R. Brown (eds.), The Acquisition of Language. Monogr. Soc. Res. Child Dev. 29:9–34.

Newcombe, N., and Zaslow, M. 1981. Do 2½-year-olds hint? A study of directive forms in the speech of 2½-year-old children to adults. Discourse Processes 4(3):239–252.

Park, T. Z. 1979. Some facts on negation: Wode's four-stage developmental theory of negation revisited. J. Child Lang. 6:147–151.

Pea, R. D. 1979. The development of negation in early child language. *In* D. R. Olson (ed.), The Social Foundations of Language and Thought: Essays in Honor of Jerome S. Bruner. W. W. Norton & Company, Inc., New York.

Piaget, J. 1970. Piaget's theory. *In* P. H. Mussen (ed.), Carmichael's Manual of Child Psychology. John Wiley & Sons, Inc., New York.

Ryan, J. 1974. Early language development: Towards a communicational analysis. *In* M. P. M. Richards (ed.), The Integration of a Child into a Social World. Cambridge University Press, London.

Searle, J. 1969. Speech Acts. Cambridge University Press, Cambridge, England.

Searle, J. 1975. Indirect speech acts. *In* P. Cole and J. L. Morgan (eds.), Syntax and Semantics, Vol. 3. Academic Press, Inc., New York.

Shatz, M. 1978a. The development of communicative understanding: An early strategy for interpreting and responding to messages. Cognitive Psychol. 10:271–301.

Shatz, M. 1978b. Children's comprehension of their mothers' question-directives. J. Child Lang. 5:39–46.

Shatz, M. S. 1979. How to do things by asking: Form-function pairings in mother's questions and their relation to children's responses. Child Dev. 50:1093–1099.

Slobin, D. S. 1966. Abstracts of Soviet studies of child language. *In* F. Smith and G. A. Miller (eds.), The Genesis of Language. MIT Press, Cambridge, MA.

Slobin, D. I., and Welsh, C. A. 1973. Elicited imitation as a research tool in developmental psycholinguistics. *In* C. A. Ferguson and D. E. Slobin (eds.), Studies of Child Language Development. Holt, Rinehart & Winston, Inc., New York.

Smith, W. J. 1977. The Behavior of Communicating. Harvard University Press, Cambridge, MA.

Tager-Flusberg, H., de Villiers, J. G., and Hakuta, K. 1982. The development of sentence coordination. *In* S. Kuczaj (ed.), Language Development: Problems, Theories and Controversies, Vol. 1: Syntax and Semantics. Lawrence Erlbaum Assocs. Inc., Hillsdale, N.J.

Tyack, D., and Ingram, D. 1977. Children's production and comprehension of questions. J. Child Lang. 4:211–224.

Winzemer, J. A. 1981. A lexical expectation model for children's comprehension of wh-questions. Unpublished doctoral dissertation, City University of New York.

Wode, H. 1977. Four early stages in the development of L1 negation. J. Child Lang. 4:87–102.

Wolff, P. 1969. The natural history of crying and other vocalizations in early infancy. *In* B. Foss (ed.), Determinants of Infant Behavior, Vol. 4. Methuen, London.

Wootten, J., Merkin, S., Hood, L., and Bloom, L. 1979. Wh-questions: Linguistic evidence to explain the sequence of acquisition. Paper presented at Biennial Meeting of the Society for Research in Child Development, San Francisco, March.

chapter 6

Children's Acquisition of Presuppositional Usages

Ganie DeHart

and

Michael Maratsos

Institute of Child Development
University of Minnesota
Minneapolis, Minnesota

Editors' Note

Presuppositions consist of the semantic and pragmatic assumptions of a speaker, as reflected in words, linguistic forms, and sentential devices. Presuppositions may include assumptions about word meaning, about what the listener knows, or about the social context in which the speaker and listener find themselves. Children seem to bring a basic ability to presuppose to the task of language acquisition, but they must learn the particular presuppositions that apply to specific usages. They gradually become more and more facile at deciding whether those presuppositions are met in a particular situation or are shared by a particular listener. Children's early use of constructions involving presupposition (e.g., definite reference, factive predicates, *wh*-questions, and negation) is often basically correct, although complete mastery of the semantic and social subtleties of the constructions is a gradual process. Through middle childhood, errors tend to be in the direction of mistakenly assuming shared presuppositions with the listener. We do not know how children learn all of the complex dimensional information necessary to appropriate presupposition, especially because many presuppositional usages involve complex meanings that apply to both speaker and listener.

Most language-disordered children have presuppositional skills similar to those of younger children. However, autistic children have special difficulties with many presuppositional constructions that are not characteristic of young normal children.

contents

ELEMENTS OF PRESUPPOSITION 240

    Basic Presuppositions of Communication 240
    Presuppositions Carried by Particular Linguistic Forms 242
    Presuppositions Carried by General Linguistic Devices 249
    Presupposition and the Roles of Speaker and Listener 250

EMPIRICAL FINDINGS ABOUT CHILDREN'S PRESUPPOSITION 252

    Early Presupposition 254
    Later Use of Particular Presuppositional Constructions 257
    Later Use of General Presuppositional Devices 279
    Gricean Conversational Principles 281

SOME BASIC THEORETICAL QUESTIONS 281

IMPLICATIONS FOR CHILDREN WITH LANGUAGE DELAYS 285

SUMMARY AND CONCLUSIONS 288

REFERENCES 289

In common usage, presuppositions are the background assumptions on which people base their behavior and speech, the things that are taken for granted at the outset. For example, a teacher of second-year German presupposes that the students in the class have taken first-year German and that they therefore already know a certain amount about the language; those presuppositions shape the material that will be presented to the students, the level at which it will be presented, and the amount of explanation that will be considered necessary to make it clear. At a more basic level, a person entering a shop in Minneapolis assumes—presupposes—that the clerk behind the counter speaks English, and he makes his requests in that language. The same person entering a shop in Paris might preface his requests with a hesitant "Do you speak English?" In the Parisian shop, he cannot presuppose that the clerk speaks English.

Linguistic presupposition is not much more complicated than that. It simply comprises the semantic or pragmatic assumptions of a speaker, as reflected in the words, linguistic forms, and sentential devices he uses. Depending on the particular word or linguistic form, presupposition may include assumptions about word meaning, assumptions about what the listener knows, or assumptions about the social context in which the speaker and listener find themselves.

Because of the variety of linguistic forms that involve presuppositions, it is complicated to discuss the development of presupposition in children. There does not seem to be a unitary ability that develops separately and is reflected uniformly in all types of presupposition. Instead, accurate and appropriate presupposition seems to result from and be reflected in the development of various linguistic and social skills, some of them quite specific. In addition, a distinction needs to be made between children's understanding of some basic communicative presuppositions and their ability to understand and observe other, more specific rules of semantic and pragmatic presupposition.

At the most basic level, some elements of presupposition, not tied to particular linguistic forms, must be present from the very beginning of children's use of language; using language for communication implies certain rudimentary assumptions about the roles of speaker and listener and the shared meaning of the words being used. Beyond such a basic ability, children develop increasing sophistication in knowing what information to put in a sentence and what to leave out, how to arrange

---

Preparation of this chapter was supported by a Sloan Foundation grant to the second author and by grants to the University of Minnesota, Center for Research in Human Learning, from the National Institute for Child Health and Human Development (T32-HD-07151 and HD-01136) and the National Science Foundation (NSF/BNS-77-22075). Authors are listed in alphabetical order.

the information so that the listener will understand what is being communicated, what social assumptions need to be reflected in speech, and what presuppositions are part of the meaning of particular words and linguistic forms.

Anecdotally, most adults can think of situations in which children show evidence of inaccurate presuppositions about the listener's knowledge of the topic at hand. A preschool child might say something like, "Remember when Fluffy died?" to a friend of the family who has no idea that Fluffy was the family cat and who certainly was not present at the unfortunate feline's demise. On the other hand, the same child might begin a story about an older sister that the family friend knows well by saying, "Mary, she's my big sister, she goes to school . . ." when a simple "Mary" would suffice. In the first case, the child provides less information about Fluffy than the listener needs; in the second, he provides more information about Mary than is necessary.

Empirical evidence about the development of presupposition comes primarily from studies of children's understanding and use of specific words that carry presuppositions. Although the evidence in some cases is either quite sketchy or apparently contradictory, three general themes emerge clearly from the empirical studies that have been done. On the one hand, children have a remarkable *basic* grasp of many presuppositional words and sentential devices at a very early age, in some cases virtually as soon as they begin to use them. However, complete facility with presuppositional usages emerges gradually, and on a usage-by-usage basis. Finally, there does not seem to be a single presuppositional ability that generalizes to all instances of presupposition.

ELEMENTS OF PRESUPPOSITION

In discussing the development of linguistic presupposition in children, it is convenient to divide presuppositional usages into three broad categories. The first category consists of basic presuppositions associated with communication; the second contains presuppositions carried by particular linguistic forms; and the third includes presuppositions carried by general linguistic devices.

Basic Presuppositions of Communication

The most basic type of presupposition involves assumptions of speakers and listeners about the rules that underlie conversation and the social use of language—rules that are not tied to any *particular* words or linguistic forms. As we have already suggested, some presuppositions seem implicit in communicative language: that language can be used to communicate, that there is something to be communicated, and that the listener and speaker share the same (or at least very similar) meanings for the words being used, for example. There is little point in talking about this basic type of presupposition as something that children develop separately from the ability to use language in the first place; intentionally communicative language would be impossible without it.

Grice (1975) formulated a set of conversational postulates that are slightly less basic than those cited above, and perhaps more susceptible to developmental influences and empirical research. He characterized conversation as a cooperative social enterprise in which some implicit or explicit purpose and direction are shared by the participants; as a result, participants in a conversation expect each other to observe certain basic principles. The most general is the Cooperative Principle— that participants in a conversation will make each of their contributions to that conversation support its general purpose and direction. This general principle subsumes several assumptions about the quantity, quality, relevance, and clarity of the participants' contributions.

Grice's principles embody particular assumptions or presuppositions that participants in a conversation share about the content of their conversation and the way in which conversations in general ought to be carried on. Such assumptions not only allow normal communication to proceed, but also make it possible for conversation partners to interpret remarks that do not seem to obey normal principles of conversation, such as sarcasm or deliberate obscurity. Suppose, for example, that a mother and father are discussing their child's Christmas present when that child suddenly walks into the room. The mother sees the child and abruptly changes the subject or begins to talk about the gift in an oblique or obscure way to keep the child from understanding what is really being discussed. Such a change would violate the father's assumptions that the mother's remarks will be clear and relevant to the topic being discussed. That violation, however, would alert the father to the child's presence and would be interpreted as an intentional shift in the way the conversation's purpose (discussing the child's present) is to be achieved. It would not be interpreted as a simple random shift in the conversation or as a loss of interest in the topic at hand.

It seems apparent that children do not understand or apply Grice's principles as well as adults do. For instance, the examples about Fluffy the cat and Mary the big sister demonstrate children's failure to observe the maxims dealing with informativeness and relevance. Piaget's (1926) famous examples of collective monologues demonstrate the difficulties young children may have being relevant, quite apart from what the monologues may have to say about egocentrism. Certainly, children are not noted for brief and orderly descriptions or for utterances free of obscurity and ambiguity. As listeners, children are not as sensitive as adults to violations of Grice's maxims. Such violations may simply go unnoticed or they may make the conversation hard for the child to understand, rather than signaling a particular implication.

It is not that children do not follow or understand Grice's principles at all, however, whereas adults always follow them perfectly. Indeed, it is clear that adults do not always volunteer exactly the right amount of true, relevant information in a completely clear, orderly way (Keenan, 1976; Lakoff, 1973). At the same time, most conversations with children are not completely unintelligible. Any conversation that is at all successful implies that at least some of Grice's principles are operating with some degree of success. It seems likely, however, that adults observe Grice's principles more consistently than do children. Children's inconsistent conversational skill may be due to imperfect understanding of a word they are using or to imperfect understanding of what another person knows about a topic. "Remember when Fluffy died?" may have been said inappropriately either because the child doesn't know that "remember" implies previous knowledge or because he doesn't realize that the listener knows nothing about Fluffy's death. The example about Mary the big sister implies that the child may understand that there is a need to be informative, but may not understand how informative to be in a particular case. Development of Gricean presupposition, then, consists of increasingly sophisticated observance of a set of principles governing conversation. That increased sophistication may be due partly to more complete understanding of particular words and partly to increased understanding of conversational conventions and what others know in particular situations.

Presuppositions Carried by Particular Linguistic Forms

In addition to the basic presuppositions that undergird the use of language to communicate, there are other presuppositions that are tied directly to the use of particular words and linguistic forms. Many cases of the latter type of presupposition are described as "semantic" because they involve words whose meanings include presuppositions about other elements *within* the sentences in which they are used. Other cases are referred to as "pragmatic" because they involve words that carry presuppositions about the social situation in which they are used.

Words and linguistic forms that carry presuppositions include words of definite reference (*the*, definite pronouns, proper nouns), factive predicates (e.g., *know, remember,* and *be happy*), *wh*-questions (those beginning with *who, what, where, when, why,* and *how*), negation, and forms of address. Much of the empirical research on children's presupposition has concentrated on their understanding and use of this set of words and linguistic forms.

Definite Reference The various forms of definite reference—definite articles, definite pronouns, and proper names—all carry similar presuppositions. In most contexts, the use of any of these forms presupposes the existence of a particular referent that can be identified by both participants in the conversation. (See MacWhinney, this volume, for a detailed discussion of the rules of definite reference.)

The definite article *the* usually presupposes the existence of a particular, identifiable member of the class denoted by the noun that follows it. For example, "I didn't see *the* dog" refers, for both speaker and listener, to a particular dog; on the other hand, "I didn't see *a* dog" might refer to any dog or to no dog at all. Notice, however, that what is presupposed in a sentence like "I didn't see the dog" is independent of what is asserted. In that sentence, the speaker presupposes the existence of a particular, identifiable dog and asserts that he did not see that dog. If the speaker were to say "I did see the dog" instead, his assertion would change, but his presupposition—the existence of the dog—would stay the same. The distinction between presupposition and assertion is a general one that can be applied to most presuppositional usages.

In the case of *the*, the particular member of the class being referred to may be physically present, it may have been introduced earlier in a story or conversation, or it may simply be previously known to both the speaker and the listener. If a mother asks her son, "Where's the dog?", for example, the particular dog to which she is referring may be the family dog, a lost dog the son has recently found, a neighbor's dog the son is taking care of, a stuffed dog that is usually on a shelf in his room, or a dog in a picture book they are reading together, to name just a few possibilities. If it is none of these, the question may not make much sense—and the son may reply, "What dog?"

Use of a definite pronoun presupposes the existence of a particular, identifiable referent that meets all the number and gender requirements of the pronoun being used. For instance, the use of *she* presupposes the existence of a particular, identifiable female; the use of *they*, the existence of a particular, identifiable group of persons or things. The referent for a pronoun may appear either as a previously introduced noun in the discourse or as a physically present member of an appropriate class. If the pronoun's referent has been introduced linguistically, the pronoun is functioning *anaphorically*, pointing back to the first usage; if the referent is physically present, the pronoun is functioning *exophorically*, pointing to the physical referent[1] (see MacWhinney, this volume, for more detail).

In some cases, more than one appropriate referent may be present, either physically or linguistically, making the pronoun potentially ambiguous. In context, it is usually possible to determine which potential referent is meant, by noticing stress or gesture or by knowing the topic of the conversation. In the sentence "Nancy took Sue home, so I didn't see her," for example, *her* could refer either to Nancy or to Sue. If the discussion is about Nancy's activities, Nancy would be the likely antecedent for *her*; however, if it is about Sue's whereabouts, Sue becomes more likely. If the listener cannot tell which potential referent was intended by the speaker, the pronoun remains ambiguous, and its use violates the presupposition of an *identifiable* referent.

Proper names are another example of definite reference because they refer to particular identifiable persons, places, or things. Thus, a sentence like "John is bald" presupposes the existence of a particular person named John who is identifiable to both speaker and listener. In practice, of course, a speaker using such a sentence presupposes that the listener both knows the person being referred to and knows that the speaker means that particular person. For the sake of identifiability, it may be necessary to say "John McGrew is bald" if the listener knows several Johns, among them John McGrew, or "John McGrew, my next-door neighbor, is bald" if the listener does not know John McGrew at all. The examples using Fluffy and Mary both involve presuppositions carried by the use of a proper name. In both cases, it can be argued either that the child does not completely understand the presuppositions implicit in the use of a proper name or that he does not know to what extent those presuppositions are shared by his listener.

Factive Predicates   A second set of words that carry presuppositions are factive predicates such as *know, remember, be happy,* and *be sad* (Kiparsky and Kiparsky, 1971). When used in a sentence with a *that*-complement, such predicates presuppose the truth of the clause that follows them. Moreover, the presupposition remains regardless of whether the assertion made by the predicate is affirmative or negative. For example, both "John knew that Mary was coming" (or "John was happy that Mary was coming") and "John didn't know that Mary was coming" (or "John wasn't happy that Mary was coming") presuppose that Mary was coming, although they make opposite assertions about John's awareness of (or sentiments about) that fact. Nonfactive verbs such as *think* and *believe*, on the other hand, carry no presuppositions

---

[1] Occasionally, pronouns are used *cataphorically*, pointing ahead to a noun used later in the sentence.

about the truth of the clause that follows them. In neither "John thought that Mary was coming" nor "John didn't think that Mary was coming" is there any presupposition about whether she was actually coming.[2]

A major difference between the presuppositions carried by definite articles and those carried by factive predicates is their scope—how much of the rest of the sentence is involved in the presupposition. In the case of definite articles, the presupposition involves only the noun immediately following the article, along with any modifiers that noun may have. In the case of factive predicates, however, the presupposition involves the entire sentential complement that follows the factive predicate.

Different factive predicates carry presuppositions of varying complexity. Both *know* and *remember*, for example, are factives when used with *that*-complements. However, *remember* carries not only a presupposition about the truth of its sentential complement, but also a presupposition about past knowledge on the part of the person named by the subject of the verb. "John remembered that Mary was coming" implies: 1) that Mary was in fact coming, and 2) that John was at one time aware of that fact. Even if the sentence is negated ("John did not remember that Mary was coming"), the presupposition that John once knew she was coming remains, regardless of his failure to call that fact to mind in the present. As we have already suggested, one possible explanation for the Fluffy the cat example may be that the child does not understand the presuppositions carried by *remember* and therefore uses the word inappropriately, i.e., when the listener has no prior knowledge of the event being discussed.

Wh-questions Questions that begin with the so-called *wh*-words (who, what, when, where, why, and how) involve presuppositions with greater scope than those discussed so far. Instead of affecting only the immediately following noun or sentence complement, the presuppositions carried by a *wh*-word apply to the entire clause in which that word appears. Questions like "Why is Mary coming?" or "When is Mary coming?" presuppose that Mary is in fact coming; what is being asked for is additional information about that presupposed fact. Ac-

---

[2] There are also counterfactive predicates, such as *pretend* and *wish*, that carry the presupposition that the clause following the predicate is false. For example, "John pretended Mary was coming" and "John didn't pretend Mary was coming" both can be taken to presuppose that Mary was in fact *not* coming. However, some authors (e.g., Macnamara et al., 1976) have pointed out that the second sentence also can be construed to mean that Mary was in fact coming and thus John didn't have to *pretend* that she was. Consequently, rather than calling the assumption that Mary was not coming a presupposition of the first sentence, some investigators would call it an *implicative* of the first sentence—that is, a component of the sentence's meaning that is not its assertion, but that is affected by negation of the sentence.

tually, different *wh*-words carry slightly different presuppositions. For example, a speaker who asks "Why is Mary coming?" presupposes that Mary is coming for a reason; one who asks "When is Mary coming?" presupposes that she is coming at some time.

Unlike the presuppositions carried by definite reference and by factive predicates, the presuppositions carried by *wh*-words do not survive negation of the sentence. "Why isn't Mary coming?" carries a presupposition (that Mary is *not* coming) that is the exact opposite of the presupposition in "Why is Mary coming?" However, the failure of presuppositions to survive negation of *wh*-questions can be attributed to the scope of those presuppositions—the entire clause in which the *wh*-word appears. The presuppositions carried by factive predicates, for example, apply to the clause that follows the predicate, not to the clause in which the predicate appears. The presupposition in "John knew that Mary was coming" does not change if the factive predicate is negated, resulting in "John didn't know that Mary was coming." However, if the clause following the factive predicate were negated, resulting in "John knew that Mary wasn't coming," the presupposition would change—from an assumption that Mary *was* coming to an assumption that she *wasn't*. In that case, the negation would be within the scope of the presupposition carried by the factive predicate, just as negation in a *wh*-question is within the scope of the presupposition carried by the *wh*-word.

If a *wh*-question is recast as a statement, the parallel becomes even more obvious. For instance, "Why is Mary coming?" can be recast as "I want to know why Mary is coming," a sentence with a factive predicate. The presupposition (that Mary is coming) remains the same regardless of whether the sentence's assertion is negative or affirmative (whether the speaker wants to know or does not want to know why). That kind of negation is not possible when the sentence is expressed as a *wh*-question; presumably, if the speaker does not want to know why Mary is coming, he won't ask. The presupposition changes, however, if the clause following the factive predicate is negated (changed from "why Mary is coming" to "why Mary isn't coming")—and it is that kind of negation that is found in *wh*-questions.

Negation Another linguistic form that carries presuppositions is negation. As in the case of *wh*-words, the presuppositions carried by negation apply to the entire clause in which the negation occurs. The particular presupposition carried by plausible negation is, curiously enough, affirmation; that is, it makes no sense to deny something that has not been at least implicitly asserted. De Villiers and de Villiers (1978) provided useful examples: it would be considered odd, they pointed out, for a person to walk into a room and remark, without prior context, "This ceiling isn't blue" or "You don't have three heads." There would be no reason to suppose that the ceiling was blue or that the person being addressed had three heads, unless an expectation to that effect had been set up in earlier conversation or experience.[3]

The prior context need not be an explicit assertion, however. An expectation could arise from something implicit in the situation in which a remark is made, or it could involve an inference from an explicit assertion. A secretary who remarks to her boss, "I'm not your maid," when he asks her to pick up his dry cleaning is not responding to a direct claim that she is his maid. Instead, she is denying something that is implicit in his request and in her working situation. Another of the de Villiers' examples illustrated denial that requires an inference from a previous statement: one person remarks, "I saw John's wife," and another replies, "He's not married." The first person has not said John is married, but anyone who knows the meaning of the phrase *John's wife* can infer the claim that he is from what has been said. Other inferences that make negation plausible may depend on knowledge shared by the speaker and listener, rather than simply on knowledge of the language being spoken. De Villiers and de Villiers illustrated this point with the following exchange: "The Williamses have gone to Maine."—"Jane hasn't left." What makes the negation in the second remark plausible is personal knowledge that Jane is one of the Williamses.

Forms of Address Forms of address involve a type of presupposition that is slightly different from those we have discussed so far. Like the basically "semantic" forms of presupposition we have considered, the assumptions carried by forms of address are tied to the use of particular words. However, forms of address do not carry presuppositions about *other* words or assertions in the sentence. Instead, they carry presuppositions about the social situation in which they are used. The focus is on the pragmatic assumptions surrounding the use of a particular word or linguistic form, rather than on its semantic effect in a sentence.

In modern English, forms of address are limited to the names used to refer to or address others—*Mom, Dad, Aunt Helen, Uncle Harry, Chuck, Mrs. Smith,* and *Dr. Jones,* for example—as well as nicknames, epithets, and terms of endearment. Use of a name to address somebody carries the presuppositions already ascribed to proper names and definite articles: that there is a particular identifiable person to whom the

---

[3] The opposite point could, of course, be made about certain affirmative statements. At times, something may be asserted because it has been implicitly denied. A person might walk into a room and say, "This ceiling is *blue*," for instance, because he had been expecting a different color.

name refers and that the individual being addressed is that person. Forms of address, however, also carry presuppositions about the social context in which they are used. For example, calling a woman *Mary* generally implies greater familiarity than calling her *Mrs. Smith*. Calling her *dear* or *honey* implies still greater familiarity, unless the speaker happens to be a waitress or a sales clerk in a dress department. Addressing her as *you twit* carries a different set of assumptions, which may depend on the context in which it is used.

In many languages, variations in forms of address also include the distinction between formal and familiar second-person pronouns. In German, for example, *du* is the familiar second-person singular pronoun, used to address a family member, a close friend, a child, an animal, or an idiot. The formal pronoun, *Sie*, is used for everyone else. The use of *du* presupposes either that the speaker and listener are quite familiar with each other or that the listener has much lower status than the speaker. Distinguishing between formal and familiar pronouns is probably a more pervasive task in language use than choosing the appropriate name to call somebody, because *you* is used much more frequently than the listener's name in most conversations.

The type of presupposition involved in forms of address is sometimes referred to as pragmatic presupposition (Keenan, 1971). Some writers (e.g., Karttunen, 1974; McCawley, 1970) have argued that all presupposition can actually be described in terms of pragmatic assumptions and that the distinction between pragmatic and semantic presupposition is not a basic one. Indeed, pragmatic assumptions do seem to be a unifying theme in all of the types of presupposition we have discussed so far, despite the differences in their semantic significance. All of them require: 1) an understanding of the assumptions implicit in the forms involved; 2) an understanding of the degree to which those assumptions need to be shared by speaker and listener; and 3) the ability to determine whether or not the necessary assumptions are in fact shared in a given situation.

Moreover, the philosophical/linguistic distinction between semantic presupposition and pragmatic presupposition may not be an important one for the language-learning child. What may be more important are the distinctions between presuppositions that are implicit in communicative language, presuppositions that are carried by particular words or syntactic forms, and presuppositions that are carried by general linguistic devices such as stress and the ordering of information. What the child has to learn about presupposition and how he might go about learning it seems to be more related to those distinctions than to the semantic-pragmatic distinction. For example, learning the pragmatic or semantic implications that are part of a particular word's meaning is probably quite different from learning how to use stress in a sentence. On the other hand, learning the meaning of a word with strong pragmatic implications may not be very different from learning the meaning of a word with strong semantic implications.

Presuppositions Carried by General Linguistic Devices

In connected discourse, presuppositions are carried by general linguistic devices, such as word order and stress, as well as by particular words and linguistic forms. For example, the distinction between topic and comment in a sentence—a distinction that parallels that between presupposed and asserted information—is not conveyed by specific words, but rather by the order in which information is presented and by the stress applied to different words in the sentence.

Basically, the topic of a sentence is what the ongoing discourse is about. It is often (but not always) the surface subject in English. For example, in a discussion of glass, it would be natural to place nouns and pronouns referring to glass in initial sentence position, with low stress: "Glass has many interesting properties. For example, it is elastic." Glass is the topic of both sentences; the comment in both cases is information about glass—that it has many interesting properties and that one of them is elasticity.

However, the topic does not always appear in initial sentence position. A discussion of elasticity, for example, might include a statement like "Well, *glass* is elastic." The stress on *glass* indicates that the surface subject of the sentence is not playing its usual role of topic. In this case, the topic of the sentence is elasticity, and the comment is an example of a substance that is elastic.

Like the presuppositions of a sentence, the topic seems to be something already given; the comment, like the assertion of the sentence, is something new. Once the topic of a discourse (or a segment of discourse) has been established, the speaker may presuppose what the topic is and shape his sentences accordingly. Notice that both speaker and listener are involved in the notion of topic; the speaker assumes not only what the topic is but also that the listener shares that assumption.

Stress can also communicate a speaker's presuppositions in ways unrelated to the topic-comment distinction. Lakoff (1971) provided the following example: "John called Mary a Republican, and then she insulted him." If the sentence is said with normal stress, then it means simply that Mary insulted John for some reason after he had called her a Republican. Suppose instead that the sentence is pronounced with increasingly contrastive stress on *John, Republican, she,* and *him*: "John called Mary a Republican, and then *she* insulted *him*." The change in stress also brings a change in meaning; instead of insulting John for some unknown reason, Mary now seems to be returning an insult. The second stress pattern carries a presupposition on the part of the speaker—that to call someone a Republican is an insult.

The very choice of what to include and what to leave out of a sentence is as much a reflection of the speaker's presuppositions as are choices about what to stress and how to order information. Ellipsis, or the omission of information, particularly in response to questions, can indicate what the speaker regards as given or presupposed either in the question itself or in the situation. Thus, in answering a question, a speaker does not have to repeat information provided in the question. The answer to "Does this bus go downtown or to the zoo?" (or, for that matter, to "Where does this bus go?") is more likely to be "Downtown," or perhaps "It goes downtown," than "This bus goes downtown" (unless there is some reason to emphasize *this bus* in contrast to another bus). Clearly, the presuppositions involved in an elliptical answer are related to those carried by the particular forms used in the question. For example, the answer "Downtown" reflects the presupposition carried by *where*—i.e., that the bus goes somewhere.

Presupposition and the Roles of Speaker and Listener

Particularly in discussing presuppositions carried by words such as *the* and *know*, it may seem reasonable to talk about the presuppositions of a sentence per se. However, as Austin (1962) pointed out, it is not sentences that have presuppositions; rather, it is the speakers who use the sentences to communicate who have presuppositions. A speaker's presuppositions affect, among other things, his word choices and stress patterns; the sentences produced by a speaker thus reflect his own particular presuppositions and not simply an abstract set of logical presuppositions tied to the forms used. Consequently, it is generally more accurate to refer to the presuppositions of speakers than to the presuppositions of sentences.

In discussing children, it is especially important to differentiate between the presuppositions normally implied in the use of a word, linguistic form, or discourse device, and the speaker's presuppositions in using it. As we have already pointed out, a child may use the verb *remember*, for example, without realizing that its use implies previous knowledge. In that case, the presuppositions that might be ascribed to the sentence in isolation would differ from the actual presuppositions of the speaker, as a result of the speaker's imperfect understanding of the meaning of one word in the sentence.

A complete analysis of presupposition in communicative situations must include not only the assumptions of the speaker, but also the assumptions of the listener. Furthermore, the speaker's and listener's knowledge of the presuppositional elements particular to a given situation must be considered. Such consideration must include: 1) the knowledge each of them has about the standard presuppositions carried by the words or linguistic devices being used; and 2) the understanding each of them has of the other's background knowledge in the situation.

Jackendoff (1972) suggested that a conversation goes best if both speaker and listener continually share the same presuppositions. However, it seems important not only for speaker and listener to share the same presuppositions, but also for them to be aware of the fact that they do—or, perhaps even more important, to know when they do not. Children often seem to have particular difficulty in judging which presuppositions their listeners share with them; they may understand the presuppositions inherent in a word like *remember* but not recognize whether their listener has the same background knowledge they do. That is, they may know that *remember* implies previous knowledge but not know whether their listener has the particular previous knowledge implied in their use of the word.

There are thus two presuppositional skills that a child must master: he must learn what presuppositions are involved in particular usages, and he must learn how to tell when those presuppositions are fulfilled in particular situations. When he uses various words or linguistic devices, a child may be perfectly aware of the presuppositions he is making, but may have trouble recognizing whether those presuppositions are fulfilled.

Karttunen (1974) pointed out that an important part of conversation is making sure that certain presuppositions are shared by the speaker and the listener. A speaker can establish common presuppositions in various ways, some more explicit than others. Sitting in a living room where there is only one stereo, a visitor might simply ask "How long have you had the stereo?" to introduce *the stereo* as a unique referent in that conversational context. In some situations, he might introduce it more cautiously, with an indefinite expression such as "I see you have a stereo." In situations where a unique referent is not immediately present, an even more explicit introduction may be necessary, as in the following example: "Do you know my sister Sue? She's moving to Rome for a year." Children may not be very skilled at using such introductions to check listeners' presuppositions, or even at knowing when introductions are necessary—as the example about Mary the big sister illustrates. Learning such skills seems to be a different kind of task from learning the presuppositions that are part of a word's meaning, however.

There are cases in which a speaker can convey new information with a usage that normally expresses presupposed information without much conversational dislocation. For example, when John asks Mary why Garth is smiling, she may answer, "Oh, he's happy that his tax refund came." For Mary, the tax refund's coming is presupposed in the use of the factive predicate *is happy*. For John, the arrival of the refund may be new information, but he can easily assimilate that information, in part because its truth is presupposed in the predicate Mary used. Besides, it is probably not startling information to John, assuming that he knows Garth is in a position to have paid taxes and possibly to receive a refund. Unexpected information, on the other hand, usually requires explicit assertion. If Mary were to reply, "Oh, he's happy that he inherited the million dollars," John might have more difficulty assimilating the information. In general, a speaker can expect a listener to understand unshared presupposed information if it is easily assimilated to knowledge the listener already has. Unexpected or uncommon information, however, should be introduced on its own before being treated as presupposed material. Again, children may lack skill in recognizing when a separate introduction is necessary and when it is redundant, because they may not know enough about the listener's knowledge to recognize information that the listener would regard as unexpected or uncommon.

EMPIRICAL FINDINGS ABOUT CHILDREN'S PRESUPPOSITION

As we have already suggested, it is probably not very useful—or very accurate—to talk about children acquiring and developing a single, uniform ability that applies to all instances of linguistic presupposition. There are several reasons why that is so. First, children need to apply presuppositional analysis to use a wide variety of linguistic constructions and devices, ranging from pronouns and articles to word order and stress. However, the particular presuppositions involved and the way in which they are expressed vary considerably across that range of forms. In addition, the time and manner of acquiring the various presuppositional constructions are influenced by factors that are not directly involved in presuppositional analysis and that are unlikely to be shared by all of those constructions.

Second, the heading "presuppositional analysis" subsumes several related but probably separate tasks: 1) understanding what presuppositions are carried by various words and linguistic devices; 2) accurately using words and linguistic devices that carry presuppositions; and 3) judging what listeners already know in a given situation. Separating those tasks to determine the cause of a child's presuppositional error may be difficult or impossible, especially because an error could be due to difficulty with any combination of them. One sense in which it might be valid to speak of the development of presupposition, however, is in discussing children's emerging skill at presuppositional analysis with particular presuppositional forms; in fact, that is what existing research evidence allows us to do with the most confidence.

Third, it seems very unlikely that the basic ability to analyze things according to presupposed and asserted content truly "develops" in the sense of being acquired, because it is hard to see how experience could be relevant to constructing such an ability. In other words, it seems unlikely that children somehow learn to presuppose. Unless it can be shown that presupposition itself can be broken down into more primitive parts for which acquisition of knowledge and analysis of experience are necessary, it can be assumed that some rudimentary type of presupposition is a given that children bring to the task of language acquisition.

We do not mean to say that children have adult competence in the various kinds and elements of presupposition from the time that they begin to use language. Instead, children begin with some basic ability to presuppose and to separate presupposition from assertion. Presuppositional analysis is then instantiated over an ever-widening range of constructions as other development takes place. For example, the use of contrastive stress to express presupposition—as in "John called Mary a Republican, and then *she* insulted *him*"—is a fairly subtle presuppositional device and, we would guess, one that is not mastered until relatively late. To use or completely understand such a sentence, a child would have to be able to interpret change, constancy of meaning, and surface structure similarity across clauses. Thus, other developments in grammar and cognition may be required before a presuppositional analysis can be successfully made; the failure of such an analysis may be due not to an inability to make or understand presuppositions, but rather to other cognitive and linguistic limitations.

The question in considering the development of presupposition in children is thus not how do children learn to presuppose, but rather how do children learn to understand and express the particular presuppositions carried by various words and linguistic devices? The process by which such development occurs seems to vary tremendously for the different elements of presupposition that we have discussed. Some basic aspects of presupposition are probably present from the very beginning of language use; however, specific presuppositions carried by particular words have to be learned as those words are acquired.

The more complicated presuppositional devices that appear in discourse may be fully mastered only after other necessary cognitive and linguistic skills have been acquired.

Early Presupposition

Surprisingly enough, some research suggests that it is possible to speak in a nontrivial way about presupposition and assertion in children's speech at the one- and two-word stages. We have already suggested that certain presuppositions about the roles of speaker and listener are inherent in the use of language to communicate. Although that assertion is probably unresearchable, there are other elements of presupposition in children's early language that are amenable to study.

Investigators such as Greenfield and Smith (1976) and Greenfield and Zukow (1978) have applied the notions of topic and comment—which, as already noted, parallel the notions of presupposition and assertion—to children's speech in the one-word stage. They point out that children at that stage usually verbalize the new or changing aspects of a situation, omitting the given or unchanging aspects. Greenfield and her colleagues interpret those early utterances as comment on a topic, with the topic being the physical element that is undergoing change or serving as the focus of attention. For example, suppose a child is putting different objects into the same bucket. In this situation, the child is likely to give the names of the changing objects, rather than the unchanging bucket, which provides a kind of background for the actions. On the other hand, if a child is putting the same objects in different locations, among them a bucket, then "bucket" is more likely to be uttered. MacWhinney and Bates (1978) cited similar observations from DeLaguna (1927), Sechehaye (1926), and Vygotsky (1962).

Such usages are similar to more complex examples of presupposition in that they involve a distinction between given and new elements. Given elements can be viewed as presuppositions and new elements as assertions. It is quite probable, however, that the given-new distinction is not learned as part of a conventional linguistic system. Rather, as Bates (1976) hypothesized, the tendency to give preference to new rather than given information probably has deeper roots; infants as young as a few days of age attend to novel stimuli more than to old background information, for example. Children who are beginning to speak probably still pay more attention to the new elements of a situation than to those that are given; consequently, they are more likely to talk about the new elements. Children do not comment on new elements because they have learned to do so as part of the structure of the language they are learning or because they presuppose that their listeners already know the given elements. Instead, they talk about what they notice—namely, the new elements in the situation. At the given-new level, presupposition is thus inherent not only in early language, but also in early experience.

There are also some linguistic uses common to early language that seem closely related to the kind of presupposition carried by particular words. For example, children in the one-word stage commonly use terms such as *allgone* and *nomore* (to denote disappearance), *more* (to denote either desired or actual recurrence), and *no* (to denote denial that something exists or rejection of something that is present). Bloom (1973) provided many examples of such usages. Used in this way, *allgone* and *nomore* carry the presupposition that something was present before disappearing, *more* carries the presupposition that some other instance of a class is already present or was present earlier, and *no* carries the presupposition of something to be denied or rejected.

All of these uses seem closer to conventional linguistic presupposition than the topic-comment analysis offered by Greenfield and her colleagues. Appropriate use of terms like *allgone, more,* and *no* cannot easily be accounted for by a general attentional mechanism. Instead, they seem to require some understanding of the conventional meanings of the terms; a semantic element is thus introduced into presuppositional analysis even at this early stage.

Recurrence and disappearance are among the most common meanings expressed during both the one- and the two-word stages (Bloom, 1973). At the one-word stage, the child's utterance includes only an assertion—that something has disappeared ("allgone") or recurred ("more"), for example. What it is that has disappeared or recurred remains an unstated presupposition. At the two-word stage, however, the child produces utterances such as "more cereal" and "allgone shoe." In those utterances, the presupposed element (cereal, shoe) and the assertion about that element (recurrence, disappearance) are expressed together.

Other early words that carry presuppositions include proper names and personal pronouns. As discussed earlier, proper names and personal pronouns carry presuppositions about the existence of particular, identifiable persons and the social roles of conversational partners. As utterances become longer, such presuppositions become more obvious. Sentences like "Lois hat" and "Lois no hat" clearly carry the presupposition that there exists someone named Lois who is known to both speaker and listener, regardless of whether she has or does not have a hat.

It seems clear that, as early as could be expected in speech, the essentials of presupposition are both understood and expressed by young children. The examples, of course, are very simple; the complex interaction of presupposition with various linguistic devices is not yet present. However, the existence of early presuppositional usages suggests that presupposition is developmentally very simple, a given primitive of analysis, not unlike such perceptual abilities as the detection of motion. The later instantiation of more complex linguistic presupposition depends on relevant syntactic and semantic development, but it is very difficult to claim that presupposition itself undergoes any marked changes over the course of the child's development.

There seems to be something more involved in presupposition, however, than the given-new or figure-ground relations that have been suggested as primitive counterparts of presupposition. One of the defining characteristics of presupposition is that the presupposed element constitutes part of the meaning of the entire construction; it is not simply a ground against which the figure moves as a complete whole. For example, the use of the predicate *be happy*, as in "John is happy that Mary came," presupposes the truth of the sentential complement and asserts someone's emotional reaction to it. When someone is happy, they are happy *about* something; that relationship is an intrinsic part of the meaning of the predicate. The role of the presuppositional element in such a sentence is thus a more integrated one than is commonly ascribed to the given or the ground. Instead, the position of a presupposed element in a sentence seems analogous to the role of the object of a sensorimotor schema such as "picking up" or "pushing aside." Obviously, the notion of "picking up" presupposes something to pick up; that of "pushing aside," something to push aside. The existence of something for the schema to operate on is inherent in the schema itself, just as a presupposed element is inherent in the meaning of a presuppositional linguistic form. In both cases, there is interaction between the given element and the operation upon it.

Although there seem to be correlates to presupposition in sensorimotor development, it does not necessarily follow that linguistic presupposition somehow grows out of early sensorimotor development. It could well be that the ability to presuppose or to separate given from new elements is basic to both sensorimotor and linguistic development, but that this ability is instantiated earlier in sensorimotor schemata because they develop earlier than linguistic ones. Similarly, linguistic presupposition is seen earlier in predicates such as *allgone* than in sentential predicates such as *be happy* because the requisite grammar and semantics develop earlier for the former type of predicate.

To summarize, our essential claim is that there is little or no development of presupposition itself with a child's increasing linguistic skill. Rather, there is an increasing instantiation of presupposition across a wider variety of constructions, some of which provide interesting developmental problems. There may, of course, be some generalization of presuppositional knowledge between related constructions. For example, a child might generalize some portion of the presuppositional analysis required by one factive predicate to other factive predicates, rather than learning them all as a list. Subtle analysis will be required to find such possibilities, however; they do not seem likely to emerge straightforwardly from empirical data.

The lack of any revealing overall sequence of development for presupposition thus stems not only from the general scarcity of empirical data but also from the lack of a unifying theoretical motivation for describing such a sequence. Whatever developmental trends may emerge are likely to be ascribable more to differences in the complexity of the linguistic constructions that convey presuppositions than to differences in the type of presuppositions being made or the child's ability to make or understand them.

Later Use of Particular Presuppositional Constructions

Much of the research on children's command of presupposition is concerned with their use and understanding of particular words and constructions that carry presuppositions. Understandably, there has been very little research that deals directly with more general notions of presupposition. Grice's (1975) conversational postulates, for example, are often cited by researchers interested in presupposition, but there has been little research directly investigating the child's awareness of Grice's postulates, probably because they are too general to be easily researched. However, much of the work with specific presuppositional constructions does relate indirectly to Grice's notions, because his postulates are partially instantiated in those specific constructions. Informativeness and relevance, for example, are partly a matter of correct usage of definite and indefinite articles, proper names, and pronouns—which in turn depends partly on the speaker's understanding of what the listener knows.

Definite Reference Among the most frequently studied words that carry presuppositions are those involving definite reference, particularly the definite article *the*. We have already discussed in some detail the presuppositions carried by *the*, proper nouns, and definite pronouns. The presuppositions carried by these words vary, but they all include reference to a particular class member that can be uniquely identified within the discourse. That referent need not actually exist or be physically present; it need only have been previously introduced or be otherwise identifiable from the discourse context.

In every case, appropriate use of a word that carries definite reference requires that the speaker not only know the general conditions for its use, but also be able to tell when those conditions are satisfied in a particular conversation. A speaker might use the definite article *the* incorrectly either because he does not realize that it has to have a particular, identifiable referent for the listener as well as for the speaker, or because he does not know that a particular referent is not identifiable for the listener.

In general, children seem to make the distinction between definite and indefinite reference very well, even in the early preschool years. Brown (1973), in a search through naturalistic records of three children, found that such uses are generally correct. Maratsos (1974, 1976) gave further evidence of young preschool children's sophistication in dealing with this distinction. In a comprehension task, children saw a boy doll go up to three dogs in cars and begin talking to one. The children were told either, "Suddenly the dog drove away," or "Suddenly a dog drove away," and were asked to indicate which dog drove away. In the first case, the correct answer is the contextually specific dog, the one the boy was talking to. In the second case, the correct answer is a contextually nonspecific dog—one of the other two dogs. Three- and 4-year-olds who used the articles in their natural speech answered accurately 85% of the time.

Maratsos also used tasks that lacked contextual support from toys. For instance, he asked children questions that were designed to elicit either definite or indefinite articles, based on short stories. One such story involved a man who goes to the jungle to find a lion or a zebra. One version ends, "He looked for a lion or a zebra everywhere. He looked and looked. Suddenly, who came running out at the man?" The correct answer, unless the child decides to introduce a new character, is "*a* lion" or "*a* zebra," because no particular lion or zebra was mentioned in the story. The other version ends, "Then the man found a lion and a zebra together. Who came running out at the man?" In this case, the correct answer is "*the* lion" or "*the* zebra," because a particular lion and a particular zebra were referred to in the story. On this task, children again demonstrated a sophisticated ability to choose correctly between definite and indefinite articles, with even the youngest children performing above a chance level on the task. However, the errors that they did make suggested that they sometimes assumed that the listener shared a common referent with them when that assumption could not truly be made.

Other empirical evidence also suggests a deficiency in children's ability to take into account the listener's knowledge in determining conversational uniqueness of reference. Brown (1973) cited exchanges such as the following in his data:

Sarah: The cat's dead.
Mother: What cat?

The mother's response indicates that she knows *the cat* should call up a particular referent for her, but it does not. Sarah may know what cat she is talking about, but she does not seem to realize that her mother does not know.

Warden (1976) used a task in which children were given pictures to describe to a listener who could not see them. He found that even preschool children almost always referred to conversationally established referents with definite articles; children as young as 7 always did so. However, preschoolers sometimes also used definite articles to introduce new referents to the listener. In fact, 3-year-olds were slightly more likely to use definite articles than indefinite ones for that purpose. Although errors in choosing between definite and indefinite articles decreased with age, 9-year-olds still used definite articles to introduce new referents 18% of the time. Thus, errors were in the direction of assuming a shared referent when none existed, with that tendency decreasing with age.

Peterson employed perhaps the most ecologically interesting task to study children's use of definite and indefinite articles (Menig-Peterson, 1975; Peterson, 1974). In her study, 3- and 4-year-olds participated individually with an adult in a play session that included a staged accident, such as a spilled glass of Kool-Aid or an escaped gerbil. A week later, the child returned to the same room, with either the same or a different adult, and was induced to tell the adult something about the previous session. Peterson found that 3-year-olds' use of definite and indefinite articles did not depend on whether the listener had been present at the events being described. Four-year-olds did make some distinction, using more definite reference with adults who had been present in the previous session than with adults who had not been present.

Karmiloff-Smith (1977) has suggested that children's earliest uses of definite articles may seem anaphoric to an adult observer, but may actually be exophoric, referring to something in the extralinguistic environment rather than to something that has already been introduced linguistically. Furthermore, her study with French-speaking children suggested that use of *the* and *a* is not usually the only linguistic means by which children make their reference unambiguous; *the same* and *another* are often used to clarify reference. If early definite article use is tied to situationally introduced referents and is not truly anaphoric, that might explain why young children often seem to be able to use definite and indefinite articles correctly within a concrete situation but overuse the definite article in referring to items that are not physically present. Children's early use of definite articles to introduce a referent in a conversation may be exophoric in the sense that the children are trying to point to the referent itself—even though it is not physically present—and are ignoring its linguistic status.

Most research on children's use of pronouns has concentrated on the deixis of first and second person pronoun usage, a somewhat different issue than the one that concerns us here. With a few exceptions, research on third person pronouns also has focused on their deictic function (Charney, 1980), rather than on their anaphoric function. However, the research that has been done on anaphoric third person pronoun usage has yielded results that parallel those obtained for definite and indefinite articles.

In a detailed study of two children, Huxley (1970) found correct use of *he*, *she*, *it*, and *they* by age 3. Those results parallel Brown's (1973) findings of early correct use of definite and indefinite articles. However, Bloom, Lightbown, and Hood (1975) found variation among 2-year-olds in the extent to which the children used pronouns; some used many pronouns whereas others used mainly nouns. Bloom et al. hypothesized that the children they studied used nouns and pronouns initially as separate systems, had individual preferences for one of the systems, and did not recognize that one could be substituted for the other. However, neither of these studies addresses the issue of whether the pronouns referred appropriately to particular, identifiable persons and things.

Chipman and de Dardel (1974) studied 3- to 6-year-olds' interpretations of the definite pronoun *it* in sentences in which *it* referred to substances or collections. The experimenters read the children sequences of sentences like "There is Play-Doh there. Give it to me" and then recorded the children's responses. They found that all of the children made the minimal anaphoric connection, understanding that *it* referred to the substance previously mentioned. However, the younger children gave the experimenter only part of the substance—a piece of the Play-Doh, for example—rather than all of it. Chipman and de Dardel concluded that the children were interpreting *it* to mean "one piece" of the substance previously mentioned, and that they did not understand that the quantifier "all" is implicit when the definite pronoun *it* refers to substances or collections.

Reanalyzing Chipman and de Dardel's results, Tanz (1977) suggested that the children might actually have been interpreting *it* as the indefinite pronoun "some," because they sometimes handed the experimenter more than one piece of the substance or collection requested. She repeated Chipman and de Dardel's experiment, giving 3-

to 5-year-olds either requests using *it*, requests using noun phrases with definite articles (e.g., "Give me the Play-Doh"), or requests using *some* (e.g., "Give me some Play-Doh"). She also added items that involved plural nouns and the definite pronoun *them*, such as "There are flowers on the table. Give them to me." She did not obtain the same results as Chipman and de Dardel for the items using *it*; even her youngest subjects nearly always gave the experimenters all of the substance or collection requested. They also usually responded appropriately to the requests using *the* and *some*. The youngest children, however, had some difficulty with the requests using *them*; sometimes they gave the experimenter only part of what had been requested. Tanz concluded that children understand the quantitative implications of definite and indefinite pronouns at an early age, with the implications of *them* understood slightly later than the implications of *it*.

Nelson (1975) found that over 90% of the pronouns used by a group of 2-year-olds referred to a person or object that was physically present or understood from the nonlinguistic context. In the cases in which pronouns referred to previously introduced nouns, those nouns were almost always from a previous sentence; almost never did the children produce a sentence like "Henry was sure he could come," in which a pronoun referred to a noun within the same sentence. Overall, pronouns were used more frequently than nouns, especially in sentences; the redundant use of nouns where pronouns would have been more appropriate was quite rare.

Van Hekken, Vergeer, and Harris (1980) examined 4- to 6-year-olds' use of potentially ambiguous third person pronouns in a play situation with another child. They found that children often used nonverbal means, such as pointing, to indicate what they intended a pronoun to refer to. Furthermore, children's pronoun usage was much more likely to be ambiguous in situations where only verbal disambiguation was possible—when the object referred to was not present, for example. These results as well as Nelson's findings seem related to Karmiloff-Smith's (1977) contention that early definite reference is exophoric rather than anaphoric.

To summarize, children as young as 2 can use pronouns correctly and seem to recognize that a pronoun can be used to refer to an already established referent. However, even older children do not always seem to be able to tell when a referent has *not* achieved unique discourse status. The errors that continue to be made seem to be mostly in the direction of mistakenly assuming a shared referent, as was the case with definite articles.

Children thus differentiate definite from indefinite reference to some extent reasonably early, but it takes some time for that differentiation to become reliable. What seems to give them the most trouble is making the correct presuppositions about their conversational partner's knowledge. For some time, they may not understand the relevance of what the listener knows to their own choice of an article or pronoun. That problem could be exacerbated by the fact that, in the earliest speech contexts, the child and those around him generally share conversational knowledge (see Snow, this volume). However, as the child begins to talk about a wider variety of topics with a wider range of people, he cannot always assume a set of shared presuppositions. At that point, the difficulties of computing the discourse status of the referents in particular situations may easily overwhelm him, and his incomplete appreciation of the connection between a listener's knowledge and definiteness of reference may result in apparently egocentric reference. The research literature on referential communication, summarized by Glucksberg, Krauss, and Higgins (1975) and by Flavell (1977), provides ample evidence of children's difficulties in adjusting all sorts of reference to the needs of particular listeners in particular situations—at least when those situations are experimental ones.

It is highly dubious, however, that the problems arise from a general inability to take into account the fact that one's own viewpoint or knowledge may differ from that of a listener. Many recent studies show not only that preschool children have knowledge of others' points of view, even when these diverge from their own (e.g., Lempers, Flavell, and Flavell, 1977), but also that they can modulate their communications accordingly (e.g., Maratsos, 1973b; Shatz and Gelman, 1973). Menig-Peterson's (1975) study, in fact, included many indices of ways in which children might vary their accounts according to the knowledgeability of their listeners. For example, they should use more elaborate descriptions of referents and simply talk more overall to unknowledgeable listeners. In fact, the children in her study did both of those things, even the 3-year-olds who did not differentiate in their article usage. The problem seemed to be not that they did not realize that the listeners' knowledge differed from their own, but that they did not know exactly *how* it differed and could not yet reliably use definite and indefinite articles to reflect their appreciation of the difference. Children's difficulties in using definite and indefinite reference can thus be explained by the complex analyses required for the appropriate use of articles and pronouns, rather than by a generalized inability to take into account the listener's viewpoint or knowledge.

Factive Predicates Another set of presuppositional words whose use and understanding by children has been heavily studied is the factive predicates, especially factive verbs such as *know* and *remember*. There have been a number of studies that have been directly concerned with children's knowledge of the factivity of these predicates (Harris,

1975; Hopmann and Maratsos, 1978; Johnson and Maratsos, 1977; Macnamara, Baker, and Olson, 1976; Scoville and Gordon, 1980) or that are relevant to the problem (Johnson and Wellman, 1980; Miscione et al., 1978; Wellman and Johnson, 1979). Most of the studies concerned with factives also have included tests of knowledge of nonfactive predicates such as *want*, *guess*, and *say*, and some have dealt with children's understanding of the additional presuppositions associated with verbs such as *remember*.

Studies of Factivity Harris (1975) examined 4- to 12-year-olds' and adults' comprehension of sentences involving factive predicates (*know* and *be happy*), nonfactive predicates (*say* and *whisper*), and counterfactive predicates (*wish* and *pretend*). Counterfactive predicates carry the presupposition that the clause following the predicate is *false* (see footnote #2). Three of the tasks that Harris used were: 1) responses to imperative sentences, 2) judgments about the truth value of sentence complements, and 3) judgments of sentence anomaly. He found that children's responses to imperative sentences containing counterfactives ("Pretend that you are stamping your foot") changed considerably from nursery school to sixth grade. The most common response among the 4-year-olds was simply to do the action called for in the complement, regardless of what the predicate was; instead of pretending or saying that they were stamping their feet, these children would actually stamp. The frequency of that error decreased with age, but it had not completely disappeared even among the sixth graders. Understanding of nonfactives lagged behind understanding of counterfactives. Second-graders performed quite well on the counterfactives, but performance on the nonfactives did not reach a comparable level until fifth grade.

Harris asked both children and adults to judge whether complements of sentences containing factive, nonfactive, and counterfactive predicates were true or false; both the predicates and the complements could be either affirmative or negative. For example, subjects would hear "David said that he was not in trouble" and then would be asked "Was David in trouble?" Subjects of all ages generally recognized the presupposed truth of the complements of factive predicates, especially when the factive predicates were affirmative. They were slightly less likely to recognize the presupposed falsity of the complements of counterfactives. Only the adults recognized that nonfactive predicates carried no presuppositions about the truth or falsity of their complements; children of all ages tended to judge the complements of nonfactive predicates to be true.

Harris also asked subjects to judge whether various sentences containing factives, nonfactives, and counterfactives were anomalous. As in the truth judgment task, predicates and complements could be either affirmative or negative. Some of the sentences contained tautological complements ("his sister was a girl"), some contained contradictory complements ("his father was a tree"), and some neutral complements ("George lived in New York"). As a result, in one group of sentences—those with factive predicates and tautological complements ("Johnny knew that his sister was a girl")—the complement was logically in accord with the presuppositions carried by the predicate. In a second group, sentences with factive predicates and contradictory complements ("Johnny knew that his father was a tree"), the complement violated the presuppositions carried by the predicate. Finally, in a third group, there was no possibility of logical conflict or accord because either the predicate carried no presuppositions about factivity ("Johnny said that his father was a tree") or the complement was logically neutral ("Johnny knew/said/pretended that George lived in New York"). Sentences in which the complement was in logical conflict with the presuppositions carried by the predicate were considered anomalous.

Recognition of anomaly improved through adulthood. All age groups showed the most accurate performance on sentences containing factive predicates and the least accurate performance on sentences containing nonfactives. Subjects of all ages seemed to base their judgments of truth value on the logical plausibility of the sentence more than on conflicts between the presuppositions carried by the predicates and the logical status of the complement. Thus, sentences such as "Johnny said that his father was a tree" were often judged anomalous even though predicates like *said* carry no presuppositions to be violated by their complements. That result may have been produced by the instructions used in the anomaly judgment task. Subjects were asked whether sentences were "funny" or not, an instruction that may have invited responses based on overall plausibility of the sentences rather than on logical consistency.

In summary, across his tasks Harris found that subjects of all ages had the most difficulty with nonfactive predicates, somewhat less with counterfactives, and the least with factives. Developmentally, children seemed to gain command of factive predicates first, followed by counterfactives, and then by nonfactives. Understanding of all three types of predicates improved from age 4 to age 12. However, 12-year-olds did not perform as well as adults did—and even adults had some difficulty, especially with nonfactives.

Hopmann and Maratsos (1978) studied 4-, 5-, and 7-year-olds' understanding of factive and nonfactive predicates, using toys for contextual support. The factive predicates in their study were *know, be surprising, be happy, be nice,* and *be sad*; the nonfactives were *think, be possible*, *desire*, *be true*, and *want*. Like Harris, they used both affirmative and negative forms of the predicates, to test whether children understood when negation of the predicate affected the truth of its complement.

In Hopmann and Maratsos' study, children were shown two toys, such as a boy doll and a girl doll, and were told that one of the two was going to do something. The child then heard and repeated a sentence that mentioned only one of the toys, such as "It's nice that the boy sleeps in the bed." For the predicates that required an animate subject, such as *know*, *be happy*, and *think*, the experimenter held a Dumbo hand puppet and used sentences like "Dumbo knows that the boy sleeps in the bed." After the child repeated the sentence, he was then asked a question that required him to tell which toy actually did whatever was described in the sentence complement—for example, "Who sleeps in the bed?" For affirmative and negative factive predicates ("It's nice/it isn't nice that the boy sleeps in the bed") and for some affirmative nonfactive predicates ("It's true that the boy sleeps in the bed"), the correct answer to the question was the toy that was mentioned in the sentence (*the boy*). For some negative nonfactive predicates ("It's not true/not possible that the boy sleeps in the bed"), however, the correct answer was the toy that was not mentioned—in this case, *the girl*. For other nonfactive predicates (*think*, *desire*, *want*, and the affirmative forms of *be possible*), the correct answer was that it was impossible to tell.

Only one of the 60 children who participated in the study ever used the "can't tell" response to the questions, which is not surprising because the instructions strongly encouraged the children to choose one of the toys. The 4-year-olds were more likely than the older children to choose the toy that was not mentioned in response to negative factive sentences such as "It isn't nice that the boy sleeps in the bed." That response was less frequent among the 5-year-olds; and the 7-year-olds were no more likely to choose the unmentioned toy in response to negative factives than in response to affirmative factives. In response to nonfactive predicates, even the youngest children were more likely to choose the unmentioned toy if the nonfactive was negative than if it was affirmative, and that distinction became more definite with age. However, nearly half of the 4-year-olds, one-quarter of the 5-year-olds, and one-sixth of the 7-year-olds never chose the unmentioned toy at all, but seemed to be basing their answers strictly on the complements of the sentences they heard. That finding is analogous to the results Harris obtained.

There were differences in the children's responses to various factive predicates. The children seemed to master the predicates *know* and *be surprising* earlier than *be nice*, *be sad*, and *be happy*. Hopmann and Maratsos suggested that the affective content of *be nice*, *be sad*, and *be happy* makes them more difficult to interpret because extra pragmatic factors are involved. In addition, *know* may be somewhat simpler than *be happy* and *be sad* because the meaning of *know* is included in the meaning of the other two predicates. Thus, "Dumbo is happy that the boy sleeps in the bed" carries two presuppositions: 1) that the boy sleeps in the bed, and 2) that Dumbo knows he does.

Hopmann and Maratsos suggested that their study may have underestimated children's comprehensions of factive and nonfactive predicates because their tasks made comprehension more complicated than it is in normal conversation. Ordinarily, a sentence like "Dumbo isn't happy that the boy sleeps in the bed" would be used in a situation in which it was already clear to both speaker and listener that the boy sleeps in the bed. The presupposition that the boy sleeps in the bed would be established before Dumbo's feelings about the boy's sleeping habits were described. In Hopmann and Maratsos' experimental task, however, the child had to infer the presupposition backward from the use of a factive predicate—i.e., because *be happy* always presupposes the truth of its sentential complement, then it must be that the boy sleeps in the bed, despite the fact that the sentence is negative. Of course, as we pointed out earlier, a shared presupposition can be established simply by the use of a factive predicate, provided that the presupposed information is not too unusual or too unexpected for the listener to assimilate. Nevertheless, the backward inference of a presupposition outside a conversational context is not the usual way children are called on to use and understand factive predicates.

Scoville and Gordon (1980) compared children's and adults' understanding of five factive and five nonfactive verbs, using a videotaped quiz show format. Their subjects were kindergartners, second, fifth, and eighth graders, and adults. The factive verbs they used were *know*, *forget*, *be sorry*, *be happy*, and *be surprised*; the nonfactives were *be sure*, *think*, *figure*, *say*, and *believe*. Subjects saw a blindfolded "mindreader" named Dr. Fact try to guess the color of balls chosen by his "assistant." After each ball was drawn, Dr. Fact would whisper something to his assistant, who would then say a sentence of the form "Dr. Fact thinks the ball is red," which the subject would repeat. An announcer would then appear on the screen and ask "Is the ball red?" The subject could respond *yes*, *no*, or *don't know*.

The sentences referring to Dr. Fact followed three patterns: affirmative main predicate/affirmative complement, affirmative main predicate/negative complement, and negative main predicate/affirmative complement. Scoville and Gordon found that adults almost always recognized that negation of factive predicates did not affect the truth of the sentence complements. Kindergartners and second graders were as likely to assume that negation of factive predicates did affect the truth of the sentence complements as to assume that it did not. However, nearly half of the responses given by those two age groups did not clearly indicate either assumption and were not reported. Although eighth graders were still not performing at an adult level, the recognition of factivity did increase with age. At the same time, the tendency to equate the negation of factive predicates with the negation of their complements decreased with age. Fifth graders were as likely to make that mistake as second graders were, but eighth graders were much less likely to do so and adults never did.

In response to nonfactive predicates, kindergartners, second graders, and fifth graders often responded as if negating the main predicate negated the complement. That response pattern was less frequent in eighth graders and almost nonexistent in adults. The tendency to respond that the truth value of the sentence complement was indeterminate increased steadily from kindergarten to adulthood. Even in adulthood, however, subjects did not always respond to nonfactive verbs as if the truth value of their complements were indeterminate. Scoville and Gordon (1980) suggested that such responses indicate a continuum of factivity in adult interpretation of verbs, rather than a clear factive-nonfactive dichotomy.

Scoville and Gordon also compared their results to those found in other studies of factive verbs. They noted that their finding of fairly late mastery of the factive-nonfactive distinction is more in line with Harris' (1975) results than with Hopmann and Maratsos' (1978). They attributed part of the age discrepancy to differences in subject populations and experimental techniques. However, they also suggested that the evidence across studies argues for gradual acquisition of the factivity distinction on a verb-by-verb basis, rather than more general, sudden, once-and-for-all acquisition.

Johnson and Maratsos (1977) examined 3- and 4-year-olds' understanding of the nonfactive verb *think* and the factive verb *know*. They told children stories in which one character hid an object and then told another character that the object was in a different hiding place. The children were then asked questions about the seeker's and the hider's knowledge of where the object was hidden—for example, "Does Mary (the seeker) know that the duck is under this box?" "Does Mary think that the duck is under this box?" "Does John (the hider) know that the duck is under this box?" "Does John think that the duck is under this box?" The questions were designed to test the children's understanding of the fact that use of the verb *know* presupposes the truth of its complement while use of the verb *think* does not. The correct answers were, of course, that the hider *knew* (and also *thought*) that the object was in its real hiding place, while the seeker *thought* that it was in the false hiding place but could not *know* that it was there—because he did not see the other character hiding the object and it wasn't really there at all.

Both the 3-year-olds and the 4-year-olds in Johnson and Maratsos' study consistently agreed that the seeker *thought* the object was in the false hiding place and that the hider *knew* the object was in the true hiding place. However, the 3-year-olds also tended to agree that the seeker *knew* the object was in the true hiding place and even that the hider *thought* the object was in the false hiding place. The 4-year-olds, on the other hand, usually recognized that the seeker did not know the object was in the real hiding place and the hider did not think it was in the false hiding place. The 3-year-olds' answers may be ascribed to a response bias—a tendency to answer "yes" to all of the questions. The children were also asked questions of the form "Does Mary/John *think* the duck is under this box or does she/he *know* the duck is under this box?" The 3-year-olds showed a slight tendency to respond *know* for both the seeker and the hider, but the 4-year-olds consistently chose *think* for the seeker and *know* for the hider. Overall, the results suggest that 3-year-olds do not fully understand the distinctions between *think* and *know*, but that 4-year-olds in some sense recognize that *know* presupposes the truth of its complement and *think* does not.

Macnamara et al. (1976) were interested in 4-year-olds' ability to understand and draw conclusions from sentences containing *pretend*, *forget*, and *know*. They drew a strict line between presuppositions (components of the meaning of a sentence that are not affected by negation of the predicate) and implicatives (sentence meaning components that are not part of the assertion of the sentence but that are affected by negation) in their examination of those three verbs. They told children stories containing a key sentence that used either *pretend*, *forget*, or *know*; then they asked questions designed to test the children's understanding of the presuppositions and implicatives of the verbs.

Macnamara et al. found that 4-year-olds showed a partial understanding of the implicative of *pretend*: that the complement in sentences such as "Robert, you're pretending you're sick" is false. [Some researchers, such as Harris (1975) refer to the falsity of complements in such sentences as a presupposition of *pretend* rather than an implicative.] Because Macnamara et al. viewed complement falsity as an implicative and not a presupposition of *pretend* sentences, they construed the negative version of that type of sentence (i.e., "Robert, you're not pretending you're sick") to mean that Robert really was sick. However, the children seemed to treat complement falsity as a presupposition of *pretend*; they often thought the sentence meant that Robert was not sick. In other words, the children acted as if negation of *pretend* did not affect the truth value of its complement. Given the logical ambiguity of negative *pretend* sentences, that result is not surprising.

In response to sentences containing *forget* (such as "Mary Jane forgot to bring the ball"), the children showed a clear understanding of both the implicative of complement falsity (Mary Jane did not bring the ball) and the presupposition of prior knowledge or expectation (Mary Jane was supposed to bring the ball). However, the sentences containing *know* yielded only weak evidence that the children understood the presupposition of complement truth associated with *know*. That may be explained by some special difficulties in the way the children's understanding of *know* was tested. First, the sentences using *know* were syntactically and conceptually complex (i.e., "Christopher said to his mother: 'Mummy, Susan knows/doesn't know that I hid the penny under the cushion of the green chair'"). Second, the question about the complement of *know* was rather indirect ("Did Christopher say the penny was there?") Third, the story containing the *know* sentences was confusing, because the penny was not really under the cushion. The complicated and conflicting information presented in the story seemed to be too much for 4-year-olds to process.

Studies Related to Factivity Another group of studies has been concerned with children's understanding of the mental verbs *remember*, *know*, and *guess*. These studies were motivated not by an interest in the verbs' factivity or nonfactivity, but by an interest in children's understanding of internal mental states. However, the results of such studies have some implications for children's understanding of factivity and for their understanding of the presuppositions beyond factivity that are associated with those verbs.

Miscione et al. (1978) studied 4-, 5-, and 6-year-olds' and adults' understanding of *know* and *guess*. The experimenters hid objects in boxes, with the subjects either watching or not watching. They then had the subjects pick which box contained the object and asked the subjects whether they knew or guessed the object's location. The boxes had false bottoms that allowed the experimenters to control whether the subjects who had not seen the object hidden were successful in finding it.

The youngest children used *know* and *guess* unsystematically, with no clear differentiation between the meanings of the two verbs. Slightly older children tended to base their use of the verbs on the outcome of their response. If they were right, they said they *knew* where the object was; if they were wrong, they said they *guessed*. Somewhere between the ages of 5 and 7, the children began to base their use of the verbs on their actual knowledge of the object's location rather than on the success of their responses; this was also the usage pattern followed by the adults.

Wellman and Johnson (1979) examined 3-, 4-, 5-, and 7-year-olds' understanding of *remember* and *forget*. They told children stories in which an object was hidden, and a character who had either seen or not seen the hiding of the object later returned and had to find the object. The children were then asked questions about the character's knowledge of the object's hiding place, including whether the character remembered where the object was and whether he forgot where it was. The 3-year-olds used the two verbs indiscriminately, just as the youngest children in the Miscione et al. study did with *know* and *guess*. The 4-year-olds began to differentiate between *remember* and *forget*, but based their use on the success or failure of the character's search for the hidden object, rather than on his previous knowledge of its location. The 5- and 7-year-olds used previous knowledge as well as search outcome in deciding whether the character remembered or forgot the object's location. The oldest children had more trouble with *forget* than with *remember*. They often said that a character who was unsuccessful at finding an object had forgotten where it was when he had never known its location, and sometimes they even said that a character who found the object without previous knowledge of its location had forgotten where it was.

Wellman and Johnson's findings say nothing directly about factivity, but they do provide evidence about children's understanding of other presuppositions carried by factive verbs. Both *forget* and *remember* carry the presupposition of prior knowledge, regardless of current performance. Thus, "John remembered that Mary was coming," "John didn't remember that Mary was coming," "John forgot that Mary was coming," and "John didn't forget that Mary was coming" all carry the presupposition that John at one time knew Mary was coming (as well as the presupposition that Mary was in fact coming). Wellman and Johnson's study indicates that children do not understand the presupposition of prior knowledge until about age 5.[4] Miscione et al.'s results with *guess* are analogous to this finding, because they indicate that children younger than 5 do not understand that *guess* carries a presupposition of *no* prior knowledge.

---

[4] An interesting utterance that one of us (Maratsos) found in a naturalistic transcript of one 3-year-old also supports this conclusion. This child said, "We hafta remember something to do," clearly meaning *think of* or *come up with*, rather than *remember* in the adult sense.

In a later study, Johnson and Wellman (1980) tested 4-, 5-, 6-, and 9-year-olds' understanding of *remember*, *know*, and *guess*. They presented the children with a series of hidden-object tasks that varied along three dimensions: whether the children saw the object being hidden, whether the children could see or infer the object's location after it was hidden, and whether the children found the hidden object. After each hidden-object task, the children were asked where the object was. Their answers formed the basis for three more questions: "Do you know it's there?", "Do you remember it's there?", and "Do you guess it's there?"

Contrary to the results reported by Wellman and Johnson (1979), the 4-year-olds did not seem to base their judgments on the outcome of their search. When they were asked "Do you know/remember/guess it's there?" they tended to respond "yes" to each question, except when they did not see the object being hidden and guessed wrong about its location. The conditions under which they agreed that they knew and remembered the location of the object included one in which they saw the object being hidden but later could not find it (because it was put in a false-bottomed box), and one in which they did not see the object being hidden and never found out where it was. Their responses may be due simply to a general bias toward answering "yes" to questions. In any case, the 4-year-olds made no distinction in their answers among *remember*, *know*, and *guess*, and thus did not seem to understand the varying presuppositions associated with those three verbs.

The 5-year-olds showed signs of beginning to appreciate the differences between the verbs, but they still affirmed that they remembered or knew where the object was in situations in which they had no prior knowledge, and they also insisted that they guessed in situations in which they did have prior knowledge. The 6-year-olds were less likely to say that they guessed when they had prior knowledge. Although they often agreed that they remembered where the object was when they had present but no prior knowledge (i.e., they could see or infer where the object was, but had not seen it hidden), they were less likely than the younger children to say that they remembered when they had no knowledge at all of the object's location. Consistent recognition that *remember* applies only to situations with prior knowledge and *guess* applies only to situations without prior knowledge showed up only among the 9-year-olds. Even in that group, *know* was almost always deemed appropriate in situations involving prior knowledge as well as those involving present knowledge. Those responses were acceptable, however, because *know* is often used in situations that actually involve remembering, and because the time lapse between the prior knowledge and the questioning was not great.

Conclusions Taken as a group, what do all of these studies suggest about children's understanding of the presuppositions associated with factive verbs? First, children seem to understand factivity before they understand nonfactivity. That is, they recognize that the complements of factive predicates are presupposed to be true before they recognize that no such presupposition is made about the complements of nonfactive predicates. That result may be due in part to pragmatic assumptions about nonfactive verbs such as *say* and *think*—for example, that what people say and think is assumed to be true (at least until proved otherwise). Second, understanding of factivity seems to come not all at once, but on a verb-by-verb basis. Verbs with affective connotations seem to be mastered later than those without such connotations, and verbs that carry additional presuppositions beyond factivity seem to be mastered later than simple factives.

There are some differences among studies in age estimates for mastery of the presuppositions associated with various verbs. All of the studies suggest basic understanding of the factivity of verbs such as *know* by age 4 or 5, followed by gradual mastery of more complicated presuppositions and nonfactivity. What the studies do not agree on is how long it takes to achieve complete mastery. Harris' (1975) and Scoville and Gordon's (1980) results suggested a gradual process that continues into adulthood. In contrast, Hopmann and Maratsos (1978) found relatively complete mastery of factives and nonfactives by age 7. The various studies of *remember*, *forget*, and *guess* agree that children begin to understand presuppositions about prior knowledge somewhere between the ages of 5 and 7, with that understanding becoming virtually complete by ages 7 to 9.

In general, we favor the lower age estimates for competence in using factive and nonfactive predicates, for two reasons. First, findings of very late competence lack plausibility when applied to children's normal conversation. In Harris' (1975) study, for example, elementary school children ascribed factivity to the nonfactive verb *say*; in other words, they interpreted *say* as presupposing the truth of its sentential complement. Extended generally, those results imply that children do not believe it is possible to talk about saying something false. They thus would not say things like, "Johnny said I hit him, but I didn't," which seems implausible. If children actually used nonfactive predicates in the way Harris' results imply they do, their speech would be bizarre for quite a long time. Remember, however, that Johnson and Maratsos (1977) found that children as young as 4 understand that *think*, a nonfactive similar to *say*, can be used to express false opinions. In addition, naturalistic transcripts suggest that preschool children actually use the verb *think* in expressions like "Do you think that . . . " about uncertain possibilities (Shatz and Gelman, 1973). In natural conversation—and even in some experiments—children seem quite skilled at using nonfactive verbs appropriately at an early age.

The second reason for our preference for early estimates is methodological. The researcher who found the latest competence (Harris) required subjects to interpret sentences out of context and then answer fairly difficult questions about their meaning. In contrast, researchers who found competence at younger ages either: 1) asked children to carry out some activity contingent on their understanding of the test sentences (e.g., Hopmann and Maratsos); 2) asked children to reason from their understanding of the sentences (e.g., Macnamara et al.); or 3) provided a context for the questions that were asked (e.g., Johnson and Maratsos). During pilot work for the Johnson and Maratsos study, attempts to make the task as clear and simple as possible, while keeping the basic distinctions, quickly resulted in a lowering of the age at which children could perform the task. Furthermore, task simplification has yielded similar results in studies of other cognitive abilities (see, e.g., Gelman, 1978).

It is quite possible, of course, that the studies that suggest late competence are tapping the young child's unstable knowledge of factive predicates. Something of the same unsystematicity and contradiction seen in children's responses to factive, counterfactive, and nonfactive predicates is probably also true of adult usage. Indeed, Scoville and Gordon's results, which show gradually developing, late competence, suggested that the factivity-nonfactivity distinction is not always clearcut, even for adults. Situational elements (including those present in Scoville and Gordon's quiz show format) may sometimes lead a listener to assign factivity to a supposedly nonfactive verb like *say*. In addition, there are special uses in which predicates like *know* lose the factivity normally associated with them. Sometimes adults say things like "He just *knew* she would come, but she didn't" or "I don't know that this is the best way to proceed." In the first case, the sentence complement of *know* turns out not to be true; in the second, the complement has an indeterminate truth value. Factivity of predicates is thus far from absolute in normal adult usage; it is no surprise that it is not entirely stable in children's usage.

Wh-Questions Although children's acquisition of *wh*-questions has been studied fairly extensively, the research was motivated by issues not directly related to presupposition. The results of some of that research, however, are indirectly related to children's understanding of the presuppositions involved in *wh*-questions.

Wh-questions carry a presupposition of the truth of the corresponding declarative sentence, with an indefinite variable substituted for the *wh*-word. That is, "Where is the dog?" presupposes that the dog is somewhere. What the question asserts is that the speaker wants the listener to supply more information about the dog's location. Most *wh*-questions also carry the presupposition that the speaker does not know the answer to the question, but thinks the listener does. In the case of "Where is the dog?" it is presupposed that the person who asked the question does not know the dog's location, but has reason to believe the listener does.

Mothers' early uses of *wh*-questions quite frequently do not follow the preceding pattern (Shatz, 1978). Instead, the mother often knows the answer and is either 1) testing the child, as in "What does the doggie say?" or 2) using the question as a directive, as in "Where's your shoe?", which may mean in context "Get me your shoe." Although *wh*-questions that are used as directives or as part of a naming routine violate the usual presupposition that the questioner does not know the answer to the question, they still carry the presupposition that the listener *does* know the answer—or at least that the questioner thinks the listener can supply an answer. *Wh*-directives and naming questions also resemble standard *wh*-questions in that they all carry presuppositions about the truth of the corresponding declarative sentence. Whether "Where is your shoe?" is asked to seek information about the location of a shoe or to direct a child to bring a shoe, the speaker still presupposes that the shoe is somewhere. "What does the doggie say?" carries the presupposition that the doggie says something, even if the question is asked to elicit a performance rather than new information.

Children do have some difficulties figuring out the semantics of particular *wh*-terms, which in turn lead to trouble with the specific presuppositions connected with each term. Ervin-Tripp (1970), studying 2- and 3-year-olds, found that the children correctly answered *why* and *who-subject* questions earlier than *how* and *where-from* questions, which in turn were mastered before *when* and *who-object* questions. Tyack and Ingram (1977) found the following order of difficulty for 3- to 5-year-olds answering *wh*-questions (easiest listed first): *where* (with intransitive verbs), *why*, *who-subject*, *where* (with transitive verbs), *what-object*, *who-object*, *when*, *how*, and *what-subject*. Cairns and Hsu (1978) found a similar order of difficulty for 3- to 5-year-olds. Tyack and Ingram (1977) also examined the production of *wh*-questions by 2- and 3-year-olds. They found that *what* and *where* questions were the most common *wh*-questions among the youngest children, that *why* and *how* questions were infrequent to start with but increased with age, and that *who* and *when* questions were infrequent among even the oldest children.

Within the limits of their mastery of the semantics of particular *wh*-words, children seem to observe the presuppositional requirements of *wh*-questions from an early age. They do not ask, "Where's the shoe?" if they do not think that there is a shoe somewhere about which it makes sense to ask the question (except perhaps as a joke, which adults may do as well; we know of no applicable data on that kind of joking). With regard to the presupposition of listener knowledgeability, children do not seem to ask questions when they do not think the listener can supply an answer—despite every parent's intuition that children ask unanswerable questions.

An understanding of the particular presuppositions carried by various *wh*-words is needed if *wh*-questions are to be used correctly in conversation. Except for the naming and directive questions asked of children, questions are usually asked to seek out information that was not provided by the speaker or not heard by the listener. For example, appropriate responses to "I bought a new car" might be "What?", "What kind?", "Why?", "Where?", "When?", or "How?", but probably not "Who?" The question "What?" is actually a shortened version of "What did you say?" and it carries the presupposition that the speaker said something that the listener did not hear. "What kind?" carries the presupposition that some kind of car was bought; "Why?" that it was bought for some reason; "Where?" that it was bought in some place, and so on.

"Who?" is not an appropriate question for several reasons. If the listener heard the speaker, then the question has already been answered. If the listener did not hear or did not understand part of the sentence, then the form of the question is inappropriate. When requesting information that was not heard (or not believed), questioners usually repeat the information that was heard (and believed), especially when the question could be ambiguous. Thus, a listener might ask "Who bought the car?" if he didn't hear the subject of the sentence. If the listener did not believe the speaker—for instance, if he had reason to think the speaker's father had actually paid for the car—he might even ask "*Who* bought the car?" with extra stress on *who*. If a listener did not hear the object of the sentence, the expected form would be "Who (or whom) did you buy?" However, that form would still be inappropriate, because *who* refers to an animate being, and—excluding discussions of bribery and white slavery—it cannot be presupposed that someone was bought. "What did you buy?" would be the appropriate form. There are thus two elements involved in the correct conversational use of *wh*-questions: an understanding of the semantics of the particular *wh*-words involved, and a recognition of their appropriateness to the conversational context and to the listener's knowledge of the situation.

Garvey (1975, 1977) has done some research on the appropriateness of preschool children's responses to each other's conversational questions, especially requests for clarification, which she calls contingent queries. For a contingent query to work properly in a conversation, both speaker and listener have to pay attention to the preceding discourse and the presuppositions it contains. The following exchange is an example from Garvey (1977):

Child Y: This is a nice place.
Child X: What?
Child Y: This is a nice place.
Child X: What's a nice place? This room?
Child Y: Yup.
Child X: Oh, yeah.

In that conversation, "What?", "What's a nice place?", and "This room?" are examples of contingent queries. Obviously, not all contingent queries are *wh*-questions, but many are.

Garvey (1977) found that 3- to 5-year-olds responded appropriately to each other's contingent queries more often than not and that even the youngest children never gave nonsensical responses, such as answering "yes" or "no" to questions like "What?" Three-year-olds were less responsive than older children to nonspecific requests for repetition ("*What?*" or "*huh?*"), ignoring them about 40% of the time. Four-year-olds ignored only 10% of such requests, and 5-year-olds ignored only 5%. Interestingly, all three age groups were more responsive to *what* than to *huh*. The 3-year-olds failed to respond to *what* only 21% of the time, the 4-year-olds only 5% of the time, and the 5-year-olds only 3% of the time. More specific contingent queries showed no such developmental trends; all three age groups ignored about 20% of such queries. Unfortunately, the *wh*-questions included in this group of queries were not analyzed separately. These findings do not tell us anything very specific about children's understanding of the various presuppositions carried by *wh*-words. What they do demonstrate is that even very young children are able to use *wh*-words appropriately in conversation without violating presuppositional constraints.

Gallagher (1981) studied 2- and 3-year-olds' responses to and use of contingent queries in conversation with adults. One of the query types she studied—requests for specific constituent repetition—involved the use of *wh*-questions. Gallagher found that slightly over half of the children in her study had a consistent response pattern to *wh*-questions of this type. With very few exceptions, they responded by correctly repeating the constituent requested, as in the following example:

Child: I got fire engine.
Adult: You got what?
Child: Fire engine.

However, requests for constituent repetition were infrequent among the children's own contingent queries; only about one-third of the children used them at all, and even those children used them much less frequently than the other types of contingent queries studied.

The major presuppositional challenges faced by children learning to ask and answer *wh*-questions are: 1) to learn the particular presuppositions associated with each *wh*-word, and 2) to learn to use *wh*-questions appropriately in conversation. Children's discourse may show evidence of semantic confusion among *wh*-words until all of them have been mastered, but their discourse does not seem to abound with *wh*-questions that are completely irrelevant or with inappropriate answers to *wh*-questions. Again, presuppositional understanding of *wh*-questions is not something that children completely lack early in their development, nor is it something that they suddenly acquire all at once. Although children add the various *wh*-words to their repertoires gradually, they seem to observe the presuppositional rules associated with each *wh*-word virtually as soon as they understand the meaning of that particular word.

Negation Like *wh*-questions, the development of negation in children's language has been studied fairly extensively, but there have been only a few studies that have dealt with the presuppositional aspects of negation. As we have already suggested, the plausible negation in discourse presupposes affirmation; it makes no sense to negate something that has not been either explicitly or implicitly affirmed.

Antinucci and Volterra (1973), in their examination of early negation, concluded that very young children (1½ to 2 years old) do not make negative statements that violate the presuppositions of plausibility. The problem with their finding, as de Villiers and de Villiers (1978) pointed out, is that it is possible to find the presupposition of affirmation in a situation after the fact, especially because the presupposition need not be explicit or even verbally implied.

Wason (1965) devised an experimental task to study the effects of context on the plausibility of negation for adults. He showed subjects a set of seven circles of one color (e.g., red) and one circle of a different color (e.g., blue); he then asked them to complete positive and negative sentences about the color of each circle—for example, "Circle 4 is _____," or "Circle 7 is not _____." He found that negative statements about the circle that was a different color (e.g., "Circle 4 is not *red*") were completed more rapidly than negative statements about the other circles (e.g., "Circle 7 is not *blue*"). Wason concluded that the subjects found negative statements about exceptions to the rule (i.e., "Circle 4 is not *red*") more plausible than negative statements about rule items (i.e., "Circle 7 is not *blue*"). Donaldson (1970) tried to replicate Wason's experiment with 5- and 6-year-olds but was unsuccessful, perhaps because the task was too abstract.

To circumvent that problem, de Villiers and Tager-Flusberg (1975) devised a more concrete procedure to study children's responses to unsupported negative sentences, using toys and drawings of objects for contextual support. For example, the child was presented with a group of several toy horses and one toy cow. In that situation, the plausible negative is to point to the cow and say, "That's not a horse," because the cow is the odd item in the group of horses. To point to one of the horses and say, "That's not a cow," is an implausible negative because there is no particular reason to expect that it would be a cow (unless, of course, someone had said or done something demonstrating that he thought it might be a cow). De Villiers and Tager-Flusberg found that some 2-year-olds could complete plausible negative sentences correctly, but not implausible ones. The syntactic and semantic complexity of negation made negative sentences in general ("That's not _____") harder for the 2-year-olds than affirmative ones ("That's a _____"). Older children also made more errors on implausible negatives than on plausible ones, and they took longer to complete them. Even 4-year-olds, who had a reasonably good command of negation and could complete plausible negative sentences nearly as fast as affirmative sentences, still took longer to complete implausible negatives.

Forms of Address and Requests There has been a great deal of research recently on the development of politeness and the marking of social differences in children's speech; but none of it, at least in English, has dealt with particular forms of address. Instead, researchers have studied topics such as the forms used to make requests and children's awareness of the social conventions associated with the use of those forms (Bates, 1976; Ervin-Tripp, 1976; Garvey, 1975). The general finding of most of these studies is that children begin to adjust their language to reflect differences in the status or familiarity of their listeners at a relatively early age, but it takes them a while to master completely the social conventions involved. A review of the literature on politeness and children's marking of social status and familiarity may be found in Gordon and Ervin-Tripp's chapter in this volume.

As stated earlier, we do not believe that the distinction between the "semantic" presupposition and the "pragmatic" presupposition involved in forms of address is an important, practical one for children learning a language. In both cases, the basic ability to presuppose, to assert something against a given background assumption, is exercised in a particular semantic domain. The "semantic" presuppositions associated with factive predicates and definite articles may seem to be basically linguistic, whereas the "pragmatic" presuppositions involved in forms of address and requests may seem to be more genuinely social. The task for the child in both cases, however, is to learn the presuppositions associated with a particular word or form and to become skilled at deciding whether those presuppositions can appropriately be made in a given situation.

Later Use of General Presuppositional Devices

Empirical evidence on children's use and understanding of the general linguistic devices that reflect presuppositions is much scantier than the evidence concerning particular presuppositional constructions. Paradoxically, such general devices appear in children's language earlier than the specific constructions we have already discussed, but they are not completely mastered until much later. The distinction between given (presupposed) and new (asserted) information, or between topic and comment, seems to be implicit in the child's earliest language; however, complete mastery of the devices used to communicate that distinction may not occur until relatively late in language development.

Word Order One way in which the distinction between presupposed and asserted, or given and new, information can be expressed is the order in which the information is presented. However, there is no hard and fast rule in English about the position of presupposed information in a sentence, and other devices such as stress often interact with word order to express presupposition. MacWhinney and Bates (1978) cited several studies of early language development that seem to suggest a preference in very young children for putting new information before given information. This early tendency can be interpreted as an extension of Greenfield and Zukow's (1978) finding that new, rather than given, information is expressed during the one-word stage of language development. However, the tendency to put new information first declines as children begin to produce three-word and longer sentences, according to MacWhinney and Bates. In fact, Bock (1977) found that adults, in a question-answering task, tended to place given information before new information in sentences. When MacWhinney and Bates asked subjects to describe pictures with elements of varying givenness and newness, however, they found that neither children nor adults consistently used word order as a means of marking givenness and newness. This result may be due in part to the interaction of word order with other sentential devices (e.g., stress) for making the distinction between given and new information.

Stress As we suggested earlier, stress can be used either: 1) to distinguish between topic and comment in a sentence by overriding the usual implications of word order (as in "Well, *glass* is elastic"); or 2) to express particular presuppositions on its own (as in "John called Mary a Republican, and then *she* insulted *him*"). Wieman (1976) found that even 2-year-olds used stress to emphasize new information in a sentence. Hornby (1971), using a task in which children had to correct descriptions of pictures, found that the children almost always used stress to mark corrections–that is, to set off the new information from that which was given or presupposed. MacWhinney and Bates (1978) found that, by the age of 3, children had begun to use stress fairly reliably to mark new information, and the use of stress continued to increase with age. Maratsos (1973a) found that children were able to use stress as a means of assigning referents to ambiguous pronouns, a process that also involves the distinction between given and new information.

Ellipsis Ellipsis, or the omission of information from a sentence, conveys presuppositions in an implicit way: what is presupposed can often be omitted, especially in an answer to a question. MacWhinney and Bates (1978) pointed out that naturalistic observations by researchers such as Greenfield and Zukow (1978), Keenan (1974), and Rodgon (1976) reveal a decreasing use of ellipsis with age. However, as children grow older they become increasingly sophisticated and selective about what may be omitted and what must be included in a sentence. That sophistication and selectivity reflect an increasing appreciation and observance of Grice's (1975) conversational principles of informativeness and relevance. Whether early replies to questions represent true ellipsis or simply the generally shorter utterances of the very young child remains to be seen. In their own study, MacWhinney and Bates found that the use of ellipsis declined from age 3 to age 5, but generally increased with increased givenness of material.

The available research evidence about the use of sentential devices such as word order, stress, and ellipsis to express presupposition does not allow us to say very much about developmental processes in children's mastery of those devices. As with more specific presuppositional constructions, the general trend in the findings seems to be for children to begin using and understanding the devices very early, perhaps as soon as they begin to use language at all, with specific refinements in their use continuing for some time.

Gricean Conversational Principles

We know of only one study that has attempted to examine directly children's understanding of Gricean presupposition; there are, of course, many others that have dealt with phenomena involving Grice's principles. Ackerman (1978) examined kindergartners' and third graders' ability to recognize violations of Gricean conversational principles and to infer correctly the pragmatic meanings of sentences on that basis. He used sentences that could be pragmatically interpreted in two very different ways, depending on the context in which they were used. Each sentence appeared in two different versions of a story. In one version, the sentence violated Grice's principles; in the other, it did not. For example, in one story a teacher said, "I know you tried very hard to be nice today" to a boy who has either given a classmate an apple or stuck her with a pin. In this case, the children were asked if the boy was trying to be friendly in the story. According to Ackerman, if the children draw the correct pragmatic inference from the story, they will recognize when normal conversational principles have been violated and the teacher is being sarcastic. If they do not draw the correct pragmatic inference, they will take what the teacher says at face value.

Ackerman found that even kindergartners were able to recognize violations of Grice's principles a good share of the time, but his study did not yield any significant developmental trends. One difficulty with Ackerman's study is that the children were given all of the information they needed to make the inference right in the story; they did not have to make a pragmatic inference at all. In the story of the boy and the teacher, for example, the question that was asked could be answered strictly on the basis of the information about what the boy did, with little regard to what the teacher said about it. A more relevant question would have been "Did the teacher think the boy was trying to be friendly?"

SOME BASIC THEORETICAL QUESTIONS

So far in our account we have provided an analysis of some presuppositional linguistic usages and a review of empirical findings about children's acquisition of them. We have suggested that children start with a basic ability to presuppose, gradually learn the particular presuppositions that apply to specific usages, and at the same time become more facile at deciding whether those presuppositions are met in a particular situation or are shared by a particular listener. We have not addressed the more basic—and thornier—question of how children are able to assign the appropriate meanings to presuppositional usages in the first place. That question is one that is shared with semantic acquisition (and grammatical acquisition) in general; stated more broadly, it becomes "How are children able to assign the appropriate meaning to any aspect of language at all?" Obviously, an answer to that question is well beyond the scope of this chapter. Some aspects of the general meaning question are particularly noticeable in connection with presuppositional usages, however.

To begin with, it is reasonable to suppose that a child's acquisition of some words is facilitated when the word's referent is salient to the child and the child's parents share his focus of attention (see Snow, this volume). In these cases, a child may learn something about the meaning of a word simply by listening to his parents refer to the salient element. For example, a parent can say to a child who is looking at lions in a zoo, "Those are *lions*." In perhaps the majority of cases, however, there is no such salient element or focus of attention to help the child learn word meanings, and that must surely be the case for the presuppositional words we have considered. Usually, presuppositions are not particularly salient. By definition, the presuppositions of a linguistic expression are conditions that must be taken for granted for the expression to be used. To understand the presuppositional content of a usage, a child must pay attention to the elements of the situation that are given or taken for granted, rather than the elements that are new, changing, or under focus.

The very fact that there is background information to be taken for granted might occasionally be salient in itself. However, this fact usually is far from salient—and salience or the lack thereof is not the condition that determines the use of a presuppositional form. Definite and indefinite articles, for example, are part of a system of obligatory use. Speakers do not decide to use them because the contextual definiteness or indefiniteness of reference to some member of a class is especially striking, interesting, or important. Instead, they must be used in many circumstances in which such meanings are of no particular interest. Many languages, such as Japanese, Chinese, and Russian, have no articles at all, with no noticeable loss of communicative efficiency. In English, definite and indefinite articles occasionally have communicative value, but usually they could be left out without ambiguity. Of course, a mature speaker of English would find their deletion disconcerting because he is used to hearing them obligatorily.

The point is that most of the time when children hear definite or indefinite articles, the subtle definite or indefinite reference they make is not particularly salient. In addition, in normal speech, articles are usually not stressed and are often present in reduced form. Thus, articles often are not very salient themselves, and are not associated with the most salient aspects of the situation in which they are used. In order to figure out the meaning and application of definite and indefinite articles—as well as any number of other linguistic elements—children cannot simply pay attention to what is interesting or salient in the situation. There apparently must also be a great deal of more or less automatic tabulation of uses and sorting of relevant hypotheses about meaning and application. Such sorting must include separating hypotheses that may be somewhat relevant to a number of uses of a construction from those that are truly the best predictors of its use.

A child who is hypothesizing meanings for presuppositional terms is hampered not only by the terms' lack of salience, but also by the complexity of their meanings and the variety of possible hypotheses. Let us consider some of the hypotheses that a child could construct for the meaning of *the* from the input he receives. First, there is the problem of deciding that article use is relevant to nouns at all, which may not be a trivial problem. In English, the initial noun phrase position in a sentence tends to be occupied by pronouns and proper names; noun phrases with articles are more likely to follow the verb. Thus, a child could conclude that the article has to do with the verb, rather than the noun. In fact, one of Brown's subjects, Adam, apparently used definite and indefinite articles for some time as meaningless phonological entities dependent on the ending of the preceding verb (Brown, 1973).

Even if the child decides that the article has something to do with the noun that follows it, he still must figure out exactly what the article refers to. He might hypothesize that it denotes something salient about the noun. For example, upon hearing "Would you like the cereal?" a child might decide *the* means *edible* or *good-tasting*. Of course, such a hypothesis would not apply to other uses of *the* and therefore would not be very enduring. What the child has to do is tabulate a number of properties of situations in which *the* is used, along with properties of the referents of the nouns it is used with, and find those that are common to all (or to many) of the uses.

A further complication is that the child has to arrive at a hypothesis that is general enough to predict correctly most uses of the form, but specific enough to exclude cases in which it is not called for. For example, the uses of *the* that a child hears early in development refer to concrete members of countable classes. However, a hypothesis that *the* means "member of a concrete, countable class" would cause the child to say things like "I want the banana" when "I want a banana" was actually called for. Another aspect of meaning common to most uses of *the* is that it refers to a class member that is distinct and well established in the mind of the speaker. A hypothesis based on distinctness in the mind of the speaker might lead the child to say "I want the banana" if he had a very clear idea of wanting a banana, even if there was not one particular banana for him to want.

In fact, errors such as these do not seem to be very common in children's language. Apparently, the process by which children arrive at a meaning for *the* is more efficient than the hypothesizing we have suggested. The actual specifications for the correct use of *the* are more complex than the hypotheses proposed so far, yet children are able to arrive at a relatively good working knowledge of the uses of *the* with very little trial and error. A complete hypothesis regarding the use of *the* that would correctly predict use and nonuse would be something like the following: *the* may be used when reference is to some member of a named class already made specific in the conversational or situational context, in a way beyond the class reference, and in the same way for both speaker and listener. To arrive at that specification, a child must be able to pay attention not only to the items being referred to but also to the discourse and situation in which the reference occurs.

Of course, it is possible that presuppositional meaning, although not especially salient in most situations, is so basic that the task of acquisition is simpler than we might expect. The presuppositional usages we have been discussing all involve questions of existence or truth, which are fairly basic even in children's early cognition. The very basicness of such meanings might make them more likely candidates for children's hypotheses than other, more salient aspects of a situation. The task for the child is not to construct the meaning of presupposition but, rather, to connect that meaning with particular usages and to discover the subtle differences among the usages. Such a task is still a formidable one, and the fact that presupposition is so basic does not entirely explain how it is possible; we must appeal for explanation to a combination of the basicness of the concepts and the efficiency of the child's analytic equipment.

In summary, the child's analysis of presuppositional uses highlights a number of problems in semantic acquisition. First, the meanings of presuppositional terms are often not very salient. In fact, attempts by the child to associate the use of these terms with the salient elements of situations would often lead to confusion. It seems more appropriate to hypothesize that the child simply registers great amounts of information about conversational situations, regardless of salience. Second, presupposed meanings are often amazingly complex. Acquisition of such complex meanings requires that the child have primitive analytic elements and combinatorial devices that are correspondingly complex, along with a means of deciding which characteristics best predict use. Third, the child must be able to construct notions of discourse, of conversational universes that include the knowledge of both speaker and listener.

It seems likely that our present formulations of children's word meaning acquisition fail to capture the necessary complexity of the child's task. The problem is seeing everything the child reasonably *could* do and explaining how he manages to do what he *does* do. Of course, there is an intuition that things cannot be so complex, because it is just children that we are talking about. It may be, however, that the efficiency and complexity of children's analytic equipment make the task seem easier than it is. For example, it is easy to show that acts of motor coordination and balance, which seem so simple to us, involve tremendous unconscious analytic and sorting equipment (e.g., see Turvey, 1977). There is little reason to suppose that semantic acquisition should be very different.

Thus, a difficulty with present considerations of empirical data on the acquisition of presuppositional terms—and on semantic acquisition in general—is that we do not have much of a framework in which to place the data. Should we be surprised that children are as quick at some acquisitions as they are? Or are they actually slow? The data seem to show early general competence with presuppositional terms, followed by term-by-term refinements. In the end, however, deciding which empirical findings are important, which are not, and what they might mean requires specific accounts of what semantic acquisition is and how it occurs at all. Such accounts are truly lacking at present; there has been little work on the necessary analytic primitives and practically no work on possible inductive and sorting systems. Careful analysis of presuppositional meanings clearly demonstrates this void. Perhaps one reason the available data on presuppositional terms tell us so little of interest developmentally is that we have not been looking at the real roots of the acquisition process. To do so would require a more powerful and detailed account of the processes involved in semantic acquisition than any presently available.

IMPLICATIONS FOR CHILDREN WITH LANGUAGE DELAYS

If the empirical evidence concerning the acquisition of presuppositional forms by normal children is somewhat scanty, the corresponding evidence for language-disordered children is even more limited. However, the recently increasing interest in the pragmatic development of children with language delays has produced an increase in studies of pragmatics in general, including some that deal specifically with presupposition. In this section, we briefly review some of the studies available on language-delayed children and discuss the implications for disordered populations of the research and theoretical considerations related to normal development. (See Snyder, this volume, for a more extensive discussion of language-delayed children's presuppositional usages.)

Snyder (1976) studied the presuppositional characteristics of the verbal and nonverbal communication of language-disordered 1- and 2-year-olds and of normal children with comparable mean lengths of utterance and vocabularies. She used a procedure designed to test the notion that, early in language development, children generally comment on the new or changing elements in a situation rather than on the given or unchanging elements. She found that both the normal and the language-disordered children's nonverbal gestures (e.g., pointing) nearly always referred to the new element in the situation (96% and 95% of the time, respectively). However, there was a significant difference between the normal children and the language-disordered children in the percentage of verbalizations that referred to the new element in the situation. Nearly all (94%) of the normal children's verbalizations referred to the new element, compared to only 69% of the language-disordered children's verbalizations.

Leonard (1979) cited several studies that suggest group differences in the ways young language-disordered and normal children maintain a topic of conversation and respond to contingent queries. In comparison to the normal children, the language-disordered children showed less sophistication or skill, rather than a total inability to maintain a topic of conversation or respond to contingent queries.

Working with a different disorder and at the other end of the developmental scale, Baltaxe (1977) found that high-functioning autistic adolescents had difficulty with various presuppositional elements of conversation. Basically, his subjects had trouble with the distinction between given and new information. They made mistakes with definite articles, and often used nouns and noun phrases instead of anaphoric pronouns to refer to previously introduced items—a tendency that is not found in young normal children. Those mistakes gave their speech the redundancy and pedantic literalness that has often been noted in the language of autistic children.

In a study of German-speaking autistic adolescents, Baltaxe and Simmons (1977) found that their subjects had trouble distinguishing between the familiar and polite forms of *you* (*du* and *Sie*). They would often use the two forms interchangeably to refer to the same person in the course of a conversation, demonstrating a lack of understanding of the presuppositions carried by familiar and polite forms of address.

The available research evidence on presupposition in non-normal populations thus suggests, not surprisingly, that a general difficulty with language includes difficulty with presuppositions. However, with the possible exception of autism, there is not yet any evidence that presupposition is particularly *central* to the general difficulty. In the case of autism, some theorists (e.g., Cromer, 1981) have suggested that the pragmatic dimension may be a focus of difficulty. In any case, the presuppositional mistakes reported by Baltaxe in his studies of autistic adolescents certainly seem to be more fundamental than the presuppositional impairments found in other language-delayed groups.

It seems reasonable to think that difficulties with presupposition can arise at any point in the course of a child's development. On the basis of the limited research available, it is impossible to be very specific about what kinds of children might have problems at what points or even about what kinds of problems actually arise. However, we can speculate about what kinds of problems *might* arise and how these problems might affect communication.

The most fundamental problem, of course, would be a disturbance in the basic ability to presuppose. Such a problem would reveal itself even on a sensorimotor level in many areas of cognition and action, and not just in language. A total inability to presuppose is hardly conceivable; a more likely problem would be an incomplete awareness of the distinction between given and new, background and foreground. Difficulties of this type, if they exist, might be hard to deal with clinically; teaching a child to presuppose would be a formidable, if not an impossible, task.

Slightly less fundamental, but still cognitively based, problems might arise in the process of attaching presuppositional meanings to linguistic forms or in the acquisition of increasingly complex forms. Difficulties at the first point could be part of a general problem with semantic acquisition—overall difficulty attaching meanings to words. As the complexity of meaning increases, the cognitive demands might become too great for some children. Purely linguistic difficulties with complex syntactic forms might also become involved. Finally, children could have problems deciding what usage is appropriate in a particular situation, either because they lack understanding of the social context or because they have difficulty recognizing when the social and linguistic context demands or allows a particular usage.

Just as it means little to talk about the development of presupposition as a separate, unitary process, so it probably also means little to talk about children having trouble with presupposition as if it were a separate aspect of communicative competence. Problems with presupposition could range from misuse or misunderstanding of specific presuppositional forms to basic cognitive presuppositional deficits, or to difficulty applying the forms in social contexts. What all types of presuppositional mistakes have in common is that they are not usually mistakes in the form of an utterance but rather mistakes in the way the utterance fits into the discourse; that fact may have implications for the treatment of children who have difficulty with presuppositional forms.

What little research exists suggests that the nonverbal communication of language-disordered children is presuppositionally similar to that of young normal children. However, the verbal communication of normal children may be more presuppositionally appropriate than the verbal communication of language-disordered children. In addition, normal children may be more skilled than language-disordered children at maintaining a topic of conversation and responding to contingent queries. Finally, the difference in usage patterns between normal and autistic children may be even greater than the difference between normal and language-disordered children. For example, autistic children tend to overuse nouns where pronouns would be appropriate and to have serious difficulty with definite articles. The underlying difficulties and hence the appropriate interventions for these two kinds of children may thus be rather different from each other.

SUMMARY AND CONCLUSIONS

The language-learning child is faced with presuppositional analysis in several forms: in the basic communicative assumptions of language, in presuppositions carried by individual words, and in presuppositions carried by general linguistic devices. In part because there is such a variety of presuppositional usages, it is not very helpful to try to describe the development of presupposition as if it were a single, separate ability. Indeed, the ability to presuppose does not seem to be something that develops in any real sense; rather, it is a basic ability that is brought by children to the task of language acquisition, and that is apparent even at the sensorimotor stage of development.

However, there are two presuppositional skills that children have to master. First, they have to learn what presuppositions are involved in particular usages; second, they have to learn how to tell when those presuppositions are fulfilled in particular situations. The classic philosophical/linguistic distinction between semantic and pragmatic presupposition does not seem to be particularly meaningful for language-learning children; it may be more meaningful to draw distinctions between presuppositional usages of varying scope and complexity.

Research on early language use suggests that, even at the one- and two-word stages, children demonstrate an ability to differentiate the given or presupposed elements of a situation from the new or asserted elements. Research on later use of presupposition has concentrated mainly on particular constructions such as definite reference, factive predicates, *wh*-questions, and negation. The general findings in these areas suggest early basically correct usage of most constructions, followed by gradual mastery of whatever semantic and social subtleties are involved. Some findings suggest that early usage may be more exophoric than anaphoric—that is, tied directly to the physically present situation more than to the preceding linguistic context.

Through middle childhood, errors in using presuppositional constructions tend to be in the direction of erroneously assuming shared presuppositions with the listener. However, there is no reason to ascribe errors of this type to a general egocentrism; they are more likely to be due to the complexity of determining the conversational status of various referents and the listener's knowledge of them.

Discussion of presuppositional usages and their acquisition make certain general questions of semantic acquisition stand out with particular sharpness. Because the meanings to be assigned to presuppositional terms are not usually prominent in a situation, salience cannot be used to explain acquisition. A better explanation would focus on the basicness of their meanings, in combination with the assumption that children bring very complex and efficient analytical equipment to the task of acquisition.

Although the evidence on presuppositional difficulties in children with language delays is not extensive, presuppositional constructions do seem to pose some problems. Research suggests that autistic children show more fundamental disturbances than do children with general language disorders. However, difficulties theoretically could arise at any point in the process of development. Just as presupposition does not seem to reflect one separate ability in normal children, so presuppositional problems do not reflect one separate disability in children with language delays.

REFERENCES

Ackerman, B. P. 1978. Children's comprehension of presupposed information: Logical and pragmatic inferences to speaker belief. J. Exp. Child Psychol. 26:92–114.

Antinucci, F., and Volterra, V. 1973. Lo sviluppo della negazione nel linguaggio infantile: Uno studio pragmatico. *In* Studi per un Modello del Linguaggio. Quaderni della Ricera Scientifica, CNR, Rome.

Austin, J. L. 1962. How To Do Things with Words. Oxford University Press, Cambridge, England.

Baltaxe, C. 1977. Pragmatic deficits in the language of autistic adolescents. J. Pediatr. Psychol. 2:176–180.

Baltaxe, C., and Simmons, J. Q., III. 1977. Language patterns of adolescent autistics: A comparison between English and German. In P. Mittler (ed.), Research to Practice in Mental Retardation, Vol. II: Education and Training. University Park Press, Baltimore.

Bates, E. 1976. Pragmatics and sociolinguistics in child language. In D. Morehead and A. Morehead (eds.), Language Deficiency in Children: Selected Readings. University Park Press, Baltimore.

Bloom, L. 1973. One Word at a Time: The Use of Single Word Utterances before Syntax. Mouton, The Hague.

Bloom, L., Lightbown, P., and Hood, L. 1975. Structure and variation in child language. Monogr. Soc. Res. Child Dev. 40, Serial No. 160.

Bock, K. 1977. The effect of a pragmatic presupposition on syntactic structure in question answering. J. Verbal Learn. Verbal Behav. 16:723–734.

Brown, R. 1973. A First Language. Harvard University Press, Cambridge, MA.

Cairns, H., and Hsu, J. 1978. Who, why, when, and how: A developmental study. J. Child Lang. 5:477–488.

Charney, R. 1980. Speech roles and the development of personal pronouns. J. Child Lang. 7:509–528.

Chipman, H., and de Dardel, C. 1974. Developmental study of the comprehension and production of the pronoun it. J. Psycholing. Res. 3:91–99.

Cromer, R. F. 1981. Developmental language disorders: Cognitive processes, semantics, pragmatics, phonology, and syntax. J. Autism Dev. Disord. 11:57–74.

de Villiers, J. G., and de Villiers, P. A. 1978. Language Acquisition. Harvard University Press, Cambridge, MA.

de Villiers, J. G., and Tager-Flusberg, H. B. 1975. Some facts one simply cannot deny. J. Child Lang. 2:279–286.

DeLaguna, G. 1927. Speech: Its Function and Development. Indiana University Press, Bloomington.

Donaldson, M. 1970. Developmental aspects of performance with negatives. In G. B. Flores D'Arcais and W. J. M. Levelt (eds.), Advances in Psycholinguistics. North-Holland, Amsterdam.

Ervin-Tripp, S. 1970. Discourse agreement: How children answer questions. In J. R. Hayes (ed.), Cognition and the Development of Language. John Wiley & Sons, Inc., New York.

Ervin-Tripp, S. 1976. Is Sybil there: The structure of some American English directives. Lang. Soc. 5:25–66.

Flavell, J. H. 1977. Cognitive Development. Prentice-Hall, Inc., Englewood Cliffs, N.J.

Gallagher, T. M. 1981. Contingent queries within adult-child discourse. J. Child Lang. 8:51–62.

Garvey, C. 1975. Requests and responses in children's speech. J. Child Lang. 2:41–63.

Garvey, C. 1977. The contingent query: A dependent act in conversation. In M. Lewis and L. A. Rosenblum (eds.), Interaction, Conversation, and the Development of Language. John Wiley & Sons, Inc., New York.

Gelman, R. 1978. Cognitive development. *In* L. W. Porter and M. R. Rosenzweig (eds.), Annual Review of Psychology, Vol. 29. Annual Reviews, Palo Alto, CA.

Glucksberg, S., Krauss, R. M., and Higgins, T. 1975. The development of communication skills in children. *In* F. Horowitz (ed.), Review of Child Development Research, Vol. 4. University of Chicago Press, Chicago.

Greenfield, P. M., and Smith, J. H. 1976. The Structure of Communication in Early Language Development. Academic Press, Inc., New York.

Greenfield, P. M., and Zukow, P. G. 1978. Why do children say what they say when they say it?: An experimental approach to the psychogenesis of presupposition. *In* K. E. Nelson (ed.), Children's Language, Vol. 1. Gardner Press, New York.

Grice, H. P. 1975. Logic and conversation. *In* P. Cole and J. Morgan (eds.), Syntax and Semantics, Vol. 3: Speech Acts. Academic Press, Inc., New York.

Harris, R. J. 1975. Children's comprehension of complex sentences. J. Exp. Child Psychol. 19:420–433.

Hopmann, M. R., and Maratsos, M. P. 1978. A developmental study of factivity and negation in complex syntax. J. Child Lang. 5:295–309.

Hornby, P. 1971. Surface structure and the topic-comment distinction: A developmental study. Child Dev. 42:1975–1988.

Huxley, R. 1970. The development of the correct use of subject personal pronouns in two children. *In* G. B. Flores D'Arcais and W. J. M. Levelt (eds.), Advances in Psycholinguistics. North-Holland, Amsterdam.

Jackendoff, R. 1972. Semantic Interpretation in Generative Grammar. MIT Press, Cambridge, MA.

Johnson, C. N., and Maratsos, M. P. 1977. Early comprehension of mental verbs: Think and know. Child Dev. 48:1743–1747.

Johnson, C. N., and Wellman, H. M. 1980. Children's developing understanding of mental verbs: Remember, know, and guess. Child Dev. 51:1095–1102.

Karmiloff-Smith, A. 1977. More about the same: Children's understanding of post articles. J. Child Lang. 4:377–394.

Karttunen, L. 1974. Presupposition and linguistic context. Theoret. Ling. 1:181–194.

Keenan, E. L. 1971. Two kinds of presupposition in natural language. *In* C. J. Fillmore and D. Langendoen (eds.), Studies in Linguistic Semantics. Holt, Rinehart & Winston, Inc., New York.

Keenan, E. O. 1974. Conversational competence in children. J. Child Lang. 1:163–184.

Keenan, E. O. 1976. The universality of conversational postulates. Lang. Soc. 5:67–80.

Kiparsky, P., and Kiparsky, C. 1971. Fact. *In* D. D. Steinberg and L. A. Jakobovits (eds.), Semantics. Cambridge University Press, New York.

Lakoff, G. 1971. Presupposition and relative well-formedness. *In* D. D. Steinberg and L. A. Jakobovits (eds.), Semantics. Cambridge University Press, New York.

Lakoff, R. 1973. The logic of politeness: Or, minding your p's and q's. Papers from the Ninth Regional Meeting of the Chicago Linguistic Society. Linguistics Department, University of Chicago, Chicago.

Lempers, J. D., Flavell, E. R., and Flavell, J. H. 1977. The development in very young children of tacit knowledge concerning visual perception. Genet. Psychol. Monogr. 95:3–53.

Leonard, L. B. 1979. Language impairment in children. Merrill-Palmer Q. 25:205–232.

McCawley, J. D. 1970. Semantic representation. *In* P. L. Garvin (ed.), Cognition: A Multiple View. Spartan Books, New York.

Macnamara, J., Baker, E., and Olson, C. L. 1976. Four-year-olds' understanding of pretend, forget, and know: Evidence for propositional operations. Child Dev. 47:62–70.

MacWhinney, B., and Bates, E. 1978. Sentential devices for conveying givenness and newness: A cross-cultural developmental study. J. Verbal Learn. Verbal Behav. 17:539–558.

Maratsos, M. 1973a. The effects of stress on the understanding of pronominal co-reference in children. J. Psycholing. Res. 2:1–8.

Maratsos, M. 1973b. Nonegocentric communication difficulties in preschool children. Child Dev. 44:697–700.

Maratsos, M. P. 1974. Preschool children's use of definite and indefinite articles. Child Dev. 45:446–455.

Maratsos, M. P. 1976. The Use of Definite and Indefinite Reference in Young Children: An Experimental Study of Semantic Acquisition. Cambridge University Press, Cambridge, England.

Menig-Peterson, C. L. 1975. The modification of communicative behavior in preschool-age children as a function of the listener's perspective. Child Dev. 46:1015–1018.

Miscione, J. L., Marvin, P. S., O'Brien, R. G., and Greenberg, M. T. 1978. A developmental study of preschool children's understanding of the words "know" and "guess." Child Dev. 49:1107–1113.

Nelson, K. 1975. The nominal shift in semantic-syntactic development. Cognitive Psychol. 7:461–479.

Peterson, C. L. 1974. Communicative and narrative behavior of preschool-aged children. Unpublished doctoral dissertation, University of Minnesota.

Piaget, J. 1926. The Language and Thought of the Child. Harcourt, Brace, and Co., New York.

Rodgon, M. 1976. Single Word Usage, Cognitive Development, and the Beginnings of Combinatorial Speech. Cambridge University Press, Cambridge, England.

Scoville, R. P., and Gordon, A. M. 1980. Children's understanding of factive presuppositions: An experiment and a review. J. Child Lang. 7:381–399.

Sechehaye, M. A. 1926. Essai sur la Structure Logique de la Phrase. Champion, Paris.

Shatz, M. 1978. Children's comprehension of their mothers' question-directives. J. Child Lang. 5:39–46.

Shatz, M., and Gelman, R. 1973. The development of communication skills: Modifications in the speech of young children as a function of the listeners. Monogr. Soc. Res. Child Dev. 38, Serial no. 152.

Snyder, L. 1976. The early presuppositions and performatives of normal and language disabled children. Papers Rep. Child Lang. Dev. 12:221–229.

Tanz, C. 1977. Learning how "it" works. J. Child Lang. 4:225–235.

Turvey, M. T. 1977. Preliminaries to a theory of action with reference to vision. *In* R. Shaw and J. Bransford (eds.), Perceiving, Acting, and Knowing: Toward an Ecological Psychology. Lawrence Erlbaum Assocs., Inc., Hillsdale, N.J.

Tyack, D., and Ingram, D. 1977. Children's production and comprehension of questions. J. Child Lang. 4:211–224.

Van Hekken, S. M. J., Vergeer, M. M., and Harris, P. L. 1980. Ambiguity of reference and listeners' reaction in a naturalistic setting. J. Child Lang. 7:555–563.

Vygotsky, L. 1962. Thought and Language. MIT Press, Cambridge, MA.

Warden, D. A. 1976. The influence of context on children's use of identifying expressions and references. Br. J. Psychol. 67:101–112.

Wason, P. C. 1965. The contexts of plausible denial. J. Verbal Learn. Verbal Behav. 4:7–11.

Wellman, H. M., and Johnson, C. N. 1979. Understanding of mental processes: A developmental study of "remember" and "forget." Child Dev. 50:79–88.

Wieman, L. A. 1976. Stress patterns of early child language. J. Child Lang. 3:283–286.

The Structure of Children's Requests

David Gordon

and

Susan Ervin-Tripp

Institute of Human Learning
University of California
Berkeley, California

Editors' Note

This chapter provides an analysis of social and situational variables and a design for analyzing instrumental language. Instrumental language attempts to get a hearer to cooperate with or carry out a goal of a speaker. When formulating an instrumental move, speakers develop a plan or select a strategy that prompts the hearer to cooperate. If the hearer's initial response is negative, a new strategy may be chosen. Social relationships and situational variables influence the choice of strategies, which in turn affects the type of instrumental act expressed—its form, nuances, and arguments.

Instrumental moves are either conventional (requests) or nonconventional (indirect or "strategic"). Indirect instrumental moves may be as direct, cognitively, as "direct" requests. Both types express the child's concepts of social motivation and social interaction. Although children have apparent knowledge of many instrumental strategies at an early age, their use of indirect forms increases through the late preschool and school years.

contents

SOCIAL AND SITUATIONAL VARIABLES 297
    Social Relations 298
    Intrusiveness and Routinality 299

INSTRUMENTAL LANGUAGE 300
    Structure of an Instrumental Sequence 300
    Conventionality in Requests 302
    Instrumental Strategies 303
    Formal Variation in Instrumental Moves 305
    Speech Acts 306
    Conventional Requests 307
    Formal Nuancing 308
    Persuasive Arguments 309

THE MEANING OF FORM AND THE "CHECKLIST" MODEL OF SPEECH 310

THE INSTRUMENTAL LANGUAGE OF FOUR-YEAR-OLD T 311
    Self-Oriented Requests (W) 312
    Requests Oriented to Rules and Norms (C) 314
    Activity- or External Goal–Oriented Requests (A) 314
    Summary of T's System 316
    Comparison with Adult Requests 316
    Indirect Speech Acts 317

REFERENCES 320

Instrumental language attempts to get a hearer to cooperate with or carry out a goal of a speaker. The speaker's success or failure in getting such cooperation depends in part on the coordination of social and linguistic knowledge. The characterization of this coordination and the causal reasoning behind it are the topics of this chapter. We discuss the social and situational factors that prompt a child to choose one verbal means rather than another to request cooperation. We discuss development only incidentally; for more detailed descriptions, see Ervin-Tripp and Gordon (in press), Ervin-Tripp (1982), and Becker (1982).

Our discussion is organized into four sections. In the first two sections, we describe two required domains of knowledge: the social and the verbal. We begin by defining important social and situational variables—features of the context—that are likely to affect what is said. We then discuss the levels and types of choices that are involved in getting instrumental moves accomplished verbally. Here we describe various strategies, acts, utterance forms, nuances, and persuasive arguments. In the last two sections, we discuss how children might coordinate different strategies, acts, and so forth with particular social and situational variables. Observational data from videotapes of a 4-year-old are used to illustrate our approach.[1]

SOCIAL AND SITUATIONAL VARIABLES

The choice of an instrumental move depends, in part, on the social relations between participants. Social relations involve power and familiarity/distance, among other factors. These determine "status" and are usually signaled in adult requests. Requests often confirm existing social relations. They can also remind partners of temporarily changed relations. For example, a child's power can change temporarily when role playing or instructing a peer, and the form of requests will change accordingly. Requests can also be used to unilaterally change social relations by making moves that increase distance, power, familiarity, or deference. Finally, requests can express attitudes such as anger, helpfulness, or cooperation. By studying requests, we may find out what aspects of social relations are important to children.

The choice of an instrumental move also depends on situational variables such as the *intrusiveness* or *routinality* of the action requested. Questions here include: Does the speaker have the *right* to

---

[1] Except when otherwise indicated, the data reported in this chapter come from our studies of middle-class mainstream American families with children ages 8 and under. These studies were funded by grants from the National Institute of Mental Health (MH-26063) and the National Science Foundation (NSF-BNS-7826539).

expect cooperation? Is the hearer *obligated* to cooperate? If the goal is an object, who *owns* the object—the speaker, the hearer, or both? Who is currently using it? Does the request *intrude* on the hearer's conversation with someone else? Will compliance *disrupt* the hearer's plans? Will compliance be *difficult*? These situational factors can be seen as differentiating a routine from an unexpected, intrusive, or disruptive act (Brown and Levinson, 1978).

Social relations and intrusiveness/routinality mediate the choice of instrumental language. Adults generally use more polite, formal, or indirect instrumental language as the status of the listener and the intrusiveness of the request increase. For example, if a person of low status wants a person of high status to do something that would disrupt the latter's current activity, asking for it will involve a high social cost, which may be "paid" for through an expression of deferential politeness. Asking for something that can be provided without serious disruption involves lower cost, and generally less deference. The following list illustrates how social relations and intrusiveness/routinality affect the selection of an instrumental move (see Ervin-Tripp and Gordon, in press, for a more detailed discussion of these variables).

Social Relations

What aspects of social relations are important to children? An examination of children's instrumental language may help us answer this question. We begin this section by citing instances of how variables related to status may affect children's use of polite instrumental moves. The section continues with a similar discussion of attitude.

Relative Status Status pertains to the relative power of speaker and addressee, and the social distance between them. Preschoolers as young as 2 years are sensitive to power and familiarity, judging from their instrumental language (Ervin-Tripp, 1982). They use significantly more imperatives to mothers than to fathers; siblings are given orders, but visitors receive polite requests.

1. *Child (2;0) to father (after several questions about milk and who it belongs to):*
    C: You want milk, Daddy?
    F: I have some, thank you.
    C: Milk in there, Daddy?
    F: Yes.
    C: Daddy, I want some, please? Please Daddy, huh?
    Same child to mother: Mommy, I want milk. (C. Lawson)
2. *Brother to younger sister:* Carrie, stop sucking your fingers.
    Sister to brother: David, you're not the boss of me. (A. Rogers)
3. *Nursery school child (5;5) to adult visitor:* Do you think you could put your foot right there? (B. A. O'Connell)

Formal politeness reflects not only power and familiarity; it also reflects social distance. Mitchell-Kernan and Kernan (1977) found that, among grade-school children, polite instrumental moves to peer group members increased when the speaker was estranged from the peer group.

Finally, studies of role playing (Andersen, 1977) and elicited requests in experiments (James, 1978) have shown that, when there are no actual costs, children use the frequency, content, and form of requests to symbolically identify roles.

Attitudes Social relations include temporary attitudes concerning the situation at hand. Like status, attitudes affect the use of deference, joking, orders, and threats:

4. Last person to talk to me like that didn't talk to me no more. (Mitchell-Kernan and Kernan)
5. *S (12;0):* Gimme that ruler.
   A (12;0): Huh?
   S: Gimme that ruler, girl.
   A: Huh?
   S: Will you please gimme that ruler before I knock you down. (Mitchell-Kernan and Kernan)

Intrusiveness and Routinality

The intrusiveness or routinality of a request also affects the type of instrumental language selected. This section begins with instances of how intrusiveness may affect children's use of polite instrumental moves. We continue with a discussion of possessions, rights, and obligations. In general, children are sensitive to roles, rights, and possessions by age 2; however, intrusiveness and task difficulty do not come into play until school age.

Intrusiveness Requests can intrude on listeners in three ways: making a request may *interrupt* an ongoing conversation; cooperating with a request may entail a *disruption* of plans or of ongoing activity; and requests may demand *valuable goods*, or *unusual* or *difficult* services. Direct imperative forms are quite normal in adult speech in situations where speaker and hearer are engaged in a cooperative activity, or where the action desired is routine, easy to carry out, or consistent with the listener's present focus of attention. However, adults are generally careful to provide a justification or use extra politeness for requests that may be intrusive. Children are aware of roles, rights, and possessions by age 2, but sensitivity to interruptions, or to what might be disruptive or difficult from the hearer's viewpoint, is generally not present until school age. Our own data indicate that, around the third grade, children begin to show verbal awareness of imposing on others when making requests (Gordon et al., 1980).

6. *Child (8;0) to adult experimenter engaged in conversation:* She told me to get a letter for my parents.
7. *Similar situation:* Do you have a green marker I could use?

Possessions By age 2, children show more deference when asking for other's property than when asking for their own. Property may involve permanent possessions, or temporary rights of usage when ownership is communal, as in schools.

8. *Nursery schooler (4;0) to peers:* Can I drive your car? (C. Garvey)
9. *Sister (4;3) to sister (5;10):* Well it's my turn after. Now it's my turn.

Rights and Obligations Rights and obligations are often related to specific social roles. For instance, mothers are expected to provide help, and nursery school teachers are expected to enforce the school routine. Less deference is required when cooperation is expected than when it is not. For example, a request that a teacher perform some service related to the school routine requires less deference than a request for the same service from a classroom visitor.

10. *Child (4;3) to mother:* This won't stick. (S. Isola)
11. *Nursery school child to adult:* Jason's trying to take my stuff. (O'Connell)
12. *Preschooler to teacher:* Jean, we didn't have a snack. (S. Isola)

As Brown and Levinson (1978) have shown for adults, a calculation of status and intrusiveness/routinality allows a speaker to select instrumental language of appropriate politeness, informality, and indirectness. At the same time, the language selected by the speaker enables the hearer to recognize the quality of social relations with the speaker and how the speaker has assessed the difficulty of the task. An analysis of children's instrumental language needs to take both the hearer's and the speaker's "calculations" into account.

INSTRUMENTAL LANGUAGE

When formulating an instrumental move, speakers develop a plan or select a strategy that will prompt the hearer to cooperate; if the partner's initial response is negative, a new strategy may be chosen. Social relationships and situational variables affect which strategy is selected, which in turn influences the type of instrumental act chosen—its form, its nuances, and the persuasive arguments employed, if any.

Structure of an Instrumental Sequence

We identify as the *domain* (Garvey, 1975) of an instrumental sequence all the speaking turns involved in it. The following dialogue has been constructed to exemplify the domain of a request.

13. A: Hey, let's play fire engine. Toot toot!
    B: This is my place (climbs next to A).
    A: I haven't got enough room. Move over! I've gotta drive the fire engine.
    B: No! Pretend I'm driving. (B remains)
    A: I'm the driver. Get behind! (pushes)

As the preceding dialogue illustrates, the domain of a request may include: attention-getters, preliminary framing moves, preliminary persuasive adjuncts, instrumental acts, post-posed persuasive adjuncts, responses, and remedies.

Attention-getters: If the addressee is not paying attention, the speaker may try to get attention by verbal and/or nonverbal means ("Hey!", hand waving, etc.). In a group, a particular addressee may be designated. An attention-getter alone can function as a request if the context makes clear what is wanted. Our research indicates that children of 4 or 5 years can assess where the attention of the addressee is focused, and redirect it if necessary.

Framing moves: If the speaker wants to set up a cooperative situation to make an instrumental move more effective, preliminary moves—such as proposing a particular kind of play—may be necessary. ("Let's play fire engine.")

Persuasive adjuncts: Instrumental moves are often prefaced or followed by reasons, promises, threats, and so forth, which serve to justify the request or persuade the hearer. ("I haven't got enough . . . "; "I've gotta drive . . . ") Persuasive adjuncts such as reasons can often stand alone as instrumental moves in themselves.

Instrumental moves: A conventional speech act may occur here ("Move over!"). The act may be qualified by the addition of politeness formulas, vocatives, and so on.

Responses: Hearer responses are also constituents in instrumental sequences. Assent, denial, excuses for noncompliance, and requests for clarification require as much attention to politeness and persuasion as do the original speaker's instrumental moves and adjuncts.

Remedies: Following a response, the speaker may repeat, alter, intensify, clarify, or add persuasive arguments to support an instrumental move that has been challenged ("I'm the driver. Get behind!"). At the earliest stages, children typically repeat what they originally said in order to remedy an ineffective or deficient request. When they do alter a request, they try to clarify it. However, school-age children tend to make repairs by adding justifications when asking for favors; and they use intensifiers or nonverbal moves when asking for what is theirs by right (Montes, 1981).

Each of the above moves is optional. For example, a hint may involve just an adjunct without any explicit request at all. "I haven't got enough room" in Example 13 is interpretable without "Get behind!" Sometimes the context is so clear than an attention-getter alone is enough to serve as an instrumental act.

Conventionality in Requests

One way of obtaining cooperation is to simply ask for it. Children do this by age 2½. This can be done through the use of conventional request forms in which the form of the utterance makes explicit the call for cooperation or obedience. Thus, an utterance such as "Could you close the door?" may be expected to get its hearer to close the door (in part) because the utterance is recognized as a request to do so. Many utterances serve instrumental goals without explicitly signaling that they are requests. Although an utterance such as "It's freezing in here" may prompt the hearer to close the door, the hearer in this case may act not because of being asked to, but rather for some other reason suggested by the statement—for example, that the addressee doesn't want the speaker to be cold or uncomfortable, or because the hearer may feel cold too, and will act for the benefit of both.

An utterance such as "It's freezing in here" is often not an attempt to get the hearer to carry out any specific action that the speaker has in mind. It may be satisfied by any action that remedies the situation. How an utterance like this would be described depends on its context. Said by a customer to a sauna operator, it might be reported as a request or a command.

A similar utterance, such as "It's noon," may get a child to start working, or to stop working and run outside to play. In either case, we would not say that the speaker told or requested the hearer to start/stop doing anything. We would expect that whatever the hearer did after hearing "It's noon" would probably be a response to the information it contained rather than a result of being asked to do something.

The point that these two examples make is that speakers in many cases use language to achieve instrumental goals without using conventional forms that can properly be described as requests, and without intending their utterances to be interpreted as requests. We refer to instrumental moves of this type as nonconventional instrumental moves, or NCIs. Among the most important reasons for using NCIs is the goal of maintaining appropriate social relationships (Brown and Levinson, 1978; Ervin-Tripp, 1976).

In practice, at least in the case of older children and adults, the reason for complying with an NCI may not be so different from the reason for carrying out a conventional request. Expressions similar to

"It's freezing in here" may be used so frequently that they are immediately interpretable as requests; and the conventional request "Could you close the door?" may be complied with because the reason behind it—i.e., that it's freezing—is immediately recognized. In many cases, of course, speakers combine such utterances to produce justified, socially appropriate requests: "Could you close the door? It's freezing in here."

However, conventional requests and NCIs are learned in different ways. Conventional requests can be learned as formulas. In fact, such formulas can be found in phrase books for foreigners. NCIs, on the other hand, cannot be mastered by learning formulas. If we want to teach someone how to produce NCIs like "It's freezing in here," we have to teach them either to find an adequate reason for the hearer to act, or to state a problem that the act might solve. This is why the development of effective instrumental acts requires cognitive and social strategies that go beyond simply learning a fixed linguistic repertoire.

Instrumental Strategies

In this section we consider possible instrumental strategies for producing NCIs, and the way they are used by children. In general, young children's strategies are based on their own focus of attention rather than the informational needs of listeners. Young children are not good at attending to the cognitive states of listeners. It is not until the middle of grade school that children gear their strategies to the states of their hearers. At the most general level there are probably three basic strategies for NCIs:

R: Identify a *reason* or cause for the hearer to carry out, or facilitate, the desired action and make the hearer aware of it (e.g., "It's your turn").

N: Anticipate an obstacle to the hearer's cooperation and *neutralize* it (e.g., "I'll give you a dollar for that").

G: Make the hearer aware of the desired *goal* situation, or some aspect of it, and hope the hearer brings it about voluntarily (e.g., "Do we have any candy?", asked when child knows "we" do).

It is unlikely that young children have general procedural rules of this nature, and it is certainly not evident that adults have such rules for NCIs either. We consider these to be descriptive frameworks under which the more specific instrumental strategies we give below may fall.

There are at least five strategies that seem to be related to the Reason approach:

R.1. *Call attention to a problem:* If the hearer's action is needed to remedy some problem, or a problem can be identified that the desired action would remedy, state the problem (e.g., "I can't find my white marble"; "The macaroni's boiling"; "This is too heavy for me").

> 14. *Girl (7;10) to sister (5;10) dyeing Easter eggs:* Well she's going to mess yours up. Well you better take yours out. (S. Isola)

R.2. *State an infraction:* If the hearer is engaged in an activity that violates a norm or creates a problem, state the infraction (e.g., "You're not supposed to do that").

R.3. *Make a correction:* If the hearer is engaged in an inappropriate action, make the hearer aware of the appropriate action (e.g., "That goes there").

R.4. *Provide preconditions:* If the hearer will carry out the desired act when specific preconditions are met, make the hearer aware that such preconditions have been, or will be met (e.g., "I'm ready now"; "The train's leaving"; "It's your turn"; "Is there any juice left?" "Is Mom there?").

R.5. *Forestall intervention:* If intervention in some activity is anticipated, identify or justify the planned activity. The effect is that of a prohibition (e.g., "That's mine" said as speaker grabs toy; "I'll get it" said as speaker runs out of room to answer phone or get some object). In a child, such verbalizations may show recognition that violation of another's territory, crossing activity boundaries, or interrupting an activity must be justified.

There are also at least three strategies that seem to be related to the Obstacle Neutralization approach:

N.1. *Anticipate counterarguments:* If the hearer may have reasons not to cooperate with the goal, identify a way to mitigate such obstacles and inform the hearer.

> 15. If I can have a kitten I'll take care of it all by myself. (Clark and Delia)

N.2. *Modify cost:* If the cost of a goal or activity is high, find a way of neutralizing it: 1) minimize cost (e.g., ask for small amount); 2) provide compensation (e.g., 42-month-old child to peer: "If you give me this for a while, you can have this for a while" [Ervin-Tripp]); or 3) increase cost of noncompliance (e.g., threaten hearer: "If you don't give it to me, I'll take my truck back").

N.3. *Change activity context:* If the framing situation or current activity is not favorable to obtaining the goal, invoke a different situation or activity (e.g., a child denied access to a toy may suggest a game or activity in which the use of the toy is routine).

16. *A 4-year-old to peer (playing mommies):* And we sit down and have a glass of orange juice. . . . And they sit on our lap with us. (J. Cook-Gumperz)
17. No, the train station is this. (B. A. O'Connell)

Successive remedies may reframe:

18. *A 4-year-old to peer:* Pretend this was my car. (B refuses)
    A: Pretend this was our car. (B refuses)
    A: Can I drive your car? (B accepts) (Garvey)

The major developmental changes in children's tactics result from the capacity of children over the age of 8 to take the perspective of their partners. This is illustrated in the examples below:

19. *Girl (8;0) to brother (4;0):* D'ya wanna be Santa Claus? Here, take these toys to the basement. (Girl ties her laundry in her nightgown, and brother carries it to laundry.)

In the next example, the brother had become whiny because he wanted to cram his tricycle into a station wagon already full of bicycles. He was wearing a Batman cape:

20. *Girl to brother:* Batman, you don't need a bike. You can *fly* over everyone faster than the bikes! (he accepts)

On both occasions, the request was part of a proposal for play in which the boy was given a desirable role. This method accommodates to his perspective, and uses a familiar pretense strategy.

Although some of the preceding strategies, such as reframing, can be realized through a variety of instrumental acts, many of the examples given would be called *hints*. They illustrate the use of NCIs that are neither clearly requests nor any other conventional instrumental act. In some cases what start off as hints may become conventionalized through repeated use in stereotyped contexts. In addition, as discussed in the next section, many conventional request forms in English appear to have their origins in NCIs.

Formal Variation in Instrumental Moves

The form an NCI takes depends on the instrumental strategy a speaker has chosen. Often the strategy chosen will be a direct outcome of ongoing activities. Thus, as part of an instructional context in which a younger child is helping set up a toy town, "These go on the roof" provides general instructions and also directs the immediate behavior of the partner.

In adult usage, NCIs or hints often have social features not available in conventional requests. Conventional requests are explicit both about what the hearer is to do and about the amount of politeness paid.

They occur when the speaker wants clarity on either or both of these features. However, there are cooperative or informal contexts in which adults find conventional polite requests to be overly formal or cold; such requests may seem to imply inappropriate doubts either about the hearer's willingness to comply or about the hearer's ability to recognize a hint in the shared context. NCIs allow the speaker not to be seen as making a direct request; they avoid formality and avoid explicitness when the hearer can be assumed to know what is going on. They also make it possible to show humor and express other social attitudes. In this way they permit the speaker to save face when noncompliance is possible; and they may increase rapport by alluding to shared knowledge and by implying familiarity or common ground (Brown and Levinson, 1978).[2]

The desire to establish or maintain deference, or to avoid an appearance of control, is often important in the choice of an NCI. When the speaker knows whose turn it is, the use of an NCI such as "Whose turn is it?"—instead of the more direct NCI, "It's your turn to make coffee, Joan"—illustrates two points. First, NCIs can be quite direct in context; second, the flexibility of NCIs allows speakers to choose strategies that serve a particular purpose, whether that purpose is to avoid the appearance of control or to address other social concerns.

Preschool children rarely use NCIs for the kind of tactfulness indicated above. By school age, however, hints are used in some contexts. Mitchell-Kernan and Kernan's (1977) school data indicate that hints may initially be most common in situations involving corrections or conflicts. They found that the use of hints instead of conventional requests was closely related to group norms about children's behavior to adults:

Children do not arrogate supervision when adults are present (e.g., 11-year-old to 8-year-old: "It's peanuts all over the floor").
Children are not supposed to beg (e.g., child to adult: "You gave Jimmy a nickel!").
Children do not request things that have already been denied them (e.g., 11-year-old to adult (after child mishandled microphone, and adult took it back): "I like to talk on the mike").

Speech Acts

Conversational texts from adults and children show that NCIs may have the appearance of many other types of speech acts. Speech acts

---

[2] There are major cultural variations both in adult preferences for conventional requests/NCIs and in how early children are trained to understand hints (Ervin-Tripp and Gordon, in press).

are categories of social action that are recognized by members of a group and identified by terms like *request, offer,* and *ask permission.* The description of an utterance as a particular speech act in indirect accounts (e.g., "And then they *offered/promised/refused* to help with the expenses") reflects social as well as formal properties. For instance, *offers* implies that the hearer has to give permission and therefore controls the completion of the exchange; *permission requests* explicitly recognize that the hearer has control over desired resources or the speaker's behavior. In identifying children's instrumental acts we often find NCIs that look like permission requests ("Can I use your car?"), claims to possession ("That's my car"), offers ("Do you want to trade this for your car?"), warnings or threats ("I'm gonna drive that!"), and other speech acts.

Conventional Requests

The boundary between what is an NCI and what is a conventional request is not always clear. Conventional forms, with the exception of syntactic imperatives, appear to have developed from NCIs that were particularly susceptible to formulaic expression. Such NCIs make possible fixed syntactic frames containing specific lexical items that identify either the instrumental action or the goal. This can be seen in the list of conventional request types given below:

Imperatives: "Gimme that!"; "Don't!" Any form with imperative syntax.
Imperative ellipsis: "More milk"; "Right here." In certain contexts (e.g., eating, shopping, joint enterprises, second tries), naming what is wanted without a verb is heard as a request with the social force of an imperative.[3]
Imbedded requests: "Can/Could/Will/Would you . . . ?"; "Why don't you . . . ?" Imbedded requests make explicit the desired action, agent, and object. By age 2½ English-speaking children begin using auxiliaries and start to mark social contrasts with the use of imbedded requests.
Permission requests: "Can/May I (have/do) . . . ?" Requests for permission to have goods are very similar to imbedded requests and are used equally early to mark social contrasts. "Can I have . . . ?" usually implies an action on the part of the hearer, and therefore is more than simply a request for permission.
Explicit need or want statements: "I want. . ." "I need. . . ."[3]

---

[3] We include these forms in our list, but leave open whether, or to what extent, they are truly conventional.

Conventionalized hints: "Is there any juice left?"; "Have you got my ball?" The production of conventionalized hints is rare in preschoolers, but increases during elementary school (Liebling, 1981; Montes, 1981). Conventionalization is specific to each social group or family, of course, as is the social meaning of the form.[3]

It is striking that conventional polite requests, with few exceptions, are interrogatives that appear to offer the hearer options in responding. Even polite noninterrogatives (e.g., "I wonder if you would/could . . .") are likely to imply questions. Conventional polite forms appear to derive from NCIs that express uncertainty and avoid the appearance of imposing claims or controlling the hearer. Of particular interest here are permission requests that ask for an object ("Can I have . . . ?") and imbedded requests that ask about volition ("Do you wanna pass that bucket over here?"). True permission requests imply that the addressee has control over the speaker, and that the speaker's wishes are subject to the hearer's approval. This is precisely the opposite of the status relations in a command. As a result, borrowing the social implications of a permission request in asking for something is a very marked way of avoiding the appearance of trying to control or impose on another. Such forms leave it up to the hearer to decide what the actual social realities are. A "Do you want to . . . ?" request is very similar in form to a conventional offer. By asking about the hearer's wishes in an offer, the speaker signals the hearer's power to choose, which again is the opposite of the roles in a command. A "Do you want to . . . ?" request appears to leave matters to the hearer's volition, and avoids the appearance of control.

These two examples illustrate the way in which the social implications of different instrumental forms may be "borrowed" for use in request contexts. As NCIs they are particularly careful and polite moves, and this may be part of the reason they were conventionalized. When NCIs become fully conventional, they may lose some of their original implications; the more conventionalized they become, the more their social meanings shift to fit the social implications of the new contexts in which they are used.

Formal Nuancing

All of the above forms can be varied or nuanced in many ways. Very young children express politeness only through the use of imbedded requests, "please," and a change of intonation. The following list illustrates different ways of nuancing requests:

Conventional politeness forms such as "please" and terms of address, which have their own range of social meanings.

21. *Two-and-one-half–year-old to father:* Daddy, I want some, please. Please Daddy, huh?

Politeness can be expressed through post-posed modals and other tags (e.g., "Open the door, would you?").

22. *Four-year-old to 2½-year-old sister:* Addie, why don't you show Gina what you wore, OK?

Expressions can be intensified or mitigated through prosodic variations such as shouting, rising versus falling pitch, angry voice, and wheedling tone.

Requests can be mitigated through displacements and minimizers, which include: utterances with displaced tense or aspect (e.g., "Would you?", "Could you?", "I wanted," "Did you want?", and "If you would"); utterances with displaced agents (e.g., "We have to take our naps now" and "Someone needs to clean his room"); and minimizations (e.g., "Give me a little of your juice").

The formal complexity of a request can be increased through a combination of conventional forms, or through forms derived from expressions frequently associated with other speech acts (see Example 3 above). Complex forms often appear to be particularly polite, as in the following teenage example:

23. *12-year-old to hostess at a party in a house:* Do you have any water that I could drink?

Persuasive Arguments

An important part of the domain of an instrumental act is the collection of supporting material, which Garvey (1975) has called "adjuncts." Adjuncts reflect the speaker's awareness of the state of mind and the motives of the addressee. They provide conditions, reasons, and justifications for a request. For example, children sometimes try to justify requests to an adult by appealing to the latter's role and obligations. This is illustrated in Examples 24 through 26, where children appeal to adults' caregiving roles.

24. *Beth (5;0) to mother:* Mommy, I want you to open all of them, the paint, so I won't have to trouble.
25. *Lisa (4;0) to researcher:* OK, we don't know all these pages, so you read 'em.
26. *Eight-year-old to mother:* If you don't give it to me right now, I won't want it later on.

Children may appeal to norms, goals, or facts about the world when addressing younger children:

27. *Eight-year-old to 4-year-old:* We only have a little more, OK? So don't use one on every Valentine.
28. *Four-year-old to 2-year-old:* Get out of my space. This is *my* space.

For our purposes, the classification of persuasive adjuncts depends less on linguistic criteria than on a recognition of the reasoning and social skills the adjuncts imply. We have classified children's adjuncts as instances of *reasons* such as external conditions ("It's lost"), internal dispositions ("I like that"), states ("He hurt himself"), plans ("I'm making another one"), history ("I chose them"), and norms ("It's lunchtime"). In addition, excuses ("I'm all messy"), threats ("I'll tell Mom"), clarifications ("The blue ones are best"), and different types of expansions and explanations occur. We find that 2- to 3-year-old children typically do not enrich their requests with extra persuasive material. By age 4, however, persuasion and justification appear, especially when stopping another's activities or making a second try in order to remedy a failure or denial.

Because there is no way to define possible persuasive adjuncts in terms of linguistic form, one cannot simply list them as part of a verbal repertoire. They can only be categorized in terms of general, context-sensitive strategies.

THE MEANING OF FORM AND THE "CHECKLIST" MODEL OF SPEECH

Our discussion of the development of instrumental language has shown that by age 5 children attend to a wide range of variables, both social and situational, and can coordinate them with a considerable variety of instrumental strategies and moves. The major issue remains, How does a child arrive at these coordinations? What social understandings do children have that make them choose one form rather than another for their instrumental moves? What, in other words, does the child's choice of form mean?

Research on instrumental language has rarely looked at the concepts behind children's choices of instrumental moves or use of social and situational variables. As a result, most findings can be accounted for by what might be called the "checklist" model of speech. According to this model, the child has a general category such as "Request" that is routinely invoked when the child's communicative goal is instrumental. Under this category, there is a list of request types each of which is paired with a set of contextual specifications. When producing speech, the child: 1) checks the current social and situational variables (e.g., addressee is younger, lower in status, familiar, not in control of desired resource, difficulty is minimal); and then 2) finds the request form that corresponds to that particular cluster of variables (e.g., an imperative). When interpreting speech, the child: 1) looks up the utterance form in a kind of mental "dictionary"; and 2) if the utterance has more than one meaning, the child compares the social/situational variables of the current context with the "dictionary" specifications for contextual features, and chooses the interpretation with matching variables. The mechanism of form choice in this view is just a matching of arbitrary forms to contextual features. The checklist model is fundamentally idiomatic and attributes no power of inference or construction to the child. In such a model, a request is hardly more than a ritual incantation that is produced according to a simple formula.

It is, of course, possible that conventional requests are sometimes selected in this way. NCIs, however, are not likely to be mere incantations because they cannot be generated formulaically, and must be adjusted to meet the demands of a given situation. Without imputing active causal reasoning and social understanding to children, it does not seem possible to account for the variations in the form and content of their NCIs. As we see it, a child who has an instrumental goal will try to cause or motivate another person to cooperate. Simple incantation might be one such means, but evidence from the earliest ages (e.g., Bates, 1976; Carter, 1974) indicates that the child relies on causal reasoning more than on word magic.

THE INSTRUMENTAL LANGUAGE OF FOUR-YEAR-OLD T

A case study is presented here to illuminate the way in which children's social reasoning may be reflected in their use of instrumental moves. We consider the instrumental language of T, a 4-year-old boy from our video study of four families. T was videotaped in naturalistic interaction with others in his home over a period of 7 months. Twelve hours of videotaping during this period yielded over 600 examples of instrumental language.

The basic distribution of T's requests, covering 90% of the examples collected, can be summarized in terms of three types of instrumental goals:

W—*Self-oriented "wants"*: In situations where T wanted an object or wanted to carry out an action himself, he said: 1) "I want . . ." or "I want to . . ." when he assumed he would get what he wanted on the basis of established routines or expectations (nearly 80% of the examples); and 2) "Can I . . . ?" or "Can I have . . . ?" when compliance could not be assumed or was urgently desired (almost 20% of the cases). T was more likely to use the latter forms if he had reason to expect that what he was requesting would not be granted, was clearly part of another's domain, or if the urgency of his desire—as we could tell from his voice—made him fear risking failure. A justification or reason for self-oriented wants was rarely given (5% of examples) regardless of the request form used.

C—Corrections (rule- or norm-oriented concerns): In situations where T wanted to change what was going on, not for direct personal gain but on normative grounds, he either stated a reason for discontinuing what had been started, or gave a reason or correction indicating the correct or appropriate act. These control moves often contained expressions such as "should," "supposed to," "have to," or "goes," which directly refer to the existence of rules or norms (e.g., "You should . . . ," "You're not supposed to . . .").

29. No, I said *three* spoonfuls.
30. That doesn't go there, it goes *there*.

T initiated almost 50% of these instrumental moves with a one-word exclamation such as "Wait!", "Don't!", or "No!"

A—Activity- or external goal–oriented requests: In situations where T's goal was not to correct something on normative grounds (C) or to obtain a self-oriented goal (W), he used: 1) a simple imperative that usually was not accompanied by reasons or justifications (persuasive adjuncts appeared in about 15% of the examples); or 2) an imbedded request form such as "Can you . . . ?", "Why don't you . . . ?", etc. (see Example 22 above). As with self-oriented requests, the imbedded forms were used when T had reason to think that his basic request form would not be complied with or when he was asking for something that was clearly in another's domain. Persuasive adjuncts rarely accompanied imbedded requests.

At first glance, it might seem that T's requests were rather stereotyped, and accord well with a checklist model that simply pairs forms with relevant social and situational variables. In support of this position, one might argue that: 1) T's "I want" statements are conventionalized request formulas; 2) except for rule- and norm-oriented requests, he infrequently elaborated his requests or gave reasons; and 3) he attended to simple social and situational variables that prompted him to choose the imbedded forms for self-oriented wants and external goal–oriented requests. As we argue in the next section, we think such an analysis does not go far enough.

Self-Oriented Requests (W)

Let us consider the self-oriented requests of T. It is highly unlikely that T's basic "I want" request is simply a conventionalized formula without any literal significance. First of all, the majority of T's "I want" requests were responses to direct or implied denials of something he desired. They usually could not be fully distinguished from reason adjuncts, especially since there are clear instances of T using expressions such as "But I want it" not as a conventional request, but as a reason for compliance in response to a denial. In addition, T certainly was aware that the "wants" of others are motivations or justifications for compliance. In a situation where his mother would not allow him to turn on the sprinklers, T said:

31. Well, G [visiting adult] wants to see the sprinklers—don't you G?

Thus, T often used "want" literally and correctly to express a state of desire and to motivate others to comply with what he, or somebody else, wished. Furthermore, T rarely supplied other reasons for wanting something, or for why a listener should go along with his requests for objects and activities. He acted as if his wanting something were a basic, and sufficient reason for compliance.[4] In general, it often seemed to be the only reason he was aware of, both for himself and for others. T's "I want," then, is not just a conventionalized form, however automatic its use. When T said "I want," he meant it.

T's understanding that certain people were oriented to his concerns was not limited to "I want" requests; it also accounted for his use of "I need" and "problem" statements:

32. Mommy, I need some cold medicine.
33. I can't see [it].

With the preceding analysis of T's use of "I want," we can now look at T's self-oriented "Can I?" requests. These were clearly conventional in form, but by no means devoid of meaning. T asked "Can I?" in a tone of voice that usually indicated either uncertainty about compliance or an urgent appeal for acquiescence. This usage indicates that "Can I?" requests probably were made in anticipation of a "You can't (have) . . ." response. In general, "Can I?" requests may be learned early because denials of other forms, such as T's "I want" statements, often contain the phrase "You can't."[5]

On the basis of tone of voice and context, it appears that T used "Can I?" in situations where what he was asking for either was not routine, and therefore might not be readily granted, or was sufficiently

---

[4] That this view might not be unique to T is suggested by Example 26: "If you don't give it to me right now, I won't want it later on." Here, the mother's assumed solicitude for the child's "wants" makes possible a rather unusual threat.

[5] Similarly, the use of "I want" for requesting is probably facilitated by parents asking very young children questions such as "Do you want. . . ?" or "What do you want?" We do not know of any input studies that have looked at question-answer pairs or other structural aspects of dialogue as a basis for the acquisition of linguistic forms.

routine but so urgently desired that he was afraid of possible noncompliance. Thus, the two situations in which T used "Can I?" were externally very different, but they produced similar psychological states—concern over the possibility of denial. These states were dealt with in a way that reflected T's focus of attention, and fully invested a conventional request form with meaning.

"Can I?" requests were rarely accompanied by reasons. This may have been because T considered his "want" to be a sufficient reason for self-oriented requests. In routine circumstances, T could focus on his state of wanting, and simply state "I want" to motivate compliance. In other cases, where he was attending to the possibility of "You can't," he had no further reason for compliance, and simply asked "Can I?"

In sum, the forms "I want" and "Can I?" occurred in contexts defined by T's psychological state of wanting to possess, use, or do something. The forms were "meaningful" to T, and were used against a background assessment of whether an individual was likely to be oriented to his concerns. Seen in this light, T's choice of request forms reflects a simple concept of the causes or motivations for behavior in another.

Requests Oriented to Rules and Norms (C)

Request type C, which contains mostly corrections, reflects T's sense of right and wrong, or correct and incorrect, and was directed at external matters. Many of the control moves in C contained expressions such as "supposed to," "have to," and "goes," which imply norms and obligations. T seemed to assume that others were oriented to doing what is "right" or "expected." An exclamation such as "Hey!", "Don't!", or "Wait!" often was used to get an immediate halt in activity; but T's basic means of getting others to do what was correct or to stop what was not correct was to simply tell them what was right or wrong. The underlying strategy here was very similar to T's use of "I want." In both cases, the willingness to act in accord with a general orientation was assumed. Only the need and goal of the activity was verbalized. Once again, then, T's choice of form was meaningful rather than ritual, and demonstrated an active concept of social causality.

Activity- or External Goal–Oriented Requests (A)

The requests of type A generally are oriented to cooperative or routine actions by others in which T's goal is not to correct something on normative grounds or obtain something for himself. T's basic form here is a simple imperative. In our transcripts of T, imperatives occurred more often than any other request form, and most of these imperative forms occurred during shared or routine activities.

A third of T's imperatives were given during imaginative game play when he was directing others in the activities that were to go on. In addition, T often used imperatives to direct activities in other contexts that he assumed were cooperative, such as the placement of video equipment or the positioning of objects that he wanted to have videotaped.

    34. *To researcher:* Okay, now put that other one . . . Where should we put that one?

Other imperatives occurred when a hearer had already begun helping him. Thus, when his mother was putting lunch on his plate, he directed: "Put—Mix it."

Because imperatives usually occurred when cooperation was assumed, supporting reasons were rarely necessary. Most of T's initiating imperatives (85%) were not supported by reason adjuncts that could be interpreted as attempts to gain compliance from the listener. Reasons for compliance apparently were considered superfluous in these contexts. Deviations from this finding were generally limited to: 1) situations in which, for personal reasons, T wanted to stop someone from doing something or warn them; 2) responses to denials; and 3) situations in which the context did not make clear his reason.

    35. Wait a minute, A, I'm putting this somewhere.
    36. Go ahead and sit down, or you might fall.

Thus, Type A requests were usually imperatives, and usually occurred in cooperative contexts. T used conventional imbedded requests in situations when there was not an established context of cooperation and he was asking for a favor or for action under the control of another.

    37. *Inviting a peer to play "airplane":* Oh, K, do you wanna be by the pilot?
         [no response]
         Why don't you sit by the pilot?

In respect to self- and rule- or norm-oriented requests, we said that T's control moves were typically carried out by providing reasons for an act that, based on simple assumptions about others' motivations, would be adequate to elicit compliance. With goal-oriented requests, however, the reasons for compliance were usually situated in the type of activity and only the relevant action needed to be made clear. This often was done directly with an imperative form. Conventionally polite requests forms were used on occasions when an established context of cooperation was not present. In this respect they were similar to the "Can I?" requests that T used for self-oriented goals.

Summary of T's System

We have maintained that T's instrumental moves involved more than simple formulaic pairings of forms with contexts. According to our findings, the primary determinant of the form for T's instrumental acts was the goal or type of action desired. Subordinate to this was T's anticipation of compliance by the addressee. T's form choices cannot be accounted for simply on the basis of the social attributes of the speaker, the hearer, or the immediate situation. T's three basic request types—self-oriented, rule/norm oriented, and external action—did not correspond to familiar social contexts as adults might define them; they were T's own constructs. Within these request types there was generally a basic form used when compliance could be expected. Conventionally polite forms were used when T was concerned about the possibility of denial. This system of form choices was based on T's understanding of social motivation and social relationships. It was imbued with meaning, but very different from the system of adults.

Comparison with Adult Requests

T, at age 4, had all the basic request types used by adults, including hints such as "Okay everybody, the airplane's starting" (so come and play "airplane"), and, to his mother, "The macaroni's boiling." His social perceptions, however, differed from those of adults. For example, T often assumed compliance and used "I want" without giving a reason when an adult would use a more polite request or offer a reason.

Adults usually do not assume that others are at their beck and call. Outside of cooperative contexts, people are to be treated as free agents. Consequently, unelaborated forms like "I want" and imperatives generally appear only in special contexts of joint activity, cooperativeness, and presupposed services (Ervin-Tripp, 1976; Gibbs, 1981).

    38. *Salesman or fast-food clerk:* What'll it be?
          Customer: I'd like two . . . ; I want a couple . . . ; Gimme a couple. . . .

In contrast to adults, T only infrequently gave reasons in support of imperatives and "I want" statements; however, he did use conventional polite requests in context where he had particular doubt about compliance.

    T's use of imperatives and type C rule-oriented requests implies that T often assumed that he was in a position of authority, even when addressing adults. T may have been able to assume this because his mother and the experimenters were routinely cooperative, and, like many Americans, did not expect respect. In similar contexts, adults generally try to avoid any appearance of claiming authority by using mitigating explanations or paralinguistic behaviors indicating uncertainty or hesitation. T, at age 4, had not yet learned the necessity of making it clear verbally that one respects the decisions and actions of others, and does not seek to impose ones own wishes or values upon them. In any case, as with most young children, T's requests contained little tactful deviousness; in general, they directly reflected his focus of attention. Evidence from other research (e.g., Gordon et al., 1980) indicates that it is not until the third grade, or upward of age 8, that American children begin to systematically incorporate considerations of face (Brown and Levinson, 1978) into their instrumental language. This is, of course, very much in line with Piaget's claim that the child moves from egocentrism to concrete operations at around 7 or 8.

T's use of polite forms was infrequent and limited to situations in which he doubted that his request would be successful. However, he probably did not choose "polite" or conventional forms because they are more effective than other forms. Our family videotape data (see Ervin-Tripp, 1982) strongly suggest that simple efficacy was not the basis for T's, or the other children's, use of conventional politeness. In fact, to our great surprise, polite forms were overall the *least successful* in gaining compliance. In our data, when we controlled form and response according to cost, rights, intrusiveness, etc., we found that there was no significant advantage to being polite, except that adults were less likely to ignore the child. From the point of view of family experience, politeness seems to be learned through modeling rather than through reinforcement.

Turning to the instrumental strategies used by 4-year-old T and comparing them to the strategies of older children, it appears that T differed from older children in that he did not anticipate counterarguments or minimize costs, unless prompted by a denial or temporizing. After denials, he sometimes changed the setting or activity. However, T did employ all the remaining strategies without prompting. Thus, developmental changes probably pertain more to the content of these strategies and to the social considerations that prompt children to choose one strategy over another than to children's strategic repertoires.

Indirect Speech Acts

The discussion of instrumental strategies brings us to the topic of direct versus indirect speech acts. This issue was originally raised within the field of linguistics (e.g., Gordon and Lakoff, 1975), and it has been treated extensively in the literature on the development of requests. Direct requests are conventional and "on record." Indirect requests are inferential. "It's cold in here," used to get somebody to close the door, is an example of what has been called an indirect request. It is indirect because it does not have the identifying form of a conventional request, it does not literally specify that any action is desired or requested, and in order to be explicitly recognized as a request it must go through some process of logical inference. Imperative and other conventional request forms are direct requests. Hints and other NCIs are indirect requests.[6]

Indirect speech acts might seem to require a good deal of logical reasoning in order to be understood or produced as requests. For a hearer to recognize "It's cold in here" as a request to close the door, it might appear that he has to go through the logical process of figuring out that the speaker is cold, that this is a state the speaker does not want to be in, that closing the door would remove the cause of this state, and that the speaker must have wanted the hearer to recognize all of this in saying "It's cold in here." Research on the development of requests has focused on the ages at which indirection and hinting can be understood and produced rather than on the logical or psychological processes that may be involved. However, general developmental principles indicate that the production or interpretation of an utterance like "It's cold in here" in the manner given above involves more than most children under 5 can routinely accomplish, yet they do produce and understand many indirect speech acts. How is this to be explained? The answer, as our preceding discussion has suggested, may lie in the way language is embedded in activity, everyday routine, social interaction, shared norms, values, and institutions of the culture or social unit.

We would agree that adults are capable of the kind of reasoning given above, and no doubt sometimes employ it when producing and interpreting indirect requests. However, in most cases for adults, and in all cases for young children, we think that the process is far simpler, and just as "direct," as that associated with the direct imperative. Consider NCIs such as:

    39. I want my special straw. (Because I want it, bring it.)
    40. I can't see [it]. (Because I can't see the picture, adjust the camera.)

---

[6] Some writers consider request forms such as "Can you. . . ?" to be indirect because they are ambiguous between requests and information questions, and may require inferential reasoning in order to be interpreted in context. Other writers consider them to be direct requests because they are formulaically recognizable as requests and they make explicit what action is desired. Experimental research by Gibbs (in press) indicates that conventional request forms are often treated as request idioms requiring minimal inferential processing.

41. The macaroni's boiling. [*Mother:* What?] It's boiling over. (Because the macaroni's boiling over, do something about it.)
42. Okay everybody, the airplane's starting. (Because the game is starting, come and take your places.)

Each of the above utterances represents an NCI that was spontaneously produced by T as a cause for somebody else to carry out some action. In each case, we would expect that T's desire for the signaled action was evoked by his awareness of the cause. When T produced the preceding NCIs, he apparently believed that whatever caused him to want the activity would also cause another to want, and therefore produce, the activity. This pattern appeared in many situations. As noted in our discussion of types W and C requests, T often assumed that others were oriented to his wants and to his evaluations of right and wrong. Thus, T simply verbalized the cause for an action, a cause of which he was well aware because it was the basis for his wishing the act in the first place.

If cause and act were connected from the start in T's mind, and T had only to mention the cause, then the mental processes involved would be quite straightforward. Indeed, the processes would be as direct as those involved in choosing an explicit imperative form because the latter requires the "selection" of a specific linguistic request convention that is distinct from the causal connection already established. Furthermore, adults often use NCIs or "indirect" forms when they are not asking for any specific action, do not have a specific action in mind, and simply want any response that removes or resolves a problem. Because imperatives necessitate specifying what the addressee must do, they may involve an added step for the speaker and they may be even more indirect in a cognitive sense than an NCI such as a hint. This suggests that requests that do not explicitly or literally specify desired actions may be *formally* defined as "indirect," when at the same time they are "logically" direct. T's "I want" statements, for example, may be formally "indirect" but logically "direct."

In arguing that our examples of indirect requests were really direct expressions from the point of view of the child, we implied that cause-action links form functional units in the child's mind. These links are formed on the basis of general experience and are not limited to requests. They are implicit in T's three basic instrumental types because the forms T used depended on his assumptions about the causes for an action. Even the imperative requests that were not accompanied by reasons seemed to be based on the assumption that the causes for compliance were already present in the current activity, or the routine nature of the request.

We think that causal links are also active when a hearer responds to instrumental language, regardless of whether the hearer is a child or an adult. If a hearer of any age receives an imperative to do something, it may be recognized as a direct order to carry out a specified action, but *compliance* with the order may require an additional assessment of the cause for the desired act, or a reason for compliance—which in some cases is just the authority of the speaker. If responses to an instrumental move involve the formulation of a cause-action link, then NCIs such as those in Examples 39 through 42 should be directly understood and responded to when the causal link assumed by the speaker is shared or recognized by the hearer.

Our experiments (Ervin-Tripp and Gordon, in press) on the use of situated directives with children indicate that children who respond appropriately to hints or indirect request forms do not need to know they are being asked to do something. All that is necessary is that they understand a situation in terms of its characteristic events and typical cause-action links. That is, a child does not have to assess the motives of a particular speaker at all in deciding on what action is called for. The child can go directly from an NCI to a recognition of the behavior that is typical or appropriate in the situation.

We have taken the position that indirect request forms may not be indirect, because they focus on precisely that information that may be most decisive for spurring action. Our purpose throughout has been to indicate the importance of looking beyond form to the nature of children's instrumental strategies, and to the relationship between strategies and underlying concepts of social motivation and social interaction.

REFERENCES

Andersen, E. 1977. Learning to speak with style. Unpublished doctoral dissertation, Stanford University, Stanford, CA.
Bates, E., 1976. Language and Context: The Acquisition of Pragmatics. Academic Press, Inc., New York.
Becker, J. 1982. Children's strategic use of requests to mark and manipulate social status. *In* S. Kuczaj and D. Palermo (eds.), Language Development. Vol. 2: Language, Thought and Culture. Lawrence Erlbaum Assocs., Inc., Hillsdale, N.J.
Brown, P., and Levinson, S. 1978. Universals in language usage: Politeness phenomena. *In* E. Goody (ed.), Questions and Politeness, pp. 356-389. Cambridge University Press, Cambridge, England.
Carter, A. L. 1974. Communication in the sensorimotor period. Unpublished doctoral dissertation, University of California–Berkeley.
Ervin-Tripp, S. M. 1976. Is Sybil there? The structure of some American English directives. Lang. Soc. 5:25-66.
Ervin-Tripp, S. M. 1982. Ask and it shall be given you: Children's requests. *In* H. Byrnes (ed.), Georgetown University Roundtable in Language and Linguistics, pp. 235-245. Georgetown University Press, Washington, D.C.

Ervin-Tripp, S. M., and Gordon, D. The development of requests. *In* R. L. Schiefelbusch (ed.), Communicative Competence: Assessment and Intervention. University Park Press, Baltimore. (in press)

Garvey, C. 1975. Requests and responses in children's speech. J. Child Lang. 2:41–63.

Gibbs, R. W. 1981. Your wish is my command: Convention and context in interpreting indirect requests. J. Verbal Learn. Verbal Behav. 20:431–444.

Gibbs, R. W., Jr. Do people always process the literal meanings of indirect requests? J. Exp. Psychol. Learn. Memory Cognition. (in press)

Gordon, D., and Lakoff, G. 1975. Conversational postulates. *In* J. Morgan (ed.), Syntax and Semantics: Speech Acts, pp. 83–106. Academic Press, Inc., New York.

Gordon, D. P., Budwig, N., Strage, A., and Carrell, P. 1980. Children's requests to unfamiliar adults: Form, social function, age variation. Paper presented at the Fifth Annual Boston University Conference on Language Development, Boston. (ERIC Document Number ED 205 053.)

James, S. 1978. The effect of listener age and situation on the politeness of children's directives. J. Psycholing. Res. 7:307–317.

Liebling, C. R. 1981. Comprehension of the directive pragmatic structure in oral and written discourse by children ages 6 to 11. Unpublished doctoral dissertation, University of California–Berkeley.

Mitchell-Kernan, C., and Kernan, K. 1977. Pragmatics of directive choice among children. *In* C. Mitchell-Kernan and S. Ervin-Tripp (eds.), Child Discourse, pp. 189–208. Academic Press, Inc., New York.

Montes, R. 1981. Extending a concept: Functioning directively. *In* Children's Functional Language and Education in the Early Years. Final Report to the Carnegie Foundation.

chapter

Grammatical Devices for Sharing Points

Brian MacWhinney

Department of Psychology
Carnegie-Mellon University
Pittsburgh, Pennsylvania

Editors' Note

Point sharing is a system used by speakers and listeners. Included in the system is point making (speakers), point using (listeners), specific devices for using point sharing, and the ways in which these devices convey instructions. The devices are guided by the functionalist approach to semantics, e.g., differences in word order, article use, ellipsis, and so on to reflect fundamental differences in the kinds of points the speaker is trying to make.

Twelve of the most prominent grammatical devices in English are discussed in terms of both a common thread of meaning and alternatives in meaning or polysemes. Data on the use of devices by children and adults are presented and the implications of the analysis are related to normal and abnormal language development. To share points effectively, the child must acquire various point-sharing devices and their polysemes. To communicate fully, the child needs a dictionary, a grammar, an encyclopedia with long-term knowledge, a diary with a referent memory and a discourse memory, and a rhetoricon. Successful use of the devices of the point-sharing system relies on these components.

contents

SEMANTIC ANALYSIS 325
    Definite Article 326
    Indefinite Article 333
    Pronominalization 335
    Ellipsis 340
    Relativization 344
    Stress 345
    Initialization 348
    Preverbal Positioning 351
    Subject-Verb Agreement 355
    Verb Selection 357
    Case Marking 358
    Particles 359
MAKING AND USING THE INSTRUCTIONS 359
LEARNING THE SYSTEM 363
CONCLUSIONS 364
ACKNOWLEDGMENTS 364
REFERENCES 365

Certain linguistic devices play a central role in facilitating the exchange of thoughts between the speaker and the listener in natural communication. These devices are designed to control the ebb and flow of knowledge, belief, narration, and assertion during both planned and unplanned discourse. The collection of such devices constitutes what I call the "point-sharing system." From the speaker's point of view, the function of point sharing is realized through point making, because each attempt by the speaker to share his thoughts with his listener involves the making of a "point." From the listener's point of view, the function of point sharing is realized through point using, because the listener takes the points that have been presented by the speaker and uses them to alter his own cognitive structures. When we wish to speak about both point making and point using, we can talk about the overall function of point sharing.

In other papers, Elizabeth Bates and I have examined the development of point sharing in children (Bates and MacWhinney, 1979) and the theoretical place of functionalist grammar within modern-day psycholinguistics (Bates and MacWhinney, 1982a). We have also reported data on children's acquisition of point-sharing devices in English, Hungarian, and Italian (MacWhinney and Bates, 1978; MacWhinney and Price, 1980) and the use of these devices by adults in sentence comprehension (Bates and MacWhinney, 1982b; Bates et al., 1982). In the present chapter, I would like to focus attention on specific devices from the point-sharing system and the ways in which these devices convey instructions to a listener that guide him in elaborating his cognitive representations.[1]

The analysis of these devices is guided by the functionalist approach to semantics—an approach that is summarized in Bolinger's (1972) observation that "when we say two things that are different we mean two different things by them." According to the functionalist perspective, differences in word order, article use, ellipsis, and so on are not arbitrary formal facts. Rather, they reflect fundamental differences in the kinds of points the speaker is trying to make. This chapter shows how both children and adults use different devices from the point-sharing system to convey different instructions to a listener.

SEMANTIC ANALYSIS

English is an extremely thrifty language. Rather than creating a new word for every new meaning or shade of meaning, our language tends

---

[1] Cross-linguistic research relating to this proposal was supported by Grant #BN57905755 from the Linguistics Program of the National Science Foundation to Brian MacWhinney and Elizabeth Bates.

to make the most of the old words already in the dictionary. For example, the word *blow* has scores of different entries in the lexicon. A person can "suffer a blow," "blow off steam," "blow balloons," "blow his last chance," "blow into town," and so forth. Many common English words have dozens of these alternative minor readings. When some thread of commonality runs through the whole series, we can say that the alternative readings are *polysemes* of a single lexical item (MacWhinney, 1982) and the rules that tell us which polyseme to pick in a given case can be called *polysemic* rules. In the next 12 sections, the polysemic structure of 12 of the most important devices of the point-sharing system are discussed: the definite article, the indefinite article, pronominalization, ellipsis, relativization, stress, initialization, preverbal positioning, subject-verb agreement, verb selection, case-marking, and particle use. Data on the use of these devices by both children and adults are examined, and the final sections of the chapter show how, by their very nature, these various devices place clear limitations on the shape of the information-processing system we use to interpret the instructions. Finally, the implications of this analysis for the study of normal and abnormal language development are considered. Because many of the data that are currently available on the various devices of the point-sharing system derive from experimental studies of either sentences in isolation or short strings of sentences, little is said about some of the more elaborate uses of devices that come into play only in longer textual structures.

Definite Article

The definite article *the* has a variety of meanings or polysemes. These polysemes are similar to each other in some ways, but different in others. They share as a common core the instruction to the listener that it is possible to compute a unique referent for the following noun (i.e., that a referent is "presupposed" or "given"). Exactly how that referent is to be computed, however, depends on the polyseme being used. There are seven different ways in which to compute a referent for a noun with a definite article: computation through exophora, anaphora, cataphora, paraphrase, partonymy, set operation, and genericalness. Whichever of these seven polysemes the listener selects as appropriate, the end result must be identification of a unique referent. In other words, all of the readings of the definite article share the semantic feature of computability of a referent. However, polysemes differ from each other in terms of the exact way in which the referent is computed.

    Exophora The first way of establishing the referent of a definite article is through exophoric deixis (*exophora*, from Greek *exo* "out"

+ *pherein* "carry," i.e., referring outside of the text). Information that is exophorically given is concretely available in the physical-perceptual situation even though it has not been mentioned verbally. As Clark and Marshall (1981) argued, reference can be achieved when there is a physical copresence of the speaker, the hearer, and the object being identified. For example, when ordering dessert pastries from a tray at a restaurant, one can say "I'd like the Sacher torte." In such a case, the identity of the referent (in this case "the Sacher torte") is exophorically given. Brown and Levinson (1978) noted that, by emphasizing his physical copresence with the listener and the object being mentioned, the speaker may also succeed in establishing a polite, cohesive social bond with the listener. For example, a visitor may enter an acquaintance's house for the first time and exclaim "Oh, this is lovely!"

Another common example of exophoric givenness occurs in the case of personal pronouns (Silverstein, 1976). For example, when we use the pronoun *I*, the referent is always the speaker. Also, the referents for the pronouns *we* and *you* may be situationally clear in many cases, but *he*, *she*, *it*, and *they* are far less likely to be exophorically given.

The act of referring to something exophorically is essentially the verbal counterpart of pointing. When we point, we are saying something like "Look at that!" Extending this analogy between gesture and speech, Lyons (1975) has argued that exophoric deixis, or pointing, provides a conceptual basis for givenness in general. This viewpoint seems intuitively satisfying because even nonexophoric givenness can be seen as directing the listener to attend to something he will find in his mind if he only looks hard enough.

Studies by Bresson (1974), Maratsos (1976), and Warden (1976) showed that children are particularly likely to overgeneralize the exophoric use of articles. In cases where the listener is blindfolded or otherwise unable to infer the referent, children may treat that referent as given when an adult would not. Moreover, MacWhinney and Bates (1978) and Warden (1976) found that, even among adults, there is a high level of exophoric use of the definite article. In such experiments, adults often correctly infer that the experimenter must have previous knowledge of the referents for the experimental stimuli. Given this presumed omniscience of the experimenter, it is often quite difficult to exclude exophoric use of the definite article.

Anaphora The second way of establishing the referent of a definite article is through anaphoric mention. Material that has been mentioned in previous discourse is anaphorically given (*ana* "back" + *pherein* "carry," i.e., referring back to earlier text). In other words, when an item is anaphorically given, the listener can identify the referent of the item simply by going back and finding the last mention of that referent in his working memory for the conversation. For example, if one speaker talks about "a dog named Clyde," the next speaker can simply refer to Clyde as "the dog" and still feel confident that all his listeners know to whom he is referring.

Haviland and Clark (1974) and Yekovich, Walker, and Blackman (1979) have shown that sentences with a definite article are easier to understand if the attached noun phrase can be matched to an anaphorically given referent. Fortunately for their listeners, speakers make frequent use of definite noun phrases with anaphorically given referents (Grieve, 1973; Osgood, 1971). Moreover, anaphoric use of the definite article is not confined to adults. Maratsos (1976) found that American children as young as 3 years old make correct use of the definite article to mark referents that are uniquely given in previous discourse. However, Karmiloff-Smith (1979) has noted that, when given a situation in which either an anaphoric or an exophoric interpretation of the definite article is possible in French, preschoolers prefer the exophoric interpretation.

Cataphora The third way of establishing givenness is through "backward anaphora" or "cataphora" (*cata* "below" + *pherein* "carry," i.e., referring to material that occurs below in the text). Material that can only be identified by referring to information in subsequent discourse is cataphorically given. In the sentence "The girl he was to marry jilted John" the phrase "the girl" is identified by material that follows it, i.e., by the phrase "he was to marry." At the same time, the word "he" is identified by the word "John," which follows it. Cataphoric givenness also occurs in phrases such as "the number seven" or "the country of Bolivia." These cases of cataphoric identification are what Donnellan (1966) calls the "attributional" use of definite reference, because the item is being identified by the following attribution.

Paraphrase A fourth way of establishing the referent of a definite article is by paraphrase. In anaphoric reference, there is a previous noun in the text that has the same lexical form as the current noun. However, it may also happen that the previous noun is actually a paraphrase of the current noun. Consider these examples based on Hawkins (1977):

1. Ed was standing by the drill press when suddenly the machine began to vibrate.
2. A man and a woman were walking down the alleyway. The couple was speaking Portuguese.

Sentences 1 and 2 involve the minimal type of inference known as paraphrase. Paraphrase makes use of the fact that lexical items have associations that specify their class membership. For example, in our lexical frame for a *drill press*, we have presumably stored the information that a drill press is a *machine*. Thus, activation of the *drill press* frame also partially activates the association that leads to the *machine* frame. In sentence 2, the inference works the other way, but again nothing more is involved than simple paraphrase. A subcase of paraphrase is the use of the definite article in phrases such as *John, the fool* where "John" is being identified as a fool.

Garrod and Sanford (1977, 1978) investigated the comprehension of sequences such as Examples 3 to 6, below. Some of the sequences involve the substitution of a superordinate for a subordinate term (i.e., a bus can be referred to as "a vehicle"), whereas others involve the use of a subordinate for a superordinate term (i.e., one type of vehicle is "a bus").

3. a. A tank came trundling down the hill.
   b. The vehicle almost hit a pedestrian.
4. a. A bus came trundling down the hill.
   b. The vehicle almost hit a pedestrian.
5. a. A vehicle came trundling down the hill.
   b. The bus almost hit a pedestrian.
6. a. Mrs. Dupont yelled at the bus.
   b. The vehicle almost hit a pedestrian.

Garrod and Sanford found that readers were quicker to understand sentence 4b than sentence 3b and that both of these were faster than sentence 5b. On the basis of these and other data, they argued that, when readers encounter an item like "a bus," that item generates an expectation for its paraphrase "vehicle." The word "tank" also generates an expectation for "vehicle," but because a bus is better than a tank as an instance of a vehicle (Rosch, 1977), the word "bus" generates a stronger expectation for "vehicle." This explains why subjects were quicker to understand sentence 4b than sentence 3b. Conversely, the word "vehicle" generates expectations for buses and tanks and so on, but these are weaker than the paraphrase use of vehicle generated by either bus or tank. As a result, subjects took significantly more time in sentence 5b than in 4b figuring out the referent of the "bus."

Garrod and Sanford also found that subjects' reading of sentence 6b was slower than their reading of sentence 4b. They took this as evidence that the *bus* frame in sentences like 6a is not activated in the same way as it is in sentences like 4a and that frames are activated more strongly for topics than for comments. However, if by "topic" they mean "the principal theme of the discourse," this cannot be strictly true because both sentences 4a and 6a occur at the beginning of the discourse. It seems more likely that the superior frame activation in 4 is due to the fact that "a bus" is the "perspective" of sentence 4a and this perspective is maintained in sentence 4b. (The notion of a "perspective" is discussed in the section on subject-verb agreement below.)

Partonymy A fifth, somewhat more complex way of establishing the referent of a definite article is by partonymy. This way of computing givenness views a current referent as a unique part or piece of some large referent or frame already under discussion. For example, Linde and Labov (1975) have shown that, when describing apartment layouts, adults regularly use definite articles to refer to major rooms whenever there is typically only one such room per apartment. Thus, they speak about "the living room" or "the kitchen." In effect, they are assuming that every *apartment* has one *kitchen*. Speakers do this even when they have not yet mentioned the room in a previous sentence and when it is not exophorically given. In such cases, speakers assume that listeners realize that the referent is unique.

Sentences 7 to 9 provide further examples of definiteness by partonymy:

7. Bill swore. The oath embarrassed his mother.
8. Mary traveled to Munich. The journey was long and tiring.
9. Bill found a prewar German novel in the Goodwill bin. Soon he discovered that some of the pages were uncut, that the author was a racist, and the content was offensive.

In sentence 7, the use of "swearing" evokes a frame that includes the execution of an "oath." Similarly, in sentence 8 the lexical frame for "traveling" presupposes a "journey"; and in sentence 9 a "book" must have "pages," an "author," and "content."

Partonymic relations extend quite pervasively throughout the lexicon. When discussing "the body" in physiology, we can also refer definitely on first mention to "the kidney," "the blood," "the lymph nodes," "the medulla oblongata," and so forth. In astronomy, we have "the sun," "the asteroid belt," "the corolla," "the Doppler shift," and so on. The importance of such systems in determining definite reference has prompted Clark and Marshall (1981) to think of definite reference as being computed out of an encyclopedia organized in a way that allows all information relevant to a given social group to be stored together. Thus astronomers, physicians, Palo Alto homeowners, or Pittsburgh school bus drivers would all have direct access to certain types of definite reference by partonymy by virtue of their active role as participants in a social group.

Sanford and Garrod (1979) have examined the role of partonymic associations in sequences like 10 and 11.

10. a. Mary was dressing the baby.
    b. The clothes were made of soft pink wool.
11. a. Mary was putting the clothes on the baby.
    b. The clothes were made of soft pink wool.

Using a self-paced reading paradigm, Sanford and Garrod found that subjects took no longer to read sentence 10b than they did to read sentence 11b. From this, they concluded that the lexical frame for *dressing* generates a presupposition for *clothes*, and that information that is presupposed in this way is just as available as information that is overtly stated.

Keenan and Kintsch (1974) gave subjects sentence pairs that contained even greater inferential leaps, supported by even weaker presuppositions. A typical sequence in their experiment on the comprehension of sentences related by partonymy is:

12. a. Gas leaked from a butane tank.
    b. The explosion leveled a nearby service station and a new home.
13. The gas leak caused the explosion.

In order to understand example 12, subjects may have relied on some weak expectations for "explosion" generated by "gas." However, these expectations were apparently quite weak. When subjects were asked immediately whether sentence 13 fit the meaning of what they had read, they were slow in making this decision if they had not actually read 13. However, after a 15-minute delay, subjects who had not read sentence 13 made this judgment just as quickly as those who had read it, indicating that both groups had "made the inference" by that point.

These studies indicate that identification of definite noun phrases relies heavily on expectations generated by earlier items. If these expectations are strong and if they match the current item, identification is strongly facilitated. If the expectations are weak, identification will take longer and other factors may come into play. Note that the most general case of definite reference is reference by partonymy. Reference by paraphrase can be viewed as a subtype of reference by partonymy in the sense that some of the associations included in the frame for a lexical item are paraphrases of that item. In a similar vein, one could view anaphoric reference as a subtype of paraphrase in which the two items just happen to be lexically identical.

Set Operation A sixth way of establishing the referent of a definite article is through the specification of an operation on a set such that the operation is guaranteed to yield a unique item. For example, if we are talking about a row of birds on a power line, we may speak about "the first," "the last," "the biggest," "the middle one," "the second from the end," or "the yellow one." In each case we specify some characteristic that allows us to operate on the set of birds to achieve unique identification. Note that certain characteristics apply by definition. If there is a line of birds, then by definition there must be one that is "the first." However, there may not always be a "yellow one." Therefore, we can distinguish two types of givenness by set operation: givenness that applies by definition and givenness that applies by assertion.

Assertion is important in the establishment of a referent for the definite noun phrases in all of the following sentences except 16:

14. Do not feed the llamas.
15. *Speaker A:* Can you recommend a good mechanic?
    Speaker B: I take the Mercedes to Dieter Neckritz.
16. Returning from his success in the Middle East, Carter was confronted by an unruly and vindictive Congress.
17. Returning from his success in the Middle East, Carter was confronted by the unruly and vindictive Congress.
18. Mary didn't know which marble to choose. Finally, she took the red one.

Sentence 14 could represent a sign posted on a fence. The fact that no llamas are visible really does not matter; their presence is being asserted by the sign itself. Note that a set operation is still involved here. A variety of other animals—including antelopes, peacocks, turtles, and giraffes—may be located behind the fence. The sign states only that one should not feed the llamas. In example 15, Speaker A may not have told the listener about his new Mercedes; but that does not matter. All Speaker B cares about is that Speaker A should know about it now. He achieves this effect by simply asserting its existence. This type of assertion of knowledge not necessarily known to the listener is often called one-upmanship. In sentence 16 the speaker is asserting that one of the moods of the Congress is a mood that is unruly and vindictive, whereas in sentence 17 no such assertion is made. The assertion in 17 is much like the assertion in example 18. In both cases, the speaker claims that the set of moods or marbles contains only one member with such and such a description. Given this fact, identification by set operation is a trivial matter. Of course, if the listener does not know this fact, it does not really matter; the very act of uttering the sentence assures that he knows it now.

The assumptions underlying the computation of givenness by set operation can vary from language to language. For example, in Haitian Creole (Jürgen Meisel, personal communication), the list of participants for a conference is only definite once the conference has begun. Before that time, one cannot really refer to "the participants."

Genericalness The definite article can also be used as a marker of genericalness. When we say "The butterfly is graceful," we may be using the definite article generically. In such cases, the referent of the noun is the whole class. It is clear that we are not referring to the individual members of the class, because we can say "The silkworm butterfly lays its eggs in the mulberry tree" or "Silkworm butterflies lay their eggs in the mulberry tree," but not "The silkworm butterfly lays their eggs in the mulberry tree." Thus, reference must be to the class and not to the individuals of the class. Uniqueness of reference is guaranteed, because there is only one class that can be the referent.

Indefinite Article

The initial introduction of an item in discourse is accomplished through the use of an indefinite pronoun or an indefinite article with a noun. The actual shape of this introduction determines the way in which the speaker may make future references to that item.

Shatz (1983) revealed one child's difficulties in learning to use the indefinite article to provide initial descriptions of referents.

> A five-year-old wrote a story beginning, "One morning the little old woman . . ." Her brother, aged 7, criticized her as follows:
> Bro: You should have said "a little old woman."
> Sis: Why? What's wrong with "the?"
> Bro: You don't know who the woman is yet. You have to use "a" when you don't know her.
>
> However, a little learning is a dangerous thing. Bro overapplied the "first mention takes the indefinite" rule to produce the following error, which Sis, a year older and wiser by this time, gleefully corrected.
> Bro: Where's a woffel? (Woffel was a nickname for the family dog.)
> Sis: "A" woffel? "The" woffel. There's only one woffel in the whole world.

Of course, even this final correction of Bro's error was an error in itself.

The basic use of the indefinite article *a/an* is to introduce a single nonunique referent. Because it introduces a singular referent, the indefinite article can only be used with countable nouns. The noun that follows the article is used to identify the class of which the referent is a member.

The indefinite article has two alternative readings, which have often been characterized as "referential" and "nonreferential." However, in order to avoid talking about such improbable things as the "referential referent" or the "nonreferential referent" of a noun, the terms "instantiated" instead of "referential" and "parameterized" (Webber, 1981) instead of "nonreferential" are used here.

Instantiated The most common use of the indefinite article is to refer to some real member of a group. Thus, in the sentence "I saw a pig" reference is being made to some real pig. Because the indefinite article and its noun refer to a single real-life instance of a pig, this is called the "instantiated" use of the indefinite article.

Parameterized The indefinite article may also be used to refer to all the individual members of a class, as in "A businessman has to have a briefcase." The parameterized reading of "businessman" produces an interpretation of the sentence that says, in effect, that "whatever businessman you choose, he has to have a briefcase." In this reading, the indefinite article uses the following noun to set clear parameters on the shape of the possible referents without actually limiting reference to a single item.

These readings of the article can be distinguished in pairs such as sentences 19 and 20:

19. Betty wants to marry a cowboy, but he is too old.
20. Betty wants to marry a cowboy, but she hasn't met one yet.

For both the instantiated and the parameterized uses of the indefinite article, the attached noun must refer to some item. In the instantiated use, the noun refers to a real-world referent. In the parameterized use, the noun "refers" not to a real-world referent, but to an item in the lexicon that sets parameters on the class of real-world referents. Alternatively, one can think of the parameterized use as referring to a whole class in terms of an enumeration of each of its individual members. For example, in the sentence, "Every man who owns a donkey beats it," the initial description (Webber, 1981) of "donkey" is parameterized. As a result, it is possible to treat the singular initial description as referentially plural, as in "Every man who owns a donkey beats it, but the donkeys are planning to get back at them."

This contrast between instantiated and parameterized initial descriptions is not unique to the indefinite article. It extends to the indefinite use of the demonstrative article *this*. As Prince (1981) noted, the demonstrative article can be used indefinitely in sentences such as "There was this hippie, you see." In such cases, the article refers to a particular instance (in the sense of sentence 19), but does so indefinitely. As is shown in the next section, the instantiated/parameterized contrast also extends to pronoun interpretation. Furthermore, Akmajian (1979, pp. 162–174) showed how this distinction has important consequences for the use of clefts and relative clauses in English.

In order to process sentences containing anaphorically definite articles or pronouns, the listener must be able to locate items either as parameters or as instances in his working memory. Thus, when processing either an indefinite article or an indefinite pronoun, the listener has to decide whether to set up a new referential instance in working memory or to simply activate a lexical item without making it refer to a real entity.

Pronominalization

Like articles, pronouns may be definite or indefinite. Definite pronouns include *he, she, it, they, that, this, these, his, hers,* and *theirs*. Indefinites include *some, one, another, somebody's, any,* and *a few*. An indefinite pronoun like *one* usually refers not to an instance, but to a class. Consider these sentences:

21. Jane likes a turtle, and Paula likes one too.
22. Jane wants a turtle, and Paula wants one too.
23. Bill likes his beer cold and Jim likes it warm.
24. Bill kicked his Bronco, and Jim kicked it too.

In sentence 21 the initial description of "a turtle" could be either parameterized or instantiated, but the pronoun "one" must be understood as parameterized. Consequently, the listener has to match "one" to the lexical category "turtle"; but once this is done, there is no need to identify a particular pragmatic referent. In sentence 22 the initial description of "a turtle" is not parameterized, but the word "one" still refers to the class. Thus, locating a pragmatic referent is again unnecessary. On the other hand, with singular definite pronouns such as "it" in sentence 23, both a lexical referent and a pragmatic instance must be identified. After matching "it" to the parameter "beer," the listener must still decide on an instantiated pragmatic referent. Reasoning that each man is probably drinking his own beer, listeners would choose "Jim's beer" as the referent of "it." In sentence 24, the lexical referent of "it" is "Bill's Bronco"; in this case, the pragmatic referent is identical to the lexical referent.

Regardless of whether or not a pronoun can be instantiated, the listener always has to match it to the correct lexical item. Two steps are involved in this matching process. First, the listener has to determine the semantic features associated with the pronoun. For example, *he* is (+ animate), (+ third person), (+ singular), and (+ nominative); whereas *ours* is (+ animate), (+ first person), (+ plural), and (+ possessive). The pronoun *that*, on the other hand, is simply (+ singular). All uses of these pronouns must maintain these "core features." However, to unambiguously match a pronoun to a referent, the listener must also decide which of the following polysemes best characterizes the speaker's meaning.

Exophora The deictic pronouns *this* and *that* have particularly strong exophoric readings. For example, a sign may say "This is Cody Springs," and point directly at the town. However, *this* and *that* are not the only pronouns that can be used exophorically. The personal pronouns *we, you, he, she, it,* and *they* also can receive exophoric readings. For instance, someone may comment to another listener on a poor joke made by the previous speaker by saying "He is silly, isn't he?"

Anaphora As in the case of the definite article, another way in which pronouns may be identified is anaphorically. In the case of anaphoric identification, the pronoun is bound to the last-mentioned noun that has the semantic features corresponding to the pronoun. Fortunately, the very last noun that was mentioned often has the required features and usually is the most likely referent for the pronoun (Charniak, 1973; Sanford and Garrod, 1979; Springston, 1977). Consider the following sequence:

> Tom was holding a red ball and a blue ball.
> He threw Hank the red ball.
> Hank was holding a green ball.
> He threw it to Bill.

In the last sentence of this sequence, the most likely referent for "he" is "Hank," because Hank is the most recently mentioned noun that also has the required features for animacy and masculinity. The relationship between a pronoun and the last-mentioned noun is particularly strong for reflexive pronouns such as *himself, itself,* and *herself.* Whereas reflexive pronouns demand that the coreferent noun be in the same clause as the pronoun, object pronouns such as *him, her,* and *it* do not have polysemes permitting coreferents within the same clause. As a result, Springston (1977) found that subjects were quick to comprehend sentences like 25, but slow at comprehending sentences like 26.

> 25. Bill made John shoot himself.
> 26. Bill made John shoot him.

In sentence 25, the candidacy of "John" as the referent of "himself" is strongly supported by the proximity of the object pronoun. In sentence 26, the candidacy of "John" as the referent of "him" is inhibited by the proximity of the object pronoun. Eventually, the less recent alternative "Bill" wins out. Ambiguity between anaphoric and exophoric uses of demonstrative pronouns can often lead to misunderstandings. For example, suppose there is a tea party and Speaker A is discussing the quality of different types of teas. The last tea he mentions is Jasmine. Speaker B then continues with "This is not really my favorite tea." At that point it may be unclear whether Speaker B intends to refer to the exophoric cup of Assam tea he is drinking or to the anaphoric Jasmine tea mentioned by Speaker A.

Cataphora Although cataphoric readings of pronouns are less common than anaphoric readings, they are governed by similar principles. It is important to realize that cataphora can serve a real communicative function in sentences like "Well, I haven't seen him yet, but John is back." The phrase "I haven't seen him yet" is taken to be background material in which knowledge of the referent for "him" is presupposed. It is in cases such as these, where background material logically precedes foregrounded material, that cataphora is most likely to occur (Mittwoch, 1979). Bickerton (1975) has suggested that a speaker may pronominalize any noun phrase as long as its referent (cataphoric or anaphoric) is not a part of the "focus," i.e., the main assertion of the sentence. To see how this principle works, consider sentences 27 to 30:

27. It was my *punching* him that annoyed Bill.
28. It was my *punching* Bill that annoyed him.
29. It was my punching *Bill* that annoyed him.
30. It was my punching *him* that annoyed Bill.

In sentences 27 and 28, the pronoun "him" can be interpreted as coreferential with "Bill." In these two sentences, the focus is on "punching," which is the main assertion of the sentence; "him" and "Bill" are parts of the presupposed background. In sentence 29, "Bill" is the focus and thus cannot be coreferential with "him." In 30, on the other hand, "him" can be coreferential with "Bill" because "Bill" is not the focus. In each of these four sentences, the flow of pronominalization is correctly predicted by Bickerton's analysis.

Metaphora The fourth way of establishing the referent of a definite pronoun is through metaphora. In cases of what we shall call metaphora (referring beyond), the speaker establishes reference to the entire discourse frame or to large pieces of that frame. In many cases, the reference is to the speech-act frame within which the point sharing is embedded or to other completed speech acts. Gensler (1976) cited the following sentence types as cases of metaphoric reference to the discourse frame:

31. If this be treason, make the most of it.
32. How do you like that?
33. OK, where should we go with this? (In response to a suggestion at an administrative meeting.)
34. It fits. And I ought to have figured it out myself.
35. The thing here would be to think of it as a network—you set it up once and then just point to it.

The uses of *this, that* and *it* in these sentences all refer metaphorically to the speech act itself. Related, but more complex, reference to speech act frames occurs with phrases such as "speaking of" (Schegloff and Sacks, 1973), frankly speaking," or "let's just say" (Cogen and Herrmann, 1976). Here, the referents are often chunks of speech in short-term memory.

Perspective The perspective is identified in English with the grammatical subject of the sentence. It is usually an animate noun and serves as the point of view from which the speaker constructs the utterance and from which the listener can best comprehend the utterance. Because utterances are often constructed of multiple clauses, there are often multiple perspectives in a sentence. However, the subject of the main clause is usually the main perspective. Pronouns may be interpreted by identification with the main perspective of the previous utterance. This interpretation process is easiest when the previous sentence contains only one animate element and consequently only one probable perspective. This is illustrated in the following sentences from Sanford and Garrod (1979):

36. The engineer repaired the television set.
    It had been out of order for two weeks.
    It was only a few months old.
    It was the last model.
    He took only five minutes to repair it.
37. The mother picked up the baby.
    She had been ironing all afternoon.
    She would not be finished for some time.
    She was very tired.

Sanford and Garrod found that subjects spent significantly more time reading the last sentence in 37 than the last sentence in 36. Note that in 36 there is only one probable perspective, whereas in 37 there are two.

Parallel Function A pronoun in a coordinate clause can also be identified by relating it to a word that serves a "parallel function" (Akmajian, 1979; Maratsos, 1974b; Sheldon, 1974; Springston, 1977) in the earlier clause. For example, in "Paula knows why Mary came, but Bill doesn't know why she did," the pronoun "she" has a syntactic function parallel to that of "Mary" in the first clause. When the sentence has unmarked intonation, "she" refers to "Mary" rather than to "Paula." However, in "Paula knows why Mary came, but Bill doesn't know *why* she did" (stress on "why"), "she" is best identified with "Paula." This is to say that, within sentences, the parallel function polyseme is stronger than the perspective polyseme, but only if stress underlines the parallelism of the clauses. In any case, the parallel function polyseme only operates within sentences.

Role Frame of an Interaction Verb Verbs like *blame, tell, ask, command, want, offer*, or *criticize* describe scenes in which a speaker interacts communicatively or socially with a listener. The message being communicated is typically placed into either a subordinate clause as in sentence 38 or a complement clause as in sentence 41:

38. Bill criticized Paul because he talks too much.
39. Bill apologized to Paul because he talks too much.

40. Paul was criticized by Bill because he talks too much.
41. Bill told Paul that he would help him.
42. Bill told Paul that he should help him.
43. Bill may scold Paul because he disobeys orders.
44. Bill must scold Paul because he disobeys orders.
45. John telephoned Bill because he wanted some information.
46. John telephoned Bill because he withheld some information.

Caramazza et al. (1977), Caramazza and Gupta (1979), Garvey, Caramazza, and Yates (1975), Grober, Beardsley, and Caramazza (1978), and Springston (1977) have found that the interpretation of the pronouns in these sentences depends in part on the "implicit causality" of the verbs. Thus, a causally reversed verb like "criticize" implicitly attributes more causality to the semantic patient of the main clause (as in sentences 38 and 40) than does a verb like "apologize," which attributes more causality to the semantic agent (as in sentence 39). Moreover, "strong" modals like "must" and "should" suggest a larger causal role for the object than weak modals like "may" and "would." Because of this, "Bill" is the preferred referent of "he" in sentences 39 and 41, whereas "Paul" is the preferred referent in sentences 38, 40, and 42.

In some cases, various forces compete with each other for the selection of a referent. When such competition occurs, the preferred referent will be the noun receiving the most support. For example, in sentence 43 the verb "scold" encourages selection of "Paul" as the referent. However, parallel function and the weak modal encourage the selection of "Bill" as the referent. Conversely, in sentence 44 "scold" and the strong modal converge to support the candidacy of "Paul" as the referent of "he," while parallel function encourages the selection of "Bill" as the referent. Similarly, in sentences 45 and 46 parallel function encourages the selection of "John" as the referent of "he." In 45 this reading is supported by the verb "want," but in 46 the strong causality of "withheld" forces a reinterpretation in which "Bill" becomes coreferential with "he." Caramazza et al. (1977) have shown that subjects take longer to find the referent of "he" in sentence 46 than in sentence 45. These results are consistent with the claim that competition among polysemes leads to longer response latencies.

Topicality In a recent study of pronominalization in Chinese, Li and Thompson (1979, p. 328) found that subjects used pronominalization to mark the reinstatement of an ongoing topic. Thus, in a series of seven or eight sentences with the same topic, subjects tended to accept the deletion of a repeated topic after the first mention. However, after about four or five sentences with deleted topics, subjects felt a need to reinstate the topic with a pronoun. In this way, speakers seem to use pronouns to bind discourse together. Pronouns can function in a similar way for the listener, allowing him to link together a series of events in memory (Lesgold, 1972).

In many cases the identification of a pronoun with the topic is the same as the identification of the pronoun with a previous perspective or the last (anaphoric) mention of the lexical item. In a few cases, however, these polysemes are not identical. Charniak (1973) presents an example in which topicality contradicts anaphora:

> Today was Jack's birthday. Penny and Janet went to the store. They were going to get presents. Janet decided to get a top. "Don't do that," said Penny. "Jack has a top. He will make you take it back." (p. 312)

Of course, it is not Jack's old top that Janet will have to return. Rather it is the new one that she wants to buy for him. Here the last-mentioned (anaphoric) top already belongs to Jack, whereas the more topical top is the one Janet wants to buy. Normally, anaphoric reference would win out over topicality, but in this case there is also something illogical about Jack asking Janet to take his old top back to the store. Sensing this, the listener reverts to identifying the pronoun *it* with the more topical "top."

Ellipsis

Material that might normally be included in a sentence but that, for some reason, is omitted is said to be ellipsed. In general, material can be ellipsed when: 1) its identity is so clear that it can be taken for granted; and 2) its identity is instantiated, not just parameterized. Consider this sequence:

> *Speaker A:* Where did you put the can-opener?
> *Speaker B:* On the refrigerator.

If Speaker B were to respond nonelliptically, he would say "I put the can-opener on the refrigerator." However, the first part of his reply is so obvious that it can be safely omitted.

Looking at descriptions of pictures in three different languages, MacWhinney and Bates (1978) observed a decline in the ellipsis of given material with age. This developmental pattern is consistent with the findings of de Laguna (1963), Greenfield and Zukow (1978), Keenan (1974), Miller (1978), Rodgon (1976), Sechehaye (1926), Sinclair (1975), Vygotsky (1962), and Weisenburger (1976).

If it is true that very young children give a low priority to the lexicalization of given material, then it follows that their sentences should begin with new information. In fact, observational studies by Bates (1976), Fava and Tirondola (1977), Leonard and Schwartz (1977), Lindner (1898), Meggyes (1971), O'Shea (1907), Park (1974), and Viktor

(1917) reported just this. In particular, Leonard and Schwartz, Lindner, and O'Shea argued that it is attentional salience that governs the order of words in early sentences. Note that, if this is true, the words that follow the first word must be viewed as afterthoughts, i.e., material that could have been omitted but that was just important enough to be lexicalized as an addendum to the main message.

When processing a sentence characterized by ellipsis, the listener must fill in the missing material with given material. However, as in the case of the definite article and the pronouns, there are several ways in which the missing material may be computed. In other words, there are several polysemes for ellipsis.

Exophora   A speaker may look at a picture and say "Beautiful." In so doing, a great deal of information that is given in the situation is ellipsed. It is up to the listener to decide how much of that information is needed to fill in the ellipsis. However, at a minimum, the utterance must mean "This thing is beautiful."

Anaphora   Ellipses may also be filled by anaphoric reference. In their study of sentence production in three languages, MacWhinney and Bates (1978) found that, across languages, ellipsis did in fact tend to increase with increased anaphoric givenness and to decrease with decreased anaphoric givenness. Dent and Greenfield (1980) and Snyder (1976) obtained similar results in experiments with English-speaking children. These data are in accord with Delis and Slater's (1977) findings that adult English speakers use more ellipsis when their listeners are familiar with the subject matter than when they are not.

Anaphoric reference for ellipsis may be computed in several ways. These techniques include parallel function, perspective maintenance, and the use of the role frame of a verb describing an interaction. Because each of these ways are fundamentally different, each is best understood as an alternative polyseme.

Parallel Function   In many cases, ellipses may be interpreted by reliance on a parallel function reading. Consider these examples from Akmajian (1979):

47. *Bill* knows why he is sick, but *Sam* doesn't.
48. *Bill* knows why *he* is sick, but *Sam* doesn't.

In order to interpret sentences like 47 and 48, the listener must figure out how to "fill in the blanks." Akmajian (1979) suggested a general principle that seems to work quite well. The idea is that all information in a previous clause can carry over to the parallel position in the next clause unless it is specifically marked as contrastive. Thus, in sentence 45 everything carries over to the ellipsis except for the contrasted term "Bill." In sentence 48, however, one additional piece of information in the first clause is excluded from the second clause because of the stress on "he." Similarly in tag-questions such as sentence 49, the auxiliary in the tag must be selected to match the auxiliary of the main clause:

    49. He did go to the store, didn't he?

In sentences like 47 to 49 there is really only one plausible way to "fill in the blank." In other words, only the parallel function polyseme is relevant in these sentences. Because of the obvious nature of this type of processing, there have been few attempts to investigate the comprehension of these types of ellipsis.

    Perspective Another way of identifying an ellipsed noun is by relating it to the perspective. When sentences are studied in isolation, the perspective is usually equivalent to the "subject." However, this relationship is probabilistic because the category "subject" is defined syntactically as the noun phrase to the left of the verb phrase (Chomsky, 1965), whereas the category of "perspective" can be given a functional definition (MacWhinney, 1977): the perspective is the point of view from which the speaker constructs the sentence and from which the listener interprets the sentence.

Perspective seems to be particularly important in ellipses arising from sentential conjunction. The comprehension of ellipsis in sentential conjunction has been examined by de Villiers, Tager-Flusberg, and Hakuta (1977), Hakuta (1979), Lust (1977), Lust and Mervis (1980), Solan (1979), and Tavakolian (1977, 1978). These studies have examined the ways children fill in the "gaps" in sentences like 50 to 54. In these sentences the symbol Ø indicates an ellipsed element:

    50. Kittens hop and Ø run.
    51. The kittens Ø and the dogs hide.
    52. Mary cooked the meal and Ø ate the bread.
    53. John baked Ø and Mary ate the bread.
    54. John ate the bread and Ø Ø the sausage.

Note that the gaps in sentences 50, 52, and 54 are filled in by looking backward (i.e., anaphorically), whereas the gaps in sentences 51 and 53 are filled in by looking forward, (i.e., cataphorically). Of particular interest here is the fact that children find sentences like 50, 52, and 54 easier to enact and imitate than sentences like 51 and 53 (Lust, 1977). Sentences like 50, 52, and 54 involve forward gapping, but they also allow the listener to use a single perspective for interpreting the sentence. The functionalist explanation for this phenomenon points to the difficulty children have in maintaining a dual perspective in movement and placement tasks (Huttenlocher, Eisenberg, and Strauss, 1968; Huttenlocher and Presson, 1973; MacWhinney, 1977).

Role Frame of Interactional Verbs Finally, as in the case of pronominalization, the computation of an anaphoric referent for an ellipsed item may depend on the role frame of the main verb, particularly if that verb describes a social interaction. To illustrate this type of computation, the use of ellipsis in infinitival complement clauses is examined. The filling of gaps in infinitival complement clauses has been examined in a series of studies (Chomsky, 1969, 1972; Goldman, 1976; Goodluck and Roeper, 1978; Gowie and Powers, 1979; Kessel, 1970; Kramer, Koff, and Luria, 1972; Maratsos, 1974b). Gaps of this type occur in sentences like 55 to 66 in which there is one noun in the main clause that is coreferential with the deleted subject of the complement clause:

55. John wants to leave.
56. John asks to leave.
57. John promises to leave.
58. *John tells to leave.
59. John wants Bill to leave.
60. John asks Bill to leave.
61. John promises Bill to leave.
62. John tells Bill to leave.
63. Bill is wanted by John to leave.
64. Bill is asked by John to leave.
65. Bill is promised by John to leave.
66. Bill is told by John to leave.

In each of these sentences, the listener has to figure out which noun in the main clause is the subject of the infinitive "to leave." There seem to be three ways for the listener to make this decision. First, Maratsos (1974b) showed how preschoolers place heavy emphasis on the fact that, if there is only one noun, it must be the missing subject of the infinitive. This solution simply carries the perspective of the main clause into the complement clause. This method works for sentences like 55, 56, and 57; however, Tavakolian (1978) has shown that, around age 3, children use perspective maintenance even for sentences like 59 where the perspective of the main clause is not the perspective of the complement.

Somewhat older children take the opposite tack and identify all gaps in complements with the patient of the main clause. This second way of computing complement ellipsis works in sentences 59, 60, 62, 63, 64, and 66. In sentences 59, 60, and 62, the ellipsed element could be interpreted by choosing the NP "closest" to the infinitive. However, Maratsos has shown that the child's interpretation is based more on semantic roles than "distance" in either deep or surface structure.

Finally, children learn to fill in the gap by relying on the specific role frames of the various main verbs. For example, for the verb "promise" (sentences 61 and 65), the child simply learns that the subject of the complement verb is the subject of the main clause. For the verb "asked," the child learns that the subject of the complement verb is the object of the main verb. In other words, when given a complement clause with an ellipsed element or a pronoun, the child has to look up the main verb in his lexicon and use its role frame to determine the correct anaphoric referent for the ellipsed element or pronoun. These specific role frames are acquired as co-occurrence patterns bound to specific lexical items. Research has shown that these co-occurrence patterns are learned very slowly with acquisition continuing until the mid-school years. For more detail on the course of these developments and for a fuller characterization of the notions of co-occurrence patterns and lexically bound patterns, see MacWhinney (1982).

Cataphora We have already noted that in sentences such as 51 and 53 gaps must be filled in cataphorically. Because cataphoric identification goes against perspective maintenance and because it places greater demands on memory (Wanner and Maratsos, 1978), it seems to be more difficult for both children and adults.

Metaphora Speakers may also use ellipsis to delete material that can be identified by reference to the whole speech scene. For example, when we say "Too bad!" we may be intending: "It is too bad that you had to go all the way downtown just to find the store closed." Note that, if we had said "That's too bad," then the pronoun *that* still would have had a metaphoric referent.

Relativization

Brown (1958) noted that the general rule governing item specification is to "be only as specific as necessary." If you can get by with ellipsis, do so. If a pronoun will suffice, use a pronoun. If not, use a definite article with a noun. Krauss and Weinheimer (1964, 1967), Olson (1970), and Osgood (1971) presented experiments demonstrating a general relation between all of the preceding devices and the need for item specification.

There are, however, some situations where pronouns and definite articles do not provide adequate specification. In such cases, speakers sometimes use adjectives and phrases as qualifiers. Thus, the item "the dog" may be further identified as "the black dog" or "the dog on the right." Karmiloff-Smith (1979, p. 78) has shown that, between the ages of 3 and 11, children make progressively more accurate use of adjectives for item specification.

A more elaborate type of specification involves the use of relative clauses. However, these clauses are used only when the preceding simpler devices are inadequate. A second qualification is that not all relative clauses can be used for item specification. There are two types of relative clauses: restrictive and nonrestrictive. Restrictive clauses are used to specify the exact identity of a referent. At the same time, they convey presupposed information. Nonrestrictive relative clauses have a quite different use; they convey material that is not presupposed but that is backgrounded in terms of the main story line.

Relatives Used for Item Specification Limber (1976) observed that relative clauses are used far more frequently with objects (i.e., comments) than with subjects (i.e., themes). Both Limber (1976) and Zubin (1979) attributed this asymmetry to the fact that subjects are most likely to be given and need no further identification, whereas comments are full of new information requiring further identification. Because comments are usually inanimate, their specification often results in the use of relative clauses with inanimate head nouns.

Although restrictive relative clauses are commonly used to specify information in the main clause that is either new or confusable, they themselves contain information that is presupposed to be true. While serving the function of item specification, they also serve the function of conveying a speaker's presuppositions. The fact that restrictive relative clauses convey presupposed information is most evident in pseudo-cleft sentences such as "The one who ate the apple was John." In this case, it is presupposed that someone ate the apple. At the same time, it is asserted that the one who ate the apple was *John*. Adjectives also can be used to convey presupposed material (Schachter, 1973). Thus, the phrase "a red fish" presupposes that there is at least one fish that is red. Similarly, "the girl that Hank dated" presupposes that Hank dated someone.

Relatives Used for Backgrounding In contrast to the preceding restrictive clauses, nonrestrictive relative clauses in sentences such as "Bill, who is a friend of Harry's, was the first to arrive" do not convey presuppositions, nor do they serve to identify or specify items. Instead, such clauses are used to convey background assertions or asides. They tell us about information that is secondary to the main plot or story line. For further discussion of the role of backgrounded information in a story line, see Hopper (1979).

Stress

The English language possesses a rich array of intonational patterns for marking emotional and informational contrasts. Of these, primary stress is the one that has the most applications to point sharing. Stress can be interpreted through a variety of polysemes. These different polysemes appear in denials, responses, questions, reversals, and clefts.

Stress in Denials The second sentence in sequence 67 illustrates how assertions can be focused in denials.

67. a. Bill seems to have taken the wrench.
    b. No, it was *Hank* who took the wrench.
    Presupposed: someone had taken the wrench.
    Asserted: the one who did so was Hank.

Following Chomsky (1971) we can analyze sentence 67b into a *focus* (the asserted element *Hank*) and a *presupposition* (the rest of the sentence). It also appears that, for sentences of this type to occur, two conversational conditions must be met:

1. The presupposition must be clear to all parties. (This is most likely to occur when the presupposition is actually stated in a preceding statement or question.)
2. The focus must be, at least implicitly, a denial of the assertion made in the previous utterance.

These conditions can be fulfilled by two types of very simple sequences—contrast and questioning. Sequence 67 illustrates how an item can be put into focus by contrastive denial. In 67a, the speaker asserts that "Bill seems to have taken the wrench." In 67b, the second speaker accepts all but one element in that previous sentence. In this sense, almost all of 67a is taken as the background for 67b. The only part that is not accepted is the part that is specifically denied. This kind of denial results in a particularly strong level of contrast or emphasis (Boadi, 1974; Bolinger, 1961).

Textual analyses by Berman and Szamosi (1972), Bolinger (1961), Gunter (1966), and Schmerling (1974) have indicated that the use of emphatic stress is closely tied to the need for marking contrastivity or focus. Experimental studies with children by Cruttenden (1974), Hornby (1971), Hornby and Hass (1970), and MacWhinney and Bates (1978) support these linguistic analyses quite clearly. However, stress is not the only device used to mark focus; word order also can be used for this purpose. Although young children initially determine the speaker's focus by relying almost exclusively on his use of stress, between the ages of 5 and 10 they shift from a reliance on stress to a reliance on word order (Hornby, 1973; MacWhinney and Price, 1980).

Stress in Questions Focusing in questions works in a way that is quite parallel to focusing in denials. Both statement-denial pairs and question-answer pairs can be best understood as simple cases of what Schenkein (1978) called "set-ups." In such sequences the structure of the first speaker's assertions and presuppositions loosely determines or "sets up" the structure of the next speaker's contribution (Hatcher, 1956; Most and Saltz, 1979). In a *wh*-question, the focus is usually the *wh*-word. Thus, in sentence 68a, the focus is on *who*.

68. a. Who chased the cat?
    b. The *dog* chased the cat.
    Presupposed: someone chased the cat.
    Asserted: the one who did so was the dog.

It is also possible to have a question in which primary stress is placed on an asserted element. Thus, if I walk into a living room and find the walls covered with tastefully executed landscapes and portraits, I might well ask, "Who's the *artist*?" with stress on *artist*. In that case, I am asserting that there is an artist and I am asking who that artist might be.

Stress in Identification Reversal A fourth possible reading of contrastive stress is one that relates primarily to pronouns. Here contrastive stress is used explicitly to state that the normal interpretations of the pronouns must be reworked. Consider examples 69 to 72:

69. Tim hit Peter and then he hit Bill.
70. Tim hit Peter and then *he* hit Bill.
71. Tim saw Peter and then *he* saw *him*.
72. Tim saw Peter and then he saw *him*.

In sentence 70 stress tells us that it is Peter rather than Tim who hit Bill. In sentence 71 the stress tells to reverse the roles of Tim and Peter. In sentence 72 the stress tells us to look outside of the sentence to find the referent of the pronoun "him." The kind of operation required by this referent reversal is particularly difficult for young children (Maratsos, 1973; Solan, 1979). One explanation for this difficulty might be that young children have problems in applying operations (i.e., transformations) to complete surface forms.

Stress in Clefts English tends to place the greatest stress on the last content word in the sentence. In order to place a contrastive element into this salient position, English speakers may use a variety of cleft and pseudocleft structures. These and other structures were included in a study by Hornby (1974). In that study, Hornby found that identification of the focus is cued by at least four factors that summate algebraically: 1) stress, 2) sentence final placement, 3) postcopular placement, and 4) placement following the agential "by" marker. Thus, the most clearly marked focus is the stressed agent in a passive pseudocleft like "The one whom the apple was eaten by was the *cook*," in which all four cues converge on the final noun. Consistent with this position, both Hornby (1974) and Carpenter and Just (1977) found that the pseudocleft structure yielded the strongest effects of focusing. In both studies, it was found that, the more clearly a sentence marks focus, the more quickly subjects can verify that sentence.

Two of the studies of cleft sentences reported by Carpenter and Just are particularly interesting because they show how focus operates within a discourse context. In one study, Carpenter and Just asked subjects to read sequences like 73 and 74:

73. a. Where is John?
    b. The one who is leading Jim is John.
74. a. Where is Jim?
    b. The one who is leading Jim is John.

They found that subjects were quicker to answer 73b than 74b. Sentence 73a serves to "set up" the focus as "John" and 73b follows along with that set-up, placing "John" in a stressed position and "Jim" in a presupposed relative clause. In sentence 74b, on the other hand, the focus is placed inappropriately in the presupposed relative clause.

Carpenter and Just detected even stronger effects of a discourse "set-up" in a second experiment with sequences like 75 and 76:

75. a. The ballerina captivated a musician in the orchestra during her performance.
    b. The one whom the ballerina captivated was the trombonist.
76. a. The ballerina captivated a musician in the orchestra during her performance.
    b. The one who captivated the trombonist was the ballerina.

Sentences like 76 took 1.444 seconds longer to comprehend than sentences like 75. In 75a and 76a "the ballerina" is given and cannot serve as the focus for the cleft. However, "musician" is new indefinite information in need of further identification. In sentence 75b the new information is identified by the focus of the pseudocleft. In sentence 76b, however, the presupposed information is identified. This is a mistake, because the material that needs to be identified is the new information, not the given information.

Initialization

In English, the beginning of the sentence is a position of particular importance. The positioning of an item at the beginning of the sentence can be used to encode a variety of grammatical functions. These include interactional indicators, vocatives, imperatives, question markers, conditions, and topics.

Interactional Regulation   When words like *alright, well,* and *now* are used to express interactional sequencing, they must occur at the beginning of the utterance.

Vocatives   When the speaker is calling the addressee by name, the summons may appear at the beginning of the sentence. This occurs most frequently with warnings, commands, questions, and other emotional communications.

Imperatives Imperative verbs must also be initialized. However, they may follow vocatives and interactional markers as in "John, now come here."

Questions Like imperative verbs, *wh*-words, and the auxiliaries in yes/no questions must be initialized.

Conditions Initialization may also be used to convey the fact that something is a condition on the applicability of the following sentence. Often the speaker wishes to describe the settings or conditions under which an event transpires. Consider the sentence "Late at night on Tuesday in Chicago in the park by the Lakeshore, one of the gorillas named Irving was seen signing to a chimp." Here there is a string of six temporal and spatial conditions. These conditions set the stage for the interpretation of the main predication. Note that this sentence is not "about" Chicago or Tuesday or the Lakeshore. Rather it is "about" a gorilla named Irving. Thus, Irving is the perspective of the predication and the various initial phrases are used to set the conditions for that predication (Dik, 1978, pp. 140–141).

State-setting conditions play a particularly important role in languages like Chinese, where they often resemble themes. Consider these sentences from Barry (1975):

77. Nèijyan shr̀   wǒ dzwò jǔ.
    That   matter I   act as boss.
    "I am in charge of that matter."
78. shū   (dāngjung), jèige   dzwèi hǎu
    book(s) among   this one most good
    "Among books, this one is the best."
79. nèiban   sywésheng (lǐ), tā dzwèi tsūngming
    that class students   in   he most smart
    "In that class of students, he is the brightest."

In both English and Chinese, preposed phrases can be used to set the stage for the main point. However, in Chinese, as in Ameslan (Grosjean and Lane, 1976) and Hungarian (Dezső, 1972), this can be done with much greater flexibility than in English because the grammar makes fewer requirements regarding prepositions, possessive markers, and participials. Nonetheless, the basic motive of conditionalization seems to be the same across these languages.

Most of the preceding examples involved preposed prepositional phrases. However, it is even more common in English to set conditions with adverbial phrases. Consider the sentence "If you mow his lawn, then Steve will pay you four dollars." Here the asserted event is that Steve will pay the listener four dollars. However, this event is guaranteed to occur only within the context of a certain frame that is understood to stay in effect for the duration of the insert (Clark and Clark,

1977). The frame is the situation in which the listener mows Steve's lawn. Thus, as Haiman (1978) argued, conditional clauses set the scene for the main predication. Other clause types that can be used as condition setters include absolutes (Berent, 1975), temporals, and parentheticals. Although all of these clause types are typically initialized, they also may occur in other positions. For example, many of them may be placed in sentence-final position as afterthoughts.

Introduction of a New Topic Initialization may also be used to introduce a new topic. When this occurs, the topicalized noun phrase usually doubles as the perspective and appears before the verb. Karmiloff-Smith (1976) has presented some clear examples of how this occurs in the context of a story description. In her study, children described a short sequence of pictures involving a child and a balloon vendor. At the beginning of the story, the children used left-dislocations such as "the boy, he . . ." Later in the story, when attention shifted from the little boy to the balloon vendor, children again used left dislocations such as "the vendor, he. . ." These results show that such structures are used not only to introduce the first actor at the beginning of the story, but also to change to a new principal actor. Karmiloff-Smith's studies were conducted in French where left-dislocations are, if anything, more common than in English. However, she also reported frequent use of right-dislocations at the same points in the story where left-dislocations are used. For example, one child said, "Then all of a sudden he lets go of it and it goes off far away, the balloon." In this case the right-dislocation was necessary to disambiguate the two uses of *il* in the French sentence "Puis tout d'un coup il le lâche et puis il part tres loin, le ballon."

All of the preceding dislocations involve topicalized noun phrases that double as perspectives. However, there are many instances in which speakers use left-dislocations when their topics cannot double as perspectives. For example, consider the left-dislocation in sentence 80:

80. The refrigerator, we're going to have to clean it up before Carole comes.
81. The refrigerator is going to have to be cleaned up by us before Carole comes.
82. We're going to have to clean up the refrigerator before Carole comes.

Having taken "the refrigerator" as a starting point, it is very difficult to finish out the sentence without a left-dislocation. Sentence 81 avoids the left-dislocation, but at the cost of some extremely clumsy wording. Sentence 82 is clearly the best alternative. However, if a speaker has for some reason already committed himself to "the refrigerator" as a starting point, then sentence 80 would be the most likely form of expression. Facts such as these have led Allerton (1978), Chafe (1976), Duranti and Ochs (1979), Karmiloff-Smith (1979), and MacWhinney (1975) to consider instances of left-dislocation in which the initial noun is not the subject of the verb as cases of "premature topics." These topics are premature in the sense that they fail to merge the role of the topic with that of the perspective.

Such premature topics seem to be particularly common in Italian (Duranti and Ochs, 1979), where they are used in competitive attempts to get the floor. Languages like Italian, German, and Hungarian allow more left-dislocation than English. This may be attributed to the fact that the former languages have fewer ways of shifting perspective within the verb (Kirkwood, 1978). In terms of our present analysis, left-dislocations are topics that the speaker has introduced before he has completely decided on the verb he plans to use in the comment (Lindsley, 1976). For the listener this type of left-dislocation can be decoded in terms of an instruction to set up a topic that is separate from the perspective.

An example of both a left-dislocation and a way to forewarn the listener of the need to set up a topic was given by Keenan and Schieffelin (1976, p. 240). In this example, the speaker uses an initialized topic-introducing phrase to forewarn the listener of an upcoming change in topics, and then a left-dislocation to identify what the new topic will be. The example involves two girls discussing the reading required for their courses. One says, "Oh I g'ta tell ya one course, the modern art, the twentieth century art, there's about eight books." Here the nominal phrases "one course, the modern art, the twentieth century art" reinstate a topic from previous discourse. This particular reinstatement utilizes the topic-introducing phrase *I gotta tell ya*. Other topic-introducing phrases used like this include *you know that, remember the, there was a,* and *this*. These topic-introducing phrases with left-dislocations alert and then instruct the listener to shift attention to a new topic. This new topic may be familiar to the listener, but it cannot be the current topic of the discourse.

Preverbal Positioning

Perhaps no other device has received more attention from psycholinguists than preverbal positioning. According to the Prague School of Functional Linguistics, elements that are given and topical are usually placed before the verb. In many sentences, the preverbal noun is also the first content word in the sentence. Mathesius (1939) held that this initial element is the item "which is known or at least obvious in a given situation and from which the speaker proceeds." Travníček (1962) went somewhat further and suggested that the initial element of a sentence is "the sentence element which links up directly with the object of thought, proceeds from it, and opens the sentence thereby." These descriptions underscore the importance of givenness in determining the selection of a starting point.

Unfortunately, the writers of the Prague School often failed to distinguish between initialization and preverbal positioning. In many cases the first noun is also the preverbal noun, the topic, and the perspective of the sentence. However, left-dislocations make it clear that, even in English, this "coalition" (Bates and MacWhinney, 1982a) can break down. In left-dislocations, the dislocated item is the initial element and the topic, but it is not always the perspective. The preverbal element, on the other hand, is the perspective and the subject of the verb. In Czech, a language that figures prominently in many of the Prague School analyses, the dissociation is clearer, because initialization codes topicality whereas preverbal positioning codes perspective. Because left-dislocations are fairly rare in English, preverbal positioning is generally used to express not only agency, focus, and perspective (MacWhinney, 1977), but also givenness and topicality. In order to clarify the ways in which preverbal positioning serves each of these functions in English, the research on givenness, topicality, focus, and agency is reviewed here. Perspective is covered later in this chapter.

Givenness Studies of actual language samples do in fact show that preverbal nouns are fairly likely to be given. For example, Limber (1976) compared preverbal and postverbal pronouns, i.e., nominal phrases that require given referents. In seven different samples of actual adult and child dialogues, Limber found that preverbal nominal phrases are pronominal 87% of the time, whereas postverbal noun phrases are pronominal 35% of the time. Similarly, definite articles are more likely to precede preverbal nouns than postverbal nouns. Finally, studies of adult acceptability judgments (Bock, 1977; Bock and Irwin, 1980; Grieve and Wales, 1973; Hupet and LeBouedec, 1975; Klenbort and Anisfeld, 1974; Wright and Glucksberg, 1976) have shown that listeners prefer sentences in which the given is placed before the new. For example, Hupet and LeBouedec (1975) found that adult subjects preferred sentence 83 to sentence 84, and 85 to 86:

83. I thought that the gangster had injured a policeman.
84. I thought that a policeman had been injured by the gangster.
85. I thought that the policeman had been injured by a gangster.
86. I thought that a gangster had injured the policeman.

Here the subjects preferred sentences in which the preverbal noun (after "I thought that") was preceded by a definite article, even if the sentence was in the passive. Thus, one possible "use" of the passive (Anisfeld and Klenbort, 1973) might be to place given material into a preverbal position, as in sentence 85.

One problem with the studies discussed in this section is that none of them have attempted to distinguish between givenness and topicality as determinants of preverbal positioning. Using frequency counts from language samples, there is no easy way to draw this distinction. Moreover, in studies of acceptability judgments, it is hard to know exactly how subjects use meaning to determine acceptability. It is not entirely clear whether, in actual sentence production, preverbal positioning has any strong relation to givenness. In fact, MacWhinney and Bates (1978) found that, as the anaphoric givenness of an element increased in their picture description task, its preverbal positioning actually decreased. However, to a certain degree, this decrease resulted from an increased ellipsis of given material.

Current Topicality The possible importance of the current discourse topic in determining preverbal positioning is illustrated in Goodenough-Trepagnier and Smith (1978). These authors have shown that subjects prefer sentences in which the preverbal element is also the discourse topic.

Data from several studies of elicited production provide general support for a hypothesized relation between topicality and preverbal positioning. Carroll (1958), Osgood (1971), Tannenbaum and Williams (1968), and Turner and Rommetveit (1967) have shown that subjects use passives to position semantic patients preverbally when presented with a discourse context in which the patient is an anaphorically given topic and the agent is new. The simplest case of this manipulation is the question test utilized by Hatcher (1956) and Most and Saltz (1979). This test is based upon the fact that items that are presupposed and topical in the question are also presupposed and topical in the answer. For example, the question "Who threw the ball?" is likely to evoke the answer "The pitcher threw the ball." However, it could also evoke the answer "The ball was thrown by the pitcher." In this second sequence, the fact that the patient (i.e., "the ball") is also an anaphorically given topic encourages use of the passive with preverbal positioning of the topical element. All of these studies have shown that passives cannot be evoked simply by making the patient exophorically given in some visual context and the agent exophorically new. Rather, it is necessary to make the patient topical.

Note that the studies reviewed in this section point to a relation between the current topic of discourse and preverbal positioning. Initialization in a left-dislocation, on the other hand, introduces a new topic of discourse.

Focus Preverbal positioning may also be used to mark newness or focus. Focusing is a process that directs the listener's attention to some item because of its surprise value or inherent interest. It is largely an attention-getting process that is independent of both the discourse topic and the perspective. In many cases, the focus is an adverbial rather than a nominal and cannot serve as the perspective from which the sentence is interpreted. For example, in generating sentences like "Never in my life have I seen such a crowd" or "Up the street trotted the dog," structure-altering "root" transformations (Hooper and Thompson, 1973) mark a focused element by positioning it before the tense-bearing verb. Moreover, in generating questions such as "Who did John see?" the *wh*-question transformation serves a similar function. In all these cases, we may say that preverbal positioning marks focus or newness. Hooper and Thompson (1973) showed that such reorderings can occur only within asserted clauses. Thus, there seems to be a close association between focusing, assertion, and preverbal positioning.

Perspective The preverbal noun usually codes the perspective. Evidence supporting this claim is examined in the section on subject-verb agreement below.

Agency In most transitive sentences in English, the agent is the NP that immediately precedes the verb. Of course, in the passive, the preverbal NP is the perspective but not the agent. In a series of studies (Beilin, 1975; Bever, 1970; Braine and Wells, 1978; Chapman and Kohn, 1978; Chapman and Miller, 1975; de Villiers and de Villiers, 1973; Dewart, 1972, 1976; Huttenlocher et al., 1968; Maratsos, 1974a; Sinclair and Bronckart, 1972) it has been shown that, in English, young children tend to assume that the noun phrase (NP) before the verb is the agent even when the sentence contains syntactic cues to the contrary. Similar results have been obtained when comprehension is evaluated from: 1) the behavioral responses of young children (de Villiers and de Villiers, 1972; Shipley, Smith, and Gleitman, 1969; Wetstone and Friedlander, 1973); and 2) sentence verification tasks with somewhat older children (Beilin, 1975; Gaer, 1969; Slobin, 1966; Suci and Hamacher, 1972; Turner and Rommetveit, 1967). Furthermore, the superiority of actives (with a preverbal agent) to passives (with a nonpreverbal agent) in adult comprehension has been demonstrated by Clifton, Kurcz, and Jenkins (1965), Clifton and Odom (1966), Gough (1965), Miller (1964), Slobin (1966, 1968), and many others.

Some authors have thought of the preverbal-NP-as-agent strategy as a first-NP-as-agent strategy. In other words, they have claimed that it is initialization rather than preverbal positioning that codes agency. In some cases, it is claimed that this use of initialization is a linguistic universal. Studies of Japanese and Tagalog (Hakuta, 1979; Segalowitz and Galang, 1976) would seem to support the relation between initialization and agency. However, the Japanese and Tagalog systems are complex and the developmental results are not fully interpretable. In other languages, such as Hungarian and Turkish, the situation is more straightforward, with one case suffix uniformly signaling who did what to whom. Under such circumstances, evidence for a universal assignment of agency to the first NP is not obtained (Aksu and Slobin, in press; MacWhinney, 1976). Furthermore, Bates et al. (1982) found no evidence for a first-NP-as-agent strategy in the enactment of VNN and NNV sentences by Italian adults. In English, there was even a tendency for adults to choose the second noun as the agent in VNN and NNV sentences.

Word Order and Lexical Availability So far, the analysis of the point-making system has focused on the ways in which devices are used to express meanings. However, it is important to remember that a speaker is constrained not only by the nature of the meanings he wishes to express, but also by the availability of information in real time. In particular, initialization or preverbal positioning might be particularly facilitated when the exact lexical item (not just a paraphrase) is already available. Testing for this possibility, Bock and Irwin (1980) found that both givenness and lexical availability make independent contributions toward encouraging the initialization of an item. In general, it seems that initialization in English operates most smoothly when a noun that is available, animate, and topical can also serve as the focus, the agent, and the perspective. In such cases, the initial item is also the preverbal item.

Subject-Verb Agreement

In English, the element that precedes the verb is also the element that governs the number of the verb. This element appears in the nominative case and is often the first element in the sentence. Thus, in English, the devices of preverbal positioning, verbal governance, nominative case marking, and initialization are all highly correlated. However, sentences like "Never have I ever seen a ruder pest" show that, even when it does not occur preverbally, the subject of the verb still codes the perspective. To see what this means, consider some examples:
- 87. The monkey is on the limb.
- 88. The limb is under the monkey.
- 89. Our son talks like our chimp.
- 90. Our chimp talks like our son.

In sentence 87 the perspective seems fairly normal, whereas in sentence 88 things seem to be topsy-turvy. Why should we talk about where the "limb" is located? It seems to make more sense to locate the monkey. In the case of sentences 89 and 90, neither sentence seems unnatural. However, the two sentences imply markedly different things and these differences are largely a function of differences in perspective.

MacWhinney (1977) argued that: 1) the subject (i.e., the NP governing the person and number of the verb) is always the perspective; and 2) speakers tend to choose as subjects those elements whose stance or perspective most closely matches their own. Of course, speakers always see themselves as highly human, highly animate, and highly active. They also tend to see themselves as conversational participants and as the instigators or causers of actions and events (DeLancey, 1981). Thus, when speakers have to select a subject and a perspective for the verb, they tend to select the element that is maximally human and animate (Jarvella and Sinnott, 1972; Turner and Rommetveit, 1967) as long as that element can also be perceived as the instigator of the action.

In order to maintain the disambiguating function of role assignment, it is crucial that the agent always be the instigator of the action and that its role be marked in some way by morphology or word order. Thus, in "Meg gave Alan the watch," Meg is the agent and the instigator of the action. If we were to abandon the rules of English word order and say "The watch gave Alan Meg," we would have no idea of who was the agent and the instigator of the action. However, languages do provide alternative ways of viewing the instigation of an action (Kirkwood, 1978). Instead of the first sentence, one can say "Alan got the watch from Meg" with "Meg" as the instigator.

Perspective also governs role assignment in comparatives. Here it is possible to distinguish two cases: the case of the figure and the case of the ground. The figure serves as the perspective or subject. For example, in a sentence like "John is bigger than Bill," "John" is the figure and "Bill" is the ground. Here, a figure is selected so that the relational predicate (i.e., *big*) is maximally compatible with the perspective that speakers like to assume in their interactions with the world. As Boucher and Osgood (1969), Clark (1973), Cooper and Ross (1975), Ertel (1977), MacWhinney (1977), and Osgood and Bock (1977) have argued, this perspective is usually one that can be characterized as *big, strong, good, kind, clean*, and so forth. Thus, speakers tend to prefer a sentence like "John is bigger than Bill," in which the figure is big, to a sentence like "Bill is smaller than John," in which the figure is small.

A similar situation arises in locative clauses where the object being located is the figure and the location is the ground. For example, in the sentence "The star is above the line," the figure is "the star" and the ground is "the line." Clark (1974) has reviewed a large body of research (including Clark and Chase, 1973, 1974; Huttenlocher and Higgins, 1971; Huttenlocher et al., 1968; Smith and McMahon, 1970) indicating that speakers and listeners prefer figures that are *above, in front of, ahead of, first, to,* and *into* over figures that take a perspective that is *below, in back of, after, behind, last, from,* and *out of.* The naturalness of the perspective of unmarked words like *above* and *first* is demonstrated in lower latencies for answering questions, following instructions, and verifying sentences. This tendency is, again, a reflection of the "preferred stance" that MacWhinney (1977) called perspective.

Verb Selection

In English, the most frequently used verbs are those that place the most active, figural, or human element in preverbal position. However, many verbs have "inverse" forms that can be used to express secondary perspectives. When there are two highly active human elements, the responsibility for an event is divided between them. This division of responsibility often is achieved through the use of an inverse verb that assigns subject/perspective status to the more active element. An example of such a division and the use of an inverse verb was given in the last section. The following sentences contain other examples of this division:

91. Bill gave Tom the scissors.
92. Tom was given the scissors by Bill.
93. Tom took the scissors from Bill.
94. Tom got the scissors from Bill.
95. Every Sunday follows a Saturday.
96. *A Saturday is followed by every Sunday.
97. A Saturday precedes every Sunday.
98. Every Saturday is followed by a Sunday.

Sentences like these display an interesting set of relationships between point sharing, syntactic structure, and the lexicon. These relationships have been studied by Bowerman (1982), Fillmore (1970), Kirkwood (1978), MacWhinney (1977), Sgall (1972), Talmy (1976), and others. Sentence 92 illustrates a patient in preverbal position, presumably because it is topical and perspectival. Sentence 93 achieves a similar effect while also promoting "Tom" to agent status. However, in sentence 93 this change in verbs also forces a change in our understanding of the event, with Bill becoming much more passive than he was in sentence 92. Sentence 94 has an interpretation lying somewhere between that of 93 and that of 92. Finally, sentence 96 is particularly interesting because it shows that sentence 95 cannot be directly passivized but must be inverted as in sentence 97. This may be due to a tendency to interpret an indefinite NP as "nonparameterized" before a passive verb. Because subjects of topics are "marked" for topicality (Anisfeld and Klenbort, 1973), it would be strange to have them parameterized.

By continuing to explore the ways in which verbs serve to place nouns into their preferred case roles, we may eventually be able to elucidate the details of the perspective system and the ways in which perspective interacts with verbal conflation, verbal aspect, and discourse structure.

Case Marking

Because English marks case only for pronouns, there has been little experimental investigation of perspective as a determinant of case marking. By contrast, linguists working with languages with more extensive systems of case marking have devoted a great deal of attention to this issue, particularly during the last few years. For example, Zubin (1979) argued that the German nominative expresses the item of maximum perspective, the dative the item with medium perspective, and the accusative the item with minimum perspective. The idea that different cases and types of transitivity show different degrees of perspective can also be found in Hopper and Thompson (1980).

Zubin also reported that, in relative clauses, writers tend to place the relative pronoun into the nominative case as a marker of givenness. In about 24% of the sentences he examined, the given item was also the perspective. However, in the other 76% of the data, perspective conflicted with givenness for use of the nominative case. When such competition occurred, perspective won out about 56% of the time and givenness dominated about 38% of the time. In about 6% of the conflicts, neither givenness nor perspective won. Thus, both perspective and givenness seem to be important possible readings of nominative case markings in German.

In a related vein, Garcia and Otheguy (1977) found that, in Spanish, when the subject was low in animacy (and hence low in perspective), the recipient of the action was likely to be in the dative case; but, when the subject was high in animacy, the recipient was likely to be in the accusative case. Similarly, in German, Zubin (1977) noted that verbs that impose strong physical contact on the object take the accusative, whereas ones with gentler contact take the dative. Hopper and Thompson (1980) have noted that many languages mark the direct object only when it might compete with the agent as a perspective, i.e., when it is definite, referential, animate, etc. It seems that languages often omit case markings when it is clear which element is the perspective. The decision to use or not use case markings is rule governed, however (Comrie, 1979).

Particles

One of the most extensive parts of the point-sharing system is the network of pragmatic adverbs and particles such as *surely, still, even, but, moreover, well,* and *maybe*, which convey instructions about how to process the assertions in the sentence and what presuppositions to make. Although no complete description of this system has yet been attempted, the articles collected by Weydt (1979) on German and English particles show how much important material is to be found in this particular area of the point-sharing system.

To illustrate some of the issues involved in the acquisition of particles, let us examine Stern's (1980) data on the use of the particle *ebe* by Swiss-German children. When used as an adjective *ebe* means "flat" or "even." But when used as a particle, *ebe* means "the following item is obviously true, as we both know." In its use as a particle, *ebe* roughly corresponds to *exactly* in the English sentence "That is exactly what I was going to say," or to *just* in the English sentence "I was going to say just that." In its use as a particle, *ebe* has two polysemes: when stressed, it refers the listener to facts in previous discourse; and when unstressed, it calls the listener's attention to presupposed facts. Stern showed that, at around the age of 6 or 7, children use *ebe* correctly to refer to presupposed knowledge but often make errors in their use of stressed *ebe* to refer to facts from the preceding discourse. This is because children can access presuppositions directly, whereas they have trouble remembering all the propositions that have been asserted in an ongoing narrative.

MAKING AND USING THE INSTRUCTIONS

In the previous sections the various alternative readings for 12 major devices from the point-sharing system were reviewed. Table 1 lists the 12 devices and their polysemes. It also provides a summary statement regarding the nature of the instructions conveyed by each polyseme.

Some of the more important results deriving from the study of functional grammar are summarized in Table 1. The various linguistic and psycholinguistic investigations reviewed in this chapter provide evidence that people make continual use of constructs such as givenness, parameterization, anaphora, perspective, backgrounding, presupposition, focus, exophora, parallel function, and contrast. In fact, one might go so far as to say that these basic components of the point-sharing system constitute a set of processing routines that provide the basic structure not only for the process of human communication, but also for much of thought itself. However, these routines and structures are not utilized separately from the overall system of human information processing, nor are they exempt from the limits and constraints common to all higher cognitive processes.

Given the analysis in Table 1, one can then ask: What kind of an information-processing system does a speaker need in order to formulate these instructions, and what kind does the listener need in order to decode the instructions? First, it is clear that both the speaker and the listener must make use of a mental "dictionary" or lexicon. This

Table 1. Point-sharing devices and polysemes

Device	Polysemes	Explanation/function
Definite article	Core: unique identifiability of a referent	
	Exophora	In the perceptual situation
	Anaphora	In the preceding discourse
	Cataphora	In the following discourse
	Paraphrase	In a lexical paraphrase
	Partonymy	As a part of a prior referent
	Set operation	By the nature of the set
	Genericalness	By generic type
Indefinite article	Core: nonuniqueness (but singularity) of a referent	
	Instantiated	Referent exists
	Parameterized	Noun sets parameters on referent
Pronouns	Core: number, sex, person, identifiability, case, etc.	
	Exophora	In the perceptual situation
	Anaphora	In the preceding discourse
	Cataphora	In the following discourse
	Metaphora	To a speech act
	Perspective	By identifying with the earlier point of view
	Parallel function	By using the role structure of the previous clause
	Role frame	By filling out the role frame of a verb
	Topicality	In the rhetorical structure of the discourse
Ellipsis	Core: lexical/referential givenness	
	Exophora	In the perceptual situation
	Anaphora	In the preceding discourse
	Parallel function	By using the role structure of the previous clause
	Perspective	By maintaining perspective
	Role frame	By filling out the role frame of a verb
	Cataphora	In the following discourse
	Metaphora	To a speech act

continued

Table 1. (*Continued*)

Device	Polysemes	Explanation/function
Relative clauses	Core: addition of information about a noun	
	Specification	To narrow the class of referents
	Presupposition	To convey presupposed material
	Backgrounding	To include background material
Stress	Core: contrast	
	Denials	Rejection of a previous point
	Questions	Specification of needed information
	Answers	Response to queries
	Reversals	Reversal of normal identification
	Clefts	Marking of sentence focus
Initialization	Core: starting point	
	Interactional	Place of communication in discourse
	Vocatives	Summons
	Imperatives	Grammatically fixed
	Questions	Grammatically fixed
	Conditions	Set frame for predication
	Topic introduction	Setting up a new discourse topic
Preverbal positioning	Core: perspective	
	Givenness	Unique identifiability
	Topicality	Continuing a discourse topic
	Focus	Attentional salience
	Perspective	Point of view of predication
	Agency	Actor-cause
Subject-verb agreement	Core: perspective	
Verb selection	Core: placement of perspective in main case role (polysemes vary with items)	
Case marking	Core: distinction between competing perspectives	
Particles	Core: discourse presuppositions (polysemes vary with items)	

lexicon provides the listener with the readings of words, and also allows the listener to find paraphrases and associates for lexical items. Paraphrase, partonymy, and identity of reference are important in the processing of definite reference. The lexicon also contains those aspects of the grammar that are bound to specific lexical items (MacWhinney, 1982); more general rules of the language are stored in the grammar.

As Clark and Marshall (1981) pointed out, a dictionary and a grammar are not enough to make a language user competent. In addition, both the speaker and the listener must possess a "diary" and an "encyclopedia." One of the many uses of the diary is to maintain, in short-term memory, notes about the current discourse. In other words, both the speaker and the listener must possess a short-term memory that stores not only the various referents (anaphoric and exophoric) but also the ways in which the predications fit together. This is to say that short-term memory involves: 1) lexical memory, 2) reference memory, and 3) discourse memory. Lexical memory is used to compute givenness in terms of the parameterized values set up by initial descriptions. Reference memory stores pointers to specific instantiated referents that have been mentioned in the discourse or are present in the real world. Discourse memory is used to compute contrast, assertion, focus, topic, metaphorical givenness, and other rhetorical operations. Initially, discourse memory organizes predications from the point of view of the perspective developed by the speaker. Eventually, the topic probably takes over the major role as the organizer of material in the diary (Reder and Anderson, 1980).

In addition to a dictionary, a grammar, and a diary, both the speaker and listener must possess a store of factual material in long-term memory. This store may be thought of as an encyclopedia. Although access to the memories in this encyclopedia is governed at least in part by the structure of the dictionary, the exact shape of the relation between the dictionary and the encyclopedia (Clark and Clark, 1977) has not yet been worked out. However, access in both systems probably involves some form of spreading activation and intersecting searches (Anderson, 1976; Collins and Loftus, 1975). Clark and Marshall (1981) have suggested that at least one way of accessing the encyclopedia is by social group membership. Access of this type could facilitate the computation of certain types of presuppositions and definite references. The material in the encyclopedia must be accessed whenever the message encodes certain facts as presupposed for a given speaker-listener pair. The listener must check his store to see if such material is actually there. If it is not, he must decide whether or not to add it. Asserted material also must be either added to semantic memory or rejected as invalid.

Finally, the speaker and the listener must both utilize a set of rhetorical structures for controlling the addition of information to the encyclopedia. These structures filter and organize information according to its credibility, utility, and relevance. Conditions set on predications, the perspective structure of the message, the asserted-presupposed contrast, and the overall shape of the argument in terms of the sequence of rhetorical acts will all influence the listener to either accept or reject the message. The system that uses rhetorical structures to add information to either the diary or the encyclopedia can be thought of as a "rhetoricon." Thus, the five basic structures needed for the processing of points are: 1) a lexicon or dictionary, 2) a grammar, 3) an encyclopedia with long-term knowledge, 4) a diary with a referent memory and a discourse/lexical memory, and 5) a rhetoricon.

LEARNING THE SYSTEM

In order to share points effectively, the child must acquire the various point-sharing devices and their polysemes. In addition, he must construct the basic structures of a dictionary, a grammar, an encyclopedia, a diary with a lexical, referent, and discourse memory, and a rhetoricon. Because successful use of the devices of the point-sharing system relies on these five systems, the child's system may not operate on the adult level even after the devices themselves have been acquired. For example, Karmiloff-Smith (1979) and Stern (1980) have found that correct interpretation of the definite article/particle *ebe* may be blocked by an inadequate or inadequately constructed discourse memory.

Regarding the acquisition of the point-sharing devices themselves, one developmental hypothesis that is consistent with the data currently available is that the polysemes of the different devices emerge in the order of their "cue validity." Thus, the first devices and the first readings the child learns are those that are used most frequently and are most unambiguous in the language. This hypothesis is also the one proposed by MacWhinney (1978) for the acquisition of morphophonolgy and by MacWhinney (1982) for the acquisition of syntax and lexical semantics. Data from a recent study by Bates et al. (1982) supported this hypothesis for the comprehension of word order cues by English-speaking and Italian-speaking children.

Bates and MacWhinney (1982a) also claimed that, when a given device serves a number of common uses, its first uses appear to be based on a prototype structure (Bates et al., 1982). This structure resembles a Venn diagram in which the central element, i.e., the prototype, has the maximum number of characteristics in common with the other members of the class. For example, the prototypical preverbal element is an agent that also serves as the perspective for the verb. Very young children comprehend preverbal nouns in terms of this prototype. Of course, simple use of the prototype will not work in the case of the passive where the perspective is not the agent. Older children will learn that a nonperspectival agent is coded with a by-clause in the passive. Over time, the child sorts out the separate functions originally merged in the prototype and learns to use additional devices for rarer constellations of meanings. This progression is analogous to the one associated with the child's acquisition of the meanings of content words (Anglin, 1977; Bowerman, 1978; Rosch, 1973; Rosch and Mervis, 1975).

Because of the difficulty researchers face in achieving experimental control over devices such as verbal conflations, particles, and participials, we know little about their use in either adults or children. As a result, current functionalist grammar (Dik, 1978) is adequate as a description of the simple sentences of a preschooler. However, the expressive capacities of the school-age child go far beyond the bounds of current theory. This means that functionalist grammar cannot yet tell teachers exactly how to improve children's command over the more expressive grammatical devices. We can identify causes of inadequate article use, pronominalization, ellipsis, and so on, but our knowledge does not extend much beyond these simple devices. Research on the school-age child's use of more elaborate devices is clearly needed. Many of the problems seen in both normal and abnormal children concern the development of ways to put together both simple and elaborate devices to form larger segments of effective and expressive discourse. To understand these developments, we would need to look more deeply into the structure of rhetorical forms and the development of written composition (Hayes and Flower, 1980). If we want to expand our understanding of the uses of human communication, the integration of functionalist grammar with rhetorical theory should be a top priority for further research.

CONCLUSIONS

The activity of sharing points is fundamental to human society, yet it is an activity that few of us have fully mastered. If we are to encourage the development of this ability, we need to understand not only the rudiments of the system, but also its more complex elaborations. This understanding will not be easy to achieve, nor will it be achieved without dispute. However, there is no reason to fear this disagreement, because, as Vygotsky (1962) reminds us, "it is not so much that collision of ideas gives birth to dispute as that disputes give rise to ideas." It is in this vein that the preceding analysis has been offered. It does not constitute a finished theory; rather, it attempts to organize our understanding of certain basic devices in human communication in a way that can give rise to new ideas.

ACKNOWLEDGMENTS

My thanks to Jim Connell, Kurt Fischer, Suzanne Gendreau, Sybillyn Jennings, Annette Karmiloff-Smith, Jan Keenan, Mary MacWhinney, Sandy McNew, Derek Price, Lynn Snyder, and David Zubin for their perceptive critiques of an earlier draft of this paper, to Richard Schiefelbusch and Joanne Pickar for their thorough and intelligent assistance in editing the draft, to Elizabeth Bates for her help in working out many aspects of the analysis offered in this paper, and to László Dezső for first introducing me to the functionalist approach to language.

REFERENCES

Akmajian, A. 1979. Aspects of the Grammar of Focus in English. Garland Publishing, New York.
Aksu, A., and Slobin, D. I. *In* D. I. Slobin (ed.), Cross-linguistic Studies of Language Development. Lawrence Erlbaum Assocs., Inc., Hillsdale, N.J. (in press)
Allerton, D. 1978. The notion of "givenness" and its relations to presupposition and to theme. Lingua 44:133–168.
Anderson, J. R. 1976. Language, Memory, and Thought. Lawrence Erlbaum Assocs., Inc., Hillsdale, N.J.
Anglin, J. M. (ed.). 1977. Word, Object, and Conceptual Development. W. W. Norton and Company, Inc., New York.
Anisfeld, M., and Klenbort, I. 1973. On the functions of structural paraphrase: The view from the passive voice. Psychol. Bull. 79:117–126.
Barry, R. 1975. Topic in Chinese: An overlap of meaning, grammar, and discourse function. *In* R. Grossman, J. San, and T. Vance (eds.), Papers from the Parasession on Functionalism. Chicago Linguistic Society, Chicago.
Bates, E. 1976. Language and Context: Studies in the Acquisition of Pragmatics. Academic Press, Inc., New York.
Bates, E., McNew, S., MacWhinney, B., Devescovi, A., and Smith, S. 1982. Functional constraints on sentence processing: A cross linguistic study. Cognition 11:245–299.
Bates, E., and MacWhinney, B. 1979. A functionalist approach to the acquisition of grammar. *In* E. Ochs and B. Schieffelin (eds.), Developmental Pragmatics. Academic Press, Inc., New York.
Bates, E., and MacWhinney, B. 1982a. Functionalist approaches to grammar. *In* E. Wanner and L. Gleitman (eds.), Language Acquisition: The State of the Art. Cambridge University Press, New York.
Bates, E., and MacWhinney, B. 1982b. Second language acquisition from a functionalist perspective: Pragmatic, semantic and perceptual strategies. *In* H. Winitz (ed.), Annals of the New York Academy of Sciences: Conference on Native and Foreign Language Acquisition. New York Academy of Sciences, New York.
Beilin, H. 1975. Studies in the Cognitive Basis of Language Development. Academic Press, Inc., New York.
Berent, G. 1975. English absolutes in functional perspective. *In* R. Grossman, L. San, and T. Vance (eds.), Papers from the Parasession on Functionalism. Chicago Linguistic Society, Chicago.
Berman, A., and Számosi, M. 1972. Observations on sentential stress. Language 48:304–325.
Bever, T. G., 1970. The cognitive basis for linguistic structures. *In* J. R. Hayes (ed.), Cognition and the Development of Language. John Wiley & Sons, Inc., New York.
Bickerton, D. 1975. Two levels of logical presupposition. *In* Papers from the Eleventh Regional Meeting. Chicago Linguistic Society, Chicago.
Boadi, L. 1974. Focus-marking in Akan. Linguistics 140:5–57.

Bock, H. K., and Irwin, D. E. 1980. Syntactic effects of information availability in sentence production. J. Verbal Learn. Verbal Behav. 19:467–484.
Bock, K. 1977. The effect of a pragmatic presupposition on syntactic structure in question answering. J. Verbal Learn. Verbal Behav. 16:723–734.
Bolinger, D. 1961. Contrastive accent and contrastive stress. Language 37:83–96.
Bolinger, D. 1972. That's That. Mouton, The Hague.
Boucher, J., and Osgood, C. 1969. The Pollyanna hypothesis. J. Verbal Learn. Verbal Behav. 8:1–8.
Bowerman, M. 1978. Systematizing semantic knowledge: Changes over time in the child's organization of word meaning. Child Dev. 49:977–987.
Bowerman, M. 1982. Reorganizational processes in lexical and syntactic development. *In* E. Wanner and L. Gleitman, (eds.), Language Acquisition: The State of the Art. Cambridge University Press, New York.
Braine, M. D. S., and Wells, R. S. 1978. Case-like categories in children: The actor and some related categories. Cognitive Psychol. 10:100–122.
Bresson, F. 1974. Remarks on genetic psycholinguistics: The acquisition of the article system in French. *In* Current Problems in Psycholinguistics. Editions de C.N.R.S., Paris.
Brown, P., and Levinson, S. 1978. Universals in language usage: Politeness phenomena. *In* E. Goody (ed.), Questions and Politeness. Cambridge University Press, Cambridge, England.
Brown, R. 1958. How shall a thing be called? Psychol. Rev. 65:14–21.
Caramazza, A., Grober, E., Garvey, C., and Yates, J. 1977. Comprehension of anaphoric pronouns. J. Verbal Learn. Verbal Behav. 16:601–609.
Caramazza, A., and Gupta, S. 1979. The roles of topicalization, parallel function and verb semantics in the interpretation of pronouns. Linguistics 17:497–518.
Carpenter, P., and Just, M. 1977. Integrative processes in comprehension. *In* D. Laberge and S. Samuels (eds.), Basic Processes in Reading: Perception and Comprehension. Lawrence Erlbaum Assocs., Inc., Hillsdale, N.J.
Carroll, J. 1958. Process and content in psycholinguistics. *In* R. Patton (ed.), Current Trends in the Description and Analysis of Behavior. University of Pittsburgh Press, Pittsburgh.
Chafe, W. 1976. Givenness, contrastiveness, definiteness, subjects, topics, and point of view. *In* C. Li (ed.), Subject and Topic. Academic Press, Inc., New York.
Chapman, R. S., and Kohn, L. L. 1978. Comprehension strategies in two- and three-year-olds: Animate agents or probable events? J. Speech Hear. Res. 21:746–761.
Chapman, R. S., and Miller, J. F. 1975. Word order in early two- and three-word utterances: Does production precede comprehension? J. Speech Hear. Res. 18:355–371.
Charniak, E. 1973. Context and the reference problem. *In* R. Rustin (ed.), Natural Language Processing. Algorithmics Press, New York.
Chomsky, C. 1969. The Acquisition of Syntax in Children from 5 to 10. MIT Press, Cambridge, MA.
Chomsky, C. 1972. Stages in language development and reading exposure. Harvard Educ. Rev. 42:1–33.
Chomsky, N. 1965. Aspects of the Theory of Syntax. MIT Press, Cambridge, MA.

Chomsky, N. 1971. Deep structure, surface structure, and semantic interpretation. *In* D. Steinberg and L. Jakobovits (eds.), Semantics. Cambridge University Press, Cambridge, England.
Clark, H. 1973. Space, time, semantics, and the child. *In* T. E. Moore (ed.), Cognitive Development and the Acquisition of Language. Academic Press, Inc., New York.
Clark, H. 1974. Semantics and comprehension. Curr. Trends Ling. 12:1291–1428.
Clark, H., and Chase, W. 1973. On the process of comparing sentences against pictures. Cognitive Psychol. 3:472–517.
Clark, H., and Chase, W. 1974. Perceptual coding strategies in the formation and verification of descriptions. Memory Cognition 2:101–111.
Clark, H., and Clark, E. 1977. Psychology and Language. Harcourt, Brace, Jovanovich, Inc., New York.
Clark, H., and Marshall, C. 1981. Definite reference and mutual knowledge. *In* A. Joshi, B. Webber, and I. Sag (eds.), Elements of Discourse Understanding. Cambridge University Press, Cambridge, England.
Clifton, C., Kurcz, I., and Jenkins, J. J. 1965. Grammatical relations as determinants of sentence similarity. J. Verbal Learn. Verbal Behav. 4:112–117.
Clifton, C., and Odom, P. 1966. Similarity relations among certain English sentence constructions. Psychol. Monogr. 80.
Cogen, C., and Herrmann, L. 1976. Interactions of the expression 'let's just say' with the Gricean maxims of conversation. *In* C. Cogen, H. Thompson, G. Thurgod, K. Whistler, and J. Wright (eds.), Proceedings of the First Annual Meeting of the Berkeley Linguistics Society. University of California Berkeley.
Collins, A., and Loftus, E. 1975. A spreading-activation theory of semantic processing. Psychol. Rev. 82:407–428.
Comrie, B. 1979. Genitive-accusatives in Slavic: The rules and their motivation. *In* B. Comrie (ed.), Classification of Grammatical Categories. Linguistic Research, Inc., Urbana, IL.
Cooper, W., and Ross, J. 1975. Word order. *In* R. Grossman, L. San, and T. Vance (eds.), Papers from the Parasession on Functionalism. Chicago Linguistic Society, Chicago.
Cruttenden, A. 1974. An experiment involving comprehension of intonation in children from 7 to 10. J. Child Lang. 1(2):221–231.
de Laguna, G. A. 1963. Speech: Its Function and Development. Indiana University Press, Bloomington. (first published in 1927)
de Villiers, J., and de Villiers, P. 1973. A cross-sectional study of the acquisition of grammatical morphemes in child speech. J. Psycholing. Res. 2:267–278.
de Villiers, J., Tager-Flusberg, H., and Hakuta, K. 1977. Deciding among theories of the development of coordination in child speech. Papers Rep. Child Lang. Dev. 13:118–125.
de Villiers, P., and de Villiers, J. 1972. Early judgments of semantic and syntactic acceptability by children. J. Psycholing. Res. 1:299–310.
DeLancey, S. 1981. An interpretation of split ergativity and other patterns. Language 57:626–657.
Delis, D., and Slater, A. S. 1977. Toward a functional theory of reduction transformations. Cognition 5:119–132.

Dent, C. H., and Greenfield, P. M. 1980. An experimental approach to the developmental study of pragmatic presupposition. *In* D. Ingram, F. C. C. Peng, and P. Dale (eds.), Proceedings of the First International Congress for the Study of Child Language. University Press of America, Lanham, MD.

Dewart, M. H. 1972. Social class and children's understanding of deep structure in sentences. Br. J. Educ. Psychol. 42:198–203.

Dewart, M. H. 1976. The role of animate and inanimate nouns in determining sentence voice. Child memory. Unpublished manuscript, Medical Research Council, London, England.

Dezső, L. 1972. Bevezetés a mondattani tipológiába (in Hungarian). TIT központja, Budapest.

Dik, T. 1978. Functional Grammar. North-Holland, New York.

Donnellan, K. 1966. Reference and definite descriptions. Philos. Rev. 75:281–304.

Duranti, A., and Ochs, E. 1979. Left-dislocation in Italian conversation. *In* T. Givón (ed.), Syntax and Semantics. Academic Press, Inc., New York.

Ertel, S. 1977. Where do the subjects of sentences come from? *In* S. Rosenberg (ed.), Sentence Production: Developments in Research and Theory. Lawrence Erlbaum Assocs., Inc., Hillsdale, N.J.

Fava, E., and Tirondola, G. 1977. Syntactic and pragmatic regularities in Italian child discourse: Grammatical relations and word order. Institute di Glottologia, Florence, Italy.

Fillmore, C. J. 1970. Subjects, speakers, and roles. Ohio State University Working Papers in Linguistics 4:31–63.

Gaer, E. 1969. Children's understanding and production of sentences. J. Verbal Learn. Verbal Behav. 3:55–59.

Garcia, E. C., and Otheguy, R. 1977. Dialect variation in leismo: A semantic approach. *In* R. W. Fasold and R. W. Shuy (eds.), Studies in Language Variation: Semantics, Syntax, Phonology, Pragmatics, Social Situations, Ethnographic Approaches. Georgetown University Press, Washington, D.C.

Garrod, S., and Sanford, A. 1977. Interpreting anaphoric relations: The integration of semantic information while reading. J. Verbal Learn. Verbal Behav. 16:77–90.

Garrod, S., and Sanford, A. 1978. Anaphora: A problem in text comprehension. *In* R. N. Campbell and P. T. Smith (eds.), Recent Advances in the Psychology of Language. Plenum Publishing Corporation, London.

Garvey, C., Caramazza, A., and Yates, J. 1975. Factors influencing assignment of pronoun antecedents. Cognition 3:227–243.

Gensler, O. 1976. Non-syntactic antecedents of frame semantics. *In* K. Whistler, J. Jaeger, M. Petruck, H. Thompson, and A. Woodbury (eds.), Proceedings of the Second Annual Meeting of the Berkeley Linguistics Society. University of California, Berkeley.

Goldman, S. 1976. Reading skill and the minimum distance principle: A comparison of listening and reading comprehension. J. Exp. Child Psychol. 22:123–142.

Goodenough-Trepagnier, C., and Smith, F. 1978, Thematization and intonation in the organization of sentences. Lang. Speech 21:99–107.

Goodluck, H., and Roeper, T. 1978. The acquisition of perception verb complements. *In* H. Goodluck and L. Solan (eds.), Papers in the Structure and Development of Child Language. University of Massachusetts, Amherst.

Gough, P. 1965. Grammatical transformations and speed of understanding. J. Verbal Learn. Verbal Behav. 4:107–111.

Gowie, C., and Powers, J. 1979. Relations among cognitive, semantic, and syntactic variables in children's comprehension of the minimum distance principle: A two-year developmental study. J. Psycholing. Res. 8:29–41.

Greenfield, P., and Zukow, P. G. 1978. Why do children say what they say when they say it?: An experimental approach to the psychogenesis of presupposition. In K. E. Nelson (ed.), Children's Language. Gardner Press, New York.

Grieve, R. 1973. Definiteness in discourse. Lang. Speech 16:365–372.

Grieve, R., and Wales, R. 1973. Passives and topicalization. Br. J. Psychol. 64:173–182.

Grober, E., Beardsley, W., and Caramazza, A. 1978. Parallel function strategy in pronoun assignment. Cognition 6:117–133.

Grosjean, F., and Lane, H. 1976. Pauses and syntax in American sign languages. Unpublished manuscript, Northeastern University, Boston.

Gunter, R. 1966. On the placement of accent in dialogue: A feature of context grammar. J. Ling. 2:159–179.

Haiman, J. 1978. Conditionals are topics. Language 54:564–589.

Hakuta, K. 1979. Comprehension and production of simple and complex sentences by Japanese children. Doctoral dissertation, Harvard University.

Hatcher, A. 1956. Syntax and the sentence. Word 12:234–250.

Haviland, S., and Clark, H. 1974. What's new? Acquiring new information as a process in comprehension. J. Verbal Learn. Verbal Behav. 13:512–521.

Hawkins, J. 1977. The pragmatics of definiteness: Part 1. Ling. Berichte 48:1–25.

Hayes, L., and Flower, L. 1980. Identifying the organization of writing processes. In L. Gregg and E. Steinberg (eds.), Cognitive Processes in Writing. Lawrence Erlbaum Assocs., Inc., Hillsdale, N.J.

Hooper, J., and Thompson, S. 1973. On the applicability of root transformations. Ling. Inq. 4:465–497.

Hopper, P. 1979. Aspect and foregrounding in discourse. In T. Givón (ed.), Syntax and Semantics. Academic Press, Inc., New York.

Hopper, P., and Thompson, S. A. 1980. Transitivity in grammar and discourse. Language 56:251–299.

Hornby, P. 1971. Surface structure and the topic-comment distinction: A developmental study. Child Dev. 42:1975–1988.

Hornby, P. 1973. Intonation and syntactic structure in the development of presupposition. Unpublished manuscript, State University of New York, Plattsburgh.

Hornby, P. 1974. Surface structure and presupposition. J. Verbal Learn. Verbal Behav. 13:530–538.

Hornby, P., and Hass, W. 1970. Use of contrastive stress by preschool children. J. Speech Hear. Res. 13:395–399.

Hupet, M., and LeBouedec, B. 1975. Definiteness and voice in the interpretation of active and passive sentences. Q. J. Exp. Psychol. 27:323–330.

Huttenlocher, J., Eisenberg, K., and Strauss, S. 1968. Relation between perceived actor and logical subject. J. Verbal Learn. Verbal Behav. 7:527–530.

Huttenlocher, J., and Higgins, E. 1971. Adjectives, comparatives, and syllogisms. Psychol. Rev. 78:487–504.

Huttenlocher, J., and Presson, C. 1973. Mental rotation and the perspective problem. Cognitive Psychol. 4:277–299.

Jarvella, R., and Sinnott, J. 1972. Contextual constraints on noun distribution to some English verbs by children and adults. J. Verbal Learn. Verbal Behav. 11:47–53.

Karmiloff-Smith, A. 1976. More about the same: Children's understanding of post-articles. J. Child Lang. 4:377–394.

Karmiloff-Smith, A. 1979. A Functional Approach to Child Language: A Study of Determiners and Reference. Cambridge University Press, New York.

Keenan, E. O. 1974. Conversational competence in children. J. Child Lang. 1:163–183.

Keenan, E., and Schieffelin, B. 1976. Foregrounding referents: A reconsideration of left-dislocation in discourse. *In* H. Thompson, K. Whistler, V. Edge, J. Jaeger, R. Javkin, M. Petruck, and C. Smeall (eds.), Proceedings of the Second Annual Meeting of the Berkeley Linguistics Society. University of California, Berkeley.

Keenan, J., and Kintsch, W. 1974. The identification of explicitly and implicitly presented information. *In* W. Kintsch (ed.), The Representation of Meaning in Memory. Lawrence Erlbaum Assocs., Inc., Hillsdale, N.J.

Kessel, F. 1970. The role of syntax in children's comprehension from ages six to twelve. Monogr. Soc. Res. Child Dev. 35, Serial no. 139.

Kirkwood, H. 1978. Options and constraints in the surface ordering of noun phrases in English and German. J. Pragmatics 2:225–245.

Klenbort, I., and Anisfeld, M. 1974. Markedness and perspective in the interpretation of the active and passive voice. Q. J. Exp. Psychol. 26:189–195.

Kramer, P., Koff, E., and Luria, Z. 1972. The development of competence in an exceptional language structure in older children and young adults. Child Dev. 43:121–130.

Krauss, R. M., and Weinheimer, S. 1964. Changes in reference phrases as a function of frequency of usage in social interaction: A preliminary study. Psychonomic Sci. 1:113–114.

Krauss, R. M., and Weinheimer, S. 1967. Effect of referent similarity and communication mode on verbal encoding. J. Verbal Learn. Verbal Behav. 6:359–363.

Leonard, L., and Schwartz, R. 1977. Focus characteristics of single-word utterances after syntax. J. Child Lang. 5:151–158.

Lesgold, A. 1972. Pronominalization: A device for unifying sentences in memory. J. Verbal Learn. Verbal Behav. 11:316–323.

Li, C. N., and Thompson, S. A. 1979. Third-person pronouns and zero-anaphora in Chinese discourse. *In* T. Givón (ed.), Syntax and Semantics. Academic Press, Inc., New York.

Limber, J. 1976. Unravelling competence, performance and pragmatics in the speech of young children. J. Child Lang. 3:309–318.

Linde, C., and Labov, W. 1975. Spatial networks as a site for the study of language and thought. Language 51:924–939.

Lindner, G. 1898. Aus dem Naturgarten der Kindersprache (in German). Grieben, Leipzig.

Lindsley, J. 1976. Producing simple utterances: Details of the planning process. J. Psycholing. Res. 5:331–354.

Lust, B. 1977. Conjunction reduction in child language. J. Child Lang. 4:257–288.

Lust, B., and Mervis, C. A. 1980. Development of coordination in the natural speech of young children. J. Child Lang. 7:279–304.
Lyons, J. 1975. Deixis as a source of reference. *In* E. Keenan (ed.), Formal Semantics of Natural Language. Cambridge University Press, Cambridge, England.
MacWhinney, B. 1975. Pragmatics patterns in child syntax. Papers Rep. Child Dev. 10:153–165.
MacWhinney, B. 1976. Hungarian research on the acquisition of morphology and syntax. J. Child Lang. 3:397–410.
MacWhinney, B., 1977. Starting points. Language 53:152–168.
MacWhinney, B. 1978. The acquisition of morphophonology. Mongr. Soc. Res. Child Dev. 43.
MacWhinney, B. 1982. Basic syntactic processes. *In* S. Kuczaj (ed.), Language Acquisition: Vol. 1. Syntax and Semantics. Lawrence Erlbaum Assocs., Inc., Hillsdale, N.J.
MacWhinney, B., and Bates, E. 1978. Sentential devices for conveying givenness and newness: A cross-cultural developmental study. J. Verbal Learn. Verbal Behav. 17:539–558.
MacWhinney, B., and Price, D. 1980. The development of the comprehension of topic-comment marking. *In* D. Ingram, C. C. Peng, and P. Dale (eds.), Proceedings of the First International Congress for the Study of Child Language. University Press of America, Lanham, MD.
Maratsos, M. P. 1973. The effects of stress on the understanding of pronominal co-reference in children. J. Psycholing. Res. 2:1–8.
Maratsos, M. P. 1974a. Children who get worse at understanding the passive: A replication of Bever. J. Psycholing. Res. 3:65–74.
Maratsos, M. P. 1974b. How preschool children understand missing complement subjects. Child Dev. 45:700–706.
Maratsos, M. P. 1976. The Use of Definite and Indefinite Reference in Young Children. Cambridge University Press, London.
Mathesius, V. 1939. O tak zvaném aktuálním členění věty (in Czechoslovakian). Slovo o Slovenost 5:171–174.
Meggyes, K. 1971. Egy kétéves gyermek nyelvi rendszere (in Hungarian). Nyelvtudományi Értekezések 73.
Miller, G. 1964. Language and psychology. *In* E. H. Lennenberg (ed.), New Directions in the Study of Language. MIT Press, Cambridge, MA.
Miller, M. 1978. Pragmatic constraints on the linguistic realization of 'semantic intentions' in early child language. *In* N. Waterson and C. Snow (eds.), The Development of Communication. John Wiley & Sons, Inc., New York.
Mittwoch, A. 1979. Backward anaphora in utterances conjoined with "but." Paper presented at the Linguistic Society of America Winter Meeting.
Most, R., and Saltz, E. 1979. Information structure in sentences: New information. Lang. Speech 22:89–95.
Olson, D. R. 1970. Langauge and thought: Aspects of a cognitive theory of semantics. Psychol. Rev. 77:257–273.
Osgood, C. E. 1971. Where do sentences come from: *In* D. D. Steinberg and L. A. Jakobovits (eds.), Semantics. Cambridge University Press, Cambridge, England.
Osgood, C. E., and Bock, K. J. 1977. Salience and sentencing: Some production principles. *In* S. Rosenberg (ed.), Sentence Production: Developments in Research and Theory. Lawrence Erlbaum Assocs., Inc., Hillsdale, N.J.

O'Shea, M. V. 1907. Linguistic Development and Education. MacMillan, New York.

Park, Tschang-Zin. 1974. A study of German language development. Unpublished manuscript, University of Berne, Berne, Switzerland.

Prince, E. 1981. On the inferencing of indefinite *this* NP's. *In* A. Joshi, B. Webber, and I. Sag (eds.), Elements of Discourse Understanding. Cambridge University Press, Cambridge, England.

Reder, L. M., and Anderson, J. R. 1980. A partial resolution of the paradox of interference: The role of integrating knowledge. Cognitive Psychol. 12:447–472.

Rodgon, M. 1976. Single Word Usage, Cognitive Development, and the Beginning of Combinatorial Speech. Cambridge University Press, Cambridge, England.

Rosch, E. H., 1973. On the internal structure of perceptual and semantic categories. *In* T. E. Moore (ed.), Cognitive Development and the Acquisition of Language. Academic Press, Inc., New York.

Rosch, E. H. 1977. Human categorization. *In* N. Warren (ed.), Studies in Cross-cultural Psychology. Academic Press, Inc., New York.

Rosch, E. H., and Mervis, C. B. 1975. Family resemblances: Studies in the internal structure of categories. Cognitive Psychol. 7:573–605.

Sanford, A., and Garrod, S. 1979. Memory and attention in text comprehension: The problem of reference. *In* R. S. Nickerson (ed.), Attention and Performance. Lawrence Erlbaum Assocs., Inc., Hillsdale, N.J.

Schachter, P. 1973. Focus and relativization. Language 49:19–46.

Schegloff, E. A., and Sacks, H. 1973. Opening up closings. Semiotica 8:289–327.

Schenkein, J. 1978. Studies in the Organization of Conversational Interaction. Academic Press, Inc., New York.

Schmerling, S. 1974. A re-examination of "normal stress." Language 50:66–73.

Sechehaye, M. A. 1926. Essai sur la Structure Logique de la Phrase. Champion, Paris.

Segalowitz, N., and Galang, R. 1976. Agent-patient word-order preference in the acquisition of Tagalog. J. Child Lang. 5:47–64.

Sgall, P. 1972. Fillmore's mysteries and topic vs. comment. J. Ling. 8:201–357.

Shatz, M. 1983. Communication. *In* J. Flavell and E. Markman (eds.), Handbook of Child Psychology, Vol. 3 (4th ed.) John Wiley & Sons, Inc., New York.

Sheldon, A. 1974. On the role of parallel function in the acquisition of relative clauses in English. J. Verbal Learn. Verbal Behav. 13:272–281.

Shipley, E., Smith, C., and Gleitman, L. 1969. A study in the acquisition of language: Free responses to commands. Language 45:322–342.

Silverstein, M. 1976. Hierarchy of features and ergativity. *In* R. Dixon (ed.), Grammatical Categories in Australian Languages. Australian Institute of Aboriginal Studies, Canberra.

Sinclair, H. J. 1975. The role of cognitive structures in language acquisition. *In* E. H. Lenneberg and E. Lenneberg (eds.), Foundations of Language Development: A Multidisciplinary Approach. Academic Press, Inc., New York.

Sinclair, H. J., and Bronckart, J. 1972. SVO—a linguistic universal?: A study in developmental psycholinguistics. J. Exp. Child Psychol. 14:329–348.

Slobin, D. I. 1966. Grammatical transformations and sentence comprehension in childhood and adulthood. J. Verbal Learn. Verbal Behav. 5:219–227.
Slobin, D. I. 1968. Recall of full and truncated passive sentences in connected discourse. J. Verbal Learn. Verbal Behav. 7:876–881.
Smith, K., and McMahon, L. 1970. Understanding order information in sentences: Some recent work at Bell Laboratories. *In* G. Flores d'Arcais and W. Levelt (eds.), Advances in Psycholinguistics. North-Holland, Amsterdam.
Snyder, L. 1976. The early presuppositions and performatives of normal and language disabled children. Papers Rep. Child Lang. Dev. 12:221–229.
Solan, L. 1979. Contrastive stress and children's interpretation of pronouns. Unpublished manuscript, University of Massachusetts, Amherst.
Springston, F. 1977. Some cognitive aspects of presupposed coreferential anaphora. Doctoral dissertation, Stanford University.
Stern, O. 1980. The evaluative function of the particle "ebe" in Swiss-German children's narratives. Papers Rep. Child Lang. Dev. 19:104–112.
Suci, G., and Hamacher, J. 1972. Psychological dimensions of case in sentence processing: Action role and animateness. Int. J. Psycholing. 1:34–48.
Talmy, L. 1976. Semantic causative types. Syntax Semantics 6:43–116.
Tannenbaum, P., and Williams, F. 1968. Generation of active and passive sentences as a function of subject or object focus. J. Verbal Learn. Verbal Behav. 7:246–250.
Tavakolian, S. 1977. Structural principles in the acquisition of complex sentences. Doctoral dissertation, University of Massachusetts, Amherst.
Tavakolian, S. 1978. The conjoined clause analysis of relative clause and other structures. *In* H. Goodluck and L. Solan (eds.), Papers in the Structure and Development of Child Language. University of Massachusetts Occasional Papers in Linguistics Psychology. University of Massachusetts, Amherst.
Travniček, F. 1962. O tak zvaném aktuálním čleveění větném (in Czechoslovakian). Slovo o Slovesnost 22:163–171.
Turner, E., and Rommetveit, R. 1967. Experimental manipulation of the production of active and passive voice in children. Lang. Speech 10:169–180.
Viktor, G. 1917. A gyermek nyelve: a gyermeknyelv irodalmának ismertetése főként nyelvészeti szempontból (in Hungarian). Nagyvárad.
Vygotsky, L. 1962. Thought and Language. MIT Press, Cambridge, MA. (first published in 1934)
Wanner, E., and Maratsos, M. 1978. An ATN approach to comprehension. *In* M. Halle, J. Bresnan, and G. Miller (ed.), Linguistic Theory and Psychological Reality. MIT Press, Cambridge, MA.
Warden, D. A. 1976. The influence of context on children's use of identifying expressions and references. Br. J. Psychol. 67:101–112.
Webber, B. 1981. Discourse model synthesis: Preliminaries to reference. *In* A. Joshi, B. Webber, and I. Sag (eds.), Elements of Discourse Understanding. Cambridge University Press, Cambridge, England.
Weisenburger, J. L. 1976. A choice of words: Two-year-old speech from a situational point of view. J. Child Lang. 3:275–281.
Wetstone, H. S., and Friedlander, B. Z. 1973. The effect of word order on young children's response to simple questions and commands. Child Dev. 44:734–740.
Weydt, H. (ed.). 1979. Die Partikeln der deutschen Sprache. Walter deGruyter, Berlin.

Wright, P., and Glucksberg, S. 1976. Choice of definite versus indefinite article as a function of sentence voice and reversibility. Q. J. Exp. Psychol. 28:561–570.

Yekovich, F., Walker, C., and Blackman, H. 1979. The role of presupposed and focal information in integrating sentences. J. Verbal Learn. Verbal Behav. 18:535–548.

Zubin, D. A. 1977. The semantic basis of case alternation in German. *In* R. W. Fasold and R. W. Shuy (eds.), Studies in Language Variation: Semantics, Syntax, Phonology, Pragmatics, Social Situations, Ethnographic Approaches. Georgetown University Press, Washington, D.C.

Zubin, D. A. 1979. Discourse function of morphology: The focus system in German. *In* T. Givón (ed.), Syntax and Semantics, Vol. 12: Discourse and Syntax. Academic Press, Inc., New York.

Section III

Children across Cultures

Cultural Variation in Children's Conversations

Bambi B. Schieffelin

Graduate School of Education
University of Pennsylvania
Philadelphia, Pennsylvania

Ann R. Eisenberg

Division of Behavioral and Cultural Sciences
University of Texas at San Antonio
San Antonio, Texas

Editors' Note

    This chapter examines cultural variation in the structure of conversations between adults and children. It is based on the assumption that the ways of speaking in every speech community are culturally patterned. Variation in the ways of speaking in different societies reflect important differences in beliefs, values, and practices. These differences enter into the organization and systematic use of language at many different levels. It follows that, when children are acquiring their language, they are being spoken to and are learning to talk to others according to the patterns of language use that reflect the beliefs and values of their particular speech community.
    There are several determinants of cultural variation in children's conversation that must be considered in any study of the development of communicative competence. These include the beliefs about the status and role of the child in a particular society, the social organization of caregiving, and the folk conceptions of how children learn language. Data from several societies are used to examine these cultural domains and the relationships that hold between them. Research questions relevant to studying the development of communicative competence are suggested.

Naturalistic conversational data collected in two societies (white middle class in Northern California and Kaluli of Papua New Guinea) are used to examine the differences in the ways in which children are socialized to talk about experiences in the past. Findings from this and other studies demonstrate that in evaluating a child's linguistic performance, it is necessary to know what constitutes communicative competence within the child's own speech community. Such knowledge should help educators understand the difficulties minority children have in adjusting to the predominantly white middle-class style of speech in American schools.

contents

DETERMINANTS OF CULTURAL VARIABILITY IN CONVERSATION 382
    Beliefs about the Status and Role of the Child in Society 382
    Social Organization of Caregiving 387
    Folk Beliefs about How Children Learn Language 390
    Research Questions 395

REFERRING TO EVENTS IN THE PAST 399
    Talk about the Past in White Middle-Class Society 400
    A Comparative Study 401

CONCLUSIONS 412

ACKNOWLEDGMENTS 415

REFERENCES 415

> A child capable of any and all grammatical utterances, but not knowing which to use, not knowing even when to talk and when to stop, would be a cultural monstrosity.
>
> (Hymes, 1967, p. 16)

Cultures vary along many dimensions: their ways of organizing groups, their ways of growing and distributing food, and their beliefs and practices with regard to health and illness. Another major area in which cultures differ is their ways of speaking. Only in recent years have the ways of speaking in different cultures been taken up as a focus of study. This has largely been through the efforts of anthropologists, in particular John Gumperz and Dell Hymes (1964, 1972).

In writing about ways of speaking in different cultures, Gumperz and Hymes called attention to an approach used in sociolinguistics and ethnography, which they called the ethnography of communication. This approach held as a major assumption and made explicit the fact that language use manifests kinds of knowledge and abilities that are largely outside the range of immediate awareness. These kinds of knowledge, "communicative competence," can be characterized just as can the competence that underlies language structure.

The notion of communicative competence was first introduced by Hymes in 1967 and grew out of his recognition of the continuity of linguistic form with the patterning of social behavior (Sapir, 1949) and a view of language as a mode of action (Malinowski, 1935). The term "communicative competence" was used by Hymes to include all modes of competence in communication.

> The acquisition of competence for use, indeed, can be stated in the same terms as acquisition of competence for grammar. Within the developmental matrix in which knowledge of the sentences of a language is acquired, children also acquire knowledge of a set of ways in which sentences are used. From a finite experience of speech acts and their interdependence with socio-cultural features they develop a general theory of the speaking appropriate to their community, which they employ, like other forms of tacit cultural knowledge (competence) in conducting and interpreting social life.
>
> In sum, the goal of a broad theory of competence can be said to show the ways in which the systematically possible, the feasible, and the appropriate are linked to produce and interpret actually occurring cultural behavior. (Hymes, 1972, p. 286)

Across cultures variation in the ways of speaking reflects important differences in beliefs, practices, values, and norms. These differences enter into the organization and systematic use of language at

---

This research was supported by National Institutes of Health National Research Service award 1T32HD07181-01 from NICHD to Dr. Schieffelin through the Department of Psychology, University of California, Berkeley.

many levels in every community. It follows, then, that when children are acquiring their language they are being spoken to and are learning to talk to others according to ways of speaking that reflect the beliefs and values of their particular speech community.

One set of beliefs inherent in the language that children hear and eventually learn are beliefs about the child's status and role. Consequently, when we examine interactions in which children participate, we should ask what are the cultural beliefs that shape members' attitudes toward the child's status and role within the society. An important issue to explore is how the beliefs held by adults in a given society affect the types of interactions in which young children are involved. A related issue is how young children learn to interact and participate, or not participate, in particular conversational sequences. For example, we may ask what a given culture's ideas are concerning how the young child learns to speak. What behaviors on the part of the child are thought to indicate comprehension, and the development of production skills? At what age is the child thought of as a co-conversationalist? Western psycholinguists have as one of their major goals the development of a theory of language acquisition. However, most societies have their own native theories of language acquisition that guide the treatment of young language-learning children. Both traditional folk theories and Western scientific theories of language acquisition must be acknowledged by individuals dealing with children from diverse cultural backgrounds. By taking into account traditional folk attitudes toward the role of language in children's interaction with adults, it is possible to interpret and understand behaviors that otherwise might not appear to display competence.

In addition to cultural beliefs about young children and language socialization, the social organization of any given society strongly shapes how children learn their roles in verbal interactions, and how they learn appropriate language use. Thus, studies of how children learn to use language should address questions such as: What role, if any, do mothers take in the process? fathers? siblings?

Children all over the world acquire their conversational skills in the context of social interaction. In these contexts they are learning not only the structure of their language, but also the culturally preferred conventions of interaction and language use. These conventions, and the child's ability to follow them, in turn help guide the acquisition of additional linguistic forms. These conventions generally reflect the values, attitudes, and beliefs held by members of the culture—in other words, the beliefs and values of members are implicit in the conventions they choose to follow. In addition, members' attitudes may also be conveyed by more explicit means during the course of an interaction. In any case, through their interactions with others, children learn a set of social and cultural values and beliefs that will *make* them members of their own cultural group and *identify* them as such. To summarize, as children become communicatively competent, they are learning not only the structure of their language, but also: 1) a set of conventions for interaction and the use of language; and 2) the values, attitudes, and beliefs of other cultural members.

In the last 15 years there has been a growing interest in investigating the development of communicative competence. The first wave of research came out of an innovative multidisciplinary approach formulated in 1967 by Dan Slobin, Susan Ervin-Tripp, John Gumperz, and others at the University of California, Berkeley. The major goals and methods of this approach are stated in *A Field Manual for Cross-Cultural Study of the Acquisition of Communicative Competence*. The approach discussed in the *Field Manual* is one of several that have been used to investigate different aspects of the development of communicative competence in American and cross-cultural contexts. (For other approaches, see Cazden, John, and Hymes, 1972; Ervin-Tripp and Mitchell-Kernan, 1977; Jordan, Au, and Joesting, 1983; Ochs and Schieffelin, 1979.) The different perspectives and approaches to the cross-cultural study of early language development have been reviewed by Blount (1975), Bowerman (1981), Ervin-Tripp (1978), and Schieffelin (1979).

In this chapter we focus on cultural variation in conversations between young children and adults. We hope to point out the importance of cultural variation as it affects the organization and systematic use of verbal and nonverbal communication. We are focusing on child-adult interactions only because they have been more adequately described in the literature than child-child exchanges. We are not suggesting, by any means, that the ways in which young children interact with adults will be identical to the ways in which they interact with other children. Just as adult-adult dialogues have certain characteristics marking them as such, so will child-adult and child-child exchanges have features that are unique to them.

Because this chapter is about cultural variation, we do not discuss register variation or individual variation in conversations. The reader is referred to Andersen (1977) and Gordon and Ervin-Tripp (this volume) for research pertaining to register variation in children's language, and to Lieven (1978a, 1978b, 1980) and Fillmore (1976) for studies on individual differences in language use.

In discussing cultural variation, we have had to draw from a wide range of reports from researchers with different perspectives. Consequently, we consider this to be a preliminary statement. Specifically, we have made a preliminary attempt to answer the following two questions: 1) What aspects of conversational exchanges are affected by cultural variation? and 2) How and why do different cultural groups organize conversations in the ways that they do? Our discussion of these two questions begins with a review of various determinants of cultural variability in child-adult conversations. We then examine the ways in which children and adults in two cultures talk about events in the past as one example of how the culture shapes language use. In discussing this issue, we compare the conversations of white middle-class English speakers (Northern California) to those of a traditional nonliterate people, the Kaluli of Papua New Guinea. Talk about past events emerged as an important source of variation in the data collected from these two groups.

DETERMINANTS OF CULTURAL VARIABILITY IN CONVERSATION

The determinants discussed here are drawn primarily from naturalistic and ethnographic research reports. These determinants include: 1) beliefs about the status and role of the child in society; 2) the social organization of caregiving; and 3) folk beliefs about how children learn language. Following our review of these determinants, we propose four sets of research questions that have been and should continue to be investigated.

Beliefs about the Status and Role of the Child in Society

In most societies children are thought to hold a special status, different from that of adults. This may range from a relatively low to a high status depending on the culture and the context. These culturally specific definitions of children's social status and role determine both what adults expect from them and how adults act toward them. This in turn affects the forms and functions of verbal interactions.

One way in which interactions vary across cultures is in the amount of talk thought to be appropriate between adults and children. Cultures vary along a continuum ranging from societies in which children are not allowed or expected to talk to adults or strangers and/or are not thought of as co-conversationalists to those in which children are actively encouraged to talk to adults, who in turn support this interaction and try to understand it. In some societies adults think it is important to elicit speech from children, socializing them in terms of production and interaction skills (e.g., Kaluli in Papua New Guinea, white middle-class American); but in other cultures children are encouraged to be quiet and speak only when spoken to (e.g., rural Louisiana Blacks, Luo in Kenya).

Researchers who have studied various cultures on this continuum have been able to identify a number of cultural differences concerning the degree to which adult-child dialogues are appropriate and encouraged. Heath (1982a), for example, described interactions between adults and children in an ethnographic study of a Black working-class community. She found that, in this community, children were not viewed as information-givers nor considered appropriate conversational partners. Although they were not excluded from adult verbal interactions, language input was not specially modified for them nor were topics addressed to them. As Heath put it, "The children did not have to be used as conversational partners; others more knowledgeable and more competent as conversants were available" (pp. 114–115). In particular, adults did not ask children special types of questions in order to engage them in conversation. Adults only rarely asked children test questions to which they already knew the answer. When adults did ask known-answer questions, their questions differed in function from the white middle-class teachers' test questions to their own children at home, i.e., requests for confirmation that the children had an objective piece of knowledge (e.g., the name of an object, its color, its size). In contrast to the Black adults, the teachers saw questions as necessary to train children, to cause them to respond verbally and to be trained as conversational partners.

In her ethnographic study of poor Black rural families in Louisiana, Ward (1971) described how the adults in the community favor "lap babies" who are not yet speaking over older children who can speak and therefore be counted on to be fresh and unpleasant. In this community, parents attend to children longer when the children are not talking than when they are talking. In general, children are responsible only for taking care of themselves and for following orders. They are not supposed to initiate conversations; when conversation is initiated by an adult, children are expected to respond by saying only the necessary minimum. Children are not expected to display their knowledge and linguistic abilities to adult friends and relatives.

Ward also found that, once conversation has been initiated, children are not supposed to direct topic selection. Since children are thought of as being unable to hold up their end of the conversation and adults are unwilling to "talk for the sake of talk," topic selection is handled by adults. Moreover, children's information-seeking questions are ignored since adults consider the questions to be unimportant. Instead, the adult chooses the topic and the child may give minimal feedback (e.g., "huh," "mm"). Rather than expanding the child's speech, caregivers expand and vary their *own* utterances, which tend to be imperatives or true information-seeking questions rather than test questions designed to evoke information already known to the adult.

To summarize, the rural Louisiana Black children described by Ward are expected to listen and follow orders instead of initiating conversation. Rather than expanding a child's speech, caregivers expand their own orders and questions presumably to facilitate comprehension. In any case, a child's quiet comprehension of language is more valued than his production of it.

In a number of societies, silence is a sign of deference reflecting the subordinate relationship that children hold with respect to adults—e.g., the Kipsigis (Harkness and Super, 1977), the Luo (Blount, 1969), and the Athabaskan Indians (Scollon and Scollon, 1981a, 1981b). The Athabaskan attitude is that parents and teachers should speak and that children should listen. The ability to learn language is not considered to be related to the child's overt production of speech. Consequently, in contrast to American caregiver-child interactions, Athabaskan interactions rarely involve long vertical constructions in which the child is encouraged to build topic-comment sequences across utterances (Keenan and Schieffelin, 1976; Ochs, Schieffelin, and Platt, 1979; Scollon, 1976). Similarly, Kipsigis mothers socialize their children for silence by infrequently using speech forms designed to evoke speech (e.g., questions).

When Blount (1969, 1972a, 1975) collected language acquisition data from the Luo in Kenya, he found that Luo children are encouraged to stay near adults, and to be silent in front of strangers. Children are not allowed to participate in adult social gatherings, except to greet and then to retreat. In addition, there is a marked separation of child and adult activities that is reinforced by language behavior. For a Luo boy, the primary source of interaction with adults comes at mealtimes, where he is expected to eat in silence while his father uses the context to apply behavioral sanctions to his sons.

Ochs (1982) described aspects of language socialization in a traditional Western Samoan village. In this highly stratified society, high status is correlated with age, generation, and title. Young children, growing up in large extended families, are considered to have the lowest status. When they interact with caregivers, the latter introduce and control the topics. Young language-learning children are neither expected nor encouraged to initiate topics of talk if the topic focuses on them. Although young Western Samoan children can and do orient speech to their mothers, the mothers do not respond directly to any of their requests. Instead, the children must wait for the mother to reallocate their requests to older sibling caregivers. Older children have the primary responsibility for daily household chores and child minding, but they need a push from above to carry out sibling requests. For example, when young children ask their mothers for food or services, the mothers turn to the older siblings and redirect the requests to them, creating in effect a triadic interaction. In time, young children learn to ask older siblings directly.

In all of the aforementioned cultures, it is primarily children who, as a reflection of their lower status, are expected to be silent in the presence of adults. Thus, in these cultures, the child's silence in adult-child interactions indicates that he is learning to act as a child. However, in other cultures, keeping silent—that is, learning when not to talk—might reflect learning that silence is valued for all members of the society. An example of such a culture is Apache. Being polite—especially in situations of uncertainty—requires being careful about what is said (Basso, 1972).

According to Fischer (1970), Japanese caregivers do not discourage speech in their children, but they are less likely than American mothers to talk with their children. However, Japanese mothers emphasize nonverbal communication more than do American mothers, and the former are more likely to anticipate their children's wants before the children verbalize their complaints. Similarly, the Japanese make more of an effort to soothe their children with physical, rather than verbal, contact (Caudill and Weinstein, 1970). Fischer suggested that Japanese mothers value silence because it helps maintain personal privacy in households where a large number of individuals live together.

Fischer (1970) also suggested that the hierarchical structure of Japanese culture creates a strict distinction between child and adult; and that this distinction "dictates" how a child is expected to talk and how others are expected to talk to him. Parents "condescend to enter the child's world as a regressive form of relaxation" (p. 115) and they view their children as "amusement" unrelated to the "serious" work of the day. When this viewpoint is combined with the belief that adult Japanese words are too difficult for young children to pronounce, the result is a favorable attitude toward baby-talk, which children are permitted to use well into the school years. Adults do not rapidly encourage children to "talk like adults," but instead allow them to use a special register to signify the continuation of their status as children. In addition, Fischer reported that, when talking to a child, adults often use the child's baby-talk words, thereby creating a feeling of intimacy with the child.

Philips (1982) stressed the importance of the visual rather than the auditory channel for all members of the Warm Springs Indian society. The way in which Warm Springs parents attempt to soothe their children suggests that this emphasis on the visual channel is present from birth. Philips pointed out that Warm Springs parents create a soothing environment for a child by covering the infants' face to cut off the visual channel. White Anglo parents, on the other hand, attempt to soothe their infants by cutting off the auditory channel (i.e., keeping things quiet). In addition, when Warm Springs parents interact with children who are speaking, they use less verbal explanation and less elicitation than do white Anglo parents. Among members of the Warm Springs society, the most common form of speech to children is the imperative, which is used to elicit action responses. Comprehension is indicated through action rather than verbal response.

Chicano children also are taught the value of silence and its association with aloofness and self-restraint. Although teasing and laughter are an important part of interactions, there are times when interpersonal relations require the use of diplomacy and tact. In such cases, silence becomes the screen behind which an individual can preserve dignity and make the relationship appear harmonious (Murillo, 1976). Silence also is associated with thoughtful composure. Thus, the virtues of being silent, of listening carefully before speaking, and of hesitating before speaking are stressed (Coles, 1977).

One final example completes the point. In her study of Tamil baby-talk, Williamson (1979) pointed out that lower middle-class speakers of Malayasian Tamil (Malaysia) think of their young children as being inferior to adults. This inferior status is manifested in a number of ways. First, in the presence of visitors, children are expected to speak only upon request. Second, adult caregivers usually use the impolite imperative to direct the activities of their children. Finally, the inferior status of children is manifested in the Tamil pronominal system. Tamil adults use animate pronouns when referring to rational beings, and inanimate pronouns when referring to either irrational beings or to children who are not yet mature speaking members of the culture. Although they regard their children as inferior, Tamil mothers do imitate and expand their children's utterances; but, like Luo and Samoan parents, Tamil mothers do not regard their children as conversational partners. Williamson explicitly states that "Tamil children are socially more inferior than American children (at least in the context of conversations with visitors)" (p. 116).

In summary, the status of the child has many repercussions on the nature of verbal interactions between adults and children. For example, the degree to which children are expected to be seen and not heard depends to a great extent on the status of the child. In some cultures, silence is seen as the only appropriate behavior for someone who is deferent and respectful.

A number of researchers also have commented on how the distribution of sentence types spoken to children reflects the social hierarchy (Blount, 1972b; Williamson, 1979). In cultures where talk between adults and children is encouraged, children tend to hear many questions that are designed to elicit answers from them. On the other hand, when adults do not see children as active conversational partners, the language directed toward them tends to be directive. Under these conditions, the children must take a more active role in initiating and maintaining interactions.

However, there are two potential problems with these analyses. One is that, in the presence of a researcher, adults may attempt to demonstrate competence either by asking questions to elicit talk or by giving commands to evoke action. What adults and children do together when unobserved is sometimes difficult to determine. In addition, members of different societies vary in the degree to which they are able to carry on "as usual" while a researcher is present.

A second problem involves the analysis of sentence types. Without a description of the functions served by different sentence types, it is difficult to evaluate the quality of the interaction. (See de Villiers, this volume, for a discussion of "form-function mappings.")

Social Organization of Caregiving

Another important determinant of cultural variation in adult-child conversations is the social organization of caregiving—that is, who talks to small children, in what contexts, and about what topics. In most Western cultures, the primary caregiver is the mother or another adult (usually female); but in many other cultures, children are cared for primarily by child-nursemaids, or they spend the majority of their time in child peer groups (Weisner and Gallimore, 1977).

When the primary caregiver is the mother—as in many white middle-class American nuclear families—young children frequently spend much of their time in focused dyadic interactions with their mothers. However, in societies where children grow up in extended families or are taken care of primarily by older children, verbal exchanges and interactions may be structured differently. Several researchers have suggested that older children do not interact with a young child in the same way that adults do (Andersen and Johnson 1973; Blount, 1975; Gleason, 1973; Harkness, 1971; Sachs and Devin, 1976). Consequently, what a child learns in verbal interaction depends on the caregiver's age and relationship to the child.

One of the differences between adult-child and child-child interactions centers on the use of baby-talk. Blount (1972a) reported that older children speaking to younger children were less likely to use baby-talk features than were adults. Among the Luo, older children were more likely to insist that a child use actual Luo words rather than baby-talk. Sibling caregivers refused to imitate or respond to the babblings of children, but coaxed them to use recognizable words instead.

Harkness (1977) reported that Kipsigis mothers in Kenya seemed to be more effective language "trainers" than were preadolescent nursemaids. Adults encouraged more language "practice" by using more utterances in which the primary intent was to get the child to produce speech. Once the children became members of a peer group and were spending most of their time with other children of the same age, the children seemed to talk less and they were talked to less (Harkness and Super, 1977). The type of speech learned or used most frequently in peer groups also may differ from that used with adults. Different situations place different communicative demands on the child. In comparison to adult-child interaction, child-child interaction generally requires more reciprocity and places a greater responsibility for initiation and maintenance on each child (Blount, 1975).

Although child-child and child-adult speech may indeed be different, there is no evidence that children who spend most of their time in the company of peers and older children learn language more slowly. Instead, as Harkness (1977) has suggested, they may learn that there are optimum styles for different situations. While interacting with adults, children may learn that they are expected to answer; while interacting with other children, they may learn to share their observations or to play language games. These situational differences may even delineate contextual expectations for the child and guide his formation of appropriate sociolinguistic rules for interacting with different-status speakers.

In addition to the child's age/relationship to the primary caregiver and the type of routine activities that constitute the child's day, the number of individuals with whom the child regularly interacts varies across cultures and ethnic groups. Children who grow up in communities where most of their interactions are dyadic and consist of focused conversations with their mothers will learn different patterns of attention getting and turn taking than children who are raised in societies where most interactions are multiparty and the child is not the assumed focus.

For example, in the Southeastern Black community described by Heath (1982a), mothers and immediate neighbors rarely addressed children directly in an effort to bring them into the conversation. However, the children in this community were exposed to a wide variety of individuals other than the nuclear family unit and immediate neighbors. Friends and kin from other parts of the community frequently came and went. These visitors again would not attempt to bring the children into a conversation, but they would often tease the children, challenging them to particular feats. By 12 to 14 months, boys in the community were regularly approached by adults and expected to respond to verbal challenges. Thus, many of their earliest utterances were phrases rather than one-word labels for objects (Heath, 1983). In addition, the teases allowed the children to take on multiple roles within the "play" frame. They learned to "boss, cuss, beg, cuddle, comfort, tend, and fuss with their elders."

The frequent comings and goings of a wide variety of individuals also affected the structure of interactions in the Mexican-American homes described by Eisenberg (1982). The majority of conversations involving adults and children were triadic rather than dyadic. Rather than asking questions to initiate conversations between themselves and young children, caregivers would help children initiate and maintain conversations with a third individual. Using the expression *dile* ("say to him/her"), the adult would give the child a message to repeat to someone else. What the adults told the children to say reflected their beliefs concerning how different individuals should be addressed. When speaking to infants, children were taught to soothe and to get the infant's attention. When speaking to peers, they were taught to be assertive, to request politely, and to tease. Speech directed to adults emphasized politeness and the importance of responding to another person's utterances.

Even when questions were asked in seemingly dyadic formats (i.e., the adult asking and the child responding), the questions were often asked for the benefit of an observing audience. Adults asked known-information questions not just to test whether the child knew a particular piece of information, but to show other adults that the child was capable of answering (Eisenberg, 1982). Adults also asked specific questions because those questions were of the type that visitors might ask. Such questions sought information that visitors would expect children to know—e.g., "What's your name?", "Where's your Daddy?", and "What's your sister's name?" Questions frequently appeared in interactions with *dile* as well. Once an adult had told the child what to say, another adult could use the information in that utterance in order to ask the right questions. Two or more adults often cooperated to create conversations.

By 4 or 5 years of age the children had become quite adept at participating in conversations with multiple participants. They had learned to monitor conversations between two or more other speakers and to insert their own relevant comments at appropriate turn junctures. They were also able to manipulate the presence of an audience for the purpose of social control. In conversations with their peers they often appealed to a higher authority (i.e., an adult) for support in their assertions and demands. They also teased their friends, parents, and siblings by addressing comments about the victim of the tease to a third individual (e.g., "Laura's really crazy, isn't she, Mommy?"). Thus, like the Southeastern Black community described by Heath (1982a), the linguistic environment of these Mexican-American children was rich and children were exposed to a variety of styles, speakers, and topics.

In summary, both the quantity and the *quality* of verbal interaction must be taken into account in any analysis. Furthermore, whatever the social organization in a community, the young child is learning culturally specific patterns of both verbal and nonverbal interaction according to the norms of that society.

Folk Beliefs about How Children Learn Language

Cultures vary in the types of theories they have about how young children learn language and in how explicit they make those theories. They range from believing that children must be explicitly taught to speak by adults (Kaluli) to thinking that children will somehow learn by themselves (Kipsigis). Of course, there are also cultures in which there is not a single accepted or stated belief. In any case, the nature of the belief system has important consequences for how adult caregivers interact with their young language-learning children.

Much of the research on the language used by adults when speaking to children has focused on the language itself (Snow and Ferguson, 1977) rather than on the underlying beliefs and assumptions that motivate that behavior. In this section we point out how examining the effects of cultural beliefs on the ways in which adults speak to children might help us to understand behaviors that otherwise may look incomprehensible or misguided. It is important to keep in mind that beliefs about language acquisition are deeply rooted in and form part of a coherent cultural and symbolic system that relates to other facets of society (e.g., notions concerning the role of language, and of course the child's status in the society).

We start with the Kaluli of Papua New Guinea. The Kaluli folk theory of language acquisition explicitly states how children learn to talk. The consequences of this belief are evident in the structure of conversations between children and adults. When asked how they thought children learn language, Kaluli adults usually replied that children have to be "shown language" (*to widan*) by other Kaluli speakers, principally the mother. The Kaluli use no baby-talk lexicon with children because it is more important for children to hear "hard language" (*to halaido*) as spoken by adults. Language is considered to have begun once the child uses two critical words: *nɔ* ("mother") and *bo* ("breast"). Small children who use other words (the names of objects and animals) are not yet said to be using language if the two critical words are lacking. This essentially social view of language emphasizes not the learning and using of words per se but learning and using those words that express the first social relationship a person has. Clearly, the notion here is that language use is not merely a verbal skill. It is also a social skill pertaining to and part of relationships between people.

Once a child is identified as having language, his language is viewed as "soft." At this point in development, the mother (and older children) try to "harden" his language by "showing" the child what to say in a variety of situations. The form this takes is as follows: when the mother wants a child to speak she says the message followed by the word *ɛlɛma*, which is a contraction of two words—*ɛlɛ* ("like this/ that") and *sama* (present tense, singular, imperative "speak/say"), i.e., "say like this/that."

Caregivers use *ɛlɛma* in dyadic interactions to tell a child to say something back to them, and in triadic interactions to tell a child to say something to a third person. In both types of interactions *ɛlɛma* serves a variety of functions; however, several important and frequently occurring functions are served only by triadic uses of *ɛlɛma*. These are teasing, shaming, threatening, asserting, and challenging claims of ownership. Although mothers never ask the child to tease or shame the mother (in dyadic interactions), they frequently tell the child to engage in such interactions with other children and adults. These speech acts, which are recognized and named by the Kaluli, are felt to be important for the child to master as a way of verbally controlling other people (see Schieffelin, 1979, for further discussion).

Most of the cross-cultural literature cited thus far does not contain specific examples of child-adult conversation. In order to give the reader a better sense of how these Kaluli exchanges are initiated and maintained, a portion of a transcript is given below.[1]

> Mother, daughter named Binalia (5 years), and female niece named Mama (3½ years) are watching Wanu (26.3 months) play with a pen top. He drops it and it falls into a hole in the floor of the house. He tries to get it but can't.
>
> 1. Binalia → Mother/Mama: I can't get it.
> 2. Mother → Wanu →» Mama: Give (me) that, ɛlɛma.
>   3. give that/
> 4. Mama: Give! (mocking the way Mother says it)

---

[1] Transcription conventions follow Bloom and Lahey (1978). The child's speech is in the right column, and utterance boundaries are indicated with a slash (/). The speech of all other participants and contextual notes are in the left column. In sequences with *ɛlɛma*, a single arrow (→) indicates speaker → addressee. The double arrow (→») indicates to whom the child speaker is to talk—e.g., in line 2 Mother tells Wanu to speak to Mama. For the Kaluli examples, English translations provide the closest possible gloss to Kaluli, but should not be used to assess the linguistic development of the child. Morpheme by morpheme glosses are in Schieffelin (in press).

5. *Mother → Wanu →»*
   Mama: Mama! ɛlɛma.
6. *Mama:* Mɛmɛ. (again mocking Mother)
7. Mama/
8. *Mother → Wanu →» Mama:* Give!
9. give/
10. *Binalia → Mother:* Mama just took it.
11. *Mama → Mother:* Not me! Binalia took it!
12. *Binalia:* Mama took it!
13. *Mama:* Binalia took it! (neither has it)
14. *Mother → $\genfrac{}{}{0pt}{}{Binalia}{Mama}$:* Don't shout!
15. *Mother → Wanu →» Mama:* Give (me) that! (pointing to pen top in hole)
16. (look at) that! Mama/
17. *Mother → Wanu →» Mama:* Give mine back to me, ɛlɛma.
18. give mine back to me/

(Mama starts to reach into the hole to get it)
19. *Mama → Mother:* And how did it fall down?

In this sequence Wanu's mother (line 2) tells Wanu to ask his cousin (Mama) to give him the pen top. He repeats the lines provided by his mother. However, when his cousin mocks Mother, Mother tells Wanu to get his cousin's attention again (line 5) by calling her name. Mother then provides a model of what Wanu is to say (line 8) and Wanu again repeats the model (line 9). After some argument between Wanu's sister and cousin, Mother tells Wanu to request the pen top again (line 15). In this utterance, as in others, the *ɛlɛma* is not explicitly stated, but it is understood from the situation that Wanu is to repeat his mother's utterance. However, Wanu does not repeat the utterance; instead, he points to the pen top. When Mother again tries to instruct Wanu (line 17) in asking for the object, he complies and so does his cousin.

In this as in many other interactions, the mother provides a model of what the child should say, followed by the instruction to "say it." By explicitly telling children when to speak, what to say, and how to say it with the appropriate rhetorical force, mothers (and older sisters) help very young children learn to get what they think the children should want. Moreover, the use of *ɛlɛma* is not limited to requests. Mothers also use *ɛlɛma* discourse routines to show children how to offer, shame, assert, challenge, tease, and threaten. Thus, young children (ages 22–40 months) are always supported and encouraged to be active participants in interactions with others.

Williamson (1979) reported that Tamil-speaking mothers say that their "children cannot learn language without the presence of family and language speakers in the environment" (p. 163). She observed Tamil caregivers trying to teach their children words by engaging the children in routines that involved labeling individuals and objects. The child was to repeat the labels after the caregiver. However, the frequency of triadic routines similar to those of the Kaluli is not clear from Williamson's report.

Blount (1972a, 1975) documented the fact that Luo caregivers say that it is necessary to teach children important lexical items. Many of the interactions between young children and their child-nursemaids focus on naming and labeling, with the child repeating what the nursemaid says. The first lexical items focused on are caregivers' names, followed by a general term to express want/need, and finally water, basic foods, names of other family members, household objects, and words for basic activities such as eating and drinking. The motivation for "teaching" these specific words is to enable children to express their needs more clearly and to participate more actively in household routines. Blount further noted that, once a Luo child begins to produce recognizable words, caregivers will no longer tolerate baby-talk and babbling, but will respond only to actual Luo words used by the child. Although Kaluli, Tamil, and Luo people all say that language must be taught, their notions of what constitutes "language" and how to organize the teaching vary in both elaboration and execution. For example, the Kaluli do not have a baby-talk lexicon, but the Luo do.

In contrast to cultures that assume that children must be taught to use language, the Kipsigis people say that children learn to talk on their own soon enough, but that they must be taught to *understand* requests and commands (Harkness and Super, 1977). As a result, commands and prohibitions are the most commonly used speech forms directed to young children.

According to Gleason and Weintraub (1975), middle-class American mothers concentrate on teaching (by explicit means) their children such routines as "say bye-bye" and "say thank-you." In addition, they also engage in fairly long and frequent sequences of "direct instruction" on cultural material. These sequences involve naming, labeling, talking about storybooks, discussing past events, and so on.

Miller (1982) studied three working-class mothers from South Baltimore, and found that they held similar beliefs about how children learn to talk. They all felt that children learn to talk by listening to those around them, but they also felt that children have to be taught to be polite, and to avoid using curse words. In addition, all of the mothers engaged their children in interactions involving displays of cultural material: reciting names, addresses, and nursery rhymes, naming body parts and family members, and looking at and talking about picture books. Finally, it appears that adults in both middle- and working-class American families often solicit information about their children's internal states, and generally treat children as interactional and conversational equals (Blount, 1975; Ochs and Schieffelin, in press; Wooton, 1974).

Many other beliefs can affect the language that children hear as well as the language they are permitted or encouraged to use. Beliefs can also affect whether adults respond to children, as well as when and how they respond to them. For example, Stross (1970) described a Tzeltal-speaking community in Mexico in which children's speech was almost always responded to because of the belief that the state of the child's soul is directly influenced by a parental response or the lack of one.

It must be stressed that these beliefs relate to a wider set of cultural assumptions and are embedded in everyday activities. It is also important to remember that any cultural differences exist along a continuum, rather than as dichotomous possibilities. As Wells (1979) has argued, societal variability cannot be reduced to an opposition between two monolithic classes because the variations that exist within a class cannot be ignored (as has commonly been done in discussions about social class differences in language use). Second, cultural practices might vary in regard to one norm, but not in regard to another. Finally, different beliefs or processes may still result in similar outcomes (see the discussion on the role of silence).

Although all cultural groups contain some variability, they do not all contain the same amount. Certain groups contain more variability than others. These differences in variability are important because it is easier to isolate and compare homogeneous cultural groups (such as the Kaluli and the Luo) than heterogeneous ones. Comparative studies conducted in urban contexts often run into problems because the variability is so great that it is difficult to delineate ethnic or cultural groups. Nowhere is this more evident than in those studies in which lower-class families and minorities in the United States are compared to what is commonly thought of as the homogeneous white middle class. Bee et al. (1969) found that, in comparison to middle-class mothers, lower-class mothers (in a laboratory setting) gave fewer elicitations and less explicit directions to their children. However, Miller (1982) found a high percentage of "direct instruction" in lower-class families, and this figure was quite similar to what is found in middle-class homes. Finally, this variability is not restricted to white Americans; Black Americans also are not a homogeneous group in their language use. Interactions of rural Louisiana Blacks (Ward, 1971) differ considerably from the interactions of both urban Blacks (Blount, 1975; Horner and Gussow, 1972) and the Appalachian Black families described by Heath (1983).

Research Questions

In the preceding sections, we discussed a variety of issues that one might keep in mind when considering cross-cultural data.[2] Many of the issues discussed thus far concern the frequency and meaning of various kinds of adult-child interactions. Relevant research questions often take the form: *How often* does interaction X occur? Other issues already discussed concern the roles played by each individual engaged in the interaction. Relevant questions here are often phrased as: *Who* performs behavior X during an interaction? Questions pertaining to *how often* and *who* are important, but so are questions concerning *how* participants achieve their respective objectives. Here researchers are interested not only in how participants take/relinquish a speaking turn, but also in how participants perform behavior X during a turn. Thus, there are four types of questions: 1) *How often does interaction X occur?*; 2) *Who performs behavior X during an interaction?*; 3) *How is turn taking accomplished?*; and 4) *How do participants perform behavior X during a turn?* It should be obvious that each of the four questions encompasses a variety of more specific questions. To illustrate the range of questions that might be investigated to promote a better understanding of cultural variation in conversation, we now list some representative *how often, who,* and *how* questions.

How often does interaction X occur? One obvious difference across societies is in the amount of verbal interaction that occurs between adults and children. Consequently, researchers often ask questions such as: How frequently do adult-child interactions occur? Do children interact more frequently with peers and older siblings than they do with adults? What proportion of the total number of interactions are verbal? How often does interaction without talk occur? Is physical proximity without talk usually a comfortable situation for all participants?

---

[2] These research questions are meant to be suggestive, not definitive or prescriptive. When doing ethnographic research, one must proceed inductively and develop research questions that grow out of the investigation. Additionally, the research questions that evolve should be relevant and meaningful to the participants under study.

When children and adults interact with each other, how many people are involved in the interactions? Do most of these interactions involve two people? Three people? Multiple parties? Do peer interactions usually involve more participants than adult-child interactions?

Related questions concern the length and scope of the conversations. How long do adult-child interactions last? Are peer interactions usually longer than adult-child interactions? Is the talk focused (e.g., on getting chores done), or do participants often engage in extended arguments and discussions?

How often do caregivers and children "make conversation" or engage in "talk for talk's sake?" When caregivers and children "make conversation," do more test questions appear than when the interactions are focused on achieving a specific objective? How often do true questions appear in comparison to test questions? How often are questions answered? How often do directives appear? Jokes?

The need to "make conversation" may also result in an unusually high incidence of labeling routines. Labeling objects or pictures in story books is a common pastime with working and middle-class Americans (Miller, 1982; Ninio and Bruner, 1978). In contrast, the Kaluli traditionally have no books and do not engage in literacy-related activities. Indeed, the Kaluli say that naming objects is talk "to no purpose." These findings demonstrate the importance of considering the relationships between the frequency of various behaviors and the folk beliefs held by members of the cultures under study. Questions concerning how folk beliefs might affect the incidence of a behavior should be asked in any study of cultural differences.

Who performs behavior X during an interaction? The second general type of question concerns the roles played by each participant in an interaction. Who is expected to do the talking, and who the listening? Are children expected to speak frequently, or are they expected to be silent and listen? How does the amount of speech produced by a participant vary: 1) with the number and status of other participants in the interaction, and 2) with the setting and purpose of the interaction?

A related issue concerns the initiation and maintenance of a conversation. Who is expected to initiate a conversation? Are children encouraged to maintain a conversation once it has begun? Answers to these questions may depend on the child's social role in an interaction. When children are expected to maintain subordinate roles, all topic initiation and maintenance may come from the dominant adult. Or, as in the case of the Athabaskan Indians described by Scollon and Scollon (1981b), children may initiate talk, but then are expected to leave the responsibility for topic maintenance to the interactive partner.

Finally, researchers interested in the roles played by various participants in an interaction have asked questions concerning the types of speech acts performed by each participant. Examples include: Who issues directives? Who does the joking and teasing? Do adults threaten children? Are children encouraged to threaten other children? Do adults ask true questions? Test questions? Do adults respond to children's questions?

How is turn taking accomplished? In order to initiate a conversation, one party must secure the attention of the other; and if both parties are expected to maintain the conversation, then some type of turn taking must occur. How is attention secured and turn taking accomplished? How do the means for securing the attention of a listener vary with the number and status of the participants in an interaction? Do low-status individuals initiate conversation only when a dominant partner signals that it is alright to do so? Can low-status individuals interrupt people with higher status? Is there much speaker overlap or do prospective speakers wait until their partners are finished speaking?

How do participants perform behavior X during a turn? The last broad question pertains to the form of a participant's interactive behavior. For example, if adults do respond to the utterances of children, how complex are the responses? Are the responses minimal, or do adults freely expand children's utterances? Are the topics of their utterances contingent upon the child's utterance?

Another domain often investigated is the use of politeness and the directness-indirectness continuum in speech. Request forms in many societies vary along a continuum of politeness. Being too direct carries with it the chance of being considered rude and socially inept; being overly indirect carries with it the risk of being misunderstood, and not getting what one wishes. All children must learn how and when to be direct as well as how and when to be indirect to achieve an objective in their own communities. A number of studies have focused on children's knowledge of this continuum (e.g., Ervin-Tripp and Mitchell-Kernan, 1977; Gordon and Ervin-Tripp, this volume) in order to answer such questions as: In what situations do children in a particular community use direct forms? When do they use indirect forms? When do they learn to match forms to situations? How do they learn when to use what form?

The reactions of others to the request forms a child uses can help the child learn what forms to use in subsequent interactions.

Hawaiian children quickly learn that they "risk a slap" if they repeat requests with increasing emphasis. Consequently, the repetitions of young children usually show decreased urgency (Boggs, 1976). In contrast, Hungarian parents appear to value an individual's manipulation of others. They train their children to engage in manipulative strategies, and the children tend to intensify successive requests (Hollos and Beeman, 1975).

According to Hollos and Beeman (1978), Hungarian children have a wide array of lexical and nonlexical forms and routines for issuing directives. Some of these devices are used with family members, whereas others are used with outsiders. Norwegian children, on the other hand, have no special linguistic devices for dealing with outsiders. In fact, they prefer *not* to issue directives at all to outsiders. Hollos (1970) pointed out that Norwegian children do not need to be able to make requests of outsiders because the general mode of indirectness—even among adults—leads to the use of a "middleman" in such interactions.

Finally, researchers interested in the form of an interaction need to consider not only its verbal characteristics, but also its nonverbal ones. Nonverbal behaviors, like verbal behaviors, vary cross-culturally. Gaze direction, for example, may have different uses and "meanings" in different cultures. Consequently, researchers need to consider the culture when analyzing the implications of a particular gaze direction. Research questions on this topic include: Where do members of a particular culture look when speaking? listening? Where do members of a particular culture look when issuing directives? questions? jokes? What gaze direction is associated with deceit? threats? How does the direction of gaze vary with the status of the participants?

When norms associated with gaze direction are violated, or when the participants in an interaction are members of different cultures and adhere to different norms, the results can be serious. Byers and Byers (1972) illustrated the problems that can occur when participants in cross-ethnic encounters have different gaze patterns. In their study of white and Black 4-year-olds, Byers and Byers found that the white children were more successful than the Black children in securing the attention of their white teacher. Consequently, they were better able to establish communication with her. The gaze behavior of the white children was timed to mesh with the adult's. When the white teacher looked at the class, the white children looked back; but the Black children often looked away. These differences in gaze patterns stem from different attitudes toward the meaning of looking directly at someone. For example, white children learn that if they do not look at the person speaking to them when they are being chastized, they will be accused of not paying attention or being disrespectful. Among Puerto Ricans and Africans, however, a person who does not look down when being chastized is seen as challenging, disrespectful, or arrogant (Byers and Byers, 1972).

Gazing behavior has special significance for Mexican-Americans (Coles, 1977). Eye-to-eye contact is important, and very young children are often held up so that they can look adults in the eye and thereby become their "equals." When adults reprimand or advise children, they often follow their verbal remarks with a stare that the child is supposed to reciprocate. Sometimes words are not even necessary because a scowl, frown, or touch often has the same effect as a verbal command. Children "ask with their eyes" to be excused from the table. Much emphasis is placed on the eyes, and parents report being able to determine what their children are feeling by looking at their eyes and faces.

As we have seen, a number of interrelated cultural and social factors affect the structure of adult-child conversations. Consequently, cultural considerations must be taken into account when describing contexts of language acquisition and the child's developing communicative competence.

REFERRING TO EVENTS IN THE PAST

In many white middle-class families, conversations between young children and adults are organized around shared past experiences. When a caregiver and child share the same experience, the caregiver has an "inside line" on what has happened and is better able to interpret and expand the young child's less-than-explicit utterances (see Snow's example, p. 84, this volume). Retelling these experiences is an important interactional context in which the caregiver can assist, prompt, and support the young child in his reconstruction of the past event, thereby facilitating the child's participation in conversation.

As children begin to engage in activities without their caregivers, they again may be asked to recount the events of the day; as they get older, children may even volunteer to report on daily events and activities that the adult has not shared. These recountings of past experiences, like earlier recountings of shared experiences, are encouraged and supported. Such discourses form an important context for the development of communicative skills in the literate white middle-class society of the United States.

In this section we review research on the emergence of the past tense and of talk about the past. Factors that may affect the success of a young child's recounting of a past experience also are discussed.

Since our ultimate intent is to analyze cultural variation in children's conversations, and the research reviewed here focuses on white middle-class society, we next examine the extent to which talking about immediate and distant past events takes place in other societies. As an example, we examine conversational data from the Kaluli of Papua New Guinea. We compare the way in which past experiences are recounted by the Kaluli to the way in which they are recounted in white middle-class society as represented by a sample from Northern California. Similarities and differences in the ways these conversations are organized and carried out are sought, as are the underlying cultural reasons for these similarities and differences.

Talk about the Past in White Middle-Class Society

Most studies of the young child's knowledge about the past tense have focused on his ability to either: 1) produce appropriate grammatical markers (Antinucci and Miller, 1976; Bloom, Lifter, and Hafitz, 1980; Bronckart and Sinclair, 1973; de Lemos, 1981; Smith, 1979); or 2) comprehend differences between tense and/or aspectual markers (Bronckart and Sinclair, 1973; Harner, 1976; Herriot, 1969). The results of such studies indicate that children first use past tense markers to encode immediately past, completive, state-changing events. The use of these markers is later extended to include any event occurring prior to speech.

Although such studies do not address questions concerning *what* past events young children talk about and how such talk gets accomplished, preliminary answers to some of these questions are available from Sachs' research (1977, 1979a). Sachs focused on the *intent* to talk about past events, rather than on the actual use of past tense morphemes. She analyzed her interactions with her daughter when the daughter was between 15 and 36 months old to determine how references to past events emerged as topics of conversation. The child talked about nonpresent objects at 15 months, and the endpoints of completed events at 22 months. At 27 months, she began using the *-ed* marker for both completive and earlier past events, but her discussions of the latter were still constrained by the limited temporal framework of the current day's activities. By 32 months, there was an increasing reference to past experiences (as well as to future plans) and the child began relating her current perceptions to previous events.

Both Sachs (1977, 1979a) and Stoel-Gammon and Cabral (1977) identified a number of features characteristic of young children's conversations about earlier past events. First, unlike adult retellings, which are generally monologues, young children talk about past events in dialogues. Much of such talk is accomplished with the aid of adult support through prompts and questions. Sachs' daughter initially recounted earlier past experiences as responses to her mother. In other words, although the child did not initiate discussions of past events herself, she did respond to her mother's initiatives. However, her earliest responses were usually imitative or unrelated to her mother's comments.

A second feature was that the adult had prior knowledge of the event being discussed. In fact, when the setting provided no extralinguistic cues that would enable the adult to ask necessary questions concerning the child's topic, the adult's prior knowledge of the event was the single most important determinant of successful communication. The need for prior knowledge has also been pointed out by Snow (1978):

> Mother in kitchen. Experimenter (CS) and Meredith (18 months) in living room.
> Meredith: Bandaid.
> CS: Where's your bandaid?
> Meredith: Bandaid.
> CS: Do you have a bandaid?
> Meredith: Bandaid.
> CS: Did you fall down and hurt yourself?
> Mother enters.
> Meredith: Bandaid.
> Mother: Who gave you the bandaid?
> Meredith: Nurse.
> Mother: Where did she put it?
> Meredith: Arm.
> Meredith and her mother continued an extensive and complicated conversation about their shared visit to the doctor's office for several more turns. It is important to note that Meredith and her mother had shared more than just the visit; they had also shared the experience of discussing the visit, with the result that the mother knew what kinds of questions Meredith could answer and Meredith knew what kinds of questions her mother was likely to ask. (pp. 254–255)

Another important determinant of success in referring to past events was the child's current interest in the event being described. Furthermore, in interactions that are not primarily dyadic, the role of other participants may contribute to the success of the exchange.

A Comparative Study

A number of important questions remain to be asked. First, what are appropriate topics and uses of the past tense in dialogues? Second, who (adult and/or child) initiates and maintains conversations about past events? Third, what linguistic forms are used by the child and the adult for initiation and maintenance? Finally, how do children and adults in non-Western, nonliterate, traditional cultures, such as the Kaluli, talk about events that occurred in the past? In this section, we hope to provide some answers to these questions.

Data Base The data reported here were collected from four English-speaking children and three Kaluli-speaking children. A brief description of these subjects and the contexts in which the data were collected is given. Afterward, we discuss our focus in comparing these data.

English-speaking Children The data from the English-speaking sample come from a large study of interactions in three white middle-class families (Susan Ervin-Tripp, principal investigator). The four target children (three girls and one boy, ages 23–33 months at the beginning of the study) were all later-borns. The children were recorded interacting with their siblings as well as with adults. Each family was videotaped at home for 1 to 2 hours during each month of the study. Data collection continued for 6 months for one family and a year for the other two.

The major caregiver in these families was the mother, but fathers were present in at least two of the samples. The target children were generally the focus of the interactions in which they participated. The mother was usually present during taping and only occasionally left to read a book, bathe a baby, or make a meal. The videotapes documented everyday activities—mealtimes, playing with toys, pretend play, and reading or talking about story books. Discussions about past events were most likely to occur: 1) when a child's older sibling was not present; or 2) when the children were all seated at the table, eating a meal, and the mother addressed questions to each of them in turn. Thus, conversations about past events were essentially dialogic with the adult initiating the topic.

Kaluli-speaking Children The data on the Kaluli children are drawn from an ethnographic study on the development of communicative competence (Schieffelin, in press). The Kaluli (population 1200) are a traditional nonliterate people who live in the tropical forest in the Southern Highlands of Papua New Guinea (Feld, 1982; Schieffelin, 1976). Except for a few of the younger men, the Kaluli are monolingual speakers of the (NonAustronesian) Kaluli language. Like other societies in Papua, reciprocity and exchange underlie the daily organization of community and small scale events. Kaluli society is highly egalitarian, and does not have chiefs, or the "Big Men" typical of the Highland societies.

Children under the age of 3 are taken care of primarily by their mothers. As they get older and begin to play in the village, the children often are under the watchful eye of older girls. Because of the small size of the villages (60–100 individuals) and the familiarity within it, children interact with many people of various ages and relationships to them.

Three children (one girl, two boys) who were just beginning to use syntax were the focus of the study. The spontaneous verbal interactions of each child in and around his home were audiotaped for 3–4 hours at monthly intervals for one year. Children were recorded during their everyday conversations with familiar people. It was assumed that this would be the most natural situation for the children, and that it would facilitate observing and recording them in the recurring social situations in which they learn language. Contextual notes were taken that described the ongoing behavior that accompanied the speech (see Schieffelin, 1979, for details of the ethnographic methodology used in the study).

Like the English-speaking children, the Kaluli children in this study were not singletons. Therefore, other children were often present during taping; siblings and cousins competed for the floor as well as the mother's attention. The language sampled in these Kaluli tapes reflects a variety of different types of speech events—extended play sequences, negotiations about who will perform chores or have access to food and other objects, and so forth. However, unlike the English-speaking children, the Kaluli have no toys or story books, and only a few objects (sticks, knives, fishing traps, food) held their attention over time. The majority of talk was about food, other people, and the activities in which people were involved.

Focus In the discussion that follows, we focus on aspects of conversation that show culturally significant differences in the two societies. In some instances, variation is in terms of degree; in others, the phenomenon is totally absent in one cultural context but highly elaborated in the other. In addition, the meaning of a particular linguistic form in one cultural context will not necessarily be the same in another. What we wish to emphasize in the discussion that follows is that there is variation in the structure of conversation as a result of the culture in which the language is used. Furthermore, culturally specific ways of speaking are evident in the earliest everyday exchanges of young children.

At this point in our analysis, we do not wish to present quantitative descriptions of the data. There are many reasons for this decision. For one, it is very difficult to make adequate quantitative comparisons across or within culture samples because of the inherent variability of naturalistic data. It is not clear at this point what such comparisons would mean. More important than the quantity of references to past events in any given sample are the *ways* in which such references are organized in conversation and help organize conversation. We are still at the stage where we need culturally contextualized descriptions of naturalistic interaction in different societies. Only when these are available can we identify many of the features that are relevant to the organization of conversation. This is an initial attempt in that direction.

Topics from Past Experience and Their Management In the discussion that follows, we examine four kinds of past events. The first kind is the shared experience—that is, an event in which both the adult and the child have participated. One way to initiate conversation about a shared experience is to ask a question, in particular "*Do you* remember . . . ?" An example of this type of question is "Do you remember what was out there?" An important aspect of such questions is that the questioner already knows the answer to the question.

A second type of question is one in which the questioner is actually seeking information that he does not know. Interactions of this sort sometimes concern the giving and taking of objects, and might begin with a question such as "Who gave it to you?" Both of these types of questions, when they appear in conversations with young children, tend to be asked by adults. However, children also may ask questions about past events. For example, they may ask for information pertaining to individuals' comings and goings with a question like "Where did my father go?"

Finally, not all discussions about past events are initiated with questions; children frequently initiate such conversations with declarative comments. Moreover, not all conversations about the past concern an event from the distant past; an event in the immediate past might also be noteworthy. For example, finding a lost block might be of sufficient importance to a child that he might attempt to initiate conversation with a statement such as "I found my blue block."

The remainder of this chapter concerns conversations about past events that are initiated in these four ways. In an effort to uncover cultural differences and similarities in regard to the management of conversations about past events, we ask whether and how English-speaking and Kaluli-speaking children and adults use these different forms.

"Do You Remember What Was Out There?" In the English speaking families, one of the most striking features of adult-child discussions of past events was the focus on *shared* experiences. In other words, adults often asked children to talk about events already familiar to the addressee. The most common way of initiating such discussions was to ask a direct question either about something that had happened in

the past or about the act of remembering itself:

> Child named Amy (30 months) is looking out a window.
> *Mother:* What cha see out the window, Amy?
>
> I 'n't know/
>
> *Mother:* You don't know?
>
> No/
>
> *Mother:* What was there the other day when Mommy tried to take a picture with the camera?... What was out there?... Do you remember?
> (whispers)
>
> Yeah/
>
> *Mother:* What?
> (Amy shakes head no)
> *Mother:* Remember the deer that were out there? And we tried to take a picture, but they got away too fast, didn't they. *Three* deer.
> *Brother:* (calls from bathroom) Who got away too fast? (x)
> *Mother:* Well, I was talking about the other day when I got—tried to get the picture of them, but they left.
>
> A deer/
>
> *Mother:* A deer.
>
> A deer came/
>
> *Mother:* Yes.

In this example, the mother reconstructs the entire event for the child, stressing all of the relevant points to be remembered—the deer (*three* of them) outside the window, her trying to take a picture, etc. The child may not actually remember any of the events, but, as her mother talks about them, they become real enough to her that she is able to construct a novel utterance about them.

Adults provide children with a large amount of positive feedback for attempting to talk about their experiences and their abilities to remember. Having a "good memory" receives a great deal of positive comment. For example,

> Mother, Amy (now 34 months), and older brother (4 years) have been discussing a woodpecker that frightened Amy when her parents were away on a vacation. Amy abruptly switches to another past event.
>
> and Daddy take the mouse down to the street and let him go/

Mother: And Daddy took the mouse down to the street and let him go. You've got a *very* good memory, Amy. That didn't happen but about a year ago.

Although adults often initiate and evoke conversations about some shared past experience, many of these conversations are not lengthy, either because the children cannot remember the event or because they are just not interested in participating in such discussions at that moment. However, some conversations about shared past experiences *are* quite long and extend over a number of exchanges. These conversations often are initiated by the child commenting on an experience known to the adult. Once the child indicates his interest by initiating the topic, the adult can extend and maintain the topic with elicitations and prompts:

Child (32 months) has been describing a doll's trip to the zoo when she changes the topic to include her own trip.

                                                    I jus' go that zoo once/
                                                    I jus' go that zoo once/
                                                    bu' I did, Mommy/

Mother: Yes, you did.

                                                    yeah/

Mother: Who else went?

                                                  um-no-not-nobody/

Mother: You went all alone?

                                                  yeah/ you and Tommy
                                                  and me/ and Daddy/

Mother: Mm. Anybody else?

                                                  don—nobody/ else/
                                                  jus' Mommy 'n' you
                                                  an' Daddy/

Mother: Mm, and what did we see at the zoo?

                                                  jus' see the e'phants,
                                                  Mommy/

Episode continues.

In this case, the child initiated the discussion. However once again, the mother helped the child reconstruct the event being discussed. Her questions not only prompted the child to recall the structure of the event, but they also provided one possible outline for telling the story. When engaged in such interactions, adults usually focus their questions on the most important elements of the text, most often who (agent) and what (action). However, adults occasionally do ask where and when, and not infrequently they ask the child for his reaction to an event (e.g., "Was it good?" when the child has mentioned having hamburgers and root beer at A&W). Without such questions, young children almost never provide more than one or two elements of a story; and only rarely (even in the later samples) do they provide more information than is explicitly requested. It is interesting to note that mothers often ask questions to which they know the answer, but children never do so in the context of remembering past events.

Remembering events in the past is a very powerful and significant aspect of ritual life for Kaluli adults. The Kaluli have elaborate poems and songs that use particular images to evoke memories of past events (Feld, 1982; Schieffelin, 1976). However, remembering and talking about shared past events is not part of the repertoire of conversational topics of Kaluli mothers and children. Moreover, events from the day also are not topic worthy because a child's day is usually predictable, routine, and amazingly like every other day (a few exceptions are discussed below). Since caregivers do not "make talk," the creation of texts about shared or everyday events in the past is usually not part of the Kaluli child's language experience. Mothers do not ask children to remember such events because there is no point in doing so according to the Kaluli.

"Who Gave It to You?" Kaluli mothers do pose questions to their children, but these questions do not function in the same way as many of the questions asked by American mothers of their young children. The most outstanding difference is that Kaluli mothers rarely ask their children test questions in order to make conversation or to display the child's knowledge to someone else. For the Kaluli, there would be no point in asking such questions since adults do not talk to children "to no purpose." Thus, the common pedagogical question that forms the basis for so many conversations in white middle-class mother-child dyads is simply nonexistent and indeed irrelevant to the Kaluli ways of speaking.

Although Kaluli mothers do not ask test questions, they do ask two other types of questions: one is rhetorical in nature and calls for no answer, and the second seeks information. Rhetorical questions are directed to children from the time they are very young as a way of controlling their behavior. Mothers use these questions to call the child's attention to an action or utterance that the mother considers inappropriate. For example, if a young child starts to take an object that is not his or hers, the mother will ask, "Who gave it to you?!" meaning, "No one gave it to you—it's not yours to take!" The purpose of this question is to confront and shame the child, who may in fact already know that the object is not available for the taking. If the child does not know this, he or she is duly informed by the very asking of the rhetorical question.

Rhetorical questions in dialogue do not lead to exchanges because the addressee cannot answer without feeling shame. In contrast to a negative imperative such as "Don't take that!", rhetorical questions have the interactional effect of giving the next turn to the addressee, who in fact cannot take it without feeling shame. On the other hand, foregoing one's turn is to admit the wrongdoing. By placing children in this bind, rhetorical questions become a powerful linguistic device for social control.

The second type of question—the information-seeking question—is conveyed by the linguistic form used for rhetorical questions, but a different intonational contour. Information-seeking questions are somewhat limited in scope since Kaluli mothers spend very little time away from their young children. As already mentioned, there is no elicited or expected retelling of the events of the day. In addition, mothers do not take more than a casual interest in the child's telling of any activity unless there is a reason for the recounting. However, mothers will inquire about a child's toileting activity because they are responsible for cleaning up after the child. They also will ask a child if he is ill. Furthermore, as shown below, mothers often ask questions to obtain information about the location of persons other than the addressee. In other words, mothers expect a child to know where other family members have gone, and they will ask if they do not know.

Another frequent information-seeking question that parents and older siblings ask young children is: "Who gave it to you?" Among the Kaluli, the giving and receiving of food and objects contributes to the development of relationships. As an information-seeking question, "Who gave it to you?" calls attention to the giver, not to the object, which is usually in plain sight. The question occurs frequently because parents like to: 1) know who has given something to a child; and 2) call a child's attention to the fact that it is important to be aware of a giver. When others ask "Who gave . . . ?", children are instructed through *ɛlɛma* sequences to provide the name and to say it correctly. In addition, when seeing food or an object it is appropriate for the owner to name the person "who gave." It is the giver that is the focus of talk, not the object or its qualities. These exchanges are limited in duration, often only 2–4 turns in length, except, of course, if clarification is necessary.

> Mɛli (age 27.3 months) is with her mother, who has just come back from another part of the house. Mɛli is playing with a rubber sandal.
> *Mother:* Who gave (it)?
> Bambi gave (it)/

Mother: Gave to you?

gave to me/

Both rhetorical and information-seeking questions are used to refer to past events; and children are actively taught how to respond to these questions as well as how to use such questions themselves to initiate conversations. The most common information-seeking questions that refer to past events are *who* and *where* questions. These questions are used by both adults and children. *Why* and *when* questions are rarely part of a dialogue between mothers and children under 4 years of age.

The Northern California families offer a striking contrast to the above Kaluli material. The parents of the California children occasionally asked questions about past events when they did *not* know the answers, but such questions were not nearly as frequent as test questions. The California parents primarily asked questions about past events when they already knew the answers. Indeed, in many cases, they actually had participated in the events with their children. Moreover, when the adults elicited information about events in which they had not participated, such events tended to be similar to events in which they had participated (e.g., trips to the museum or to a friend's house). Thus, they again were likely to have some ideas about possible answers to their questions. Occasionally, however, adults did ask questions concerning events that were totally unfamiliar to them. These rarely led to topic elaboration because the adults often did not know enough about the events to ask the "right questions" (see Snow's example, p. 85, this volume).

California children were similar to their parents in that they rarely initiated discussions about past events in which the adult had not participated. When they did, the adults often requested clarification from the young child's older sibling who had participated in the activity. However, when a knowledgeable sibling was not available, the adults had difficulty identifying the referents involved. An added complication is that young children do not use expressions such as "remember when" to mark the fact that they want the addressee to locate something in memory (see Keenan and Schieffelin, 1976). In any case, on those rare occasions in which the children talked about events that were unfamiliar to adults, the adults often had great difficulty simply establishing the topic of conversation. Consequently, the adults usually were unable (or unwilling) to elicit topic elaborations in order to sustain the conversation.

"Where Did My Father Go?" A large proportion of Kaluli child-initiated utterances about immediate or distant past events concern the locations or the comings and goings of individuals in the village. Children become aware at an early age (from adult conversation around

them) that comings and goings are topic worthy. They also learn to pay attention to how people respond to questions about where others have gone. Through direct instruction (with *elɛma*) they learn to use the names of different garden, water, and forest sites to refer to specific places (e.g., "at the spring of the Sulu stream"). For the Kaluli, place names are extremely important and carry a great deal of cultural information. They are used as reference points for various activities that involve specific people at a particular point in time. One recalls events to mind primarily through the use of place names in the tropical forest (Feld, 1982; Schieffelin, 1979).

In responding to children's questions such as "Where did my father go?", caregivers provide ground names to help familiarize the child with the land that belongs to his or her family. Often the child is encouraged to repeat the name followed by the caregiver's acknowledgment. These place names become more significant as the child gets older; familiarity with them is crucial. The act of asking about one person's whereabouts often leads to an elaborate sequence in which the child asks about the location of other family members and the adult supplies the appropriate ground names. Kaluli are not concerned with whether their children can name objects, but they are concerned about the children knowing the names of places.

The English-speaking children asked true information-seeking questions about past events, but such questions constituted only a very small proportion of the utterances that contained a past tense verb. These children never elicited information about other individuals' past experiences. However, one child asked who started the fire that her older brother was talking about (from a description of a drawing). The few questions that the English-speaking children did ask concerned where someone had gone (after just leaving a room), whether someone had found a missing object, and what had happened to broken objects. Children's information-seeking questions about past events were almost always responded to, but such discussions were never extended beyond one exchange.

"I Found My Blue Block" The majority of the English-speaking children's references to past events were in child-initiated sequences in which the form of the initiation was a declarative ("I found my blue block"), and the event of interest had either just occurred or its consequence was still evident in the context. In general, the child's utterance drew the adult's attention to an activity in which the child was engaged or had at least observed. The most frequently mentioned actions were associated with a child's finding or acting on an object, but children also called attention to their own injuries ("I hurt myself")

as well as to the mishaps of other individuals or objects ("The chair fell, Mommy").

The ways in which the English-speaking children talked about immediate past events were not radically different from their talk about more distant events. As previously mentioned, most initiations were declaratives and the children rarely used more than one past tense verb in referring to an event.

The greatest difference between discussions focusing on immediate past events and those focusing on more distant past events was the way in which adults responded to the children's initiations. Declarative utterances that referred to immediate events were much less likely to receive a response than those that referred to distant events. Almost all declarative utterances concerning distant past events evoked a response. On the other hand, to get a response to an utterance concerning an immediate past event, children often had to repeat the utterance a number of times.

Moreover, when the adults did respond to utterances concerning immediate past events, the *form* of the responses differed from responses to statements about more distant past events. Adults never elicited additional information when children talked about the immediate past, and exchanges on the topic were short-lived. The most common response was a repetition or expansion of the child's utterance. These responses often were uttered with a rising intonation and sometimes were phrased as tag questions. An acknowledgment (e.g., "yeah" or "uh-huh") usually preceded the repetition or expansion. Such conversations might consist of two or three exchanges with the child "confirming" the adult's repetition of the initial utterance:

Child (28 mos.) stands up on chair at kitchen table
I go pee-pee/ I go pee/
Mommy, I go pee-pee/

Mother: You did?

yeah/

Mother: Oh, that's nice

In these episodes, adults rarely referred to other aspects of the situation that would be relevant to the child's reconstruction of the event. The only item ever added to the child's report was an affective comment, reflecting the way the child should feel about the event (e.g., "I bet you liked that").

Although Kaluli children comment on observed, immediate past events from the time that they first begin to speak, such comments are rare. Some of the references to the immediate past concern objects that have fallen, disappeared, spilled, or been broken. The children infrequently talk about what they themselves have done, and, when they do, these sequences are short and unelaborated. Like the Northern California mothers, Kaluli mothers do not elaborate utterances concerning the immediate past. Except for an occasional affective comment or question, the mothers simply acknowledged the children's utterances or requested clarification if they did not understand the children:

> Meli (29 mos.) with her mother; She has just finished eating the tail of a small animal. To her mother:
>
> I ate/ I ate (the) tail/ x/x/x
>
> *Mother:* You ate (the) tail?
>
> yes/
>
> *Mother:* Was it good?
>
> it was good/

When they appear, these kinds of references to immediate past events are organized very similarly in the two cultural contexts under consideration. In both cultures, children can and do initiate discussions about the immediate past, and they receive acknowledgments from their caregivers. The cultural differences here are in the frequency of talk about the immediate past and the children's use of comments to initiate such discussions. The Kaluli children usually initiated conversations about immediate past events with questions, whereas the American children initiated with declarative comments.

CONCLUSIONS

Patterns of speaking, like other forms of social and symbolic behavior, vary in culturally specific ways. In the first part of this chapter, we explored some of the determinants of cultural variation in verbal interactions between young children and adults. We suggested that, in studying children's language use and communicative competence, researchers should consider how the organization and structure of adult-child conversation is affected by: 1) the child's status and role in society; 2) the social organization of caregiving; and 3) folk beliefs about language acquisition. Information about these three determinants—together with transcriptions of spontaneous verbal interactions—are needed for a culturally contextualized analysis of the ways in which young children acquire the appropriate use of language.

In the second part of this chapter, we explored how two societies organize talk about events in the past. Talk about the past occurs in all speech communities, but the kinds of past events discussed will vary, as will the frequency and form of such discussions. For example, when middle-class English-speaking children from Northern California were asked to recount past events, they created stories that they might repeat in other conversations. Kaluli children, on the other hand, were not asked to retell events that were known to their caregivers. That would be considered talk "to no purpose." Instead, the children were held accountable for knowing who gave them objects and where the people they lived with had gone during the day. Thus, people and their locations were stressed in the earliest conversational exchanges about past events.

Culturally based studies of different aspects of communicative competence have many implications for teachers, clinicians, and researchers who work in multicultural contexts. One of the most important implications of these studies is that, even when members of different ethnic groups speak the "same" language, they do not necessarily share the same assumptions concerning what constitutes appropriate language use (Gumperz, 1977; Philips, 1972). The rules of language use are culturally specific and largely out of our awareness (Silverstein, 1981), but individuals use their knowledge of these rules to interpret utterances. Thus, faulty communication can occur when individuals from different ethnic groups interact.

In the United States, as in other countries, children from a variety of cultural backgrounds come together for schooling. Their differences in language use and communicative style often look like and may be interpreted as deficits in competence or intellectual ability. Failure to perform according to the expectations of the teacher may result in a child being denied access to various activities, may affect how the teacher deals with that student, and may affect the student's chances for opportunities and success (see Cazden et al., 1972; Michaels and Cook-Gumperz, 1979).

Adaptation to the discourse patterns used in schools is a task faced by all children (Scribner and Cole, 1973), but the transition may be easier for some children because of their early language experiences in the family. In other words, the adjustment to school may be minimal if the linguistic patterns that children learn in the home are similar to the organization of discourse in school (Gumperz and Cook-Gumperz, 1981). Therefore, in order to evaluate a child's linguistic performance, it is first necessary to know what constitutes competence within the child's own speech community. If educators and policymakers acquire a better understanding of the cultural patterning of verbal interactions, they may be able to understand the difficulties minority children have in adjusting to the predominantly white middle-class style of speech used in American schools. In fact, they may be able to integrate the speech patterns of a minority group into the classroom itself, thereby facilitating learning for one group of children and providing variety in the ways of speaking for another group (Jordan et al., 1983).

However, in order to determine how children from different cultural and social groups organize their conversational exchanges, we need studies of language use that are culturally contextualized. For example, the ethnographic studies by Heath (1982a, 1982b, 1983) documented differences in the ways in which rural Southern Black and white children use language at home and in school. Additionally, the sociolinguistic research by Michaels and Cook-Gumperz (1979) and Collins and Michaels (1980) uncovered differences in the narrative structures of urban first graders from Black and white families. These researchers have analyzed how children from different ethnic groups structure and organize discourse in different interactional contexts. They seek to understand the role of language for children in everyday interactions, and they look for both continuities and discontinuities between home and school.

Ethnographic and sociolinguistic studies can provide detailed descriptions of the communicative skills considered to be necessary by members of a given speech community. The importance of an ethnographic perspective in studying language use is that it enables one to find out the meanings of events for the participants. The rules of verbal interaction are largely out of awareness (Silverstein, 1981). They cannot be determined out of context. In order to discover rules of use, speakers must be systematically observed in a variety of situations, and their language must be tape-recorded and transcribed. Since members of any group are continually "informing and conforming each other to whatever it is that has to happen next" (McDermott, Gospodinoff, and Aron, 1978, p. 246), spontaneous verbal exchanges provide an excellent source of contextualized data on what should or should not be, is or is not, said or done. Children, especially, are often corrected for speaking "out of turn" or inappropriately. Thus, the rules of speaking that members of a group follow, and encourage or teach their young children to follow, can be uncovered through ethnographically sensitive observation and analysis.

It is through the use of ethnographic studies that we are able to do comparative work in which we understand what differences in language use mean. It is clear from the studies reviewed and the data presented here that making comparisons across cultures is only meaningful when the features being compared are contextualized, and their communicative functions are known and understood. For example, it looks (from the transcripts) as if Kaluli mothers ask their children a great many questions, but the majority of these questions are in fact rhetorical in nature and call for no answer. They are used to shame a child and to control undesirable behavior. Thus, they are interactionally different from other types of questions (e.g., information questions and clarification requests). Knowing the underlying cultural beliefs, attitudes, expectations, and values that prompt caregivers to interact in particular ways with their children enables researchers to determine the meanings that those behaviors might have for the individuals involved.

Language use is embedded in a complex cultural system and it has culturally specific communicative functions and meanings. In order to understand the meanings behind cultural variations in conversation, careful attention must be given to the ways of speaking in each society and to the acquisition of both linguistic and cultural knowledge.

ACKNOWLEDGMENTS

The authors thank Perry Gilmore, Patricia Clancy, and Elinor Ochs for comments on an earlier draft of this chapter.

REFERENCES

Andersen, E. 1977. Learning to speak with style: A study of the sociolinguistic skills of children. Unpublished Ph.D. dissertation, Stanford University.
Andersen, E. S., and Johnson, C. E. 1973. Modifications in the speech of an eight-year-old to younger children. Stanford Occasional Papers in Linguistics (Stanford University, Stanford, CA) 3:149–160.
Antinucci, F., and Miller, R. 1976. How children talk about what happened. J. Child Lang. 3:167–189.
Basso, K. 1972. To give up on words: Silence in western Apache culture. In P. Giglioli (ed.), Language and Social Context. Penguin Books, New York.
Bee, H. L., Van Egeren, L. F., Streissguth, A. P., Nyman, B. A., and Lechie, M. S. 1969. Social class differences in maternal teaching strategies and speech patterns. Dev. Psychol. 1:726–734.
Bloom, L., and Lahey, M. 1978. Language Development and Language Disorders. John Wiley & Sons, Inc., New York.
Bloom, L., Lifter, K., and Hafitz, J. 1980. Semantics of verbs and the development of verb inflections in child language. Language 56(2):386–412.
Blount, B. G. 1969. Acquisition of language by Luo children. Unpublished Ph.D. dissertation, University of California, Berkeley.
Blount, B. G. 1970. The prelinguistic system of Luo children. Anthropol. Ling. 12:326–342.
Blount, B. G. 1972a. Aspects of Luo socialization. Lang. Soc. 1:235–248.
Blount, B. G. 1972b. Parental speech and language acquisition: Some Luo and Samoan examples. Anthropol. Ling. 14:119–130.
Blount, B. G. 1975. Studies in child language: An anthropological view. Am. Anthropol. 77(3).
Blount, B. G. 1977. Ethnography and caretaker-child interaction. In C. E. Snow and C. A. Ferguson (eds.), Talking to Children. Cambridge University Press, New York.

Blount, B. G., and Padgug, E. J. 1977. Prosodic, paralinguistic and interactional features in parent-child speech: English and Spanish. J. Child Lang. 4:67–86.
Boggs, S. 1972. The meaning of questions and narratives to Hawaiian children. *In* C. B. Cazden, V. P. John, and D. Hymes (eds.), Functions of Language in the Classroom. Teachers College Press, New York.
Boggs, S. 1976. From the mouths of babes: Reflections of social structure in the verbal interaction of part-Hawaiian children. *In* K. A. Watson-Gegeo and J. L. Seaton (eds.), Adaptation and Symbolism. University of Hawaii Press, Honolulu.
Boggs, S. 1978. The development of verbal disputing in part-Hawaiian children. Lang. Soc. 7:325–344.
Bowerman, M. 1981. Language development. *In* H. C. Triandis and A. Heron (eds.), Handbook of Cross-cultural Psychology. Allyn & Bacon, Inc., Boston.
Bronckart, J. P., and Sinclair, H. 1973. Time, tense, and aspect. Cognition 2:107–130.
Byers, P., and Byers, H. 1972. Nonverbal communication and the education of children. *In* C. B. Cazden, V. P. John, and D. Hymes (eds.), Functions of Language in the Classroom. Teachers College Press, New York.
Caudill, W., and Weinstein, H. 1970. Maternal and infant behavior in Japanese and American urban middle class families. *In* R. Hill and R. Konig (eds.), Families in East and West. Mouton, The Hague.
Cazden, C. B., John, V. P., and Hymes, D. (eds.). 1972. Functions of Language in the Classroom. Teachers College Press, New York.
Coles, R. 1977. Growing up Chicano. *In* R. Coles (ed.), Eskimos, Chicanos, Indians. Little, Brown, & Company, Boston.
Collins, J., and Michaels, S. 1980. The importance of conversational discourse strategies in the acquisition of literacy. *In* Proceedings of the Sixth Annual Meeting of the Berkeley Linguistics Society, Berkeley, CA.
de Lemos, C. 1981. Interactional processes in the child's construction of language. *In* W. Deutsch (ed.), The Child's Construction of Language. Academic Press, London.
Eisenberg, A. R. 1981. Family and early language experience. Paper presented at the American Anthropological Association Meetings, Los Angeles, CA.
Eisenberg, A. 1982. Language development in cultural perspective: Talk in three Mexicano homes. Unpublished Ph.D. dissertation, Dept. of Psychology, University of California, Berkeley.
Ervin-Tripp, S. 1978. Whatever happened to communicative competence? *In* Studies in the Linguistic Sciences, Vol. 8, No. 2. University of Illinois Press, Champaign.
Ervin-Tripp, S., and Mitchell-Kernan, C. (eds.). 1977. Child Discourse. Academic Press, Inc., New York.
Feld, S. 1982. Sound and Sentiment: Birds, Weeping, Poetics, and Song in Kaluli Expression. University of Pennsylvania Press, Philadelphia.
Fillmore, L. W. 1976. The second time around: Cognitive and social strategies in second language acquisition. Unpublished Ph.D. dissertation, University of California, Berkeley.
Fischer, J. L. 1970. Linguistic socialization: Japan and the United States. *In* R. Hill and R. Konig (eds.), Families in East and West. Mouton, The Hague.

Gleason, J. B. 1973. Code switching in children's language. *In* T. E. Moore (ed.), Cognitive Development and the Acquisition of Language. Academic Press, Inc., New York.

Gleason, J. B., and Weintraub, S. 1975. The acquisition of routines in child language. Papers Rep. Child Lang. Dev. (Linguistics Department, Stanford University) 10:89–96.

Gumperz, J. J. 1977. Sociocultural knowledge in conversational inference. *In* M. Saville-Troike (ed.), Linguistics and Anthropology, Georgetown University Press, Washington, D.C.

Gumperz, J. J. 1979. The retrieval of sociocultural knowledge in conversation. Poetics Today 1:273–286.

Gumperz, J. J., and Cook-Gumperz, J. 1981. Ethnic differences in communicative style. *In* C. A. Ferguson and S. B. Heath (eds.), Language in the USA. Cambridge University Press, New York.

Gumperz, J. J., and Hymes, D. (eds.). 1964. The ethnography of communication. Am. Anthropol. 66(6), Part II.

Gumperz, J. J., and Hymes, D. (eds.). 1972. Directions in Sociolinguistics. Holt, Rinehart & Co., New York.

Gumperz, J. J., and Tannen, D. 1979. Individual and social differences in language use. *In* C. F. Fillmore, D. Kempler, and W. S. Y. Wang (eds.), Individual Differences in Language Ability and Language Behavior. Academic Press, Inc., New York.

Harkness, S. 1971. Cultural variation in mothers' language. Word 27:495–498.

Harkness, S. 1977. Aspects of social environment and first language acquisition in rural Africa. *In* C. A. Ferguson and C. E. Snow (eds.), Talking to Children. Cambridge University Press, New York.

Harkness, S., and Super, C. M. 1977. Why African children are so hard to test. Ann. N.Y. Acad. Sci. 285:326–331.

Harner, L. 1976. Children's understanding of linguistic reference to past and future. J. Psycholing. Res. 5:65–84.

Heath, S. B. 1982a. Questioning at home and at school: A comparative study. *In* G. Spindler (ed.), Doing the Ethnography of Schooling: Educational Anthropology in Action. Holt, Rinehart & Winston, Inc., New York.

Heath, S. B. 1982b. What no bedtime story means: Narrative skills at home and at school. Lang. Soc. 11(1):49–76.

Heath, S. B. 1983. Ways with Words: Language, Life and Work in Communities and Classrooms. Cambridge University Press, London.

Herriot, P. 1969. The comprehension of tense by young children. Child Dev. 40:103–110.

Hollos, M. C. 1970. Community, family and cognitive development in rural Norway. Unpublished Ph.D. dissertation, University of California, Berkeley.

Hollos, M., and Beeman, W. 1975. "If you please:" The development of directives among Norwegian and Hungarian children. Unpublished manuscript.

Hollos, M., and Beeman, W. 1978. The development of directives among Norwegian and Hungarian children: An example of communicative style in culture. Lang. Soc. 7:345–356.

Horner, V. M., and Gussow, J. D. 1972. John and Mary: A pilot study in linguistic ecology. *In* C. B. Cazden, V. P. John, and D. Hymes (eds.), Functions of Language in the Classroom. Teachers College Press, New York.

Hymes, D. 1967. Models of the interaction of language and social setting. J. Soc. Issues 23:8–28.
Hymes, D. 1972. On communicative competence. *In* J. B. Pride and J. Holmes (eds.), Sociolinguistics. Penguin Books, Baltimore.
Jordan, C., Au, K. Hu-pei, and Joesting, A. K. 1983. Patterns of classroom interaction with Pacific Island children: The importance of cultural differences. *In* M. Chu-Chang (ed.), Asian- and Pacific-American Perspectives in Bilingual Education. Teachers College Press, New York.
Keenan, E. O., and Schieffelin, B. B. 1976. Topic as a discourse notion: A study of topic in the conversations of children and adults. *In* C. Li (ed.), Subject and Topic. Academic Press, Inc., New York.
Lein, L. 1975. "You were talkin' though, oh yes, you was." Black American migrant children: Their speech at home and school. Council on Anthropol. Educ. Q. 6:1–11.
Lein, L., and Brenneis, D. 1978. Children's disputes in three speech communities. Lang. Soc. 7:299–323.
Lieven, E. V. M. 1978a. Conversations between mothers and young children: Individual differences and their possible implication for the study of language learning. *In* N. Waterson and C. E. Snow (eds.), The Development of Communication. John Wiley & Sons, Inc., New York.
Lieven, E. V. M. 1978b. Turn-taking and pragmatics: Two issues in early child language. *In* R. Campbell and P. Smith (eds.), Recent Advances in the Psychology of Language. Plenum Press, New York.
Lieven, E. V. M. 1980. Language development in young children: Children's speech and speech to children. Unpublished Ph.D. dissertation, Cambridge University.
McDermott, R. P., Gospodinoff, K., and Aron, J. 1978. Criteria for an ethnographically adequate description of activities and their contexts. Semiotica 24:245–275.
Malinowski, B. 1935. Coral Gardens and Their Magic, Vol. II. Allen & Unwin, London.
Michaels, S., and Cook-Gumperz, J. 1979. A study of sharing time with first grade students: Discourse narratives in the classroom. *In* Proceedings of the Fifth Annual Meetings of the Berkeley Linguistic Society, Berkeley, CA.
Miller, P. J. 1982. Amy, Wendy, and Beth: Learning Language in South Baltimore. University of Texas Press, Austin.
Mitchell-Kernan, C., and Kernan, K. T. 1975. Children's insults: American and Samoa. *In* M. Sanches and B. Blount (eds.), Sociocultural Dimensions of Language Use. Academic Press, Inc., New York.
Murillo, N. 1976. The Mexican American family. *In* C. A. Hernandez, M. H. Haug, and N. N. Wagner (eds.), Chicanos: Social and Psychological Perspectives. C. V. Mosby Company, St. Louis.
Ninio, A., and Bruner, J. 1978. The achievements and antecedents of labeling. J. Child Lang. 5:1–16.
Ochs, E. 1982. Talking to children in Western Samoa. Lang. Soc. 11(1):77–104.
Ochs, E., and Schieffelin, B. B. (eds.). 1979. Developmental Pragmatics. Academic Press, Inc., New York.
Ochs, E., and Schieffelin, B. B. Language acquisition and socialization: Three developmental stories and their implications. *In* R. Shweder and R. LeVine

(eds.), Culture Theory: Essays on Mind, Self, and Emotion. Cambridge University Press, New York. (in press)

Ochs, E., Schieffelin, B. B., and Platt, M. 1979. Propositions across utterances and speakers. *In* E. Ochs and B. B. Schieffelin (eds.), Developmental Pragmatics. Academic Press, Inc., New York.

Philips, S. U. 1972. Participant structures and communicative competence. *In* C. Cazden, D. Hymes, and V. John (eds.), Functions of Language in the Classroom. Teachers College Press, New York.

Philips, S. U. 1982. The Invisible Culture: Communication in Classroom and Community on the Warm Springs Indian Reservation. Longman, Inc., New York.

Sachs, J. 1977. Talking about the there and that. Papers Rep. Child Lang. Dev. (Linguistics Department, Stanford University) 13:56–63.

Sachs, J. 1979. (a) Talking about the there and then: The emergence of displaced reference in parent-child discourse. *In* K. E. Nelson (ed.), Children's Language. Gardner Press, New York.

Sachs, J. 1979. (b) Topic selection in parent-child discourse. Discourse Processes 2:145–153.

Sachs, J., and Devin, J. 1976. Young children's use of age-appropriate speech styles in social interaction and role-playing. J. Child Lang. 3:81–98.

Sapir, E. 1949. Language. *In* D. Mandelbaum (ed.), Selected Writings of Edward Sapir. University of California Press, Berkeley, CA.

Schieffelin, B. B. 1979. Getting it together: An ethnographic approach to the study of the development of communicative competence. *In* E. Ochs and B. B. Schieffelin (eds.), Developmental Pragmatics. Academic Press, Inc., New York.

Schieffelin, B. B. How Kaluli Children Learn What To Say, What To Do, and How To Feel: An Ethnographic Approach to the Study of Communicative Competence. Cambridge University Press, New York. (in press)

Schieffelin, E. L. 1976. The Sorrow of the Lonely and the Burning of the Dancers. St. Martin's Press, New York.

Scollon, R. 1976. Conversations with a One-Year-Old: A Case Study of the Developmental Foundation of Syntax. University of Hawaii Press, Honolulu.

Scollon, R., and Scollon, S. B. K. 1981a. The literate two-year-old: The fictionalization of self. *In* R. O. Freedle (ed.), Narrative, Literacy and Face in Interethnic Communication. Vol. VII: Advances in Discourse Processes. Ablex Publishing Corp., Norwood, N.J.

Scollon, R., and Scollon, S. B. K. 1981b. Abstracting themes: A Chipewayan two-year-old. *In* R. O. Freedle (ed.), Narrative, Literacy and Face in Interethnic Communication. Vol. VII: Advances in Discourse Processes. Ablex Publishing Corp., Norwood, N.J.

Scribner, S., and Cole, M. 1973. Cognitive consequences of formal and informal education. Science 182:553–559.

Silverstein, M. 1981. The limits of awareness. Working Papers in Sociolinguistics #84. Southwest Educational Development Laboratory, Austin, TX.

Slobin, D. I. 1975. On the nature of talk to children. *In* E. H. Lenneberg and E. E. Lenneberg (eds.), Foundations of Language Development. Academic Press, Inc., New York.

Slobin, D. I. (ed.). 1967. A Field Manual for the Cross-Cultural Study of the Acquisition of Communicative Competence. Language Behavior Research Lab, University of California, Berkeley.

Smith, C. S. 1979. The acquisition of complex sentences: Evidence from temporal reference. Paper presented at the New England Child Language Association Meeting, October.

Smith, C. S. 1980. The acquisition of time talk: Relations between child and adult grammars. J. Child Lang. 7(2):263–278.

Snow, C. E. 1978. The conversational context of language learning. In R. N. Campbell and P. Smith (eds.), Recent Advances in the Psychology of Language. Plenum Publishing Corp, New York.

Snow, C. E., and Ferguson, C. A. (eds.). 1977. Talking to Children. Cambridge University Press, New York.

Stoel-Gammon, C., and Cabral, L. S. 1977. Learning how to tell it like it is: The development of the reportative function in children's speech. Papers Rep. Child Lang. Dev. (Linguistics Department, Stanford University) 13:64–71.

Stross, B. 1970. Verbal processes in Tzeltal speech socialization. Paper presented at the American Anthropology Association Meetings.

Ward, M. C. 1971. Them Children: A Study in Language Learning. Holt, Rinehart & Winston, Inc., New York. (reprinted by Irvington Press, 1982)

Weisner, T. S., and Gallimore, R. 1977. My brother's keeper: Child and sibling caretaking. Curr. Anthropol. 18:169–190.

Wells, G. 1979. Variation in child language. In P. Fletcher and M. Garman (eds.), Language Acquisition. Cambridge University Press, New York.

Williamson, S. G. 1979. Tamil baby talk: A Cross-cultural study. Unpublished Ph.D. dissertation, University of Pennsylvania, Philadelphia.

Wooton, A. J. 1974. Talk in the homes of young children. Sociology 8:277–295.

Section IV

Developmentally Different Children

chapter 10

Communicative Competence in Children with Delayed Language Development

Lynn S. Snyder

Department of Speech Pathology and Audiology
University of Denver
Denver, Colorado

Editors' Note

   This chapter concerns the acquisition of communicative competence by normal as well as language-disordered, mentally retarded, and autistic children. The focus is upon their ability to interpret and formulate a variety of speech acts; to presuppose and take on the listener's point of view; to process, initiate, develop, and regulate conversations and narratives; and to interpret and use nonverbal signals. The possible bases of communication deficits are considered in relation to a multiple resources model that accommodates both deficient and efficient communication. The issues of parallel processing and concurrence benefits are especially relevant to an analysis of language processing.
   The complex issues of communicative competence are compared to a symphonic production in which the child is the composer, conductor, musician, and audience. The task presented to the developing child far exceeds that presented to the developing musician. Fortunately, the curriculum that enables the child to achieve competence allows for missing sections in the orchestra. Even though the symphony must then be played somewhat differently, it need not stop. It will simply sound or appear somewhat differently.

contents

ACQUISITION OF COMMUNICATIVE COMPETENCE: A CLOSER LOOK 427

LANGUAGE-DELAYED CHILDREN 430

SPEECH ACTS 431

    Language-Disordered Children 432
    Mentally Retarded Children 436
    Autistic Children 437

PRESUPPOSITION 440

    Language-Disordered Children 441
    Mentally Retarded Children 447
    Autistic Children 451

DISCOURSE: CONVERSATIONAL SKILLS 452

    Language-Disordered Children 454

NONVERBAL COMMUNICATIVE DEFICITS 457

    Language-Disordered Children 457
    Autistic Children 458

EFFECT OF SPECIFIC DEFICITS ON FUNCTIONAL COMMUNICATION 458

    Input: The Social and Verbal Environment 459
    Specific Cognitive Abilities 460
    Attention 463
    Perception 465
    Levels of Processing 466
    Language 466
    Individual Differences 467

A MULTIPLE RESOURCES MODEL 468

SUMMARY 471

ACKNOWLEDGMENTS 472

REFERENCES 472

Communication is the symphony of our species. Under his own direction, man coordinates the use of his communicative instruments to convey his message. The point or theme of the message is carried by the instrument of language in its direct and indirect forms. At times it is supported and expanded by the nonlinguistic instruments of body posture, movement, and proximity; facial movements; vocal signals such as throat clearing, grunts, and intonational contours; and other nonlinguistic cues such as timing and pauses. Some of these same instruments may provide a counterpoint to the linguistic message. Timing and crescendo can be built with rate, loudness, linguistic strings, and kinesics. The same melody may emerge in countless themes and variations.

Like the musical composition, the composition of discourse has its underlying structure. It, too, begins with an overture or introduction; it establishes the major theme, topic, or gist of the composition or conversation. The message or messages are played out in episodes or movements in which complications or the twists of events are described. Finally, major and minor themes are ended or closed with the finale or resolution of events and the cultural conventions of parting.

Unlike the orchestra, which plays the composition of some master musician, people create their own symphony. The orchestra can play the same classics every season; a person rarely has the same conversation twice. Although the underlying structure of discourse remains constant and a person's intentions or discourse goals may be the same in two situations, it is unlikely that he will generate identical series of nonlinguistic signals. Musicians often perform better when they perceive an appreciative audience. People, too, attend and respond to their listeners' signals. However, a person can take greater liberties with his composition than the musician. He can choose the communicative code appropriate for his listener and vary the formulation of both linguistic and nonlinguistic elements of his message in response to linguistic and nonlinguistic listener cues.

Like the musical symphonic production, communication is most effective when the message of a master composer is played by a full, well-tuned orchestra, under the direction of a competent conductor, before an attentive audience. Conversely, both musical and communicative productions may be hindered by a flawed composition, an incomplete or poorly tuned orchestra, insensitive direction and coordination, or an inattentive audience. These components contribute to the success of a symphony. Thus, each must be considered when examining both the musical and communicative symphony.

The musical symphonic production, then, requires conductor, composer, musician, and audience. Each person involved in the musical symphony needs to demonstrate competence in one or two roles. The conductor may know how to play some instruments but not all of them. The musician may also know how to compose but not conduct. By contrast, each person involved in communication must demonstrate competence in all of the roles required of the communicative symphony. He not only needs to know how to compose the symphony, he also needs to know how to conduct and play it and be an audience or listener for his own composition and those of others.

The task presented to the developing child far exceeds that presented to the developing musician. The young musician need only learn to become competent at one or two roles of the musical symphony. The child, however, must learn to demonstrate competence in all of the roles of the communicative symphony. He needs to learn to compose, conduct, play, and interpret linguistic symphonies. Specifically, the child needs to learn how to formulate and convey a message with sequences of linguistic symbols as well as nonlinguistic and paralinguistic signals. He needs to learn which sequences are most effective in what settings. Finally, he must also learn to interpret the symphonies of others.

Just as the musician must realize his latent talent with interest, instruction, and practice, the child must also embark upon a program of learning experiences. Unlike the musician, who must often wait several years before beginning his studies, the child begins his communicative curriculum almost immediately. Yet he does so with little direct instruction. It is as if the child must learn to play by ear, through incidental observation of others. Both the musician and the child are encouraged to practice and improve their skills. However, the child has some advantages. Music lessons are usually given for an hour at a time a few times a week; communication can be observed and experienced through much of the day. Furthermore, beginning musicians are usually encouraged to practice for an hour or two a day; children are encouraged to communicate throughout the day. Children, then, have greater opportunities available to them.

Indeed, when presented to the normal child, these opportunities interact with his developing cognitive, social, and communicative abilities to produce some rather dramatic outcomes. Although the composer and/or musician rarely achieves mastery at his craft until adulthood, the child achieves this remarkable level by adolescence. By that time, he has not only acquired basic communication skills, he has learned to exploit them.

Having briefly considered the task presented to the child, his communicative curriculum is now examined in greater detail, continuing the musical analogy.

THE ACQUISITION OF COMMUNICATIVE COMPETENCE: A CLOSER LOOK

To communicate effectively with others, the child needs to become a competent composer, conductor, musician, and listener. As a composer and conductor, the child needs to learn at least four sets of rules and conventions associated with the production of a message in his language and his culture. He must learn which phonetic signals represent objects, states, and events in the world, i.e., he must learn the linguistic symbols. He then must learn to sequence linguistic symbols to form grammatically acceptable sentences. For example, the child needs to learn the morphological rules associated with the addition of suffixes to indicate plurality and tense; he also needs to learn the syntactic rules for producing a question. Although there are many rules of this sort, most children have mastered the majority of them and can produce grammatically acceptable sentences by the age of 4.

As a composer and conductor, the child also needs to learn various conventions regarding the arrangement of individual sentences to form larger units of discourse. He must learn the underlying structure of discourse as well as methods for initiating a conversation, developing a topic or theme, and closing or ending a discourse. For example, the child needs to learn to use "closers" such as "It has been nice talking with you" to signal the end of a conversation. Because this basic structure entails several steps, and embellishments are often necessary, children usually do not begin producing complete and well-structured sequences of discourse until preadolescence.

Thus far, we have dealt with just the linguistic instruments in a child's orchestra. A full orchestra, however, contains more than linguistic instruments; it also contains nonlinguistic and paralinguistic instruments. Consequently, the success of a person's symphony depends not only on how well he sequences linguistic forms, but also on how well he coordinates the linguistic, nonlinguistic, and paralinguistic instruments in his orchestra. In order to facilitate listener comprehension while avoiding unintentional offense, contradiction, and overstatement, a child needs to learn how to coordinate all of the instruments in his orchestra according to the conventions of his language and culture. For example, an English-learning child should learn that questions are accompanied by a rising terminal intonation, but statements require a falling pitch; he should also learn what kinds of facial expressions might augment—and what kinds might contradict—specific linguistic expressions of emotion. Thus, learning linguistic forms and how to sequence them is only one step in the process of acquiring communicative competence; a child must also learn the nonlinguistic and paralinguistic signals that will harmonize with different linguistic sequences. Examples of such harmony are plentiful, and many of them appear very early.

Finally, the last set of conventions a child must learn as a composer and conductor pertain to the setting in which a message is conveyed. Just as there are conventions for combining signals from various instruments, there are also conventions for selecting the combinations most appropriate for specific settings. In English, there is not always a one-to-one correspondence between meanings and the combinations of symbols and signals used to convey meanings. Different combinations are used in different settings to convey the same meaning. The particular combination used to convey a meaning partly depends on the knowledge and social status of one's listeners. For example, a listener's knowledge of a referent determines when a speaker can use deictics appropriately; and the listener's social status affects how a speaker can request an object. A child may request a cookie from a familiar younger child by issuing an imperative: "Gimme cookie!" However, when speaking to an unfamiliar adult, a request for a cookie is conventionally conveyed through: 1) a need statement such as "I need a cookie"; 2) a permission directive, as in "May I have a cookie?"; 3) a question directive such as "Have you got any cookies?"; or 4) a hint, as in "I'm hungry" (Ervin-Tripp, 1977).

This lack of one-to-one correspondence between meanings and the forms used to convey meanings also has a reverse implication: the same form can have one meaning in one setting, and a different meaning in a different setting. In other words, the lack of one-to-one correspondence implies that: 1) in different settings, the same meaning (e.g., request for a cookie) might be conveyed by different forms; and 2) in different settings, different meanings might be conveyed by the same form (e.g., a speaker might use a question to request information in one setting, and to request an object in a second setting). For example, the question "Can you make change for a quarter?" might be interpreted as a request-command for an exchange of money if the speaker is standing in front of a pay telephone booth, a request for information if said by a teacher after a lesson on our money system, or a humorous remark if the listener is carrying an armful of bundles.

Thus, in his role as a composer and conductor, the child must learn four sets of rules and conventions. One set concerns the construction of grammatically acceptable strings. A second set pertains to the choice and arrangement of sentences to form larger units of discourse. A third set concerns the coordination of linguistic symbols with nonlinguistic and paralinguistic signals. The last set pertains to the selection of coordinated forms for different settings.

Although a child learns to follow these four sets of rules and conventions at different times, he eventually learns them all and even becomes capable of relating one set of rules to another set. For example, when coordinating the symbols and signals from different instruments, the child learns to consider both the setting and the discourse function of an utterance. Although such coordination requires a great deal of skill, it is achieved in a relatively short time. By the time a child has entered adolescence, he has learned all of these rules, and can interrelate them to compose and conduct a well-structured communicative symphony.

However, the child's responsibilities do not end when he learns how to compose and conduct a symphony, for he also must learn how to play one. As a composer and conductor, he learns how to sequence words to produce grammatically acceptable sentences that are appropriate to both the setting and the topic, but, as a musician, he must learn how to articulate these words intelligibly. As a composer and conductor, the child learns how to combine words and gestures; as a musician, he must learn how to produce gestures with a look of natural spontaneity and grace. Thus, to produce a successful symphony, the child must learn how to play three roles: that of composer, conductor, and musician.

Finally, in addition to learning how to produce a symphony, a child must also learn how to interpret those produced by others. This task requires that a child learn to interpret a variety of forms and sequences to handle the variety of meanings conveyed even in one setting. Moreover, the need for an extensive repertoire increases when many speakers are encountered, because, even if they have the same meaning and their interactions are observed in the same setting, speakers may still produce different forms to convey their meaning. Communication may be man's symphony, but the symphonies produced by men will differ.

Fortunately for the child, his efforts to interpret the messages of others often reap double benefits. In addition to enhancing his ability to decode a variety of messages, the child's interpretive efforts may also affect his ability to encode such messages. What and how much a child can learn from listening to others will vary depending upon factors such as how attentively the child listens, his existing knowledge of the rules and conventions of discourse, and how well the current conductor/composer has followed these rules and conventions. In any case, a child's experience as a listener in the audience is often reflected in his performance as a composer, conductor, and musician.

Having discussed what a child needs to learn, and a little bit about how he learns, it is necessary to return to the issue of when a child learns to communicate with others. By the time most children are adolescents, they have mastered all of the basic communicative skills and are able to exploit these skills to achieve their goals. In an effort to learn more about this remarkable achievement, researchers have studied the acquisition of many of the specific skills involved in communication. Their results suggest that many children follow the same general developmental schedule. In other words, children often resemble one another in the ages at which they develop the components of communicative competence. However, there are some groups of youngsters for whom many of these achievements are elusive. Language-delayed children are one such group, because they seem to acquire some communicative skills later than is predicted by the overall schedule.

LANGUAGE-DELAYED CHILDREN

Language-delayed children are those youngsters whose language does not develop commensurately with their advancing years. Such youngsters include the diagnostic subgroups of language-disordered, language- and learning-disabled (i.e., school-age language-disordered), mentally retarded, and autistic children.

All of these children have difficulty acquiring communicative competence, but the nature of their problems and the scope and source of their difficulties vary. The most common problem observed among delayed children is their difficulty in acquiring linguistic forms. Such children may not have all the semantic, morphological, and syntactic instruments needed to produce varied messages to convey their varied meanings.

Another problem often seen among delayed children involves the production and interpretation of nonlinguistic signals. Indeed, one of the distinguishing characteristics of autism seems to be a general lack of eye contact (Simmons and Tymchuk, 1973). However, Baltaxe and Simmons (1977) reported that autistic children also have difficulty interpreting the nonlinguistic signals of others. In this regard, however, autistic children are not alone. Johnson and Myklebust (1967), Lerner (1971), and Wiig (personal communication, 1980) have reported that some language- and learning-disabled youngsters also cannot interpret facial expressions and gestures, nor can they utilize environmental elements from the context in interpreting or producing a message.

Finally, recent findings in developmental psycholinguistics suggest that the acquisition of language and communicative competence may be related to the onset of *specific* cognitive abilities (Bates, 1976; Bates et al., 1979). Interestingly, recent studies of language-disordered children have reported that these children are delayed or deficient in the acquisition of cognitive abilities such as symbolic play schemas (Brown et al., 1975; Lovell, Hoyle, and Siddall, 1968), means-end relations (Snyder, 1978), and anticipatory imagery (Johnston and Ramstead, 1978; Savich, 1980). Some studies of mentally retarded children have also demonstrated these deficits (Oller, Tharp, and Coleman, 1978), as well as a delayed ability to take on the listener's perspective or engage in role taking (Monson, Greenspan, and Simeonsson, 1979). Finally, autistic children have been described as sustaining some highly specific cognitive deficits in precisely those abilities related to communicative competence (Curcio, 1978). *Inasmuch as samples of language-delayed children have demonstrated delays or deficits in specific social and cognitive abilities as well as language, it may be that their communicative competence—a skill that requires linguistic, social, and cognitive knowledge—is similarly affected.* (See Rice, this volume, for a somewhat different analysis of the research done in this area as well as a discussion of the problems involved in assessing the preceding relationship.)

In this chapter, I examine the literature on the communicative competence of language-disordered, mentally retarded, and autistic children. I examine their ability to: 1) interpret and formulate a variety of speech acts; 2) presuppose and take on the listener's point of view; 3) process, initiate, develop, and regulate conversations and narratives; and 4) use and interpret nonverbal signals. Finally, I consider the possible bases of communicative deficits in relation to a model that addresses both deficient and efficient communication.

SPEECH ACTS

The notion of a speech act was first described in Austin's work (1962), *How To Do Things with Words*. Austin used the term "speech act" to refer to the function or use of an utterance to convey an intended social meaning. A speech act does not focus upon the form of an utterance, but rather upon the function(s) it serves in different settings. For example, "Do you think that there's enough chocolate in my milk?" might be interpreted as a request for information. However, when spoken by a child to his mother in the context of a luncheon meal, it might also be interpreted as a request for action, i.e., as an indirect directive. Or, if the mother had put too much chocolate syrup in the milk, the sentence could serve as the sarcastic humor of an older child.

The range of functions served by language is large. A speaker's utterance can serve as a request for information, an object, attention, action, or acknowledgment; an utterance can also convey facts, attitudes, and beliefs, as well as promises and threats. Normally, developing children acquire the various functions of language as well as their forms. They acquire many of them with their earliest symbols (Bates, 1976) and are able to formulate a wide range of speech act types by the time they begin first grade (Ervin-Tripp, 1977).

Language-Disordered Children

Recently, investigators have begun to study the speech act behavior of language-disordered children—i.e., those children who, despite normal intelligence and emotional development, experience difficulty in acquiring language. Initially, it seems important to determine whether these children have problems understanding or interpreting a variety of speech act types. Current research data clearly suggest that speech act comprehension is not problematic for language-disordered children. Prinz (1977, in press) studied the processing and production of requests by language-disordered youngsters. He found that they had no difficulty comprehending a variety of request forms during structured conversations with the examiner.

However, as Shatz, Bernstein, and Shulman (1980) have noted, the linguistic context that precedes an utterance may affect its interpretation. For example, when a request for action, e.g., "Come get the telephone," precedes the speech act "Can you talk on the telephone?", the latter will also be interpreted as a request for action. However, when the initial request is for information, e.g., "Can Mommy talk on the telephone?", then the sentence "Can you talk on the telephone?" is likely to be interpreted as a request for information.

To study the effect of the context on the interpretation of speech acts, Shatz et al. (1980) varied elements of both the linguistic and nonlinguistic context in two experiments. In both experiments, Shatz and her colleagues examined the ways in which five language-disordered subjects from 5 to 6 years of age interpreted requests.

In the first experiment, the children were presented with five sets of toys. As they played with each set, subjects were given two direct requests and three indirect requests that, in a neutral context, could be interpreted either as requests for action or as requests for information. These speech acts were interspersed with filler sentences. An analysis of the data revealed that the subjects usually interpreted ambiguous indirect requests as requests for action. These results suggest that language-disordered children respond to such stimuli by acting upon whatever referents they can identify. Such findings are consistent with those reported by Shatz (1978) for normal 2-year-olds.

In their second experiment, Shatz et al. examined whether the linguistic context might affect a child's interpretation of an utterance.

To study this question, Shatz and her colleagues constructed sequences in which each indirect speech act was preceded by either a direct request for action or a request for information. The experimenters found that, as a group, the language-disordered subjects responded to an indirect speech act preceded by a request for action by acting upon whatever referents they could identify; they responded to an indirect speech act preceded by a request for information by providing information. However, the action response was still the preferred mode of response. The effect of a contextual request for action on action responses was more consistent than the effect of a contextual request for information on informative responses. These results are again much like those reported by Shatz (1978) for normal 2-year-olds, but are most similar to those obtained from the linguistically less advanced 2-year-olds in her sample.

When we look at those studies directed at the delayed child's ability to produce speech acts, we find greater evidence of deficient communicative skills. In an experimental study, Snyder (1975, 1978) examined the speech acts served by the early words and communicative gestures of samples of normal and language-disordered children who were matched for mean length of utterance (Brown, 1973) and screened for normal intelligence. Two tasks were administered to the children. The first task was designed to elicit a declarative verbal or gestural speech act. It involved engaging the child in a repetitive play schema, e.g., putting blocks into a pail, and then handing the child a new object with which to execute the schema. The other task was designed to evoke an imperative or request-command. During this task, the examiner held or placed a desirable object (e.g., a cookie) within the child's visual field but just out of his reach. The results revealed that the language-disordered children performed significantly worse than their normal counterparts in the number and level of declarative and imperative speech acts produced. Language-disordered subjects tended to use gestural performatives more frequently than words even though they had the appropriate words in their lexicons. Moreover, the developmental level of their gesturing was significantly lower than that of the younger, normal children. In general, the language-disordered children failed to mobilize their communicative resources to achieve social goals within the experimental contexts. These children demonstrated functional as well as structural communicative deficits at a very early stage of language development.

Communicative deficits were also noted in a naturalistic study conducted by Geller and Wollner (1976). They observed the communicative behaviors of three language-disordered children between 3 and 5 years of age who were just making the transition into multiword speech. Using Dore's (1977) classification of speech act types, Geller and Wollner compared the performances of their subjects with those of the 3-year-olds studied by Dore (1977). They found that the language-disordered children used fewer speech act types than the normal children in Dore's sample. Thus, the results from Geller and Wollner's study also point to deficient communicative skills in language-disordered children.

The work of Prinz (1977, in press) focused upon one category of speech acts: requests. He examined the comprehension, production, and metapragmatic politeness judgment of requests by taking samples of language-disordered children. In his first study (1977), Prinz compared the performance of normal 3- to 5-year-old children on the preceding parameters. Only his findings regarding their ability to produce and interpret requests are reported here. Prinz observed all subjects during free play with a peer and during an experimental situation designed to evoke polite requests. In the latter condition, he used hand puppets representing an older woman and a young child to which each subject was instructed to address requests.

In the free play condition, Prinz found that the language-disordered children were able to produce a number of indirect requests, with requests for action predominating. However, they differed from the normal subjects in structural forms mobilized for requests. The language-disordered children used fewer declarative hints and relied more heavily upon interrogative strategies than the normal children. During the experimental condition, Prinz observed that the language-disordered children also used fewer formal linguistic devices such as contrastive stress and conditional mood to form polite requests. In contrast to these group differences in production, the language-disordered subjects did not differ from their normal counterparts in the accuracy with which they interpreted requests. In other words, the language-disordered children could accurately interpret as many types of requests as the younger normal children with whom they were matched, but they could not formulate request forms with the range of strategies and devices that were available to the normal children.

In his second study, Prinz (in press) studied 30 language-disordered children ranging from 3½ through 8 years of age. Each subject was observed interacting with a peer during free play, and again under experimental conditions that assessed the subject's production and comprehension of request forms. The data from the play condition confirmed Prinz's earlier conclusion that language-disordered subjects are indeed able to produce a variety of indirect requests. However, the proportion of indirect requests obtained from children of increasing age varied as a function of the method used to collect the data. It has been reported (e.g., Ervin-Tripp, 1977; Garvey, 1975) that normal children demonstrate increased use of indirect requests with advancing age. However, the language-disordered children in this study performed as predicted only in the experimental condition. During free play, the proportion of indirect requests decreased, while direct requests increased, with age.

Prinz's findings may be related to the stimuli given to the children during play: a "doctor" kit. Studies of requests produced during role playing of this type (Andersen, 1978) have demonstrated that high proportions of direct requests or imperatives are associated with specific roles. Thus, the higher proportions of imperatives produced by the older language-disordered children during play may have reflected their growing sensitivity to the sociolinguistic constraints on role playing. In short, the frequent use of imperatives by older children underscores the importance of contextual variables in evaluating the forms that children use.

In another investigation of the speech acts produced by language-disordered children, Fey et al. (1978) examined the communicative intentions expressed by eight language-disordered children during play. They observed each subject interacting with an age-matched normal child and again with a younger normal child to whom the subject had been matched for mean length of utterance (MLU). The data were coded for communicative intent, using an adaptation of Dore's categories (1977). The language-disordered children expressed a variety of speech acts. The distribution of their communicative intentions was similar to that of the younger normal children with matching MLUs. When compared to the normal age-matched children, the language-disordered subjects differed from the former group primarily in the number of speech acts performed. The normal age-matched children produced significantly more speech acts than did the language-disordered subjects.

In summary, the literature indicates that, although language-disordered youngsters can respond to a variety of request types embedded in differing linguistic contexts, some have difficulty doing so in a consistent manner. Moreover, some samples of language-disordered children have difficulty mobilizing their prelinguistic and early linguistic forms in functional communication (Snyder, 1978), formulating indirect requests with declarative sentence forms (Prinz, 1977), and using language to express a variety of intentions (Geller and Wollner, 1976). However, other samples of language-disordered children do not demonstrate such deficits. Thus, impaired functional communicative skills may be characteristic of some language-disordered children, but not others.

Mentally Retarded Children

Although some language-disordered children show differences or deficits in their speech act behavior, we cannot assume that children from other diagnostic categories of language delay will show similar handicaps. Even though language-disordered children exhibit impaired functional communication skills, their intelligence is within the normal range. Mentally retarded children, on the other hand present a somewhat different picture. These youngsters demonstrate significant cognitive deficits. It is generally thought that their language structures develop in much the same way as do those of normal children, but at a much slower rate (Berry, 1976). However, studies that relate the language performances of retarded children to those of normal children with comparable mental ages have offered equivocal results (Milgram, 1973). Some experimenters have observed similar language performance, whereas others have noted deficient performance in the retarded children. The nature of the communicative competence of retarded children is far from clear.

In a longitudinal study, Oller et al. (1978) examined the speech acts produced by groups of normal and mentally retarded children. Language was sampled and recorded for all subjects over 23–25 play sessions. The data were analyzed functionally, semantically, and syntactically. The results indicated that the retarded children were similar to the normal children in the kinds of semantic information conveyed. Moreover, the two groups of children used similar kinds of syntactic constructions, and performed similar kinds of speech acts. However, the subjects differed in how they performed specific speech acts. The normally developing children used a much higher proportion of advanced speech act strategies (e.g., indirect requests), than did the retarded children. This finding suggests a very real difference in the communicative competence of this sample of mentally retarded children.

Greenwald and Leonard (1979) studied the performance of young normal and mentally retarded Down's syndrome children using Snyder's (1975, 1978) declarative and imperative tasks. Their subjects were matched for stage of sensorimotor intelligence on the means-end, operational causality, and relating-to-objects scales from the Uzgiris-Hunt *Ordinal Scales of Psychological Development* (1975). Greenwald and Leonard found no significant difference in the imperative speech acts of normal and Down's syndrome children at the same sensorimotor stage. However, the normal children at sensorimotor Stage 5 performed significantly better than their Down's syndrome counterparts on the declarative tasks. (Very few responses were made to the declarative tasks by any of the Stage 4 subjects.) Moreover, the experimenters observed that, in general, the Stage 5 Down's syndrome subjects did not combine vocalizations with gestures as often as did the normal subjects.

When the performances of the chronologically older and younger Stage 5 mentally retarded subjects were compared, Greenwald and Leonard found that the older subjects achieved higher levels of functional performance. They noted that this finding is consistent with Miller, Chapman, and Bedrosian's (1977) observations. Greenwald and Leonard point out that "chronological age and/or the amount of time spent in a sensorimotor stage may also have a bearing on the degree to which sensorimotor and communicative abilities are related in Down's syndrome children" (p. 302). In conclusion, Greenwald and Leonard found a similarity between the communicative performance of Down's syndrome and normal children for imperatives, but not for declaratives. Second, older Down's syndrome children performed significantly better than younger ones at the same level of cognitive development.

Thus, there are some studies that support the notion of deficient communicative competence in mentally retarded children. However, some of these differences seem to diminish when the retarded children are rigorously matched with normal children for cognitive level.

Autistic Children

Of all of the diagnostic categories of language delay, autism presents the most dramatic instance of impaired functional communication. Autism, a category of childhood psychosis, is best described by its major behavioral characteristics: impaired interpersonal relationships resulting from a lack of eye contact and decreased physical contact, deficient social play and self-help behaviors, stereotyped behaviors, specific cognitive impairments, and disturbances of speech and language (Simmons and Tymchuk, 1973).

Some autistic children are linguistically competent, but they do not appear to use this competence to communicate with others. It is not unusual for autistic children to generate linguistically well-formed sentences that seem to bear little relation to the context or the situation. Some of these utterances can be characterized as delayed echolalia or the repetition of sentences or utterances heard previously. For some time, professionals regarded this linguistic behavior as devoid of communicative value, and counterproductive to the communicative exchange. Consequently, both delayed and immediate echolalia (the immediate repetition of a preceding utterance) have been either ignored by clinicians or subjected to a series of therapeutic manipulations in an effort to reduce the frequency with which they occur.

However, Wolff and Chess (1965) have proposed that delayed echolalia can be classified into communicative and noncommunicative repetition depending upon the uses to which it is put. A good example of delayed echolalia taking on a communicative function is found in Ricks and Wing (1975). They described an autistic child who always requested a biscuit with "Do you want a biscuit?" Other such examples can be found in their work and in accounts by Fay and Schuler (1980). Noncommunicative echolalia involves the repetition of a phrase such as "tie my shoes" when there is no discernible need for further attention, interaction, or action of any kind from the listener or the speaker.

Instances of communicative repetition are probably not even limited to autistic children. Keenan's (1977) study of normal language acquisition has identified a variety of communicative functions for repetition in normal children. Normal children use repetition to respond to questions, make comments, imitate, self-inform, match a claim, make a counterclaim, request clarification, return a greeting, and reverse the direction of a request or command. Thus, the clinical bias to view echolalia as noncommunicative behavior may run counter to its function in the interactions of normal children.

Baltaxe and Simmons (1975) took up Wolff and Chess' notion that some of the delayed echolalia of autistic children may be communicative and suggested that it served a labeling function. Thus, the child may use whole utterances such as "blow your nose" to refer to a tissue, or "soup's on" to refer to a pot. Baltaxe and Simmons reasoned that an autistic child's difficulty with syntactic and semantic information may lead him to interpret these phrases as labels. Perhaps closer scrutiny of contextual conditions will reveal an even wider range of functions for delayed repetition.

Recently, Schuler (1980) reported several instances in which the delayed echolalia of autistic children served a function other than labeling, i.e., to request food. Furthermore, Schuler cites evidence to suggest that at least some of the remaining noncommunicative repetitions may be shaped into intentional acts of communication. Thus, at least some of the delayed echolalic behavior of autistic children seems to be communicative, and other instances of such behavior can be shaped to that end.

In a pioneering work, Prizant (1978) examined the immediate echoes of four autistic children over an 8-month period. His pilot studies and other literature on echolalia (e.g., Buium and Steucher, 1974; Fay and Coleman, 1977; Shapiro and Lucy, in press; Voeltz, 1977) indicate that four factors should be considered when differentiating or discriminating among children's repetitions: 1) all aspects—linguistic and nonlinguistic—of the communicative context; 2) the structural characteristics of the echo as compared to the speaker's utterance; 3) the latency of the echo; and 4) the behaviors that precede, accompany, and follow the repetition.

Prizant used the first factor, communicative context, to obtain information about the presence of communicative interaction. For example, if a child gazed at his listener, the accompanying echo could be regarded as communicative. The second factor, the structure of the echo in comparison to that of the model, gave information about the intentionality of the utterance. If the linguistic and prosodic characteristics of the echo and the model were identical, the repetition could be regarded as more automatic and nonintentional (see Fay and Coleman, 1977, for further discussion of this issue). Prizant used the third factor, the latency of the echo, to determine whether the function of the echo duplicated the function of the model. Finally, the child's behaviors were used to infer comprehension. The literature and Prizant's pilot studies indicate that changes in the child's behavior can provide evidence for some degree of comprehension of the model utterance. For example, if the child understood the command "Go find the ball," he might repeat the command while searching for the ball.

Prizant classified each instance of immediate echolalia by its function, using the following seven categories: turn taking, declarative, yes-answering, request, rehearsal, self-regulation, and a nonfocused category. Instances of all but the last category seemed to serve some function for the child; and instances of the first four categories appeared to be communicative in nature.

Prizant's analysis also revealed that all of the children repeated more often when they comprehended the speaker's utterance than when they did not. Behavioral evidence of comprehension consisted of contextually appropriate gestures or actions. For example, if the child understood "I'm cleaning up," he might repeat the sentence while putting toys back into a toy box.

Finally, echoes that were accompanied by evidence of comprehension often were: 1) produced in forms that varied from those of their models; and 2) produced only after latencies that were longer than those in which no evidence of comprehension was observed. The variance in form suggests that the echoes were intentional rather than automatic acts, and the longer latencies indicate that they may have served communicative functions different from those of the models. Thus, Prizant's work suggests that the echolalic behaviors of autistic children may in some cases be intentional acts of communication that serve functions different from those of their models.

Hurtig, Ensrud, and Tomblin (1980) took a somewhat different approach to the problem of determining the pragmatic function of utterances produced by autistic children. Specifically, they sought to determine the function of the excessive and often seemingly inappropriate questions produced by five autistic children. Hurtig et al. engaged each subject in conversation in which the adult systematically varied his response to the child's questions. The investigators then studied the frequency with which the children maintained the conversation associated with each type of adult response. They found that when the adult provided a minimal response, approximately half of the children's subsequent turns were appropriate. However, when the adult provided an elaborate response that contained additional topic information, almost three-fourths of the children's subsequent turns were appropriate. An even greater effect was found when the adult either asked a child a question or reversed the child's own question. Under these conditions more than 90% of the children's subsequent turns were appropriate. Hurtig et al. suggested that these data support the notion that the excessive, repetitive questioning of many autistic children serves the communicative function of initiating conversation.

To summarize, we have often considered the verbalizations of autistic children to be devoid of communicative intent, but recent evidence suggests that their immediate and delayed echolalia as well as their excessive questions can be communicative. Careful observation of the contextual conditions in which echolalia occurs has documented as many as four communicative functions (Prizant, 1978). Therefore, although studies of the speech acts produced by some language-disordered children have highlighted their communicative deficits, the same focus and methodology have also identified communicative abilities previously overlooked in autistic children.

PRESUPPOSITION

Communicative competence also includes the ability to consider the listener's knowledge, expectations, and beliefs. The knowledge, expectations, and beliefs that the speaker thinks that he shares with his listeners are *presuppositions*. When a listener does indeed have the world knowledge presupposed by the speaker, such knowledge may enable the listener to interpret an utterance as intended by the speaker, even when the preceding utterances do not contribute the information that would usually be needed to afford such an interpretation (Bates, 1976). Shared knowledge may enable a speaker to utter a single word instead of a sentence without any loss of meaning. Speakers usually presuppose or assume that their listeners have some knowledge of the conversational topic, and their utterances reflect this assumption. For a more comprehensive discussion of presupposition, the reader is referred to DeHart and Maratsos' chapter in this volume.

Psycholinguists have observed that, during the early years of language acquisition, children cannot fully understand or appreciate that the listener may have a different point of view or may lack information about the conversational topic. Yet, even at the very onset of referential language, children's utterances sustain remarkable success. This may be related to Greenfield and Smith's (1976) observation that children tend to comment upon that element of the context that is novel, uncertain, or in the process of change. In most cases, children at the single-word stage take the topic of conversation for granted, and comment on the most uncertain or changing aspect of the topic, such as what it is doing or where it is currently located. Bates (1976) has suggested that this phenomenon may have its underpinnings in the child's attentional system: children attend to, or orient to, new or novel stimuli in any context. Thus, the linguistic mapping of novel information as a comment upon an unstated topic is the result of activity within the child's attentional system. In other words, the informativeness of a child's early utterances may have its basis in attention.

Fortunately for the child, his attentional mechanism initially allows him to bypass difficulties associated with considering the listener's point of view. Thus, the normal child's early communicative experiences are generally positive, and improve as his developing cognitive abilities enable him to consider or take on the listener's point of view (Petersen, Danner, and Flavell, 1972). As children learn to take a listener's point of view, they then become better able to formulate messages and jokes that accurately reflect the extent of a listener's knowledge; they also become able to revise their messages in the face of communicative failure.

Language-Disordered Children

What, then, can be said of language-disordered children? Their attentional problems have been well documented in both the clinical (Berry, 1969) and experimental (Mackworth, Grandstaff, and Pribram, 1973) literature. Might these difficulties affect the informativeness of their early speech acts? Furthermore, might underlying difficulties in taking the view or role of another (Muma, 1975) affect a child's later ability to formulate a message that accurately reflects the extent of a listener's knowledge?

The first question has been addressed by Snyder (1975, 1978). In the earlier-cited study, she examined the informativeness of her subjects' declarative one-word and gestural speech acts. Under Snyder's experimental conditions, the Greenfield and Smith (1976) notion of informativeness would predict that subjects would comment upon those new objects introduced into each experimental context. For example, it would predict that, when a child engaged in throwing blocks into a pail was given a small doll figure to throw, he would comment on or name the new object, i.e., the doll figure. Thus, Snyder's subjects should have commented upon information that was new or had changed in the context. This prediction was overwhelmingly confirmed for the normal subjects. The normally developing children verbally encoded the most informative element of the context approximately 94% of the time, and the children's nonverbal behaviors (e.g., pointing) signaled this element 96% of the time. Although the language-disordered subjects employed nonverbal signals appropriately 95% of the time, their verbalizations symbolized the most informative element only 69% of the time. Group differences in the informativeness of the subjects' nonverbal signals were not statistically significant, but differences regarding the informativeness of their verbalizations were highly significant. The language-disordered subjects named old objects almost as often as they named new ones. Because these subjects did not consistently use their language to inform their listeners about the most uncertain or novel element of the context, the communicative efficiency of their single-word messages was compromised. However, there may have been some trade-off in the language-disordered children's deployment of resources because their gestural signals efficiently marked informativeness. The retrieval of words may not have been as automatic a skill for them as for their normal counterparts. Thus, the increased effort required to locate lexical items may have exhausted the resources that they brought to the task. Consequently, they may have been more apt to choose a less informative word.

More recently, Skarakis and Greenfield (1979) have compared the frequencies with which normal and language-disordered children encode new or changing information using multiword utterances. Each child was shown four sets of pictures with three pictures in each set. For each set, the examiner described the first two pictures and then asked the child to describe the last picture. The pictures showed continuous events, with the last one differing from its predecessor by only one element. Skarakis and Greenfield found no significant differences in the frequencies with which the normal and language-disordered children verbally encoded new or changing information. Perhaps the behavior of the younger language-disordered children studied by Snyder was a sign of early lexical access problems in that particular sample.

So far discussion of presuppositions has focused on the situational context of an utterance. Speakers presuppose that their listeners can infer certain information just by attending to the events preceding an utterance. However, to be successful a speaker must consider more than the situational context; he must also consider the social context. A speaker needs to estimate his listeners' linguistic competence, age, social status, occupation, and so forth to find those forms or the specific register that will best convey a particular message to that listener. In other words, the selection of a register is often based on the speaker's presuppositions or expectations of what is needed to convey specific information to a specific listener whose presupposed social status and linguistic competence may be quite different from—or similar to—those of the speaker.

Normal preschoolers show some ability to consider the social status of their listeners. They can change their registers in relation to both the age (Shatz and Gelman, 1973) and the role or occupation (Andersen, 1977, 1978; Bates, 1976; Ervin-Tripp, 1977) of a listener. However, children who typically find it difficult to manipulate linguistic forms may be unable to orchestrate the register variations required to communicate effectively with different types of listeners. Can such children reduce the complexity of their language when they talk to very young children? Can they use expressions of politeness when speaking to adults, particularly unfamiliar adults?

Fey, Leonard, and Wilcox (1981) studied the ability of language-disordered children to modify their speech styles in relation to the age of a listener. They examined the children's spontaneous conversational language during two types of dyadic interactions. One interaction was with an age-matched normal peer and the other was with a much younger normal child matched for MLU. Fey et al. found that the language-disordered children used shorter preverb utterances and asked more internal state questions when speaking to younger children whose MLUs matched their own. In addition, the language-disordered subjects produced fewer back channel responses (e.g., "yeah," "uh-huh") and sentence completions (Dittmann, 1972, 1977), when they talked with the younger children. Although they did not systematically alter the total length of their utterances or vary the directness of their speech acts, the language-disordered children did demonstrate the ability to make some structural changes in relation to their listener's age.

Messick and Newhoff (1979) also examined language-disordered children's abilities to consider their listeners. They focused on: 1) the children's abilities to vary the forms of their requests when speaking to listeners with different roles; and 2) their abilities to identify photographs of listeners that were associated with particular request forms. Comparing the language-disordered children's performance with that of normal children matched for linguistic level, Messick and Newhoff found that the two groups did not differ significantly in the number of different request forms produced. However, the groups demonstrated marked differences in the frequencies with which the children were able to associate specific request forms with specific listeners. Most of the time, the normal children associated direct imperatives with requests addressed to children and politeness markers (e.g., "please") with requests addressed to adults. By contrast, the language-disordered children associated both request forms with various listeners in a random manner. Messick and Newhoff suggested that the language-disordered children may not have developed rules relating the form of a request to the age of a listener.

Meline (1978) also studied normal and language-disordered children's (matched by linguistic level) abilities to consider the listener. He compared their abilities to communicate information about novel referents to an adult listener in a referential communication paradigm. Each child communicator and adult listener had a pegboard and blocks printed with novel figures. Separated by a screen, the child had to tell the adult how to stack his blocks so that they matched the child's block pattern. The effectiveness of the children's responses were analyzed according to whether the listeners chose the correct referents. Meline found that the language-disordered children communicated more successfully than did the linguistically matched normal children. However, when a proportion was created between the quantity of verbal output and communicative effectiveness, there were no significant differences between the groups. Furthermore, preliminary data on chronologically matched normal children revealed that these normal children performed better than did language-disordered children. It was suggested that the language-disordered children's extra years of communicative interaction gave them an advantage over the younger, but linguistically similar, normal children. However, this advantage ceased when a preliminary comparison was made with chronologically similar normal youngsters.

If a child's initial presuppositions about a listener fail, a new set of assumptions must be developed before the message can be effectively revised. The child must be able to estimate how and why his initial utterance failed before he can correct it. After studying the problem, the child may revise or paraphrase his utterances and/or he may add new information. Such revisions are powerful communicative strategies that change developmentally. As the child becomes increasingly sensitive to his listener's needs, and as he gains greater control over verbal forms, he begins to utilize more extensive strategies for revision. He progresses from merely restating his original utterance to altering his vocabulary, syntax, and even the sequence of propositions and their cohesion. Because language-disordered children typically experience difficulty formulating effective messages, they need to have a variety of revision strategies at their disposal. However, do they know these strategies? Do they at least have the same arsenal of revision strategies as normal children?

Hoar (1977) examined these revision skills in a comparative study of normal and language-disordered children from grades one, three, five, and seven. After matching the children for grade, sex, and nonverbal intelligence, Hoar studied their abilities to produce and recognize paraphrases. The production task required that each subject paraphrase a total of 18 sentences containing transitive verbs, intransitive verbs, and verbs with direct as well as indirect objects. Each type of sentence was presented in two syntactic variations. For example, the transitive sentences were presented in both the active and passive forms. Responses were categorized as instances of lexical paraphrase, syntactic paraphrase, both lexical and syntactic paraphrase, or nonparaphrase.

Hoar found that the language-disordered children produced significantly fewer correct paraphrases than did the normal children with whom they had been matched. The language-disordered subjects produced paraphrases that were antonyms of the stimulus sentences more often than did the normal children. In some instances, they reversed subject and indirect object nouns in a sentence. Other times, they substituted words that were polar opposites, e.g., "fat" for "thin."

Hoar's qualitative analysis revealed that the less accurate performance of the language-disordered children was accompanied by a greater use of sentence repetition (i.e., a strategy in which no alterations are made) in all grades. Furthermore, when the first- and third-grade language-disordered children did modify a sentence in a paraphrase, they tended to use lexical or word substitution. Normal children did not use this strategy in the third grade; instead, they began to use a more extensive revision strategy involving syntactic modification of sentence structure.

In addition to studying the children's abilities to produce paraphrases, Hoar also studied their abilities to recognize paraphrases. Recognition was assessed by asking the children to judge whether lexical and syntactic paraphrases and nonparaphrases had the same meaning as a target sentence. Hoar found that the language-disordered children were significantly less accurate at recognizing paraphrases than were the normal children. Her analyses revealed that some language-disordered children used a quantitative strategy to judge instances of paraphrase. If the paraphrased sentence was longer than the stimulus sentence, these children would not consider it an acceptable paraphrase. Thus, the language-disordered children studied by Hoar not only used less extensive paraphrase strategies than did the normal children, but they also had greater difficulty recognizing paraphrases of sentences.

Paraphrasing behavior has been studied in two other experiments, using quite different methodologies. One study (Gallagher and Darnton, 1978) employed a naturalistic setting and the other (Meline, 1978) used a classic experimental role-taking manipulation. Gallagher and Darnton (1978) examined the revision behaviors of language-disordered children at Brown's syntactic Stages I, II, and III. In a replication of Gallagher's (1977) experiment with normal children, the investigator pretended to misunderstand a child's utterance, asking "What?" 20 times during an hour-long conversation, or approximately every 3 minutes, regardless of the structural features of the child's utterance. The children's responses were recorded, analyzed, and compared with the data from Gallagher's earlier study (1977) of normal children at a similar linguistic level.

The results of the comparative analysis yielded rather interesting findings. All children engaged in revision strategies. However, the language-disordered children differed markedly from the normal children in the distribution of strategies employed at each developmental stage. The normal children demonstrated a profile of revision strategies that changed as a function of linguistic level. Stage I children relied most heavily on phonetic revision, i.e., articulating a more accurate phonetic realization of the target word—making it "sound" better. The revisions of Stage II normal children incorporated more constituent reduction or the deletion of a word(s), as well as constituent elaboration or the addition of morphemes. Finally, the revisions of Stage III normal children were characterized by greater reliance on constituent substitution or the substitution of words. Although all three strategies were observed at each stage, the frequency of their occurrence changed in relation to the child's level of linguistic development. Presumably, the children's increasing control over linguistic form made strategies such as constituent elaboration and substitution more available to them.

By contrast, the language-disordered children demonstrated a profile of revision strategies that did not change with advanced linguistic skill. The frequency with which these children used phonetic change, constituent elaboration, and constituent reduction did not change as the children progressed through stages I, II, and III. Although the language-disordered subjects made minimal use of the most advanced strategy (i.e., constituent substitution), the level of their performance at the earliest stage was developmentally superior to that of their normal counterparts. Because the language-disordered children were older than the normal subjects, the added communicative experiences of the former children, together with their more frequent need to deal with communicative failure, may have sensitized the language-disordered Stage I children to some of the more advanced revision strategies, e.g., constituent elaboration.

Meline's (1978) study, discussed earlier, examined the ability of normal and language-disordered children (matched by linguistic level) to make revisions in a referential communication paradigm. Each child gave an adult listener, located on the other side of a screen, information regarding the selection of patterned blocks. After the child had completed his instructions, the listener solicited additional information or a revision by requesting the child to tell him more. Meline observed no significant group differences in the frequency of revisions or the success of these revisions. Normal and linguistically matched language-disordered children issued roughly equal numbers of revisions and experienced comparable success following their revisions.

To summarize, accurate presuppositions concerning the knowledge of a listener enable a speaker to mobilize the language content and structures needed to convey information efficiently. Snyder (1975, 1978) observed a sample of very young language-disordered children who, in comparison to normal children, had significant difficulty mobilizing those linguistic elements that would be maximally informative. However, subsequent studies with older samples of language-disordered children have often reported "no significant group differences." By and large, the results of these latter studies indicate that language-disordered children can consider their listener and can mobilize language to effectively inform a listener. However, language-disordered children may differ from normal children in the linguistic structures or forms that they mobilize, particularly when their listeners ask them to revise a message.

Mentally Retarded Children

When a child's communication and cognition develop at a very slow pace, as seen in mental retardation, he will spend longer periods of time at each developmental stage. Thus, he will be exposed to more communicative experiences per stage than the nonretarded child. These extended experiences can differentially enhance the language development of some retarded children (Miller et al., 1977) relative to other less experienced children at the same cognitive stage. As a result, the language development of the experienced children may be more advanced than their cognitive development, but less advanced than their chronological age would predict. Because the cognitively influenced ability to presuppose the listener's needs interacts with the ability to mobilize specific content and linguistic forms, that interaction may be particularly vulnerable to the effects of dysynchronous development. Furthermore, if—as Bates (1976) has argued—presupposition has its early bases in the attentional system, the prevalence of attentional problems in mentally retarded children (Alabiso, 1972; Bower and Tate, 1976; Crosby, 1972) may significantly affect the development of presupposition in this diagnostic subgroup.

In an effort to examine the informativeness of the lexical usage of retarded children, Leonard, Cole, and Steckol (1979) conducted two experiments. In their first experiment, 12 mentally retarded subjects—with a mean chronological age of 34 months and a mean mental age of 18 months on the Bayley Scales of Infant Development—were asked to play a game similar to the declarative task devised by Snyder (1975, 1978). During the course of the game, subjects were given 18 objects, with three exemplars of each object, to place in a container. Prior to the experiment itself, all subjects had demonstrated that they knew the name of each object used in the experiment.

During the experiment, subjects were asked to name one exemplar of each object. The exemplars were sequenced so that the elements named were familiar and redundant in the first condition, novel and nonredundant in the second condition, and familiar but nonredundant in the last condition. Six different objects, with three exemplars of each object, were used in each condition. In the familiar and redundant condition, the exemplars of each object were presented in succession, and subjects were asked to label each object upon its third presentation. Thus, the object was familiar to the subjects from the presentations preceding the tested exemplar, and the tested exemplar was redundant in that it essentially duplicated the object immediately preceding it. In the novel and nonredundant condition, the three exemplars of each object were again presented in succession, but subjects were asked to label the object on its first presentation. Thus, the object was novel to the subjects in that none of the preceding presentations contained an exemplar of the object, and the tested exemplar was nonredundant because the immediately preceding element was not from the same object category as the tested exemplar. Finally, in the familiar but nonredundant condition, the three exemplars were not presented in succession, but instead were shown randomly to subjects. As in the first condition, however, subjects were asked to label each object upon its third presentation. Thus, the object was familiar from the presentations preceding the tested exemplar, but the tested exemplar was nonredundant because the immediately preceding element was not from the same category as the tested exemplar.

The results indicated that the subjects produced a significantly greater number of labels when a nonredundant referent was novel than when it was familiar; and more labels were produced when a familiar referent was nonredundant than when it was redundant. The second condition evoked the most labeling (mean of 3.58 out of 6, followed by the third condition (mean of 1.75), with the first condition evoking the fewest number of labels (mean of 0.67).

In their second experiment, Leonard et al. studied a group of retarded children similar in chronological and mental age to the sample studied in the first experiment. This second study retained the three object presentation conditions of the earlier investigation, but changed the items. This time Leonard et al. used a set of objects whose names were *not* known to the children. In each condition, the critical exemplar was accompanied by the experimenter's use of a nonsense name (e.g., *pim*). However, rather than counting the number of times subjects labeled the objects when questioned about them, the dependent measure became the number of times subjects imitated the nonsense labels.

The results of this second experiment agreed with those obtained from the first study. The subjects imitated significantly more nonsense labels in the second condition than they did in the third condition, and they imitated more labels in the latter condition than they did in the first condition. Thus, subjects labeled objects when questioned about them and imitated nonsense labels most frequently when the objects were novel and nonredundant with the situational context. These results are consistent with those reported by Leonard et al. (1979) on the labels used by normal children. Instead of labeling static and predictable objects, both the normal and young retarded children in these studies tended to label objects that had been subjected to change.

The Leonard et al. studies reported above dealt with children's tendencies to focus and comment upon elements that varied in familiarity and redundancy. The young children in these studies labeled unfamiliar and nonredundant elements presumably because their attention was directed to those elements. At their developmental level, it is unlikely that they were intentionally considering their listeners. However, older, more competent children do seem to consider their listeners. Longhurst and Berry (1975) studied the presuppositional abilities of three groups of mentally retarded adolescents with mean IQs of 78, 63, and 47. These investigators had their subjects select an abstract design and describe it to their listeners so that the latter could locate the same design in an array. (Each subject was also given the opportunity to play the role of a listener, but those results are not discussed here.)

When the descriptions obtained from the three groups of retarded subjects were compared, the results indicated that subjects with higher IQs considered the needs of their listeners more frequently than did subjects with lower IQs. The higher level subjects responded more frequently to listener cues that signaled the necessity for additional information. Moreover, the revisions from higher level subjects were more informative than those from lower level subjects.

After reviewing Longhurst and Berry's results, Beveridge and Tatham (1976) noted that the reported group differences are difficult to interpret. Rather than reflecting increased sensitivity to the listener, the superior performance of the higher level subjects might instead reflect their increased linguistic competence. The higher level subjects probably had more descriptive terms at their disposal, and thus could describe designs more explicitly than could the lower level subjects. Furthermore, the use of abstract designs may have biased the sampling because those subjects who could not deal with nonsense stimuli were excluded from the experiment.

Consequently, Beveridge and Tatham repeated the Longhurst and Berry study using the same experimental paradigm, but with concrete meaningful stimuli and subjects comparable to those in Longhurst and Berry's lowest level group. The results indicated that even children with IQs in the 40s can describe designs informatively when the stimuli are concrete and meaningful. Beveridge and Tatham also noted that the quality of a subject's performance as a speaker was related to his performance as a listener. When a subject's performance improved over trials in one role, it also improved in the other interlocutory role.

The preceding two studies focused on the informativeness of the subjects' instructions, and the subjects' willingness to revise instructions when the need arises. However, researchers also have studied the strategies retarded children use in revising a message. There seems to be some early evidence that the revision behaviors of retarded children may be similar to those of nonretarded children. Using language samples from a variety of settings, Stoel-Gammon and Coggins (1977) examined the revision behaviors of Down's syndrome children at Brown's Stage I, the beginning of combinatorial speech. They examined the samples for repetitions of utterances as well as for structural revisions, including both phonological revisions and utterance elaborations that involved the addition of new semantic information to disambiguate the original utterance. Their data revealed that all subjects could modify their original utterances. All but one used all types of revision strategies. However, the profile of proportional and absolute frequencies of these strategies differed from child to child. Stoel-Gammon and Coggins suggested that these were similar to the frequencies observed by Garvey (1977), but they cautioned against a strong interpretation because the number of subjects was small.

To date, the literature suggests that, like normal children, mentally retarded children respond informatively initially by attending to novel/nonredundant events, and later by attending to the needs of the listener. Retarded children also have been observed using appropriate revision behaviors, again reflecting their sensitivity to a listener's needs.

Autistic Children

The autistic child's ability to organize his comments in an informative way, i.e., to take his listener into account and to revise his utterances in response to listener feedback is now considered. Although there seems to be no direct experimental study of the autistic child's presuppositional behavior, the literature is filled with descriptive data that speak to this point; these observations suggest that autistic children do not consider their listeners. Whereas normal children usually talk about objects and events present in the context and observed by their listeners (Greenfield and Smith, 1976), autistic children often talk about topics unrelated to the context and of little interest to their listeners. Moreover, these children make little effort to relate their utterances to the context or to evoke interest in their listeners even when they are well acquainted with their listeners. Ricks and Wing (1975) have reported that autistic children will talk *ad nauseam* about a topic that is only of interest to themselves. Their communication has also been described as rather repetitive, with little new information being introduced. Thus, the informativeness or communicative efficiency of their comments tends to be low.

Just as autistic children seem to convey less relevant information, they often attend to less informative and/or less relevant stimuli in a task or situation. For example, when presented with an experimental task in which dolls' heads were systematically changed, autistic children's responses were guided by the doll's jacket (Schriebman and Lovaas, 1973). Their performance contrasted with that of the normal children studied, who used the doll's clothing *and* the doll's head to determine their response. Because one can reasonably expect that a child's comments will reflect that to which he attends, the apparent lack of informativeness in the utterances of autistic children may result from attentional differences.

Autistic children also have difficulty revising their utterances in response to a listener's feedback. Baltaxe (1977) has observed that autistic adolescents make few revisions in their utterances. Furthermore, those revisions that they do make often take the form of phonetic repetition, a very early developmental strategy. Here, too, autistic children are astoundingly deficient.

In summary, autistic children are reported to have particular difficulty producing comments that are informative and reflect consideration of the listener. They also tend to ignore listener cues that signal the need for revision. However, the significance of their deviant behavior might be reduced if we investigate the informativeness of their delayed echolalia. Just as Baltaxe and Simmons (1975), Schuler (1980), and Prizant (1978) observed primitive communicative functions in such utterances, we may find that the autistic child's echolalic utterances are more informative than our initial reactions may have led us to believe.

DISCOURSE: CONVERSATIONAL SKILLS

Up to this point, the discussion has focused upon pragmatic structures observed in normal and delayed child language, using the utterance as the primary level of analysis. However, interlocutors rarely exchange isolated utterances that are unrelated to the utterances that have preceded them. Rather, each utterance is an orchestrated movement of some larger unit, i.e., the discourse. As the speaker tries to make and share his points (see MacWhinney, this volume), successive utterances may share the same topic, or they may digress from that topic. In other words, utterances A and B may both share the topic of C (coordinate subtopics); or A may share B's topic, so that only B shares the topic of C (embedded subtopics); or finally, A and/or B may be digressions from the topic of C. Thus, the discourse may be hierarchically structured with subtopics embedded in more global topics (Bates and MacWhinney, 1982) and the entire array ordered under the major topic or the gist of the discourse; or the discourse may show a combination of linearly embedded and coordinated topics together with brief digressions from the main topic.

The hierarchical structuring is evident in at least two types of discourse: the narration of stories and social conversation. Story narratives have their own internal structure (Kintsch, 1974; Kintsch and Kintsch, 1979; Labov and Waletzky, 1967; Mandler and Johnson, 1977; Stein and Glenn, 1979). In their most general form they consist of an exposition or setting, a complication or twist of events, and a resolution. However, as in other forms of discourse, this basic structure is often expanded through embedding and the coordination of two or more basic elements (i.e., some complications do not have immediate resolutions, but are followed by other twists of events). Instances of embedding and coordination appear in both the stories told to children and, subsequently, in the stories told by them (Botvin and Sutton-Smith, 1977). The importance of story structure is evident from the studies of comprehension and recall done in the last five years. This research indicates that internal structuring facilitates both the comprehension and subsequent recall of narrative discourse.

The second type of discourse in which hierarchical structuring often appears is social conversation. Social conversations are usually sequenced to contain initial greetings, followed by "openers" or topic-setting questions and remarks that are bids or gambits to establish the major topic of discussion. These are generally followed by a logical development or exploration of the topic. Once the topic has been exhausted, the conversation is closed with a series of exchanges that signal its resolution. At this point, one of the interlocutors may wish to initiate a new topic and a new "opener" might be offered. Or, in the course of the conversation one of the interlocutors may have digressed and introduced a new topic or embedded one within another. Once the new topic is resolved, the interlocutors may return to the earlier topic after one of them has given an "opener" to indicate his desire to redirect and resume discussion of the earlier theme or question. When a topic has been resolved and/or an interlocutor wishes to discontinue the conversation, a "closer" is typically offered. Closers are remarks that signal the ending of a conversation—for example, "It's been nice talking to you," or "My, it's late. I really must go," or "Well, I had better let you go now." These, in turn, are typically followed by closing routines, e.g., "Good-bye."

Thus, social conversation also has an underlying hierarchical structure (see Goffman, 1976, and Keenan, 1974, for more complete discussions of this structure). Constraints on this structure originate from social and cultural conventions. Basically, these conventions caution speakers to be clear and polite to their listeners. In regard to the clarity of an utterance, Grice's (1975) conversational postulates require that speakers be both informative and relevant. Consequently, a person cannot walk up to an acquaintance and remark, "The rebels are losing ground." Without prior topical context and development, this sentence would be irrelevant and uninformative.

Even if the above hypothetical remark were somehow understood, listeners would still consider it a rude initiation of an exchange. Rules of politeness (Lakoff, 1973) say that speakers should not impose themselves on listeners. Cordial greetings as well as "closers" are needed, and their omission may bring criticism from one's peers. Most of us would be annoyed if an acquaintance approached us and initiated discourse without so much as a greeting. We would be similarly annoyed if our interlocutor turned on his heel and left us at the resolution of the conversational topic—without so much as a "closer" or "goodbye."

Control over these parameters and the acquisition of discourse structures emerge by adolescence in the normal child (Ochs and Schieffelin, 1979). What, then, of language-disordered children? Is their acquisition of discourse structures delayed?

Language-Disordered Children

This discussion focuses on the discourse skills of language-disordered children—first, on their abilities to comprehend and remember narratives, and then on their abilities to structure and produce conversation. Researchers interested in the narrative processing of delayed children usually have studied school-age children with reading problems. Most of these children probably had a language disorder as well; there is considerable agreement that the overwhelming majority of reading-disabled children have some form of language disorder (see Vellutino, 1979, for a comprehensive review).

Smiley et al. (1977) studied the ability of good and poor readers to recall stories read to them as well as those that they had read. Under both conditions—listening and reading—the poorer readers recalled less information from the narratives. A detailed analysis of their performance revealed that the poor readers could not use their knowledge of the underlying structure to help them organize and retrieve information.

Recently, Weaver and Dickenson (1979) compared the discourse processing of normal and reading-disabled children between 9 and 15 years of age. Stories were read to the children and they were asked to recall them. The data were analyzed for the number of ideas recalled and the number of inferences made by the children. The results of a quantitative analysis revealed no significant differences between the two groups for the number of ideas recalled. However, when they looked within the reading-disabled group, Weaver and Dickenson found that poor readers with high verbal ability recalled significantly more ideas than did those with low verbal ability. Qualitative analyses of all children's performance revealed that the reading-disabled subjects as a group had greater difficulty with verbatim recall than did the normal subjects. In addition, the disabled subjects made fewer of the inferences necessary for story comprehension. Thus, there are data to support the notion that reading-disabled children—especially those with low verbal abilities—may have difficulty organizing, recalling, and inferring information from narratives.

Snyder and Haas (in preparation) also studied the discourse processing of normal and reading-disabled sixth graders. They compared the number of propositions or ideas recalled and the number of inferences made by the children after listening to stories. When normal listeners are presented with two successive ideas that lack a cohesive relation, they infer or supply the missing relation. For example, take the sentence: "There was an explosion at the chemical factory last night. The fire could be seen for miles." Listeners mobilize their world knowledge to infer the relationship between the explosion and the fire. The preliminary results of Snyder and Haas' study indicate that the reading-disabled children recalled significantly fewer correct propositions and made fewer appropriate inferences than did the normal controls.

Moreover, the reading-disabled children generated a significantly greater number of perspective intrusions in their recall of the stories. That is, they changed the story line to reflect their personal circumstances. Indeed, one reading-disabled child even changed the major proposition of a story to reflect his own wishes. He told the examiner that the story character was a boy who loved dogs and always wanted to have one, but his parents would not allow it. However, the actual major proposition or gist of the story was that the character was *afraid* of dogs! Not only did these sixth-grade reading-disabled children have difficulty remembering ideas from the story and connecting them with inferences, some of them also had difficulty appreciating the protagonist's perspective. Thus, there are trends in recent research that suggest that some school-age reading-disabled children—most of whom are language disordered—have difficulty processing narrative discourse.

Narrative processing, however, is only part of the picture. We also need to consider the language-disordered child's skill as an active conversational participant. As Bates and Johnston (1977), Rees (1978), and others have noted, over time the child learns to observe the rules for discourse. He learns to take conversational turns; to be polite by mastering routines such as "hi," "good-bye," and "thank you" (Berko-Gleason and Grief, 1979); to give his listener just enough but not too much information (lest he be boring); to maintain and develop the conversational topic (Rees, 1978); to mark a shift of topic; and to tell the truth. Conversational competence develops early (Garvey, 1975) and continues to develop throughout the concrete operational period as the child becomes more effective in role taking or considering the listener's perspective (Muma, 1978).

What happens when a language-disordered child becomes engaged in conversation? Watson's (1977) study provides us with some insight. She observed linguistically matched normal and language-disordered preschoolers engaged in conversations with their parents during a story-telling activity. Watson analyzed all child utterances that were not responses to parental bids for speech. This analysis involved categorizing utterances as back channel, main channel, or unintelligible responses, after Duncan (1972, 1973). Main channel responses convey the speaker's intentions and meanings. Back channel responses are those verbal and nonverbal signals that indicate a listener's attention to and understanding of main channel utterances. Watson observed that both the normal and language-disordered children took conversational turns, but that the language-disordered subjects took the role of a passive responder more frequently than did the normal children. Similarly, both groups used back channels, but the normal children signaled their attention and understanding by completing an utterance more frequently than did the disordered children. The language-disordered subjects tended to rely on more primitive signals such as "yeah" and "uh-uh," with the utterance completion appearing less frequently. Therefore, although the language-disordered children were responsive participants, the level of their responses was lower than that of their normal counterparts.

The Fey et al. (1981) study described earlier also analyzed the proportion of back channel responses produced by language-disordered children. Fey et al. found that their disordered subjects produced almost twice as many back channel responses when they talked with agemates than when they talked with younger children. Moreover, they could not find one instance in which a language-disordered child completed a partner's statement. This last result confirms Watson's earlier observations.

Also looking at discourse, but using a somewhat older age group, Donahue, Bryan, and Pearl (1980) compared the conversational strategies of 54 learning-disabled and 46 control children from grades 3 through 8. Observing each child in a triad with two randomly selected same-sex normal classmates, Donahue et al. involved the children in a decision task in which the triad had to reach a group consensus.

A comparison of the children's conversational strategies indicated no significant group differences in the percentage of conversational turns taken by the subjects, and no significant differences in the percentage of topics initiated. However, the learning-disabled youngsters differed from their peers in that they were more likely to agree and less likely to disagree with the others' opinions and arguments. By contrast, the control group were more likely to monitor the triad's progress at the task, and to attempt to hold the conversational floor. Thus, the learning-disabled children were relatively unassertive conversational partners.

Thus far, the study of language-disordered children's abilities to process narrative discourse suggests that some of them may have difficulty using their world knowledge to organize their recall of narratives and to make inferences or the implicit bridges that relate ideas to one another. Language-disordered children also may have difficulty separating their own perspective from that of the protagonist in a story. Furthermore, when we examine their active conversational participation, we find that, although young language-disordered children are responsive, they do not take the conversational floor as actively as do their normal counterparts. Older language-disordered children do seem to take their share of active conversational turns. However, they are less assertive than their normal peers in this interaction. Again, an element of passivity seems to pervade their conversational exchanges.

NONVERBAL COMMUNICATIVE DEFICITS

At the outset of this chapter, the characterization of communicative competence took communication beyond language. It emphasized the construction and/or interpretation of the linguistic message against a background of nonlinguistic and paralinguistic signals. Nonlinguistic signals include such things as: facial expressions, head nods and shakes, body postures (Birdwhistell, 1970), and the actual spatial distance between speaker and listener (Hall, 1959). Paralinguistic cues include pauses, intonational contours, variation of rate, and so forth. Both nonlinguistic and paralinguistic signals may reinforce, contradict, supplement, substitute for, or maintain the message expressed linguistically (Svenson, 1971). There is limited evidence to suggest that language-delayed children not only have difficulty dealing with linguistic symbols, but also may have problems with nonlinguistic and paralinguistic signals.

Language-Disordered Children

Some—but not all—language-disordered children have been reported (Johnson and Myklebust, 1967; Lerner, 1971; Wiig and Semel, 1977) to have difficulty interpreting nonverbal communicative signals. Johnson and Myklebust's (1967) and Lerner's (1971) accounts suggest that some of these youngsters have particular problems interpreting facial expressions, and respecting their interlocutor's intimate space zone.

Bryan (1977) compared the performance of 23 learning-disabled third, fourth, and fifth graders with that of 11 normally achieving youngsters at corresponding grade levels on a test of comprehension of nonverbal communication. The measure consisted of a film that contained scenarios depicting expressions of positive and negative affect as well as dominant and submissive attitudes. The film was presented under two modalities: silently and accompanied by an audiotape in which the speech was degraded. The children were shown each scenario and asked to select the test sentence that best described the scenario. Two test sentences were devised for each scenario. The test sentences were distributed in standardized questionnaires, and each sentence was read aloud for the children by the examiner.

The analyses of the data indicated that the learning-disabled children scored significantly lower than the control children on the test. The results from the two viewing conditions showed that the degraded audio condition was significantly more difficult for both groups. The results of this study, taken together with the clinical reports in the literature, suggest that some language-disordered children find it difficult to handle the nonverbal aspects of communication.

Autistic Children

Because autistic children typically have problems handling transient stimuli (Lovaas et al., 1971), they might have difficulty interpreting and producing transient nonverbal cues. Indeed, Baltaxe and Simmons (1977) have reported that the autistic adolescents they studied were not able to interpret their partner's nonverbal back channel cues. These subjects did not consider the compliance states, interest levels, or nonverbal affective reactions of their listeners. Moreover, their failure to consider nonverbal cues was accompanied by a failure to produce such cues. The autistic adolescents neither interpreted nor produced nonverbal signals of interest. Thus, there are observations suggesting that autistic children also may have problems handling the nonverbal aspects of communication.

EFFECT OF SPECIFIC DEFICITS ON FUNCTIONAL COMMUNICATION

The deficiencies discussed in the previous sections are group data norms for particular diagnostic populations. Not all children in each diagnostic category will show the deficiencies mentioned. This diversity suggests that we must look beyond the surface manifestation of the deficit. Given the multifaceted nature of communicative competence and the complexity of human information processing, there may be many potential sources as well as many kinds of underlying deficiencies. Taking a cue from Johnston's (1980) exploration of the bases of child language disorders, the possible effects of attentional, perceptual, environmental, and cognitive deficits on the communicative processing of language-delayed children are considered here. In addition, some other factors, such as the nature of the resources used and the levels of processing, are considered.

Input: The Social and Verbal Environment

The normal child's development from a somewhat passive dyadic partner into an independent communicator takes place rapidly. The notion that a child learns a great deal about the communicative process from within the framework of parent-child interaction is intuitively appealing and well supported (see, e.g., Bruner, 1975; and Snow, this volume). However, there are limits on how much and when these interactions can affect development. In other words, the significance of social and verbal input cannot be denied (see, e.g., Spitz, 1965), but it is difficult to argue that discrete differences in the quality and/or quantity of verbal interaction are entirely responsible for the child's eventual communicative skills. For example, the work of Bretherton et al. (1979) suggests that the relationship between early language development and attachment is not strong. More recently, Kaye's (1981) longitudinal study of 50 children indicated that the quality and quantity of the infant's prelinguistic social interactions do not seem to be related to later language development. Instead, current research suggests that a child's acquisition of linguistic forms is positively influenced by his mothers' speech only when the child has already formulated the underlying concepts (Bowerman, 1978). Thus, the verbal environment of the child can influence his mastery of linguistic forms, but only under particular conditions.

What, then, is the nature of the social and verbal environment of language-delayed children? A study of the home environments of age-matched normal and language-delayed preschool children was conducted by Wulbert et al. (1975). Assessing these children's environments with the Caldwell Inventory, a measure that includes both a parental interview and a home observation, Wulbert et al. found significant differences between the two groups of subjects. The mothers of the language-disordered subjects interacted less frequently with their children, and provided fewer emotional and verbal responses and less variety of experiences. Similar results have been obtained in studies of the home environments of Down's syndrome children (Cicchetti and Sroufe, 1976).

However, one might question whether the verbal environment of the language-disordered child might not still be appropriate to his linguistic level. Millet and Newhoff (1978) addressed this question in their comparative study of communicative interactions that occur in mother-child dyads containing either young normal or preschool-age language-disordered children. Unlike previous studies, Millet and Newhoff matched the children for linguistic level. Their results indicated that, even when the children had similar MLUs, the mothers of the language-disordered children provided fewer semantically related responses to their children's utterances. By contrast, Silverman and Newhoff's (1979) subsequent study of father's verbal interactions with normal and language-disordered children at similar ages did not yield these differences. They found that fathers of language-disordered children were not significantly different from fathers of normal children in regard to the number of semantically related responses produced. In a subsequent analysis of these data, Newhoff, Silverman, and Millet (1980) found that, when the mothers and fathers of the language-disordered subjects were compared, 20% of the mothers' utterances were semantically related responses, whereas such responses constituted only 8% of the fathers' utterances. A similar trend was observed in their comparison of the mothers and fathers of the normal children. Thus, mothers seem to be more sensitive than fathers to children's semantic intentions. Although mothers of language-disordered children are less sensitive than mothers of normal children, the lower sensitivity of the former mothers may not, as Johnston (1980) has pointed out, cause the child's delay. Indeed, the relationship might operate in the reverse direction. The parents might be responding to the impoverished or unintelligible communication of the delayed child. However, their responses may confound the problem, providing the delayed child with less rich and/or motivating language data.

Specific Cognitive Abilities

Research in child language disorders has often focused on the relationship between these disorders and the child's conceptual or cognitive ability. Two possible relationships have been proposed: 1) the child's linguistic communicative deficits reflect an underlying general representational deficit that affects the child's performance on both linguistic and nonlinguistic tasks (Morehead, 1972); and 2) communicative deficits are related to deficiencies in the specific cognitive abilities needed to perform particular linguistic and nonlinguistic operations. (See Bates and Snyder, 1982, Rice, this volume, Savich, 1980, and Snyder, 1975, for more complete discussions of these hypothesized relationships.) In an attempt to resolve the controversy regarding which proposed relationship best represents the assumed source of a language-disordered child's problems, researchers have investigated a variety of cognitive abilities including those needed to: 1) perform various Piagetian tasks; 2) engage in symbolic play; 3) solve problems requiring anticipatory imagery; and 4) take on the perspective or role of another person.

Piagetian Tasks Studies of young language-disordered children and mentally retarded children have often focused on the relationship between a subject's communicative performance and his performance on a series of Piagetian tasks taken from the Uzgiris-Hunt *Ordinal Scales of Psychological Development* (1975). In a study of 87 mentally retarded children, Miller et al. (1977) found that the communicative skills of almost all of their subjects were commensurate with or below the level of their cognitive skills. However, a few of the chronologically older subjects demonstrated the converse pattern. This reversal among older children also appeared in a study by Greenwald and Leonard (1979). Like Miller et al., Greenwald and Leonard reported that the communicative skills of their older subjects exceeded the levels predicted by the means-end, relating-to-objects, and operational causality subtests from the *Ordinal Scales of Psychological Development*.

Because many of the studies that have attempted to relate a child's communicative development to his cognitive development have used several measures from the *Ordinal Scales* to evaluate the child's level of cognitive development, researchers have questioned whether some of these tasks might be more predictive of a child's communicative development than other tasks. Snyder (1975, 1978) found that, when children at the single-word stage of linguistic development were administered all six tasks from the *Ordinal Scales*, the means-end subtest predicted their level of communicative skill better than did any of the other tasks. However, the research of Bates (1976) and Bates et al. (1979) suggested that the relationship between means-end abilities and communication appears to obtain only when children are engaged in using gestural performatives and making the transition into single words. In keeping with these results, Folger and Leonard (1978) found that means-end abilities did not predict the transition from one- to two-word utterances. When Folger and Leonard administered only the means-end and relating-to-objects tasks, they found that "language-disordered children producing single- and two-word utterances did not differ in their performances on either the means-end or relating-to-objects scale. When age was controlled, the same held true for normal children" (p. 525). For a more comprehensive treatment of this issue, see Bates and Snyder (1982).

Amount and Complexity of Symbolic Play Comparative studies of preoperational language-disordered and normal children have also pointed to concomitant deficits in symbolic play. Lovell et al. (1968) examined the play and verbal interactions of age-matched normal and language-disordered preschoolers. They found significant differences between the groups in the amount of time spent in symbolic play. Qualitative analyses revealed a greater dependency on concrete contextual support in the symbolic play of the language-disordered children. Furthermore, this deficit in symbolic play does not disappear when subjects are matched by linguistic level. Morehead (1972) compared the symbolic play of normal and language-disordered children matched for linguistic level. Despite the fact that the language-disordered children were somewhat older than their normal counterparts, they had greater difficulty generating symbolic play with items that were less contextually related. Finally, Brown et al.'s (1975) observations also revealed lower complexity of symbolic play in preschool language-disordered children as compared with that of their age-matched peers.

Problem Solving Studies of school-age language-disordered children have examined aspects of their problem solving. Inhelder's work (1963, transl. 1966, 1976) has demonstrated that these children have difficulty symbolizing the critical aspects of problems. Although the language-disordered children were able to mobilize operative strategies to solve problems, they could not complete the tasks accurately when the solution was dependent upon the symbolization of critical dimensions. Furthermore, a longitudinal study conducted by de Ajuriaguerra et al. (1965, transl. 1976) resulted in similar observations. Even after two years, language-disordered children continued to have difficulties symbolizing the critical aspects of problems, although they developed normally in the operative domains.

Experiments by Johnston and Ramstead (1978) and Savich (1980) support and extend the preceding conclusions. Johnston and Ramstead's study of school-age language-disordered children revealed a specific profile of problem-solving deficits that centered around difficulty handling anticipatory imagery. Savich's (1980) study confirmed these findings. She found that school-age language-disordered children performed significantly worse than their age-mates on problem-solving tasks involving anticipatory imagery and analytic constructions. By contrast, there were no significant group differences in their performance of static visual tasks. Savich has argued that anticipatory imagery is a task that involves successive transformations of the stimuli, and therefore requires a symbolic representation of that information. She inferred that the language-disordered child's difficulty in accomplishing certain kinds of problem-solving tasks might be related to his linguistic deficit. (See Bates and Snyder, 1982, for a more comprehensive discussion of this issue.)

Role Taking The intrusions in language- and learning-disabled children's recall of discourse narratives (Snyder and Haas, in preparation) suggest cognitive deficits in the form of role-taking difficulties. It is possible that some children have difficulty narrating a story accurately because they cannot distinguish their perspective from that of the protagonist. However, before any firm conclusions can be reached regarding the presence of role-taking deficits and their relationship to the recall of narratives in language-disordered children, it is necessary to find a measure of nonlinguistic role taking and assess its predictive relationship to the narrative recall of these children.

Thus, the literature does suggest some relationship between specific cognitive deficits and the communicative competence of language-delayed children. However, this relationship fails to account for the handful of older mentally retarded children reported by Miller et al. (1977) and Greenwald and Leonard (1979) whose linguistic performance exceeded their cognitive performance. Both studies observed that these children had spent longer periods of time at the same linguistic level. The children's increased exposure to language stimulation programs may have reinforced their use of more advanced linguistic forms. Whatever the reason, these data must also be considered.

Attention

Earlier in this chapter, Bates' (1976) suggestion of a possible relationship between attention and the informativeness of an utterance, was discussed. Briefly put, Bates suggested that the child's encoding of new or changing information represents a developmental growth in the ability to orient toward and differentiate novel from familiar stimuli. Other aspects of communicative competence can also be considered to require attentional focus. For example, the ability to maintain and develop a conversational topic may reflect the child's ability to focus on and retrieve micropropositions that relate to a major topical proposition. Similarly, the ability to follow a topic being developed in conversation may also rest on attentional factors.

The above relationships were discussed here only as theoretical possibilities. Unfortunately, there is little actual evidence relating specific communicative deficits to the lack of attentional vigilance or focus. On the other hand, the very nature of some of these deficits makes attention a good theoretical possibility. For example, an inability to focus on critical elements could reasonably account for Snyder's (1975, 1978) finding that some learning-disordered children do not encode the most informative element as predictably as normal children. Furthermore, among autistic children, a lack of attention could account for their reported (Baltaxe and Simmons, 1977) difficulty in perceiving transient stimuli such as nonverbal facial expressions (Schuler, 1980). However, until more research is available with which to assess the role of attention in specific communicative deficits, it is difficult to know whether attentional deficits have some direct relationship to children's communicative deficits.

However, attention is a more broadly conceived processing component than vigilance or focus. It includes the more global concept of resources or capacity. Current capacity theories of human information processing (Kahneman, 1973; Norman, 1976) have suggested that an individual's performance in a given instance will be affected by the information available to him, and the resources (i.e., effort or attention) that can be allocated to perform a task. Thus, performance can be data limited and/or resource limited, respectively (Norman and Bobrow, 1975). If an individual is asked to repeat sentences spoken to him, he may be able to do so with ease. However, if he is asked to do so in an environment in which the signal-to-noise ratio is such that the noise masks the signal, he will be unable to perform the task. His performance will be *data limited*. The amount of noise limits the information available to complete the task. On the other hand, the individual's performance may also be limited if he is asked to repeat sentences while adding columns of figures. In this case, his performance will be *resource limited*. Because he will have to deploy his attentional resources to both tasks, some of the resources needed for one task will be used to accomplish the other. The individual's performance on the sentence repetition task will improve if/when he can deploy more resources to it. (See Kintsch, 1977, for a more comprehensive discussion of these and the point that follows.)

Schneider and Shiffrin (1977) and Shiffrin and Schneider (1977) have suggested that two modes of processing are available to the individual: automatic and controlled. Automatic processes are operations that: 1) are triggered by specific stimuli; 2) have usually developed through response repetition; 3) are difficult to suppress; and 4) use little or no attentional resources. The use of formulaic routines like those observed in answering a telephone or the neuromotor programming of speech-sound articulation can be considered automatic processes. In contrast, controlled processes are triggered when automatic processes are not available to meet the task demands. However, controlled processes demand that the individual allocate attentional resources to their execution. The decision to hedge in an answer to any uncomfortable question or the formulation of a propositional string are examples of the use of controlled processes.

These notions can be applied to the communicative deficits of language-delayed children. Communicative tasks may pose resource allocation problems for these youngsters. When a child cannot perform a specific communicative operation automatically or with relative ease, he may need to allocate more resources to performing the operation. Given the notion of limited capacity (Kahneman, 1973), the child may then find himself resource limited. Having deployed a larger than average amount of resources to perform an operation, he may find he has drawn upon all of the resources in his account. He may not have a sufficient fund of resources left to accomplish other necessary operations. For example, a child with an oral apraxia may expend a great many resources on the motor planning dimension of a communicative task. In so doing, he may find himself without sufficient resources to hold on to the topic of discourse or to formulate a well-formed indirect directive. On the other hand, he may adapt to his deficit and compensate by using a formulaic, holistically learned indirect phrase that has been committed to automatic processing. Unfortunately, this formulaic phrase may not have the specificity needed to be effective.

Because most children in each diagnostic category have limited capacities and a variety of specific communicative deficits, it seems fair to infer the presence of resource allocation problems. When, for some reason, children need to deploy more resources than are normally required to perform one communicative operation, they may have insufficient resources left with which to attend to other necessary operations. Language-delayed children may appear to sustain attentional vigilance problems simply because their resources have been allocated to perform tasks with controlled processes that normal children can perform with automatic processes. Thus, rather than studying the children's ability to maintain vigilance and focus, it might be more productive to examine the resources they bring to tasks, the type or degree of processing used for these tasks (controlled or automatic), and their allocation of resources.

Perception

Traditionally, the information-processing paradigm has included perception, or the ability to attach meaning to sensory stimuli. Communication—because it relies on the processing of many stimuli, including visual, auditory, linguistic, nonlinguistic, and paralinguistic events—may be vulnerable to the effects of deficient or inefficient perceptual processing. That is, one could reason that almost any perceptual deficit sustained by the language-delayed child may seriously affect his communicative performance. Reasoning in this manner would suggest that visual perceptual deficits may affect the ability to interpret gestural, postural, and facial cues. Similarly, difficulty with auditory stimuli that occur in rapid succession (Tallal, 1976) may affect the ability to interpret auditory, linguistic, and paralinguistic messages. Or, one might alternately argue that some language-delayed children may allocate controlled processes to perceptual stimuli that normal children can process automatically. The resource allocation problems that could result from such extensive use of controlled processes may impair communicative performance.

Levels of Processing

Another factor that must be considered are the levels of information processing being activated for specific tasks and the direction of the flow of information. "Bottom"-level operations are considered to be perceptual or data-driven processes that involve feature extraction and analysis. By contrast, "top"-level operations are considered to be conceptual or knowledge-driven processes. (See Norman, 1976, for a more comprehensive discussion of these operations.) One can "top-down" listen to a conversation, using one's world knowledge and knowledge of language structure to predict words and phrases yet to come. These predictions can then be compared with the results of the actual perceptual analyses of the stimuli to either confirm or refute one's guesses. Thus, context can facilitate perceptual processing (Marslen-Wilson, 1975). Or, one can process an isolated word "bottom-up" by extracting and analyzing its auditory features. Finally, processing can also occur in parallel, with higher and lower levels interacting and affecting one another in a reciprocal manner (Rumelhart, 1976).

Language-delayed children may sustain discrete deficits at different levels of processing. Some children may have difficulty with bottom-up processing, whereas others have problems with top-down processing. The nature of the communicative task, the type and quantity of communicative signals and context available, and the child's development and allocation of resources may alternately or additively affect his communicative performance.

Language

Given that language-delayed children often have linguistic as well as communicative deficits, it is reasonable to ask whether a child's communicative deficiencies are caused by his not knowing the linguistic rules well enough to comprehend and produce complex linguistic structures, or whether his deficiencies are caused by not knowing when to apply the rules he does know. It would appear that some communicative deficits may be related to inadequate linguistic knowledge, whereas others are the result of inadequate or inappropriate use of this knowledge. For example, some language-delayed children may fail to revise an ineffective statement to meet their listeners' needs because a linguistic deficiency prevents them from using alternative semantic and/or syntactic structures; others may fail to revise a statement because they are not aware of their listeners' facial expressions, and so do not take the time to apply the knowledge they have to meet the listeners' needs.

Regardless of the nature or the source of a child's communicative difficulties, it is important to remember that these difficulties may increase the severity of the linguistic deficiencies. In other words, just as deficient linguistic skills may result in deficient communicative performance, the reverse may also be true. Because listeners are often unwilling to engage in inefficient exchanges, deficient communicative performance may limit the child's opportunities for interaction, thus further delaying the child's acquisition of linguistic skills.

Finally, even if the child's deficient communicative performance is related to a linguistic deficiency, either one or both of these deficiencies may be accompanied by resource allocation problems and/or specific cognitive deficits that make any type of successive analytic activity difficult. The complexity of this situation has made it difficult to isolate the source of a communicative disorder. Unfortunately, the confusion becomes even greater when one considers the probability of individual differences.

Individual Differences

If we examine clinical and educational methods of appraisal and intervention, we find that some professionals assume and try to deal with differences between diagnostic groups (e.g., autistic, retarded) as well as differences within each group. They attempt to construct profiles of communicative abilities and disabilities, and then use these profiles to determine intervention strategies, select materials, and group children for therapy. These profiles may not be as specific as needed, but they do represent an attempt to deal with the child as a unique individual, regardless of his diagnostic label.

Although some clinicians have focused on the uniqueness of the child, this approach has had little impact on researchers. Researchers have tended to concern themselves with group means, ignoring the variability surrounding these means—as well as the fact that skills not tested may show similar group differences. The majority of comparative studies using language-disabled children are single-factor studies. Investigators typically compare the performance of normal and delayed subjects in one or possibly two domains. If the delayed children show any significant group deficiencies in the domain(s) tested, it is often assumed that such deficiencies are primary characteristic(s) of the diagnostic category as a whole. Researchers may lose sight of the fact that: 1) on the domain tested, the performance of some subjects in the delayed group may actually be very similar to that of some subjects from the normal group; and 2) if tested on a different skill, the performance of these same delayed subjects might be very different from that of previously similar normal children.

To deal with the variability that is often found in both normal and delayed groups of children, researchers will need to begin: 1) testing a variety of skills in each child; and 2) partitioning the variance to reflect common sources and common problems. The second suggestion implies the existence of subgroups within each of the larger diagnostic categories. Members of each subgroup may be similar to normal children on some tasks, but resemble delayed children on other tasks. The possibility of finding individual differences within a diagnostic category, and specific similarities between categories, has already received some investigation and support. For example, Aram and Nation (1975) investigated a variety of language disorders in mentally retarded children in an attempt to group the children according to the kind of disorder exhibited. The work of Miller et al. (1977) with retarded children has suggested the presence of subgroups based on both cognitive and linguistic deficits. Recently, Miller (1981), using a comprehension/production dichotomy, identified nine subtypes of language delay in a large sample of developmentally disabled subjects. Finally, Snyder and Haas' (in preparation) findings identified distinct subgroups of language- and learning-disabled children with reading disorders.

Thus, significant variability in both the underlying basis for communicative deficits and the nature of the deficits may be encountered within each diagnostic category. Children within each of the large categories may be differentially affected by selective deficits, resulting in the development of qualitatively different communicative strategies.

A MULTIPLE RESOURCES MODEL

The heterogeneity of the language-delayed population presents serious problems for the educator, clinician, and researcher. Even after finding a significant relationship between a specific communicative deficit and a diagnostic category, the variability within this category makes it difficult to apply one's knowledge of the overall group relationship to a specific instance in order to plan a therapy program. However, if we can develop a model of communicative competence that can accommodate the diversity of communicative output, its processing, and the competitive and collaborative use of resources within the system, we might make more realistic assumptions and predictions about children's communicative competence. If we consider the subject and task characteristics as well as the resources that can be used to perform various communicative tasks, we may be able to unmask some of the puzzling inconsistency in the language-delayed child's communicative performance.

It is not unusual for professionals to observe that some language-delayed children perform better at multimodality tasks (i.e., tasks requiring multiply integrated processes) than they do at tasks requiring a single modality or process, whereas other youngsters may perform better under single modality conditions (Johnson and Myklebust, 1967). By considering the possibility that people may have multiple resources available to them, each of which has its own capacity, we can begin to explain the vagaries of communicative processing. The multiple resource model of Navon and Gopher (1979) suggests that some tasks must be executed with preestablished proportions of specific resources and nothing else will suffice. For example, if a language-disordered child is asked to solve a set of analytic construction problems without manipulating the materials, the child must use anticipatory imagery and symbolic resources. Because his symbolic resources are deficient, he is likely to fail. Conversely, other tasks may be accomplished by using various combinations of resources in varying proportions.

In other words, if there is more than one way to solve a problem, then the child who has difficulty mobilizing his symbolic resources may still be able to solve the problem by using combinations of other resources. Indeed, if the same language-disordered child is allowed to solve the first set of construction problems in a trial-and-error manipulative manner, he can often arrive at the desired solutions. Similarly, some communicative tasks may require a specific resource, but other tasks may be accomplished by using either: 1) a combination or a simultaneous collaboration of different resources; or 2) a sequential scheduling of different resources, some of which may be reactivated after their initial service.

A multiple resource model also makes it easier for parallel processing to occur within the system. If different processes or operations tap different resources, the operations can be executed in parallel. For example, decoding a verbal message and perceiving facial expressions presumably require different resources. Consequently, a child should be able to process incoming verbal signals and nonverbal facial expressions at the same time. This parallel processing is both efficient, and, in some cases, absolutely necessary. For instance, a complex indirect request may exhaust the resources usually used for decoding verbal messages, or these resources may be deficient at the outset. In either case, knowledge of the speaker's facial expression may be needed to comprehend the utterance.

Another example of parallel processing as well as a collaboration among resources is the handicapped person's use of sign language. Experienced users of American Sign Language encode information by using an integrated combination of manual signs, facial expressions, gaze, and body posture. Wilbur (1976) noted that the "use of facial expression in modern signing is analogous to intonation in spoken languages; it conveys question, uncertainty, affirmation, negation, etc. . . . " (p. 447). Moreover, a signer's "body language" can delimit the intended meaning, add nuances, and actually contribute to the content being signed. Moreover, "body language" and facial expressions are not the only resources used to supplement the meanings conveyed by manual signs. Some experienced signers also mouth and sometimes vocalize the words being signed. Thus, decoding a signed message might be accomplished by reading the signer's lips, or more accurately by reading his signs, but most accurately by reading both his lips and his signs. However, regardless of whether the message is decoded from lip movements and/or manual signs, the signer's "body language" and facial expressions must be processed in parallel with the other movements read. To accomplish this parallel processing efficiently, many people claim that they focus on the face of the signer while they look at the manual signs out of the corners of their eyes (Dittmann, 1978; Riekehof, 1978).

Although parallel processing is often essential, there may be some costs involved in its use. According to the multiple resource model, both the speaker and the listener may have to "pay" when two or more resources are used concurrently, because additional resources may be needed to coordinate and integrate the activity. These charges constitute *concurrence costs*. For example, take the individual's role in discourse. The speaker must not only know and remember what his listener said during previous turns, he must also process back channel responses and "body language" as he constructs informative messages that maintain and develop the topic of conversation. If the topic is a particularly sensitive one, it is likely that the required integration will cost the speaker additional resources.

Conversely, there are occasions when the deployment of more than one resource may benefit the system. The utilization of two resources simultaneously may cost less than would be required if the resources were deployed individually. This constitutes a *concurrence benefit*. For example, a dancer may find it easier to remember a sequence of steps if he hums the music or sings the song, or a baby may find it easier to remember the appropriate greeting when it is embedded in a hand-waving routine. Thus, some information may be stored together within the system. It will take more resources to retrieve and use that information separately than to use it together.

SUMMARY

In summary, language-delayed children may exhibit selective strengths and deficits in one or more resources. If profiles of these strengths and weaknesses could be constructed, they might delineate subgroups of delayed children. Furthermore, these subgroup profiles should remain constant across diagnostic categories because the types of resources within our species and the types of information to be processed remain constant. Thus, a multiple resource approach to communicative competence would enhance and capture the efficiency with which man operates as a processor.

Efficiency, however, can be found external to the processor as well as internal to it. Efficiency exists in both the language system and the processing of this language system. As Bates and MacWhinney (1982) have so elegantly demonstrated, the topic-comment system in language is constrained by competition and collaboration. Some linguistic forms may map more than one type of information, e.g., human agents tend to be the topic of informal discourse more than 80% of the time. Other kinds of information may be marked by separate linguistic devices. For example, pragmatic information may be carried by specific word choice while case roles are mapped by word order. Those forms collaborating within the language may be learned earlier and processed more easily than those that compete. Thus, communicative efficiency is facilitated by efficiency both within the processor and within the information to be processed.

Just as the orchestra plays a symphony by drawing upon the resources of many instruments in various combinations, people communicate information with various combinations of the means at their disposal. The cello and viola can collaborate to create one mood in a symphonic sequence just as a person can use eye contact and language to create one communicative effect. Conversely, the cello and viola can execute different, competing moods and nonharmonizing sequences just as the communicative effect of the linguistic message can be changed by competing nonlinguistic signals. Moreover, just as the absence of two violins and a French horn may alter the sound of the symphony being played, the language-disordered child's syntactic and phonological deficits may alter his communication. However, just as the symphony conductor may compensate for missing instruments in the orchestra by increasing or changing the roles of the existing instruments, the central nervous system of the language-delayed child will allow him to compensate for some of his linguistic deficits by increasing his use of nonverbal signals. Thus, missing sections from an orchestra will not stop the symphony from being played; it will just be played somewhat differently. Likewise, the language-delayed child's deficits will not halt his communication; his messages will simply sound somewhat different.

ACKNOWLEDGMENTS

I wish to thank Brian MacWhinney, Elizabeth Bates, and Inge Bretherton for their comments and suggestions on an earlier draft of this chapter.

REFERENCES

Alabiso, F. 1972. Inhibition functions of attention in reducing hyperactive behavior. Am. J. Ment. Defic. 77:259–282.
Andersen, E. 1977. Young children's knowledge of role-related speech differences: A Mommy is not a Daddy is not a Baby. Papers Rep. Child Lang. Dev. 13:91–98.
Andersen, E. 1978. Will you don't snore please? Directives in young children's role-play speech. Papers Rep. Child Lang. Dev. 15:140–160.
Aram, D., and Nation, J. 1975. Patterns of language behavior in children with developmental language disorders. J. Speech Hear. Res. 18:229–241.
Austin, J. 1962. How To Do Things with Words. Harvard University Press, Cambridge, MA.
Baltaxe, C. 1977. Pragmatic deficits in the language of autistic adolescents. J. Pediatr. Psychol. 2:176–180.
Baltaxe, C., and Simmons, J. 1975. Language in childhood psychosis: A review. J. Speech Hear. Disord. 40:439–458.
Baltaxe, C., and Simmons, J. 1977. Language patterns of adolescent autistics. In P. Mittler (ed.), Research to Practice in Mental Retardation, Vol. II: Education and Training, pp. 267–278. University Park Press, Baltimore.
Bates, E. 1976. Language and Context: Studies in the Acquisition of Pragmatics. Academic Press, Inc., New York.
Bates, E., Benigni, L., Bretherton, I., Camaioni, L., and Volterra, V. 1979. The Emergence of Symbols. Academic Press, Inc., New York.
Bates, E., and Johnston, J. 1977. Pragmatics in normal and deficient child language. Short course presented at a meeting of the American Speech and Hearing Association, Chicago.
Bates, E., and MacWhinney, B. 1982. Functionalist approaches to grammar. In L. Gleitman and E. Wanner (eds.), Language Acquisition: The State of the Art. Cambridge University Press, New York.
Bates, E., and Snyder, L. 1982. The cognitive hypothesis in language development. In I. Uzgiris and J. McV. Hunt (eds.), Research with Scales of Psychological Development in Infancy. University of Illinois Press, Champaign-Urbana.
Berko-Gleason, J., and Grief, E. 1979. Hi, thanks and good-bye: More routine information. Paper presented at the Child Language Research Forum, Stanford University, Palo Alto.

Berry, M. 1969. Language Disorders of Children. Appleton-Century-Crofts, New York.
Berry, P. 1976. Language and Communication in the Mentally Handicapped. University Park Press, Baltimore.
Beveridge, M., and Tatham, A. 1976. Communication in retarded adolescents: Utilization of known language skills. Am. J. Ment. Defic. 81:96–99.
Birdwhistell, R. 1970. Kinesics and Context. University of Pennsylvania Press, Philadelphia.
Botvin, G., and Sutton-Smith, B. 1977. The development of structural complexity in children's fantasy narratives. Dev. Psychol. 13:377–388.
Bower, A., and Tate, D. 1976. Cardiovascular and skin conductance correlates of a fixed-foreperiod reaction time task in retarded and nonretarded youth. Psychophysiology 13:1–9.
Bowerman, M. 1978. Semantic and syntactic development. *In* R. L. Schiefelbusch (ed.), Bases of Language Intervention. University Park Press, Baltimore.
Bretherton, I., Bates, E., Benigni, L., Camaioni, L., and Volterra, V. 1979. Relationships between cognition, communication, and quality of attachment. *In* E. Bates, L. Benigni, I. Bretherton, L. Camaioni, and V. Volterra (eds.), The Emergence of Symbols. Academic Press, Inc., New York.
Brown, J., Redmond, A., Bass, K., Liebergott, J., and Swope, S. 1975. Symbolic play in normal and language impaired children. Paper presented at a meeting of the American Speech and Hearing Association, Washington, D.C.
Brown, R. 1973. A First Language. Harvard University Press, Cambridge, MA.
Bruner, J. 1975. The ontogenesis of speech acts. J. Child Lang. 9:1–19.
Bryan, T. 1977. Learning disabled children's comprehension of nonverbal communication. J. Learn. Disabil. 10:501–506.
Buium, N., and Steucher, H. 1974. On some language parameters of autistic echolalia. Lang. Speech 17:353–357.
Cicchetti, D., and Sroufe, L. 1976. The relationship between affective and cognitive development in Down syndrome infants. Child Dev. 47:920–929.
Crosby, K. C. 1972. Attention and distractibility in mentally retarded and intellectually average children. Am. J. Ment. Defic. 77:46–53.
Curcio, F. 1978. Sensorimotor functioning and communication in mute autistic children. J. Autism Child. Schizophrenia 8:281–292.
de Ajuriaguerra, J., Jaeggi, A., Guignard, F., Kocher, F., Maquard, M., Roth, S., and Schmid, E. 1965. Evolution et pronostic de la dysphasie chez l'enfant (in French). Psychiatr. Enfant 8:391–452. (Partially translated by Morehead, D., Morehead, A., and Cooper, K. 1976. The development and prognosis of dysphasia in children. *In* D. Morehead and A. Morehead (eds.), Normal and Deficient Child Language. University Park Press, Baltimore.)
Dittmann, A. 1972. Developmental factors in conversational behavior. J. Commun. 22:404–423.
Dittmann, A. 1977. The development of conversational behavior. *In* N. Freedman and S. Grand (eds.), Communicative Structures and Psychic Structures. Plenum Publishing Corp., New York.
Dittmann, A. 1978. The role of body movement in communication. *In* A. Siegman and S. Feldstein (eds.), Nonverbal Behavior and Communication. Lawrence Erlbaum Assocs., Inc., Hillsdale, N.J.

Donahue, M., Bryan, T., and Pearl, R. 1980. Learning disabled children's conversational strategies in a decision-making task with peers. Paper presented at the First Symposium on Research in Child Language Disorders, University of Wisconsin, Madison, June.

Dore, J. 1977. "Oh them Sheriff": A pragmatic analysis of children's responses to questions. *In* S. Ervin-Tripp and C. Mitchell-Kernan (eds.), Child Discourse. Academic Press, Inc., New York.

Dowty, D., Wall, R., and Peters, S. 1981. Introduction to Montague Semantics. D. Reidel Publishing, Boston.

Duncan, S. 1972. Some signals and rules for taking speaking turns in conversations. J. Personality Soc. Psychol. 23:283–292.

Duncan, S. 1973. Toward a grammar for dyadic conversation. Semiotica 9:29–46.

Ervin-Tripp, S. 1977. Wait for me, Roller Skate! *In* S. Ervin-Tripp and C. Mitchell-Kernan (eds.), Child Discourse. Academic Press, Inc., New York.

Fay, W., and Coleman, R. 1977. The human sound transducer/reproducer: Temporal capabilities of a profoundly echolalic child. Brain Lang. 4:396–402.

Fay, W., and Schuler, L. 1980. Emerging Language in Autistic Children. University Park Press, Baltimore.

Fey, M., Leonard, L., Fey, S., and O'Connor, C. 1978. The intent to communicate in language impaired children. Paper presented at the Third Annual Boston University Conference on Language Development, Boston, September.

Fey, M., Leonard, L., and Wilcox, K. 1981. Speech style modifications of language impaired children. J. Speech Hear. Disord. 46:91–96.

Folger, M., and Leonard, L. 1978. Language and sensorimotor development during the early period of referential speech. J. Speech Hear. Res. 21:519–527.

Gallagher, T. 1977. Revision behaviors in the speech of normal children developing language. J. Speech Hear. Res. 20:303–318.

Gallagher, T., and Darnton, B. 1978. Conversational aspects of the speech of language disordered children: Revision behaviors. J. Speech Hear. Res. 21:118–135.

Garvey, C. 1975. Requests and responses in children's speech. J. Child Lang. 2:41–60.

Garvey, C. 1977. The contingent query: A dependent act in conversation. *In* M. Leis and L. Rosenblum (eds.), Interaction, Conversation and the Development of Language. John Wiley & Sons, Inc., New York.

Geller, E., and Wollner, S. 1976. A preliminary investigation of the communicative competence of three linguistically impaired children. Paper presented at the New York State Speech and Hearing Association, Grossingers.

Goffman, E. 1976. Replies and responses. Lang. Soc. 5:257–313.

Greenfield, P., and Smith, J. 1976. The Structure of Communication in Early Language Development. Academic Press, Inc., New York.

Greenwald, C., and Leonard, L. 1979. Communicative and sensorimotor development in Down's syndrome children. Am. J. Ment. Defic. 84:296–303.

Grice, H. 1975. Logic and conversation. *In* P. Cole and J. Morgan (eds.), Syntax and Semantics, Vol. 3: Speech Acts. Academic Press, Inc., New York.

Hall, E. 1959. The Silent Language. Fawcett World Library, New York.

Hoar, N. 1977. Paraphrase capabilities of language impaired children. Paper presented at the Second Annual Boston University Conference on Language Development, October.
Hurtig, R., Ensrud, S., and Tomblin, J. B. 1980. Question production in autistic children: A linguistic pragmatic perspective. Paper presented at the First Symposium on Research in Child Language Disorders, University of Wisconsin, Madison, June.
Inhelder, B. 1963. Observations sur les aspects opératifs et figuratifs de la pensée chez des enfants dysphasiques (in French). Prob. Psycholing. 6:143–153. (Partially translated by Inhelder, B. 1966. Cognitive development and its contribution to the diagnosis of some phenomena of mental deficiency. Merrill-Palmer Q. 12:299–319. Translated by Morehead, D., Morehead, A., and Cooper, K. 1976. Observations on the operational and figurative aspects of thought in dysphasic children. In D. Morehead and A. Morehead (eds.), Normal and Deficient Child Language. University Park Press, Baltimore.)
Johnson, D., and Myklebust, H. 1967. Learning Disabilities: Educational Principles and Practices. Grune & Stratton, New York.
Johnston, J. 1980. The language disordered child. In N. Lass, J. Northern, D. Yoder, and L. McReynolds (eds.), Speech, Language and Hearing. W. B. Saunders Company, Philadelphia.
Johnston, J., and Ramstead, V. 1978. Cognitive development in pre-adolescent impaired children. In M. Burns and J. Andrews (eds.), Selected Papers in Language and Phonology. Institute for Continuing Professional Education, Evanston, IL.
Kahneman, D. 1973. Attention and Effort. Prentice-Hall, Inc., Englewood Cliffs, N.J.
Kaye, K. 1981. The Mental and Social Life of Babies. University of Chicago Press, Chicago.
Keenan, E. 1974. Conversational competence in children. J. Child Lang. 1:163–183.
Keenan, E. 1977. Making it last: Repetition in children's discourse. In S. Ervin-Tripp and C. Mitchell-Kernan (eds.), Child Discourse. Academic Press, Inc., New York.
Kintsch, E., and Kintsch, W. 1979. The comprehension of texts. In R. McLens (ed.), Reading. Deakin University Press, Belmont, Victoria, Australia.
Kintsch, W. 1974. The Representation of Meaning in Memory. Lawrence Erlbaum Assocs., Inc., Hillsdale, N.J.
Kintsch, W. 1977. Memory and Cognition. John Wiley & Sons, Inc., New York.
Labov, W., and Waletzky, J. 1967. Narrative analysis: Oral versions of personal experience. In J. Helm (ed.), Essays on the Verbal and Visual Arts: Proceedings of the 1966 Annual Spring Meeting of the American Ethnological Society. University of Washington Press, Seattle.
Lakoff, R. 1973. The logic of politeness: Or, minding your p's and q's. Papers from the Ninth Regional Meeting of the Chicago Linguistic Society. Linguistics Department, University of Chicago, Chicago, IL.
Lerner, J. 1971. Children with Learning Disabilities. Houghton Mifflin Company, Boston.
Leonard, L., Cole, B., and Steckol, K. 1979. Lexical usage of retarded children: An examination of informativeness. Am. J. Ment. Defic. 84:49–54.
Leonard, L., Schwartz, R., Folger, M., Newhoff, M., and Wilcox, M. 1979. Children's imitations of lexical items. Child Dev. 50:19–27.

Longhurst, T., and Berry C. 1975. Communication in retarded adolescents: Response to listener feedback. Am. J. Ment. Defic. 80:158–164.

Lovaas, O., Schreibman, L., Koegel, R., and Rehm, R. 1971. Selective responding by autistic children to multiple sensory input. J. Abnorm. Psychol. 77:211–222.

Lovell, K., Hoyle, H., and Siddall, M. 1968. A study of some aspects of the play and language of young children with delayed speech. J. Child Psychol. Psychiatry 9:41–50.

Mackworth, N., Grandstaff, N., and Pribram, K. 1973. Orientation to pictorial novelty by speech disordered children. Neuropsychologia 11:443–450.

Mandler, J., and Johnson, N. 1977. Remembrance of things parsed: Story structure and recall. Cognitive Psychol. 9:111–151.

Marslen-Wilson, W. 1975. Sentence perception as an interactive parallel process. Science 189:226–228.

Meline, T. 1978. Referential communication by normal and deficient language children. Paper presented at a meeting of the American Speech and Hearing Association, San Francisco.

Messick, C., and Newhoff, M. 1979. Request form: Does the language-delayed child consider the listener? Paper presented at a meeting of the American Speech and Hearing Association, Atlanta.

Milgram, N. 1973. Cognition and language in mental retardation: Distinction and implications. In C. Routh (ed.), The Developmental Psychology of Mental Retardation. Aldine Publishing Company, Chicago.

Miller, J. 1981. Individual differences in the language acquisition of retarded children. Paper presented at the Second Symposium on Research in Child Language Disorders, University of Wisconsin, Madison, June.

Miller, J., Chapman, R., and Bedrosian, J. 1977. Defining developmentally disabled subjects for research: The relationship between etiology, cognitive development, language and communicative performance. Paper presented at the Second Annual Boston University Conference on Language Development, Boston, September.

Millet, A., and Newhoff, M. 1978. Language disordered children: Language disordered mothers? Paper presented at a meeting of the American Speech and Hearing Association, San Francisco.

Monson, L., Greenspan, S., and Simeonsson, R. 1979. Correlates of social competence in retarded children. Am. J. Ment. Defic. 83:627–630.

Morehead, D. 1972. Early grammatical and semantic relations: Some implications for a general representational deficit in linguistically deviant children. Papers Rep. Child Lang. Dev. 4:1–12.

Muma, J. 1975. The communication game: Dump and play. J. Speech Hear. Disord. 40:296–309.

Muma, J. 1978. The Language Handbook. Prentice-Hall, Inc., Englewood Cliffs, N.J.

Navon, D., and Gopher, D. 1979. On the economy of the human information processing system. Psychol. Rev. 86:214–255.

Newhoff, M., Silverman, L., and Millet, A. 1980. Linguistic differences in parents' speech to normal and language disordered children. Paper presented at the First Symposium on Research on Child Language Disorders, University of Wisconsin, Madison.

Norman, D. 1976. Memory and Attention. (2nd ed.). John Wiley & Sons, Inc., New York.

Norman, D., and Bobrow, D. 1975. On data-limited and resource-limited processes. Cognitive Psychol. 7:44–64.

Ochs, E., and Schieffelin, B. 1979. Developmental Pragmatics. Academic Press, Inc., New York.

Oller, D., Tharp, T., and Coleman, D. A. 1978. Natural logic of pragmatic function of language. Paper presented at the Third Annual Boston University Conference on Language Development, Boston.

Petersen, C., Danner, R., and Flavell, J. 1972. Developmental changes in children's responses to three indications of communicative failure. Child Dev. 43:1463–1468.

Prinz, P. 1977. The comprehension and production of requests in language disordered children. Paper presented at the Second Annual Boston University Conference on Language Development, Boston, October.

Prinz, P. Requesting in normal and language disordered children. *In* K. Nelson (ed.), Children's Language, Vol. 3. Gardner Press, New York. (in press)

Prizant, B. 1978. An analysis of the functions of immediate echolalia. Unpublished Ph.D. dissertation, State University of New York, Buffalo.

Rees, N. 1978. Pragmatics of language. *In* R. L. Schiefelbusch (ed.), Bases of Language Intervention. University Park Press, Baltimore.

Ricks, D., and Wing, L. 1975. Language, communication and the use of symbols in normal and autistic children. J. Autism Child. Schizophrenia 5:191–221.

Riekehof, L. 1978. The Joy of Signing. Gospel Pub., Springfield, MO.

Rumelhart, D. 1976. Toward an interactive model of reading. Technical Report #56. Center for Human Information Processing, University of California, San Diego.

Savich, P. 1980. A comparison of the anticipatory imagery and spatial representation ability of normal and language-disabled children. Unpublished Ph.D. Dissertation, University of Colorado.

Schneider, W., and Shiffrin, R. M. 1977. Controlled and automatic human information processing I. Detection, search and attention. Psychol. Rev. 84:1–66.

Schriebman, L., and Lovaas, O. 1973. Over-selective responses to social stimuli by autistic children. J. Abnorm. Child Psychol. 1:152–168.

Schuler, A. 1980. The interaction of social, linguistic and cognitive development in childhood autism. *In* W. Fay and A. Schuler (eds.), Emerging Language in Autistic Children. University Park Press, Baltimore.

Shapiro, T., and Lucy, P. Echoing in autistic children: A chronometric study of semantic processing. J. Child Psychol. Psychiatry. (in press)

Shatz, M. 1978. On the development of communicative understandings: An early strategy for interpreting and responding to messages. Cognitive Psychol. 10:217–301.

Shatz, M., Bernstein, D., and Shulman, M. 1980. The responses of language disordered children to indirect directives in varying contexts. Appl. Psycholing. 1:295–306.

Shatz, M., and Gelman, R. 1973. The development of communication skills in the speech of young children as a function of the listener. Monogr. Soc. Res. Child Dev. No. 38.

Shiffrin, R., and Schneider, W. 1977. Controlled and automatic human information processing II. Perceptual learning, automatic attending and a general theory. Psychol. Rev. 84:127–190.

Silverman, L., and Newhoff, M. 1979. Father's speech to normal and language delayed children: A comparison. Paper presented at a meeting of the American Speech and Hearing Association, Atlanta.

Simmons, J., and Tymchuk, A. 1973. The learning deficits in childhood psychosis. Pediatr. Clin. North Am. 20:665–679.

Skarakis, E., and Greenfield, P. 1979. The role of old and new information in the linguistic expression of language-disabled children. Paper presented at the Fourth Annual Boston University Conference on Language Development, Boston, September.

Smiley, S., Oakley, D., Worthen, D., Campione, J., and Brown, A. 1977. Recall of thematically relevant material by adolescent good and poor readers as a function of written vs. oral presentation. J. Educ. Psychol. 69:381–387.

Snyder, L. 1975. Pragmatics in language disordered children: Their prelinguistic and early verbal performatives and presuppositions. Unpublished Ph.D. dissertation, University of Colorado.

Snyder, L. 1978. Communicative and cognitive abilities and disabilities in the sensorimotor period. Merrill-Palmer Q. 24:161–180.

Spitz, R. 1965. The First Year of Life. International Universities Press, New York.

Stein, N., and Glenn, C. 1979. An analysis of story comprehension in elementary school children. In R. Freedle (ed.), New Directions in Discourse Processing. Ablex Publishing Corp., Hillsdale, N.J.

Stoel-Gammon, C., and Coggins, T. 1977. Making yourself understood: A study of self-correction strategies in the spontaneous speech of Down's syndrome children. Paper presented at the Second Annual Boston University Conference on Language Development, Boston, September.

Svenson, C. 1971. Introduction to Interpersonal Relations. Scott, Foresman & Company, Glenview, IL.

Tallal, P. 1976. Rapid auditory processing in normal and disordered language development. J. Speech Hear. Res. 19:561–571.

Uzgiris, I., and Hunt, J. McV. 1975. Assessment in Infancy: Ordinal Scales of Psychological Development. University of Illinois Press, Champaign-Urbana.

Vellutino, F. 1979. Dyslexia: Theory and Research. MIT Press, Cambridge, MA.

Voeltz, L. 1977. Syntactic rule mediation and echolalia in autistic children. Unpublished manuscript, University of Hawaii.

Watson, L. 1977. Conversational participation by language deficient and normal children. Paper presented at a meeting of the American Speech and Hearing Association, Chicago.

Weaver, P., and Dickenson, D. 1979. Story comprehension and recall in dyslexic students. Bull. Orton Soc. 29:157–171.

Wiig, E., and Semel, E. 1977. Language Disabilities in Children and Adolescents. Charles E. Merrill Publishing Co., Columbus, OH.

Wilbur, R. 1976. The linguistics of manual languages and manual systems. In L. Lloyd (ed.), Communication Assessment and Intervention Strategies. University Park Press, Baltimore.

Wolff, S., and Chess, S. 1965. An analysis of the language of fourteen schizophrenic children. J. Child Psychol. Psychiatry 6:29–41.

Wulbert, M., Inglis, S., Kriegsmann, E., and Mills, B. 1975. Language delay and associated mother-child interactions. Dev. Psychol. 11:61–70.

chapter

Communication in Infancy and the Emergence of Language in Blind Children

Cathy Urwin

Child Care and Development Group
University of Cambridge
Cambridge, England

Editors' Note

The preverbal communicative skills and cognitive abilities of blind infants are considered in relation to their language development. Predictions are examined in light of available evidence, including a longitudinal description of three congenitally blind children. The language literature on sighted children is also examined as a means for better understanding the developmental problems of blind children. Finally, the longitudinal study of blind children is analyzed to determine areas of needed research as well as the kind of guidance that can be given to parents of young blind children.

The primary message of this chapter is that the effects of blindness on language development must be studied in two ways: 1) through the apparent social and cognitive requirements of normal children in acquiring language, and 2) through the apparent developmental anomalies of blind children. These two issues lead to the conclusion that research on the language of sighted children should be augmented by similar research on blind children in which investigators search for specific developmental prerequisites that apply to their language resources.

contents

**IMPLICATIONS OF BLINDNESS FOR THE
DEVELOPMENT OF PREVERBAL SKILLS
AND COGNITIVE ABILITIES** 484

    Parent-Child Interactions during the Preverbal Period 485
    Attachment Behavior and Sensorimotor Intelligence 489

**EARLY LANGUAGE DEVELOPMENT IN
BLIND CHILDREN** 490

    Onset of Language 490
    Imitation 493
    Emergence of Pronouns 494
    Alternative Routes to Competence: Uses of Language 496
    Need for Further Research 498

A LONGITUDINAL STUDY 500

    Subjects 500
    Objectives and Procedures 501
    Results 503
    Suzanne's Later Development 511

CONCLUDING DISCUSSION 518

REFERENCES 521

For blind children, the importance of acquiring language as a system of communication can hardly be overestimated. Because opportunities for eye contact and other forms of nonverbal communication are absent or considerably reduced, language makes it possible for them to sustain contact with other people and to express and share emotions. It also enables them to seek information about what is going on around them and may play an important role in their coming to know the world as others know it. Ultimately, the success with which blind children master the use of language will be a major factor in determining their acceptance within the wider sighted community.

Given its relative importance, there has been remarkably little research on how blind children use language, and even less on how they acquire it. This is partly due to the nature of the blind child population, which is extremely small compared to many other handicaps. The population is also highly heterogeneous. Statutory definitions of *blindness* generally encompass a broad range of visual defects and degrees of visual loss, and an increasing proportion of blind children have additional handicaps.[1] Finally, the age at which blindness is diagnosed varies considerably. As a result of these considerations, systematic research into the development of preschool blind children is extremely difficult.

Another reason for the paucity of research may be the lack of adequate theoretical tools for conceptualizing and comparing the nature of the tasks facing blind and sighted children. For example, it is notable that the evidence that is available largely comes from a few insightful but obviously limited case histories (e.g., Burlingham, 1961; Wills, 1979), and from cross-sectional and longitudinal surveys (e.g., Fraiberg, 1977; Norris, Spaulding, and Brodie, 1957; Wood, 1970) that rely heavily on normative scales. These kinds of scales allow only very crude comparisons to be made with sighted children, and their limited scope makes it difficult to examine language acquisition in relation to other developmental processes.

Research on language acquisition in blind children is sparse, but research on the same topic with sighted children is abundant. Although

---

[1] In England, where the research reported in this chapter was carried out, blindness in children is defined in terms of educational need, the statutory definition being "Requiring education by methods not involving the use of sight." That is, such children have insufficient sight to allow them to read print, even with the help of special aids. They have to be taught to use braille. In practice, this definition encompasses a range of visual defects and degrees of visual loss similar to that of the definition used in the United States. In England and Wales there are roughly 2,000 children registered as blind. It has been estimated that more than half of these children have additional handicaps (Vernon, 1972). This chapter is principally concerned with legally blind children who do not have additional handicaps, although some of the points that I make also apply to additionally handicapped blind children and their parents.

the data are not directly comparable, the two bodies of literature do complement each other in at least two ways. First, researchers studying language acquisition in sighted children have recently reported a number of findings that make language development in blind children a subject of particular theoretical interest. Many of these findings are well represented in other chapters of this book. Second, the sighted child literature has raised important questions about the kinds of differences that might exist between blind and sighted children. For example, given the general emphasis on the communicative functions of language, one is immediately prompted to ask whether blind children use language in the same way as do sighted children, or exploit certain language functions as a consequence of their particular needs for speech. As Burlingham (1961) put it, perhaps blind children find "uses for speech which sighted children do not require." Because the importance of language for communication also applies to the blind child's parents, one might imagine that the parents also might be called upon to find different or additional uses for language.

Perhaps the clearest predictions that can be made from the sighted child literature come from a number of studies that stem from a general concern for the relationship between language development and other aspects of the child's functioning. This relationship has been proposed in two ways, depending upon whether infant development is operationalized in terms of cognitive development, or the development of preverbal communication is given priority. The first approach has yielded a relationship between cognitive development in infancy and the earliest stages of language development (e.g., Bloom, 1973; Nelson, 1973). The second approach has sought to demonstrate continuities between preverbal and verbal communication (e.g., Bates, Camaioni, and Volterra, 1975; Bruner, 1975, 1978). The significance of these possible continuities has contributed to a change of emphasis in mother-infant interaction studies. Such studies are now attempting to characterize the development of early social relationships in terms of a growing capacity for communication (see, e.g., Bullowa, 1979; Schaffer, 1977).

As I have argued elsewhere (Urwin, 1979b), despite their differing priorities, each of these approaches suggests that blindness in infancy may have important consequences for early language development because, implicitly or explicity, each has assumed the dominance of vision. For example, most of the studies dealing with the cognitive underpinnings of language have leaned heavily on Piaget's (1951, 1953, 1955) theory. It has been argued that changes in word usage and lexical development through the one-word stage reflect concurrent developments in sensorimotor intelligence (Bloom, 1973). Investigators have also proposed that cognitive achievements in the sensorimotor period can account for apparent universals in the conceptual relations that underlie the first word combinations (e.g., Bowerman, 1973; Brown, 1973; Edwards, 1973; Slobin, 1973).

Piaget's theory is often interpreted as giving vision a primary role; indeed, Piaget's own writings seem to imply that a lack of vision will "slow down" cognitive development in infancy (Piaget and Inhelder, 1969). If a lack of vision does delay a child's cognitive development, and if the latter is related to the child's language development, then one might predict that: 1) the emergence of language will be delayed in blind children; and/or 2) during the single-word stage, blind children's use of words will be limited; and/or 3) blind children's first word combinations will reflect a restricted set of conceptual relations.

The sighted child literature also suggests that a lack of vision will impose as great and perhaps even greater constraints on the development of preverbal communication than those on the development of cognition and early word usage. Despite considerable variations in theoretical orientation, researchers who have tried to clarify the nature of preverbal communication and its relationship to language have concentrated on just those communication systems that the blind child lacks (Rowland, 1980). These systems include: 1) the use of eye contact and mutual gaze in the regulation of heightened social play in the early months (e.g., Brazelton, Koslowski, and Main, 1974; Stern, 1974); 2) the role of the visual channel in monitoring mutual attention to distal objects, an activity that is considered important in establishing a shared frame of reference (e.g., Bruner, 1977; Collis and Schaffer, 1975); and 3) the use of gestures such as pointing and reaching to communicate various intentions both before and after the acquisition of prosodically marked words (e.g., Bates et al., 1975; Carter, 1979a; Dore, 1975; Griffiths, 1979).

The priority that these studies give to visually based communication systems implies that, at the very least, blindness in infancy may pose considerable problems for parent-child communication. For example, it suggests that the parents of a blind child may need to adjust to the limited opportunities for monitoring their baby's attention. In addition, if communicative means established in the preverbal period are indeed important for the emergence of language, then constraints on the development of preverbal communicative means may either contribute to delays in the acquisition of language or limit the kinds of communicative intentions that blind children subsequently are able to express.

However, there are alternative or additional possibilities. Even if visually based communication systems play as important a role in parent-infant communication as the sighted child literature suggests, this does not mean that the dominance of vision is necessary. Blind infants and their parents may be able to circumvent the need for vision by relying on alternative communication systems. For example, they might use physical contact to regulate mutual attention and signal communicative intent. In other words, blind children might use communication systems with their parents that are rarely used by their sighted counterparts.

My objective in preparing this chapter has been to analyze the preceding predictions and possibilities. My analysis is organized in the following way. In the first section I discuss the available evidence on the implications of blindness for the development of preverbal communicative skills and cognitive abilities in infancy. In the second section I summarize findings from previous research on the language development of blind children. In addition, because the sighted child literature has generated certain predictions concerning the language development of blind children, I also examine the extent to which these predictions are supported by the available research on blind children. The third section of this chapter contains a description of a longitudinal investigation into the development of three congenitally blind children. These children were studied throughout a large part of the preverbal period as well as the early stages of language development (Urwin, 1978a). Compared to the majority of blind children, these children's language and overall development has progressed extremely well. In the conclusion to this chapter, I discuss the extent to which recent research into language development in sighted children may prove useful in understanding blind children's development. Also discussed are the implications of the findings from the longitudinal study for the kinds of research that are needed, and the kind of guidance that might be given to parents and clinicians working with young blind children.

IMPLICATIONS OF BLINDNESS FOR THE
DEVELOPMENT OF PREVERBAL SKILLS AND COGNITIVE ABILITIES

Broadly speaking, the assumption that blindness may seriously delay development in infancy is endorsed by the available evidence on the early development of blind children. Most of this evidence is clinical and comes from the work of two groups of child psychoanalysts and clinicians. The first group includes Dorothy Burlingham, Doris Wills, and their colleagues at the Hampstead Child Therapy Clinic, London; the second group consists of Selma Fraiberg and her colleagues in the United States. Working independently, both of these groups have emphasized the considerable problems that congenital blindness may pose for the development of early social relations and for the construction of an object world beyond the infant's immediate sphere of action (Burlingham, 1961, 1964; Fraiberg, 1977; Wills, 1970). However, these researchers also stress the fact that parents may play a very important role in helping their blind children overcome some of these difficulties. Unfortunately, this does not necessarily occur automatically. When parents are coping with shock, grief, and other feelings associated with the knowledge that their baby is blind, the provision of anything extra on their part may demand too much from them.

Parent-Child Interactions during the Preverbal Period
Even when parents have accepted their child's blindness, they still may find it difficult to provide the kind of social contact and opportunities for exploration that their child will need. In this section, I discuss some of the problems typically encountered during the preverbal period. When the available literature suggests ways to solve these problems, the possible solutions are also discussed. The discussion focuses on problems associated with: 1) the establishment of an emotional relationship between mother and child; 2) the regulation of attention; and 3) the initiation of interaction by the child. Finally, arguments for parental counseling and support are given.

Problems and Some Possible Solutions Without opportunities for eye contact and reciprocal gazing, blind infants and their mothers are deprived of one of the communication systems normally regarded as crucial for drawing mother and child together in the early stages of their developing relationship (Ainsworth, Bell, and Stayton, 1974; Robson, 1967; Stern, 1974). Can we thus conclude that a lack of vision will seriously affect the development of a relationship between mother and child? Is there any other communicative system that might draw mother and infant together? One possible compensatory mechanism on the part of the infant is the smile (Rowland, 1980). Smiling to the mother's voice has been observed in blind infants as young as 4 weeks (Fraiberg, 1977; Freedman, 1964). Furthermore, Rowland (1980) reported that the frequency of facial expressions in 1–3-year-old blind children was comparable to the frequency of such expressions in sighted infants; but most other observers have found that smiling in blind infants is muted and fleeting compared to sighted infants. Finally, Fraiberg (1977) noted that a smile may offer parents considerable encouragement, but its appearance required some prior initiative from the parent, who then must work hard to sustain it.

In terms of an ongoing interaction, the infant's smile may be one element in a cycle that often must begin with the parent. Parental efforts to initiate an interaction may evoke smiles from the infant. The resulting smiles may evoke further parental efforts, which in turn may evoke additional smiles, and so on. Thus, infant smiling might perpetuate interactions initiated by a parent (Rowland, 1980). Conversely, when parents do not initiate much interaction, few smiles are likely to be observed. The absence of infant smiles might further discourage parents from initiating the necessary interactions. In other words, the lack of smiles might depress parental initiatives and thereby constrain the development of a relationship between parent and child.

However, the drawing together of mother and child is not the only problem encountered here. Once the mother initiates an interaction, how does she determine what the infant wants to do? This calls for a discussion of the ways in which blind and sighted children reveal attention and interest. The regulation of attention is often attributed to the visual system in the sighted child literature (e.g., Bruner, 1977; Collis and Schaffer, 1975). By following the infant's line of regard, the mother of a sighted child may gain information as to the object of a child's attention; by the end of the first year, corresponding behavior may be observed in the infant (Churcher and Scaife, 1979).

The sighted infant's orientation toward a person or object is often accompanied by gesturing. These gestures may further specify the object/activity of interest. Prior to the onset of words sighted children indicate/demand specific objects of interest by pointing and/or reaching (Bates et al., 1975; Carter, 1979b; Sugarman, this volume). Blind children, on the other hand, do not reach to demand objects, nor do they point to things in the environment. They also do not spontaneously offer or show objects as sighted children do in the last quarter of the first year (Rowland, 1980). Even raising the arms to be picked up, if it occurs at all, may not emerge until the third year or later.

If parents of blind children are given neither visual nor gestural cues as to the children's preferred objects and activities, then how can parents determine the children's preferences? One possibility is that they learn to appreciate the significance of cues associated with listening. However, in comparison to visual and gestural cues, behavior associated with listening can be extremely ambiguous; this ambiguity is often heightened by the fact that blind children's frequently nonstandard response to sound often contradicts what sighted people are likely to expect when a person is attending to a sound coming from an object. Instead of turning to face the direction of the sound source, blind infants may drop their heads or slowly swing their heads from side to side. Similarly, when spoken to, they may either fail to raise their heads or they may turn to one side, thereby returning their mothers' initiatives with cues that are in some ways paradoxical and excluding.

The parent-child interactions discussed thus far have all been initiated by the parent. However, sighted children not only respond to the initiatives of their parents, they also show such initiatives themselves. Sighted children often initiate interactions by vocalizing and gesturing. Many blind children, on the other hand, rarely initiate interactions. Although there may be marked individual differences (Rowland, 1980), researchers have often reported that young blind children tend to emit few vocalizations (Fraiberg, 1977; Wills, 1979; Wood, 1970). Furthermore, as previously mentioned, their use of gestures is sparse.

Blind infants' ability to gesture in demanding or indicating objects depends, of course, on their knowing that there is an object there. Here we find that the development of preverbal communication between parents and blind infants may be further restricted by the difficulties that blindness poses for the development of cognition in infancy. Both the Hampstead group and Fraiberg have emphasized the importance of encouraging blind infants to explore their environment actively. Here the development of coordinated reaching for sound-making objects is regarded as crucially important, "as the outward and visible sign of the blind child's becoming aware that objects in the noncontiguous world have substantiality" (Wills, 1970). However, for reasons that are not well understood, coordinated reaching for sound-making objects appears to be a more complex operation than visually guided reaching. The former reaching does not emerge before 9 to 10 months in both blind and sighted infants (Bower, 1974; Fraiberg, 1977). In many blind children, this development may not be consolidated until considerably later (Wills, 1970). In addition, opportunities for active exploration are further hampered by the fact that mobility is typically delayed in blind children (Fraiberg, 1977; Norris et al., 1957).

The implications of limited active exploration for cognitive development are discussed below. Here it is important to note that the relatively slow emergence of reaching and independent mobility may further enhance the parents' feeling that their children are uninterested in things, or are oblivious to what is going on around them.

Thus, the literature on blind infant development suggests that young blind infants rarely use standard communicative means to initiate interaction with their parents, and parental efforts to locate the object of a child's attention often meet with ambiguous infant responses. Given their reported lack of initiative, blind infants are crucially dependent on other people to initiate entertainment and to provide them with objects to hold and investigate. However, with relatively few signs of initiative or attention from the infants, it is all too easy for parents to let them listen passively to the sounds going on around them. This lack of parent-child interaction may in turn lead to an increase in passivity, with critical consequences for development. Stereotyped behaviors—such as rocking, head swaying, and eye poking—typically emerge at this time; the children's attention also may become increasingly absorbed in their own bodies (Fraiberg, 1977; Wills, 1970). Because such behavior may appear bizarre and meaningless to the mothers, it may lead them to withdraw from their children, which in turn exacerbates the children's depression.

Parental Counseling and Intervention   Wills (1977) expressed a view that is shared by many clinicians: "It is the exceptional mother who can help her blind child circumvent this major handicap without counseling." Such counseling was a central aspect of Fraiberg's (1977) longitudinal intervention study of 10 otherwise neurologically intact, totally blind infants. This study was aimed specifically at promoting interaction between mother and child in an effort to study the effects that such interaction might have on blind infants' development. Interaction was largely achieved by helping the mothers discover: 1) alternative cues to their babies' attention and involvement; and 2) ways of maintaining contact with their infants.

For example, Fraiberg (1974, 1977) helped the mothers discover how the blind infant's body movements can convey affect and attention. Mothers were also encouraged to learn how to use the child's stilling and anticipatory finger movements as cues to his or her attention to sound-making objects prior to the establishment of auditorily guided reaching. Second, parents were given guidance in how to use touching, tickling, and other gross forms of physical contact to maintain an interaction with their infants. In order to maintain contact across distances, parents were encouraged to talk as much as possible to their children. Although there were considerable individual differences in how easily the mothers were able to talk to their blind infants when the infants showed little initiative, Fraiberg (1968) still observed:

> Among our blind babies we have excellent examples of 'dialogues' with the mothers around the end of the first year, or 'questions and answers' between mother and baby following speech cadences in a parody of English. (p. 276)

In order to assess the relative value of early intervention, Fraiberg assessed the development of her 10 subjects in relation to the findings reported by Norris et al. (1957) in their survey of preschool blind children. Fraiberg's study is the largest of its kind to date and is generally taken to be adequately representative of the blind child population as a whole. Fraiberg found that, after intervention, the children in her sample were more advanced in most areas than were Norris' subjects. Thus, Fraiberg's study testifies to the value of early intervention. However, despite the children's relatively satisfactory development, Fraiberg suggested that there were some areas that remained problematic. In particular, like the literature in general, she stressed the general restrictions on available means for initiating interaction. The occurrence of vocal "dialogues," for example, seemed to depend on some prior initiative from the mothers, and not all the infants in the sample vocalized in response to the mothers' initiatives. Moreover, Fraiberg (1977) reported that even the "high vocalizers" in the group vocalized considerably less than do sighted infants at a similar age.

As previously mentioned, other investigators have similarly observed that some blind infants appear to be remarkably silent during the first year (Wills, 1979; Wood, 1970). For her group, Fraiberg suggested that the infants' silence was due to their lack of access to the kinds of events (e.g., the appearance of the mother's face above the cot, and dynamic changes or movements in objects) that are likely to evoke vocalization in a sighted infant.

Attachment Behavior and Sensorimotor Intelligence

Given that many blind children have difficulty initiating interactions, and that their parents often have difficulty locating the object of their attention, it is not surprising that many blind children show delays in the development of attachment behavior and sensorimotor intelligence. Fraiberg (1968, 1974, 1977) emphasized how important it was to the mothers in her sample that their babies were coming to know them as distinct from strangers. Except for the children's reactions to prolonged separation, the development of attachment behavior closely paralleled the course observed in sighted children. Prolonged separations, however, produced acute panic and regression; a reunion produced persistent clinging and other manifestations of extreme distress.

In regard to the development of sensorimotor intelligence, Fraiberg argued that all the children in her sample showed substantial delays in achieving a Stage 6 level of object permanence (Piaget, 1953). This conclusion was based on the finding that none of the children were observed initiating a sustained search for an object in the absence of prior tactile or sound information (Fraiberg, 1977).

Another area in which Fraiberg reported substantial delays was in the development of symbolic play. Symbolic play usually emerges in sighted children by the end of the second year (Piaget, 1951); however, like other investigators (Rowland, 1980; Wills, 1965), Fraiberg noted an initial lack of interest in imaginary activity on the part of her blind subjects at the end of their second year. For example, she stressed that none of the young children in her sample engaged in spontaneous doll play, or role play in which the children used objects to reconstruct acts that they had observed habitually or that others had directed toward them. However, this situation did improve after Fraiberg told the parents of her subjects how important it was for them to encourage their infants to play with objects and explore the environment. Thus, symbolic play was eventually observed in some of the subjects after a considerable delay and after the children had received deliberate tutoring from their parents.

Overall, Fraiberg (1977) concluded that, despite the children's relatively satisfactory development and the clear benefits of intervention, the children in her sample showed substantial delays in the development of representational intelligence. She suggested that this delay accounts for the extreme reactions to separation, and testifies to the "extraordinary problem posed by blindness in constituting a self and object world."

EARLY LANGUAGE DEVELOPMENT IN BLIND CHILDREN

This is the background against which language emerges and begins to develop. Language use seems to be a skill that parents of blind children invariably encourage, because it promises a form of contact that they missed (Burlingham, 1961).

Onset of Language

Parents may need to wait longer than usual, however, for the onset of language in blind children. Given that the continuities between preverbal and verbal communication reported for sighted children might also apply to blind children, it is not surprising that many blind children are initially delayed in acquiring words and in using them productively in communication. Some blind children will only produce words that they already know in response to parental efforts to evoke an imitation. Another group will repeat standard words to themselves in their own play, but fall silent when anyone attempts to engage them in conversation (e.g., Urwin, 1978b; Wills, 1979; Wood, 1970).

There is also a third major tendency. Children in this last group rapidly amass words associated with caregiving and familiar routines. Although the initial appearance of these words may depend on some prior initiative from the parent, the children use these words from the outset to sustain the attention of others. The existence of these children is evident from Fraiberg's (1977) report that many of the children in her sample fell close to the Bayley (1969) language development norms for second-year sighted children. However, Fraiberg suggested that these children were more advanced than is typical of the blind child population as a whole.

Despite their relatively rapid language development, Fraiberg noted that, in comparison to sighted children, her blind subjects had few object names in their early vocabularies. The initial use of object names occurred within the age range given by Bayley, but the children subsequently either failed to acquire additional object words or rarely used those available to them. Fraiberg (1968) stated that: "In the second year when we expect to see a rapid acquisition of new words . . . in the child's vocabulary, the blind child lags behind for a period." Similarly, Burlingham (1961) observed: "The mothers tell us that between sixteen and eighteen months their children seem to forget the few words that they had learned already, or at least do not increase them."

Although not specifically discussed by Fraiberg, there is also some evidence to suggest that the use of words to demand objects also may emerge relatively late in blind children. Wills' (1979) observations, for example, indicate that requests for food and for activities centering on the child's own body may emerge considerably earlier than requests for objects. Wills also suggested that the discovery that words can "get you things" may mark a crucial step forward for children who are initially slow in speaking.

Apart from an initial delay in acquiring words for naming objects, Fraiberg (1977) also noted that, relative to the Bayley norms, her blind subjects showed a delay in the use of word combinations. However, once the children's increasing mobility brought them into contact with distant objects and events, the majority of the children in Fraiberg's sample rapidly began to acquire object names and to produce novel combinations. Fraiberg reported that these combinations were similar to those first produced by sighted children; unfortunately, she does not discuss communicative intentions or the kinds of semantic relations that the blind children were most likely to express.

Fraiberg (1977) related the delay in acquiring words for naming objects and the comparative paucity of naming behavior to the delayed emergence of object permanence. Similarly, she proposed that the delay in producing word combinations was related to the delayed onset of mental representation. This line of argument suggests that the reported delay in the use of words to demand objects may also be due to a representational deficit. The child has to "know" of an object out there before he or she can ask for it. However, delayed mental representation may be only one of the factors contributing to the reported language delay. In sighted children the first uses of names and requests for objects are generally accompanied by gestures, the latter being consolidated before the emergence of language. This suggests that blind children's limited use of gesture in the preverbal period may contribute to limitations in the ways in which they initially can use language to communicate.

Fraiberg's (1977) study represents the most complete source of information available on blind infants' development. However, less extensive studies of these children have been done with varying results. Some investigators have suggested that, by the age of 3, the blind child's vocabulary may be within the normal range (Norris et al., 1957; Wood, 1970). Burlingham (1961), for example, observed that:

> When the toddler stage is over, our children seem to have picked up speech very quickly and it is one of their accomplishments that they speak fluently and have large vocabularies in which they even outdo the seeing. (pp. 135–136)

Although the third year may be a turning point for some blind children, a second group of children show continued delays. Indeed, initial delays may persist such that, by the end of the third year, a child's vocabulary might consist of only a few social words, such as "Mum," "Dad," and "tea." It is important to appreciate that these kinds of delays may occur even in cases where object skills and mobility are apparently developing well (Wood, 1970).

A third group of blind children exhibit what one might describe as a mixed developmental pattern. They show delays in the acquisition of a broad vocabulary, but a rapid acquisition of some kinds of words and phrases. For example, this group of blind children may be delayed in acquiring object names but rapidly learn words and phrases associated with their own body movements; or they may quickly pick up ready-made phrases that they have heard repeatedly, such as "Time for tea," "Shut the door," "Mummy carry you," and "Don't bang your head." Some of these children use ready-made phrases when playing, but rarely use them to initiate interaction. However, other children repeatedly use the phrases to draw attention to themselves and to produce some acknowledgment from the parent.

> Shaun [2 years;5 months(0 days)] is not yet mobile and still gives little indication of being able to put together his own sentences. However, he uses "Cuppa tea, yeah. Cuppa tea, yeah," to ask for a drink when he hears the clatter of tea things. These words are not accompanied by a gesture or any other discernible communicative means.
>
> Sam [2;4(2)], who was mobile relatively early for a blind child, is sitting on his rocking horse. With a rising intonation he uses a phrase that his mother has often said to him in this situation. He repeats it again and again until she answers.
> *Sam:* Sam go riding on a rocking horse?
>   Sam go riding on a rocking horse?
>   Sam go riding on a rocking horse?
> *Mother:* Yes, Sam go riding on the rocking horse.

Sam [2;9(0)] is bouncing up and down on his trampoline.
Sam: Mummy watch you.
Mummy watch you.
Mother: Yes, I'm watching you. I'm watching you.

Imitation

Parents of blind children often deliberately encourage their children to imitate. This encouragement may induce the children to repeat and subsequently acquire complete phrases. Some children imitate phrases that they hear around them but that are not actually directed toward them. Other children repeat only what is directed toward them; with a variable understanding of the relationship between the words and the preceding context, these children can keep a conversation going by repeating what the adult has just said to them. More extreme forms of echolalia are also fairly common. As in autistic children, the intonation patterns of this speech are flat or hollow, and the effects produced are bizarre and disturbing to the listener.

Excessive imitation or "parroting" in the early stages is often considered a danger signal. For example, Wood (1970) found that language development sometimes became "stuck" after a great deal of imitation in the early stages. Some of the early imitators in Wood's study later repeated things incessantly until someone answered. To the parents, this language seemed tedious and stilted and they were not sure how much their children understood. These kinds of difficulties are usually resolved by the end of the nursery school period. However, a tendency to rely on "prepackaged" forms of speech may persist into the early school years and even into adult life. Among any sample of school-age blind children, one can find examples of children in whom an apparent verbal precosity conceals gaps in their understanding of the physical world. In some cases, these children's speech has a "feel" of shallowness about it, as if they are talking for talking's sake (Langan, 1970; Urwin, 1978b).

Although excessive imitation may be a danger signal, children who rapidly acquire a productive use of language often show a marked tendency to imitate. Some children begin using language by imitating prolifically and may even show echolalia, but their later productive language proves highly adequate (Wills, 1979). This finding suggests that an activity that may give considerable pleasure to both parents and children should not necessarily be discouraged. Furthermore, the very predominance of imitation in blind children suggests that it might be highly functional for the children. These questions are discussed further when I review the results from the longitudinal study. (Also see Snyder, this volume, for a discussion of the communicative uses of imitation in other delayed children.)

Emergence of Pronouns

An aspect of language development that Fraiberg claimed is universally delayed in blind children is the emergence of "I" as a stable pronoun, and by implication the ability to use "you" to refer to the other party in an interaction. Although not discussed by Fraiberg, confusions in the use of other personal pronouns also appear to be common (Wood, 1970).

The ability to handle the "I-you" distinction in language implies that: 1) the child has established a basic distinction between the roles of self and other in an interaction; and 2) he understands something about the substitutability, or the reversibility, of these roles. In sighted children, there has been little systematic study of the precursors to this distinction. Bruner (1975) has speculated that ritualized joint action sequences such as "give-and-take" games in the preverbal period may help equip the child with notions of reversible roles that later are handled linguistically with the deictic shifters "I" and "you." After the preverbal period, but prior to the acquisition of personal pronouns, the basic distinction between the roles of self and other may appear again in early word combinations where the child refers to: 1) his own agency (e.g., "Sam push"); or 2) the agency of another person (e.g., "Mummy push"); or 3) the reciprocal relationship between parties, as when one party is the beneficiary of the actions of the other (e.g., "Mummy push me").

How the ability to express these semantic roles eventually relates to the mastery of "I" and "you" is not clear. There is some evidence to suggest that certain strategies for combining words in the early stages are associated with more rapid acquisitions of pronoun usage than are other strategies (Bloom, Rocissano, and Hood, 1976; Nelson, 1973). However, even children who use one of the slower strategies normally begin using deictics by the middle of the third year (Clark, 1978; Huxley, 1970; Maratsos, 1979).

Although it is commonly assumed that sighted children initially have problems in handling these terms, cases of genuine reversal (e.g., when the child switches "I" or "me" with "you") are comparatively rare and are generally short lived where they do occur. However, in blind children confusions and instability in the use of personal pronouns are often prolonged, sometimes persisting into the early school years. Confusions and inappropriate usages may take a number of forms that can affect either comprehension or production. For example, on the comprehension side, when asked "Where's my nose?" blind children may indicate their own noses rather than the speaker's. It is difficult to know whether a particular child would perform the appropriate action if the speaker's name were substituted for "my." Research indicates that the performance of some children would improve with the substitution, but the performance of others would not. On the production side, perhaps the most common source of confusion occurs in conjunction with the previously mentioned tendency to use ready-made phrases. For instance, when Sam was playing on the trampoline [at 2;9(0)], his repetition of the phrase "Mummy watch you" resulted in a misapplication of "you." Similarly, some children repeat their own names or a third person pronoun when reproducing phrases that other people have said to them or about them. Sam, at 2;4(2), saying "Sam go riding on a rocking horse?" is an example of this behavior.

It is important to note that, in addition to illustrating frequent kinds of reversals, the preceding examples also indicate that inappropriate usages do not necessarily mean that the user has no appreciation of his agency or that of other people. Even when blind children understand the concept of agency, they still may be confused over which pronoun to use when indicating their own agency and which to use when marking a listener's agency. This, again, may be related to the tendency to acquire ready-made phrases.

Fraiberg traced how the stable use of "I" developed in some of the children in her advantaged group (Fraiberg, 1977; Fraiberg and Adelson, 1975). She suggested that the delayed ability to use "I" appropriately was caused by the blind children's delayed capacity for self-representation. She based this conclusion on the fact that each child in her sample showed a delay in the representation of self in imaginative play. When body games were used to draw the children's attention to the relationship between their own body parts and those of other people, the children began to play imaginatively with dolls; in each case, the use of dolls to represent the self coincided with the stable use of "I," "me," and "you."

However, Fraiberg's analysis of her subjects' linguistic development is limited in many ways. For example, she did not provide any data on whether or not her subjects showed reciprocal relations in their first word combinations, nor do we know the extent to which these children relied on ready-made phrases. Finally, although the proposed relationship between the stable use of "I" and the capacity for self-representation is interesting, it would be useful to have more information on what other aspects of the children's experience and development were changing over the period in which they began to use "I" and "you." For example, it is possible that changes in the interaction that accompanied the tutoring of symbolic play can explain the observed changes in language better than can Fraiberg's appeal to a representational capacity (see Urwin, 1981).

Alternative Routes to Competence: Uses of Language

Despite the preceding limitation, Fraiberg's (1977) study draws attention to important differences between blind and sighted children. These differences in turn raise several questions concerning the alternative routes that may be available to blind children.

Symbolic Play Fraiberg's definition of symbolic play demands that the form of a blind child's play be like that of a sighted child. One might well question this requirement, and the resulting conclusions. Fraiberg claimed that her subjects did not show symbolic play until relatively late and only after deliberate tutoring. However, a closer examination of what blind children do when they do not receive instruction from sighted adults might reveal that young blind children do indeed engage in symbolic play, albeit in a form that reflects a nonvisual access to the environment. This possibility was in fact suggested by some of Fraiberg's own observations. These observations indicate that language itself can serve as a medium for early representational play. The following example shows how, in pretend play, a blind child might use language to represent alternate roles well before the child begins to play with dolls in the way that sighted children do:

> (Kathie, 2;0(23), is sitting in a toy bath tub)
> As she squatted in the tub, pushing herself up and down in the water, she began to carry on a dialogue in two voices: 'swimming in the water'. 'Mama look at that'. 'Whee, whee!' 'Can you feel it?' 'O.K. You sit in the water.' Very clearly one voice in this speech belonged to Kathie and one voice to her mother, bathing Kathie. (Fraiberg, 1977, p. 256)

It is not clear why Fraiberg did not consider such playful uses of language when defining symbolic play. However, she does appear to separate play with language from play with objects. Indeed, she even argued that instances of play such as the one just cited are not sufficient to ensure the appropriate use of "I" and "you," for which the application of some intermediary object is necessary to symbolize the self. Whether or not Fraiberg is correct in this regard remains unclear from the available evidence. Either way, it is possible that pretense involving dialogue may play an important role in enabling blind children to establish a distinction between "self" and "other."

Alternative Ways To Explore the Environment and To Make Contact with People Fraiberg's case history of emergence of "I" is instructive in other ways. In considering the differences between early pretend play in blind and in sighted children, we must recognize that much of sighted children's early pretense is based on what they have seen and/or imitated. However, blind children's access to what is going on around them is limited. For example, there are many objects in the children's environment that cannot be touched and that do not make sounds. This in turn may limit what blind children can talk about, contributing to further delays in language development. On the other hand, if the children are given enough opportunities for exploration to allow their language to begin in the first place, the entry into language may provide them with an alternative way of exploring the environment. That is to say, conversation with other people might allow blind children to become aware of those aspects of the environment to which their access is limited.

There are a number of examples in the literature that suggest that, by the end of the preschool years, some blind children use language to explore and comment upon objects in the environment. For example, they might ask questions to gain information about the characteristics that differentiate people and objects in the environment. In general, questioning enables blind children to extend their understanding of what is going on around them. It also is not hard to find comments that reflect connections based on the blind child's nonvisual experience of the world. However, as illustrated by the second example given below, sighted individuals are not always quick to appreciate the significance of a blind child's remarks:

> Caroline [4;0(0)] has been asked whether she would like to touch the guinea pig in the nursery. She backs away.
> *Caroline:* No, I don't like it. It feels like a horse. (Burlingham, 1964)
> Simon [4;3(0)] is lifting a metal torch out of his play box.
> *Simon:* Coldy, coldy ice cream.
> *Mother:* Don't be silly. It's not an ice cream.

As far as interaction with other people is concerned, the ability to ask questions is perhaps one of the most significant developments for blind children. This ability is usually well developed by the end of the preschool years. Indeed, by this age many blind children seem to ask questions almost incessantly. This continual questioning has one disadvantage, but many advantages. The disadvantage is that a long series of questions (e.g., "What's your name?" "Where do you live?" "Have you got children?" "What are their names?" "Where are they?" "Why have you come?") may seem strange and disturbing to strangers. Some observers (e.g., Maxfield, 1936) have suggested that these questions reflect the blind child's insecurity. One advantage of asking questions has already been discussed. Questions enable the child to gain information about the environment. However, blind children also use questions to check on the presence and attentiveness of a presumed listener, and to find out whether an object is accessible to both of them. Many blind children also ask questions to facilitate orientation and mobility (Burlingham, 1961). When the child gets a reply to his question, he can use the other person's voice as a reference point.

Other forms of questioning may emerge later as the children become increasingly aware of the fact that the seeing know what is unknown to them (Burlingham, 1961). They may ask about objects that the sighted use in order to find out how to use the objects themselves. They may even ask whether they will be able to see when they grow up. Talking about their blindness may go some way toward releasing them from an inexplicable sense of limitation and frustration, thereby increasing their potential for active participation in the social world.

Summary The use of language may help blind children overcome many of the problems posed by their handicap. However, the number and kinds of limitations removed by language varies among children. This variability results in a broad range of differences in developmental progress, but similarities among children also exist. For example, children often show more extensive delays and language difficulties in the early stages of development than they do in the later ones. In general terms, the frequent occurrence of these early delays supports predictions drawn from recent studies of the relationship between preverbal communication, cognitive development, and the emergence of language in sighted children.

Need for Further Research

There still remain many unanswered questions. There has been no systematic study of the early syntactic development of blind children as far as I am aware. The use of syntax emerges late in many blind children; but Fraiberg (1977) reported that, when syntactic structures did finally appear in her subjects' speech, the structures closely resembled those of sighted children.

Second, from the available evidence it is not possible to distinguish the effects of restricted opportunities for social interaction from the effects of similar restrictions on the exploration of the inanimate environment. It is the latter source of constraint that has been given the most attention. For example, Fraiberg suggested that in some cases initial restrictions on the use of words for naming objects and the delayed production of word combinations may reflect cognitive constraints due to limitations on active exploration during the first two years. Limitations on active exploration and the resulting "cognitive delay" also may be responsible for the fact that no observer has reported that blind children overgeneralize words in the single-word period. Finally, I have suggested above that the delay in requesting objects may similarly be due to cognitive constraints.

In general, the preceding relationships all suggest ways in which exploration and cognitive change might contribute to a child's acquisition of language. However, cognitive development cannot totally explain the acquisition of language. Whereas many blind children rapidly develop language once their mobility permits active exploration of the environment, there still are other children whose language fails to progress even after mobility is established. Reasons for this lack of progress are at present unknown.

Here, I would suggest, more attention needs to be given to the possible effects of constraints on the development of preverbal communication. I have already suggested that the absence of gestural demands may contribute to the blind child's limited exploitation of these speech functions in the early stages. More generally, evidence that some blind children are relatively slow to "latch on" to the communicative functions of language again directs attention to the relation between preverbal communication and language.

In any case, it is clear that many blind children are, for some reason, late in using words to communicate. For example, in her longitudinal study of five infants with ages that initially ranged from 11 to 32 months, Rowland (1980) reported that only one of these infants (a 15-month-old) used words. One year after the initiation of this project, none of the other infants in Rowland's sample had even begun to use words consistently.

Even after acquiring a vocabulary, blind children do not always use the acquired words to communicate with others. Some blind children verbalize to themselves during play, but fall silent when anyone attempts to engage them in conversation (Urwin, 1978b; Wills, 1979; Wood, 1970). Although these difficulties sometimes disappear by the age of 3, there are also cases in which delays persist. By the end of the third year, some blind children have only a few social words in their vocabularies and others show persistent problems in relating their speech to the ongoing context of interaction. Here we need to know more about how blind children can gain access to what is going on around them, and what sighted people can do to aid them in this respect.

Despite the frequent reports of delayed language in blind children, we cannot conclude that language difficulties are a necessary consequence of blindness. It is clear from the available evidence that some blind children cope with the task of acquiring language considerably better than do others. For example, the children in Fraiberg's (1977) intervention study appear to be more advanced than the majority of blind children. Yet there is no reason to suppose that the developmental progress of Fraiberg's subjects represents a ceiling on what blind children can do. Furthermore, judging the blind child's linguistic progress according to criteria derived from studies of sighted children may be to ignore the blind child's particular needs for language, and the possible consequences of these needs on the acquisition process.

A number of examples have been given that suggest that some blind children find ways of using language that are not likely to be observed extensively in sighted children. These include: 1) the use of language in fantasy play; 2) the expression of connections based on nonvisual sensory experience; and 3) the use of questions to prompt interaction and obtain information about the social and physical environment. Although these adaptive uses of language may not appear until relatively late, their eventual production often results in substantial benefits to the child. Indeed, the use of language may enable the blind child to develop competencies by taking "alternative routes" that circumvent some of the handicaps posed by blindness. Because blind children's opportunities for learning through observation are obviously reduced, the children may depend on verbal interaction for information about the environment and for feedback on what they themselves are doing. Thus, the acquisition of language might be even more important for blind children than it is for sighted children.

A considerable amount of research into language development in blind children is clearly needed before we can understand what might constitute general sources of difficulty and how certain factors might contribute to individual differences in developmental progress. However, researchers attempting to deal with these issues should consider the blind children's needs rather than just comparing their progress with the course of development assumed to be typical of sighted children.

A LONGITUDINAL STUDY

As a first step toward obtaining the needed information, an intensive longitudinal study was conducted on three congenitally blind children. These children were observed throughout a large part of the preverbal period as well as during the early stages of language acquisition (Urwin, 1978a).[2]

Subjects

The three children—Steven, Jerry, and Suzanne—are all legally blind but have no additional neurological impairment. Steven and Jerry are firstborn children. Suzanne has a sighted sister Elaine who is 2 years older than she. Jerry and Suzanne are totally blind through optic atrophy. As the result of a malformation, Steven has no sight in his right

---

[2] The research described was undertaken in fulfilling the requirements for a Ph.D. I was financed by the Social Science Research Council for two years and through King's College Cambridge Studentship for one year.

eye. However, he does have a little sight in his left eye, in which he has glaucoma and aniridia.[3]

Steven's minimal vision gave him considerable advantages over the other two children. In particular, toward the end of his sixth month he became capable of reaching for objects if they were presented within a few inches of his "good" eye. The emergence of this visually guided reaching, of course, sets Steven apart from the totally blind children. On the other hand, his mobility was delayed, as is typical of blind infants, and his early language showed biases that distinguished him from fully sighted children.

I studied Steven and Jerry's development until they were approximately 21 months old. Suzanne's development, on the other hand, was followed during her first year by Dr. Michael Tobin from the Institute of Research into the Visually Handicapped, Birmingham. Dr. Tobin made his videotapes and other records available to me. My own study of Suzanne began when she was 15 months old, and ended when she was 27 months old. The study of Suzanne thus spans a wider age range than in the other two cases. According to Brown's (1973) criteria, she was entering Stage III at the final visit.

Objectives and Procedures

The objectives of this study were to describe patterns of parent-child communication that can emerge when the child is blind and to identify cognitive changes that occur during the preverbal period and early stages of language acquisition. In addition, because the issue of continuity between preverbal and verbal forms of communication is a major issue in the sighted child literature, attention was given to the possibility that regularized forms of interaction might become identifiable prior to speech, and that the ability to express communicative intent might emerge in a different form than it does in sighted infants. To fulfill the preceding objectives, developments in the children's lexicons and use of language were examined in relation to changes in: 1) their social interactions; 2) their knowledge of objects; and 3) their parent's use of speech.

The children were observed at regular intervals in their homes. Steven and Jerry were observed every other week. I observed Suzanne at monthly intervals until she was 21 months old. Subsequent observations were made at 24 and 27 months. During each observational

---

[3] Optic atrophy involves a degeneration of the optic nerve. Glaucoma involves a swelling of the eyeball because of a build up of excess fluid. Aniridia is a condition in which the iris fails to develop. In all three children described, the cause of blindness was unknown.

session, the child's interactions with either parent (generally the mother) were recorded on audiotape. Video recording was done monthly. Because Jerry's father was often at home during the daytime, there were more opportunities to observe father-child interaction in Jerry's case than there were for the other children.

The audio recordings and supplementary written records of contextual information provided many samples of parental speech, and eventually the children's own use of language. However, the video recordings were used as the major data base for the descriptive analysis of parent-child communication. This analysis concentrated on how the children's activities—in certain preselected contexts or situations—related to the parents' activities, and vice versa. These contexts were distinguishable by their implicit and explicit content, as well as by what was required of the participants. The contexts included episodes of: 1) *social play*, which was loosely defined as affectively motivated and obviously pleasurable interaction that depended on a high degree of mutual attention and reciprocal coordination and, for convenience, excluded situations in which objects were incorporated; 2) *joint action involving objects*, which might be either task oriented or playful and open-ended; 3) *the child's own object projects*, i.e., situations in which the child was engaged in exploring or manipulating an object when the parent was not acting on the object; and 4) situations involving joint attention or explicit reference to objects and events in the *distal environment*, i.e., outside the immediate sphere of action of both parent and child.

In each situation, my objectives required analyzing both the parents' speech and the children's speech when it emerged. A number of the categories used to analyze the parents' speech were taken from studies of mothers' speech to sighted children. These categories were used to permit a comparison of the speech that these mothers used with their blind children to the speech typically used by mothers with sighted children.

In order to make comparisons with research done on sighted children (or parental interactions with sighted children), I also needed to assess the blind children's cognitive development in terms of Piaget's theory. Because traditional Piagetian tests involve presenting materials visually, the assessment process was far from straightforward. Rather than attempting to adapt the Piagetian tests, I used Fraiberg's (1977) method of inferring changes in the infants' cognitive functioning from observations of their spontaneous explorations of toys and objects. Some informal experiments were also included to allow a more detailed exploration of certain aspects of development, such as the ability to search for objects. Consistent with Fraiberg's guidelines, an infant who sustained a search across various locations for an inaudible lost object was granted the acquisition of mental representation. (A more detailed account of methodology can be found in Urwin, 1978a.)

To summarize, the literature on preverbal communication in sighted children suggests that certain consequences might arise from the infants' lack of vision. In line with these predictions and the previously cited work on development in blind infants, the study examined how and to what extent the lack of eye contact and absent or reduced nonverbal communication might result in the parents making adjustments, and the children using "alternative routes."

Results

My report of the results obtained from this study begins with a comparison of the ways in which the three sets of parents interacted with their children. Here I discuss both similarities and differences among the families studied. Second, I compare the communicative skills and interactions of each child with those of chronologically similar sighted children. Similarities and differences are again discussed; differences are analyzed developmentally. I cover differences that appeared during the preverbal period first; following this there is a discussion of differences associated with the children's early verbalizations. Because Suzanne was observed longer than the other two children, I then go on to discuss her later development. Here I describe initial difficulties that eventually were resolved and cite factors contributing to this resolution. I also discuss limitations existing at the end of the study and suggest some reasons for their continued existence.

A Comparison of the Three Families Studied The children's home environments differed considerably and the parents held different beliefs about how they could or should contribute to their children's development. Steven's mother, for example, believed that toys were an invaluable aid to the child's learning, and she spent a considerable proportion of each observation session engaged in various activities involving joint action on objects. Jerry's parents saw the value of toys somewhat differently. As soon as he was capable of retrieving objects for himself Jerry's parents let him play with things on his own. However, they put far more emphasis on the child's becoming mobile than did the other parents, because they felt that mobility was an achievement that would ensure Jerry's independence. Through the use of activities such as body play, they encouraged Jerry to stand alone and to take steps, and by the end of the first year Jerry was beginning to walk independently. This mobility at one year contradicts the literature, which suggests that blind children inevitably are delayed in becoming mobile (Fraiberg, 1977).

Suzanne's parents also emphasized the value of body play. As Suzanne's mother put it, "We soon found out what she likes." However, Suzanne's mobility was not as advanced as Jerry's and she did not begin to walk independently until the eighteenth month. In the provision and use of objects, Suzanne's parents were different from both Jerry's and Steven's. Suzanne was given toys and other objects to play with far more frequently than was Jerry, and her mother would comment on what the child was doing with them in her object projects. On the other hand, Suzanne's mother, unlike Steven's mother, engaged in little joint action involving objects until the final months of the investigation.

Despite the preceding environmental differences, all three children have developed extremely well in comparison to the blind child population as a whole. This relatively satisfactory development was largely achieved through the adaptive use of alternative communication and sensory systems. The use of these systems depended on the parents' ability to appreciate alternative cues to their infant's attention, as well as on their discovering ways of using alternative communicative systems themselves. For example, during episodes of social play in the first year, all the mothers would work to find some sign of attention or responsiveness that they could take as a "reply" to their initiatives. In spite of the fact that the babies could not see them, the mothers would watch their faces intently and verbally mirror any changes of mood or fluctuations in the infants' attention in their own speech. The mothers also showed a marked tendency to imitate or dramatize the infants' preverbal vocalizations, and they encouraged the infants to take turns vocalizing with them by questioning and prompting the children. Finally, all the mothers repeatedly used touching, tickling, and more exuberant forms of body play. Here Jerry's parents appeared to be particularly attuned to the communicative significance of their child's body movements. For example, they would mark his excitement, anticipation, and gross changes of body position in their own speech. In this way, they effectively provided the child with information about the effects of his actions on those who watched him.

To summarize, the three sets of parents differed on the importance of mobility and play with objects, but were similar in their use of alternative communication and sensory systems. These similarities and differences were reflected in the children's development. The children developed different early vocabularies and uses of language, but, as described below, there were similar developmental changes in the ways in which they interacted with others. They also showed similar developments in their understanding of objects. Regardless of the developmental style chosen, there were striking parallels between the course of development followed by these blind children and that reported for sighted children. These parallels contradict many of the assumptions about the inevitability of a developmental delay in blind children.

Similarities between Blind and Sighted Children An analysis of the infants' social interactions through the preverbal period revealed changes in participation that closely parallel those described for sighted children. For example, the ability to regulate interaction emerged in the blind children at approximately the same time that it does in sighted children. The findings from this study together with the results of similar research on sighted children (Bates et al., 1975; Sugarman, this volume; Sugarman-Bell, 1978; Trevarthen and Hubley, 1979) indicate that during the last quarter of their first year both groups can begin to sustain interaction by: 1) repeating procedures that were previously successful in gaining adult attention; and 2) coordinating people with actions and objects.

Additional similarities to sighted children appeared as the children grew older. For example, the manner in which the single-word stage emerged and developed in the three blind children resembled the manner in which it develops in sighted children. Each of the blind children's first words clearly originated in affective, well-routinized forms of interactions within which the child had already gained some measure of active control. Furthermore, the children's early words were supported by distinctive prosodic markings and/or action procedures that were established prior to speech. This usage is consistent with claims for continuity between preverbal and verbal communication in sighted children (see Bates et al., 1975; Bruner, 1975; Carter, 1979a; Dore, 1975).

The single-word stage of development in sighted children is a period in which words often serve multiple functions. Like the early words of their sighted counterparts, Steven, Jerry, and Suzanne's first words did serve multiple functions. A related characteristic of the one-word stage in sighted children is the occurrence of frequent overgeneralizations. That is, the early words of sighted children serve more functions than the rules of the "adult" language generally permit. However, the literature on blind children's language development reveals no such behavior. Does this void in the literature mean that young blind children do not have the capacity for overgeneralization? The results of the present study do not support such a conclusion. The three blind children studied were similar to sighted children insofar as they extended words into new contexts.[4]

Another parallel to sighted children was evident in the onset of word combinations. At around 18 months, the vocabularies of the blind children expanded rapidly and they began to produce their first word combinations. In each case, these developments co-occurred with the beginnings of symbolic play and changes in search behavior, which indicated that the children knew of the continued existence of objects apart from their own actions.

The emergence of symbolic play and mental representation at 18 months conflicts with the common assumption that blind children are inevitably delayed in developing sensorimotor intelligence. These findings also indicate that the blind children in this study were relatively advanced compared to the children in Fraiberg's (1977) sample.

Finally, the development of attachment behavior in Suzanne, Steven, and Jerry closely paralleled the course observed in sighted children. None of these three children showed the extreme reactions to separation that Fraiberg described.

Differences between Blind and Sighted Children: Preverbal Period
Although the course of development for the three blind children was similar in many respects to that reported for sighted children, differences were also apparent. That is, the children's limited or absent vision did have some effects on their communicative initiatives and on their parent's contributions to the interactions. My discussion of these effects begins with an analysis of the preverbal period.

As the literature suggests, the fact that these children could not look toward their mothers meant that before the emergence of speech the blind infants' opportunities to evoke adult attention and interaction were limited. By the end of the first year, each infant was capable of prompting and controlling the parent's actions once interaction was underway, but the exercise of this ability generally depended on physical contact, and hence on the parents' prior decision to put themselves at the infant's disposal.

Another difference between these children and sighted children centers on the use of gestures. Studies of preverbal communication in sighted children have focused on the use of reaching and pointing gestures to request and indicate objects in the last quarter of the first year. Along with offering and exchanging objects, the preceding interactions

---

[4] Steven was also the only one of the three children for whom I was able to identify clear cases of overextension based on a perceptual similarity (Bowerman, 1978; Clark, 1973). This may indicate an area of relative restriction in the blind children's language. Alternatively, it might reflect my own inability to appreciate their making connections based on nonvisual sensory information.

mark the child's coordination of people with actions and objects (Bates et al., 1975; Sugarman, this volume; Trevarthen and Hubley, 1979). Although the blind children observed in this project demonstrated such coordination at an age comparable to that reported for sighted children, the means they used were very different from the ritualized gestures employed by sighted children. With little or no opportunity for eye contact, the blind children relied on vocal exchanges and sophisticated forms of body play rather than gestures. For example, Steven would clap to prompt his mother to clap in sequence. Jerry would sustain long imitative sequences in which he banged on objects to produce sounds, and, while standing by his father's knee, Jerry would ask to be picked up by using a demanding vocalization and a ritualized "jerk" of his body. Other differences between the blind children and chronologically similar sighted children were that by the end of the first year: 1) none of the blind children indicated distal objects; and 2) as far as I could observe, none of them spontaneously offered objects to partners. However, offers of objects did emerge after deliberate training from the parents; in Suzanne's case, this was not until the beginning of the third year.

The children's lack of clear communicative forms constrained their access to activities. Initially, for example, the children's requests for body play depended on physical contact, and such requests were confined to demanding "more" of the game already initiated by the parents. Thus, the children could not request different forms of body play. For the two totally blind children, this situation continued until the children began using movements from well-established body games to control their parent's actions from a distance. For example, Jerry would clap his hands to start a clapping game with his mother. This development did not occur until the second year (see Urwin, 1979a).

Differences between Blind and Sighted Children: Early Verbalizations
Differences were not confined to the preverbal period. The early verbalizations of the blind children contained additional restrictions. These later restrictions were most evident in the children's use of people's names, object names, and function words.

At 18 months the totally blind children frequently used a person's name to call him. However, none of the children at this time produced another person's name to comment upon the agent of an action. The expression of agency is not an early development even in sighted children. Nevertheless, the two sighted children in Greenfield and Smith's (1976) longitudinal study did begin to refer to other people as agents of actions by the end of the single-word period.

In regard to the use of object names, all the children had acquired a number of words for naming objects by 20 months. However, the totally blind children, particularly Jerry, produced these words relatively infrequently. Occasionally, the children would name familiar objects if they were audible; and Steven would announce the names of things when they came within his visual range. In general, however, the children had to be in physical contact with an object before they would name it.

Finally, there were several restrictions with respect to the function words delineated by Bloom (1973), including *there, more, no,* and *gone*. Function words were acquired relatively early, but the words were initially given only limited meanings. By 18 months, Steven (the child with limited vision) was the only one of the three to use *there* and *more* to comment on or request the occurrence or re-occurrence of objects. Similarly, he was the only one to use *no* or *gone* to refer to the non-existence of an object when its presence was expected.

A paucity of references to distant objects and a sparse use of function words to request objects may well be common if not general characteristics of young blind children. In any case, these limitations appear to be consistent with the cited evidence on the blind child population as a whole. However, given the competence that Suzanne, Steven, and Jerry displayed in searching for objects at the end of the single-word period, an adequate explanation for their limitations is difficult to find. Restrictions in their early use of language cannot be conveniently explained in terms of a simple notion of "cognitive delay."

An alternative explanation may be that the nature of the immediate context is different for blind and sighted children. If such differences exist, then the appearance of similar linguistic phenomena might require a higher level of cognitive functioning when the child is blind than when he is sighted. The fact that the children studied did not use function words like *more* and *gone* in the way that sighted children do, for example, may have been the result of an inability to meet the additional cognitive requirements imposed when a child is given only limited access to the range of contrasts that are potent elicitors of such comments in sighted children. In other words, the lack of visual exposure to members of the same class of objects may have been at least partially responsible for the blind children's limited use of *more*; and the fact that they never saw objects disappear may have been related to their restricted use of *gone*. In support of this argument, research on sighted children of this age indicates that references to distal events and requests for objects are largely, if not entirely, evoked by things that the children can see. Perhaps the nearest approximation to the blind child's situation is the sighted child's reference to absent or concealed objects with only minimal support from ongoing events. The fact that this way of using language is observed rarely in sighted children in the early stages (Huxley and Urwin, unpublished data) is certainly consistent with the preceding arguments concerning the source of the blind child's difficulties.

Restrictions on the use of people's names, object names, and function words were not the only differences between these children's use of language and that of sighted children. However, many of the remaining differences had beneficial effects on the children's development. Indeed, these children were already showing adaptive uses for language that were similar to those described for some older blind children in the previous section. In particular, each child showed an unusually early mastery of basic procedures for sustaining conversation. This development originated in the preverbal period when the children discovered adaptive uses for the vocal system.

By the end of the first year, the parents and children studied here were able to sustain a conversation by repeating vocalizations and/or imitating those produced by their partners. Jerry's quasi-dialogues were highly significant in this respect. Indeed, they might last up to 15 minutes at a time. As the following examples suggest, Jerry at age 0;11(8) also showed exquisite control over his mother's subsequent responses, such that, as Jerry's mother put it, you could "have, like, a conversation with him."

> *Mother:* Are you poor babba? Yeah?
> *Jerry:* Er
> *Mother:* Mm (following the child)
> *Jerry:* Er
> *Mother:* Mm
> Hm (taking the lead)
> *Jerry:* Er
> *Mother:* Mm
> *Jerry:* Er
> *Mother:* Hm
> *Jerry:* Er
> *Mother:* Hmm!
> *Jerry:* Er!
> ... and so on.

Sometimes the child would vary the form or stress himself as if he were conducting an "experiment" in controlling his mother:

> *Jerry:* Huh
> *Mother:* Huh
> *Jerry:* HUH!
> *Mother:* Huh
> *Jerry:* Er—uh
> *Mother:* Aa—aa
> *Jerry:* Er—uh

> *Mother:* Aa—aa
> *Jerry:* Huh
> *Mother:* Hm
> ... and they continue.

The preceding kinds of interactions were clearly important for keeping mother and child in contact with each other. In addition, the interactions paved the way for an early acquisition of simple procedures for allocating "turns" in conversation. This was particularly true for the two totally blind infants, who rapidly began using a rising intonation to evoke replies from their parents. Indeed, a rising "Ay?" was one of Suzanne's first words as well as her most frequently produced single word. Her use of this word in any context virtually guaranteed that her mother would speak again.

Over the course of the single-word period, other devices for initiating, maintaining, and closing a conversation emerged. For example, Jerry began to use "Hello" and "Bye-bye" to open and close encounters before the end of the study. Similarly, at 17 months, Suzanne began using the standard conversation opener: "Mummy?" In response to this opener, Suzanne's mother would ask an open-ended question such as: "Yes, Suzanne?", thereby encouraging the child to maintain the conversation. At first, the majority of Suzanne's subsequent utterances were inarticulate, but the mother would continue the conversation by interpreting the replies as comments on what the child was doing. However, by 21 months, Suzanne was beginning to throw the onus back on her mother by following her mother's acknowledgments with "Where are yer?"

Repetition, calls, acknowledgments, greetings, and farewells are all simple procedures for allocating turns in conversation; they carry with them a basic reversibility or the potential for introducing the other party into the conversation even when "the other party" is not actually present. For example, Suzanne and Jerry took the role of the other party in their play when they reconstructed past conversations and repeated that person's contribution. Although all recorded examples of Steven's early pretend play involved transforming an object for use in some activity that he had seen, the two totally blind children at this stage rarely transformed objects in their play. Instead, the first recorded instance of their pretend play involved the use of language itself. By 20 months these two children were engaging in the kind of play through language that Fraiberg (1977) observed in older children, as described in the previous section.

The following example shows Jerry at age 1;6(2) reconstructing an event 2 hours after it occurred. The event was a game that I called "Are you sure?" It evolved over a period of several months as Jerry's father attempted to encourage the child's mobility. Using his own voice for himself and a "gruff" voice for his father, Jerry represented the two roles in a mock dialogue:

(Jerry is rambling around the room while both parents are elsewhere)
'Father's voice': Are you sure?
Jerry's voice: I sure Dad.
'Father's voice': Are you sure?
Jerry's voice: I sure Dad.
'Father's voice': You sure?
Jerry's voice: I sure Dad.
I sure Dadda.
. . . and bursts of hysterical laughter.

One implication of the preceding discussion is that the speech of the totally blind children differed from that of some sighted children (but see Snow, 1977) in the extensive use of imitation. However, it is important to appreciate the many functions that imitation may have served for the blind children. Imitation allowed parent and child to convey the fact that they were attending to one another, and it also ensured that a topic of conversation could be kept alive when cues from the supporting context were minimal. Indeed, imitation may well have consolidated the basic dialogue procedures themselves. Finally, at least in Jerry's case, imitation appeared to aid the child's mobility because he used the parent's voice as a reference point.

Suzanne's Later Development

Resolution of Early Problems: Later Verbalizations Because Suzanne was followed to an older age, it was possible to explore how the early restrictions in her use of language were eventually resolved, and the extent to which the early mastery of conversational procedures contributed to this process.

Suzanne's language development was more advanced than that of the other two children. Consistent with behavioral evidence indicating the emergence of mental representation, Suzanne had produced examples of all of Brown's (1973) basic set of two-term semantic relations by 21 months. However, some relations occurred rarely; locative relations were particularly infrequent. Indeed, prior to her second birthday, I did not observe Suzanne referring to the place of things when they were outside of her own immediate sphere of action. The majority of her utterances were classified as agent-action, agent-object, and action-object constructions, which are the dominant relations expressed by sighted children at Stage I (Brown, 1973).

Suzanne often used the pronoun "I" when referring to herself as an agent in the first two types of relations. This early use of "I" distinguished Suzanne from other blind children. Although the appearance of "I" is not, of course, the same thing as mastery of the "I"–"you" distinction, its appearance still suggests some differences between Suzanne and the children studied by Fraiberg, who were late in acquiring this pronoun. In contrast to her widespread use of "I," Suzanne's use of the pronoun "you" was confined to the ready-made phrase "Where are yer?" Thus, the vast majority of Suzanne's two-word and longer constructions referred to her own agency rather than to that of other people. This finding is consistent with her verbalizations at the one-word stage. As reported earlier, none of the children commented on the agency of others at the single-word stage.

When Suzanne was last observed at 27 months, many of her earlier problems had been resolved. She was referring to distal objects and locations. She was also marking recurrence and making requests for objects. In her dialogues, exact imitation appeared to have given way to a strategy whereby she would extend a conversational theme by incorporating all or part of her mother's preceding utterance into her own subsequent utterances. Semantically, she would reconstruct her mother's explanations about past or habitual events; she would talk about absent people; and, in the immediate context, she would comment explicitly on what her older sister Elaine was doing when those actions were familiar to her. Her use of "I" remained stable throughout, and she was now beginning to use "you" appropriately. In addition, she was showing the extensive use of questions usually found only in older blind children.

Reasons for Suzanne's Progress The development of independent mobility was one of the most important factors contributing to Suzanne's progress. Mobility made new kinds of social activities available and opened new contexts in which talk could take place. Another important factor was Suzanne's cognitive development. An increasing ability to categorize objects and to sustain a goal over space and time was most evident in her requests for objects. Even when cues indicating the existence of an object were minimal, Suzanne would now demand one if it was necessary to complete some plan already underway; also, while playing with one toy, she might demand another toy related to the first one in some way. In addition, at 27 months, Suzanne was apparently better able to use surrounding sounds than she was at 15 months. Upon hearing her sister play with a particular toy, for example, she could identify the toy and demand it. Similarly, upon hearing her sister go into the adjoining room, Suzanne could recognize where Elaine was going, what she was doing, and even insist that she be allowed to go there, too.

Although improved mobility and cognitive functioning were important to Suzanne's language development, more opportunities for cooperative play with objects and developments within the discourse mode itself also contributed to her progress. In both cases, her mother played an important role. By actively encouraging Suzanne to play cooperatively with objects and by responding to the child's communicative efforts, her mother may have promoted Suzanne's progress.

By interpreting the child's communicative intentions and sustaining dialogue sequences through expansions, incorporations, and prompts, Suzanne's mother's speech showed characteristics found in mothers' speech to sighted children with relatively advanced syntax. On the other hand, her use of language also showed several innovations that were well suited to Suzanne's individual needs. First, Suzanne's mother showed a marked tendency to follow the child's utterances with questions. This was a particularly useful strategy because it invited Suzanne to speak again. Second, her mother's use of language seemed especially well suited to extending Suzanne's access to what was going on around her.

Snow's (1977) longitudinal study of how two mothers spoke to their sighted infants yielded several categories that were used in analyzing the maternal speech directed to Jerry and Suzanne. The results revealed that, except for occasional references to absent people, the mothers' speech generally centered on their children for much of the second year. That is, the mothers talked more about their children and less about objects and events in the surrounding context than they might have done if their children had been sighted. A paucity of references to anything in the context other than the child was especially noticeable in Jerry's mother's speech because she seldom commented on her son's play with objects. I have argued elsewhere that the tendency to comment upon the child instead of objects in the context was partly due to the lack of cues regarding the blind infants' attention to distal objects and events, and/or to the mothers' difficulties in actually appreciating these cues when they were present (Urwin, 1978a).

However, maternal speech that was not centered on the child began to increase at the end of the one-word stage, because by then the mothers were responding to the language that the children were using and to apparent changes in what the children understood. For example, maternal references to absent people began to increase when the children themselves began using other people's names. At 21 months, Suzanne began to produce her grandmother's name, as well as the names of the children next door. In response, her mother would weave a dialogue around these utterances by telling the child where the person was, what she was doing, or when she might be expected to call. These kinds of descriptions were similar to the ones Suzanne herself began to reconstruct in the final months of the study.

In the final months of the study, Suzanne's mother also increased her use of Elaine's name when speaking to Suzanne. Throughout the investigation, the mother was greatly aided by the presence of Elaine, in that she could familiarize Suzanne with some event taking place outside of the child's own sphere of action by referring to Elaine and her activities. Like the names of absent people, the mother's use of Elaine's name increased in response to Suzanne's initiatives. Toward the end of the study, when Suzanne herself began to initiate interaction with her sister by calling out her name, the mother showed a corresponding increase in her own use of Elaine's name.

Other changes in the mother's speech were associated with changes in the child's understanding of objects. As Suzanne progressed, her mother made more demands on her. For example, in the one-word stage, any object references concerned materials that the child was currently investigating or attending to in her own object projects; but, once it became evident that Suzanne was beginning to search for lost objects, her mother would encourage the child to explore the space around her with "Where's X?" questions. These kinds of questions were appropriated by the child in her early requests for objects.

Finally, developments in Suzanne's mobility also produced changes in her mother's speech. Toward the end of the study, Suzanne's mother seldom responded to the child's requests for objects by providing them herself. Instead, she would specify their location relative to the child or to some familiar landmark within the room: "It's by the door," "This way," "That way," "It's in the bedroom," or "It's on the table." In this way, changes in the mother's speech both reflected Suzanne's needs and extended the child's access to the surrounding context. These changes prefigured developments in Suzanne's own use of language.

Persistent Limitations and Some Reasons for Them   Despite Suzanne's progress, some of the restrictions evident at 21 months persisted through the end of the study. In particular, at 27 months Suzanne was still producing comparatively few constructions in which she referred explicity to others as agents of an action. When they did occur, the majority of Suzanne's references to the agency of others concerned events from the past. These events were reconstructed by the child according to the description originally given by the mother. In the immediate context, most of Suzanne's explicit references to the agency of others occurred in the third person, but involved Elaine and her activities. There were only two clearly novel second-person references in the corpus obtained at the final session, even though Suzanne often used language to request some action from a listener and to manipulate her addressee's attention. Both of these second-person references occurred in situations in which mother and child were acting jointly on an object. In one instance, Suzanne protested her mother's shutting the door to prevent the child from leaving the room.

> Suzanne [2;3(0)] is trying to leave the room. The mother restrains her by pushing the door closed while Suzanne is pulling the handle.
> *Suzanne:* Mummy, let me open the door, Mum.
> *Mother:* What do you want me to open the door for?
> *Suzanne:* Mummy!
> *Mother:* What?
> *Suzanne:* You shut the door!

The other instance of "you" occurred in pretend play when both mother and child were putting a doll to bed. This kind of cooperative activity was a relatively new enterprise for Suzanne and her mother because, as previously mentioned, the mother seldom participated in object play with the child until the final months of the study. In the episode described here, Suzanne used "you" to request a specific action from her mother:

> *Mother:* Here's another cover. (She gives Suzanne a sheet)
> Cover her up.
> (Suzanne takes the sheet and then raises it towards her mother)
> *Suzanne:* Will you put this sheet in?
> *Mother:* Mm?
> *Suzanne:* Will you put this sheet in?
> *Mother:* O.K.
> (The mother takes the sheet and covers the doll)
> There we are.

Suzanne was not followed long enough to permit a thorough analysis of the I-you distinction. Nevertheless, the fact that one of Suzanne's first recorded productions of "you" occurred in pretend play with dolls is consistent with Fraiberg's (1977) claim that the capacity for symbolic representation of the self is a necessary precondition for the emergence of the I-you distinction. However, because Suzanne was also engaging in language-based pretend play without the support of objects, it remains unclear whether the incorporation of objects in play is a prerequisite for the correct use of "I" and "you."

In any case, symbolic play involving alternate roles does not itself guarantee that the child can apply "I" and "you" in conversation. Despite her occasional use of a relatively sophisticated utterance such as "Will you put this sheet in?", Suzanne rarely produced utterances containing the pronoun "you." There may be several reasons for this.

Reasons for Suzanne's Restricted Use of Pronouns First, the persistent restrictions on Suzanne's access to the surrounding context clearly limited the child's opportunities for commenting on what her addressee was doing. Given this limitation, the strategy whereby she would incorporate all of her mother's utterances into her own utterances and reconstruct her mother's descriptions may be one way in which she could organize her understanding of what was going on around her. Ultimately this understanding should increase the number of occasions in which she has cause to produce "you."

Besides her restricted access to the immediate context, there were other factors that contributed to Suzanne's difficulties with "you," and with pronouns in general. One factor may have been her use of ready-made phrases. In comparison to many blind children, Suzanne did not rely heavily on such phrases. However, when the phrases were produced, the resulting errors suggest specific deficits in Suzanne's productive abilities.

The most common sorts of errors were: 1) the use of a proper name where an adult would use a pronoun; and 2) reversals of first and second person pronouns. For example, while resisting her mother's attempts to withdraw her support, Suzanne at 24 months produced "Hold Mummy's hands" rather than "Hold your hands"; and, in anticipation of her mother's protest at the child provocatively standing on her toe, Suzanne at 27 months used the ready-made phrase "On me toe" instead of saying "On your toe." Although these two errors are not unusual even for sighted children, they are still highly significant in this study. They represent the only recorded occasions in which Suzanne's meanings required that she refer to other people as beneficiaries of her own actions. This raises the question of why she so rarely had occasion to produce such utterances.

In addition to imitating ready-made phrases that had once been directed to her, Suzanne occasionally repeated phrases that other people often used in talking about her among themselves. Her use of such phrases may have contributed to some of the remaining pronoun errors and substitutions of proper names for pronouns. Suzanne's use of her own name rather than the pronoun "I" is a good example. Suzanne's mother claimed that, toward the end of her second year, Suzanne went through a phase of using "Suzanne" instead of "I" in making requests. In trying to get out of the room, for example, she would repeat "Suzanne's by the door" with a demanding intonation, until someone opened the door for her. However, she continued to use "I" in other contexts; and, with one exception, she stopped using her own name in making requests by the end of her second year.

The exception poses three additional reasons for the occurrence of errors involving the substitution of a proper name for a pronoun. In the final session, Suzanne [age 2;3(0)] used her own name as she turned to me for help after a request for a biscuit had been refused by her mother.

Suzanne: I want a biscuit, Mum.
Mother: I haven't got any, love.
Suzanne: I want a biscuit. Cathy?
Cathy: Yes?
Suzanne: Suzanne wants a biscuit. Cathy. I want a biscuit, Cathy.

One possible explanation for the substitution is that the ineffective use of "I" led Suzanne to fall back on the more primitive use of her name. Another explanation is that, in using "Suzanne" to refer to herself, the child was attempting to represent herself as a beneficiary of an implicit action rather than as the initiator of a request. (Difficulties in referring to *other* people as beneficiaries were, of course, indicated above.) A final possibility concerns the fact that this episode involved both the investigator and the mother. Communicating with two people at the same time may have posed special problems for Suzanne. This possibility is given some additional support from an episode that occurred at 27 months.

Suzanne [2;3(0)] has demanded bricks. The mother acts on the demand and Suzanne turns to C.U. to report on the event.
Mother: I'm going to get the bricks.
Suzanne: Cathy?
Cathy: Yes?
Suzanne: Mummy's going to fetch you. Mummy fetch you the bricks.

In this episode, Suzanne used "you" where "me" was required as the beneficiary. This episode is significant not only because it again illustrates the difficulty that a child might have in interacting with two people at the same time, but also because it represents the only recorded instance in which Suzanne even attempted to refer explicitly to someone else as an agent with her being the beneficiary of their actions. She produced no utterances containing either her own name or "me" as a beneficiary. Indeed, she never used her own name or "me" in any sort of object or indirect object relationship. Examples of such utterances would be: "Mummy wash me," "He hit me," and "Give (it to) me." These hypothetical utterances implicitly or explicitly attribute agency to another party. Suzanne's failure to produce such constructions, and her failure to refer to other people as beneficiaries of *her* actions, may indicate that she had little occasion to make these relationships explicit. On the other hand, it also suggests that there may have been deficiencies in her understanding of reciprocal roles in interaction.

More research with sighted children is obviously needed to establish when and under what conditions sighted children produce constructions containing pronouns in various roles. This research would enable us to discover the extent to which Suzanne's lack of such constructions is unusual. For the present, the speculations made by Bruner (1975) might enhance our understanding of Suzanne's acquisition of pronominal reference. In discussing the communicative functions established in the preverbal period, Bruner has suggested that forms of joint action that involve the use of objects, (e.g., "give-and-take" games) may equip the child with notions of reversible roles that later may be handled in language with "I" and "you." In general terms, it is not clear how such a relationship could ever be proved. However, for Suzanne the conjecture draws attention to specific restrictions in her opportunities for interaction. Like the two other blind children, Suzanne did not spontaneously offer objects at the beginning of the study. Although talking about an object allowed Suzanne and her mother to establish its mutual accessibility, the two initially engaged in little joint action with objects and the child's own explorations of objects were largely independent of the actions of other people at the beginning of the study. Given that what she did would affect what she talked about, Suzanne's lack of experience with interchangeable or complementary roles in object play may have been a major factor contributing to her failure to express these roles in language.

However, by the end of the study this situation was beginning to change. After deliberate training Suzanne began to offer objects, and, perhaps because of an increase in the child's comprehension, her mother was actively engaging Suzanne in more joint action with objects. This play may have been partly responsible for the child's eventual use of the pronoun "you." Excluding the familiar questions for sustaining phatic exchange (e.g., "How are you?"), appropriate uses of "you" were observed only in situations involving joint action on objects. These observations are far from conclusive, but they do suggest that utterances in which Suzanne refers to the agency of other people as well as to herself and others as beneficiaries may increase as she is given further experience in cooperative activity with objects. The acquisition of questions such as "What are you doing?" and "Where are you going?" may also facilitate a more extensive use of the second person pronoun, as well as promoting the child's overall development.

CONCLUDING DISCUSSION

After reviewing the current evidence on language development in blind children, it was proposed that restrictions in the children's early language may be related to the problems that a lack of vision poses for the development of social interaction and cognitive functioning in infancy. In other words, lack of vision may limit a child's early social interaction and cognitive functioning, and the resulting difficulties may in turn restrict the child's language development. In order to understand how this indirect relationship operates, we first need to understand the kinds of social interactions and cognitive functioning that sighted children require for the development of language. Thus, a review of the literature on sighted children might be of some benefit in analyzing the problems of blind children. On the other hand, it also might be misleading. There are many problems in using theories of "normal' development to either predict the likely consequences of blindness or to gauge the blind child's progress.

One problem is that theories of normal development foster the assumption that difficulties will be inevitable, because they seldom if ever contain precise descriptions of the form that alternative routes may take. Blind and sighted children may follow different routes in acquiring language. Suzanne, for instance, developed early conversational skills that incorporated uses for language that rarely appear in either sighted children or blind children at such a young age. By capitalizing on her skill at conversation, Suzanne was subsequently able to resolve many of her initial linguistic difficulties. Of course, there is no necessity for blind children to follow this particular "alternative route." Other possible routes may involve the use of imitation, ready-made phrases, social rituals, and even echolalia. Before these behaviors are judged as impoverished or downgraded versions of similar phenomena observable in sighted children, researchers need to investigate their potential or actual functions for the blind children themselves. To summarize, the existence of these alternatives suggests that it may be inappropriate to rely entirely on norms for sighted children in gauging the blind child's progress. We also need to consider the apparent anomalies that commonly occur among the blind child population as a whole.

A second reason for exercising caution in using norms from sighted children to gauge the progress of blind children is that prerequisite levels of functioning for a particular development may differ in blind and sighted children. We cannot assume that similar linguistic achievements, such as the ability to request objects, necessarily require similar levels of cognitive functioning in blind and sighted children.

The preceding considerations lead to the following recommendations for research. First, a fuller appreciation of blind children's problems and the solutions that may be available to them will only be gained by augmenting the research on sighted children with similar research on blind children. Second, investigators should search for specific developmental prerequisites rather than assuming that the prerequisites for one group apply to the other. Finally, our understanding of language acquisition in both blind and sighted children would improve if researchers studying blind children stressed what the children *have* rather than just what they lack. In other words, we need to give more attention to the alternative communicative systems and ways of coming to know the world that may be available to blind children.

Reviewing the reported similarities and differences, Steven, Jerry, and Suzanne's developmental patterns were in many respects strikingly similar to those of sighted children. For example, the three children began coordinating people with actions and objects (Bates et al., 1975; Sugarman, this volume; Trevarthen and Hubley, 1979) at approximately the same time that sighted children show such coordinations. Also, the ontogeny of the blind children's first words was similar to that of sighted children. The results of this study and findings from research on sighted children indicate that early words from both groups of children are particularly likely to emerge in affective, well-routinized forms of interaction that have already given the children some measure of active control. Finally, word combinations emerged in the blind children at an age similar to that usually reported for sighted children; this event coincided—as it often does in sighted children—with the appearance of symbolic play and systematic search for objects. These similarities indicate that many of the language difficulties that have been cited in the blind child literature are not a necessary consequence of blindness.

However, there were certain undeniable restrictions in the three blind children's use of language relative to chronologically similar sighted children. For example, prior to the onset of speech, the blind infants had difficulty evoking adult attention and interaction. Furthermore, the means they used to coordinate people with actions and objects differed from the means frequently used by sighted children. The early verbalizations of the blind children also showed restrictions. These later restrictions were most evident in the children's use of people's names, object names, and function words. However, many of these limitations were resolved as the children began to engage in conversation with their parents. In the case of Suzanne, particular limitations at the end of the study involved the use of pronouns to specify beneficiaries and the agency of others.

Overall, the findings from this study lead to the following recommendations for helping parents. First, the parents of a blind child will often require considerable encouragement and support, especially during the child's first two years. Second, it would be useful if parental counseling could help parents learn to: 1) read alternative signs of their babies' attention and involvement, and 2) use alternative communication systems themselves (see Fraiberg, 1974, 1977). It may also be useful to tell the parents about the important role that their speech can play in sustaining contact with their children, in providing the children with feedback concerning the effects of their actions, and in extending the children's access to the environment.

Many of the difficulties caused by blindness can certainly be circumvented. However, it is clearly inappropriate to think in terms of providing parents with "recipes" for promoting their child's development. Any attempt to give support to parents must take into account their own beliefs about children and development as well as their particular living situations. Perhaps the most useful perspective is one that will enable the blind child's parents to view the raising of their child as a process of discovery.

REFERENCES

Ainsworth, M., Bell, S., and Stayton, D. 1974. Infant-mother attachment and social development: "Socialization" as a product of reciprocal responsiveness to signals. *In* M. P. M. Richards (ed.), The Integration of a Child into a Social World. Cambridge University Press, Cambridge, England.

Bates, E., Camaioni, L., and Volterra, V. 1975. The acquisition of performatives prior to speech. Merrill-Palmer Q. 21:205–226.

Bayley, N. 1969. Bayley Scales of Infant Development. The Psychological Corporation, New York.

Bloom, L. 1973. One Word at a Time: The Use of Single Word Utterances before Syntax. Mouton, The Hague.

Bloom, L., Rocissano, L., and Hood, L. 1976. Adult-child discourse: Development interaction between information processing and linguistic knowledge. Cognitive Psychol. 8:521–552.

Bower, T. 1974. Development in Infancy. W. H. Freeman & Company, San Francisco.

Bowerman, M. 1973. Early Syntactic Development: A Cross Linguistic Study with Special Reference to Finnish. Cambridge University Press, Cambridge, England.

Bowerman, M. 1978. The acquisition of word meaning: An investigation into some current conflicts. *In* N. Waterson and C. Snow (eds.), The Development of Communication. John Wiley & Sons, Chichester.

Brazelton, T. B., Koslowski, B., and Main, M. 1974. The origins of reciprocity: The early mother-infant interaction. *In* M. Lewis and L. Rosenblum (eds.), The Effect of the Infant on It's Caregiver. John Wiley & Sons, Inc., New York.

Brown, R. 1973. A First Language: The Early Stages. Harvard University Press, Cambridge, MA.

Bruner, J. S. 1975. The ontogenesis of speech acts. J. Child Lang. 2:1–19.

Bruner, J. S. 1977. Early social interaction and language acquisition. *In* H. R. Schaffer (ed.), Studies in Mother-Infant Interaction. Academic Press, London.

Bruner, J. S. 1978. From communication to language: A psychological perspective. *In* I. Markova (ed.), The Social Context of Language. John Wiley & Sons, Chichester.

Bullowa, M. (ed.). 1979. Before Speech: The Beginning of Interpersonal Communication. Cambridge University Press, Cambridge, England.
Burlingham, D. 1961. Some notes on the development of the blind. Psychoanal. Study Child 26:121–145.
Burlingham, D. 1964. Hearing and its role in the development of the blind. Psychoanal. Study Child 26:95–112.
Carter, A. 1979a. From sensori-motor vocalizations to words: A case study of the evolution of attention-directing communication in the second year. In A. Lock (ed.), Action, Gesture and Symbol: The Emergence of Language. Academic Press, Inc., New York.
Carter, A. 1979b. Prespeech meaning relations: An outline of one infant's sensorimotor morpheme development. In P. Fletcher and M. Garman (eds.), Language Acquisition. Cambridge University Press, Cambridge, England.
Churcher, J., and Scaife, M. 1979. How infants understand spatially oriented gestures. Paper presented at the British Psychological Society Developmental Section Conference, Southampton.
Clark, E. 1973. What's in a word? On the child's acquisition of semantics in his first language. In T. Moore (ed.), Cognitive Development and the Acquisition of Language. Academic Press, Inc., New York.
Clark, E. 1978. From gesture to word: On the natural history of deixis in language acquisition. In J. S. Bruner and A. Garton (eds.), Human Growth and Development. Wolfson College Lecture, 1976. The University Press, Oxford, England.
Collis, G. M., and Schaffer, H. R. 1975. Synchronisation of visual attention in mother-infant pairs. J. Child Psychol. 16:315–320.
Corrigan, R. 1978. Language development as related to Stage 6 object permanence development. J. Child Lang. 5:173–189.
Cross, T. 1977. Mother's speech adjustments: The contribution of selected child listener variables. In C. E. Snow and C. Ferguson (eds.), Talking to Children: Language Input and Acquisition. Cambridge University Press, Cambridge, England.
Dore, J. 1975. Holophrases, speech acts and language universals. J. Child Psychol. 2:21–40.
Edwards, D. 1973. Sensory-motor intelligence and semantic relations in early child grammar. Cognition 2:395–434.
Fraiberg, S. 1968. Parallel and divergent patterns in blind and sighted infants. Psychoanal. Study Child 23:264–300.
Fraiberg, S. 1974. Blind infants and their mothers: An examination of the sign system. In M. Lewis and L. Rosenblum (eds.), The Effect of the Infant on Its Caregiver. John Wiley & Sons, Inc., New York.
Fraiberg, S. 1977. Insights from the Blind. Souvenir Press, London.
Fraiberg, S., and Adelson, E. 1975. Self representation in language and play. Observations of blind children. In E. Lenneberg and E. Lenneberg (eds.), Foundations of Language Development: A Multidisciplinary Approach, Vol. 2. Academic Press, Inc., New York.
Freedman, D. 1964. Smiling in blind infants and the issue of innate versus acquired. J. Child Psychol. Psychiatry 5:171–184.
Greenfield, P., and Smith, J. 1976. The Structure of Communication in Early Language Development. Academic Press, Inc., New York.
Griffiths, P. 1979. In P. Fletcher and M. Garman (eds.), Language Acquisition. Cambridge University Press, Cambridge, England.

Huxley, R. 1970. The development of the correct use of subject personal pronouns in two children. *In* G. B. Flores d'Arcais and W. J. M. Levelt (eds.), Advances in Psycholinguistics. North Holland Publishing Company, Amsterdam.

Langan, W. 1970. The assessment of children with visual and perceptual difficulties. *In* P. Mittler (ed.), The Psychological Assessment of the Handicapped Child. Methuen, London.

Maratsos, M. 1979. Learning how to use nouns and determiners. *In* P. Fletcher and M. Garman (eds.), Language Acquisition. Cambridge University Press, Cambridge, England.

Maxfield, K. E. 1936. The spoken language of the blind preschool child: A study of method. Arch. Psychol. 201.

Nelson, K. 1973. Structure and strategy in learning to talk. S.R.C.D. Monograph 149, 38, Nos. 1–2.

Norris, M., Spaulding, P. J., and Brodie, F. H. 1957. Blindness in Children. University of Chicago Press, Chicago.

Piaget, J. 1951. Play, Dreams and Imitation. Routledge & Kegan Paul, London.

Piaget, J. 1953. The Origin of Intelligence in the Child. Routledge & Kegan Paul, London.

Piaget, J. 1955. The Child's Construction of Reality. Routledge & Kegan Paul, London.

Piaget, J., and Inhelder, B. 1969. The Psychology of the Child. Routledge & Kegan Paul, London.

Robson, K. S. 1967. The role of eye-to-eye contact in maternal-infant attachment. J. Child Psychol. Psychiatry 8:13–25.

Rowland, C. 1980. Communicative strategies of visually impaired infants and their mothers. Unpublished Ph.D. dissertation, University of Oklahoma.

Schaffer, H. R. (ed.). 1977. Studies in Mother-Infant Interaction. Academic Press, London.

Slobin, D. 1973. Cognitive prerequisites for the development of grammar. *In* C. Ferguson and D. Slobin (eds.), Studies of Child Language Development. Holt, Rinehart & Winston, Inc., New York.

Snow, C. E. 1977. The development of conversation between mothers and babies. J. Child Lang. 4(1):1–22.

Stern, D. N. 1974. Mother and infant at play: The dyadic interaction involving facial, vocal and gaze behaviors. *In* M. Lewis and L. Rosenblum (eds.), The Effect of the Infant on Its Caregiver. John Wiley & Sons, Inc., New York.

Sugarman-Bell, S. 1978. Some organizational aspects of preverbal communication. *In* I. Markova (ed.), Social Context of Language. John Wiley & Sons, Chichester.

Trevarthen, C., and Hubley, P. 1979. Secondary intersubjectivity: Confidence confiding and acts of meaning in the first year. *In* A. Lock (ed.), Action, Gesture and Symbol: The Emergence of Language. Academic Press, Inc., New York.

Urwin, C. 1978a. The development of communication between blind infants and their parents: Some ways into language. Unpublished Ph.D. Thesis, University of Cambridge, Cambridge, England.

Urwin, C. 1978b. Early language development in blind children. Br. Psychol. Soc. Occasional Papers 2:2.73–2.87.

Urwin, C. 1979a. The development of communication between blind infants and their parents. *In* A. Lock (ed.), Action, Gesture and Symbol: The Emergence of Language. Academic Press, Inc., New York.

Urwin, C. 1979b. Preverbal communication and early language development in blind children. Papers Rep. Child Lang. Dev. 17:119–128.

Urwin, C. 1981. The contribution of non-visual communication systems and language to knowing oneself. *In* M. Beveridge (ed.), Children Thinking Through Language. Edward Arnold, London.

Vernon, M. 1972. The Education of the Visually Handicapped. Department of Education and Science Report, Her Majesty's Stationery Office, London.

Wills, D. 1965. Some observations on blind nursery school children's understanding of their world. Psychoanal. Study Child 20:344–364.

Wills, D. 1970. Vulnerable periods in the early development of blind children. Psychoanal. Study Child 25:461–480.

Wills, D. 1977. The ordinary devoted mother and her blind baby. Paper presented at Paediatric Opthalmology Study Group Conference, University of Nottingham, April, 1977.

Wills, D. 1979. Early speech development in blind children. Psychoanal. Study Child 34:85–120.

Wood, M. 1970. Problems in the development and homecare of preschool blind children. Unpublished Ph.D. Thesis, University of Nottingham.

Afterword

Assisting Children To Become Communicatively Competent

Richard L. Schiefelbusch

Bureau of Child Research
University of Kansas
Lawrence, Kansas

contents

A POINT OF VIEW 527
ASSISTING THE CHILD 529
    Infants and Toddlers 529
    Preschool Children 530
    Schoolchildren 531
SUMMARY 532
REFERENCES 533

In the Introduction we asked, *How do children acquire communicative competence?* This question forces us to look more closely at communication events in early childhood, to consider possible developmental antecedents more carefully, and to consider the changing environments during the early years of childhood.

We now ask a somewhat different but related question: *How can we assist a child to become communicatively competent?* The word *assist*, rather than other terms such as *teach*, *promote*, or *stimulate*, emphasizes that the child learns in an individualized, active manner while being influenced by a varied, complex set of environmental events. No single teaching agent can do more than assist, although that assistance can be instrumental to the acquisition process.

A POINT OF VIEW

This book focuses on the transactions between the child and the persons in his life. One view of these events is that they expand and shape the child's communicative behavior in contextually appropriate ways. Another view is that competence emerges as cognitive knowledge is mapped in the form of codes used in communication. The language codes, in turn, may contribute to the acquisition of cognitive knowledge.

Still another view is that language rules, in the formal sense, evolve because the infant is born with an innately determined human capacity for learning a language. This view of acquisition focuses upon the individual's innate proclivities for acquiring a language.

Credence can be given to all these positions. The child learns a language because he has special processing and acquisition aptitudes. The learning also unfolds because of sensorimotor and subsequent cognitive and perceptual development and because of numerous experiences with caregivers and others who induce him to attend to and respond to language events. In normal children, this complex learning process unfolds, seemingly without mishap, because natural aptitudes and communicative experiences bring about the anticipated competencies. The language learner seems most often to develop competencies in a fail-safe system.

Yet, as explained by Snyder, Sugarman, Snow, Rice, and Urwin, many children do not achieve the range and level of competencies of their age peers. This volume has discussed the language of the developmentally delayed or disordered child both individually and categorically. Learning disruptions are produced by organic impairments or environmental deficiencies or both. The impaired child is more likely than the normal child to experience environmental deficiencies.

Schieffelin and Eisenberg pointed out that every culture has its own folk concepts about how children acquire language. The Kaluli of Papua New Guinea, for example, hold that children must be taught by direct instruction. They see talk as being purposeful and achieving social ends. Because they do not consider very young children to be conversational partners, they do not engage in conversation "to no purpose." The cultural assumptions regarding language acquisition shape the organization as well as the content of language instruction.

A culture's considerations for its handicapped children may vary from the ways in which normal children are treated. There is little research about cross-cultural practices and attitudes toward handicapped children. However, within Western cultures, as explained by Urwin, parents of blind children have difficulty establishing mutually orienting responses, such as person-object functions, apparently because the parent is inclined to seek visual orientations and does not easily shift the focus to shared auditory or tactual orientations. Likewise, parental expectations for social transactions may be upset by the aloofness and the inconsistencies of the autistic child or by the limited response repertoires of the retarded child. Also, there are possibilities that parental responses will be constrained or largely nullified by bizarre or limited cues of impaired infants. If so, the early preverbal communication experiences will be limited.

The possible differences between the communication experiences of the normal and the impaired infant, in any culture, might be considered in terms of the amount of communication experienced. Urwin, Snyder, and Snow suggested that parents should be encouraged, instructed, and supported to attend more often and play more actively with an impaired child. In addition, the parents should learn alternative possibilities for mutual responding. Visually oriented play or auditorily oriented play can be augmented with tactual or kinesthetic routines. Communication responses can be formatted in different ways while retaining responsiveness to social cues.

The urgency for frequent communication experiences with handicapped children was emphasized by Snow: "the child who is, for whatever reason, at risk for language delay or disability cannot develop normally without optimum access to the crucial features of social interaction. . . ." She explained that a normally developing child seems to be buffered in many ways against a suboptimal environment and, consequently, may show no noticeable deficits even when provided only intermittent episodes of attention or play. However, many handicapped children seem to have lost their buffering. They need an optimal social environment.

ASSISTING THE CHILD

Unfortunately, it is difficult to prescribe an optimal social environment for a handicapped child. We should first acknowledge that children vary greatly in the range and nature of their deficiencies and that they differ in age. What is optimal at one age may not be optimal at another; young children usually do not thrive in an environment that has been designed for older children and vice versa. We consider here environmental issues for infants and toddlers, preschool children, and school children.

Infants and Toddlers

Snow would have us start with the adult caregivers who should be available to engage in *contingent social interaction*. The contingent responsiveness of the adult, even when the intentions of the infant are not clearly presented, help create a system of reciprocal interaction (Brazelton, 1982). Snow advocated an environment that is attentive to the child's special modes of responding so that the child can engage in frequent communication activities. She speculates that a young handicapped child must have a more intensive set of experiences to compensate for greater difficulty in learning from experience. The issue may be one of the need of more time to practice and to experience the transactions than is needed by normal children.

Additional experiences should be introduced as early as possible. Caregivers should have a general guide to the object and person-object sequences that a preverbal child goes through in reaching the early stages of language use (Bruner, 1982). The importance of communication experience during the early stages of object and person-object play was emphasized by Snow, Sachs, and Urwin. They provided evidence that handicapped children have difficulty exploring their environment and responding to objects. Also, impaired children may be reluctant to engage in play activities with caregivers; an optimal environment encourages such activities. Sugarman reported that object and person interactions frequently precede the person-object schemas, which, in turn, precede first words. Urwin reported that these schemata (together with social play and symbolic play activities) are often delayed for blind children. This means that the interest in pretend play activities that emerges for normal children by the end of the second year may emerge later for blind children.

The early developmental sequences noted by Sugarman, Snow, Sachs, and Urwin might be combined into an informal design for orienting parents of handicapped children. For instance, the sequence could include object play or person play → object-person play → increasing social play → symbolic play → role play. These activity stages were discussed by Sugarman and Sachs.

In addition to discussions of normal acquisition stages Sugarman provided an in-depth discussion of the development of institutionalized infants and an autistic child. Urwin discussed normal and blind children. Snow considered normal infants during the first year using an anecdotal description of one child, and de Villiers discussed the perlocutionary, illocutionary, and locutionary stages (Bates, Camaioni, and Volterra, 1975) as they pertain to the infant's development of negation and interrogatives. Interestingly, each discussion sketches similar sequences and, at least indirectly, each recommends that all normal and handicapped children experience a great amount of mutual responding.

Also, Sachs described how social, symbolic, and role play at early stages of development can promote mutual responding. The forms of play progress from simple social interactions between parent and child (social play) to subtle adaptations to novel discourse and social contexts (role play). Between these two forms of play is symbolic play, during which the child may have a range of make-believe experiences. During this time, the development of language and make-believe play are closely interrelated. It is valuable social experience for children to engage in both make-believe and role play with both children and adults so they can participate in social roles that they might not experience in real life.

As Rice explained, the child's environment should provide rich and diverse ideational experiences. The play experiences discussed by Sachs should contribute greatly to this objective. In addition, Rice recommended that sociolinguistic rules be taught in relation to familiar sequences so the rules can then be extended to other less familiar contexts and in less frequently experienced sequences. The child also can help plan sequences of events and roles that enact social participation. Rice also recommended that observational as well as participatory learning contexts be arranged. All experiences leading to expanding social skills can best be ordered in relation to the child's emerging concepts.

Preschool Children

The assistance provided by adults during the preschool period may be divided into two types of activities. The first might be called *instruction* and the second *semantically contingent responding*. The two are related and each denotes a class of assistance.

An illustration of instruction is the parent instructing a child how to play. However, instruction may also include modeling, imitation training, storytelling, and role playing. Our assumptions are that, even in creative play where the scene, the topic, and the roles are chosen by the child, the parent may still need to instruct as the play activities unfold.

Instruction can vary from the most formal tactics of training to the most indirect and informal. Any event that is "proposed" by the parent as information, corrections, suggestions, or rules is instruction. Instructions provide the framework within which the child's play activities are maintained and that, from time to time, are restructured and elaborated. Thus, tea parties and other creative activities may be planned and acted out from instructions.

Semantically contingent responding may be described as the relationship of adult speech (in semantic content) to the immediately preceding child speech (see Snow, p. 85). This class of events differs in that the adult is directly or indirectly responding to the initiatives of the child. In other words, the child is given the opportunity to determine the topic, and is given help in expressing intentions. Snow pointed out that a caregiver who is familiar with a child will be more accurate in interpreting the child's utterances correctly and thus is more likely to respond in a semantically contingent fashion. Semantically contingent speech might include "repetitions of child utterances, expansions of child utterances, responses to child questions, clarification questions (also called occasional questions and contingent queries), and acknowledgments or confirmations of child assertions" (p. 86).

Adult uses of semantic contingencies encourage and support the child's further development of both language and communication—especially if used to extend conversational topics initiated by the child. A skillful adult can combine the two tactics in relating to the child's changing interests and creative repertoires. The adult can teach and encourage the child during pretend and role play (as discussed by Sachs), in asking questions (de Villiers), in making requests, including indirect ones geared to the causes of compliance (Gordon and Ervin-Tripp), and even in how to presuppose (DeHart and Maratsos). In fact, during the preschool years the child learns much of the point-sharing system discussed by MacWhinney. Preschool children vary greatly in the range of their learning. However, whatever the level and rate of the child, the adult can learn to assist the child.

Schoolchildren

The importance of semantic contingencies discussed by Snow for preschool children apply to school-age children as well. Under the heading "Who should control the interaction?", Bowerman (1978) pointed out that "accepting" adults are more facilitative than adults who attempt to closely monitor, correct, and instruct. She concluded that children should be allowed to select their own topics and that adults make their greatest contribution through indirect support.

This issue poses a serious question for teachers and specialists who work with children in the classroom. Children who share points effectively, and who have discourse skills for polite conversation, fare relatively well. Children who are less developed socially find classrooms to be poor contexts for learning additional skills. What social experiences do socially ineffective children need? What conditions should be recommended for home and school?

Possibly, the child should be included in social groupings in which he can be an active participant. The child's passive, silent manner is evidence enough that the context is wrong for him. Perhaps a different arrangement for the child, at least part of the day, will permit him to experience a social role that is more active and instrumental. Small groups offer possibilities for the child to test his presuppositions about the views of other children and attending adults as well as possibilities for turn taking, requesting, and information sharing. The opposite experience is for the child to be largely an observer while others gain the experience of doing.

Classroom experiences can combine the roles played both at home and at school. The more familiar and supportive the contexts the more likely the child is to gain positive experiences. In the social designs of both home and school, adults should provide: 1) a variety of experiences; 2) socially appropriate communication embedded in familiar sequences of events; and 3) participatory as well as observational learning contexts (see Rice, this volume).

Schieffelin and Eisenberg suggested that teachers, clinicians, and researchers who work in multicultural contexts give more attention to culturally based studies. Different ethnic groups may engage in faulty communication because of language rules that are culture specific. Teachers may perceive differences of communicative style as deficits of intellectual ability. The child may even find reduced classroom opportunities if his adjustments to the teacher's expectations are inappropriate. The communication style of predominately white, middle-class American schools may contrast strongly with the style in a minority child's home. However, Heath (1983) has demonstrated that different cultural styles can be bridged and that educational settings can be contexts in which children from contrasting ethnic backgrounds can thrive together.

SUMMARY

We have focused on developmental phases of communicative competence in assisting the child to become more effective. For instance, during the infant/toddler period, person play, object-person play, social play, symbolic play, and role play can provide opportunities for the adult to engage in contingent social interaction.

Preschool children also may respond favorably to contingent responding by adults. The familiar social activities of preschool children (storytelling, play school, tea parties, etc.) can provide opportunities for semantically contingent adult responses. The quality of the preschool child's social experience can also be enhanced by instructions.

School-age children also need continued contingent responding from adults. However, they need appropriate social contexts with both peers and adults in which they can be active, successful participants. Children from different cultures may find our school contexts to be strange or threatening. Also, children with limited language skills need contexts in which extra portions of practice and experience can be arranged. These arrangements, of course, should be designed for handicapped children as early as posssible and should be extended across all stages of childhood.

REFERENCES

Bates, E., Camaioni, L., and Volterra, V. 1975. The acquisition of performatives prior to speech. Merrill-Palmer Q. 21:205–226.

Bowerman, M. 1978. Semantic and syntactic development: A review of what, when and how in language acquisition. In R. L. Schiefelbusch (ed.), Bases of Language Intervention. University Park Press, Baltimore.

Brazelton, T. 1982. Joint regulation of neonate-parent behavior. In E. Z. Tronick (ed.), Social Interchange in Infancy: Affect, Cognition and Communication. University Park Press, Baltimore.

Bruner, J. 1982. The organization of action and the nature of the adult-infant transaction. In E. Z. Tronick (ed.), Social Interchange in Infancy: Affect, Cognition and Communication. University Park Press, Baltimore.

Heath, S. 1983. Ways with Words. Cambridge University Press, Cambridge, England.

index

Activity-oriented requests, 312, 314–316
Address, forms of
  in blindness, 494–495
  presuppositions in, 244, 247–249, 255, 256, 278–279
  in language disorders, 286–287
Adult-child interactions
  cultural variations in, 379–415
    in references to past events, 399–412
  see also Parent-child interactions
Age
  of caregiver, and language acquisition in child, 387–388
  and communicative development
    after third year, 91–93
    in first year, 30–51, 72–84
    in second and third years, 84–91
  and language delays, 421–524
    in infants and toddlers, 529–530, 533
    in preschool children, 530–531, 533
    in school-age children, 531–532
  and play activities, 118–119
Anaphoric references
  of definite articles, 259, 327–328
  in ellipsis, 341
  of negatives, 197–198, 199
  of pronouns, 243, 336
Animal communication studies, 204–205
Apache families, status and role of children in, 385
Appropriateness of communication, for context, see Contextual appropriateness of communication
Articles
  definite, use of
    acquisition of, 282–283
    anaphoric, 259, 327–328
    cataphoric, 328
    exophoric, 326–327
    generic, 332–333
    paraphrasing in, 328–330
    partonymic associations in, 320–321
    in point sharing, 326–333
    polysemes in, 326–333, 360
    presuppositions in, 243, 257–260
    set operation in, 331–332
  indefinite, use of
    instantiated, 333–334
    parameterized, 334
    in point sharing, 333–334
    polysemes in, 333–334, 360
Assertion, in point sharing, 332
Assistance toward communicative competence, 525–533
  see also Therapy activities
Assumptions, and presuppositions, 237, 239
  see also Presuppositions
Athabaskan Indian families, role of children in, 384
Attachment behavior, in blindness, 489
  compared to sighted children, 506
Attention, and communicative competence, 463–465
  in blindness, 486, 487, 488, 520
Attention-getters, in requests, 301
Attitudes
  cultural variations in, see Cultural variations
  and form of requests, 299
Autism, 14–15, 16, 51–60, 430
  cognitive deficit in, 431, 437
  echolalia in, 14, 437–439, 440, 452
  imitation and modeling in, 55, 56, 96
  nonverbal communication in, 458
    in eye contact, 53, 55, 56, 57, 58, 430, 437
  parent-child interactions in, 528
  presuppositional usage in, 286–287, 289, 290, 451–452
  preverbal communication in, 26, 51–60, 61–62
  questioning in, 440
  revision strategies in, 451–452
  sensitivity to listener in, 451–452
  speech acts in, 437–440

Baby talk by adults, 74–75
  cultural variations in, 385, 387, 390
Background information, relative clauses used for, 345
Black families
  communication in, 398, 414
  variability of, 395
  role of children in, 382, 383
  social organization of caregiving in, 388–389
Blind children, 15, 62, 479–524, 530
  attachment behavior of, 489, 506
  cognitive development of, 482–483, 502, 512, 518–519
  compared to sighted children, 509–511, 519–520
  early language development of, 490–500
  future research on, 498–500
  later verbalizations of, 511–518
  longitudinal study on, 500–518
  parent interactions with, 15, 483, 484–489, 528
  see also Parent-child interactions, blind children in
  parental counseling and intervention in, 488–489, 520–521
  play activities of, 94, 100, 500, 503–504, 507, 513
    role playing in, 489–490, 510–511, 518
    social play in, 502, 504
    symbolic play in, 489–490, 495, 496, 506, 515, 520
  preverbal communication of, 94, 483, 484–490, 499, 501, 503, 504, 505, 506–507, 520
  pronoun use of, 511–512, 515–518, 520
  sensorimotor intelligence of, 489
  social interactions of, 93, 94, 95, 100
Book reading, see Reading

Caregiver-child interactions
  age of caregiver affecting, 387–388
  cultural variations in, 387–395, 396
  see also Parent-child interactions

Case marking in point sharing, 358–359
  polysemes in, 358–359, 361
Cataphoric references
  of definite articles, 328
  in ellipsis, 344
  of pronouns, 336–337
Categorical knowledge
  and communicative development, 141, 145, 148–153, 165–166
  compared to event knowledge, 166
  object-based, 148–153
  social, 162–165, 168, 181, 182
Cerebral palsy, communicative development in, 16
Clarification of speech, semantically contingent, 85, 86, 88
Classroom experiences
  cultural factors affecting, 413–414, 532
  in language delays, 531–532, 533
Cleft sentences, stress patterns in, 347–348
Cognitive aspects of communicative development, 8–9, 113, 141–189
  in blindness, 482–483, 502, 508, 512, 518–519
  environmental sources of, 170–179
  event knowledge in, 165–169
  see also Event knowledge
  in interrogatives, 218–219, 229–230
  in language delays and disorders, 179–184, 430–431, 460–463
  mapping problems in, 145, 150, 152, 170, 171, 174
  mental representation in, 141, 2145–148, 152
  in mental retardation, 436, 461
  in negatives, 206–208, 212
  nonlinguistic knowledge in, 143, 144–170, 171, 174
  object-based knowledge in, 141, 145–153, 159–160, 169
  person knowledge in, 157–162, 169
  in play activities, 118, 120
  in presuppositional usage, 287

Cognitive aspects of communicative development—*continued*
  preverbal, 29–30, 45–46, 61–62
  in autism, 59
  social knowledge in, 153–165, 168, 169
  in two-year-olds, 87
Combination speech
  in blindness, 491, 495, 498
  compared to sighted children, 506, 520
  in play activities, 116, 120
Communicative competence, definition of, 3–5
Constructive-interactional model of language acquisition, 112
Contextual appropriateness of communication, 113, 114, 143, 181
  in autism, 439, 440
  in language training programs, 183, 184
  in play activities, 121
  in requests, 297–300, 305–306, 310–311, 316
  in social interactions, 155–165
Contingency of speech, semantic, *see* Semantic contingency
Conventional requests, 11, 17, 295, 302–303, 305–306, 307–308, 318
Conversations, 452–457
  in autism, 451
  in blindness, 509–510, 512, 519
  cooperative principle on, 241
  cultural variations in, 382–387, 395–397, 399–412
  Gricean principles on, 241–242, 257, 281
  initiation of, *see* Initiation of conversation
  introduction of new topics in, 87–91, 350–351, 442
  in language disorders, 286, 288, 442, 454–457
  on past events, 399–412
  point sharing in, *see* Point sharing
  politeness in, 453–454
  premature topics in, 351
  presuppositions in, 249, 255, 362
  preverbal positioning in, 351–355
  pronoun interpretation in, 335–340
  semantic analysis of, 85–87, 325–359
  situational appropriateness of, 113, 114
  structure of, 453
  turn taking in, 397, 414
  with preverbal children, 77–78
Cooperative principle in conversation, 241
Counterfactive predicates, 245, 263, 273
Crying, parent interpretation of, 76
Cues
  to categories of social relationships, 164
  and hints in requests, 308, 318
  in parent-child interactions, 7, 8, 75
    with blind child, 94, 486, 488, 504
    with hearing-impaired child, 93
    with preverbal child, 75, 486, 488
Cultural variations, 4, 5, 12, 17, 375–420, 528
  in attitudes toward handicapped children, 528
  and classroom experiences of ethnic groups, 413–414, 532
  in communicative competence, 379
  in folk beliefs on language acquisition, 390–395, 396
  in nonverbal communication, 385
  in parent-child interactions, 380, 383, 384, 385–386, 387–390
    in first year 74–75
  in reading ability, 92–93
  in references to past events, 399–412
  research questions on, 395–399
  in speech styles in role play, 127, 133
  in status and role of children in society, 380, 382–387, 396–397
  in value of silent children, 384, 385, 386
  see also Foreign languages

Deafness, *see* Hearing impairment
Decontextualization of language, in play, 121

Definite articles, *see* Articles, definite, use of
Definite reference words, presuppositional usage of, 243–244, 245, 257–262
Delay of language, *see* Language delays and disorders
Denials, *see* Negatives
Developmental factors in communicative competence, 6–10, 21–189
  cognitive aspects of, 8–9, 141–189
  parent-child interactions in, 6–7, 69–107
  play activities in, 7, 8, 109–140
  preverbal communication in, 6, 23–67
Developmentally different children, communicative competence of, 12–16, 421–524
Directives, parental forms of, 228
Disorders of language, *see* Language delays and disorders
Down's syndrome
  development of communicative competence in, 13–14
  revision strategies in, 450
  social and verbal environment in, 93, 94, 459
  speech acts in, 436–437

Echolalia
  in autism, 14, 437–439, 440, 452
  in blindness, 493
Egocentricity of children, 157–158
Elicited communication
  in assessment of interrogatives, 214–216
  preverbal, 36, 37, 41
  in role playing, 127–128
Ellipsis, 340–344
  anaphoric reference to, 341
  cataphoric reference to, 344
  exophoric reference to, 341
  metaphoric reference to, 344
  parallel function readings of, 341–342
  perspective affecting comprehension of, 342
  polysemes of, 340–344, 360
  and presuppositions, 250, 280–281
  in requests, 307

  and role frame of interactional verbs, 343–344
Environmental influences on communicative competence, 5, 141, 170–179, 459
  in blindness, 496–497, 500, 502
  cultural variations in, 375–420
    see also Cultural variations
  in home, 26, 30–46
    see also Home environment
  in institutions, 26, 46–51, 60, 71, 530
  in language delays, 459–460, 529–533
  suboptimal, 100, 117
  supportive and facilitative, 99–100, 117
  television in, 173, 175–177
Ethnic variations, 375–420
  see also Cultural variations
Event knowledge, 165–169
  associated with roles, 167, 168
  and communicative development, 165–169
  and interpretation of interrogatives, 230
  and interpretation of negatives, 212
  in language disorders, 181, 183
  in language training program, 183
Exophoric references, 244
  of definite articles, 326–327
  in ellipsis, 341
  of pronouns, 335
Expansion of speech, semantically contingent, 85, 86, 88, 89, 90
Eye contact
  in autism, 53, 55, 56, 57, 58, 430, 437
  cultural variations in, 398, 399
  and language acquisition in blindness, 15, 94, 479–524
  in preverbal communication, 94, 205

Facial expressions, in blindness, 485–486
Factive predicates, presuppositional usage of, 244–245, 246, 256, 257, 262–263
  in early language, 256, 257
  studies on, 263–272

538   Index

Folk beliefs on language acquisition, 390–395, 396
Force of speech, illocutionary, 193–236
  hypothesis about, 196
  of interrogatives, 219–222, 230
  of negatives, 199–203
Foreign languages
  articles in, definite and indefinite, 282
  case marking in, 358
  forms of address in, 248
  initialization in, 349, 351
  negative sentences in, 197, 198, 201–202
  particles in, 359
  preverbal positioning in, 352, 355
Forget, children's understanding of, 270
Form of speech, 193–236
  hypotheses about, 196
  of interrogatives, 212–219
    related to functions of, 224–227, 231, 232
  of negatives, 196–199, 211–212
    related to functions of, 208–209, 231
Framing moves, in requests, 301
Framing role of interactional verbs, 338–339, 343–344

Games, *see* Play activities
Gaze, in preverbal communication, 78, 81
  see also Eye contact
Gestures, in preverbal communication, 80, 205
  in blindness, 486, 487, 506–507
  in interrogatives, 223
  in negatives, 206, 208
Givenness, and preverbal positioning, 352–353
Goal-oriented behavior, preverbal, 60
Grammatical form of speech, 193–236
  and communicative competence, 143, 427
  environmental sources of, 172–173
  in interrogatives, 212–219
  in language disorders, 179, 180
  in negatives, 196–199
  in point sharing, 323
Gricean conversational principles, 241–242, 257, 281
Guess, children's understanding of, 269–272

Handicapped children, 7–8, 12–16, 17
  assistance toward communicative competence for, 525–533
  autistic, *see* Autism
  blind, *see* Blind children
  cultural variations in attitudes toward, 528
  play activities of, 134–135
  preverbal communication of, 26, 51–60
  social routines learned by, 83
Happy, presuppositional usage of, 244, 256, 264, 265, 266
Headshakes, in preverbal negative, 206, 208
Hearing impairment
  in children
    communicative development in, 15–16, 63, 71, 93–94, 95, 100
    reading ability in, 92
    social interactions in, 93–94, 95, 100, 164
  in parents, and language development in hearing children, 71, 112, 172, 175
"Here and now" emphasis, in play activities and language, 121, 131
Hints in requests, 308, 318
Home environment, 26, 30–46, 459
  cultural variations in, 375–420
  and language delays, 459–460
  and literacy skills, 7
  parent-child interactions in, 69–107
    see also Parent-child interactions
  and person-object coordination, 30–46
  preverbal communication in, 26, 30–46, 60

Hungarian families, communication in, 398

Illness and stress, infant behavior in, 41
Illocutionary force of speech, 193–236
  hypotheses about, 196
  of interrogatives, 219–222, 230
  of negatives, 199–203
Illocutionary stage in communicative development, 204, 205
Imbedded requests, 307, 308
Imitation and modeling, 84, 95–99, 111
  in autism, 55, 56, 96
  in blindness, 490, 493, 511, 516, 519
  delayed, 97
  in first year of life, 76
  functions of, 97
  in interrogatives, 214–216
  in language therapy, 97–99
  in play activities, 123
Imperatives in speech
  cultural variations in, 386
  initialization of, 349
  in language disorders, 435
  in mental retardation, 436, 437
Indirect learning of language, 171–174
  television in, 173, 175–177
  in training program, 183–184
Infants and toddlers
  in home environment, 26, 30–46
  in institutional environment, 26, 46–51
  language delays in, 529–530, 533
  parent-child interactions affecting, 6–7, 69–107
  person-object coordination in, 30–51
  preverbal communication of, 6, 9, 23–67
  see also Preverbal communication
Initialization, 348–351, 352
  in foreign languages, 349, 351
  in introduction of new topic, 350–351
  polysemes of, 348–351, 361

Initiation of conversation
  acquisition of skill in, 427
  in blindness, 487, 488–489, 514
  cultural variations in, 383, 384, 386, 387, 389, 396–397
  on past events, 404, 406, 410–411
Institutional environment, and language development, 71, 530
  preverbal, 26, 46–51, 60
Instructional activities in language delays, 530–531
Instrumental language and moves, in requests, 295, 297, 299, 300–310
  case study on, 311–320
  variations of, 305–306
Intelligence quotient, and style of transaction, 14
Intention of communication, 27, 195
  in autism, 57–58, 59, 61, 438–439, 440
  in interrogatives, 220–222
  in negatives, 199–203
  preverbal, 27–29, 44, 63–64, 203, 204
    in autism, 57–58, 59, 61
    parent interpretation of, 74, 76–77, 79, 80–81, 82, 204, 205
Interactional indicators, 348
Interrogatives, 10, 84, 193, 195–196, 212–232
  acquisition of skill in, 427
  in autism, 440
  in blindness, 497–498, 500, 512, 514
  cultural variations in, 383, 384, 386, 389, 396, 397, 414–415
  on past events, 404–405, 407–410
  elliptical answers to, 250
  forms of, 212–219, 232
    auxillary placement in, 213–218
    canonical and noncanonical, 229–230
    cognitive complexity of, 218–219
    elicited imitation in assessment of, 214–216
    related to functions of, 224–227, 231, 232

540   Index

Interrogatives—*continued*
    functional categories of, 220–222
        forms used with, 224–227, 231, 232
    hypotheses about, 222–230
    illocutionary force of, 219–222
    initialization of, 349
    interpretation of, 229–230
    in parent-child interactions, 227–229, 232, 274
    presuppositions in, 245–246, 249, 273–278
    in preverbal communication, 222–224, 231–232
    in requests, *see* Requests
    and social status, 428
    stress of voice in, 346–347
    structure of, 295–321
    in *wh-* questions, 212–219
        see also Wh- questions
Intonation of voice
    acquisition of, 425, 427
    in blindness, 510
    in interrogatives, 212–213
        development of, 222–223
Intrusiveness of requests, 297, 298, 299–300, 313–314
Item specification
    restrictive relative clauses used for, 345
    set operation in, 331–332

Japan, social status and role of children in, 385
Jokes, 111, 275
    cultural variations in, 396, 397

Kaluli families
    communication in, 414–415, 528
        on past events, 400, 402–412
    folk beliefs of, on language acquisition, 390–393, 396
    status and role of children in, 382
Kipsigis families
    folk beliefs of, on language acquisition, 390, 393
    social organization of caregiving in, 387–388

Know
    children's understanding of, 269–271
    presuppositional usage of, 244, 245, 266, 267–268, 269–271

Language delays and disorders, 13, 423–478
    attention in, 463–465
    in autism, 430
        see also Autism
    in blind children, 490–492, 498
    cognitive aspects of, 179–184, 430–431, 460–463
    conversational skill in, 454–457
    environmental aspects of, 459–460, 529–533
    identification and assessment of, 13, 179–182
    imitation and modeling in, 97–99
    individual differences in, 467–468
    information processing in, 466
    linguistic competence in, 466–467
    in mental retardation, 430, 431
    multiple resources model of, 468–471
    narrative processing in, 454–455, 457
    nonlinguistic knowledge in, 179–182, 183
    nonverbal communication in, 286, 288, 430, 433, 457–458
    object knowledge in, 529
    parent-child interactions in, 83, 93–99, 100, 459–460, 529, 530–531
    perception in, 465–466
    play activities in, 528, 529–530, 531, 533
        amount and complexity of, 461–462
    point sharing in, 531
    presuppositional usage in, 237, 285–288, 289, 441–447
    problem-solving skill in, 462
    reading skills in, 92, 454–455
    requests in, 432–435, 443–444
    resource allocation problems in, 464–465, 466
    revision strategies in, 444–447

role taking in, 462–463
in school-age children, 531–532, 533
semantic contingency of speech in, 531, 533
social and verbal environment in, 93–95, 100, 459–460, 528–533
speech acts in, 432–436
therapeutic activities in, 182–184, 525–533
see also Therapeutic activities
Language onset, 60
age at time of, 43–44
in autism, 58, 61
in blindness, 490–493, 498
in home environment, 43–44, 46, 49
in institutional environment, 48–49, 50, 51
and play activities, 83
prerequisite skills for, 61–62, 63–64
Learning disabilities, language delay in, 430
Lexicon
in point sharing, 355
variations in, 154
Linguistic competence, 3, 4, 5, 143, 144
compared to communicative competence, 128–129
and expression of nonlinguistic knowledge, 143, 144–145
in language delays, 466–467
Listener, speaker awareness of
in autism, 451–452
in language disorders, 441–444
in mental retardation, 449–450
and presuppositional usage, 250–252, 262
Literacy skills, home environment affecting, 7, 92–93
Locutionary stage in communicative development, 204
Luo families
folk beliefs of, on language acquisition, 393
social organization of caregiving in, 387
status and role of children in, 382, 384, 386

Mapping problems, 145, 150, 152, 170, 171, 174
Mean length of utterances, 121
Memory
of objects, 146, 147, 152, 159–160
of past events, cultural variations in references to, 399–412
and point sharing, 362, 363
Mental representation
in blindness, 506, 511
and communicative development, 141, 145–148, 152
and language disorders, 181
and object permanence concept, 146, 147
and symbolic play, 146, 147
Mental retardation
cognitive abilities in, 436, 461
communicative competence in, 13–14
individual differences in, 468
language delay in, 430, 431
parent-child interactions in, 528
presuppositional usage in, 447–451
revision strategies in, 450, 451
sensitivity to listener in, 449–450
speech acts in, 436–437
Metaphoric references
to ellipsis, 344
pronouns in, 337
Mexican-American families
communication in, 399
social organization of caregiving in, 389
status and role of children in, 386
Minorities, variations in communication styles of, 12
see also Cultural variations
Modeling, in language acquisition, 95–99
see also Imitation and modeling

Names, in forms of address
in blindness, 494–495
presuppositions in, 244, 247–249, 255, 256, 278–279
in language disorders, 286–287
Narrative skills, 452–453
in language disorders, 454–455, 457
in play activities, 123–124, 128

Negatives, 10, 193, 195–212
  in foreign languages, 197, 198, 201–202
  forms of, 196–199
    anaphoric, 197–198, 199
    canonical and noncanonical, 211–212
    related to functions, 208–209, 231
    stages in development of, 197–198, 199
  functional categories of, 202, 203
    cognitive complexity of, 206–208
    forms used with, 208–209, 231
    hypotheses about, 203–212
    illocutionary force of, 199–203
    interpretation of, 212
    in parent-child interactions, 199, 208, 209–211, 212, 232
    presuppositions in, 246–247, 277–278, 346
  in preverbal communication, 206
  stress of voice in, 346
Neutralization approach to requests, 304–305
Nonfactive predicates, 263, 264, 265, 266, 267, 272–273
Nonlinguistic knowledge, 145–170, 171, 174, 457
  acquisition of, 425, 427–428
  and language disorders, 179–182
  in language training program, 183
  object-based, 145–153, 159–160
  social, 153–165
Nonverbal communication, 17, 457–458
  acquisition of, 425, 427
  in autism, 53, 55, 56, 57, 58, 430, 437, 458
  in blindness, 485–486, 487, 504, 506–507
  cultural variations in, 385, 398, 399
  eye contact in, *see* Eye contact
  in interrogatives, 223
  in language delays and disorders, 286, 288, 430, 433, 457–458, 469–470
  in negation, 206, 208
  parallel processing of, 469–470
  preverbal development of, 23–67, 72–84, 205

Norm-oriented requests, 312, 314
Norwegian families, communication in, 398
Nouns, preverbal positioning of, 351–355

Object knowledge
  in blindness, 489, 491, 501, 502, 508, 514, 518, 520
  categorical, 148–153
  compared to social knowledge, 162, 163–164
  in language delays, 529
  and language development, 145–153, 169
  mental representation of, 145–148
  on permanence of object, 146, 147, 152, 159–160, 489
Object-oriented behavior, 16, 29, 30
  in autism, 51–60
  and cognitive development, 45
  and communicative development, 6, 8–9
  in parent-child interactions, 77–78
  preverbal, 28, 51–60
    in institutionalized infants, 47
    simple and complex, 34, 35
    trends in, 41–43
Obligations, and appropriateness of requests, 297–298, 300, 314
Obscenities, child use of, 157, 173
Observational learning of language, 171–174, 426
  in language training program, 183–184
  television in, 173, 175–177
One-word stage of language development
  in blindness, 505, 508, 512, 514, 520
  presuppositional usage in, 254–255
Onset of language, *see* Language onset
Orientation of preverbal communication
  in autism, 51–60
  in home environment, 30–46
  in institutional environment, 46–51
Overregularization in speech, 130

Paralinguistic features of
  communication, 457
  acquisition of, 427–428
Parallel functions
  of ellipses, 341–342
  in multiple resources model of
    language delays, 469–470
  of pronouns, 338
Paraphrasing
  in language disorders, 444–446
  in point sharing, 328–330
Parent-child interactions, 6–7, 15,
    16, 69–107
  after third year, 91–93
  in autism, 528
  baby talk of parent in, 74–75
  blind children in, 15, 483,
    484–489, 520–521, 528
    longitudinal study on, 501–518
    and parental counseling,
      488–489, 520–521
    in preverbal period, 485–489
  cues in, 7, 8, 75
    see also Cues, in parent-child
      interactions
  cultural variations in, 12, 74–75,
    380, 383, 384, 385–386,
    387–395
  first verbal, 43–44, 46
  in first year of life, 72–84
  imitation and modeling in, 76,
    95–99
  interrogatives in, 227–229, 232,
    274
  in language delays, 83, 93–99,
    100, 459–460, 529, 530–531
  and literacy skills of child, 92–93
  in mental retardation, 528
  negatives in, 199, 208, 209–211,
    212, 232
  and person-object coordination,
    30–46
  in play activities, 8, 81–83, 109,
    111, 112–113, 133–134
    parent modeling in, 123
    in social play, 114–118
    in symbolic play, 118, 122–124
  in preverbal period, 30–46, 72–84
    blind children in, 485–489
    elicited communication in, 36,
      37

  notation symbols for, 32
  scoring categories of, 33–36
  spontaneous behavior in, 31–41
  Uzgiris-Hunt scales in
    assessment of, 36
  role playing about, 125–127, 133
  in second and third years of life,
    84–91
  semantic contingency in, 85–87
  in social routines, 83–84
  socialization in, 77
  vocabulary acquisition in, 87–91
Particles
  in point sharing, 359
  polysemes of, 359, 361
Partonymy, in use of definite
  articles, 330–331
Past events, cultural variations in
  references to, 399–412
Peer group interactions, and
  language acquisition, 388
Perception, and language delays,
  465–466
Perlocutionary stage in
  communicative development,
  203, 204, 205
Permission requests, 307, 308
Person knowledge
  and communicative development,
    157–162, 169
  and language disorders, 181, 182
Person-object coordination, 6, 7,
    8–9, 28, 29, 30–51
  in autism, 51–60
  and cognitive development, 45–46
  in home environment, 30–46
  in institutional environment,
    46–51
  preverbal, 28, 29, 41–43, 60, 61,
    63
Perspective
  and comprehension of ellipsis, 342
  in language disorders, 457
  and preverbal positioning, 354
  and pronoun interpretation,
    337–338
  and subject-verb agreement,
    356–357
Persuasive adjuncts in requests, 301,
    309–310

Phonology
  competence in, 128, 129
  in game routines, 82–83
  in language disorders, 179, 180
Pitch of voice, in play activities, 125, 126, 127, 133
Play activities, 15–16, 17
  abstraction of invariant features in, 129–130
  in autism, 52, 53, 55, 56–57
  in blindness, 94, 100
    see also Blind children, play activities of
  child-child, 134
  and cognitive development, 118, 120
  and combinatorial speech, 116, 120
  and communicative development, 7, 8, 109–140
    limitations in, 131
    stages of 130–131
  cultural variations in, 388–389
  in Down's syndrome, 94
  in first year of life, 81–83
  in hearing impairment, 93
  "here and now" emphasis in, 121, 131
  in language delays, 93, 94, 95, 433, 434–435, 529–531, 533
    instruction on, 530–531
  linguistic materials in, 111
  mean length of utterances in, 121
  mental representation in, 146
  narrative skills in, 123–124, 128
  necessary, typical, and optimal, 117–118
  overregularization of speech in, 130
  parent-child, 8
    see also Parent-child interactions, in play activities
  planned sequences of, 120
  preverbal communication in, 81–83
  role-related, 8
    see also Role playing
  social, 8
    see also Social play
  social development studied in, 133, 156
  speech styles in, 125–126, 130, 133, 134, 156, 173–174
  symbolic 8
    see also Symbolic play
  as therapy, 134–135
  turn-taking skills in, 115, 116
  word-action combinations in, 116
Point sharing, 11–12, 17, 323–373
  acquisition of skill in, 363–364
  anaphoric references in, 327–328, 336, 341
  assertion in, 330
  case marking in, 358–359
  cataphoric references in, 328, 336–337, 344
  definite articles in, 326–333
  devices used in, 326–363
  ellipsis in, 340–344
  exophoric references in, 326–327, 335, 341
  generic references in, 332–333
  grammatical devices in, 323
  indefinite articles in, 333–334
  initialization of, 348–351, 352
  introduction of new topic in, 350–351
  in language delays, 531
  lexical availability affecting, 355
  metaphoric references in, 337, 344
  paraphrasing in, 328–330
  particles in, 359
  partonymy in, 350–351
  perspective affecting, 337–338, 342, 354, 356–357
  polysemes in, 326–359, 360–361
    parallel function of, 338, 341–342
  presuppositions in, 362
  preverbal positioning in, 351–355
  pronominalization in, 335–340
  relativization in, 344–345
  role frame of interactional verbs in, 338–339, 343–344
  semantic analysis of, 325–359
  set operation in, 331–332
  stress of voice in, 345–348
  subject-verb agreement in, 355–357
  topics in, 339–340, 350–351, 353
  verb selection in, 357–358
  word order in, 355

Politeness of speech, 453–454
  cultural variations in, 385, 389, 397
  in language disorders, 444
  and obscenities used by children, 157, 173
  and presuppositions in forms of address, 278
  in requests, 298–299, 305–306, 308–309, 315, 316, 317
Polysemes, 11, 326
  in case marking, 358–359, 361
  of definite articles, 326–333, 360
  in ellipsis, 340–344, 360
  of indefinite articles, 333–334, 360
  in initialization, 348–351, 361
  of particles, 359, 361
  in point sharing, 326–359, 360–361
  of preverbal positioning, 351–355, 361
  of pronouns, 335–340, 360
  of relative clauses, 344–345, 361
  in stress of voice, 345–348, 361
  in subject-verb agreement, 355–357, 361
  in verb selection, 357–358, 361
Possessions, requests about, 300
Predicates
  counterfactive, 245, 263, 273
  factive, 244–245, 246, 256, 257, 262–273
  nonfactive, 263, 264, 265, 266, 267, 272–273
Preschool children
  language delays in, 530–531, 533
  see also Infants and toddlers
Presuppositions, 10–11, 237–293, 440–452
  in autism, 286–287, 289, 290, 451–452
  carried by general linguistic devices, 249–250
  carried by particular words and linguistic devices, 242–249
  in definite reference word use, 243–244, 245, 257–262
  development of, 252–281
    in early language, 254–257
    in later language, 257–281
  elements of, 240–252
  and ellipsis, 250, 280–281
  empirical findings about, 252–281
  in factive predicate use, 244-245, 246, 256, 257, 262–273
  in forms of address, 244, 247–249, 255, 278–279, 286–287
  and Gricean conversational principles, 241–242, 257, 281
  in interrogatives, 245–246, 249, 273–278
  and introduction of unshared information, 251–252, 279–280, 442
  and language delays, 13, 237, 285–288, 289, 441–447
  in mental retardation, 447–451
  in negation, 246–247, 277–278, 346
  and partonymy, 330–331
  in point sharing, 362
  pragmatic and semantic, 248–249, 288
  in relative clauses, restrictive, 345
  on social roles, 443–444
  of speaker and listener, 250–252, 262
  and stress placed on words, 249–250, 253, 280
  theoretical questions on, 281–285
  and word order in sentence, 245–246, 249, 279–280
Pretend, understanding usage of, 268–269
Pretend play, 8
  see also Symbolic play
Preverbal communication, 6, 9, 16, 23–67
  in autism, 26, 51–60, 61–62
  in blindness, 94, 483, 484–490, 499, 501, 503, 504
    compared to sighted children, 505, 506–507, 520
  and cognitive development, 29–30, 45–46, 59, 61–62
  conceptual and methodological issues in, 26–30
  crying in, 76
  elicited, 36, 37, 41
  in first year of life, 30–51, 72–84
  gaze in, 78, 81
  gestures in, 80
    see also Gestures, in preverbal communication

Preverbal communication–*continued*
  in hearing impairment, 93–94
  in home environment, 26, 30–46, 60
  in institutional environment, 26, 46–51, 60
  intention of, 27–29, 44, 63–64, 203, 204
    in autism, 57–58, 59, 61
    parent interpretation of, 74, 75–76, 77, 80–82, 204, 205
  interrogatives in, 222–224, 231–232
  negatives in, 206
  notation symbols for, 32
  object-object coordination in, 41–43
  in play activities, 81–83
  scoring categories of, 33–36
  in social routines, 83–84
  spontaneous behavior in, 31–41
    frequency of, 36–38
    trends in, 38–41
  stages of, 203–204
  Uzgiris-Hunt scales in assessment of, 36
Preverbal positioning, 351–355
  agency affecting, 354–355
  in focusing process, 354
  in foreign languages, 352, 355
  givenness affecting, 352–353
  perspective affecting, 354
  polysemes of, 351–355, 361
  topic determining, 353
Problem-solving skill, in language delays, 462
Pronominalization, in point sharing, 335–340
Pronoun use, 335–340
  anaphoric, 336
  in blindness, 511–512, 515–518, 520
    emergence of, 494–495
  cataphoric, 336–337
  cultural variations in, 386
  exophoric, 327, 335
  metaphoric, 337
  parallel function of, 338
  perspective of, 337–338
  polysemes in, 335–340, 360
  presuppositional, 243–244, 245, 255, 256, 260–261
  and role frame of interactional verbs, 338–339
  stress affecting interpretation of, 347
  topic affecting, 339–340
Pronunciation
  and communicative effectiveness, 85
  variations in, 154
Property, requests about, 300
Propositional meanings of language, 144, 152, 153, 154
Prosody, 130, 132
  in requests, 309
  variations in, 154
Psychosocial development, and communicative competence, 157–162, 461
Puns and jokes, 111, 275, 396, 397

Questions, 212–230
  see also Interrogatives

Reading
  by children
    home environment affecting, 92–93
    in language delays and disorders, 92, 454–455
  by parents to children, 91, 92
Reason approach to requests, 303–304, 312, 314, 315
Referential language, 141, 143, 144, 153, 154
  and person knowledge, 161–162
  and social categories, 165
Register variations, 381
  cultural factors in, 385
  in language disorders, 443
  in role playing, 124–127, 133, 156
Regularities
  categorization of, 148–153
  child knowledge about, revealed in play activities, 129–130
  and overregularization of speech, 130
Rehabilitation in language delays, 182–184
  see also Therapy activities

Relative clauses, 344–345
  for backgrounding, 345
  for item specification, 345
  polysemes of, 344–345, 361
  restrictive and nonrestrictive, 344–345
Remember
  children's understanding of, 269–272
  presuppositional usage of, 240, 245, 251, 262, 269–271
Remembering, *see* Memory
Repetition of communication
  in autism, 14, 437–439, 440, 452
  in blindness, 493
Requests, 11, 17, 295–321
  about possessions, 300
  activity or external goal-oriented, 312, 314–316
  attention-getters in, 301
  for behavior, 220
  in blindness, 491, 507, 517
  comparison of adult and child, 316–317
  compliance with, 320
  conventional, 11, 17, 295, 302–303, 305–306, 307–308, 318
  for correction of situation, 312
  cultural variations in, 12, 397–398
  domain of, 300–301
  forms of, 222, 226–227
  framing moves in, 301
  functional categories of, 220, 221
  hints in, 308, 318
  imbedded, 307, 308
  ineffective, remedies for, 301
  for information, 220
  instrumental language and moves in, 295, 297, 299, 300–310
    case study on, 311–320
    variations in, 305–306
  intrusiveness and routinity of, 297, 298, 299–300, 313–314
  in language disorders, 13, 432–435, 443–444
  in mental retardation, 436
  nonconventional, 11, 17, 295, 302–307, 308, 317–320
  oriented to rules and norms, 312, 314

  for permission, 307, 308
  persuasive adjuncts in, 301, 309–310
  politeness of, 298–299, 305–306, 308–309, 315, 316, 317
  presuppositions in, 276–277, 278
  preverbal, 222–224
  responses to, 301
  rights and obligations affecting, 297–298, 300, 314
  self-oriented, 311, 312–314
  social and situational variables in, 295, 297–300, 310–311, 316, 428
  speech acts in, 306–307
    indirect, 317–320
  strategies related to, 303–305
    in neutralization approach, 304–305
    in reason approach, 303–304, 312, 314, 315
Responses to speech
  in requests, 301
  semantic contingency of, 85–90
Revision of communication, 444–447
  in autism, 451–452
  in mental retardation, 450, 451
Rights and obligations, and appropriateness of requests, 297–298, 300, 314
Ritualized communication, 205
Role(s), social
  and appropriateness of communication, 163–164
  in forms of address, 278–279
  in requests, 297, 298–299, 300, 305–306, 316, 428
  of child, cultural variations in, 380, 382–387, 396–397
  event knowledge associated with, 167, 168
  knowledge of
    in blindness, 494
    from television, 177
  play activities related to, *see* Role playing
  and presuppositions in language disorders, 443–444
Role frame of interactional verbs, 338–339, 343–344

548 Index

Role playing, 8, 17, 109, 111, 114, 125–128
  abstraction of invariant features in, 129–130
  as baby, 126–127, 133
  in blindness, 489–490, 510–511, 518
  as caregiver, 125–126, 133
  child-child interactions in, 134
  and communicative development, 8
  in contrasting roles, 124, 127
  in language delays and disorders, 435, 462–463, 530
  limitations in, 131
  parent-child interactions in, 133–134
  social development studied in, 133, 156
  speech styles in, 125–126, 130, 133, 134, 156
    observational learning of, 173–174
  spontaneous and elicited, comparison of, 127–128
  stereotyping in, 130
Routinality of requests, 297, 298, 299–300, 313–314
Routines, social, *see* Social routines
Rule-oriented requests, 312, 314

Samoa, social status and role of children in, 384, 386
Schema theory, 166
School-age children
  cultural factors affecting, 413–414, 532
  language delays in, 531–532, 533
Self-oriented requests, 311, 312–314
Semantic analysis of point sharing, 325–359
Semantic competence, 128, 129
  in play activities, 130
Semantic contingency, 7, 85–87
  in imitation and modeling, 98
  in language delays, 531, 533
  studies on, 88–90
Sensorimotor development, and language acquisition, 113, 146, 147, 148, 151, 159
  in blindness, 489, 506
  in mental retardation, 436–437
Sentence structure, word order in, 279–280
  see also Word order
Sequential knowledge
  and communicative development, 165–169
  in language disorders, 181, 183
Set operation in point sharing, 331–332
Sign language, 470
Silence, cultural variations in value of, 384, 385, 386
Situational appropriateness of communication, *see* Contextual appropriateness of communication
Smiling, by blind children, 485–486
Social interactions
  after third year of life, 91–93
  appropriateness of speech in, 143, 155–165
  in requests, 11, 297–300, 305–306, 310–311, 316
  in autism, 14–15
  in blindness, 497, 498, 500, 505, 506, 518–519
  in constructive-interactional model of language acquisition, 112
  cultural variations in, 12, 380, 382–387, 396–397
  and event knowledge, 165–169
  in first year of life, 30–51, 72–84
  imitation and modeling in, 95–99
  knowledge about, *see* Social knowledge
  and language acquisition, 134–135, 459
  in language delays, 83, 93–99, 100, 459–460, 528–533
  in language training programs, 182–184
  parent-child, 69–107
    see also Parent-child interactions
  and person knowledge, 157–162, 169
  person-object coordination in, 30–51

play activities related to, *see*
  Social play
 and preverbal communication,
  23–67
  in autism, 51–60
  in home environment, 30–46
  in institutional environment,
   46–51
 routine, *see* Social routines
 in second and third years of life,
  84–91
Social knowledge
 categorization of, 162–165, 168,
  169, 181, 182
 and communicative development,
  141, 153–165
 in hearing impairment, 164
 and interpretation of
  interrogatives, 230
 and interpretation of negatives,
  212
 and language disorders, 180–182,
  183
 measured in role playing, 133, 156
 psychological awareness in,
  157–162
 television affecting, 177
Social play, 8, 17, 109, 111, 114–118
 in blindness, 502, 504
 in language delays, 529, 530
 parent-child interactions in,
  114–119
Social routines
 in autism, 55–56
 cultural variations in, 388
 event knowledge associated with,
  167
 in first year of life, 83–84
 of language handicapped children,
  83
 requests in, 297, 298, 299–300,
  313–314
Social roles, *see* Role(s), social
Socialization
 and cultural variations in
  communication, 375–420
 in parent-child interactions, 77
Socioeconomic status, and reading
  ability, 92–93
Sociolinguistic knowledge, 153–157
 and language disorders, 180–181,
  182, 183

 in language training program,
  182–184
Sounds, prespeech, 26, 27, 73–74,
  76
 parent interpretation of, 74, 76,
  79, 80–81
Speaker awareness of listener, *see*
  Listener, speaker awareness
  of
Speech acts, 431–440
 in autism, 437–440
 in mental retardation, 436–437
 in requests, 306–307
  indirect, 317–320
Speech onset, *see* Language onset
Speech styles in role playing,
  125–126, 127, 130, 133, 134,
  156
 observational learning of, 173–174
 overregularization in, 130
Spelling skills, home environment
  affecting, 92
Spontaneous behavior
 preverbal, 31–41
  frequency of, 36–38
  trends in, 38–41
 in role playing, 127–128
Status, social, *see* Role(s), social
Stress, emphatic
 in cleft sentences, 347–348
 in denials, 346
 in point sharing, 345–348
 polysemes of, 345–348, 361
 and presuppositions, 249–250,
  253, 280
 and pronoun interpretation, 347
 in questions, 346–347
 in word order, 346
Stress and illness, infant behavior
  in, 41
Subject-verb agreement
 in point sharing, 355–357
 polysemes of, 355–357, 361
Swear words, childhood use of, 157,
  173
Symbolic play, 8, 17, 109, 114,
  118–124
 in blindness, 489–490, 495, 496,
  506, 515, 520
 and communicative development,
  147

Symbolic play—*continued*
  in language delays, 529, 530
    amount and complexity of,
      461–462
    mental representation in, 146
Syntax
  in blindness, 498
  competence in, 128, 129, 132
  of interrogatives, 212–219, 232
  in language disorders, 179, 180
  of negatives, 196–199
  of parent speech, child
    comprehension of, 87–91
  in play activities, 130
  variations in, 154
  and vocabulary size and content,
    91, 99

Tamil families
  folk beliefs of, on language
    acquisition, 393
  social status and role of children
    in, 386
Television, and communicative
    development, 173, 175–177
The
  children's understanding of,
    283–284
  presuppositional usage of, 243,
    257–259
Therapy activities, 182–184,
    525–533
  cognitive aspects of, 179–184
  imitation and modeling in, 97–99
  play in, 134–135
Topic of conversation, 452, 453
  see also Conversations
Training procedures in language
    disorders, 182–184
Turn-taking
  in conversation, cultural
    variations in, 397, 414
  in play activities, 115, 116

Uzgiris-Hunt scales, 31, 36

Verbs
  children's understanding of,
    269–273
  polysemes of, 357–358, 361
  presuppositional usage of,
    262–273
  and preverbal positioning in point
    sharing, 351–355
  role frame of interactional,
    338–339, 343–344
  selection of, in point sharing,
    357–358
  subject agreement with, 355–357
Vocabulary acquisition, 87–91,
    282–285
  in blind children, 492
  compared to sighted children,
    505, 506, 507–508, 520
  imitation and modeling in, 96
  increasing complexity of, 87–91,
    99
  observational learning of, 173–174
  in social play, 115
  and television watching, 177
Vocatives, 348
Voice, intonation of, *see* Intonation
  of voice

Warm Springs Indian children,
    social status and role of,
    385–386
Wh- questions, 212–219
  cultural variations in, 407–410
  presuppositions in, 245–246, 249,
    273–278
  stress in, 346–347
Word order
  for emphatic stress, 346
  in point sharing, 355
  presuppositions carried by,
    245–246, 249, 279–280
  in preverbal positioning, 351–355

Yes/no questions, 212–218